Economics

Third Edition

A Tool for Understanding Society

Economics
Third Edition

A Tool for Understanding Society

TOM RIDDELL
SMITH COLLEGE

JEAN SHACKELFORD
BUCKNELL UNIVERSITY

STEVE STAMOS
BUCKNELL UNIVERSITY

with contributions by
BILL COOPER

ADDISON-WESLEY PUBLISHING COMPANY
Reading, Massachusetts   Menlo Park, California
Don Mills, Ontario   Wokingham, England   Amsterdam   Sydney
Singapore   Tokyo   Madrid   Bogotá   Santiago   San Juan

Library of Congress Cataloging-in-Publication Data

Riddell, Tom, 1944–
    Economics: a tool for understanding society.

    Bibliography: p.
    Includes index.
    1. Economics. I. Shackelford, Jean A. II. Stamos,
Steve, 1947–   . III. Title.
HB171.5.R43   1987   330   86-14043
ISBN 0-201-06368-9

ABCDEFGHIJ-DO-89876

Contents

Foreword

In the middle 1980s, the United States finds itself faced with a number of intriguing economic problems and puzzles. The 1981–1982 recession, the most severe since the Great Depression of the 1930s, has been followed by a modest economic recovery. Total economic activity increased steadily during 1983 and 1984, but slowed down in 1985. In mid-1986, the economy was sputtering. The unemployment rate, having reached 10.6 percent at the end of 1982, had fallen to 7.5 percent by the end of 1984. At the end of 1985, it was still over 7 percent. Investment spending by corporations, long dormant, seems to have been revived somewhat by the combination of tax cuts and the recovery itself. Spending by consumers by mid-1986 also led the revival of the economy. And, despite this acceleration of business, inflation has been reduced to its lowest rates since the mid-1960s.

Yet the overall picture has some dark spots. Unemployment remains at historically high rates, especially during a period of economic growth. Many banks have failed or had to be bailed out by government intervention. Federal deficits persist at record levels and contribute to interest rates that limit construction and investment activity in the private sector. The growth and fragility of international debt threaten

Bloom County by Berke Breathed. © 1983, Washington Post Writers Group, reprinted with permission.

the very stability of the international financial system (as well as U.S. banks). The United States faces continued sharp competition in domestic and world markets from other advanced nations and from some of the newly industrialized countries. And, at home, discrimination against women and minorities robs them of the chance to attain their full potential and contributes to economic inequality.

This list of problems is not all-inclusive. But it is suggestive. It highlights the reality of the U.S. economy in the mid-1980s, what might be called a "fragile boom." This combination of strengths and weaknesses provides fertile ground for politicians, the media, the public-at-large, and economists to try to understand what is going on. What accounts for our economic successes and failures? How can we address our economic problems and preserve long-run economic growth and stability?

The recent experiences of the U.S. economy, as well as their historical roots, have produced ferment in the field of economics. There are many competing explanations for our successes and failures. There is even disagreement among economists about what to call a problem. Supply-side economists have their explanations about what's been wrong with the economy and how their policies will correct it. Monetarists chime in with their own theories and suggestions. Keynesian economists focus on the problems inherent in the approach of the supply-siders and the monetarists, and then they offer their solutions. Further to the left, other economists have begun to argue for industrial policy, public ownership, democratic economic planning, and increased attention to economic equality based on their own assumptions and economic perspectives.

These debates are not sterile. They are a part of the public dialogue in this country—in the media, in political campaigns, in communities—about important problems and what to do about them. An informed position on these issues requires following events, paying attention to the discussion, and developing an understanding of how the economy works. In this environment, the study of economics can contribute to our efforts to understand our society and to work actively toward improving its performance in the future.

This introductory economics textbook is dedicated to assisting that effort. It attempts to develop fundamental economic tools of analysis in clear, simple, and understandable terms. It is designed to encourage the application of those tools to developing an appreciation and understanding of the most important economic issues facing the country, the world and its peoples. And it emphasizes the variety of theories and ideas that economists and others have developed in explaining U.S. and world economic events. We believe that the approach of this text encourages students to become interested in economic problems and to develop their ability to understand and analyze them. It is readable, it emphasizes relevant concerns, and it does not avoid controversy. It is "user-friendly."

A REVISED AND EXPANDED THIRD EDITION

This edition of *Economics: A Tool for Understanding Society* responds to the success of the first two editions, as well as the need to constantly update economics textbooks with current information and changing economic issues. We have also relied on feedback from colleagues, students, and faculty who have used the text to guide our revisions. Their criticisms, suggestions, and advice have been instructive and helpful.

We have also expanded the textbook. Our intention has been to supplement our presentation of the basic tools of economic analysis with wider and deeper coverage. It is still basically a one-semester text; but with this more extensive treatment, it may be appropriate for use in some full-year introductory economics courses. The scope of the book is still less than that of most full-length texts. It does not try to cover everything. We emphasize the basic fundamentals of economics, focus on relevant applications of those concepts, and do not try to intimidate through volume. It is our experience that too much information, too much qualification, and too much supplementary material can get in the way of a solid foundation in the essential and relatively simple concepts. Furthermore, there are adequate examples from contemporary economic events reported in the press every day to complement and enrich textbook economics.

Our objective has been to retain simplicity while at the same time expanding our treatment of the basic micro- and macroeconomic concepts. Consequently, we are convinced (both in theory and in practice) that this text is suitable for use in either one-semester or full-year long courses. The Preface to the Instructor contains suggested outlines for one-semester or two-semester courses.

The first two parts of the text have been only slightly revised. The part on microeconomics, however, has been reorganized and expanded. Chapters 9 and 10 still concentrate on scarcity and the supply-and-demand model. Chapter 11 on the competitive model now contains a treatment of both short-run and long-run cost curves, thus providing for more sophistication in the presentation and for a more informed foundation for students who go on in economics. Chapter 12 is a new one on models of imperfect competition—monopoly, monopolistic competition, and oligopoly—where we go into more detail than in the first two editions. Chapter 13 incorporates information and analysis on the distribution of income into a model of resource markets. Chapter 14 is on corporations and labor unions and is only slightly revised from the previous edition. Chapter 15 is a separate chapter on the role of the public sector in the economy that builds on the treatment in the second edition.

Part IV on macroeconomics has been revised to reflect the experiences of the early 1980s in the performance of the U.S. economy, the changes in economic policy, monetary regulation, the role of monetarism, and the effects of Reaganomics. There is also a new chapter on the economics of supply. The international section of the text has been updated and revised to reflect recent international economic and financial events and trends. In addition, we have split the chapter on developing nations and comparative economic systems into two chapters. Finally, the concluding section, The Future, contains a chapter on the environment and a revised chapter on the status of Keynesian economics in the mid-1980s. The final chapter offers a consideration of the current debates about the possible resolutions of the economic difficulties facing the United States—a return to Keynesianism, a continued experiment with supply-side economics and monetarism, a formation of industrial policy, or a new dedication to a more democratic and egalitarian economy?

Throughout the text, we have continued to supplement the development of the basic economic concepts with cartoons and articles. We have reduced the number of reproduced articles based on the conclusion that current economic events and requiring students to read a paper offer ample examples. We have retained the questions for students as they read through the text. This is a unique feature of our book, and one that we feel provides a strong pedagogical contribution.

ACKNOWLEDGMENTS

Once again staff members at Addison-Wesley have been supportive in their assistance, advice, and cooperation in this edition of *Economics: A Tool for Understanding Society*. We appreciate their contribution. The institutions where we have taught have provided support for our work—Bucknell University, the University of Massachusetts/Amherst, and Smith College. Colleagues have offered helpful criticisms and suggestions for improving the text, including Charles Sackrey, John Pool, Adrienne Birecree, and Frank Slavik. Reviews of the text from Robert Drago, Larry Simmons, James Cobbe, Richard B. Hansen, Ned C. Pearlstein, Teresa Amott, Norris Clement, Tom Maddox, Steve Hickerson, Claron Nelson, Dale Warnke, and Stewart Long were very helpful. Letitia Sloan, Ruth Wynkoop, Bob Brown, Tony John, and Diane Collins provided valuable research and preparation assistance. And our students over the past decade have given us the insights of their own learning process to help us in assessing our teaching experiences and translating that into our text. We thank them for what we have learned from them.

Finally, we would like to dedicate this edition of our book to our children, in order of appearance, Peter Lawrence-Riddell, Michael Lawrence-Riddell, Brian Shackelford-Brinkman, Barry Sierra Stamos, and Lisanna Stamos.

Northampton, Massachusetts   T.R.
Lewisburg, Pennsylvania   J.S.
                                                                   S.S.

Preface to the Instructor

In recent years, there has been a good bit of dissatisfaction with the available textbooks among teachers of introductory economics. Not surprisingly, this has led to a surge of new textbooks—for both the one-semester and two-semester courses. Most of these new books, but not all, have attempted to cut down on the encyclopedic nature of the Samuelson and McConnell type of text, and many have introduced readings and problems that are up-to-date and relevant to the current population of introductory economics students. This book is also in that tradition. Its singular contributions are that it is intended to be a one-semester book, that it focuses on a particular set of basic economic concepts, that it emphasizes active learning on the part of the student, that it includes different perspectives, and finally, that it places a good bit of responsibility for teaching the course on the instructor.

This last aspect addresses another concern that has recently surfaced among teachers of introductory economics. Many of the textbooks that were popular in the 1950s and 1960s were relatively easy to teach from; it was all there, it was all relatively straightforward, and the material was all familiar to anyone with a graduate degree in economics. Certainly, there was room for classroom innovation and experimentation to make the learning of economics exciting and lively. But the form and content of the two-semester textbook made it only too easy to lecture on the development of the theory in the text.

However, in the context of the continuing turmoil and confusion of the 1960s and 1970s, many economics teachers became dissatisfied with this approach to introductory economics. They wanted more relevance and applicability of economic concepts. Many were concerned with the lack of balance in the texts—one particular "brand" of economics would be emphasized to the exclusion of others; these teachers wanted more controversy and exposure to different points of view in their courses. They wanted less scope and less depth in the development of theory. They wanted to take a more active role in teaching their courses. It is with these kinds of concerns that we began the effort of writing this textbook.

In the 1980s with continuing economic difficulties, the resurgence of monetarism, the rise of supply-side economics, and expanding economics enrollments, a "countermovement" occurred. Many one-semester courses were replaced by full-year courses. Full-year textbooks proliferated in the market. They strove for comprehensiveness, relevance, applications, and, sometimes, balance. In essence, they mimicked the Samuelson model; they tried to cover every new issue, every new theory and policy, and to do so in-depth. This revised edition of *Economics: A Tool for Understanding Society* resists that current and maintains its commitment to focus on the most important, essential, and useful economic concepts. It does seek a broader and up-to-date coverage, but not at the expense of overkill.

This text obviously does not cover every possible topic or economic concept that one might want to teach in the ideal introductory course. Nor are the articles and examples we have chosen the ones that would be selected by everyone. The questions for the students as they read through the text might not be the ones that you would choose to emphasize the essence of a particular concept. However, we do feel that the book will help students to learn and practice economics and the economic way of thinking as they progress through your course. And it is essentially *your* course. We feel that this book leaves room for and, indeed, requires a substantial amount of imagination, work, and dedication on the part of the instructor. You will have to teach economics; and we hope this text will help you in your task.

We have found the material in this book to be useful to us in teaching economics. Our students seem to have enjoyed working with and learning from it. However, we have chosen to supplement it (at Bucknell) in a variety of ways. In each of our own sections of the course, we have emphasized different parts of the book more than others, based on our own interests and conclusions about what is important. We have used different examples in explaining a certain concept. Some of us rely heavily on lecturing. Some attempt to actively involve the students in discussions and in solving problems in class. In addition, each week we meet with the entire group of students taking the course for a "common hour," or laboratory. During this session, we have shown movies and slide shows; we have had guest speakers; and we have presented mock debates. The purpose of these sessions is to encourage the students to grapple with economic problems and to utilize their growing knowledge of economics to understand them. And often other media and another face help to do this.

One of the most important innovations that we have made in the teaching of our course is to require the students to read a daily paper. Because of our location and the College Service it offers, we have used the *New York Times* in this way. The *Wall Street Journal*, the *Christian Science Monitor*, and the *Washington Post Weekly* are also good supplementary resources and are mailed all over the country. Having students read the paper helps them to use and reinforce their economics—to formulate questions in class, to discuss controversial events or proposals, and to provide real, current examples of economic problems and the light that can be thrown on them by economics. Using a paper also allows the instructor to keep the course relevant and up to date.

We hope this text will encourage you and help you to continue to be creative and imaginative in the way that you teach introductory economics. It has been a lot of work for us—including many headaches and failed experiments. But then it has also been fun, exciting, and rewarding. Teaching's like that, isn't it?

Do you know what time it is, kids? It's time for Uncle Bob's Economics 324 lecture.

SUGGESTED ONE-SEMESTER COURSE OUTLINE (14 WEEKS)

Part I	Chapters 1–3	Week 1	
	Chapters 4–8	Week 2	
Part II	Chapters 9–10	Week 3	
	Chapters 11–12	Week 4	
	Chapters 13–14	Week 5	
	Chapters 15 & 29	Week 6	Exam # 1

Part III	Chapters 16–17	Week 7	
	Chapters 18–19	Week 8	
	Chapters 20–21	Week 9	
	Chapters 22–23	Week 10	Exam # 2
Part IV	Chapters 24–25	Week 11	
	Chapters 26–27	Week 12	
Part V	Chapter 28	Week 13	
	Chapter 30	Week 14	Final Exam

SUGGESTED ONE-SEMESTER MICRO COURSE OUTLINE

Part I	Chapters 1–2	Week 1	
	Chapters 3–6	Week 2	
	Chapters 7–8	Week 3	Exam # 1
Part II	Chapter 9	Week 4	
	Chapters 10–11	Week 5	
	Chapter 12	Week 6	
	Chapter 13	Week 7	
	Chapter 14	Week 8	
	Chapter 15	Week 9	Exam # 2
Part III	Chapters 24–25	Week 10	
	Chapters 26–27	Week 11	
	Chapter 28	Week 12	
	Chapter 29	Week 13	
	Review	Week 14	Final Exam

SUGGESTED ONE-SEMESTER MACRO COURSE OUTLINE

Part I	Chapters 1–2	Week 1	
	Chapters 3–6	Week 2	
	Chapters 7–8	Week 3	Exam # 1
Part II	Chapters 16–17	Week 4	
	Chapter 18	Week 5	
	Chapter 19	Week 6	
	Chapter 20	Week 7	
	Chapter 21	Week 8	
	Chapter 22	Week 9	
	Chapter 23	Week 10	Exam # 2
Part III	Chapters 24–25	Week 11	
	Chapters 26–27	Week 12	
	Chapter 28	Week 13	
	Chapter 30	Week 14	Final Exam

Preface to the Student

ECONOMICS—WHAT'S IN IT FOR YOU?

Two hundred years after the beginnings of the United States as an independent nation, we Americans live in one of the most technologically and economically advanced countries in the world. Our complex economic system produces and distributes goods and services to us daily and provides us with a high standard of living. And yet we are not satisfied, because we, personally and collectively, have many economic problems. Can we find and keep a job that provides us with the income to support ourselves and our families? Can we find a job that we like? Inflation, unemployment, energy problems, discrimination, deficits, debt, poverty, pollution, resource shortages, underdevelopment in the Third World, and corruption in business and politics are problems that have dominated the headlines in the newspapers in the 1960s, 1970s, and 1980s. We have had our successes and our failures, and we continue to experience this mixed performance.

Economics, as one of the social sciences, is intended to help us in understanding, thinking, and forming opinions about and developing responses to these economic aspects of our social experience. Economics can be a tool that aids us in defining what our successes and our failures are and in preserving success and correcting failure. In an increasingly complex and confusing world, this tool can be of service to us personally and collectively as we strive to be responsible citizens of our communities, our nation, and our world. This book is dedicated to attempting to help you acquire that tool.

We want to make economics as important as baseball and football scores. The minds are out there. It's a question of getting the attention.

> —Robert P. Keim, President of the Advertising Council, commenting on a new public service campaign to "improve public understanding and awareness of the system," 1975.

Acting is a business—no more than that—a craft, like plumbing, or being an economist; it's been a good living.

> —Marlon Brando, actor, in a television interview with Dick Cavett, 1973.

An inhabitant of cloud-cuckoo land; one knowledgeable in an obsolete art; a harmless academic drudge whose theories and laws are but mere puffs of air in face of the anarchy of banditry, greed, and corruption which holds sway in the pecuniary affairs of the real world.

> —A definition of "economist" that won an award from the *New Statesman* in England, 1976.

---

1. Would you like to be an economist? Why or why not?
None of the questions in this book are rhetorical. Each is intended to make you pause and think. Try to answer each question as you go along.

COLLEGE ECONOMICS COURSES AT THE INTRODUCTORY LEVEL

Introductory economics courses in colleges across the United States have undergone significant changes in recent years. During the 1950s and 1960s most schools offered a two-semester introduction to economics course. "Everyone" wanted to or was required to learn economics in the postwar era of American prosperity. Many textbooks appeared on the market to meet the demands from expanding enrollments. Paul Samuelson of M.I.T., a Nobel Prize winner in economics, became a millionaire through the sales of his widely used and heralded *Economics*. His book became almost a bible and influenced thousands of fledgling economists.

DOONESBURY   BY GARRY TRUDEAU

As the enrollments increased and new postwar economic problems emerged, though, the textbooks, in an effort to remain relevant, became encyclopedic. They were also pretty dry. The books all tried to convey almost everything there was to know on an introductory level about all of economics. Some texts seemed purposely to make economics as hard as possible to learn—to complicate and mystify. Ph.D. students have been known to use Samuelson's book to study for their doctoral exams! But the hitch in this approach was that not everybody was going to be a Ph.D. in economics—or even an economics major as an undergraduate. Not all students wanted to have 1000 pages of textbook economics crammed into their heads. Much of it was "irrelevant" to the students who went on to become "noneconomists." It was abstract and not related very well to real-world problems. Most of it was forgotten. Very few of the economic concepts presented—beyond supply and demand—were retained for day-to-day use by most graduates of introductory economics.

In addition, real-world events forced change. In the late 1960s and early 1970s, as the problems of race and poverty in the United States and the problem of development in the Third World became highlighted by riots in the U.S. cities and wars in Indochina, students of economics demanded less abstraction and more relevance in their courses. This trend continued with the economic upheavals of the late 1970s and early 1980s. Consequently, many college economics departments began to change their approach to introducing students to economics and economic problems. They attempted to make their courses more interesting and more relevant. Many used a historical approach. Many attempted to teach only the core of elementary economic theory (to avoid getting overly abstract and technical). Many colleges and universities retreated to a one-semester introductory course that would be more attractive and useful to the student who might never take another economics course—as well as provide a foundation for those who would take more courses as nonmajors or as majors. And many new economics textbooks came along to meet these new demands.

This textbook, which we originally developed in connection with the introductory course at Bucknell University, is one of this new breed. This book emerged from a series of changes in that course to make it more effective in teaching introductory economics to college students. The basic goal was to create an "experimental" one-semester course that enhanced the teaching and learning process in introductory economics. In this text, we have tried to compile a quality, nonencyclopedic approach that deals with the basics and doesn't overwhelm students with volume. We have tried to consistently relate these basics to real-world problems, and we have tried to use uncomplicated language to simplify and demystify your study of economics. And we have included many conflicting ideas and controversial subjects to stimulate thought and to encourage critical thinking. In our courses, we have also experimented with different approaches to teaching economics, including the use of movies and slide shows, outside speakers, newspapers, and other classroom innovations. The combination of these innovations seems to have worked in making it fun to teach and learn introductory economics.

The economic events of the 1970s and 1980s themselves, as well as the employment uncertainties they produced, resulted in increasing enrollments in economics courses on campuses across the country. Many states are even beginning to require high school students to take an economics course before they graduate. In response to this increased demand, even more economics textbooks flooded the market. And, given the increasing complexity of the problems of economic growth and stability facing the United States in the 1980s—not to mention the ferment and debates among different schools of economists—courses and textbooks tried to do it all. They became full-year courses again, went over all the theories, and tried to be relevant. Many of them, we believe, overshot the mark. This text can be used in both one-semester and two-semester courses, and it is consciously intended not to confuse by trying to teach you everything there is to know about economics. There's either plenty of time for more later on, or this is it. In either case, too much is too much. We hope you enjoy this book and your course, and we trust you'll learn a lot in the process.

2. **Why are you taking economics? Do you think you should "have fun" while you do?**

3. **"Economics has always been a countercyclical discipline; it flourishes when the economy founders, and vice versa." Why do you suppose that's so? And is it a correct observation?**

OBJECTIVES, OR WHAT WE'VE TRIED TO DESIGN THIS BOOK TO ACCOMPLISH

Before we begin our formal study, we'd like to share the following list of what we feel are the most important objectives of an introduction to modern economics:

1. To produce some "cognitive dissonance." What we mean by this is that we hope to present you with some ideas, facts, and ways of thinking that are new or different to you. It is hoped these will challenge you to think, to work a little, and to learn. *Is capitalism better than socialism?* It might be, but then again, it might not be! We hope to open your minds to thinking about alternatives. What is "investment"? It is *not* simply buying a share of stock in a corporation! Introductory economics may shake up some of your preconceived ideas and beliefs! And it may reorganize them into a *system* of thought.

2. To give you some perspective on the historical *changes* in the material conditions, economic institutions, and social relations of human society. We haven't always been affluent, and capitalism hasn't always existed.

3. To *introduce* you to a system of economic theories and ideas about the economic institutions of societies—and how those ideas and theories have changed over time. Even the conservative Republican, Richard Nixon, became a Keynesian in the 1970s. But in the 1980s, Ronald Reagan's successful campaign was based on a critique of Keynesian economic policy.

4. To convey to you *some* of the economic theories that economists, or groups of economists, regard as being accurate descriptions and predictors of economic activity. We do *not*, however, intend to attempt to give you a survey of all of economics. We want *rather* to expose you to some of the most basic and useful *economic concepts*. There is too much of economics to try to do all of it in one semester or even a year; time is *scarce* (that's an economic concept).

5. To focus on some contemporary economic problems—inflation, unemployment, growth, resource shortages, the energy crisis, the ecological crisis, poverty, multinational corporations, economic growth and development, and others.

6. To expose you to the various, and contending, "schools" of economic thought. Not all economists agree on theories or even on which problems are the most important. We hope that you will at least appreciate the variety of economic opinion—no matter which, if any, particular set of economic ideas appeals to you.

7. To give you *practice* using economic concepts. We don't want you to just "tape" the concepts in your head and play them back on tests. We hope that this text gives you opportunities to use economic concepts in solving real-world problems. Our intention is to provide you with numerous case studies that allow you to apply economic concepts, ideas, and theories so that you may come to better understand the world you live in (and perhaps to change it!). We encourage you to read a daily newspaper. Reading the paper on a regular basis ought to provide numerous real-world examples of economic problems (to integrate theory and reality). And applying economic concepts to them ought to help us understand them and figure out their implications. We may even be able to suggest solutions to some of these problems. How would you eliminate inflation?

8. To provide you with a minimum amount of economic "literacy." You should be able to interpret some of the *jargon* of professional economists. You should also be able to identify the variables, ramifications, and possible explanations of and solutions to a variety of economic problems. We hope you develop a facility to critically evaluate economic ideas.

cpf*

*cpf is a graphics exchange network for original artwork and that used in community, organizational, and other publications. Community Press Features is part of Urban Planning Aid, 120 Boylston St., Boston, Mass. 02116.

9. To *demystify* economics so that you do not feel that the economy and its problems are too complex to understand and solve. Economics ought not to be left only to the economists.

10. To provide a foundation for future and continued learning. It is a complex world. But economics ought to be able to assist you in thinking critically and independently about that world you live in. It should be one more tool that allows (and encourages) you to assume a creative stance in your community, your society, and your world. Our hope is that we can turn you on to economics enough so that it becomes a useful and creative tool that you will continue to use in achieving a rich and meaningful life.

4. Are there any objectives we've missed? Do these make sense to you? Is this what you expected introductory economics to do for you?

Economics
Third Edition

A Tool for Understanding Society

INTRODUCTION TO ECONOMICS AS A SOCIAL SCIENCE: THE EVOLUTION OF ECONOMIES AND ECONOMICS

Will capitalism survive? How did the United States come to have a free enterprise economic system? In the near future, will the economic system of the United States be fundamentally altered? Will we return to laissez-faire capitalism? Will there be some form of national economic planning or "industrial policy"? Who will do the planning? For whom?

Is inflation a threat in the United States and in Western Europe? Why are interest rates so high? Can they be reduced?

Why is unemployment so high now? Can it be reduced? Can we produce a job for every American who wants one? Why is the United States so affluent? Will it continue to be, especially if there are more shortages of such materials as oil? Can the United States develop energy self-sufficiency? Have we licked pollution, or will it get worse? What can we do with toxic wastes? Why do we still have poverty? Is there a reason for a black person's being more likely than a white person to be poor and unemployed? Why do women earn, on average, only 60 percent of what men earn? Why do we spend so much on arms? How come the United States produces so much food? What should we do with it—sell it to the Soviets? Give it to the world's starving and poor? Will *you* be employed? Rich? Poor?

1

These are all predominantly economic questions that affect each and every one of us in our day-to-day lives—either directly or indirectly. We read about these problems in the newspapers, we hear about them on the radio and the television, politicians talk about them, and we discuss them with our friends and neighbors. They are important and interesting. We have opinions about them—and answers to some or all of them.

Economics is essentially an organized body of knowledge about all of these issues—some of which are current and some of which are perpetual. It seeks to understand and explain these problems and to assist us in solving them. It helps us to think about these problems by indicating important variables and relationships. It develops for us a way of approaching such problems. It is hoped that, in this course, you will learn to use economics to consider those problems that interest and/or affect you.

In the following, we will focus first of all on the subject matter of economics— the operation of economic systems. All societies must organize themselves to produce the goods and services needed for their survival. We will examine, in a general way, the different types of economic systems that human societies have developed and how these have changed. The economic system of the United States has not always existed and has changed dramatically over the last 200 years. Its history is important to developing an informed perspective on its current operation and development. These will be the subjects of Chapter 1. In Chapter 2, we will

Economics in the news. (Photograph by Tom Riddell.)

concentrate on economics, or political economy, *as a social science*. Human beings have developed a body of knowledge to help them understand and shape their economic systems. Over time, these economic theories and ideas have also changed. In addition, since economics deals with the social affairs of *homo sapiens*, we will discover that there is and has been controversy and disagreement among economists.

The Evolution
of Economic Systems

INTRODUCTION

The first premise of all human history is, of course, the existence of living human individuals. Thus the first fact to be established is the physical organization of these individuals and their consequent relation to the rest of nature. . . .

. . . The writing of history must always set out from these natural bases and their modification in the course of history through the action of men.

Men can be distinguished from animals by consciousness, by religion or anything else you like. They themselves begin to distinguish themselves from animals as soon as they begin to *produce* their means of subsistence, a step which is conditioned by their physical organization. By producing their means of subsistence men are indirectly producing their actual material life.

The way in which men produce their means of subsistence depends first of all on the nature of the actual means of subsistence they find in existence and have to reproduce. This mode of production must not be considered simply as being the reproduction of the physical existence of the individuals. Rather it is a definite form of activity of these individuals, a definite form of expressing their life, a definite *mode of life* on their part. As individuals express their life, so they are. What they are, *therefore,* coincides with their production, both with *what* they produce and with *how* they produce. The nature of individuals thus depends on the material conditions determining their production.

—Karl Marx, *The German Ideology* (1845–1846).

Every society is faced with the problem of providing for the day-to-day survival of its people. Production of goods and services on a systematic basis is necessary for the continuance and development of any society or nation. Institutions, traditions, rules, methods, and laws are developed to determine what goods and services will be produced, how they will be produced, and how they will be distributed among the people. According to Marx, the ways in which people organize themselves for the production and distribution of goods and services—the **economic system**—constitutes "the mode of life" of any society. Individuals and organizations engage in economic activity for particular reasons and according to accepted procedures. This activity is a central and necessary aspect of all human life and societies. It provides us with food, shelter, clothing, and the other necessities of life. The production and distribution of goods and services transforms nature into human uses for survival and sustenance. The actions made by people in this process determine, to a large extent, their daily contacts and relationships with other people. The results of economic activity—what gets produced and how it gets produced—organized through an economic system, condition the nature, history, and development of a society and its people. Understanding the economic system, then, is fundamental to understanding that society.

To "know" the United States, it is necessary to acknowledge the importance of private production and consumption in providing for our day-to-day survival. Consequently, we would want to examine the roles of specialization, division of labor,

Karl Marx, 1818–1883.

and markets in the operation of our economic system. It is also important to realize that American institutions, productive methods, and material conditions have changed over time. Corporations and labor unions have emerged and developed. The standard of living has advanced remarkably. Mass production has led to the assembly line and automation. The government has accepted more direct responsibility for the health of the economy. In other words, the economic system has evolved.

Over time, all economic systems change. The present American economic system, its institutions, and its conditions, developed out of previous methods of production and distribution. The historical background lies largely, but not exclusively, in American and European experience. For example, our market system has its roots in the emergence of trade in the Middle Ages in Europe; the modern corporation has its roots in the development of earlier European and American business enterprises. If we understand this background, perhaps we will gain some useful perspective on our current economic system.

1. **Do you agree with Marx that the "mode of production" of a society constitutes "a definite mode of life on [its] part"? How does the "mode of production" in the United States affect life in the United States?**

2. **"The nature of individuals thus depends on the material conditions determining their production." What does this mean? Do you think it's true? How are Americans affected by "the material conditions" of production?**

FROM FEUDALISM TO CAPITALISM

From time to time, economic change is so wrenching that major transformations occur and completely new economic systems emerge, with new institutions, rules, methods, and laws. Such was the transition from **feudalism** to **capitalism** in Western Europe from the 12th to 18th century. The change occurred over several centuries but accelerated in the later periods. In the following, we will concentrate on the highlights of this transition to illustrate economic change and to show the historical roots of modern capitalism.

As we have said, all societies must organize themselves for production, distribution, and consumption. Perhaps if we are clear on what these economic activities are, we will be able to focus on the major differences among economic systems. **Production** refers to the activity that takes the **factors of production** (resources) and transforms them into goods and services. The factors of production include land, labor, and capital. **Land** includes raw materials and the land where productive activity takes place (i.e., farmland or the land on which a factory is located). **Labor** is the physical and mental effort of men and women that is necessary for all production. **Capital** refers to the technology, buildings, machinery, and equipment that are used in production, as well as the financial resources necessary to organizing production. **Consumption** is the purchasing and using up of produced goods and services. **Distribution** refers to the manner in which goods and services are apportioned among the people of a society. As we will see, feudalism accomplished all of these with institutions and methods much different from those of capitalism.

> **3. All societies must be able to organize themselves for production, distribution, and consumption. What other economic goals should a society have? List at least five.**

The ancient empires of Egypt, Greece, and Rome were the precursors of modern Western societies. They were largely agricultural societies that struggled to produce enough food for continued subsistence. Tradition and custom were primarily responsible for organizing production and distribution. Things were done the way they always had been done. Sons followed their fathers into occupations and daughters assumed their mothers' roles as gatherers and homemakers. Slaves remained slaves. Peasants were agricultural producers tied to the land. The priests, kings, and lords continued in the role of the elite upper class removed from production. As economist Robert Heilbroner has described them in *The Making of Economic Society*, these societies had "a mode of social organization in which both production and distribution were based on procedures devised in the distant past, rigidified by a long process of historic trial and error, and maintained by heavy sanctions of law, custom, and belief."

As a result of the inability of these societies to produce much more than was needed for subsistence, they were unable to support a large nonfarming population. Throughout history, the ability to produce an agricultural and economic **surplus** (i.e., to produce more than is needed for subsistence consumption) has been a source of growth and power. The existence of an agricultural surplus allows for a geographically separate urban population. Obviously, cities did exist in Egypt, Greece, and Rome, but they were not extensive enough to allow for a significant amount of nonagricultural production. Instead, the cities of ancient times were relatively parasitic and lived off the surplus of the rural area. What surplus the cities were able to produce themselves resulted from trade with other cities and from the institution of slavery, with its ability to exploit unpaid labor. With a largely rural population tied to tradition and an urban economy based on the unstable slave system, the ancient empires were economically stagnant—they were unable to amass economic surplus and to grow. Because of this base of internal weakness, each of these ancient empires eventually crumbled. They were replaced by feudalism during the Middle Ages.

Before we examine feudalism, it is worthwhile to pause and consider an additional aspect of economic surplus. As we have seen, if a society can produce more than it needs for consumption, it can use this excess to support an urban population that can pursue nonagricultural production, and it can devote resources to increasing further production. The surplus can be used to further a division of tasks within an economic system and thus to spur economic growth.

By forgoing current consumption, a society can use resources to increase its ability to produce goods and services in the future. A simple example would be using

Environmental Action, June 5, 1976.

excess grain to feed oxen (instead of eating it) so that more grain could be produced in the future. Another example would be transporting food to an urban area where artisans would fashion simple tools for agricultural production.

Although the surplus can thus be a source of growth, how a society uses its surplus and who controls its use tell us a lot about that society. Egypt, Greece, and Rome did succeed in producing surplus, but most of it was not used in attempting directly to further economic production. The surpluses of these societies were controlled by religious and military elites to build temples, pyramids, sphinxes, magnificent roads, and buildings that are still with us today. Little of the surplus, however, went to the slaves, peasants, or artisans who were the producers of consumable goods and services, nor was the surplus directed toward improving the productive potential of these sectors of the economic systems. As a result, these societies stagnated because they were not able to generate economic growth.

4. What does the United States do with its "economic surplus"? Who determines how it is used?

Feudalism

Feudalism was an economic system that dominated Western Europe throughout the Middle Ages. What exactly was feudalism? What were its major institutions, methods, and customs? The following selection by economic historian E. K. Hunt, from his book *Property and Prophets,* provides us with a concise description of feudalism.

FEUDALISM

E. K. Hunt

The decline of the western part of the old Roman Empire left Europe without the laws and protection the empire had provided. The vacuum was filled by the creation of a feudal hierarchy. In this hierarchy, the serf, or peasant, was protected by the lord of the manor, who, in turn, owed allegiance to and was protected by a higher overlord. And so the system went, ending eventually with the king. The strong protected the weak, but they did so at a high price. In return for payments of money, food, labor, or military allegiance, overlords granted the fief, or feudum—a hereditary right to use land—to their vassals. At the bottom was the serf, a peasant who tilled the land. The vast majority of the population raised crops for food or clothing or tended sheep for wool and clothing.

Custom and tradition are the key to understanding medieval relationships. In place of laws as we know them today, the *custom of the manor* governed. There was no strong central authority in the Middle Ages that could have enforced a system of laws. The entire medieval organization was based on a system of mutual obligations and services up and down the hierarchy. Possession or use of the land obligated one to certain customary services or payments in return for protection. The lord was as obligated to protect the serf as the serf was to turn over a portion of his crop or to perform extensive labor for the lord. . . .

The extent to which the lords could enforce their "rights" varied greatly from time to time and from place to place. It was the strengthening of these obligations and the nobleman's ability to enforce them through a long hierarchy of vassals and over a wide area that eventually led to the

(continued)

—Abridged from pp. 5–8 in *Property and Prophets: The Evolution of Economic Institutions and Ideologies* (2nd ed.) by E. K. Hunt. Copyright © 1972, 1975 by E. K. Hunt. Reprinted by permission of Harper & Row, Publishers, Inc.

By permission of Johnny Hart and News America Syndicate.

emergence of the modern nationstates. This process occurred during the period of transition from feudalism to capitalism. Throughout most of the Middle Ages, however, many of these claims were very weak because political control was fragmented.

The basic economic institution of medieval rural life was the **manor** [boldface added], which contained within it two separate and distinct classes: noblemen, or lords of the manors, and serfs (from the Latin word *servus,* "slave"). Serfs were not really slaves. Unlike a slave, who was simply property to be bought and sold at will, the serf could not be parted from either his family or his land. If his lord transferred possession of the manor to another nobleman, the serf simply had another lord. In varying degrees, however, obligations were placed upon the serfs that were sometimes very onerous and from which there was often no escape. Usually, they were far from being "free."

The lord lived off the labor of the serfs who farmed his fields and paid taxes in kind and money according to the custom of the manor. Similarly, the lord gave protection, supervision, and administration of justice according to the custom of the manor. It must be added that although the system did rest on reciprocal obligations, the concentration of economic and political power in the hands of the lord led to a system in which, by any standard, the serf was exploited in the extreme.

The Catholic church was by far the largest owner of land during the Middle Ages. . . . This was also an age during which the religious teaching of the church had a very strong and pervasive influence throughout western Europe. These factors combined to make the church the closest thing to a strong central government throughout this period.

Thus the manor might be secular or religious . . . but the essential relationships between lord and serfs were not significantly affected by this distinction. There is little evidence that serfs were treated any less harshly by religious lords than by secular ones. The religious lords and the secular nobility were the joint ruling classes; they controlled the land and the power that went with it. In return for very onerous appropriations of the serf's labor, produce, and money, the nobility provided military protection and the church provided spiritual aid.

In addition to manors, medieval Europe had many towns, which were important centers of manufacturing. Manufactured goods were sold to manors and, sometimes, traded in long-distance commerce. The dominant economic institutions in the towns were the **guilds** [boldface added]—craft, professional, and trade associations that had existed as far back as the Roman Empire. If anyone wanted to produce or sell any good or service, he had to join a guild.

The guilds were as involved with social and religious questions as with economic ones. They regulated their members' conduct in all their activities: personal, social, religious, and economic. Although the guilds

(continued)

did regulate very carefully the production and sale of commodities, they were less concerned with making profits than with saving their members' souls. Salvation demanded that the individual lead an orderly life based on church teachings and custom. Thus the guilds exerted a powerful influence as conservators of the status quo in the medieval towns.

5. **What were the dominant institutions of feudalism?**

6. **How does the feudal "custom of the manor" differ from our modern system of contracts?**

7. **What did the "religious lords and secular nobility" do with the economic surplus that they controlled?**

The Breakdown of Feudalism

As feudalism developed, several new economic activities and trends emerged that eventually created the preconditions for a new economic order, capitalism. For brevity's sake, we will simply list and describe them. Taken together over several centuries, these factors engendered **the transition from feudalism to capitalism.**

Changes in Technology.   In agriculture the widespread introduction, about the 11th century, of the three-field system of crop rotation, replacing the two-field system, allowed for a more productive use of agricultural land. In this system, all parcels of land would lie fallow every third year, preventing the land from becoming depleted by constant planting. This simple change increased the agricultural surplus and encouraged the use of more grain in supporting field animals. Agricultural production increased even further with greater use of oxen and horses, and later, with consolidation of agricultural lands. In addition, transportation of agricultural goods was facilitated by more horses and improvements in wagon technology.

Urbanization.   The increasing agricultural surplus supported an expanding and more urbanized population. Larger urban centers fostered specialization in economic production; the early medieval towns and cities began to concentrate on trade and manufacturing. This specialization led to further increases in production and stimulated trading among the cities and between the cities and the countryside.

The Medieval Merchants.   Given different specializations of agricultural and manufacturing production in different areas throughout Western Europe, individual merchants during the 10th to 14th century began traveling from place to place, buying, selling, and trading goods. These transient merchants exposed self-sufficient manors to the variety of products from the rest of Europe and Asia and created interdependencies that whittled away at the traditional patterns of feudal life. This

very trade further encouraged the development of regional and urban-rural specialization—a source of increasing economic surplus. It also laid the roots for the later
sophistication of European commerce. Traveling merchants were replaced by permanent markets in commercial cities by the 15th century.

The Crusades and Exploration.   Between the 11th and 13th centuries, the Crusades
brought Europeans into contact with a civilization much more concerned with
trading and money-making. It also exposed them to the wealth of the Orient and its
goods. This exposure encouraged an effort to expand the trading periphery of
Europe. The nations of Europe began to explore Africa and Asia. These explorations
ultimately led to the discovery of the New World. The example of money-making was
not lost either. Merchants financed and profited from the Crusades, while European
nations used their new-found exploring capability to establish colonies and reap from
them raw materials and precious metals. These new forms of economic surplus
financed further development and created fledgling capitalist institutions. In fact, the
inflow of gold and silver produced such rapid growth that a great price inflation
occurred during the 16th century in Europe.

The Nation-State.   An additional factor that broke down feudalism and, in fact,
supported exploration was the creation of the nation-state. The self-sufficient and
decentralized nature of feudalism began to hamper trade as manors attempted to levy

From "The History Book," a movie available from Tricontinental Films, 333 Sixth Avenue, New York
City.

tariffs and tolls on merchants. However, as centralization of political power became the goal of certain nobles and lords, these forces were joined by the commercial merchants in the cities. This coalition of economic and political power ensured the emergence of nation-states. By the 16th century these newly unified *nations* within Europe were encouraging trade within and among their countries and exploring across the Atlantic and the Mediterranean. The new nation-states possessed the economic, political, and military power that formed the basis for a new economic order and increased economic growth.

The Decline of the Manor.   One of the most significant trends in the transition from feudalism to capitalism occurred on the manor. Increasingly, the feudal obligations between lords and serfs became monetized. As trade expanded, the need for money caused feudal lords to sell their crops for cash and to put their serfs on money payments for work. In turn, the serfs paid rents to the lords for the use of land. This conversion to a monetary system eventually destroyed the feudal manor as the lords were squeezed by inflation and the inability of the serfs to pay their rents regularly. Eventually the serfs lost their feudal rights to the land. The *enclosure movement* from the 13th through the 18th century sealed the fate of the manorial system. Robert Heilbroner describes this process as follows in *The Making of Economic Society*:

> Starting as early as the thirteenth century, the landed aristocracy, increasingly squeezed for cash, began to view their estates not merely as the ancestral fiefs, but as potential sources of cash revenue. In order to raise larger cash crops, they therefore began to "enclose" the pasture which had previously been deemed "common land." Communal grazing fields, which had in fact always belonged to the lord despite their communal use, were now claimed for the exclusive benefit of the lord and turned into sheepwalks. Why sheepwalks? Because a rising demand for woolen cloth was making sheep-raising a highly profitable occupation.
>
> The enclosure process in England proceeded at an irregular pace over the long centuries; not until the late eighteenth and early nineteenth centuries did it reach its engulfing climax. By its end, some ten million acres, nearly *half* the arable land of England, had been "enclosed"—in its early Tudor days by the more or less high-handed conversion of the "commons" to sheep-raising; in the final period, by the forced consolidation of tenants' strips and plots into tracts suitable for large-scale commercial farming, presumably for fair compensation.
>
> From a strictly economic point of view, the enclosure movement was unquestionably salutary in that it brought into productive employment land which had hitherto yielded only a pittance. But there was another, crueler side to enclosure. As the common fields were enclosed, it became ever more difficult for the tenant to support himself. At first slowly, then with increasing rapidity, he was pressed off the land, until in the fifteenth and sixteenth centuries, when the initial enclosure of the commons reached its peak, as many as three-fourths to nine-tenths of the tenants of some estates were simply turned off the farm. Whole hamlets were thus wiped out. Sir Thomas More described it savagely in Book I of his *Utopia*.

Your sheep that were want to be so meek and tame, and so small eaters, now, as I hear say, be become so great devourers and so wild, that they eat up and swallow down the very men themselves. They consume, destroy and devour whole fields, houses and cities. For look in what parts of the realm doth grow the finest, and therefore dearest wool, there noblemen and gentlemen, yea and certain abbots, holy men Got wot, not contenting themselves with the yearly revenues and profits that were wont to grow to their forefathers and predecessors of their land . . . leave no ground for tillage, they enclose all into pastures, they throw down houses, they pluck down towns and leave nothing standing, but only the church to make of it a sheep house. . . .

The enclosure process provided a powerful force for the dissolution of feudal ties and the formation of the new relationships of a market society. By dispossessing the peasant, it "created" a new kind of labor force— landless, without traditional sources of income, however meagre, impelled to find work for wages, wherever it might be available.

—Robert L. Heilbroner, *The Making of Economic Society* (2nd ed.), © 1968, pp. 59–60. Adapted by permission of Prentice-Hall, Inc., Englewood Cliffs, N.J.

8. What similarities and/or differences do you see between the enclosure movement in Europe and the modern replacement of family farms in the United States by agribusiness corporations?

The Breakdown of the Guilds.   The process of creating a laboring class of people and the extension of the market for labor services was also accelerated by the replacement of the guilds by the *putting-out system*. Here, as in the enclosure movement, a new kind of labor force was created: a "free" labor force in which work was not a guarantee, and the individual was free to seek work for wages determined by emerging market forces.

Under the guild system of production, independent craftspeople used their own tools and shops to produce their products. The products were then sold to merchants. Production and sales were overseen by the guilds. As trade expanded and the production of manufactured goods increased, the putting-out system began in the 16th century to replace the guilds. In this arrangement, a merchant-capitalist gained control of the tools, raw materials, and work place and would hire, for wages, skilled individuals to produce the final product. Eventually this system led to the establishment of centralized industrial factories.

There were two major elements of this new system that differentiated it from the feudal guild system. First of all, production was controlled by the capitalist—the owner of tools, buildings, and other resources involved in production (i.e., the capital). This person would also arrange for the sale of product items. The goal was monetary profit. The guild no longer influenced the production and sale of the goods.

Second, this new system created a labor force that was dependent on the capitalist for work. The craftspeople no longer owned capital; they had only their skills and labor power to sell to the capitalist.

As this system further developed, markets for goods and resources determined profits for capitalists. Based on these calculations and on market relationships, rather than on the custom and tradition of feudal relations, decisions were made about who would work and for what wages, and how the work would be performed. In this way, industrial production was organized on a capitalist, rather than feudalist, basis.

The combination of the enclosure movements and the putting-out system created a new class of individuals who controlled the productive land and resources of Western Europe and whose goal was profit. In both the countryside and the city, this centralization of control and ownership resulted in increases in economic production. In addition, a new class of landless, propertyless individuals was created—people no longer tied to their hereditary lands or their crafts. This "free" labor force responded to the forces of change by attempting to sell their only resource, their labor power, at

Property rights were established following the Norman Conquest of Britain by building a castle such as this one in York. It overlooks two rivers and is perched high on a hill. Its vantage point assured the property holders that no invaders were sneaking up on them. (Photograph by Bill Cooper.)

the best possible wage. Most of these people gravitated to the cities and formed the emerging urban working class.

The Rise of Protestantism and Individualism.   The final factor contributing to the decline of feudalism concerned a change in the philosophy of much of the European population as well as a decline in the power of one of feudalism's most powerful institutions, the Catholic church. The Catholic church emphasized in its teachings a concern with afterlife and de-emphasized material life. In fact, the Church argued against lending money for interest (usury) and profit making; if people were poor, that was their station in this life (it was God's will!). This philosophy supported the role of the Church in the society and economic system, and downplayed the importance of the individual. The rise of the Protestant challenge to Catholicism weakened the controlling role of the Catholic church's feudal society. In addition, it offered a philosophy more directed toward individual salvation. Calvinism, in fact, provided a justification of profit-making as demonstrating service to God in one's "calling." Working hard, earning profits, and plowing those profits back into the business constituted circumstantial evidence that one was among God's chosen. This new religious idea and the Protestant churches as institutions, along with an increased emphasis on political freedom and liberty, supported the creation of a new *individualism*. This spirit, in turn, prompted much of the behavior necessary to the establishment of capitalist institutions.

These factors and others, as sources of change over centuries of time in Western Europe, eventually led to the destruction of feudal institutions and relationships. These were replaced by a new set of institutions and relationships that we have come to label **capitalism.**

9. **From the preceding material, list the feudal relations and institutions that were destroyed by the centuries of change in Western Europe between 1000 and 1800.**

10. **List the new relationships and institutions that were emerging to form capitalism.**

Emergent Capitalism

E. K. Hunt has provided a succinct description of what these centuries of change had wrought in terms of creating a new form of economic system. In *Property and Prophets*, he discusses the key elements and historical roots of capitalism:

Profits were accumulated as capital. *Capital* refers to the materials that are necessary for production, trade, and commerce. It consists of all tools, equipment, factories, raw materials and goods in process, means of transporting goods, and money. The essence of the capitalist system is the existence of a class of capitalists who own the capital stock. It is by virtue of their ownership of this capital that they derive their profits. These profits are then plowed back, or used to augment the capital stock. The further accumulation of capital leads to more profits, which leads to more accumulation, and the system continues in an upward spiral.

The term *capitalism* describes the system of profit-seeking and accumulation very well. Capital is the source of profits and hence the source of further accumulation of capital. But this chicken—egg process had to have a beginning. The substantial initial accumulation, or *primitive accumulation,* of capital took place [during feudalism]. The four most important sources of the initial accumulation of capital were (1) the rapidly growing volume of trade and commerce, (2) the putting-out system of industry, (3) the enclosure movement, and (4) the great price inflation. There were several other sources of initial accumulations, some of which were somewhat less respectable and often forgotten—for example, colonial plunder, piracy, and the slave trade.

During the sixteenth and seventeenth centuries the putting-out system was extended until it was common in most types of manufacturing. Although this was not yet the modern type of factory production, the system's increased degree of specialization led to significant increases in productivity. Technical improvements in shipbuilding and navigation also lowered transportation costs. Thus during this period capitalist production and trade and commerce thrived and grew very rapidly. The new capitalist class (or middle class or bourgeoisie) slowly but inexorably replaced the nobility as the class that dominated the economic and social system.

By the late 15th and early 16th century in England, France, Spain, Belgium, and Holland, capitalism was emerging, and modern nation-states involving monarchs and merchant capitalists had effectively eliminated the decentralized power of the feudal system. This new system would also change and develop, although even today it retains its basic elements of private ownership, profit making, and markets. In the following, we will briefly trace some of the most important periods in the development of Western capitalism.

MERCANTILISM

Mercantilism was a policy of the new nation-states to build and consolidate their political, economic, and military power. Trading was seen as the foundation of the nation's power and prestige. The object of trading was the accumulation and retention of gold and silver bullion. These stores of precious metals could in turn be used to finance further trade or to enhance the political and military power of the nation. Obviously, this concern led to exploration to discover and hoard more precious metals. It also led to policies designed to maximize the flow of money into the nation and minimize the flow of money out. Consequently, mercantilism developed trade monopolies to minimize the prices of imports and maximize the prices of exports, controlled importing and exporting, levied tariffs on imports, subsidized exports, and controlled shipping extensively. The state, thus, took a large degree of responsibility in geographic expansion and in controlling economic activity. At first, this sponsorship obviously aided some nascent capitalists, but the overriding control by the state over the economy eventually began to burden increasing numbers of individualistic and profit-motivated businesspeople.

THE RISE OF CLASSICAL LIBERALISM AND THE INDUSTRIAL REVOLUTION

Mercantilist restrictions gave rise in the 18th and 19th centuries to an opposition that ultimately prevailed and drastically reduced the amount of direct interference in economic affairs by the state. The movement to end mercantilism was spearheaded by a new philosophical and economic body of thought—**classical liberalism.** In 1776, the Scottish philosopher Adam Smith published *The Wealth of Nations,* in which he argued very strongly that mercantilist policies interfered with the ability of private individuals and markets to produce maximum social welfare. Smith felt that, although everyone was basically out to maximize his or her own welfare, private *competition* in production and consumption would ensure the best possible outcome for all. Therefore Smith argued forcefully that the state should not be involved in economic activity, and that beyond providing for law and order, national defense, and some public goods like highways, the state should take a laissez-faire attitude toward the economic system. Individuals would guide production and consumption.

This philosophy was seized by the emerging capitalist class in Western Europe and used eventually to legislate an end to most mercantilist restrictions on trade and other economic activity. Left to their own devices and the profit motive, English capitalists took early advantage of the technological advances of the Industrial Revolution. The introduction of more sophisticated machinery in textiles, transportation, iron production, and other industries led to a fantastic increase in the productive capacity of the English economic system. The Industrial Revolution, as well as the entrepreneurs who financed and led it, spread throughout Western Europe and to North America. However, the increase in production was not all the Industrial Revolution and emergent capitalism brought with them, as Heilbroner explains:

> We must pay heed to another immediate and visible result of the industrial revolution in England. We can characterize it as the transformation of an essentially commercial and agricultural society into one in which industrial manufacture became the dominant mode of organizing economic life. To put it more concretely, the industrial revolution was characterized by *the rise of the factory to the center of social as well as economic life.* After 1850, the factory was not only the key economic institution of England, but it was the economic institution that shaped its politics, its social problems, the character of its daily life, just as decisively as the manor or the guild had done a few centuries earlier.

The factory provided not merely a new landscape but a new and uncongenial social habitat. . . . For the peasant, this transfer requires a drastic adjustment. No longer does he work at his own pace, but at the pace of a machine. No longer are slack seasons determined by the weather, but by the state of the market. No longer is the land, however miserable its crop, an eternal source of sustenance close at hand, but only the packed and sterile earth of the industrial site.

Distasteful as was the advent of the factory itself, even more distasteful were the conditions within it. Child labor, for instance, was commonplace and sometimes began at age four; hours of work were generally dawn to dusk; abuses of every kind were all too frequent.

It was a grim age. The long hours of work, the general dirt and clangor of the factories, the lack of even the most elementary safety precautions, all combined to give early industrial capitalism a reputation from which, in the minds of many people of the world, it has never recovered. Worse yet were the slums to which the majority of workers returned after their travail. A government commissioner reports on one such workers' quarter in Glasgow called "the wynds."

> The wynds . . . house a fluctuating population between 15,000 and 30,000 persons. This district is composed of many narrow streets and square courts and in the middle of each court there is a dunghill. Although the outward appearance of these places was revolting, I was nevertheless quite unprepared for the filth and misery that were to be found inside. In some bedrooms we visited at night we found a whole mass of humanity stretched on the floor. There were often 15 to 20 men and women huddled together, some being clothed and others naked. There was hardly any furniture there and the only thing which gave these holes the appearance of a dwelling was fire burning on the hearth. Thieving and prostitution are the main sources of income of these people.*

—Robert L. Heilbroner, *The Making of Economic Society* (2nd ed.) Copyright © 1968, pp. 81–82. Adapted by permission of Prentice-Hall, Inc., Englewood Cliffs, N.J.

11. Why were capitalists and classical liberals opposed to mercantilism?

12. Why was early capitalism so unmindful of the social effects of industrialization brought on by the Industrial Revolution?

The emergence of capitalism and a free market for labor encouraged, as well as fed on, the Industrial Revolution. These forces produced rapid economic growth and the factory system, as well as urban slums and adverse working conditions. Central to

*Quoted in F. Engels, *The Condition of the Working Class in England in 1844* (New York: Macmillan, 1958), p. 46.

these changes was the spread of markets for goods and services throughout Western Europe and the world. With the diminution of the roles of tradition, custom, and the state in the economic affairs of Western Europeans, capitalism relied increasingly on *markets* to organize production and distribution.

As factors of production, land, labor, and capital all became commodities that were bought and sold on markets for prices. This required the emergence of a market system in which producers made calculations, based on prices of resources and products and directed toward the accumulation of profits. Economic activity was thus directed through the operation of these markets and the determination of prices in them. Again, land, labor, and capital became commodities. This was in contrast to the feudal system, wherein land and labor were part of the social organization of communities (feudal manors and guilds) and were regulated by social custom, tradition, and institutions. With the emergence of capitalism, land and labor became subject to the market for their occupation and use. In this way, as the late historian Karl Polanyi has argued in *The Great Transformation,* capitalism required the subordination of social considerations to the economic dictates of the private market system. Production and distribution were organized, for the society, through markets.

13. What is the significance of markets to capitalism?

THE DEVELOPMENT OF CAPITALISM IN THE UNITED STATES

As capitalism was forming in Europe, many of its institutions and relationships were transplanted to the American colonies. When the colonists eventually removed the yoke of English political and economic control during the American Revolution, the way was cleared for the formation and development of the United States' own form of capitalism. However, the Americans retained their debt to Western civilization, thought, and institutions. This lineage was important to the establishment of emerging capitalist attitudes and institutions in the colonies and their continuance after the Revolution. Most of the colonists were Protestants who emphasized individualism and hard work. Private ownership of rural and urban production was the dominant form of economic organization. International and domestic trade flourished with the goal of private gain and profit. Markets developed and guided production. In the early years of the new nation, the government utilized mercantilist policies of controlling international trade to foster economic development and to protect the emergence of the United States as a Western nation-state.

Economic Development

Before we proceed with a brief overview of the economic history of the United States, it is important to define the term **economic development.** As was suggested at the beginning of this chapter, all societies must organize themselves for the production and distribution of goods and services. The methods and institutions for accomplishing these tasks constitute a society's economic system. Over time, as we have seen in the transition from feudalism to capitalism, economic systems change. Economic development represents progressive changes in the ability of a society to meet its economic tasks of production and distribution. Economic development contains two key elements. One concerns the total amount of goods and services that are produced and available for consumption, and the other concerns institutions. Economic development occurs when a society is able to increase its total output; it experiences economic growth through the generation and usage of its economic surplus. Very often a society's ability to produce such growth is a function of the second element of economic development. This concerns the changes in the economic institutions, relationships, and methods of the society. If the society experiences changes in its economic institutions, relationships, and methods that make it better prepared to produce a growing volume of goods and services for its people, then development will occur. The discovery of new resources will encourage economic development, as will technological improvements in the methods of production. The spread of education and attitudes toward work may facilitate the ability of a society to produce goods and services. Economic development is obviously of crucial importance to any society and its continued survival. We will now turn to a brief consideration of the development of capitalism in the United States.

The Sources of U.S. Development

Throughout its first hundred years as a nation, the United States was primarily an agricultural economy. Through the mid-1870s, agricultural output accounted for more than half of total production, but by the mid-1880s the value of manufactured goods surpassed the value of agricultural goods in total U.S. production. It was also at this time that the nonagricultural portion of the labor force first outnumbered those who worked on farms. It wasn't until about 1920 that the nation's urban population surpassed the rural population. Despite the country's being primarily rural and agricultural, the development of industry began early in the 19th century. Industrial production accelerated during the middle years of the 19th century, stimulated in part by the demands of the Civil War. By the turn of the century, the United States was the world's leading producer of both manufactured and agricultural goods.

What accounts for this tremendous economic achievement? One important source of American economic development, which is often neglected, was the role of the government. In the formative years of the nation, the government played a crucial role in the construction of a federal system in which economic trade flowed freely from one state to another. Indeed, this concern with encouraging trade within the United States was one of the primary reasons behind the construction and ratification of the Constitution. In addition, the government passed tariffs to protect infant industries, it established a national currency, and it created a legal framework that governed economic transactions. In the 19th century, federal, state, and local governments financed and encouraged the development of different forms of transportation that facilitated the internal trade in the expanding nation.

Another source of growth was the vast supply of land and resources available to the United States. The country expanded westward throughout the 18th century. This expansion was made possible by conquering one after another of the Native American tribes, by the purchase of land from France and Russia, and by military conquest over Mexico and several European countries that still controlled land in North America. Through what Americans called Manifest Destiny, the United States eventually controlled the middle part of the North American continent from coast to coast. This expanding geographical territory supplied space for expansion and raw materials for increasing agricultural and industrial production. It also supplied an expanding volume of cotton and wheat exports for sale to Europe. This international market encouraged further agricultural production and made possible imports that facilitated industrial production.

At the end of the 19th and the beginning of the 20th century, the United States joined Western European countries in the process of expansion beyond their borders. American imperialism, as the nation pursued Manifest Destiny beyond the North American continent into the Pacific, Asia, and Latin America, provided raw materials, markets, and investments that fueled further economic expansion.

The American people themselves, both the original colonists and the later immigrants, proved to be an important source of growth and development. Strongly individualistic and dedicated to hard work, they took risks, organized productive activities, educated themselves, invented, and conquered. The United States became a thriving and growing economy through a primarily private economic system based on the efforts of individuals and groups of individuals tied together through an expanding system of national markets for goods and services.

Coincident with all of these sources of growth, many institutions emerged to stimulate development. The banking system, retail and wholesale organizations, and the transportation system facilitated the expansion of economic activity with improved organization and lower costs. Related to the development of these sectors of the economy was the emergence of one of the foremost institutions of American capitalism and economic production, the corporation. A legal combination of individuals, the *corporation* was a successful device for amassing resources for organizing and engaging in production. And in several leading industries—oil, the railroads, banking, steel, automobiles, and so on—large corporations led the advance of American growth. In a sense, the history of the American corporation and its development is the history of modern American capitalism.

By the middle of the 20th century, the United States was the dominant economic, political, and military country in the world. It was the most advanced nation in terms of manufacturing and agricultural techniques and production. It had the highest standard of living, on the average, for its almost 200 million citizens. And it was still a nation that valued individual economic and political freedom. For the most part its development had been a success story.

Negative Aspects of U.S. Development

However, throughout its history, there have also been some negative aspects in American economic development. The conquest and exploitation of the American

Indians must be counted as—and remain as—a black mark in our history. Slavery throughout the colonial period and until the Civil War relied on the inhuman subjugation and exploitation of human beings as sources of increased production. As both economic and political power became more concentrated, scandals of political and economic corruption have been rife throughout our history. The latter part of the 19th century was marked by the industrialization of the U.S. economy, but it also witnessed the abuses of the "robber barons." The robber barons were entrepreneurs who were generally successful as well as ruthless in their business practices. In the process of consolidating the leading industries of the economy, promoting technological developments, building giant corporations, and amassing great personal fortunes, such men as Jay Gould, Andrew Carnegie, J. P. Morgan, and John D. Rockefeller bilked their partners, eliminated their competitors, underpaid their workers, and/or overcharged many of their customers. In addition, throughout U.S. economic history, there have been instances when private economic power has led to political corruption, ranging from the Crédit Mobilier affair of the 1870s to the Teapot Dome scandal of the 1920s to more recent instances of illegal corporate campaign contributions in the United States and bribery abroad.

During the development of the American economy through the present, our country has been plagued by a host of problems that are of an economic origin or at least have an economic dimension. These include poverty, commercialism, pollution, militarism, racism, and sexism. These problems continue to challenge our economic institutions, relationships, and methods.

An additional negative aspect of American capitalist development has been its instability. Throughout the late 19th and early 20th centuries, the United States suffered through repeated depressions in economic activity. Periods of prosperity and boom were regularly followed by periods of depression and bust. Figure 1.1 graphically depicts this pattern.

During these depressions, unemployment and economic hardship for many people increased dramatically and tragically. The worst of these depressions occurred in the 1930s, when the decrease in economic activity spread around the world. In 1933, almost one-third of the work force in the United States was without employment. The Great Depression was deep and lasted throughout the 1930s.

This depression and our "escape" from it with the increased production and employment brought about by World War II, in fact, engendered one of the more recent alterations in the American form of capitalism. Given the historical instability of capitalism's growth process, the U.S. government since the 1930s has taken a more direct responsibility for the overall health of the economy. It has attempted to prevent extremes in the cycles of boom-and-bust. Some would call this mixed capitalism; others might call it state capitalism. Still others, noting the role of the state and the role of large corporations in the economy, call it monopoly capitalism. At any rate, this expanded economic role of the state constitutes one more major change in the continuing development of American capitalism as an economic system.

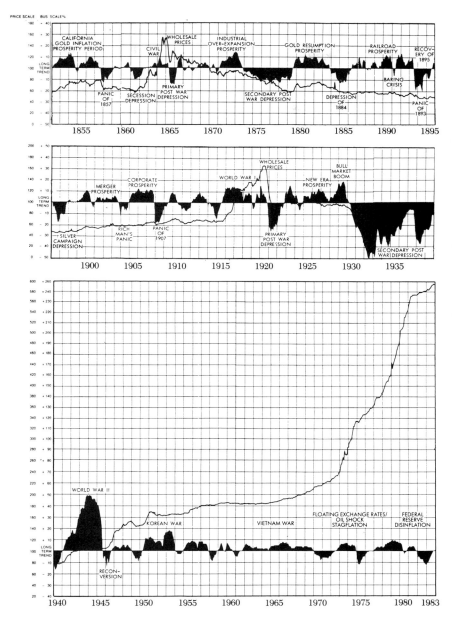

Figure 1.1   Economic instability in the United States. The chart shows the fluctuations around the long-run trend of growth in per-capita output for the United States. Also shown are the changes in the wholesale price index (1926 = 100).

(From *American Business Activity from 1790 to Today*, Ameritrust, Cleveland, Ohio.)

14. On the basis of your conception of the American economic system, list its five most important attributes. Are these positive or negative attributes? Are they results of the system? Or are they fundamental characteristics of it?

15. What's your name, or label, for our economic system? Why do you call it that?

Post—World War II Experience

Following the demobilization of the economy after World War II, the United States experienced a quarter century of almost unprecedented economic growth and prosperity. During this time, there were of course periodic recessions, but the average standard of living increased at a rate of about 3 percent per year. There were several bases to this era of prosperity. One was that the country emerged from the war as the world's leading military, economic, and political power, with its production base fully intact. From this position, it became the leader in establishing a new international economic trading and financial system that stimulated U.S. and Western economies. Following the Depression and the war, the federal government, partly based on Keynesian economics (see Part IV), assumed increased responsibility for the general health of the economy and for maintaining prosperity. Building on the labor legislation of the New Deal, which granted labor unions the right to organize and collectively bargain, and the labor peace of the war period, big business and organized labor adopted a system of labor relations that minimized conflict and disruptions in production. Corporations themselves became larger and vigorously pursued profit-making possibilities both here and abroad. The result of these and other conditions was vigorous economic growth and the world's highest standard of living.

However, beginning in the late 1960s and early 1970s, the bases of this postwar prosperity began to break down, and specific events undermined the overall health of the U.S. economy. Consequently, at the beginning of the 1980s, we found ourselves plagued with stagflation—high unemployment (stagnation) and high inflation—an energy crisis, and a general economic malaise. The causes of this "crisis" in the economy were many, and they will be explored to some extent in the remainder of this book. But it would be useful to mention a few of them briefly here. The United States had lost power in the world, partly as a result of its defeat in Vietnam, but also because of the increased power of other countries in the world, including Germany, France, Japan, and the Soviet Union. The United States encountered more effective competition in world markets. Third World countries assumed increased independence, nationalizing some American corporations and adopting independent economic policies. Along these lines, the actions of the OPEC (Organization of Petroleum Exporting Countries) countries forced the United States to come to grips with expensive and scarce energy resources. The commitment to avoid depressions through the use of governmental economic policies had given the economy an inflationary bias. The relationship between big business and big labor also contributed to an inflationary spiral, with prices and wages moving ever upward. Inflationary expectations further fueled inflation. And there were many other problems as well, including declining productivity, the tax revolt, deregulation, racial and sexual discrimination, continued poverty, and so on.

The Early 1980s

In evaluating the operation of the economy and how it changes over time, economists try to measure different types of economic activity. By measuring economic activity over time, we can develop a sense of how the economy is performing. During the rest of this text, we will identify many different economic variables—the unemployment rate, the rate of inflation, gross national product, investment spending, productivity, and many others. Table 1.1 contains information on some important economic variables for the United States and how they changed over the post–World War II period.

As Table 1.1 indicates, the U.S. economy performed much less successfully in the 1970s than it had in the 1950s and 1960s. The unemployment rate and the rate of inflation were both higher, on average, than they had been in the previous two decades. Average gross weekly earnings, after taking inflation into account, actually decreased during the 1970s. The rate of increase of total output per labor hour and the rate of increase of real total output both decreased. The economy was growing at a slower rate, and the rate of profit for corporations was lower than it had been in

Table 1.1 SELECTED MEASURES OF ECONOMIC PERFORMANCE IN THE 1950s, 1960s, AND 1970s

	1950s	1960s	1970s
Unemployment rate (annual average, percent)	4.5	4.8	6.2
Rate of inflation (annual average increase in consumer prices, percent)	2.0	2.3	7.1
Average gross weekly earnings (annual average increase, in constant dollars, percent)	2.1	1.3	−0.8
Output per labor hour (annual average increase, percent)	2.6	2.8	1.6
Real output per capita (annual average increase, percent)	1.2	3.3	2.2
Rate of profit, after taxes (annual average, as percent of fixed capital stock)	7.7	8.3	6.2
Rate of net investment (annual average, as percent of net national product)	7.7	7.2	6.0

Sources: Economic Report of the President, 1984, and Bureau of Economic Analysis, Department of Commerce.

both the 1950s and the 1960s. In addition, net investment, one of the most important sources of economic growth, was declining as a percent of total output.

Consequently, as the United States entered the 1980s, its economic system was plagued with high unemployment and inflation and low rates of economic growth. For 1979–1981, real output grew by less than 2 percent per year. The unemployment rate was above 7 percent. Consumer prices were increasing at a rate of 12 to 13 percent a year. The real average weekly earnings for nonagricultural workers in 1980 were less than they had been in 1963. Interest rates were at historic highs. In 1981, the rate that banks charged their best corporate customers for loans was close to 20 percent! The federal deficit was beginning to increase and reached the $50 billion range in 1980 and 1981. And the value of the dollar in international exchange was at its lowest levels for the entire post–World War II period.

These various economic difficulties became a primary concern of economists and the centerpiece of the 1980 presidential campaign. The "Reagan Revolution" utilized the analysis of monetarist and supply-side economics to explain the slowdown in the economy and to develop a package of economic policies that came to be known as "Reaganomics." (In Parts IV, V, and VI, we will go into much more detail about the recent performance of the U.S. economy, the various explanations for it, and different suggestions for improving its results.)

Very simply, Reagan argued that the country's economic difficulties were a result of too little economic growth. The source of the problem, he argued, was the excessive role of the government in the economy. There was too much regulation of business, there was too much government spending on social programs, taxes were too high on corporations and individuals, and there was too rapid an increase in the money supply. All of this resulted in too much demand for output and not enough production to meet that demand—hence, slow growth and inflation. The solution was to increase the incentives and the rewards for the private sector. This would unleash corporations and individuals, and we would witness a massive surge in work and investment. The economy would grow more rapidly; we would have economic prosperity with price stability once again.

The policies that President Reagan instituted and passed through Congress included a three-year tax-cut package on both individual and corporate income taxes, reductions in federal spending on a variety of social programs, deregulation in a variety of industries and business practices, a slowdown in the rate of growth of the money supply (actually the responsibility of the Federal Reserve System; see Chapter 22), and an increase in military spending to restore American power in the world. What have been the results of this program?

The immediate result of tighter money and cutbacks in federal spending was a severe recession in 1981 and 1982. Real output actually declined in 1982, and the unemployment rate rose above 10 percent during 1982. In 1983, however, the economy began to recover. Real output increased steadily throughout 1983, 1984, and 1985, and the unemployment rate began to decline very slowly. Along with the recession, the rate of inflation dropped precipitously to just below 4 percent, but workers' average wages also continued to fall. With the recovery, the rate of productivity growth (output per hour) increased and investment spending also began to increase. As a result of the recession, the tax cuts, and the massive increase in military spending, however, the federal deficit mushroomed to annual levels of close to $200 billion for 1983–1985. All of these measurements suggest that there has been some improvement in the economy but that there are significant problems as we head into the late 1980s.

During the remainder of the 1980s, we will continue to discuss and debate these issues and what to do about them. Was the 1983–1985 recovery the result of Reaganomics? Or was it just a normal expansion in a typical business cycle? What will be the results of the enormous federal deficits? Will inflation be rekindled as the economic expansion continues? Will we persist in increasing military spending and in reducing social spending? Should taxes be increased or decreased? Should businesses and their activities be further deregulated? All of these economic questions, and others, were actively debated by Ronald Reagan–George Bush and Walter Mondale–Geraldine Ferraro during the 1984 presidential election. And they will remain with us through the rest of the 1980s and into the 1990s.

The American economy has come a long way in the 200-year history of our independent nation. It has largely been a history of successful development—not, however, without negative aspects and events. The United States has the world's largest and most industrialized economy. As we entered the 1980s, however, stagflation, the energy crisis, and the role of major institutions in the economy shook our confidence and raised serious questions about the future health and progress of the U.S. economy. It is certain that the politics of the rest of the 1980s will be focused on the future development of U.S. capitalism.

With this brief introduction to the roots and evolution of our economic system, we will now turn our attention to "economics." What is economics? Now that we know something about economic systems, what they do, and how they change, what can economists tell us about them?

KEY CONCEPTS

economic system
feudalism
capitalism
production
factors of production—land, labor,
    capital
consumption
distribution

surplus
manor
guilds
the transition from feudalism to
    capitalism
mercantilism
classical liberalism
economic development

REVIEW QUESTIONS

1. Discuss the distinguishing characteristics of ancient economic systems.

2. What must an economic system accomplish? Why?

3. Why is surplus a source of economic growth?

4. Explain the transition from feudalism to capitalism, and identify the main differences between the two systems.

5. What is the importance of markets to a capitalist economic system?

6. What accounts for the success of the American economy?

7. Given Hunt's description of capitalism in this chapter, do you think the United States today has a capitalist economy? What are the major characteristics of capitalism?

8. Reread the passage by Karl Marx at the beginning of the chapter. Paraphrase his point in the last paragraph. Do you agree with his argument? Why or why not?

9. "The results of economic activity—what gets produced and how it gets produced—organized through an economic system, condition the nature, history and development of a society and its people." Give examples from the recent history of the United States. Give examples from your own experience.

10. "Economic development is obviously of crucial importance to any society and its continued survival." Why is this *obvious*? What would happen to a society if it didn't experience economic development? What are the advantages of economic development? Do you think that economic development has advantages for you? What are they?

SUGGESTED READINGS

Douglas Dowd, 1977. *The Twisted Dream: Capitalist Development in the U.S. since 1776*, Winthrop. A critical but extensive treatment of the development of the U.S. economy.

Robert Heilbroner, 1980. *The Making of Economic Society*, Prentice-Hall. This is a relatively brief introductory historical treatment of the emergence and development of Western capitalism, from its roots in feudalism to its modern manifestations. Very well written and readable.

Robert Heilbroner and Aaron Singer, 1984. *The Economic Transformation of America*, Harcourt, Brace, Jovanovich. A very readable economic history of the United States, with a good section on the industrialization period.

E. K. Hunt, 1981. *Property and Prophets*, Harper & Row. Also an introductory history of the roots of modern economic institutions. In addition, this work concentrates on the relationship of social and economic change to the development of ideas.

Douglass C. North, 1983. *Growth and Welfare in the American Past*, Prentice-Hall. A brief economic history of the United States, chock-full of interesting data detailing the economic progress of the country.

Karl Polanyi, 1973. *The Great Transformation*, Octagon. A more advanced treatment of the withering of feudalism and the introduction of the market as one of the central foundations of the capitalist economic system.

William Appleman Williams, 1973. *The Contours of American History*, New Viewpoints. An extended social, political, and economic history of the United States written from a critical perspective.

2

Chapter

Economics as a Social Science

INTRODUCTION

Now that we have briefly examined some economic history, what is economics? And what can it do for us?

Economics is the study of how the productive and distributive aspects of human life are organized. It studies the history of production, distribution, and consumption of goods and services in different societies and countries *and* how these aspects have changed over time. Economics, as a social science, is thus an accumulation of human knowledge about one particular segment of social life. It seeks to help us to understand the complexities and confusions of our economic system in the modern world.

In this chapter, we will examine the elements of economics as one of the social sciences. We will be concerned with its goals and its methods, as well as its relevance to our lives. In addition, we will introduce briefly the different branches of economics and the kinds of things that economists do. Finally, we will see that *economists* have some disagreements about what economics is and ought to be.

WHAT IS ECONOMICS?

In recent years, teachers of economics have become concerned about how best to teach economics. Their concern stems from the importance of economic knowledge in the modern world and from their occasional inability to teach that knowledge to students in a way that will prove useful to them. Out of this concern, many economists have attempted to define precisely what the key elements of economic understanding are and to concentrate on teaching these. Several of these economists, working with the Joint Council on Economic Education, have published a booklet called *A Framework for Teaching Economics: Basic Concepts*.* In this piece, they point out the following key elements of economic understanding: practicing a reasoned approach, mastering the basic concepts, possessing an overview of the economy, identifying the issues, applying these elements to particular issues, and reaching decisions on economic issues.

These elements provide some insights into what economics is. Economics is the study of how the productive and distributive aspects of human life are organized. In addition, economics is a body of knowledge and a way of thinking about the economic aspects of social life. It is concerned with "practicing a reasoned approach"; that is, economics presents an organized and logical way of thinking about economic reality. It utilizes many basic concepts that focus our attention on key variables in economic activity. It provides us with an overall appreciation of the structure and complexity of the economic system in our country, as well as in others. It should help us to identify the issues that will be important to us in our individual and social lives. In addition, economics help us to reason and to draw conclusions about specific economic problems, their ramifications, and possible solutions.

One of the central concerns of economics in attempting to accomplish all of these tasks is the development of **economic theory.** This relates to the *method* of economics. While it is concerned with social life and the vagaries of human beings, it also attempts as nearly as possible to be scientific.

The Method of Economics

Economists attempt to measure and collect facts about economic activity. In doing so, they try to discover certain similarities in the relationships between different components of economic life. These similarities can, when they are accepted as expressing a constant relationship (in normal circumstances), become economic theories. An example of such a theory would be the theory of supply and demand. We can use this economic theory to gain insight into the nature of certain goods and services—how they are valued by society's members, how costly they are to produce, and what *price* they will sell for in the society, given different circumstances.

The function of economic theory, therefore, is to allow us to examine certain limited aspects of economic life, to discover more or less constant relationships between different economic variables, and to predict possible economic events in the future. For example, the theory of supply and demand tells us that, most of the time,

---

*W. Lee Hansen, Chairman; G. L. Bach, James D. Calderwood, and Phillip Saunders. *A Framework for Teaching Economics: Basic Concepts*, Joint Council on Economic Education, 1977.

THE METHOD OF ECONOMIC THEORY

Milton Friedman, a Nobel Prize winner in economics, has argued for a particular method in the construction of economic theory. It is what he calls "positive economics." This methodology has four basic components.

1. The process begins with a set of reasonable *assumptions* about some aspect of economic behavior. For example, in Part III of this text, one of the most important assumptions that we will make is that the primary objective of firms is the maximization of their profits.

2. Next, we identify some important economic *concepts* and construct some variables to measure them. For the firm, we will identify profits, costs, revenues, marginal costs, marginal revenues, and others. These variables are all functions of the economic activity of the firm.

3. Based on the assumptions that we have made and the concepts that we have identified, we proceed to the development of some *hypotheses* and logical deductions about economic behavior. In the case of the firm, we theorize that profits are maximized when the firm's marginal costs are equal to its marginal revenues. In Part III, we will demonstrate this.

4. The final step is to *test the theory*. Does the hypothesis conform with observable events? When marginal costs do not equal marginal revenues, does the firm alter its decisions so it can increase its profits?

Friedman emphasizes that this method produces abstract economic theory; it simplifies and generalizes. The purpose, however, is to create a model of the economy that will assist us in evaluating and analyzing the real world economy. A model is an abstraction, or a simplification, of the economy, not an exact replica of it.

a desired article in short supply will command a relatively high price. From this, we can conclude (theorize) that *if* the supply of that article is reduced, its price is likely to go up even further. Note that such statements are based on an **assumption**—an *if* statement—followed by a conditional conclusion. Economists love to make assumptions. Much of their theory is based on similar assumptions. In the final analysis, however, their theories must be judged by whether their conclusions and predictions conform with what actually happens in economic reality.

In the case of supply-and-demand theory, there are frequent examples that enable us to check out the validity of the conclusions and predictions of economic theory. For example, in 1973, when the Arab oil-producing countries embargoed shipments of oil to the United States, Western Europe, and Japan, the supply of oil

I'd like you to meet Marty Thorndecker. He's an economist but he's really very nice.

Drawing by Ed Arno. Copyright © 1974, The New Yorker Magazine, Inc.

decreased and the price *did* increase. Likewise, when there are good crops of wheat in the United States, the price of wheat is likely to go down; or when crops are bad because of the weather, the price of wheat goes up. In 1980, because of a hot spell, the peanut crop was reduced in supply, and the price of peanut butter skyrocketed! In 1983, a freeze reduced the supply of Florida oranges, and this was followed by an increase in the price of oranges. In each of these cases, economic reality conforms with economic theory.

This aspect of economics highlights its *relevance*. Economics and economic theories are concerned with problems and activities that are crucial and/or important to all of us as individuals and to our societies. The scope of economics can be national, international, regional, local, or personal. The problems and activities that are the subject matter of economics include the following: inflation, productivity, supplies of natural resources, efficiency, debt, unemployment, technological development, product distribution, advertising, poverty, alienation, the allocation of scarce resources, income redistribution, taxation, war, and a host of others. Economics identifies such economic problems, describes their ramifications, hypothesizes about their causes, predicts their future development, and prescribes solutions to them. Economics seeks to build up our understanding of and knowledge about the fundamental economic aspects of our social lives.

Economics and Economists

There are many branches of economics, some of which will be introduced in this book. Economic history focuses on how and why economic activity has changed over time. Urban economics focuses on analyzing the economic operation and problems of cities. Microeconomics is concerned primarily with the activities of smaller economic units, such as the household or the firm. Macroeconomics has the much broader subject of the operation and health of an entire national economy. International economics deals with economic relationships and activities on a global scale. Economic thought treats the development of ideas by economists through the years. Economic development concentrates on theories and problems associated with the economic growth and maturation of national economies. Public policy economics is concerned with the analysis of proposals for dealing with public problems. Political economy highlights the relationships between economic and political institutions and how they affect each other. This by no means exhausts the list of the different branches of economics.

Given this wide variety of branches of economics, there are lots of different things that economists do. Many people trained in economics as a discipline become teachers of economics in high schools, colleges, or universities. Many work in businesses attempting to inform decision makers on current and future economic realities. Since World War II, an increasing number of economists have found employment in government at the state, local, and federal levels. Economists also work for consulting firms, labor unions, public interest or lobbying groups, and international organizations.

With this diversity of employment experiences (and hence allegiances and perspectives), it should not be very surprising that there is a healthy amount of "confusion" within the social science of economics. Economists, despite their efforts to build economic theory, often disagree among themselves and fall into different camps. They may differ about which problems are most important (or even, sometimes, that there *are* problems!), about what the causes of a problem are, and about which solutions to a problem are the best. Controversy in economics reflects controversy in life.

Nevertheless, there is also a large core of economic ideas that is accepted by most economists. We will study many of these ideas in this book. In addition, economists are unified by the goal of economics: building knowledge about the economic aspects of life.

Much of the debate among economists about what economics is and should be concerns its scope. The famous English economist Alfred Marshall (1842–1924) thought that economics could be one of the most precise and scientific of the social sciences because it dealt with observable and measurable data in the form of prices, quantities produced and sold, and incomes. In his *Principles of Economics*, he wrote:

> The advantage which economics has over other branches of social science appears then to arise from the fact that its special field of work gives rather large opportunities for exact methods than any other branch. It concerns itself chiefly with those desires, aspirations and other affections of human nature, the outward manifestations of which appear as incentives to action in such a form that the force or quantity of the incentives can be estimated and measured with some approach to accuracy; and which therefore are in some degree amenable to treatment by scientific machinery. An opening is made for the methods and the tests of science as soon as the force of a

person's motives—*not* the motives themselves—can be approximately measured by the sum of money, which he will just give up in order to secure a desired satisfaction; or again by the sum which is just required to induce him to undergo a certain fatigue.

—Alfred Marshall, *Principles of Economics,* Macmillan Publishing Co., Inc., 1948.

Other economists, however, have been less convinced by this argument. They point out that economics, as one of the social sciences, cannot divorce itself from the society in which it exists. The efforts of human beings to understand reality must necessarily be influenced by morality, ideology, and value judgments. In other words, economics cannot be totally scientific because the economist's understanding of the subject matter is affected by his or her evaluation of, opinions about, and conclusions concerning social reality. Economics as a body of thought functions to preserve, to protect, and/or to challenge existing social reality—as well as to help us to understand it. For some economists, then, economics should be a part of the effort to understand *and to improve* social existence. Joan Robinson (1903–1983), another English economist, wrote in *Freedom and Necessity*:

The methods to which the natural sciences owe their success—controlled experiment and exact observation of continually recurring phenom-ena—cannot be applied to the study of human beings by human beings. So far, no equally successful method of establishing reliable natural laws has been suggested.

Certainly, the social sciences should not be unscientific. Their prac-titioners should not jump to conclusions on inadequate evidence or pro-pound circular statements that are true by definition as though they had some factual content; when they disagree they should not resort to abuse like theologians or literary critics, but should calmly set about to in-vestigate the nature of the difference and to propose a plan of research to resolve it. . . .

The function of social science is quite different from that of the nat-ural sciences—it is to provide society with an organ of self-consciousness.

Every interconnected group of human beings has to have an ideolo-gy—that is, a conception of what is the proper way to behave and the permissible pattern of relationships in family, economic, and political life.

—Joan Robinson, *Freedom and Necessity,* Pantheon Books, 1970.

For Robinson, then, economics must attempt to be scientific and rigorous; but since it is also concerned with the effort to create a better society, it must also devote itself to exploring areas that are more philosophical in nature. It must recognize its ideological elements.

Along these lines, economists often divide themselves between "economics" and what is called "**political economy**." Economics is more concerned with explaining what can be measured and with developing theories about "purely" economic rela-tionships. Political economy, on the other hand, is more concerned with the rela-tionships of the economic system and its institutions to the rest of society and social development. It is sensitive to the influence of noneconomic factors such as political and social institutions, morality, ideology, and so on in determining economic events. Economics has a narrower and political economy a broader focus.

1. **"The function of social science . . . is to provide society with an organ of self-consciousness." What does this mean? How does economics do this?**

2. **What, according to Robinson, is an ideology? What role do ideologies play in social development?**

3. **What does Robinson think is the task of economics as a social science? Do you agree with her or not? Would Alfred Marshall?**

PARADIGMS AND IDEOLOGIES

As we have seen, economists disagree about what economics is and should be. Furthermore, they often disagree about what economic problems are important, what theories are correct, and what economic policies are best. This is especially true over time, as the economic problems a society is likely to face *change* with changing conditions. Along with changes in economic problems and economic institutions over time, economic theories have also changed. This aspect of changing economic theory and of differences among economists has two results that will be useful to keep in mind while studying economics. The first is that there are different and sometimes contesting kinds of economic theory, and the second is that there are different kinds of economists with different goals, values, and beliefs.

The Realm of Theory

First of all, different periods of economic history (and different economic systems) have given rise to different types of economic theories. That is, new types of economic conditions and economic institutions have required different systems of thought and explanation.

For example, as capitalism emerged as an economic system, so did classical liberalism as an economic theory. Stated slightly differently, as crises developed in economic matters as the old gave way to the new, economic institutions changed; and finally, economic thought also changed. The previous theories and notions were inadequate to explain the new conditions and problems. Thomas Kuhn, in *The Structure of Scientific Revolutions,* has referred to such changes in scientific theory as changes in **paradigms.** This concept can be applied to the natural sciences as well as to the social sciences. A paradigm serves to structure thought about a certain aspect of nature, life, or society. A paradigm delineates the questions to be asked about a certain subject and what things are to be explained (i.e., the scope of the discipline). It further establishes the criteria by which explanations are accepted (i.e., the method of the discipline).

Paradigms are usually *widely accepted* as providing a coherent and correct understanding of some aspect of life. However, as time passes, natural and social conditions change, new interpretations and new facts become known, and the existing paradigm may be challenged or may be inadequate to explain reality. If this happens, eventually a new and more widely accepted paradigm will be developed. An example of this in the scientific world was the replacement of the Ptolemaic by the Copernican conception of astronomy and the universe. The Copernican conception is now widely accepted, because it conforms with what we know and observe—that the planets revolve around the sun. In physics, there is a pre-Newtonian system and a Newtonian system. And now physicists are speculating about the existence of sub-atomic particles (quarks) as the basis of physical reality. Still another example is our debt to Christopher Columbus because he was sure that the earth wasn't flat!

In addition to changing paradigms over time, there is the possibility that two contending paradigms will seek to explain the same aspect of reality. Examining the same events and facts but differing on the use of key concepts and relationships, these contending paradigms will offer sometimes conflicting (or at least differing) interpretations of reality. At one time or another, or in different places, one or the other might be dominant. Marxian economists and orthodox economists have different interpretations of American business cycles and other economic phenomena. But in the United States, orthodox economics is dominant.

This process of changing and conflicting paradigms will also be emphasized in our study of economics. As economic crises occur and economic conditions change, one economic paradigm will replace another. Keynesian economics emerged as the dominant economic theory out of the Great Depression of the 1930s, replacing classical economics. Classical economics argued that a laissez-faire, self-regulating market economic system would eliminate instability through the flexibility of markets. If there was overproduction of goods and, consequently, a decrease in production and an increase in unemployment (that is, a depression in economic activity), then the markets would respond to correct the situation. Wherever there was an oversupply of goods, prices would fall and stimulate consumption of those goods, thus eliminating the surplus. Likewise, wages would fall and stimulate the hiring of unemployed workers by business. Classical economics relied on Say's law, developed by the French economist J. B. Say (1767–1832), which held that supply created its own demand, to explain why overproduction or underconsumption would be unlikely in a laissez-faire market economic system. Say theorized that incomes paid out in the process of production would always be sufficient to buy what was produced. Furthermore, the flexibility of prices and wages in self-regulating markets would ensure the result.

However, as we have seen, capitalist economies were and have been very unstable, with alternating periods of prosperity and depression. The weakness of Say's law was especially pronounced in the severity and persistence of the Great Depression. Consequently, a new theory, a new paradigm, Keynesian economics (about which we will learn more in Part IV) emerged to explain why depressions do occur and what can be done about them. Many economists currently argue that Keynesian economics is inadequate for an explanation of modern stagflation and further suggest the need for a new paradigm. This has given rise to supply-side economics and the resurgence of monetarist theories.

An example of conflicting paradigms is the contrast between Marxian economics and orthodox economics. **Orthodox economics** accepts the institutional setting of the economy and builds a theory around how it works. **Marxian economics** assumes a critical stance toward the existing economic system and attempts to discover how it will and can be changed. Orthodox economics accepts capitalism, and Marxian economics criticizes capitalism and argues for socialism. Another example of conflicting paradigms occurs within orthodox economics: it is the difference between the Keynesian and monetarist approaches. The Keynesian view contends that it is most important to focus on aggregate demand to understand economic events. The monetarist view rejects this approach and argues that only through monetary changes can we understand the economy. Throughout this book, we will encounter these conflicting paradigms as they attempt to explain economic reality. But this brings us to our second point: There are different kinds of economists.

The Realm of the Economist

There are different kinds of economists. Economists are human beings with differing ideas, theories, assumptions, and ideologies. As economic conditions and institutions have changed, so have economist's ideas, theories, assumptions, and ideologies. In different times and spaces, economists have differed. And in the *same* time and space, economists still disagree. Perhaps one way of clarifying this is to examine **ideology.**

E. K. Hunt, in *Property and Prophets*, defines an ideology as a set of "ideas and beliefs that tend to justify morally a society's social and economic relationships. Most members of a society internalize the ideology and thus believe that their functional roles, as well as those of others, are morally correct, and that the method by which society divides its produce is fair. This common belief gives society its cohesiveness and vitality. Lack of it creates turmoil and strife—and ultimately revolution if the differences are deep enough."

Thus at different times, different ideologies may be dominant. At one time, Confucianism was the ideology of China. Later the dominant ideology in China was Maoism and socialism. Catholicism and a concern with the next world once dominated Western Europe; later individualism and materialism held sway. Ideologies, in turn, influence the development of theory. For example, the ideology of individualism promoted the development of the economic theory of classical liberalism, and both accompanied the emergence of capitalism as an economic system. More recently, the combination of the ideologies of liberal democracy, the benevolent state, and individualism have promoted the acceptance of Keynesian economics along with the emergence of welfare or state capitalism.

Additionally, different ideologies concerning the goals of a society and an economic system may conflict. One convenient way of illustrating this is to note that there are three broad groups of Western economists today. Each group has its own ideas, theories, and ideologies. **Liberal economists,** in a liberal Western world, accept the main structures of the economic system but recognize its weaknesses and limitations. They offer reforms to alleviate the problems of capitalism. **Conservative economists** either favor the status quo or argue for a return to more laissez-faire types of capitalism; they are in favor of minimizing the role of the state in the economy. **Radical economists** are more critical of the existing system. They say that the problems are endemic to the system itself; thus solutions require systemic change. They offer new ideas and new institutions; they are in favor of revolutionary changes. Adam Smith, in his day, was a radical. Karl Marx was a radical. John Maynard Keynes offered a liberal solution to the 1930s crisis of capitalism. Milton Friedman, of the Hoover Institution in Palo Alto, California, is a contemporary conservative.

4. **What is your ideology?**

5. **Compare and contrast Hunt's definition of ideology with that of Joan Robinson.**

6. **Which set of economic ideas do you think is dominant in the United States today?**

CONSERVATIVE, LIBERAL, AND RADICAL ECONOMICS

What are some of the essential elements of conservative, liberal, and radical ideologies and theories? What are the differences among them? How do they interpret different economic issues, and what different solutions do they offer for economic problems?

Conservative economists focus on the operation of markets in a capitalist, free-market economic system. They argue that private ownership of resources under capitalism assures economic and political freedom for individuals in that society. Markets, where goods and services are exchanged, will then operate to produce economic well-being and growth for the society and all of the individuals within it. Markets, through the action of competition, enforce a result that is the best for everyone and uses resources efficiently. Consequently, conservatives see the profit motive as being one of the most important and positive aspects of capitalism. Firms, out for their own interests, are regulated by competitive markets to produce exactly what consumers want at the lowest price. One further implication of conservative economics is that, since markets operate efficiently and produce economic growth, then there is no necessity for the government to take an active role in the operation of the economy. In fact, most conservatives argue that active government intervention in the economy is the source of many of our economic problems.

The roots of conservative economics can be found in 18th century classical liberalism. We have already encountered the emergence of this body of thought in the origins of capitalism in Western Europe; in both Parts II and III, we will explore this theory in some more detail. Modern examples of conservative economics include "free-market" economics, supply-side economics, and monetarism. Conservative economists include Milton Friedman, author of *Capitalism and Freedom* and, with Anna Rose Friedman, *Free to Choose* (which was also a TV series on PBS in the early 1980s); Martin Feldstein, who was one of President Reagan's economic advisers; David Stockman, who was one of the architects of Reaganomics as the Director of the Office of Management and Budget; and other officials in the Reagan Administration. Ronald Reagan is an obvious example of a politician who believes in the ideas and the theories of conservative economics. Much of the advertising and educational efforts of corporate America utilize the logic and conclusions of conservative economics. The *Wall Street Journal* is a publication that takes a very consistently conservative position in its editorials.

Liberal economists accept the structure of the capitalist economic system and its basic institutions of private property and markets. Also, they agree with conservatives that, for the most part, this free-market system tends to produce efficiency and economic growth and that it protects individual freedom. However, they admit that the operation of the market system inherently tends to produce a number of problems. For example, it fosters an unequal distribution of income and economic power, it often neglects some of the by-products of economic production and exchange such as pollution, it sometimes fails to provide necessary goods and services that can't be produced profitably, and it can't guarantee economic stability. Liberals then usually point out that there is a solution to these problems that does not interfere with the basic structure of the economic system; it gives the responsibility for addressing these problems to the government. The federal government, in particular, can attempt to redistribute income through its taxation and spending system; it can also attempt to regulate the production of pollution in the economy; all levels of government can provide "public" goods such as parks, roads, schools, and police and fire protection; and, finally, the federal government can take responsibility for trying to achieve economic prosperity and price stability and to avoid economic depressions. For liberals, the market works economic wonders, but they are qualified wonders; the active involvement of governments in the economy can improve its performance.

The theoretical underpinnings of most liberal economists can be found in Keynesian economics. Some liberals also find the ideas of Thorstein Veblen and other institutionalist economists to be helpful in framing their understanding of the economy. We will encounter these theories again in Parts II and IV. John Kenneth Galbraith of Harvard University has written a number of important books about economics and the economy from a Keynesian and institutionalist perspective, has also had a TV series on PBS, and has served in the federal government as an economic adviser. Lester Thurow, who teaches at MIT, is another liberal economist and the author of *The Zero-Sum Society* and *Dangerous Currents*. Robert Reich, who has written books about industrial policy and advised several of the 1984 Democratic presidential contenders, is a noted liberal economist. Jimmy Carter, Gary Hart, and Walter Mondale are politicians who utilize the ideas and the theories of liberal economics. *Business Week* magazine usually follows a relatively liberal editorial policy.

Radical economists tend to be very critical of the structures, operation, and results of capitalist economic systems. They do not deny that capitalism has been quite successful over the past several centuries in increasing the productive capacity of Western nations and the average standard of living for their inhabitants. However, radical economists suggest that the very operation of the market system based on private ownership creates different classes of people in capitalist societies. On the one hand, there are those who own productive resources and organize and control productive activity. Their goal in that process is to earn profits for themselves. On the other hand, there are other people who do not own any productive property and who rely on the sale of their mental and/or physical labor to earn a living. Radicals are quick to point out that there are inherent conflicts between these two groups over wages, working conditions, product safety, and economic power. It is this basic class structure of the society, radicals argue, that produces economic inequality, exploitation, and alienation. In addition, they conclude that the inability to provide for public goods, the ignoring of the social costs of productive activity, and economic instability are inherent aspects of capitalist production and growth. Consequently, the efforts of the state (all levels of government) to deal with these problems are merely "band-aid" solutions because they do not address the root causes—private ownership, production for profit, and a class society. Radical economists, then, point to more fundamental solutions to modern economic problems such as poverty, income inequality, discrimination, pollution, and so on. They suggest alterations in the basic economic institutions of the society. Many radicals believe in nationalization, many do not worry about limiting the existing power of corporations, many would advocate much more significant redistribution of income in the United States, and some even call for social ownership and control of productive resources in pursuit of social goals of production.

Radical economics finds its roots in both institutional and Marxian economics. Although many radicals find the ideas of both Keynesian and conservative economics useful in understanding how capitalism and markets work, radicals depart in their evaluation of the operation and results of capitalism. For them, the negative aspects outweigh the positive. Samuel Bowles, David Gordon, and Thomas Weisskopf are radical economists who have written *Beyond the Wasteland: A Democratic Alternative to Economic Decline*. This book contains their analysis of recent U.S. economic experience and presents a radical economic program for restructuring the economy and addressing many of its long-run and more recent problems. Barry Bluestone and Bennett Harrison, authors of *The Deindustrialization of America*, have focused on the problem of plant closings and runaway shops from a radical perspective and have offered some solutions. *Mother Jones, In These Times*, and *The Guardian* are examples of periodicals that contain a radical point of view. Many of the ideas about economic priorities and policy articulated by Jesse Jackson in his 1984 presidential campaign—for instance, increased income redistribution, significantly reduced military spending, and the promotion of full employment—are compatible with radical economics.

From these brief descriptions of conservative, liberal and radical economics, it should be possible to identify the basic approach that each would take to understanding a particular economic problem and suggesting solutions for it. But let's develop a single example. Conservatives tend to argue that poverty exists because of the particular attributes of individuals and their inability to earn high incomes in labor markets. Either they have the wrong skills, few skills, or they don't try or work hard enough. The solution, then, is either "It's appropriate that their economic rewards are low," or "they need to develop their marketable skills." If the society decides that it wants to facilitate the reduction of poverty, the most appropriate way might be through public education.

Liberals recognize that, very often, the poverty of individuals is a result of circumstances beyond their control. Consequently, not only would they support a public role for education to increase people's marketable skills, but, in addition, they would be in favor of direct income redistribution to increase the purchasing power of poor people. This would reduce the burdens of poverty, but it also might create the chance for people to move out of poverty. Liberals would support food stamps and welfare for the poor. Conservatives tend not to support these programs because they represent government interference with markets and conservatives think that poverty can be reduced effectively only by the participation of responsible individuals in free markets.

Radicals generally would support governmental redistribution programs and certainly would oppose efforts to take economic benefits away from poor people. However, they would argue that redistribution programs have a very limited effect in eliminating poverty. Governmental programs have reduced poverty, but given the source of unequal incomes in private ownership of productive resources and the fundamental individualism of capitalism, the system cannot tolerate the amount of redistribution that would be necessary to eliminate poverty. Only massive redistribution of income to poor people or a radical restructuring of the institutions and goals of the economic system could significantly reduce the incidence of poverty in the United States.

The analyses of current economic problems are very distinctive based on different ideologies and theories. And these differences are reflected in the variety of proposed solutions to them. One of the fascinating aspects of modern economics is the controversy that rages over our understanding of, debates over, and efforts to deal with these problems. Conservative, liberal, and radical economics have all contributed to that process.

7. **Paul Sweezy, an American Marxist economist, has written: "It seems to me that from a scientific point of view the question of choosing between approaches can be answered quite simply. Which more accurately reflects the fundamental characteristics of social reality which is under analysis?" Critically evaluate each of the different perspectives with respect to that statement. How are your answers affected by your own beliefs?**

8. **What is the difference between theory and ideology?**

Having seen that there are many different branches of economics, that economists do many different things, and that there is a substantial amount of disagreement among economists on many different issues, in the next part of this book we will briefly examine the history and development of economic thought.

KEY CONCEPTS

economics
economic theory
the role of assumptions
political economy
paradigm
orthodox economics

Marxian economics
ideology
liberal economists
conservative economists
radical economists

REVIEW QUESTIONS

1. What is economics? Is that what you thought economics was (or should be)?

2. What is the goal of economic theory? What is the test of an economic theory?

3. Why do economists disagree?

4. What is a paradigm? In your life have you ever replaced one paradigm with another?

5. What are the main differences among conservative, liberal, and radical economists?

6. Paradigms can offer contending explanations of the same reality. Sometimes the contention between them can reflect intense political, social, and economic struggles. Think hard and develop some examples of new paradigms, and the people suggesting them, having been subjected to neglect, harassment, ridicule, or even punishment.

SUGGESTED READINGS

E. Ray Canterbury, 1976. *The Making of Economics*, Wadsworth. An insightful book on the development of economics: "what [it] has been and what it is becoming."

Robert B. Carson, 1983. *Economic Issues Today*, St. Martin's. Contrasts radical, liberal, and conservative positions on a variety of current economic issues.

Richard Edwards, Michael Reich, and Thomas E. Weisskopf (eds.), 1978. *The Capitalist System* (2nd ed.), Prentice-Hall. A radical analysis of the American economic system, its institutions, its laws of motion, and its problems by over twenty members of the Union of Radical Political Economics.

Milton Friedman, 1981. *Capitalism and Freedom*, University of Chicago Press. A conservative defense of the capitalist system and market theory by a Nobel Prize winner.

John Kenneth Galbraith, 1977. *The Age of Uncertainty*, Houghton Mifflin. The "text" accompanying Galbraith's recent BBC series on the development of modern economic ideas and institutions.

Robert Heilbroner, 1981. *The Worldly Philosophers,* Simon and Schuster. A classic elementary treatment of the ideas and personal lives of past economic thinkers.

Institute for Labor Education and Research, 1982. *What's Wrong With the U.S. Economy?* South End Press. An introduction to the economy—how it works, the current economic crisis, and policy options from a radical perspective.

Robert Lekachman, 1976. *Economists at Bay,* McGraw-Hill. A critical study of the state of economics today—its inability to explain and deal with combined unemployment and inflation as well as other problems. Lekachman also presents what he thinks must be the new direction for economics.

Thomas R. Swartz and Frank Bonello (eds.), 1984. *Taking Sides: Clashing Views on Controversial Economic Issues,* Dushkin. A reader with conflicting analyses by conservatives, liberals, and radicals on a variety of current economic issues.

THE DEVELOPMENT OF MODERN ECONOMIC THOUGHT

Modern economic thinking has been influenced by many economists, among them Adam Smith, Thomas Malthus, David Ricardo, J. B. Say, John Stuart Mill, W. S. Jevons, Alfred Marshall, John Maynard Keynes, Joan Robinson, P. J. Proudhon, Thorstein Veblen, and Karl Marx. Many of the economists who contributed to the growing body of economic knowledge were British. Britain's emergence as one of the first capitalist powers, through the spread of its colonial empire and the coming of the Industrial Revolution, accounts for this influence. We can trace many of our theories and ideas about the economy back to these early economists.

This book cannot study all of the ideas of all of the economists who have made significant contributions to the history of modern economic thought; in this part, we will focus on the development of a few selected and persistent ways of thinking about an economy. We will concentrate on some *fundamental economic concepts,* many of which we sometimes don't give much thought to. What gives products *value?* Where did *private property* come from? What is the role of the *division of labor* in the wealth of nations? How is the *distribution* of goods and services determined? What role does *laissez-faire* play in economic activity? What is the basis of the *Marxian critique* of capitalism? There are many other important concepts that we could focus on, including capital, entrepreneurship, poverty, efficiency, and so on. We will touch on these in this part and elsewhere in the text, but here we will focus on a limited number of concepts and how they have been treated by economists in the past. By no means, however, will we be presenting a complete treatment of the history of modern economic thought. Your own understanding of the economy may become clearer as you agree or disagree with some of the most important ideas formulated by past economists.

By examining some of the ideas of these economists as they developed, we can gain insights on economic concepts and changing economic institutions, ideas, and theories. Some of this will help us directly in understanding our current economic reality. And it will give us perspective on how the thoughts of past economists have influenced the development of economic systems as well as our understanding of the economy today.

3

Chapter

The Setting—What Is Property?

INTRODUCTION

All forms of life are sustained by the world, but much of the world is owned by only some of the people. What person or institution determines who owns the world, and why does he, she, or it have the authority to define property rights? Who settles disputes over **ownership?** Who disputes ownership? Why are some people defined as outlaws? Individuals may evaluate identical economic situations in different ways because they have different perceptions of the situation and different personal interests. For example, slaves and slaveholders had a different relationship to and ideas about slavery.

As population increases and requires increasing productivity from the land, the land becomes relatively scarce and **property rights** become more important to owners. The distribution of property ownership is a significant determinant of the relative size of income received by the inhabitants of countries that stress the sanctity of **private property** rights.

THE DEVELOPMENT OF PROPERTY IN ENGLAND

Great Britain is an island with a total area (England, Wales, and Scotland) less than that of Pennsylvania and New York. Celts occupied early Britain, followed by the

Romans, who arrived in 55 B.C. and departed about A.D. 410. Angles, Saxons, and Jutes arrived in the 5th century.

In 1066 William the Conqueror, with the approval of the pope, invaded England. With his Norman followers, he slew King Harold at the Battle of Hastings, burned houses, and destroyed crops and cattle. William conquered England.

William and the Normans confiscated all the land, and William became the chief lord. He redistributed land titles to his favorite Norman subjects, reorganized the church, and substituted his selection of foreign prelates for the English bishops.

About 1085–1086 William ordered a detailed survey of every piece of land in England that was to include information about the rights by which the land was held. This survey is the *Domesday Book*. William planned to use this information for tax purposes.

Almost two centuries later, in 1215, the barons (landholders), who felt threatened by the Crown, compelled King John to sign the Magna Carta, which would ensure the barons' rights from the encroaching authority of the king. This was a rebellion of feudal lords. The peasants and artisans were not rebelling, and the Magna Carta neither improved nor protected their rights.

Robert Jordon, in commenting about these times on the BBC, said, "A pattern of building was part of *the system* or, as we would call it, the Establishment. It began when William of Normandy parcelled out England to his Norman subjects. It was confirmed by King John at Runnymede—Magna Carta being not the bastion of our liberties, only a landowner's guarantee."

A few centuries later, Henry VIII (1491–1547) established the Church of England. He closed the Catholic monasteries and abbeys, took all of their land, and appointed his own church officers. As British historian Maurice Keen notes in *The Outlaws of Medieval Legend*, "After that the way was clear for the biggest event in our agrarian history—the distribution of all monastery lands to the Tudor millionaires. These landowners—merchants now rather than barons or earls—built themselves . . . superb mansions. . . ."

1. **In what ways might these events help shape the kind of economic system that developed in Britain?**

2. **What is a property right? What determines a property right?**

Private property emerged in England over the course of several centuries. Its roots lie in violent conquest by foreign armies under the leadership of individuals who became the medieval nobility. Later on, land was appropriated by kings and distributed to vassals, barons, and the church. This process was enforced by a combination of military power and monarchical or religious legal authority, and was often sanctioned by the church. As we have seen, the enclosure movement in the later Middle Ages accelerated this formal transfer of land to private owners (see Chapter 1).

THE SIGNIFICANCE OF PROPERTY

Through conquest, appropriation, and legislative act, land in England came to be privately owned. This was one of the bases for the private ownership of productive resources—one of the foundations of capitalism as an economic system. Under private ownership of property, an individual (or a group of individuals, as in a modern corporation) owns and controls a piece of land (or a factory, machine, or product). With that ownership, the property can be used, rented to someone else, or even sold. The decision about what to do with it, though, rests with its owner. If we assume that individuals are out to maximize their own self-interest, the property will be used in its most productive or profitable way. The property owner determines a use for the property based on his or her motivations, but also based on the operation of markets—for the property itself, either sold or rented, or for the outputs that it can produce. The property can be used, then, to maximize the economic return to the owner. The owner has a right to the use and control of that property. And the existence of markets allows owners to seek out the most productive and profitable use for their property.

One necessary implication of property and property rights is that both must be defined within a particular society. Property implies possession and control. It was, and could still be, determined by force and conquest. Property can be appropriated, willingly or unwillingly. In modern capitalist societies, we have legal documents that convey ownership—deeds, registrations, wills, and stock certificates. In addition, there are legislative, administrative, and judicial dimensions to the definition of property and property rights. Land is surveyed, counties record deeds of land and home ownership, communities pass zoning laws that regulate the use of property, and courts adjudicate disputes among property owners and enforce contracts. Property is an institution that is central to the functioning of markets in a capitalist economy, but it is also an institution that gets its essence from the social and political processes of the society.

A recent Supreme Court case provides an example of how property rights and ownership can be altered by the public process. In May 1984, the Supreme Court upheld a land reform law passed by the Hawaiian state legislature. In the mid-1960s, 18 landowners held over 40 percent of the private land in Hawaii. In reaction to this, the legislature passed a law that allowed the state to take property away from some owners in return for fair compensation and then to distribute it to tenants. The purpose of the law was to reduce the concentration of land ownership, and the state used its rights of eminent domain to achieve what it regarded as an important public purpose. The Supreme Court upheld the law in a unanimous opinion.

(continued)

Following the land redistribution, property use will be determined by decisions made by its new owners in the context of Hawaiian markets.

Another example of a national controversy over property derives from the early policies of the Reagan Administration's Department of the Interior under James Watt. The Federal Government owns vast tracts of land throughout the United States in national forests, wildlife preserves and federal reservations. From the time he came into office, Watt was interested in making arrangements to increase the opportunities for private industry to use that land for mining, foresting, grazing, and other economic activities. Watt's argument was that those resources should be available for private use and that they would contribute to the output of goods and services for the whole economy. Opponents, primarily conservationists and environmentalists, argued that valued national treasures would thus be opened for exploitation and that the sites themselves as well as the wildlife could never be reclaimed. This issue, while it focused on the conservation or the exploitation of land and its resources, was fundamentally about property—its ownership and use in our society and economy. And, like most controversial issues, it was decided in the public sector.

Given the determination of what property is and what property rights are, it is clear that this institution is an important foundation in the operation of productive economic activity in advanced capitalist economic systems.

THOSE WITHOUT PROPERTY—THE PEASANTS

During the early Middle Ages, the serfs on feudal manors seem to have accepted their lot in life. There was security and certainty to their lives, if there was also hard work and poverty. What complaining there was seems to have been confined to individual peasants or manors. In the later centuries of the Middle Ages, however, as feudal institutions began to undergo change and to be replaced by emergent capitalist institutions, the peasants began actively and widely to oppose their rulers.

Beginning in the late 14th century and continuing through the 16th century, peasant revolts sprang up all over Western Europe. In most cases, the peasants were resisting change and attempting to secure their places in the feudal order of things. They opposed increasing mechanization of agricultural work, the consolidation of plots, the **enclosure movement,** the seizure of lands, and many of the other changes that signaled the rise of the landed gentry—and the demise of the peasants' rights to land and protection. All of these rebellions were brutally put down by the well-armed nobility. The peasants were leaderless, unorganized, and poorly armed. Their actions, however, did reflect a deep sense of outrage at the costs borne by them as a result of fundamental changes in the economic, political, and social order of their day. Out of this history came the legends of Robin Hood and other outlaws of the

THE WIZARD OF ID — by Brant parker and Johnny hart

By permission of Johnny Hart and News America Syndicate.

Middle Ages. Maurice Keen, in *The Outlaws of Medieval Legend*, has noted the attraction of these stories at the time:

> But though these risings were doomed to failure before they started, they do reveal just that background of widespread popular unrest which would make men listen, and admire the stories of an outlaw whose defiance of the law was more successful than their own.
>
> Modern historians who have examined the causes of these revolts have diagnosed them in economic terms. But because the rebels were medieval men living in an age which tended to see everything in terms of law, their demands were largely legal, which is what we would expect from the outlaw poems with their persistent bitterness against the men of law.

The legal demands of the peasants, however, were primarily concerned with the ownership and use of property, and with their rights to have land and reside on the manors.

> **3. "Modern historians who have examined the causes of these revolts have diagnosed them in economic terms." What were the economic roots of the peasant rebellions?**

During this period, British people in rural England were totally dependent on the productivity of the land. Those who lived in villages used common land to raise their crops, keep their bees, graze their livestock, and gather their firewood. Without access to land they would have been without any means to sustain their lives.

Over an extended period of time a series of parliamentary acts converted many of the commons into private property. Whole villages were deserted; people who were independent when they could use the common lands became either vagrant or dependent for employment on those who owned the land. English historian Raymond Williams describes this change and its implications in *The Country and the City*:

By permission of Johnny Hart and News America Syndicate.

There is no reason to deny the critical importance of the period of parliamentary enclosures, from the second quarter of the eighteenth century to the first quarter of the nineteenth century. By nearly four thousand Acts, more than six million acres of land were appropriated, mainly by the politically dominant landowners: about a quarter of all cultivated acreage. But it is then necessary to see the essential continuity of this appropriation, both with earlier and with later phases. It is necessary to stress, for example, how much of the country had already been enclosed. . . . Indeed in history it is continuous from the long process of conquest and seizure: the land gained by killing, by repression, by political bargains.

Again, as the economy develops, enclosure can never really be isolated from the mainstream of land improvements, of changes in methods of production, of price-movements, and of those more general changes in property relationships which were all flowing in the same direction: an extension of cultivated land but also a concentration of ownership into the hands of a minority.

The parliamentary procedure for enclosure made this process at once more public and more recorded. In this sense it was directly related to the quickening pace of agricultural improvement in the late eighteenth and early nineteenth centuries. . . . The social importance of enclosures is then not that they introduced a wholly new element in the social structure, but that in getting rid of the surviving open-field villages and common rights, in some of the most populous and prosperous parts of the country, they complemented and were indeed often caused by the general economic pressure on small owners and especially small tenants. . . . It can be reasonably argued that as many people were driven from the land . . . by the continuing processes of rack-renting and short-lease policies, and by the associated need for greater capital to survive in an increasingly competitive market, as by explicit enclosure.

The number of landless, before this period of enclosure, was in any event high: in 1690, five landless labourers to every three occupiers, as compared with a proportion of five to two in 1831. . . .

By the eighteenth century, nearly half of the cultivated land was

owned by some five thousand families. As a central form of this predomi-
nance, four hundred families, in a population of some seven or eight
million people, owned nearly a quarter of cultivated land. Beneath this
domination, there was no longer, in any classical sense a peasantry, but
an increasingly regular structure of tenant farmers and wage-labourers: the
social relationships that we can properly call those of agrarian capitalism.
The regulation of production was increasingly in terms of an organized
market.

—From *The Country and the City* by Raymond Williams. Copyright © 1973 by
Raymond Williams. Reprinted by permission of Oxford University Press, Inc., and
Chatto and Windus, Ltd.

4. **What are the "social relationships" of agrarian capitalism?**

5. **"The regulation of production was increasingly in terms of an organized market." What does this mean?**

6. **What would you predict happened to the distribution of income in England as a result of these changes in property ownership?**

CONCLUSION

The formation of truly private property can be traced to this early history of England.
It is one of the fundamental prerequisites of capitalism. As feudalism faded at the end
of the Middle Ages, the notion of property in England was defined in legal terms.
Laws conferred or acknowledged the right of ownership and protected the owner's
control over the use of property. From the perspective of the owner, such property
rights and legal protection allowed for maximum earnings from the land and ensured
their dominant position in society. From the perspective of the peasants, on the
other hand, control of land was torn from them out of their own adversity and
weakness through violent conquest and legal manipulation. This ensured their
position at the bottom of society. It also forced them into "vagrancy" or a dependence
on wage labor for income. Out of this sense of frustration, peasants revolted against
the emergence of private property throughout the late Middle Ages. Control of the
land was a dominant concern in England's emerging capitalist economy. Economic
ideas were implicit in the struggle for control of the land.

However, as capitalism moved into its adolescent stage with the coming of the
Industrial Revolution in the 18th century, economic thinking became significantly
more sophisticated.

KEY CONCEPTS

ownership   private property
property rights   enclosure movement

REVIEW QUESTIONS

1. What is property? Why is it important?

2. What is the origin of private property in the United States?

3. Who or what defines an outlaw? Was Robin Hood an outlaw?

4. Why is it important to know something about the history of economic thought?

SUGGESTED READINGS

Maurice Keen, 1977. *The Outlaws of Medieval Legend*, Routledge-Kegan. Traces the stories of early opposition to the emergence of modern private property.

Karl Polanyi, 1973. *The Great Transformation*, Octagon. A classic treatment of the emergence of private property in Western Europe along with the development of early capitalism.

E. P. Thompson, 1966. *The Making of the English Working Class*, Random House. A classic history of the emergence of capitalism and its creation of a working class in Great Britain.

Raymond Williams, 1973. *The Country and the City*, Oxford University Press. Highlights the relationship between urban and rural areas in England as capitalist institutions developed.

The Coming of Adam Smith— the Division of Labor

INTRODUCTION

How did we happen to organize work in the way that we have? People didn't always have the same sense of mechanistic time that obsesses us. Does anybody really know what time it is? Assembly lines have existed for less than 100 years. And clocks to control the hours of work are not all that much older. Could we have the same division of labor and specialization without assembly lines and clocks? Is the way in which labor is divided desirable from the viewpoint of the worker?

Much of our current thinking about specialization and the division of labor has been influenced by the writings of Adam Smith (1723–1790). In turn, many modern productive methods, including the assembly line, were derived from the early development of capitalism during the Industrial Revolution—the time when Adam Smith was writing.

ADAM SMITH AND THE DIVISION OF LABOR

The year of 1776 is significant in our history because Adam Smith's great—in size and fame—book *An Inquiry into the Nature and Causes of the Wealth of Nations* was

Adam Smith, 1723–1790.

published. It was the first comprehensive treatise about economics. However, there had been many books and essays about economic matters before Adam Smith, and he used ideas from them in his book. He brought them all together and created a fairly complete picture of his understanding about the way an economy behaved and why it behaved that way in 1776. His observations coincided with the acceleration of the Industrial Revolution and the increasing importance of both domestic and international markets to British capitalists.

The following article from the March 9, 1976, *New York Times*, marking the 200th anniversary of *The Wealth of Nations*, suggests its importance in economic history and economic thought:

ADAM SMITH LED 1776 REVOLUTION IN ECONOMICS

Soma Golden

Two revolutions were begun in 1776.

One was by an outraged group of upstart colonists, armed for battle with Britain and determined to win political freedom. The other was by a lone Scottish scholar, Adam Smith, aged 53, armed only with ideas. This revolution, too, was about freedom—but economic, rather than political.

On March 9, 1776, four months before the Americans fired their Declaration of Independence at the British establishment, Adam Smith fired his own salvo—a gigantic work entitled, *An Inquiry into the Nature and Causes of the Wealth of Nations*. It was the 1097-page fruit of a decade's constant labor and a lifetime of study, a book that has shaped economic thinking from that day until this.

Although the American Revolution has generated a hurricane of activity this year, the bicentennial of the publication of "The Wealth of Na-

(continued)

tions" is a more subdued affair, the subject of a few scholarly lectures and articles in the United States and somewhat more elaborate academic festivities later this year in Britain.

SLOWER-PACED EVENT

But at another level, the ideas of Adam Smith—known as the ideologist of laissez-faire capitalism, the apostle of the industrial revolution, and the first economic philosopher—are enjoying something of a revival in the United States this election year.

The campaigns of President Ford, of former Gov. Ronald Reagan of California and of the Democratic former Governor of Georgia, Jimmy Carter, are Smithian at their core—calling for less interference by Washington in the lives of the citizens and the operations of business.

For "The Wealth of Nations," in its perceptive and exhaustive examination of late 18th Century socioeconomic life, also is . . . a critique of the heavy hand of government regulations and a paean to the power of economic freedom, checked by competition, to generate maximum wealth of nations and of individuals. . . .

Although the notion of reducing governmental power may sound conservative, rather than radical, in the late 20th century, 200 years ago, the idea was far to the left of center. "Adam Smith was a radical, not a reactionary," says Robert Lekachman, economic historian and professor at Lehman College of the City University of New York. . . .

However, the dust of history and hyperbole have done much to hide the fine lines of Smith's radicalism from today's generation. More often than not, the doctrines of the Scottish thinker are unfurled to defend the freedom of big business rather than the freedom of all individuals.

"In 1976," Professor Lekachman wrote in his recent book, *Economists at Bay,* "the natural heirs of Adam Smith are not the presidents of giant corporations who speak on public occasions in favor of competition which they have done their best to suppress."

Economists find it difficult to summarize in a few pithy thoughts the vast and complex tapestry that Smith wove into *The Wealth of Nations.* The book is no abstruse textbook only for economists to absorb. It is a rich, theoretical and political discussion, aimed at statesmen and kings in the fading days of British mercantilism, at the dawn of the industrial revolution.

The book debunks the mercantilist notion that the wealth of a nation, such as Britain, could only grow at the expense of other nations, through stringent limits on Britain's imports, forced-growth of her exports, and the resulting accumulation of hoards of gold.

To Smith, wealth depended not on a mountain of rare metals piled up in the British Treasury, but on efficiency and productive power of the

(continued)

nation. He explains how that kind of wealth could be generated to a maximum by nations freely trading together to the economic betterment of all.

SCHOLARLY REFERENCES

The book's carefully written pages are weighted with scholarly references to ancient empires, theology, history, morality and much more. . . .

Smith first gained fame as a professor of moral philosophy at Glasgow University. . . .

Smith's fundamental idea—which still has enormous force among politicians and economists—is that a democratic society, driven by the self-interest of its people competing against one another, can generate more wealth than the same society, ruled by a government that tries to regulate the minute details of economic life.

Britain's mercantilist government had bent the entire economy to the state's needs, weaving a tight web around individual economic activity—tighter, historians say, than anything the West has seen since then, except during wartime. But the people had begun to writhe against the endless regulation of wages, apprenticeship rules, state monopolies, import duties and the like.

And Smith, looking over the entire jumbled scene from the quiet beach of Kirkcaldy, fit the pieces of the past and present together like a giant puzzle and offered a rationale for unraveling the mercantilist system and an ideology for the rising business class that would dominate the next century.

The hatchet that Smith used to chop away at the British system was reason, not rhetoric. Mercantilism, he said, was undoing the natural order of things, interfering with progress for the nation and the people, stifling initiative and hobbling growth. . . .

The famous metaphor that Smith used to denote that order—mentioned only once in the book's many pages—is the "invisible hand."

Politicians apparently did not take long to get the message. Some members of Parliament came to Scotland to consult the famed author. Others soon quoted him in chamber.

Economists, too, were quick to note Smith's work inasmuch as *The Wealth of Nations* presents a vast spectrum of economic theory, some well-developed, some in germ, some the product of the author's own intelligence, some the refined product of an earlier, lesser-known theorist.

Tucked away in its pages are explanations of capital as a store of wealth; of labor as a source of value; of the productivity to be gained by economies of scale and the division of labor, illustrated by the famous example of the pin factory. Smith also explored the idea of external economies, supply and demand, price determination, worker alienation, comparative advantage, free trade, and even modern equilibrium theory.

(continued)

Being a pragmatist as well as a theorist, Smith filled his book with policy prescriptions derived from his more abstract thoughts including a recommendation, somewhat tardy, that Britain peacefully sever its colonialist ties with America. He scorned the exclusive trading arrangement that Britain had forced on the colonies and said the mother country derived "nothing but loss" from the relationship.

After 200 years, much of Smith is still surprisingly relevant. Although Smith's professional progeny have criticized him for the sins of superficiality, omission or error, economists generally applaud him for his masterly exposition of the logic and virtues of laissez-faire capitalism in a competitive world.

The loudest applause, perhaps, comes from the so-called Chicago school of economics, which orbits around the University of Chicago, where many of the laissez-faire prescriptions of the 18th-century philosopher are viewed as suitable for the 20th-century economy.

"There have been thousands of minor improvements on Smith, but no one has damaged the validity of his central thought," said George J. Stigler, a Chicago professor and noted expert on the history of economic thought. "We are still basically in a Smithian age," he said.

This proposition, however, is challenged by some economists today who think Smith's description of the market is brilliant in theory, but obsolete in practice. Smith, they say, did not anticipate the proliferation of giant private companies that now dominate the skyline of modern American industry.

Thus he saw no need for an activist government antitrust policy. The giant state-backed trading companies that held monopoly power in his day, Smith thought, would be eliminated if the state merely stopped offering them protection.

Another side of Smith that today's liberals cite, is the scholar's worry about the future of the capitalism he championed. Smith did not entirely trust the budding businessmen to compete rather than collude behind closed doors. And he worried about the moral deterioration and alienation of workers that could result from the division of labor he viewed as necessary for economic growth.

In a strongly worded passage, Smith seems to worry that even democracy itself could be undermined by the advent of the modern factory system, where workers would be forced to repeat a simple mind-numbing operation from dawn to dusk.

The "torpor" of the worker's mind, Smith wrote, makes such a man incapable of "forming any just judgment concerning many even of the ordinary duties of private life. Of the great and extensive interests of his country he is altogether incapable of judging."

The rock upon which Smith builds his entire scheme is the desire of all individuals—workers, businessmen, and statesmen—to pursue their

(continued)

competing economic self-interests or, in his words "to truck, barter and exchange one thing for another."

Walter Bagehot, the British economist, wrote long ago that Smith seemed to imagine each infant born with a tiny Scotsman inside to direct him along the proper path. Even economists who criticize Smith today concede, in the words of one, that "there's a little Adam Smith inside us all."

Smith begins *The Wealth of Nations* with this classic description "Of the Division of Labour" in the context of emerging capitalist production:

The greatest improvement in the productive powers of labour, and the greater part of the skill, dexterity, and judgment with which it is any where directed, or applied, seem to have been the effects of the division of labour.

The effects of the division of labour, in the general business of society, will be more easily understood, by considering in what manner it operates in some particular manufactures. . . .

To take an example from a very trifling manufacturer: but one in which the division of labour has been very often taken notice of, the trade of the pin-maker; a workman not educated to this business (which the division of labour has rendered a distinct trade), nor acquainted with the use of the machinery employed in it (to the invention of which the same division of labour has probably given occasion), could scarce, perhaps, with his utmost industry, make one pin in a day, and certainly could not make twenty. But in the way in which this business is now carried on, not only the whole work is a peculiar trade, but it is divided into a number of branches, of which the greater part are likewise peculiar trades. One man draws out the wire, another straights it, a third cuts it, a fourth points it, a fifth grinds it at the top for receiving the head; to make the head requires two or three distinct operations; to put it on, is a peculiar business, to whiten the pins is another; it is even a trade by itself to put them into the paper; and the important business of making a pin is, in this manner, divided into about eighteen distinct operations, which, in some manufactories, are all performed by distinct hands, though in others the same man will sometimes perform two or three of them. I have seen a small manufactory of this kind where ten men only were employed, and where some of them consequently performed two or three distinct operations. But though they were very poor, and therefore but indifferently accommodated with the necessary machinery, they could, when they exerted themselves, make among them about twelve pounds of pins in a day. There are in a pound upwards of four thousand pins of a middling size. Those ten persons, therefore, could make among them upwards of forty-eight thousand

Catchpenny Prints

pins in a day. Each person, therefore, making a tenth part of forty-eight thousand pins, might be considered as making four thousand eight hundred pins in a day. But if they had all wrought separately and independently, and without any of them having been educated to this peculiar business, they certainly could not each of them have made twenty, perhaps not one pin in a day; that is, certainly, not the two hundred and fortieth, perhaps not the four thousand eight hundredth part of what they are at present capable of performing, in consequence of a proper division and combination of their different operations.

1. Were Adam Smith's perceptions conditioned by time when he wrote this part of the book?

With this description of the **division of labor,** Adam Smith highlighted the role of **specialization** in significantly increasing productive potential. He attributed this great increase in productivity to three factors. "First, the improvement of the dexterity of the workman necessarily increases the quantity of work he can perform; and the division of labor, by reducing every man's business to some one simple operation, and by making this operation the sole employment of his life, necessarily increases very much the dexterity of the workman." Second, the worker would gain time that used to be lost in moving from one type of work to another. And, third, labor would be made more productive by the application of machinery that would facilitate the division of labor. Thus specialization and the application of new technologies during the Industrial Revolution of the late 18th and early 19th centuries contributed to rapidly expanding output.

An important result of this increase in output accompanying the division of labor was that each worker "has a great quantity of his own work to dispose of beyond what he himself has occasion for." Since every worker is in the same position, **exchange** will take place. Smith puts it this way: "He supplies them abundantly with what they have occasion for, and they accommodate him as amply with what he has occasion for, and a general plenty diffuses itself through all the different ranks of the society." Through the division of labor, economic output will increase; and the existence of exchange will facilitate and further encourage this growth in output. The extension of **markets** throughout the world, the technological revolution and the division of labor mutually reinforced one another.

---

2. **"And the division of labor, by reducing every man's business to some one simple operation, and by making this operation the sole employment of his life, necessarily increases very much the dexterity of the workman."**

   a) **How would you feel about having one simple operation made the sole employment of your life?**

   b) **Would the people on an assembly line agree with your answer?**

Smith traced the emergence of the division of labor in production to the fact that people do exchange goods and services. "It is the necessary, though very slow and gradual, consequence of a propensity in human nature which has in view no such extensive utility: **the propensity to truck, barter, and exchange** one thing for another" [boldface added]. Because there is a tendency for exchange, people will begin to specialize in what they do best and to trade with others for the other things that they need. Through this process, the division of labor will proceed and economic output will increase. Historically, the rapidly spreading and more sophisticated markets in Western Europe tremendously accelerated the development of the division of labor.

Adam Smith further argued that all of this great economic progress derived from the seeking of **self-interest** by individuals. Individuals entered markets for exchange to benefit themselves. But out of this quest for self-gain, a general good developed in the form of increasing prosperity for all.

> But man has almost constant occasion for the help of his brethren, and it is in vain for him to expect it from their benevolence only. He will be more likely to prevail if he can interest their self-love in his favour, and shew them that it is for their own advantage to do for him what he requires of them. Whoever offers to another a bargain of any kind, proposes to do this. Give me that which I want, and you shall have this which you want, is the meaning of every such offer; and it is in this manner that we obtain from one another the far greater part of those good offices which we stand in need of. It is not from the benevolence of the butcher, the brewer, or the baker, that we expect our dinner, but from their regard to their own interest. We address ourselves, not to their humanity but to their self-love, and never talk to them of our own necessities out of their advantages.

General prosperity and economic growth—the wealth of the nation—resulted from the pursuit of self-interest organized through the division of labor and markets. This is the essence of Smith's "invisible hand."

3. **Adam Smith thought that the division of labor derived from people's "propensity to truck, barter, and exchange one thing for another." Do you agree with Smith's reasoning here? Why or why not?**

4. **"But man has almost constant occasion for the help of his brethren, and it is in vain for him to expect it from their benevolence only. He will be more likely to prevail if he can interest their self-love in his favour, and shew them that it is for their own advantage to do for him what he requires of them."**

   a) **Do you agree with Smith's assumption about the nature of people's behavior? How did Smith arrive at this conclusion?**

   b) **If it is an accurate assumption about present behavior, do people have any choice about behaving in any other way?**

SIDE EFFECTS OF THE DIVISION OF LABOR

Adam Smith focused on the relation of the division of labor, specialization, exchange, and markets to the wealth of nations. He also showed sensitivity to some side effects of the division of labor. The first of these is a problem that we still experience today in the alienation and boredom of manual labor and the assembly line. Smith wrote about this problem bluntly and graphically in this passage from *The Wealth of Nations*:

> In the progress of the division of labour, the employment of the far greater part of those who live by labour, that is, of the great body of the people, comes to be confined to a few very simple operations, frequently to one or two. But the understandings of the greater part of men are necessarily formed by their ordinary employments. The man whose whole life is spent in performing a few simple operations, of which the effects too are, perhaps, always the same, or very nearly the same, has no occasion to exert his understanding, or to exercise his invention in finding out expedients for removing difficulties which never occur. He naturally loses, therefore, the habit of such exertion, and generally becomes as stupid and ignorant as it is possible for a human creature to become. The torpor of his mind renders him not only incapable of relishing or bearing a part in any rational conversation, but of conceiving any generous, noble, or tender sentiment, and consequently of forming any just judgment concerning many even of the ordinary duties of private life.
>
> His dexterity at his own particular trade seems, in this manner, to be acquired at the expence of his intellectual, social, and martial virtues. But in every improved and civilized society this is the state into which the labouring poor, that is, the great body of the people, must necessarily fall, unless government takes some pains to prevent it.

The division of labor. (Photograph by Carol Ingald.)

An additional consequence of this tendency is that the guidance of society must be left to the few, the elite, who are not stupefied by the repetitiveness of their labors. In fact, the division of labor under capitalism not only increased efficiency, it also promoted the control of the capitalist over the work process and the workers. This can be seen in the emergence of the putting-out system and later the factory system (see Chapter 1). This process effectively splits society into classes—the educated elite and the "great body of the people."

CONCLUSION

The division of labor that Adam Smith saw developing in the new and larger factories in late 18th-century England was another prerequisite in the development of capitalism. It entailed a new method of production, which allowed for large increases in production per worker. Adam Smith saw this process in operation and theorized about its benefits. He also, in turn, advocated the use of the division of labor to promote "the wealth of nations." However, other changes in economic institutions supported, and were required by, the spread of specialization resulting from the division of labor. Exchange and markets were needed so people could trade for what they did not produce. As capitalism developed further, all of these institutions—the division of labor, specialization, exchange, and markets—matured and contributed to further development and growth.

Smith also noted that there were some drawbacks to the introduction of the division of labor. These concerned the effects on workers. Boredom from dull, specialized work and limitations on the ability to function as a full member of society were to be expected. Such results pointed to possible future problems in the development of capitalism.

What other kinds of economic thoughts did Adam Smith and other economists who followed him offer? And what other kinds of economic concepts did they analyze? In the next chapter we will examine some of their thoughts on value.

KEY CONCEPTS

division of labor	the propensity to truck,
specialization	barter, and exchange
exchange and markets	self-interest

REVIEW QUESTIONS

1. Would production activity in the United States be as advanced as it is without assembly lines and the division of labor?

2. What is the relationship of private property (in the form of factories) to the division of labor? Are they necessary to each other?

3. Does specialization normally result in workers who are "as stupid and ignorant as it is possible for a human creature to become"? How was this statement of Smith's conditioned by time? Do you agree with it? Why or why not?

SUGGESTED READINGS

Robert Heilbroner, 1981. *The Worldly Philosophers*, Simon and Schuster, Chapter 3. A nice concise chapter on the development of Smith's economic thought as well as some interesting biographical information.

Adam Smith, 1776. *The Wealth of Nations*, Reprint 1937, Modern Library Edition, Random House. Go straight to the original and read the classic treatise on how economic progress takes place. Despite its length, it makes fascinating reading; Smith was a real scholar!

Creating Value—Producing Goods and Services

INTRODUCTION

What is value? Why do goods and services have value? What determines *how much value* a good or a service possesses? How is value created? Value is a complicated economic, and philosophical, concept. But it is one that economists have been concerned with because it motivates the economic activities of production and consumption. It becomes particularly relevant when exchange emerges in markets as the mediator between private production and consumption.

Some people think that value is created by labor; others think that value is determined by the utility of the product to the consumer. The problem is further complicated by the use of capital in production—in addition to direct labor.

1. Before you read through this chapter, think carefully about what you mean when you say that an object has value. Select an object that has value—a table, an orange, a computer, a chair, a desk, a pair of shoes, a hamburger, a book, a dormitory, a sweater, a gallon of gasoline—and explain as clearly as you can why it has value. What gives it value?

SMITH AND RICARDO ON VALUE

When economics was first being developed as a body of thought (which was not really so long ago), attention was directed to the concept of **value.** This became a special problem as exchange and markets became more complex. Goods were exchanged for money and had prices. Did price reflect value?

We will begin our consideration of value with Adam Smith and the labor theory of value from *The Wealth of Nations:*

> The value of any commodity . . . to the person who possesses it, and who means not to use or consume it himself, but to exchange it for other commodities, is equal to the quantity of labour which it enables him to purchase or command. Labour, therefore, is the real measure of the exchangeable value of all commodities. . . .
>
> Labour, therefore, it appears evidently, is the only universal, as well as the only accurate measure of value, or the only standard by which we can compare the values of different commodities at all times and at all places. We cannot estimate, it is allowed, the real value of different commodities from century to century by the quantities of silver which were given for them. We cannot estimate it from year to year by the quantities of corn. By the quantities of labour we can, with the greatest accuracy, estimate it both from century to century and from year to year.

> **2. In your own words, state your understanding of what Adam Smith said about value.**

The **labor theory of value** seemed simple enough: the value of a good depended on the amount of labor used in producing it. However, Smith also noted that the concept of value can be slippery. Specifically, there are two different meanings to value. We can measure exchange value by the labor content of a good. These goods have **value in exchange.** But there is another group of goods which have **value in use.** The problem is that, while use values may or may not require labor, some cannot be exchanged for other goods. Smith gave the following example:

> The things which have the greatest value in use have frequently little or no value in exchange; and on the contrary, those which have the greatest value in exchange have frequently little or no value in use. Nothing is more useful than water: but it will purchase scarce any thing; scarce any thing can be had in exchange for it. A diamond, on the contrary, has scarce any value in use; but a very great quantity of other goods may frequently be had in exchange for it.

Consequently, some goods that have use values may not have exchange values. The problem is further complicated by the fact that some goods with use values (and

Shakespeare's value. (Photograph by Robert Bostwick.)

without exchange values) may also be produced by labor. Do these goods have value, then? Obviously, *most* goods in a market system have *both* use and exchange values.

3. **Can you explain why a diamond seems to have a very high exchange value?** *Could* **water have a high exchange value?**

4. **Can you think of a good or service that has use value, requires labor, but has no exchange value?**

David Ricardo (1772–1823), another Englishman who was a major contributor to economic thought, read Adam Smith's ideas on value and decided to try to clarify them. The following passage is from his *Principles of Political Economy and Taxation*, published in 1817:

> It has been observed by Adam Smith that "the word Value has two different meanings, and sometimes expresses the utility of some particular object, and sometimes the power of purchasing other goods which the possession of that object conveys. The one may be called value in use; the other value in exchange. The things," he continues, "which have the greatest value in use, have frequently little or no value in exchange; and, on the contrary, those which have the greatest value in exchange, have little or no value in use." Water and air are abundantly useful; they are indeed indispensable to existence, yet, under ordinary circumstances, nothing can be obtained in exchange for them. Gold, on the contrary, though of little use compared with air or water, will exchange for a great quantity of other goods.
>
> *Utility* then is not the measure of exchangeable value, although it is absolutely essential to it. If a commodity were in no way useful—in other words, if it could in no way contribute to our gratification—it would be destitute of exchangeable value, however scarce it might be, or whatever quantity of labour might be necessary to procure it. Possessing utility, commodities derive their *exchangeable value* from two sources: from their scarcity, and from the quantity of labour required to obtain them.
>
> There are some commodities, the value of which is determined by their scarcity alone. No labour can increase the quantity of such goods, and therefore their value cannot be lowered by an increased supply. Some rare statues and pictures, scarce books and coins, wines of a peculiar quality, which can be made only from grapes grown on a particular soil, of which there is a very limited quantity, are all of this description. Their value is wholly independent of the quantity of labour originally necessary to produce them, and varies with the varying wealth and inclinations of those who are desirous to possess them.
>
> These commodities, however, form a very small part of the mass of commodities daily exchanged in the market. *By far the greatest part of*

those goods which are the objects of desire are procured by labour [italics added]; and they may be multiplied, not in one country alone, but in many, almost without any assignable limit, if we are disposed to bestow the labour necessary to obtain them.

Once we have delimited those goods that have exchange value, we can proceed to examine the economic laws governing their exchange in markets. This represents the vast majority of goods and the ones that we are most interested in as we examine economic activity. Prices ultimately reflect relative exchange values, and hence labor content, among different goods. Ricardo makes this point as follows:

In speaking, then, of commodities, of their exchangeable value, and of the laws which regulate their relative prices, we mean always such commodities only as can be increased in quantity by the exertion of human industry and on the production of which competition operates without restraint. . . .

If, among a nation of hunters, for example, it usually cost twice the labour to kill a beaver which it does to kill a deer, one beaver should naturally exchange for, or be worth, two deer. It is natural that what is usually the produce of two days' or two hours' labour should be worth double of what is usually the produce of one day's or one hour's labour.

That this is really the foundation of the exchangeable value of all things, excepting those which cannot be increased by human industry, is a doctrine of the utmost importance in political economy; for from no source do so many errors, and so much difference of opinion in that science proceed, as from the vague ideas which are attached to the word value.

If the quantity of labour realised in commodities regulate their exchangeable value, every increase of the quantity of labour must augment the value of that commodity on which it is exercised, as every diminution must lower it.

5. Do Ricardo's ideas differ from those of Smith?

6. Does your family pay a water bill? Why or why not?

If we think only a little about labor as a theory of value, we will recognize the oversimplification of the deer-and-beaver illustration. Our definition of value isn't so simple. What about three men who might be trimming equal amounts of a hedge: one has a pair of hand scissors, the second has a manual hedge trimmer, and the third has an electric hedge trimmer. We know who will trim the hedge in the shortest time—with significantly less labor. Here we have introduced a complication that seems to limit the applicability of the labor theory of value. Is having your hedge trimmed by hand scissors more valuable than having it done with an electric hedge trimmer because it takes more labor? Not so fast, says David Ricardo, the value of implements is accounted for in the labor theory of value:

All the implements necessary to kill the beaver and deer might belong to one class of men, and the labour employed in their destruction might be furnished by another class; still, their comparative prices would be in proportion to the actual labour bestowed, both on the formation of the *capital* and on the destruction of the animals. Under different circumstances of plenty or scarcity of capital, as compared with labour, under different circumstances of plenty or scarcity of the food and necessaries essential to the support of men, those who furnished an equal value of capital for either one employment or for the other might have a half, a fourth, or an eighth of the produce obtained, the remainder being paid as wages to those who furnished the labour; yet this division could not affect the relative value of these commodities, since whether the profits of capital were greater or less, whether they were 50, 20, or 10 per cent, or whether the wages of labour were high or low, they would operate equally on both employments.

If we suppose the occupations of the society extended, that some provide canoes and tackle necessary for fishing, others the seed and rude machinery first used in agriculture, still the same principle would hold true, that the exchangeable value of the commodities produced would be in proportion to the labour bestowed on their production; not on their immediate production only, but on all those implements or machines required to give effect to the particular labour to which they were applied.

Ricardo introduced the notion that the value of capital depends on its labor content. He defined **capital** to be "that part of the wealth of a country which is employed in production, and consists of food, clothing, tools, raw materials, machinery, etc., necessary to give effect to labour." According to Ricardo's definition, then, the labor theory of value explains the exchange value of all goods. Everything that is used in production requires labor; consequently, the value of a good will reflect its labor content. Therefore goods will exchange for one another based on their labor content.

7. **What does Ricardo mean by "necessary to give effect to labour"?**

8. **If your family owns a house, is it a form of capital?**

9. **Are the clothes you are wearing capital?**

JOHN STUART MILL ON SMITH AND RICARDO

John Stuart Mill (1806–1873), a later English economist, accepted Smith's and Ricardo's ideas on value. He restated the ideas, however, in a refreshing way that emphasized the complicated problem of precisely estimating the exact contribution of any one worker to production. In the following, from his *Principles of Political Economy* (1848), he is concerned with the value of a loaf of bread.

> The labour which terminates in the production of an article fitted for some human use, is either employed directly about the thing, or in previous operations destined to facilitate, perhaps essential to the possibility of, the subsequent ones. In making bread, for example, the labour employed about the thing itself is that of the baker; but the labour of the miller, though employed directly in the production not of bread but of flour, is equally part of the aggregate sum of labour by which the bread is produced; as is also the labour of the sower, and of the reaper. Some may think that all these persons ought to be considered as employing their labour directly about the thing; the corn, the flour, and the bread being one substance in these different states. Without disputing about this question of mere language, there is still the ploughman, who prepared the ground for the seed, and whose labour never came in contact with the substance in any of its states; and the ploughmaker, whose share in the result was still more remote. All these persons ultimately derive the remuneration of their labour from the bread, or its price: the ploughmaker as much as the rest; for since ploughs are of no use except for tilling the soil, no one would make or use ploughs for any other reason than because the increased returns, thereby obtained from the ground, afforded a source from which an adequate equivalent could be assigned for the labour of the ploughmaker. If the produce is to be used or consumed in the form of bread, it is from the bread that this equivalent must come. The bread must suffice to remunerate all these labours, and several others; such as the carpenters and bricklayers who erected the farm buildings; the hedgers and ditchers who made the fences necessary for the protection of the crop; the miners and smelters who extracted or prepared the iron of which the plough and other implements were made. These, however, and the ploughmaker, do not depend for their remuneration upon the bread made from the produce of a single harvest, but upon that made from the produce of all the harvests which are successively gathered until the plough, or the buildings and fences, are worn out. We must add yet another kind of labour; that of transporting the produce from the place of its production to the place of its destined use: the labour of carrying the corn to market, and from market to the miller's, the flour from the miller's to the baker's, and the bread from the baker's to the place of its final consumption. This labour is sometimes very considerable: flour is transported to England from beyond the Atlantic, corn from the heart of Russia; and in addition to the labourers immediately employed, the waggoners and sailors, there are also costly instruments, such as ships, in

the construction of which much labour has been expended: that labour, however, not depending for its whole remuneration upon the bread, but for a part only; ships being usually, during the course of their existence, employed in the transport of many different kinds of commodities.

To estimate, therefore, the labour of which any given commodity is the result, is far from a simple operation. The items in the calculation are very numerous—as it may seem to some persons, infinitely so; for if, as a part of the labour employed in making bread, we count the labour of the blacksmith who made the plough, why not also (it may be asked) the labour of making the tools used by the blacksmith, and the tools used in making those tools, and so back to the origin of things? But after mounting one or two steps in this ascending scale, we come into a region of fractions too minute for calculation. Suppose, for instance, that the same plough will last, before being worn out, a dozen years. Only one twelfth of the labour of making the plough must be placed to the account of each year's harvest. A twelfth part of the labour of making a plough is an appreciable quantity. But the same set of tools, perhaps, suffice to the ploughmaker for forging a hundred ploughs, which serve during the twelve years of their existence to prepare the soil of as many different farms. A twelve hundredth part of the labour of making the tools, is as much, therefore, as has been expended in procuring one year's harvest of a single farm: and when this fraction comes to be further apportioned among the various sacks of corn and loaves of bread, it is seen at once that such quantities are not worth taking into the account for any practical purpose connected with the commodity. It is true that if the toolmaker had not laboured, the corn and bread never would have been produced; but they will not be sold a tenth part of a farthing dearer in consideration of his labour.

All that productive activity and all those markets for a loaf of bread!

We are thus left with the labor theory of value intact as the explanation for the determination of relative values of goods. The labor content that goes into the production of goods, both directly and indirectly, determines their exchange values.

However, it is no easy matter to measure that value because of the complexity of the total productive process. Theoretically, though, Smith, Ricardo, and Mill thought that relative prices for goods reflected their relative labor contents.

> **10.** If value is as complicated as Mill indicates, is it possible to determine what anyone's share of production should be if we adopt the principle that income should be directly related to personal contributions to production?
>
> **11.** If we don't adopt that principle, what principle can we use to determine a person's share of income?

THE CONTRIBUTION OF JEVONS

The second half of the 19th century brought a change in emphasis in regard to developing an explanation or theory of value. One of the early contributors to the change was William Stanley Jevons (1835–1882). His writing and thinking moved in the direction of **abstractions,** in contrast to descriptions of real-life examples used by Adam Smith or John Stuart Mill. Jevons was obsessed with statistical information. He withdrew himself from social relations and plotted his collection of quantified facts, always searching for their explanation of past, present, and future (or probable) behavior. This was the period of **neoclassical economics.**

In another way we might think about Jevons as a contributor to a materialistic and hedonistic psychological behavior theory of economics. This followed in the tradition of philosopher Jeremy Bentham's utilitarianism. Jevons was not alone in this revised approach. Economists in other parts of Europe and America were working in the same direction using similar methods—quantitative abstractions and mathematical analysis—in developing economic theory.

In his theory of value, Jevons emphasized the value of a **commodity** as perceived by the consumer, as opposed to the value of a product contributed by the producers. In the following passage from his *Theory of Political Economy* (1871), he presents his theory of value:

> Pleasure and pain are undoubtedly the ultimate objects of the **Calculus of Economy** [boldface added]. To satisfy our wants to the utmost with the least effort to procure the greatest amount of what is desirable at the expense of the least that is undesirable—in other words, to maximise comfort and pleasure, is the problem of Economy. But it is convenient to transfer our attention as soon as possible to the physical objects or actions which are the source to us of pleasures or pains. A very large part of the labour of any community is spent upon the production of the ordinary necessaries and conveniences of life, food, clothing, buildings, utensils, furniture, ornaments, & c.; and the aggregate of these objects constitute, therefore, the immediate object of our attention.

[handwritten margin note: GREATEST GOOD FOR GREATEST NUMBER & MAXIMIZE HAPPINESS]

By a commodity we shall understand any object, or, it may be, any action or service, which can afford pleasure or ward off pain. The name was originally abstract, and denoted the quality of anything by which it was capable of serving man. Having acquired, by a common process of confusion, a concrete signification, it will be well to retain it entirely for that signification, and employ the word *utility* to denote the abstract quality whereby an object serves our purposes, and becomes entitled to rank as a commodity. Whatever can produce pleasure or prevent pain may possess utility.

But it is surely obvious that Political Economy does rest upon the laws of human enjoyment; and that, if those laws are developed by no other science, they must be developed by economists. We labour to produce with the sole object of consuming, and the kinds and amounts of goods produced must be governed entirely by our requirements. Every manufacturer knows and feels how closely he must anticipate the tastes and needs of his customers: his whole success depends upon it; and, in like manner, the whole theory of Economy depends upon a correct theory of consumption.

12. **"Whatever can produce pleasure or prevent pain may possess utility." Is this true for you in regard to a T-shirt? Coca-Cola? Cigarettes? Beer? A chair? A car? A TV? A record?**

13. **What does Jevons mean when he says he will "employ the word *utility* to denote the abstract quality" as opposed to its "concrete signification"?**

Thus, for Jevons, the theory of value focuses on the utility of a product to the consumer. The abstract ability that products have to satisfy our pleasures (or ward off pains) determines their value. Consequently, products that give us more pleasure have more utility and thus possess more value. This theory, therefore, is significantly different from the classical theory, which held that value was determined by the concrete amount of labor that went into the production of a good. For the classical economists, value came from the production of goods and services for consumption. For Jevons and the neoclassical economists, produced goods and services had value because they had utility for consumers. Later economists, as we shall see in Chapter 10, put these two elements together in a supply and demand model of a market in which *prices* were determined by the conditions of both production and consumption. However, the contribution of Jevons to the development of economic thought was to shift economic theory away from the labor theory of value.

CONCLUSION

We can see how elusive the quality of value has become. With the contribution of Jevons, we have moved from the realm of labor content in production to abstract notions of utility in consumption. The focus of attention and analysis of economists who followed Jevons' work centered on consumption; this focus was based on his conception of value. This approach, therefore, dismissed from concern the labor theory of value derived from the exploration of productive activity. (Karl Marx, however, as we shall see in Chapter 8, accepted the labor theory of value and continued to examine the productive sphere of economic activity.) This change, which relied very heavily on abstraction, signaled the emergence of neoclassical economics. This branch of economics utilized mathematics, statistics, and abstraction to refine economic theory during the latter part of the 19th century and the beginning of the 20th century.

Neoclassical economics developed after the Industrial Revolution and the full-blown emergence of Western capitalism. It focused narrowly and intensely on the theoretical operation of a free-market system and the decisions that producers, resource owners, and consumers made within it as economic actors. It demonstrated conclusively with abstract theory that markets produced economic efficiency and that consumers and producers maximized their own well-being through participation in markets. (We will develop this theory in some depth in Part III.)

Neoclassical economists wrote at a time when markets had reached maturity. They were more removed from the creation of markets during the transition from feudalism to capitalism in Western Europe. Smith, Ricardo, and Mill, as classical economists, all wrote in a tradition that utilized historical information and, consequently, had a perspective on the importance of human labor in originally producing goods and services and *then* bringing them to markets. In this way, we can see that different experiences and institutions in different periods of time can give rise to economic theories that are dissimilar. And both classical and neoclassical economics have had an effect on the development of modern economics.

In the next chapter, we will explore ideas concerning the distribution of values that were produced and were to be consumed.

KEY CONCEPTS

value
labor theory of value
value in exchange
value in use
capital

abstractions
neoclassical economics
commodity
calculus of economy

REVIEW QUESTIONS

1. How does the neoclassical conception of value differ from those of the early British economists?

2. What is the relationship between the value of a good or a service and its price?

3. What is the source of value?

SUGGESTED READINGS

E. K. Hunt and Howard J. Sherman, 1981. *Economics* (4th ed.), Harper & Row. An introductory economics textbook with a very good chapter (Chapter 16) on the labor theory of value.

Joan Robinson, 1962. *Economic Philosophy*, Anchor Books. The first three chapters deal with the early development of economic thought and ideas on value and utility.

6

Chapter

Dividing Value—Income Distribution

INTRODUCTION

Economic production creates value—goods and services for exchange on markets. Once produced, how is this value divided among the people? Economists are always attempting to explain why national products are divided as they are. Early economists, such as Smith, who were beginning to think of economics as a social science, defined and classified income receivers as they appeared at that time. It is income that determines how the output will be divided.

In their explanations of the shares received by each factor of production, economists offer reasons for relating the **distribution of income** to contributions to production.

DISTRIBUTING THE GOODS

Chapter 5 directed your attention to the creation of value, especially for commodities. Later modifications in economic thought included the value of services in addition to the commodities, so we can think about a large number of goods and services being produced every day by the people throughout the world. Usually economists think about counting all of these goods and services within the political boundaries of a nation during any selected period of time—a day, a month, or a year. Imagine the huge pile of goods—and services—that are created within the United States during a year: cars, houses, planes, schools, clothes, food, drinks, drugs, books, oil products, doctors' services, bombs, highways, lawnmowers, paper, and miscellaneous junk.

1. **How would you divide the yearly national production of goods and services among the people? To those who produced according to their contribution? Large shares to those who have the most and smaller shares to those who have the least? Let everyone grab what he or she can? More to people who have been good and less to people who have been bad? Let the President decide? Some other way?**

Economists have thought about how to divide these goods and services, and although they have never been in complete agreement—even though they have been very scientific—they have classified the receivers of the shares of output into categories. The receivers are (1) **laborers,** (2) **landowners,** and (3) **owners of capital.** Economists have also named the shares of income that each receives:

1. Labor receives **wages.**

2. Landowners receive **rent.**

3. Owners of capital receive **profits.**

Each of these shares is received in money, but the money is only a claim for the real goods and services and would have no value if there were not those goods and services to claim as the money holder's share. Thus income distribution determines the distribution of products.

2. **There was a time long ago before there were economists with their neat categories. (Maybe it was about the time of the Garden of Eden.) In what order were each of these categories imagined and named? Which developed first, second, and third, and why?**

3. **Another way of thinking about money in relation to claims on the shares of production is to imagine each dollar in the hands of the income receivers (labor, landowners, and capital owners) as a draft of people's labor. Are there dollar drafts on your labor? Can you refuse to be drafted? Who might be exempt from the dollar draft? If drafted, when do you have to perform your service?**

SMITH ON INCOME DISTRIBUTION

Adam Smith wrote about the division of the shares of the national product. You will remember Smith was writing at the beginning of the Industrial Revolution in England. The source of the quotations below is *The Wealth of Nations* (1776). Smith begins by contrasting distribution before and after the introduction of private property:

> But this original state of things, in which the labourer enjoyed the whole produce of his own labour, could not last beyond the first introduction of the appropriation of land and the accumulation of stock. It was at an end, therefore, long before the most considerable improvements were made in the productive powers of labour, and it would be to no purpose to trace further what might have been its effect upon the recompense or wages of labour. As soon as land becomes private property, the landlord demands a share of almost all the produce which the labourer can either raise, or collect from it. His *rent* makes the first deduction from the produce of the labour which is employed upon land.

4. **Why, in your opinion, did the landlord receive a share of the products in the form of rent?**

5. **What determined the size of the share received by the landlord?**

Adam Smith elaborated on the nature of this payment to the landowner as follows:

> Rent, considered as the price paid for the use of land, is naturally the highest which the tenant can afford to pay in the actual circumstances of the land. In adjusting the terms of the lease, the landlord endeavours to leave him no greater share of the produce than what is sufficient to keep up the stock from which he furnishes the seed, pays the labour, and purchases and maintains the cattle and other instruments of husbandry, together with the ordinary profits of farming stock in the neighbourhood. This is evidently the smallest share with which the tenant can content himself without being a loser, and the landlord seldom means to leave him any more. Whatever part of the produce, or, what is the same thing, whatever part of its price, is over and above this share, he naturally endeavours to reserve to himself as the rent of his land, which is evidently the highest the tenant can afford to pay in the actual circumstances of the land.

6. **Why did the tenant pay rent to the landlord? What would have happened if the tenant refused?**

7. **What did the landlord contribute personally to the nation's production?**

Smith calls the next receiver of income the "master." He may be the master of a farm or of a manufacturing firm. He owns the "stock," or what we have defined as the capital. The control of capital earned profit for the master. This form of income emerged with the advance of the division of labor. As Smith explained, the specialization of production required that **stocks** of goods and raw materials be maintained to support people in their productive activities. People were dependent on others for the things they no longer directly produced. This accounts for the share of the product that goes to the "master":

> It seldom happens that the person who tills the ground has wherewithal to maintain himself till he reaps the harvest. His maintenance is generally advanced to him from the stock of a master, the farmer who employs him, and who would have no interest to employ him, unless he was to share in the produce of his labour, or unless his stock was to be replaced to him with a profit. This profit makes a second deduction from the produce of the labour which is employed upon land.
>
> The produce of almost all other labour is liable to the like deduction of profit. In all arts and manufactures the greater part of the workmen stand in need of a master to advance them the materials of their work, and their wages and maintenance till it be completed. He shares in the produce of their labour, or in the value which it adds to the materials upon which it is bestowed; and in this share consists his profit.

8. Why is the following true? "It seldom happens that the person who tills the ground has wherewithal to maintain himself till he reaps the harvest." Who has the "wherewithal"? Where did the one who has the "wherewithal" get it?

Finally Smith takes us to the third party who shares in the **national product.** By this time you have guessed who it is—the laborer. Smith wants to have labor receive an adequate share, now that the landlord and capital owner have had a cut of the pie, because it is good for society: "No society can surely be flourishing and happy, of which the far greater part of the members are poor and miserable. It is but equity,

besides, that they who feed, clothe and lodge the whole body of the people, should have such a share of the produce of their own labour as to be themselves tolerably well fed, clothed and lodged."

What the share will be depends on the amount that is agreed upon by the parties—the master (capital owner) and the laborer. As Smith says, "In every part of Europe, twenty workmen serve under a master for one that is independent; and the wages of labour are every where understood to be, what they usually are, when the labour is one person, and the owner of the stock which employs him another." Smith is quite specific about what this means:

> What are the common wages of labour depends every where upon the contract usually made between those two parties, whose interests are by no means the same. The workmen desire to get as much, the masters to give as little as possible. The former are disposed to combine in order to raise, the latter in order to lower the wages of labour.
>
> It is not, however, difficult to foresee which of the two parties must, upon all ordinary occasions, have the advantage in the dispute, and force the other into a compliance with their terms. The masters, being fewer in number, can combine much more easily; and the law, besides, authorises, or at least does not prohibit their combinations, while it prohibits those of the workmen. We have not acts of parliament against combining to lower the price of work; but many against combining to raise it. In all such disputes the masters can hold out much longer. A landlord, a farmer, a master manufacturer, or merchant, though they did not employ a single workman, could generally live a year or two upon the stocks which they have already acquired. Many workmen could not subsist a week, few could subsist a month, and scarce any a year without employment. In the long run the workman may be as necessary to his master as his master is to him, but the necessity is not so immediate.

If we suggested to Smith that this division of the national product into shares must bring about some harsh conflicts among the three groups of share receivers, he would tell us:

> Envy, malice, or resentment, are the only passions which can prompt one man to injure another in his person or reputation. . . . Men may live together in society with some tolerable degree of security, though there is no civil magistrate to protect them from the injustice of those passions. But avarice and ambition in the rich, in the poor the hatred of labour and the love of present ease and enjoyment, are the passions which prompt to invade property, passions much more steady in their operation, and much more universal in their influence. Wherever there is great property, there is great inequality. For one very rich man, there must be at least five hundred poor, and the affluence of the few supposes the indigence of the many. The affluence of the rich excites the indignation of the poor, who are often both driven by want, and prompted by envy, to invade his possessions. It is only under the shelter of the civil magistrate that the

owner of that valuable property, which is acquired by the labour of many years, or perhaps of many successive generations, can sleep a single night in security. The acquisition of valuable and extensive property, therefore, necessarily requires the establishment of civil government.

The shares of the national product, then, are distributed unequally, primarily because of the unequal distribution of private property (land and capital). While this may lead to conflicts among the different groups of share receivers because each wants to maximize its own share, the government protects private property and, hence, its share of the output.

9. "The acquisition of valuable and extensive property, therefore, necessarily requires the establishment of civil government." Is the purpose of government to protect the rich from the poor?

In addition to the role played by the state in minimizing the conflict over the division of national output, the operation of markets also resolves the conflict. Each group is out to maximize its position, its own share of production. However, all economic transactions take place in markets for goods and services and, as a result, are regulated by the operation of competition. A worker will not work for a lower wage when he knows that he can get a higher wage from another master. A person will not buy a product at a price greater than that of another seller. Smith explains this in the following passage on the **"invisible hand"**:

> Every individual is continually exerting himself to find out the most advantageous employment for whatever capital he can command. It is his own advantage, indeed, and not that of the society, which he has in view. But the study of his own advantage naturally, or rather necessarily leads him to prefer that employment which is most advantageous to the society.
> But the annual revenue of every society is always precisely equal to the exchangeable value of the whole annual produce of its industry, or rather is precisely the same thing with that exchangeable value. As every individual, therefore, endeavours as much as he can both to employ his capital in the support of domestic industry, and so to direct that industry that its produce may be of the greatest value; every individual necessarily labours to render the annual revenue of the society as great as he can. He generally, indeed, neither intends to promote the public interest, nor knows how much he is promoting it. By preferring the support of domestic to that of foreign industry, he intends only his own security; and by directing that industry in such a manner as its produce may be of the greatest value, he intends only his own gain, and he is in this, as in many other cases, led by *an invisible hand* to promote an end which was no part of his intention. Nor is it always the worse for the society that it was no part of it. By pursuing his own interest he frequently promotes that of the society more effectually than when he really intends to promote it.

Despite the apparent conflict and the motivation of self-gain, the operation of the economic system produces the greatest good for the greatest number. According to Smith, social good results, even though "society . . . was no part" of directing the activity. Rather, it results from everyone's seeking his or her own advantage.

10. **What does Smith mean when he says, "he is in this, as in many other cases, led by *an invisible hand*"? What is an "invisible hand"?**

11. **Do you agree with Smith when he says, "But the study of his own advantage naturally, or rather necessarily leads him to prefer that employment which is most advantageous to the society"?**

CONCLUSION

We now have the three share receivers, who are also perceived by economists as the **factors of production.** In theory they receive their shares because of their contribution to production. They participate in and make a contribution to output. As a result, they earn income. The distribution of that income, in turn, determines the distribution of products among the population.

Factors of Production	*Shares Received*
Labor	Wages
Land	Rent
Capital	Profits

In the next chapter, we will examine the development of another concept introduced by the early economists: laissez-faire.

KEY CONCEPTS

distribution of income
laborers
landowners
owners of capital
wages
rent

profits
stocks
national product
"invisible hand"
factors of production

REVIEW QUESTIONS

1. What is the relationship between the creation of value and its distribution? How would the answer of Smith differ from that of Jevons?

2. Why is income in the United States distributed unequally?

3. Should income be distributed more equally? Why or why not?

SUGGESTED READINGS

Maurice Dobb, 1973. *Theories of Value and Distribution since Adam Smith,* Cambridge University Press. A somewhat difficult book on difficult subjects.

Lars Osberg, 1984. *Economic Inequality in the United States,* M. E. Sharpe, Inc. Theoretical perspectives on income distribution and data.

Stephen J. Rose, 1983. *Social Stratification in the United States,* Social Graphics Company. A brief booklet (and poster) on income distribution in the United States, with lots of interesting data.

Lester C. Thurow, 1975. *Generating Inequality,* Basic Books. A study of income distribution in the United States.

7 Chapter

The Rise of Laissez-Faire

INTRODUCTION

Laissez-faire, free-market ideas were promulgated at the end of the 18th century by a new school of economists who wished to transfer control of their national economies from the aristocratic ruling classes to the direction of a self-equilibrating free-market system. Such a policy, it was argued, would produce rapid economic progress. As laissez-faire ideas were adopted, growth did take place; but it was accompanied by poverty and business cycles.

J. B. Say assured economists in 1803 that if markets were left free, there could be only temporary and minor problems of unemployment. This was because production always created its own demand, and demand created production. Known as **Say's law,** this doctrine was widely accepted by most economists throughout the 19th century.

However, some economists attempted to call attention to continuing unemployment problems and suggested various ideas about ways to respond to the problems. These socialistic economists were either ignored or viewed as dangerous radicals by the dominant school of economists in the universities and the ruling classes.

By 1926 John Maynard Keynes was convinced that laissez-faire was no longer an appropriate way of thinking about unemployment. Others had noticed this from 50 to 100 years earlier, but it was Keynes's contribution that ultimately signaled the fall of laissez-faire.

THE FLOW OF ECONOMIC ACTIVITY

We have seen that three factors of production are combined to create the national product. Each receives a share of the total product transformed conveniently into money. The money is used to claim output by each of the controllers of the three productive factors—landlords, laborers, and capital owners. Some classical economists of the 19th century claimed that the demand for the product would always be equal to the supply. The reason seemed self-evident. Those who constitute each of the three factors of production receive claims on shares for everything they supply in the production process. These claims become the demand for part of the total product. Therefore demand for the products is created in the process of supplying the product. Figure 7.1 illustrates this flow of economic activity.

J. B. SAY AND GLUTS

Jean Baptiste Say (1767–1832), a French economist who studied, modified, and amplified the ideas of Adam Smith, stated this idea in *A Treatise on Political Economy* (1803):

> It is worthwhile to remark that a product is no sooner created, than it, from that instant, affords a market for other products to the full extent of its own value. When the producer has put the finishing hand to his product, he is most anxious to sell it immediately, lest its value should vanish in his hands. Nor is he less anxious to dispose of the money he may get for it; for the value of money is also perishable. But the only way of getting rid

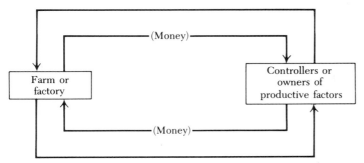

Figure 7.1 Label the outside connecting lines with the following words: *land, labor, supply of product, capital.* Use all the words. Label the inside lines with the appropriate words: *demand for products, rent, wages, profits.* Use all the words.

of money is in the purchase of some product or other. Thus, the mere circumstance of the creation of one product immediately opens a vent for other products.

However, a few economists were concerned about unemployment resulting from more production than people might demand. What if some wrong products are produced, and they are not all purchased? Won't there be unemployment because of insufficient demand in those industries? What if there is more production generally than the people are able to purchase? Economists called this situation a **glut** in the market. These gluts create unemployment and poverty that lead to terrifying social conditions and great suffering. Wouldn't that be of concern to economists?

Thomas Robert Malthus (1766–1834), a British economist, was one of the few economists concerned about these possible "gluts." In his *Principles of Political Economy* (1820) he says:

> It has been thought by some very able writers, that although there may easily be a glut of particular commodities, there cannot possibly be a glut of commodities in general; because, according to their view of the subject, commodities being always exchanged for commodities, one half will furnish a market for the other half, and production being thus the sole source of demand, an excess in the supply of one article merely proves a deficiency in the supply of some other, and a general excess is impossible. M[onsieur] Say, in his distinguished work on political economy, has indeed gone so far as to state that the consumption of a commodity by taking it out of the market diminishes demand, and the production of a product proportionably increases it.
>
> This doctrine, however, as generally applied, appears to me to be utterly unfounded, and completely to contradict the great principles which regulate supply and demand.
>
> It is by no means true, as a matter of fact, that commodities are always exchanged for commodities. An immense mass of commodities is exchanged directly, either for productive labour, or personal services: and it is quite obvious, that this mass of commodities, compared with the labour with which it is to be exchanged, may fall in value from a glut just as any one commodity falls in value from an excess of supply, compared either with labour or money.
>
> In the case supposed there would evidently be an unusual quantity of commodities of all kinds in the market, owing to those who had been before engaged in personal services having been converted, by the accumulation of capital, into productive labourers; while the number of labourers altogether being the same, and the power and will to purchase for consumption among landlords and capitalists being by supposition diminished, commodities would necessarily fall in value compared with labour, so as very greatly to lower profits, and to check for a time further production.
>
> But this is precisely what is meant by the term glut, which, in this case, is evidently general not partial.

1. Why has demand decreased according to Malthus?

Say and others countered the argument set forth by Malthus by claiming that whenever a glut of a particular product emerged, markets would immediately adjust through price changes and the reallocation of resources. If one product was over-produced, its price would fall and resources would go elsewhere. Activity would shift to those products "most in request." Consequently, gluts would soon be eliminated through the operation of the market system. This reasoning supported the idea of laissez-faire.

LAISSEZ-FAIRE

J. B. Say won the argument with Thomas Malthus. There were significant reasons for this victory, in spite of the prevalence of repeated gluts, unemployment, poverty, and economic depressions in capitalist nations.

Economists and businessmen were convinced that the self-adjusting qualities of the economy, free from government controls, was the best system for generating profits and growth. This was Smith's concept of an "invisible hand" directing a free economy to prosperity at work. The idea of "laissez-faire" (from the Physiocrats in France) was similar to this "invisible hand"—*laissez-faire* meaning "let it happen," or "let it be." Businessmen wanted to run their own affairs without—well, almost without—government interference.

The "laissez-faire" idea is to permit market forces *under competitive conditions* to operate unhindered. Economists said that if the market was permitted to work on its own, it would be most efficient and most advantageous to society. People would demand the products they wanted as they spent their income. This would determine which products would be produced. Doesn't that seem to be better than having an individual or group of powerful people decide which products will be produced?

Laissez-faire, said the economists, has additional benefits: All of the owners of the factors of production will be directed into the most effective use of the factors of production by the market. It will be to their greatest advantage to produce the products for which there is a demand in the marketplace. If the owners of the productive factors use them to produce only what they themselves want, no one will purchase the products. There will be no shares given in the national pie of products to those productive factor owners who don't follow market demand.

Therefore let the market be, *laissez-faire;* don't interfere with it. It is controlled by an "invisible hand." It will regulate itself. Furthermore, markets will eliminate any gluts and unemployment.

All of this is based on the assumption that people will work for their own **self-interest.** We have already been assured by Adam Smith about the validity of this assumption.

self-interest regulate market

2. **What is your evaluation of the *laissez-faire* idea?**

3. **What are your assumptions about people's behavior? Are they consistently selfish? Are they consistently altruistic? (*Altruism:* Regard for others as a principle of action.) Which are you? Were you born selfish or altruistic? Have you been educated to be selfish or altruistic?**

4. **Would Adam Smith think it is more patriotic to be selfish or altruistic?**

As mercantilist policies were abandoned and laissez-faire policies were adopted in England, the Industrial Revolution and the emergence of capitalist institutions proceeded. Essentially it was a period in which business sought freedom from state control, and prospered. However, not everyone was happy with the course of events, as this passage from Thomas Fleming's *1776, Year of Illusions* suggests:

There was a constant fear of the uneasy, often resentful poor. Workmen regularly smashed up new machines in the manufacturing towns. In 1765, the pitmen of the Tyne went on violent strike, wrecking the mining machinery and setting fire to the coal under ground. A few years later, riots swept Lancashire as the poor attacked spinning jennies and other machinery that they thought were depriving them of jobs. In 1773, the sailors of Liverpool staged something very close to a revolution, training their cannon on the town's stock exchange, wrecking and looting the houses of prominent shipowners, and even hoisting a "bloody flag."

On July 10, 1776, a mob marched on the town of Shepton Mallet to destroy some new weaving machines. Three justices of the peace ordered the crowd to disperse. They refused, and when two of the justices went home, the mob attacked the poorhouse where the machines had been operating, destroyed the machines, and all but wrecked the building. The remaining justice called out the local regiment of the army, and five ringleaders were arrested. The mob rioted as they were being led to jail. The troops, after firing two rounds over the heads of the mob, let it have a full volley, killing one man and seriously wounding six others. The coroner ruled the death "accidental."

When parliament convened in the fall of 1775, a pamphlet urged the people of London to rise and prevent the corrupt members from continuing to defraud them. The government rushed additional troops into the city.

Protesting the American war had nothing to do with this threatened uprising. America was too far away and the grievances of the poor in the city of London too real and immediate to make the Americans a primary concern for most Englishmen in the early days of 1776.

—Reprinted with permission from Thomas Fleming, *1776, Year of Illusions,* W. W. Norton & Co., Inc., 1975.

---

5. If you had been a member of Parliament during 1776, what kinds of legislation would you have introduced and supported? Would you have been an advocate of laissez-faire?

It was probably in response to the situation in England that Adam Smith decided it would be better to transfer control of the economy from the self-interest of the ruling class to individual self-interest as expressed in the marketplace. His preference for nontraditional direction led him to perceive the market as an impartial control of resource allocation and income distribution. He hoped the market was impartial, but was it? Smith was aware of the difficulties in his solution. He knew about the ability of combinations of employers to overwhelm the bargaining power of workers, but he continued to support markets free from government controls— laissez-faire.

What he may not have fully perceived was that the transfer of market controls from the self-interest of the ruling class to the self-interest of those who had the control of the largest quantities of productive resources was not necessarily the ideal solution for a sick economy. But it may have been an improvement in 1776.

Adam Smith thought it would be when he wrote in *The Wealth of Nations* about the allocation of capital by an individual:

What is the species of domestic industry which his capital can employ, and of which the produce is likely to be of the greatest value, every individual, it is evident, can, in his local situation, judge much better than any statesman or lawgiver can do for him. The statesman, who should attempt to direct private people in what manner they ought to employ their capitals, would not only load himself with a most unnecessary attention, but assume an authority which could safely be trusted, not only to no single person, but to no council or senate whatever, and which would nowhere be so dangerous as in the hands of a man who had folly and presumption enough to fancy himself fit to exercise it.

LAISSEZ-FAIRE AND THE POOR: THE SOCIALIST CRITIQUE

The conditions of some members of the economy were improving with laissez-faire, but the fate of some others was extreme poverty. Why weren't conditions for the poor improving as well? As markets and private property emerged in Western

Europe, most people became dependent on wage labor for income. Work was not always available, and many peasants ended up in urban areas where they inhabited emerging slums and, if possible, worked in the developing factories. Living and working conditions were extremely poor. And with so many competing for jobs, wages were very low. The growing working class during the Industrial Revolution paid the social cost of industrialization in the cities and the factories of Western Europe.

Pierre Joseph Proudhon (1809–1865), a French economist, came to a conclusion about the continuing situation of low income that he stated forcefully in his essay "What Is Property?" (1840):

> If I were asked to answer the following question: *What is slavery?* and I should answer in one word, *It is murder,* my meaning would be understood at once. No extended argument would be required to show that the power to take from a man his thought, his will, his personality, is a power of life and death; and that to enslave a man is to kill him. Why, then, to this other question: *What is property?* may I not likewise answer, *It is robbery,* without the certainty of being misunderstood; the second proposition being no other than a transformation of the first?
>
> Reader, calm yourself: I am no agent of discord, no firebrand of sedition. I anticipate history by a few days; I disclose a truth whose development we may try in vain to arrest; I write the preamble of our future constitution. This proposition which seems to you blasphemous—*property is robbery*—would, if our prejudices allowed us to consider it, be recognized as the lightning-rod to shield us from the coming thunderbolt; but too many interests stand in the way! . . . Alas! philosophy will not change the course of events; destiny will fulfill itself regardless of prophecy. Besides, must not justice be done and our education be finished?
>
> The proprietor, the robber, the hero, the sovereign—for all these titles are synonymous—imposes his will as law, and suffers neither contradiction nor control; that is, he pretends to be the legislative and executive power at once. Accordingly, the substitution of the scientific and true law for the royal will be accomplished only by a terrible struggle; and this constant substitution is, after property, the most potent element in history, the most prolific source of political disturbances. Examples are too numerous and too striking to require enumeration.

6. *"What is property? . . . It is robbery."* True or false?

Proudhon is careful to differentiate **property** from **possessions**. He has no quarrel with people owning *personal* possessions—homes, farms, tools, livestock, furniture, or any of the things we might own and use. He protests the ownership of *impersonal* property that is not used by the owner except to collect rents on land and interest and profits on capital that are produced by others. There is an important difference between property and possessions to many socialist authors. Here is Proudhon's statement about the difference:

> Individual possession is the condition of social life; five thousand years of property demonstrate it. Property is the suicide of society. Possession is a right; property is against right. Suppress property while maintaining possession, and, by this simple modification of the principle you will revolutionize law, government, economy, and institutions; you will drive evil from the face of the earth.

7. To demonstrate your understanding of Proudhon's definition, write five currently familiar examples of "possessions" and five of "property."

Proudhon was only one of many who were sufficiently uncomfortable with economic conditions to want to try something entirely different. America seemed to be a country in which some of these dissatisfied people could experiment. A proliferation of various utopian communities developed in America. After all, wasn't America envisioned as a country for people with hopeful spirits? These people were seeking new forms of a social and political paradise. These communities practiced everything from communism to fascism, from celibacy to communal sexual intercourse and selective human breeding, and from anarchistic decentralization to dictatorial centralization. But what they had in common was a vision of a political and economic situation preferable to what they were experiencing.

Not all of the discontented people emigrated to America. Many participated in political action to change their home economies and governments. There were general strikes with all workers striking at the same time, revolutions, and political education activities working toward evolutionary change.

John Stuart Mill in his *Principles of Political Economy* envisioned a different kind of economy from the one of which he was writing in England in 1848.

> The form of association, however, which if mankind continue to improve, must be expected in the end to predominate, is not that which can exist between a capitalist as chief, and workpeople without a voice in the management, but the association of the labourers themselves on terms of equality, collectively owning the capital with which they carry on their operations, and working under managers elected and removable by themselves.

8. How would you evaluate these mid-19th-century comments of John Stuart Mill?

The **socialist critique** of 19th-century capitalism was developed further in a piece also published in 1848. In this year Karl Marx (1818–1883) and Friedrich

DOONESBURY   by Garry Trudeau

Copyright © 1975, G. B. Trudeau/Distributed by Universal Press Syndicate.

Engels (1820–1895) wrote *The Communist Manifesto* for the Communist League, an association of working people in Germany. Marx and Engels argued forcefully that the capitalist system itself was the source of the poverty and instability experienced by the growing working class. They urged workers to organize themselves for their own protection and to fight for socialism. We will explore Marx's ideas in more detail in the next chapter.

THE FLOWERING OF LAISSEZ-FAIRE

Despite the conditions of the poor and the socialist critique, laissez-faire capitalism flourished in 19th-century England and throughout Western Europe.

Queen Victoria reigned from 1837 to 1901 and gave her name to the Victorian Age, an "age" that is more than a simple designation of time in history. This was the age of increasing commercial dominance over formal and informal institutions that affected social values and behavior. Transportation and communication were revolutionized by railway expansion and the telegraph, thereby quickening the pace of life. People began to illuminate their homes with electricity. The first cars were on the roads. The Carnegies, Vanderbilts, and Rockefellers were accumulating their enormous wealth. Coal and oil displaced animals and waterpower as sources of energy.

As the pace quickened, production increased, and more people attempted to be successful in business. A few individuals began to wonder about where all of this movement might lead. In 1864 John Ruskin questioned the "ideal of human life" in an essay named "Traffic," in which he describes the worshippers of the "Goddess of Getting-on." Ruskin was one of the great thinkers and writers in the Victorian Age. His works about art, architecture, and political economy have continuing relevance today.

> Your ideal of human life then is, I think, that it should be passed in a pleasant undulating world, with iron and coal everywhere underneath it. On each pleasant bank of this world is to be a beautiful mansion, with

two wings; and stables, and coach-houses; a moderately-sized park; a large garden and hot-houses; and pleasant carriage drives through the shrubberies. In this mansion are to live the favoured votaries of the Goddess; the English gentleman, with his gracious wife, and his beautiful family; he always able to have the boudoir and the jewels for the wife, and the beautiful ball dresses for the daughters, and hunters for the sons, and a shooting in the Highlands for himself. At the bottom of the bank is to be the mill; not less than a quarter of a mile long, with one steam engine at each end, and two in the middle and a chimney three hundred feet high. In this mill are to be in constant employment from eight hundred to a thousand workers, who never drink, never strike, always go to church on Sunday, and always express themselves in respectful language.

> **9. Write a paragraph about your ideal of human life discussing the same kinds of subjects mentioned by Ruskin: houses, environment, transportation, recreation, family, and industry.**

The majority of people in England didn't share the same dream. Their reality was one of poor housing, unemployment or low wages, and urban squalor. Poor people were still around all through the Victorian Age, and the people in the mansions were uneasy about their presence. It was a time of general economic growth but also of continuing economic disparity. The implications of that disparity offered a potential threat to the existing social, political, and economic order.

Walter E. Houghton published an illuminating book, *The Victorian Frame of Mind*, in 1957 that helps us understand this period. His book has become an essential work for people who are interested in the opinions and ideas of the 19th century.

> To think it strange that the great age of optimism was also an age of anxiety is to overlook the ambivalent reaction which the main social and intellectual tendencies of the period provoked. Expanding business, scientific development, the growth of democracy, and the decline of Christianity were sources of distress as well as of satisfaction. But since optimism was expressed more often than anxiety (partly because it was more widely felt, and partly because any pessimistic attitude toward the human situation was considered weak or unmanly), we are still unaware of the degree to which the Victorian consciousness—and especially the

subconsciousness—was haunted by fear and worry, by guilt and frustration and loneliness.

Bertrand Russell tells us that his grandfather, lying on his deathbed in 1869, "heard a loud noise in the street and thought it was the revolution breaking out." The incident is symbolic. For all its solid and imposing strength, Victorian society, particularly in the period before 1850, was shot through, from top to bottom, with the dread of some wild outbreak of the masses that would overthrow the established order and confiscate private property.

The possibility that it might happen here was abundantly supported, a priori, by the spread of radical propaganda, both political and religious, among the working class. The two most influential books, Tom Paine's *The Rights of Man* and *The Age of Reason,* hardly seem dangerous now, for the former did not go beyond democracy nor the latter beyond deism. But democracy, to consider that first, carried connotations much like those of communism today.

Another source of alarm came from quite a different quarter. The decline of Christianity and the prospect of atheism had social implications which now seem curious (though they may have more bearing on our contemporary situation than we suppose). It was then assumed, in spite of rationalist denials, that any collapse of faith would destroy the sanctions of morality; and morality gone, society would disintegrate. Mill described the age as one in which the opinion that religious belief was necessary for moral and social purposes was universal, and yet real belief was feeble and precarious—a situation well calculated to arouse anxiety. But just such doubts were being raised on every side. Even so honest and courageous a thinker as Henry Sidgwick was reluctant to publish his skeptical views about immorality because the loss of such a hope, "from the minds of average human beings as now constituted, would be an evil of which I cannot pretend to measure the extent,"—if not the actual "dissolution of the existing social order," at least the increased danger of such a catastrophe.

What gave edge to these general speculations on the causal relationship of disbelief and disorder was their particular application to the lower classes. For "everyone" agreed that any discarding of the Christian sanctions of duty, obedience, patience under suffering, and brotherly love was obviously "fraught with grievous danger to property and the State." Nothing could illustrate that assumption more tellingly than the reviews of *The Descent of Man* (1871) in the most important newspapers, where Darwin was severely censured for "revealing his zoological [anti-Christian] conclusions to the general public at a moment when the sky of Paris was red with the incendiary flames of the Commune."

—Reprinted with permission from Walter E. Houghton, *The Victorian Frame of Mind,*
Yale University Press, 1957.

10. **Are wealthy people in the United States today worried about democracy? Why or why not?**

11. **Would the wealthy people in America today be alarmed if the poorer people abandoned religion? Why or why not?**

THE SITUATION IN THE UNITED STATES

In the United States, the Industrial Revolution occurred in the last half of the 19th century. By the beginning of the 20th century, the United States was the world's leading producer of both agricultural and manufacturing goods. American capitalism and markets spread across the North American continent and began to reach out to the rest of the world. Economic output increased dramatically—but this success was not unchallenged. Poverty was not eliminated, a militant labor movement emerged along with a growing working class, periodic financial crises and depressions disrupted the path of growth, and there were continuing problems associated with Native American tribes and the end of slavery. The development of the American economic system was full of successes *and* difficulties.

Thorstein Veblen (1857–1929) was one of the first economists to develop a comprehensive critique of American capitalism. He wrote during a period marked by continuing industrialization and growth, but also by increasing business concentration and recurrent economic depressions. One of his first books, *The Theory of the Leisure Class* (1899), noted the rise of a new class of people in American society accompanying the economic progress of the industrial revolution. These propertied people were privileged to engage in "conspicuous consumption" as testimony to their success. Veblen, in a very sarcastic but penetrating style, offered numerous examples of the new leisure class seeking status through the purchase of houses, clothing, and other goods. His tone and insight about "pecuniary emulation" also called attention to the fact that, as in Europe, the American industrialization process did not enrich everyone, although it did subject the entire society to the influences of heightened materialism.

In later works, most notably *The Theory of Business Enterprise* (1904) and *Absentee Ownership* (1923), Veblen identified some trends that characterized American economic experience with laissez-faire capitalism. These trends were part and parcel of the American economic success, but they also suggested some future difficulties. Veblen saw a distinction between business and industry. In *Absentee Ownership,* he wrote, "The industrial arts are a matter of tangible performance directed to work that is designed to be of material use to man. . . . [The] arts of business are arts of bargaining, effrontery, salesmanship, make-believe, and are directed to the gain of the business man at the cost of the community, at large and in detail."

This distinction was important to his interpretation of the primary trends in U.S. economic development: a tendency toward business concentration, rapid technological advance, and a constant difficulty with depression. Monopoly resulted from the business instinct to eliminate competition as one of the most effective ways to secure profits. But technological progress also was caused by the business drive for profits. The problem arose because technology constantly pushed the ability of the industrial arts to produce more, but monopoly held back production to get higher prices and profits. The consequence, according to Veblen, was a constant tendency toward depression. The depressions of the 1870s and 1890s in the United States provided real evidence that Say's law should be suspect, and that Veblen's concern with explaining the frequency of high levels of unemployment, if not exactly correct, was at least worth pursuing.

Veblen was an **institutionalist.** The institutionalists were critical of the neoclassical school of economics. They argued that the focus of such economists as Marshall and Jevons was too narrow and that their method was too abstract. The neoclassical economists didn't pay enough attention to the influence of other factors in affecting economic behavior. Specifically, the institutionalists, and Veblen as one of their leading figures, argued that it was important to take account of history, institutions, and the complexity of human motivation in analyzing economic events. The following passage from Veblen's *The Place of Science in Modern Civilization* (1919) demonstrates the institutionalist critique of the neoclassical theory of markets and its assumptions about consumer behavior:

> The psychological and anthropological preconceptions of economists have been those which were accepted by the psychological and social sciences some generations ago. The hedonistic conception of man is that of a lightning calculator of pleasures and pains, who oscillates like a homogeneous globule of desire of happiness under the impulse of stimuli that shift him about the area, but leave him intact. He has neither antecedent nor consequent. He is an isolated, definitive human datum, in stable equilibrium except for the buffets of the impinging forces that displace him in one direction or another. Self-imposed in elemental space, he spins symmetrically about his own spiritual axis until the parallelogram of forces bears down upon him, whereupon he follows the line of the resultant. When the force of the impact is spent, he comes to rest, a self-contained globule of desire as before.

[handwritten margin note: INDIVIDUALS DO NOT EXIST IN A VACUUM — AFFECTED BY OTHERS, HISTORY, ETC.]

12. Are you a "self-contained globule of desire"?

THE KEYNESIAN CRITIQUE OF LAISSEZ-FAIRE

John Maynard Keynes (1883–1946), a British economist, followed the classical tradition, but in 1926 he began to write about his departure from the classical ideas held by most economists. By 1929 he was advising the British government to spend freely on public works programs to promote employment. President Franklin Roosevelt, confronted by millions of families without any income because laissez-faire capitalism was unable to provide employment in the 1930s, increased the influence of government in the American economy.

KEYNES

During the prosperous 1920s, Keynes wrote about "The End of Laissez-Faire." In this essay he challenged the notion that the search for private interests always led to the greater good for the society as a whole. In particular, he was convinced that capitalism did not automatically produce full employment. He rejected Say's law. He offered the suggestion that perhaps it was necessary for the state to assume some responsibility for the overall health of capitalist economies. Capitalism might be stronger, he argued, if some decisions were left in private hands; but some others, which were social in nature, ought to be the responsibility of the state.

Keynes thus began to explore the idea that laissez-faire did not always necessarily result in the greatest social good. He argued, in fact, that the state should take an active part in certain economic matters. This emerging argument and the Great Depression of the 1930s signaled the end of laissez-faire. Keynes, while accepting capitalism as an economic system, rejected the classical notion of laissez-faire. His primary argument in reaching this conclusion was that the laissez-faire capitalist economic system could easily result in chronic unemployment and instability, just as Malthus had argued more than 100 years earlier. In Part IV we will examine in more detail the Keynesian body of thought on instability and the proper role for the state in the economy.

13. What would Adam Smith think about Keynes' argument? Why?

KEY CONCEPTS

laissez-faire	"possessions" and "property,"
Say's law	difference between
glut	socialist critique
self-interest	institutionalist
altruism	Keynesian critique of laissez-faire

REVIEW QUESTIONS

1. What are the strengths of laissez-faire capitalism both in theory and in practice?

2. What have been the major shortcomings in the operation of laissez-faire capitalism?

3. What reasons can you think of that would cast doubt on Say's law that supply always creates its own demand?

SUGGESTED READINGS

E. Ray Canterbury, 1976. *The Making of Economics*, Wadsworth. See Chapter 7 on Keynes.

Douglas F. Dowd, 1964. *Thorstein Veblen*, Washington Square Press. A comprehensive and readable summary of Veblen's life, times and economic thought.

Douglas F. Dowd, 1977. *The Twisted Dream: Capitalist Development in the United States Since 1776*, Winthrop. An economic history of the United States relying heavily on the analysis of Marx and Veblen.

Robert Heilbroner, 1981. *The Worldly Philosophers*, Simon and Schuster. See Chapter 7 on the Victorian world and Chapter 9 on Keynes.

E. K. Hunt, 1981. *Property and Prophets*, Harper & Row. See Chapter 5 on early socialist critics of capitalism.

The Marxian Critique of Capitalism

INTRODUCTION

As capitalism developed in Western Europe and the United States, a critique of some of its results began to emerge. As we have seen in Chapter 7, some economists and historians noted the spread of poverty and the recurrence of depressions, and others theorized on these problems. One of the first systematic analyses and critiques of capitalism was made by Karl Marx (1818–1883) in the mid- and late 1800s. Marx's system provides a comprehensive and consistent framework for understanding, evaluating, and criticizing the structure and development of capitalism. For that reason alone, it would be important to summarize Marx's system of thought concerning capitalism. In addition, Marxian economics has been important to the development of economic thought, and Marxism as a political movement has become increasingly widespread in the modern era.

John Gurley of Stanford University has said the following about why it is important to study Marxism:

> Many Americans . . . are unaware of Marxism as a philosophical
> world-outlook, a useful framework for understanding much of what is
> going on in the world. In a way, this is strange, inasmuch as hundreds of

millions of people around the world know and use Marxism, at least to some degree; it is probably the most prevalent set of ideas in the world today. A study of Marxism is not only useful for understanding the robustness of the continuing attacks on capitalism and the Western way of life, but it is also helpful, almost indispensable, for understanding capitalism itself. Marxism offers new and surprising insights into this subject.

—John Gurley, *Challengers to Capitalism,* San Francisco Book Company, 1975.

We will encounter Marxist analysis elsewhere in this book. This chapter will provide a brief introduction to Marxist analysis.

KARL MARX: POLITICAL ECONOMIST AND REVOLUTIONARY

Marx was born in 1818 in Trier, in what is now West Germany. His father was a successful lawyer, and Marx began his college career in legal studies. However, he soon switched to philosophy, in which he earned a Ph.D. at the age of 23. Having already become a radical in his student days, he was unable to secure a teaching position. Instead he became the editor of the *Rheinische Zeitung*, in Cologne. However, this journal was suppressed by the Prussian government in 1843, and Marx with his new wife, Jenny von Westphalen, moved to Paris. In Paris, Marx was active in left-wing journalism and in the workers' movement. It was there that he met Friedrich Engels and first began to study political economy and capitalism.

Over the latter half of the 1840s Marx's radicalism continually got him in trouble with governments. In 1845, he was expelled from France and moved to Brussels. There he wrote *The German Ideology* and *The Communist Manifesto* with Engels. In 1848–1849 several workers' revolutions occurred in Europe, and Belgium sent Marx packing. He first went to Paris and then to Germany. He was soon kicked out of Germany and then out of France, again. Finally, in 1849 his family settled in London, where he was to remain for the rest of his life.

In London, Marx devoted himself to studying political economy and writing. His years there were spent in constant poverty, but he received substantial support from his friend Engels, who had a family interest in a manufacturing firm in Manchester. Marx developed into one of the most profound and widely known critics of capitalism in mid-19th-century Europe. His work had two basic elements: one was his study and writing, and the other was his political activism. He was a correspondent for the *New York Daily Tribune* and published numerous books, the most famous of which is *Capital*. His political activism was as a socialist and communist in the workers' movement. He helped organize the International Working Men's Association—the First International—and was active in workers' struggles throughout the rest of his life.

MARX'S GENERAL SYSTEM OF THOUGHT

Marx's political activism and his analysis of capitalism were both based on his general system of social development. This system amounted to a theory of history and of social change. As he put it in *The Communist Manifesto*, "The history of all hitherto existing society is the history of class struggles." This expressed his "materialist conception of history," which emphasized the role of the economic aspects of life in social development. This conception is central to Marx's system of thought and his analysis of capitalism, and we will explore it briefly here.

Dialectics

Marx's general system was based on two philosophical notions: dialectics and materialism. Dialectics was borrowed by Marx from the German philosopher Hegel (1770–1831). It emphasizes the idea that all things change and that all things contain not only themselves but their opposites. Dialectics is the study of the contradictions within the essence of things. A rock is a rock; but it is also, at the same time, "not a rock" because it could become a million grains of sand. And consequently, development becomes the struggle of opposites — things becoming other things. Capitalists cannot be capitalists without their opposites, the workers (and vice versa); and both capitalists and workers will develop as they interact with and influence each other. Out of this struggle of opposites comes change in which both elements, capitalists and workers, and the thing itself, capitalism, are transformed into something else. Ultimately, Marx thought that capitalism would develop into socialism and then communism. Dialectics, then, emphasizes change, contradiction, and the struggle of opposites. It thus constitutes a challenge to formal logic that concentrates on things as they are and their interrelationships. Marx wrote the following in his Preface to *Capital* (1867):

> Dialectic . . . in its rational form is a scandal and abomination to bourgeoisdom and its doctrinaire professors, because it includes in its comprehension and affirmative recognition of the existing state of things, at the same time, also, the recognition of the negation of that state, of its inevitable breaking up; because it regards every historically developed social form as in fluid movement, and therefore takes into account its transient nature not less than its momentary existence; because it lets nothing impose upon it, and is in its essence critical and revolutionary.

1. **Develop your own example that emphasizes the dialectical nature of some thing or process.**

2. **Why is the dialectic "critical and revolutionary"?**

Materialism

Materialism concerns the notion that what is basic to the real life of human beings is their activity in the world. To understand the world, we must focus on real people and their day-to-day activities — especially those concerned with production for continued survival in this world. To Marx, materialism concerns "real, active men, and on the basis of their real life-process demonstrates the development of the ideological reflexes and echoes of this life-process." To know the world we must study things and their development. In addition, we must study the interrelationships of *things*: "Things come into being, change and pass out of being, not as separate individual units, but in essential relation and inter-connection, so that they cannot be understood each separately and by itself but only in their relation and inter-connection." To know the United States, we must study its productive process and how that relates to its laws, beliefs, social classes, patterns of consumption, and so on. Additionally, we must study the history of how all these elements have changed over time and developed. Materialism contrasts with the notion that change takes place through the development of *ideas*. For Marx, the source of change rests, ultimately, in actual productive activity.

> **3. How else could we "know" our world other than through its material aspects?**

The Materialist Conception of History, or Historical Materialism

From these two philosophical bases, Marx developed his theory of history—the materialist conception of history, or **historical materialism.** Productive activity is fundamental to human beings and to their societies. Consequently, the organization of production, the economic structure, forms the basis of all societies. All other social institutions and ideas are derived from the economic structure of the society. If the economic structure changes, all other aspects of the society will also change.

Marx formalized his analysis in the following way. The economic structure, or base, was the **mode of production** and consisted of the **forces of production** and the **relations of production.** The **forces of production** included all the things that were necessary to produce goods and services: tools, machines, factories, means of transportation, raw materials, human labor, science, technology, skills, and knowledge. Over time, obviously, the forces of production changed. The **relations of production** were determined by the relationship of people to the productive process. When the forces of production are organized in a certain way, there will be different classes of people defined by their relationship to production. The relations of production, therefore, will be determined by patterns of ownership of productive resources, the nature of property relations, and the division of labor. These will determine a class structure of society. A certain mode of production, then, consists of specific forces of production and specific relations of production (that is, a specific **class structure**). In addition, the mode of production is accompanied by the **superstructure** of society. The superstructure consists of the ideas, institutions, and ideologies of the society, including laws, politics, culture, ethics, religion, morals, esthetics, art, philosophy, and so on. The purpose of the superstructure is to support the economic base of society. For example, feudalism organized production with certain methods and institutions, and it had its own class structure and superstructure.

MODE OF PRODUCTION ⌐ FORCES OF PRODUCTION: TOOLS, LABOR, MATERIALS, ETC
               └ RELATIONS OF PRODUCTION: RELATION OF PEOPLE TO PRODUCTION
↓ CLASS STRUCTURE / SUPERSTRUCT. OF SOCIETY   WORKERS & OWNERS

CHANGE TECH.
OR MEANS OF PRODUCTION,
∴ CHANGE SOCIAL CLASSES
∴ CHANGE SUPERSTRUCTURE OF
SOCIETY.

8: The Marxian Critique of Capitalism   **107**

Within this framework is Marx's theory of historical change. Oversimplifying somewhat, when the forces of production change, the relations of production—social classes—will also change; this brings about a new mode of production that will, in turn, develop its own specific superstructure. It is in this context that class struggle takes place; different classes have different interests and visions and thus will do battle over the organization of production and hence, society. The "old" classes will fight to preserve the old mode of production, and the new will fight for change. One of the most fundamental aspects of this "materialist conception of history" is that people, through acting on the forces of production, create their own history. Marx sums up his historical materialism in this passage from the *Critique of Political Economy* (1859):

> In the social production which men carry on they enter into definite relations that are indispensable and independent of their will; these relations of production correspond to a definite stage of development of their material powers of production. The sum total of these relations of production constitutes the economic structure of society—the real foundation on which rise legal and political superstructures and to which correspond definite forms of social consciousness. The mode of production in material life determines the general character of the social, political, and spiritual processes of life. It is not the consciousness of men that determines their existence, but, on the contrary, their social existence determines their consciousness. At a certain stage of their development, the material forces of production in society come into conflict with the existing relations of production, or—what is but a legal expression for the same thing—with the property relations within which they had been at work before. From forms of development of the forces of production these relations turn into their fetters. Then comes the period of social revolution. With the change of economic foundation the entire immense superstructure is more or less rapidly transformed. In considering such transformations the distinction should always be made between the material transformation of the economic conditions or production which can be determined with the precision of natural science, and the legal, political, religious, aesthetic, or philosophic—in short, ideological forms in which men become conscious of this conflict and fight it out.

4. **Apply the "materialist conception of history" (historical materialism) to the transition from feudalism to capitalism.**

5. **"It is not the consciousness of men that determines their existence, but, on the contrary, their social existence determines their consciousness." What does this mean? And how does it mean that human beings create their own history?**

Marx's model of social change thus focuses on the relationships and contradictions among the forces of production, social classes, and the general institutions and ideologies of society. This complex process, according to Marx, determines the development of societies. In that process, the forces of production are of primary importance, but class struggle and ideology are also extremely influential.

THE MARXIAN ANALYSIS OF CAPITALISM

It was from this view of social change and history that Marx proceeded to develop his analysis and critique of capitalism. His conclusion was a condemnation of capitalism and its results, as well as a scientific appraisal of its likely future development and eventual replacement by socialism. Here we will very briefly review Marx's theory of capitalist development.

Capitalism uses advanced methods of production including factories, transportation, and technology and, as it expands, has access to greater supplies of raw materials. Accompanying this mode of production are its own relations of production. Basically, according to Marx, with the advance of the division of labor and private property, there were two social classes in capitalism. They were defined by their relationship to the productive process. First of all, there were the capitalists, or the bourgeoisie, who owned the means of production, controlled productive activity, and earned profits from the sale of produced goods in markets. Second, there were the workers, the proletariat, who had nothing to sell in markets but their own labor power and, as a result, had to work for wages to survive. The history of capitalism, then, can be seen as the history of the struggle between these two classes. Marx condemned capitalism because it reduced social relations to impersonal market relations, or the "cash nexus." As he and Engels argued in *The Communist Manifesto* (1848):

> It has pitilessly torn asunder the motley feudal ties that bound man to his "natural superiors," and has left remaining no other nexus between man and man than naked self-interest, than callous "cash payment." It has drowned the most heavenly ecstasies of religious fervour, of chivalrous enthusiasm, of philistine sentimentalism, in the icy water of egotistical calculation. It has resolved personal worth into exchange value, and in place of the numberless indefeasible chartered freedoms, has set up that single, unconscionable freedom—Free Trade. In one word, for exploitation, veiled by religious and political illusions, it has substituted naked, shameless, direct, brutal exploitation.

Workers and capitalists would struggle over wages, the length of the working day, the intensity of work, and working conditions.

Additionally, since workers were forced to work for capitalists for wages, and since the capitalists controlled production, capitalism produced **alienation**. The following is from one of Marx's early critical works, *The Economic and Philosophic Manuscripts of 1844*:

What, then, constitutes the alienation of labour? First, the fact that labour is external to the worker, i.e., it does not belong to his essential being; that in his work, therefore, he does not affirm himself but denies himself, does not feel content but unhappy, does not develop freely his physical and mental energy but mortifies his body and ruins his mind. The worker therefore only feels himself outside his work, and in his work feels outside himself. He is at home when he is not working, and when he is working he is not at home. His labour is therefore not voluntary but coerced; it is *forced labour.* It is therefore not the satisfaction of a need; it is merely a *means* to satisfy needs external to it. Its alien character emerges clearly in the fact that as soon as no physical or other compulsion exists, labour is shunned like the plague. External labour, labour in which man alienates himself, is a labour of self-sacrifice, or mortification. Lastly, the external character of labour for the worker appears in the fact that it is not his own, but someone else's, that it does not belong to him, that in it he belongs, not to himself, but to another. . . . As a result, therefore, man (the worker) no longer feels himself to be freely active in any but his animal functions—eating, drinking, procreating, or at most in his dwelling and in dressing up, etc.; and in his human functions he no longer feels himself to be anything but an animal. What is animal becomes human and what is human becomes animal.

[margin, handwritten:] ONLY WORKING FOR A WAGE — HAS NO PERSONAL STAKE IN THE WORK/HE HE IS DOING.

6. Did Marx deplore the "cash nexus" because it destroyed feudal relationships?

7. According to Marx, why is labor alienated?

From this early condemnation of capitalism, Marx went on to develop a detailed and lengthy analysis of capitalism in such works as *Wage Labour and Capital* (1849), *The Grundrisse* (1859), *Theories of Surplus Value* (1863), and *Capital* (1867).

Marx accepted **the labor theory of value** as it was developed by Smith and Ricardo but turned it to his own purposes. For Marx it became a way of demonstrating the opposition of capitalists and workers and the exploitation of labor in capitalism. Marx contended that the value of all goods and services was a function of the labor (both direct and indirect) that went into them. Labor, in turn, was paid by capitalists to produce goods and services. However, since the capitalists controlled the productive process and the final output, they could earn **surplus value.** The trick was that the exchange value of goods and services, or what the capitalist sold, could be greater than the exchange value of labor power, or what the capitalist bought from the workers. The difference between these values was surplus value (the source of profit) that was appropriated by the capitalist. The exchange value of labor power, because of the existence of a mass of unemployed workers, *the industrial reserve army* of the unemployed, would always hover around "subsistence" (the value of goods and services necessary for continued survival and the reproduction of the working class). Workers could produce enough value in only part of the working day to cover their subsistence needs. The rest of the day they labored to produce surplus value for the capitalist. The more labor that capitalists could get out of the labor power they purchased from workers, the greater the surplus value for the capitalist. As a result, the very structure of capitalism and its social relations produced **exploitation of labor.** Labor accounted for the value of all goods and services, but it received in return only a portion of that value because it did not own productive assets or control the production process.

Since capitalists derive surplus value and profits from production, and since they operate in a competitive environment in which other capitalists also attempt to earn profits from the same type of activity, they are forced to accumulate capital. **Capital accumulation** is the driving force of capitalism. Profit is used to increase the capital and hence the productive activity of capitalists. This capital accumulation results in additional profits, which, in turn, will be reinvested in more capital. Capitalists, if they wish to stay in business, have no choice about this. If they do not reinvest their profits in new and better forms of capital, they will be driven out of business by their competitors. (For a more detailed treatment of the Marxian theory of profit, see the Appendix to this chapter).

This process of capital accumulation forms the basis of Marx's understanding of **capitalist instability.** Capital accumulation produces economic growth, but it does so in cycles with periods of prosperity followed by depression. When production is expanding, capitalists will buy more machines and raw materials and other forms of capital. But this also requires them to hire more workers. Doing so depletes the reserve army of the unemployed and consequently begins to drive up wages. This, however, tends to reduce profits. Consequently, capitalists would introduce new methods of production that would save on the use of labor; more capital-intensive production allowed them to produce more with less labor (substitution of capital for labor). In addition, workers would lose jobs and the wage would go down as the reserve army was replenished.

This course of action was not without its own contradictions. With more workers out of jobs and with lower wages, it was more difficult to sell what was produced. This tended to reduce capitalists' profits. In addition, with more capital-intensive methods of production, the capitalists reduced relatively the source of profits in production, surplus value generated by labor. This also tended to produce a declining rate of profits. With profits reduced, capital accumulation would slow down. All of these effects combined to produce depressions in economic activity as goods went unsold, profits decreased, workers lost jobs, and capital accumulation slowed. In true dialectical fashion, the expansion out of its own internal workings turns into its opposite, a depression. With wage rates depressed, though, capitalists will eventually rehire workers because they can once again produce surplus value and profits for the capitalists. And out of the depression comes an expansion of economic activity. Capitalism, Marx argued, grew in starts and spurts. The great mass of the people under capitalism, the working class, was dependent on this unstable process for its livelihood and subsistence.

In addition to this cyclical instability, Marx thought that there were secular tendencies that would exacerbate the opposition between the capitalist class and the working class. Because of competition, **economic concentration** tended to occur as capitalists bought each other out or went bankrupt during depressions. The strong survived and came to dominate certain industries. As this occurred, the capitalist class became relatively smaller, as well as relatively more wealthy. Meanwhile, the working class became relatively larger and relatively poorer, as it remained near "subsistence." Marx called this the **immiserization** of the proletariat. And all the while, the capitalist retains control and the workers are powerless. As a result of continuing instability and these secular tendencies, which reinforce the class structure of capitalist society, the workers will organize for their own class interests. Ultimately, Marx argued, the working class organizations would overthrow the capitalist system.

The political requirement for workers in the Socialist and Communist movement was described by Marx and Engels as follows at the end of *The Communist Manifesto*:

> In short, the Communists everywhere support every revolutionary movement against the existing social and political order of things.
>
> In all these movements they bring to the front, as the leading question in each, the property question, no matter what its degree of development at the time.
>
> Finally, they labour everywhere for the union and agreement of the democratic parties of all countries.
>
> The Communists disdain to conceal their views and aims. They openly declare that their ends can be attained only by the forcible overthrow of all existing social conditions. Let the ruling class tremble at a Communistic revolution. The proletarians have nothing to lose but their chains. They have a world to win.

However, this social revolution would not be easy. As Marx emphasized from his general system of social development, capitalism supports itself with its superstructure. The institutions, ideologies, and beliefs of the society defend capitalist economic institutions and social relations. Perhaps most important in this connection is the state. The state, according to Marxian analysis, serves as the "executive committee of the ruling class." The state protects private property and property rights and thereby the class structure of the system. It is in the camp of the capitalists and will actively oppose the workers' movement with all the resources at its command.

8. **Evaluate Marx's analysis of capitalism. Does it describe economic reality and the historical development of capitalism? Does it help you understand how capitalism works?**

9. **Why do you suppose Marx kept getting kicked out of European countries?**

SOCIAL REVOLUTION

Marx argued that workers would be exploited, alienated, and condemned to subsistence standards of living under capitalism. He further argued that in their association at work and in their communities, they would be able to analyze objectively their reality and the reasons for their oppression. Consequently, they would organize themselves and transform the whole capitalist system. (Indeed, Marx spent much of his time in political activity with workers.) In *Capital*, he describes the process of **social revolution** as follows:

> Along with the constantly diminishing number of magnates of capital, who usurp and monopolize all advantages of this process of transformation, grows the mass of misery, oppression, slavery, degradation, exploitation; but with this too grows the revolt of the working class, a class always increasing in numbers, and disciplined, united, organized by the very mechanism of the process of capitalist production itself. The monopoly of capital becomes a fetter upon the mode of production, which has sprung up and flourished along with, and under it. Centralization of the means of production and socialization of labour at last reach a point where they become incompatible with their capitalist integument. This integument is burst asunder. The knell of capitalist private property sounds. The expropriators are expropriated.

Once the death knell of capitalism sounded, what would the socialists, communists, and workers create? What would they do? Although Marx never wrote extensively on this question, a hint at the answer is contained in *The Communist Manifesto*:

> The distinguishing feature of Communism is not the abolition of property generally, but the abolition of bourgeois property. But modern bourgeois private property is the final and most complete expression of the system of producing and appropriating products, that is based on class antagonisms, on the exploitation of the many by the few.
>
> In this sense, the theory of the Communists may be summed up in the single sentence: Abolition of private property.
>
> We Communists have been reproached with the desire of abolishing the right of personally acquiring property as the fruit of a man's own labour, which property is alleged to be the groundwork of all personal freedom, activity and independence.
>
> Hard-won, self-acquired, self-earned property! Do you mean the property of the petty artisan and of the small peasant, a form of property that preceded the bourgeois form? There is no need to abolish that: the development of industry has to a great extent already destroyed it, and is still destroying it daily.
>
> Or do you mean modern bourgeois private property?
>
> The proletariat will use its political supremacy to wrest, by degrees, all capital from the bourgeoisie, to centralise all instruments of production

in the hands of the State, *i.e.,* of the proletariat organised as the ruling class; and to increase the total of productive forces as rapidly as possible.

Of course, in the beginning, this cannot be effected except by means of despotic inroads on the rights of property, and on the conditions of bourgeois production; by means of measures, therefore, which appear economically insufficient and untenable, but which, in the course of the movement, outstrip themselves, necessitate further inroads upon the old social order, and are unavoidable as a means of entirely revolutionising the mode of production.

These measures will of course be different in different countries.

Nevertheless in the most advanced countries, the following will be pretty generally applicable.

1. Abolition of property in land and application of all rents of land to public purposes.

2. A heavy progressive or graduated income tax.

3. Abolition of all rights of inheritance.

4. Confiscation of the property of all emigrants and rebels.

5. Centralisation of credit in the hands of the State, by means of a national bank with State capital and an exclusive monopoly.

6. Centralisation of the means of communication and transport in the hands of the State.

7. Extension of factories and instruments of production owned by the State; the bringing into cultivation of wastelands, and the improvement of the soil generally in accordance with a common plan.

8. Equal liability of all to labour. Establishment of industrial armies, especially for agriculture.

9. Combination of agriculture and manufacturing industries; gradual abolition of the distinction between town and country, by a more equable distribution of the population over the country.

10. Free education for all children in public schools. Abolition of children's factory labour in its present form. Combination of education with industrial production, &c., &c.

---

10. **Would the communists take your personal possessions away from you? What kinds of property would they "wrest" away?**

11. **In Marx and Engels's ten-point program, which are accepted in the United States? Which are partially accepted? Which are rejected?**

AN ASSESSMENT OF MARX

Marx died (1883) over a century ago. What can we say today about the relevance of his analysis of social change and capitalism? Most Americans either reject Marxism or never really study it. The rejection is often based on the fact that several of Marx's predictions have not transpired: the overthrow of advanced capitalism by socialism; the separation of society into only two classes, capitalists and workers; and the creation of a unified and political working class. In addition, Marxism is often associated with the repressive Soviet Union, and socialism as Marx described it has never really been put in place. Socialism and Marxism also offer a direct challenge to two of the basic economic foundations of U.S. society—private ownership of productive property and economic freedom for capital.

On the other hand, Marxian analysis is used by many economists in the United States and the rest of the world to understand economic events. There are some aspects of Marxism that offer continuing assistance in explaining the structure and development of capitalism. There remain conflicts between workers and capitalists over workplace health and safety, other working conditions, wages and fringe benefits, and the length of the workweek. This conflict is built into the different interests that they have in the very structure of the economic system. Capitalists seek profits, and workers' demands often limit profits. Although the rapid expansion of the middle class has mediated this structure, there are opposing class interests in the operation of the economy, and the classes do struggle over real economic issues in workplaces, bargaining, and public policy. Furthermore, while these struggles have not led to the collapse of capitalism, they have brought about significant changes in its institutions and operation. Marx's analysis of exploitation, surplus value, and class relations can help us to understand this dynamic of American capitalism.

One of the most long-lived aspects of Marxian economic analysis is its theory of the capital accumulation process. In this treatment, Marx explained capitalism's tendencies toward business cycles, economic concentration, and market expansion. By focusing on the importance of profits and the centrality of capital accumulation,

Marx developed a framework that is still useful in understanding recessions and expansions, merger waves, and U.S. penetration of world markets.

Nevertheless, Marx's system retains some limitations and weaknesses. Marx did not anticipate the tremendous increase in the average standard of living in the United States (and Western Europe) that went along with economic growth. A good portion of the increasing surplus was in fact apportioned to the middle class and some segments of the working class. The social revolution in advanced capitalist countries anticipated by Marx required more than his prediction: It also necessitated political organization by the working class in the real world. (To his credit, although it is often not included in discussions of Marx, he did recognize this political fact; much of his life was spent in active working class political organizing.) Even though there have been communist and socialist parties in the West and in the United States, they have never been strong enough to organize a transition to socialism. Of course, they have not been unopposed. Socialism, instead, has emerged where capitalism has been weaker, in the developing world. Marx himself would also probably be disappointed with the divergence of his ideal of socialism and its reality in much of the present world. Even so, his ideas have definitely influenced the development and the progress of socialism and the pursuit of social goals in the Soviet Union, China, Cuba, Vietnam, Mozambique, and other socialist nations (see Chapter 28).

CONCLUSION

In this chapter we have briefly presented Marx's system of thought—his "materialist conception of history" and his analysis of capitalism. We have not tried to apply it strictly to the actual historical development of capitalism in Western Europe and the United States. We have also not traced its theoretical and political development by the followers of Marx, nor have we examined the arguments of its critics. However, its strength and validity must ultimately be tested by its ability to help us understand the world and by its congruence with actual economic and social events.

KEY CONCEPTS

historical materialism
the mode of production
the forces of production
the relations of production
class
superstructure
alienation
surplus value

labor theory of value
exploitation of labor
capital accumulation
capitalist instability,
    Marxian theory of
economic concentration
immiserization
social revolution

REVIEW QUESTIONS

1. Why do people in the United States tend to reject Marxism?

2. Why is it that an increasing number of newly independent countries in the world have Marxian governments (i.e., politicians and leaders who rely on Marxian analysis)?

3. What do you feel is the weakest part of the Marxian argument?

4. What do you feel is the strongest part of the Marxian argument?

5. What is the purpose of Marxian economics?

SUGGESTED READINGS

Richard Edwards, Michael Reich, and Thomas Weisskopf (eds.), 1978. *The Capitalist System* (2nd ed.), Prentice-Hall. An excellent reader on Marxian analysis and its application to the U.S. economy.

John Gurley, 1976. *Challengers to Capitalism,* San Francisco Book Company. Chapters 2 and 3 contain very readable treatments of Marx's theory of history and analysis of capitalism.

E. K. Hunt, 1975. *Property and Prophets,* Harper & Row. See Chapter 6 on Marxian economics.

Karl Marx and Friedrich Engels, 1848. *The Communist Manifesto,* China Books and Periodicals. A classic piece of Marxist analysis and propaganda.

David McClellan, 1975. *Karl Marx,* Penguin Books. A short biography of Marx.

Robert C. Tucker, 1978. *The Marx-Engels Reader* (2nd ed.), Norton. An excellent selection of writings by Marx and Engels, including *The Communist Manifesto,* parts of *Capital,* and *The Critique of the Gotha Program,* in which Marx briefly discusses postcapitalist society.

APPENDIX 8A
The Marxian Theory of Profit

Adam Smith argued that competitive markets produce social welfare through the "invisible hand." In Chapter 11, we will examine the orthodox, neoclassical theory of the firm in a competitive market. In the long run, the results suggest that competition produces maximum social welfare (efficiency, consumer sovereignty, and the invisible hand) and that firms earn only "normal" profits. From a Marxian perspective, the operation of competitive capitalism is shown to have results that are much less attractive. Marx concludes that there is inherent conflict between capital and labor, that the source of profits lies in the exploitation of labor, and, furthermore, that the orthodox analysis hides the source of profits and the social relationships in capitalist production.

Marx's analysis focuses on the process of production within the **capitalist mode of production.** According to Marx, the value of all goods and services is determined by their labor content—both the direct labor of active labor power by workers and the embodied labor of past labor power in raw materials and capital goods. Consequently, Marx's interpretation of the behavior of firms has its roots in the **labor theory of value.** In addition, Marx assumes that firms are in business to earn profits through the process of capital accumulation (indeed, competition forces firms to seek profits). They do this by producing goods and services and selling them in markets as commodities. Finally, productive activity within capitalism has inherent in it certain **social relations of production**—specifically, there are two basic classes of people: capitalists, who own and control the means of production, and workers, who must sell their labor power to capitalists to earn a living.

Given this Marxian framework of analysis, we can proceed to examine the behavior of firms. Our analysis will concentrate on the source of capitalist profits, the determinants of the prices of products, and the relationships between capitalists and workers.

The capitalist owns the means of production and the capital necessary for the organization of production. There are two forms of this capital: **constant capital** and **variable capital. Constant capital** refers to those "factors of production" that have embodied labor in them, e.g., the factory itself, the machinery and equipment in it, and the raw materials used in production. Theoretically, it is possible to place a value on this constant capital. For example, for purposes of simplifying the analysis, let us assume that we can determine the value of one unit of labor power at $5. This assumes that we can value all labor in terms of some abstract unit of average labor. As a result, then, this $5 price for one unit of labor represents the value of the commodities necessary (at least) for the sustenance and the reproduction of this one unit of labor power. Let's assume that the constant capital (machines, raw materials, etc.) used up in production has embodied in it six units of abstract labor; therefore the constant capital is valued at $30 in our example. **Variable capital** refers to the capitalist's outlay of money for the purchase of the active labor power required, along with constant capital, to produce his or her product. It is variable in the sense that workers can work more or less time and more or less hard during the working day. Let's assume that the capitalist hires 14 units of living labor to engage in production; therefore the variable capital (labor) is valued at $70.

What about the capitalist's share? This enters the picture via Marx's concept of **surplus value.** Capitalists hire labor to put into motion constant capital and the production process. Capitalists must pay both constant and variable capital according to the value of the labor embodied in them and required to enable them to work, respectively. However, in the process of production, additional value is created. The ultimate value of the product will depend upon the amount of labor contained in it. Capitalists must be able to organize production in such a way that the value of the final product *exceeds* the value of constant and variable capital. This occurs as a natural result of the operation of capitalist production.

The capitalist controls production and, specifically, the length of the working day. Let's assume that the working day is 10 hours long. During the working day, workers can produce value equivalent to the value of their abstract labor power in 6 hours. During the remaining 4 hours, the workers produce value over and above the value necessary for the purchase of their labor power. This is surplus value which derives from surplus labor that is unpaid. Consequently, the 14 units of labor power are used to produce commodities embodying more than 14 units of labor power. Only 6 hours of labor are required to produce commodities necessary to cover the costs of the value of the labor power itself. The remaining 4 hours of labor produce surplus value. The proceeds from the surplus value go to the capitalists when they sell the products for the value contained in them. The 6 hours of labor produce commodities with a value of $70 (the value of variable capital). The 4 hours of surplus labor produce commodities with a value of $46⅔ (the value of surplus value— $70 × ⅘).

The 14 units of living labor power produce commodities embodying 14 units of labor power (the value of variable capital) *and* commodities embodying 9⅓ units of labor power (the value of surplus value— 46⅔ ÷ 5). The 6 units of labor embodied in the constant capital produced commodities with 6 units of labor embodied in them.

What is revealed in this analysis (which is quite simple compared with Marx's original contribution) is that the source of profits for the capitalists, surplus value, results from the capitalists' control of the production process and their ability to pay living labor (variable capital) less than the full value of what it produces. Hence labor is exploited, since it has little control over the production process (the essence of which is human labor) and since it does not receive compensation commensurate with what it adds to the value of social production. What's more, it is obvious that inherent in this mode of production is *conflict* between capitalists and workers. Workers will prefer to work fewer hours, less hard, and for more money; capitalists would prefer workers to work longer, harder, and for less money. Capitalists and workers will struggle with each other over the length of the working day, the intensity of work, working conditions, and the division of the fruits of variable capital (the return to variable capital vs. surplus value). The operation of the capitalist system in Marx's view thus involves differing class interests. In fact, the source of capitalists' profits is the **exploitation of labor.** This is hardly Smith's picture of the invisible hand, which leads to the greatest social welfare for all.

We can formalize this analysis in several ways. The objective of capitalist production is to earn profits and to accumulate capital. The capitalist begins with money and purchases the commodities of constant and variable capital (machines, equipment, raw materials, labor power) in markets. These resources of production are then combined and organized in a production process that requires the application of human labor. The production process results in commodities (goods and services) to be sold on markets. These commodities are sold for money. The source of profits is the production process, wherein human labor produces enough value to cover constant and variable capital, as well as surplus value, which is appropriated by the capitalist.

We can characterize this process as follows:

$$M \to C \ldots P \ldots C' \to M',$$

where M = money, C = the value of commodities used in production, P = the production process, C' = produced commodities for sale, and M' = the money value of sales. If M' exceeds M, then the capitalist earns profits. In the next round, the capitalist can use profits to accumulate more capital and earn additional profits. Notice that there is no certainty that the capitalist will, in fact, earn profits. Capitalists are all in competition with one another. If resources cost too much, if workers don't work hard enough, if the production process isn't well-organized, or if what gets produced doesn't get sold, the capitalist might not make any profits at all.

In addition, we can express the total value of any product as being equal to the sum of the various forms of embodied labor in it. Total value = constant capital + variable capital + surplus value. For example, from our analysis above,

$29\frac{1}{3}$ units of labor = 6 units of labor + 14 units of labor + $9\frac{1}{3}$ units of labor.

If the value for one unit of labor power is $5, then

$146\frac{2}{3} = \$30 + \$70 + 46\frac{2}{3}$.

From an orthodox perspective, we can view this as follows:

total sales = costs of fixed resources and variable resources (excluding labor) + costs of labor + profits.

Or from the Marxian perspective:

total value = constant capital + variable capital + surplus value.

So far, we have concentrated on the capitalist production process with the example of the single firm. However, because the same process of capital accumulation and the extraction of surplus value occurs in the economy as a whole, we can also develop an economy-wide example.* Let's say that the total output of the society in one year is valued at $500 billion (this means that the output of goods and services multiplied by their prices = $500 billion). Part of the money received for this output has to be used to cover the costs of replacing the equipment and the raw materials used up in the production period. Assume this replacement cost is $100 billion. This sum of money then allows for the purchasing of these resources for the next period of production. The total output minus the replacement cost equals the net output of the society.

Total output – replacement cost = net output,
$500 billion – $100 billion = $400 billion.

The net output of the society is divided into two parts. Workers get a portion of this output, which they purchase with their wages. Let's say labor's wages total $300 billion. They use their wages to buy goods and services so that they can survive and continue to offer their labor power in the next round of production. The remainder of the net output goes to capital as profits—$100 billion, in this case. So

net output   = wages + profits,
$400 billion = $300 billion + $100 billion.

---

*This section relies on the curriculum of the Summer Institute for Popular Economics prepared by the Center for Popular Economics, Box 785, Amherst, MA 01004.

And

profits = net output – wages.

Profits, consequently, depend on the total value of net output and the wage bill. The higher the net output and the lower the wage bill, the higher capitalists' profits will be.

Perhaps an easier way to focus on Marx's insights about class relations and profits in capitalism is to identify the **rate of profit.** The rate of profit for capitalists depends on the profits that they receive in comparison to the value of their investment in production. Their investment is the value of capital assets (the total monetary value of those assets—machines, equipment, buildings, etc.). In our example, if this capital is worth $300 billion, then the profit rate is

profit rate = profits/capital assets,
33⅓%   = 100/300.

We can also put this in per worker terms, by dividing the right side of this equation

$$\text{profit rate} = \frac{\text{net output} - \text{wages}}{\text{capital assets}}$$

by the total number of workers. So

$$\text{profit rate} = \frac{\text{net output per worker} - \text{average wage of each worker}}{\text{capital per worker}}.$$

We can use this formulation to see that there are a number of aspects of capitalism that operate to keep profits and the profit rate positive. The average wage of the worker is determined by what is necessary to enable workers to purchase goods and services that provide them with an acceptable standard of living. This allows them to participate in production and to have enough income for food, shelter, and clothing for themselves and their families, allowing in turn for the reproduction of the working class. This wage is determined by historical experience and by the struggle between capital and labor over the level of wages. But the higher the wage, the lower the profit rate. Workers can organize to get higher wages, but capital has the power to hire and fire, as well as to organize and control the production process. Furthermore, the existence of unemployment (the reserve army) constantly puts downward pressure on wages. The dynamic relationship between wages and profits, in fact, accounts for much of the instability in capitalist growth. If wages get too high, profits are reduced and capitalists slow down the accumulation process. But when wages are low and profits are high, economic booms occur.

Net output per worker is analogous to productivity. If capitalists can increase output without raising wages, profits and the profit rate will go up. This could be accomplished by increasing work intensity, increasing supervision over work, speeding up the work pace, or through technological innovations. On the other hand, because workers' demands to improve working conditions do not increase output for sale, such demands tend to reduce profits.

If nothing else changes, an increase in capital per worker would decrease the profit rate. This may result because capital replaces labor, and the exploitation of labor is the source of surplus value. But if net output per worker increases faster than capital per worker (i.e., productivity increases along with increased capital), then profits and the profit rate could go up.

Consequently, many factors have an influence on the generation of profits and the rate of profit in capitalism. The pace of capital accumulation and the level of economic activity will be determined by changes in profits. Specifically, the higher (lower) profits, the greater (lower) the rate of economic growth will tend to be.

These relationships determining the rate of profit suggest, once again, from the Marxian perspective, the inherent instability of capitalist production. Over time, the rate of profit will tend to be equalized through competition (the rate of profit in this sense is comparable to the "normal" profits we will identify in Chapter 11). However, Marx preferred to emphasize the tendency toward instability as profits rose and fell in the process of capitalist accumulation and production.

One additional aspect of Marx's analysis of the operation of the firm that is worth pointing out is the tendency toward **economic concentration** that results from long-term capital accumulation and the pursuit of profit. Firms become larger through capital accumulation, and the process of instability bankrupts some firms, so fewer firms remain in an industry. Historically, this theoretical tendency has accounted for the disappearance of competitive markets in capitalist systems.

Finally, one of the strengths of the Marxian analysis of capitalism is its integration of the micro and macro aspects of economic activity. Profits flow from the organization and control of the capitalist mode of production. The process of capital accumulation and the production of surplus value, in turn, provide the framework within which economic crises are engendered under capitalism.

KEY CONCEPTS

capitalist mode of production	exploitation of labor
labor theory of value	surplus value
social relations of production	$M \rightarrow C \ldots P \ldots C' \rightarrow M'$
constant capital	rate of profit
variable capital	economic concentration

REVIEW QUESTIONS

1. Is the labor theory of value valid? Why or why not?

2. Marx's theories were originated over 100 years ago. Was labor exploited then? Is it now? Why or why not?

3. Obviously, in the United States *most* people are not living on "subsistence" wages. What is the source of the increased wages for variable capital in many industries in the United States?

4. What is the *source* of profits according to the Marxian interpretation? Criticize this explanation.

5. Given the production of surplus value in the production process, capitalists cannot realize profits unless they sell their products for more than the value of constant and variable capital (or for more than the value of replacement costs and wages). In fact, sometimes capitalists will experience losses. What kinds of behavior will capitalists pursue in order to ensure the realization of profits?

SUGGESTED READINGS

John Gurley, 1980. *Challengers to Capitalism*, Norton. Chapter 3 provides a relatively simplified introduction to the Marxian analysis of capitalist production and the theory of profit.

Karl Marx, "Wage Labour and Capital," in Robert C. Tucker (ed.), 1978. *The Marx-Engels Reader* (2nd ed.), Norton. One of Marx's early attempts to develop and outline the extended analysis of capitalist production in *Capital*.

Joan Robinson, 1966. *An Essay on Marxian Economics*, St. Martin's. An attempt by a leading English economist to summarize Marx's analysis of the distribution of income between labor and capital and to connect that analysis with the causes of economic crises.

Paul Sweezy, 1968. *The Theory of Capitalist Development*, Monthly Review Press. Part I on value and surplus value represents an attempt by a leading American Marxist to explain the labor theory of value and surplus value.

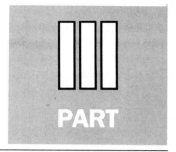

MICROECONOMICS

Now that we are about to begin studying modern economic theory, we might pause to ask ourselves what economic theory should do. Ideally, it should have *explanatory value* to help us understand how economic forces work, *predictive power* to help us understand what might happen in the future, and *relevance* so that it helps us to solve the economic problems that we face. Keep these criteria in mind as you learn economic theory in Parts III, IV, and V.

As we have seen in our account of the transition from feudalism to capitalism, markets have emerged in the Western world as a method of organizing society's production. Markets exist for all of the factors of production and for final consumption goods. Through the information transmitted by markets, producers make decisions about what factors of production to use, and consumers decide what to consume. The information appears in the form of prices. On the basis of these decisions made by various economic agents in the society, resources will be used in certain ways to produce certain goods and services. From their participation in production, people will earn certain incomes and will spend them, which will determine how goods are distributed in the society. We also have seen how early economists developed theories and concepts to explain these economic activities. The early development of economic thought provided a foundation for modern microeconomics.

Microeconomics is concerned with describing how the economic system operates to allocate resources, to determine incomes, and to organize production. Consequently, it focuses on the decision-makers—firms, consumers, the government—who determine how resources will be used. Microeconomics is fundamentally concerned with the major problem of all economies: that there are not enough resources available to satisfy all the desires of all the economic agents. Scarcity is the supreme economic fact of life. Given scarcity, microeconomics also concentrates on how the market system allocates resources by valuing them. Therefore it examines the operation of markets and price determination. Finally, microeconomics is concerned with evaluating how well society allocates its scarce resources. Ideally, society should use resources efficiently. **Efficiency** means minimizing the use of scarce resources to achieve that mix of output most highly valued by society.

In Chapter 9, we will begin with a consideration of the basic microeconomic problem and develop some economic concepts useful in helping us to understand the consequences of scarcity. In Chapter 10 we will examine the microeconomic theory of competitive markets. In Chapter 11 we will explore the theoretical results of the operation of competitive markets. In Chapter 12 we will introduce the economic reality that many productive units in our economic system are not competitive, and we will develop a theory of imperfectly competitive markets. In Chapter 13, we will examine the operation of resource markets and income determination. Chapter 14 focuses on a more institutional consideration of some of the dominant units in the American economy—corporations and labor unions. In Chapter 15 our subject will be yet another important force in the economy—the government.

Scarcity: "You Can't Always Get What You Want"

INTRODUCTION

Beginning in the 1970s, Americans began to be very sensitive to the energy crisis. Prices for oil, natural gas, and gasoline increased dramatically. Shortages of petroleum-related products developed and, at times, were serious—forcing long lines at gas stations and even shutdowns of factories and schools. In addition, the shortages of energy supplies are predicted to become even more serious in the future. It has in fact been suggested that at some point we may even run out of these resources that are so vital to us as individuals and to the operation of our entire economic system.

In 1975 the National Academy of Sciences issued a report warning of future shortages of important resources for advanced industrial societies. They noted that the United States would continue to depend on oil imports for the next half-century and that even the Middle East's oil reserves might be depleted. Other resources in possible short supply included asbestos, tin, copper, helium, and mercury. The Academy went on to urge not only conservation of energy and other resources but also efforts to increase supplies, substitution and recycling.

> Because of the limits to natural resources as well as to means for alleviating these limits, it is recommended that the federal government proclaim and deliberately pursue a national policy of conservation of

material, energy and environmental resources, informing the public and the private sectors fully about the needs and techniques for reducing energy consumption, the development of substitute materials, increasing the durability and maintainability of products, and reclamation and recycling.

Nearly a decade later, the Worldwatch Institute, in its first annual report on worldwide energy, land, water, and environmental management, concluded that the world cannot sustain the rate at which it is using up its resources. Every year 23 billion tons of topsoil are depleted, world population growth is accelerating, forests are being decimated in the Third World, and there is inadequate progress in the use of renewable energy and recycling. The report recommended increased funding for family planning, tree planting, and soil conservation.

1. **Why are there shortages? What factors play a role in creating shortages?**

2. **What sorts of actions could be taken to alleviate these projected shortages?**

SCARCITY: A FUNDAMENTAL ECONOMIC FACT OF MODERN LIFE

Scarcity is one of the fundamental economic facts of modern life. All societies must develop methods and institutions to produce goods and services and to distribute them to people for consumption. However difficult that task is, it is further complicated by the overriding reality of scarce resources and unlimited human wants and needs. Human societies, and the individual people within them, have certain physical needs for short- and long-run survival. Food, shelter, and clothing must be provided. With the desire to live beyond subsistence and to experience a richer life, the wants of a society are subject to constant expansion.

But the physical and mental resources that can be used to provide for material needs are not subject to constant expansion. This limitation is especially true if we concentrate on the short run—the present and the immediate future. The mental capabilities of humans are at a certain stage of development. Physical resources are at a fixed level. There are just so many people who can labor. There is just so much wheat, corn, coal, gas, bauxite, copper, etc. With more time, of course, science, technology, and exploration can expand the available resources. Even in the long run, though, the problem of scarcity governs the decisions that must be made; society must still concern itself with using its possibly expanding resource base in the best way possible to meet its needs.

3. **Are human wants/needs unlimited? Why or why not? What determines human wants and needs?**

4. **If wants are not unlimited, does scarcity still exist?**

The problem for society is using the resources that are available in the best way possible to meet as many of the needs and wants of its people as it can. A society will be better off if it uses its resources efficiently. This is an incredibly difficult and complicated task. How much of our resources should be used to develop nuclear energy? Should we devote more or less to exploring the possibilities of solar energy? Should more resources go to housing or to transportation? Should we build automobiles for private transportation or buses for public transportation? Because of scarcity, *we must make choices*. Society must, in addition to deciding how to organize itself for production and distribution, develop mechanisms and institutions for making **economic decisions** about how best to use the resources that are available to it. How can we make sure that resources are allocated in the best way possible? **Efficiency** in the **allocation of resources** is the economic objective. Different societies resolve and have resolved this task in different ways.

In our largely private economic system, many of these decisions are made through markets. Cars are produced because people demand them and are willing to buy them for the prices charged by producers. The prices reflect the costs to the producers for the resources that are used in production. Based on price information and individual tastes and preferences, people make decisions about what to spend money on. We will examine the workings of markets in a bit more detail in Chapters 10 and 11 to see how they allocate resources.

Public choices must also be made about the use of resources. For example, every society desires to protect itself from foreign enemies. Some countries do this through the establishment of a military force; the threat of physical reaction is intended to forestall aggressive actions by others. In the event of attack or hostile action, military force can be used to protect the interests and possessions of the society. The construction of military force, however, requires the use of resources. Resources devoted to the production of a military potential are automatically unavailable for other uses. The **opportunity cost** of using resources to produce guns, tanks, planes, etc., is that those resources cannot be used for other purposes. Society must make a choice, then, about how much of its resources to devote to producing military goods and services, with the realization that the cost of doing so is forgoing the opportunity to use resources in the production of nonmilitary goods and services. Obviously, different societies have made different choices about the size of their military establishments, and thus over how to use their scarce resources.

THE PRODUCTION POSSIBILITIES CURVE

The **production possibilities curve** is a device developed by economists to illustrate the concepts of scarcity and opportunity cost. Economic choices, necessitated by scarcity, have costs. The following presentation concentrates on the public choice between military and civilian goods. This same analysis could also be applied to other public choices about how to use tax moneys: Should we build more highways? Should we overhaul the railroad system? Should we increase welfare spending? And so on. It can also be applied to analyzing the results of decisions usually made in the private sector: Should we produce more big cars? Or more little cars? Should we produce

Screaming Yellow Zonkers? Or Fruit Roll-Ups? Or more housing? The point is that choices must be made—and choosing to use resources in a specific way means that they can't be used for other purposes.

5. What is the opportunity cost of not using resources for a particular purpose?

Every society possesses resources and uses those resources to produce goods and services. But a society cannot have all of the goods and services it desires because resources are *scarce*. The production possibilities curve is a useful way of illustrating this concept. We will make the following assumptions:

ASSUMPTIONS 1. The economy is experiencing full employment of all its resources.

2. The supplies of the factors of production are fixed at one point in time.

3. Technology is constant (again, at one point in time).

We will make one further assumption. The economy produces consumer goods and military goods (or "butter and guns"), and the resources can be used to produce both types of goods (although some resources will be better than others at producing one type of goods).

Here is the problem. With our resources (and our assumptions) we can make only limited amounts of both types of goods. We must then make a choice about how much of each type of good to produce. Since our resources are fully employed and limited, we can produce more of one type of good only by producing less of the other. That is, if we decide to produce more military goods, we can do it only by taking resources away from the production of civilian goods and thus produce fewer consumer goods. The **opportunity cost** of producing more military goods is that we will have fewer civilian goods.

This is shown graphically in Fig. 9.1. If we produce *only* military goods (using all our resources to do so), we can have M_1 of them. On the other hand, if we produce only consumer goods, we can have C_1 of them. Let's assume that the economy is at A.

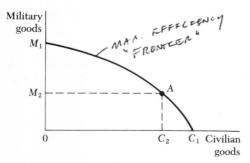

Figure 9.1   The production possibilities curve.

Then we produce C_2 of consumer goods and M_2 of military goods. However, there is a whole range of different *combinations* of military goods and consumer goods that we could have. The locus of all those possible combinations gives us a production possibilities curve. The important point here is that, at a given moment in time, whenever a society chooses to have more of one type of good, it must sacrifice some of the other type of good. To have more military goods (moving toward M_1) means that the society will have fewer resources to devote to the production of civilian goods.

This problem, obviously, can be alleviated over time somewhat by the discovery of new resources or by the institution of new technology that allows us to get more production from our resources. In either case, the entire curve would move outward.

> **6. Can you show graphically and explain why the production possibilities curve will move outward with (1) more resources available or (2) an improvement in technology that increases *efficiency?***

GRAPHS, EQUATIONS, AND WORDS

Economists like to use graphical representations. The production possibilities curve is one example of this pedagogical technique, and you will encounter many others in this book. Economic theory seeks to establish relationships among economic variables. Economists often use three different techniques to explain these relationships. First, they use words. Second, they use graphical illustrations to show the relationships. And finally, they sometimes utilize mathematical equations. In our production possibilities curve, we have discussed in words the notion of the opportunity costs between military goods and civilian goods. We have also illustrated this same relationship on a graph. If we wanted to proceed, we could write an equation, $M_x = f(C_x)$, showing that the amount of military goods (M_x) the society has will depend on the amount of civilian goods (C_x) it has (*given* all of our assumptions).

On the graph, the amount of military goods is measured on the vertical axis and the amount of civilian goods on the horizontal axis. Thus any point on the graph represents a single combination of civilian goods and military goods. And every point represents a *different* combination.

> **7. Explain what it would mean if society were at a point inside its production possibilities curve.**

The production possibilities curve is shaped the way it is (concave to the origin) because resources are not completely adaptable to other uses. For example, the more consumer goods we sacrifice (moving toward M_1), the fewer and fewer military goods we will be able to *add* to military production (for each marginal loss of consumer goods). (Can you show this on the graph?) The reason is that some resources are best suited for producing consumer goods and not suited for military production (e.g., pacifists). As more of these resources are transferred to military production, the *addition* to military goods will decline. (The reverse is true, too. If we disarmed, some generals might not be too good at producing consumer goods.)

THE USE OF GRAPHS IN ECONOMICS

Economic theory identifies important economic variables and attempts to explain their relationships. Economists frequently rely on graphs to illustrate these relationships. This book contains numerous graphs, so it is important to be clear about how they are constructed and what they show.

Let's take a simple example of the relationship between the amount of oil a household uses and how much it costs. During a particular period of time, say a month, a household could use different amounts of oil. Depending upon how much oil is used, the cost to the household will vary. Let's say oil (for heating and/or hot water) costs $1 per gallon. Table 9.1 gives information on the costs of using different amounts of oil.

We can illustrate this same information on a graph. In Fig. 9.2 we measure increasing amounts of oil as we move out from the origin on the horizontal axis, and increasing costs of oil as we move up from the origin on the vertical axis. (Generally, the independent variable is placed on the horizontal, or *x*, axis and the dependent variable is put on the vertical, or *y*, axis. Here, the amount of oil is the independent variable, and the cost is the dependent variable. The cost depends on the amount of oil used, *given* price.) Each combination of oil and its cost is represented by a point on the graph. When we connect all the different points, we have a graphical representation of the relationship between different amounts of oil used and the respective costs.

(continued)

Table 9.1 THE COST OF OIL FOR A HOUSEHOLD PER MONTH

POINT	AMOUNT OF OIL USED (GALLONS PER MONTH)	COST ($)
—	0	0
a	20	20
b	40	40
c	60	60
d	80	80
e	100	100

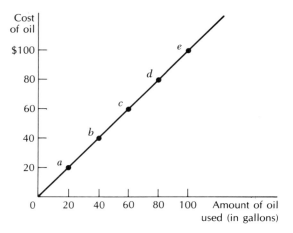

Figure 9.2 A household's relationship between amount of oil used and cost of oil.

The graph provides a picture of the relationship between the amount of oil used and the cost to the household. It tells us that the cost goes up as the household uses more oil per month. It represents exactly the same information contained in the table (and it's certainly not a terribly surprising conclusion!), but the graph presents the relationship in summary form. It's an efficient way to express the relationship between these two variables. Such illustrations will be very useful in developing economic theory about the more complicated relationships among economic variables.

In Fig. 9.2, the graph tells us that there is a positive relationship between oil used and cost—as oil use increases so does cost. If there is a positive relationship between two variables, the graph will slope upward to the right. If there is a negative relationship between two variables—as one increases the other decreases—the graph would have a negative slope (downward to the right). For example, if a household also uses wood for heat, its use of oil would decrease. We can represent this relationship in a table and in a graph (Table 9.2 and Fig. 9.3).

(continued)

Table 9.2 AMOUNTS OF OIL AND WOOD USED FOR HEAT PER MONTH

WOOD (IN CORDS)	OIL (IN GALLONS)
0	60
¼	50
½	40
¾	30
1	20

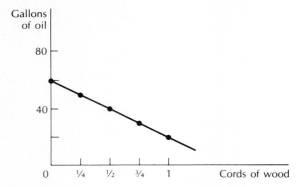

Figure 9.3 A household's relationship between amount of oil used and amount of wood used.

The slope of a graph tells us precisely how one variable changes with another. The slope is the change in the dependent variable over the change in the independent variable, or the height over the base of the line between two points, or the rise over the run. For example, the slope of the graph in Fig. 9.2 is equal to the ratio of the change in the cost over the change in the amount of oil used. In moving along the line from point *b* to point *c*, the change in cost equals $20 and the change in the amount of oil used is 20 gallons:

$$\text{slope} = \frac{\text{change in cost}}{\text{change in oil used}} = \frac{\$20}{20} = \$1.$$

(Often the symbol Δ is used to denote the change in a variable.) In this case, the slope is equal to 1. (What's the slope of the graph in Fig. 9.3?)

Graphs of the relationships between economic variables can also be curved lines, as in panels (a), (b), and (c) in Fig. 9.4. In these cases, the slope changes as we move along each line. (The slope can be approximated by drawing a line tangent to each point on the curve.) For example, in Fig. 9.4(a) the positive slope of the line becomes less steep as we move
(continued)

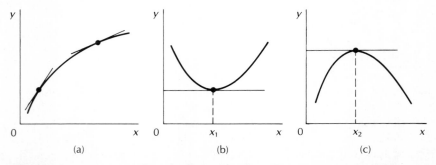

Figure 9.4 Some examples of relationships between economic variables.

to the right. In Fig. 9.4(b) from 0 to x_1, the slope is negative (y decreases as x increases); and beyond x_1 the slope is positive. At x_1, the slope of the line is zero and y is at its minimum value. In Fig. 9.4(c) the slope is positive to x_2 and negative beyond x_2. At x_2, the slope of the graph is zero and y is at its maximum value. These graphs are similar to those of economic relationships that we will encounter in Parts III and IV of this text.

MILITARY VERSUS CIVILIAN PRIORITIES

A particularly controversial example of the problem of scarcity in recent years has been the debate about national priorities. Perhaps the sharpest focus of this debate has been on military spending vs. spending on civilian priorities. Proponents of military spending want more resources for producing military goods. They argue that more is needed because of the potential military capabilities of our enemies and because they feel that military power is the best way to assure national security. Critics argue that too many of our resources are devoted to defense (more than $2 trillion since World War II!) and that military spending deprives us of the use of resources for domestic purposes (e.g., education, health, etc.).

The arguments on both sides have become more sophisticated and complex over the years, but at the heart of the matter is an economic choice about how best to use scarce resources. In this public issue, though, it is not simply an economic question. It is also a question concerned with philosophy (how best to resolve conflicts?) and with international and domestic politics.

> **8. What is national security? What determines whether a nation is secure or not?**

In 1970 the United States spent about $80 billion for national defense. This amounted to almost 10 percent of the total output of the U.S. economy. By 1980, the United States was spending $130 billion on defense, but this use of resources had shrunk in the post–Vietnam War period to about 5 percent of total output.

Throughout most of the 1970s, following the Vietnam War, the military budget decreased in real terms, that is, military spending increased slower than the rate of inflation. The national defense budget also decreased as a percent of total output. The military share of total federal spending went from 40 percent in 1970 to 24 percent a decade later. Beginning in the late 1970s during the Carter Administration and in the early 1980s under President Reagan, the United States began to increase military spending both in real terms and as a proportion of total output. By 1985, the national defense budget amounted to almost $260 billion and accounted for just over 6.5 percent of total output and about 30 percent of total federal spending. Table 9.3 details recent and projected military spending by the United States.

Table 9.3 U.S. MILITARY SPENDING, 1975–1990

YEAR	MILITARY SPENDING, BILLIONS OF CURRENT DOLLARS	PERCENTAGE ANNUAL RATE OF GROWTH, REAL TERMS
1975	84.9	−0.6
1978	103.0	0.3
1980	130.0	4.8
1981	157.5	4.8
1982	185.3	8.3
1983	209.9	8.4
1984	227.4	4.9
1985	252.7	7.3
1986	265.8	2.3
1987	282.2	2.4
1988	299.1	2.0
1989	322.3	3.9
1990	344.8	3.5

Sources: Lawrence J. Korb, "The Fiscal Year 1981–1985 Defense Program: Issues and Trends," American Enterprise Institute, *Foreign Policy and Defense Review* 2 (July 1980); Defense Budget Project, *The FY1986 Defense Budget: The Weapons Buildup Continues,* Center for Budget and Policy Priorities, 1985; and Defense Budget Project, "The FY1987 Defense Budget Preliminary Analysis," Center for Budget and Policy Priorities, 1986. Figures for 1987–1990 are based on Reagan Administration plans.

What does all this money buy? About 25 percent of the annual budget of the Department of Defense goes to pay for the personnel costs of past and present service people and civilian workers for the Pentagon. About 50 percent of it is used to purchase military supplies, equipment, and weapons: uniforms, food, planes, petroleum, ammunition, nuclear warheads, etc. Just over half the military budget supports U.S. conventional forces here and abroad, while about 20 percent covers the costs of U.S. nuclear forces. The remainder provides for the general support costs of the entire American military establishment.

Beginning in 1978, the Carter Administration began a military buildup designed to increase military spending in real terms at a rate of 3 percent per year. This was also intended to increase the military's share of total output from about 4.6 percent to just over 5 percent. Prior to the election of President Reagan, the Carter White House had issued another plan to accelerate the pace of the buildup to a rate of just under 5 percent a year. From 1980 to 1985, it called for spending a total of $1 trillion on the military and would have increased military spending to about 6 percent of total output.

The Reagan Administration came into office promising an even faster acceleration of military spending. Their plans called for increasing national defense budgets at a rate of 8 to 9 percent annually in real terms, spending more than $1.6 trillion from 1981 through 1986, and increasing the military share of total output to just over 7 percent. Reagan's plans called for increases in military pay in order to attract recruits and keep experienced personnel in the all-volunteer services, in spending for conventional forces to build up the Rapid Deployment Force for overseas combat missions, and in the procurement of advanced and expanded strategic forces, possibly including a new manned bomber, an MX missile system, an ABM system, neutron bombs, and orbital laser battle stations. Primarily the buildup involved a rapid expansion in the procurement of both conventional and strategic (nuclear) weapons. Weapons-procurement budgets increased at a rate of about 16 percent per year in real terms during the first Reagan Administration. It is a military buildup that rivals the impact of the Vietnam war in its increased claims on the output of the country.

The expansion in military spending under the Reagan Administration was accompanied by reduced spending by the federal government on nondefense programs. Food stamp, job training, welfare, education, and other programs experienced significant budget cutbacks. The $100 billion in increased military spending from 1981 to 1985 was just about matched by the decreases in spending on social programs. In 1980 the national defense budget constituted 24 percent of federal spending, and social programs (other than Social Security, Medicare, and Unemployment Compensation) accounted for 32 percent of the budget. By 1985, the military budget's share was 30 percent, while the share of other social programs was reduced to just over 20 percent.

The context for these increases in the use of resources for military purposes was the perception of deteriorating American military power in the 1970s. By the end of the decade, the Soviet Union had achieved strategic equality with the United States. While the United States had close to 10,000 deliverable, long-range nuclear warheads in its arsenal, the Soviets had a larger number of launching vehicles (missiles, submarines, and bombers). The Soviets also had large megaton bombs, while the U.S. arsenal was generally more sophisticated and accurate. In addition, each side had about 20,000 short-range, tactical nuclear devices. The SALT agreement of 1972 did not halt the arms race between the two superpowers, nor did it prevent the Soviet Union from pursuing an aggressive policy of adding to its nuclear arsenal. It was also during the 1970s that the United States lost the war in Vietnam and then suffered a series of foreign policy setbacks, including the success of Marxist revolutions in Angola, Mozambique, and Zimbabwe; the seizure of the hostages in Iran, following the ouster of the U.S.–supported Shah; and the Soviet intervention in Afghanistan. It was against this background that first Carter and then Reagan began calling for increased military spending.

What are the arguments for and against this use of the scarce material and labor resources of the United States? Ronald Reagan and his supporters have argued that the United States must maintain clear military superiority over the Soviet Union in order to prevent nuclear war and to be able to bargain with the Soviets for arms control. Moreover, they argue, larger military power will prevent the Soviet Union from fostering political instability in the Third World and will enable the United States to protect its vital interests in the Persian Gulf and other regions of the world.

The rest of the world must perceive that the United States is strong and that it is willing to use its force. In this way, the United States can contribute to international stability and world peace.

Caspar Weinberger, Secretary of Defense in the Reagan Administration, also justified the military buildup as a means of improving the readiness and preparedness of U.S. forces to fight wars, increasing the mobilization capacity of the defense industrial base so that it can gear up for "any number of long wars," and improving the "antiquated and debilitated" defense acquisition process. If all of these objectives are to be accomplished, it will require the use of an increasing amount and share of scarce national resources throughout the remainder of the 1980s.

The opponents of this view argue that both the Soviet Union and the United States already have the capability to blow up the world, that building more nuclear weapons only stimulates the arms race, and that the threat of nuclear war will be increased if the United States accelerates its strategic weapons buildup. Many of these critics support the nuclear freeze proposal and note that the current acceleration of the nuclear arms race hasn't resulted in any arms control. In terms of foreign policy, they argue that military power is not the most powerful weapon in promoting peace or American interests in the rest of the world. Rather, the United States should resign itself to the trend toward increased political and economic independence and recognize that it cannot be the world's dominant power any longer. Finally, they suggest that the national security of a country is determined at least as much by internal health as by military might. Consequently, spending more money on the military and denying resources, as a result, for domestic priorities will actually undermine the national security of the United States. What good is it to be first in military power when you're tenth in life expectancy and thirteenth in infant mortality?

Without a doubt, this debate over the use of scarce resources will continue to rage in the 1980s as it did throughout the late 1960s and 1970s. The decision about how much to spend on military priorities will be determined by continuing public debate and, ultimately, by the Congress of the United States.

9. **What are the opportunity costs of increased military spending? What are the possible opportunity costs of not increasing military spending?**

10. **How do you feel about this general debate concerning the use of our society's scarce resources? Focus your response on the economic ramifications of the various choices.**

11. **The Congressional Budget Office has estimated that the federal government could increase its spending on the nation's deteriorating infrastructure—highways, bridges, water and sewer systems, etc.—by $10 billion each year from 1985 to 1993. Would you support reducing the military budget to do so? Why or why not? Could the federal government spend more on both military and infrastructural programs?**

Bloom County by Berke Breathed. © 1984, Washington Post Writers Group, reprinted with permission.

APPLYING THE CONCEPT OF CHOICE TO PERSONAL DECISIONS

As is implicit in all of the foregoing, when making decisions about using society's resources, what we do is to compare the costs and the benefits of a particular use of resources. Included in the costs are the opportunities forgone by not using resources for alternatives. This balancing of costs vs. benefits also occurs in the economic decisions made by individuals. These include choices about work vs. leisure, type of work, consumption, and so on.

Consumers will weigh the benefits of buying a particular good (say, a used car) against its cost (that is, its price). They can also compare the benefits of purchasing a used car against the opportunity costs of not buying other goods (what could have been bought for the same price as the car, e.g., a fancy new personal computer). On the basis of such judgments, consumers make decisions about what goods to purchase in markets. (Those decisions, in turn, are taken into account by producers; and resources are allocated through markets to the production of particular goods and services.) An example of one such decision is whether to go to college or not.

In making such a decision, an individual must weigh the benefits of going to college against the opportunity costs of doing so. It costs money to go for room and board, tuition, travel, books, etc., and that money can't be used for anything else. If you're in college, you aren't working, getting experience, or earning income from a full-time job. On the other hand, a college education will develop your abilities, enrich your later life, and may qualify you for various types of employment. It's also a privileged period of time and space for growing and maturing in your experiences (curricular and extracurricular) and developing a philosophy of life.

A college education usually prepares people for white-collar, professional, higher-paying jobs. People with college educations, on the average, earn more than nongraduates. In the 1970s, however, several factors began to minimize the advantages of going to college for many young Americans. With noncollege training available in computers and other business skills, other routes developed to white-collar jobs and advancement. The growth of higher education in the post–World War II period produced a relative glut of college graduates, and a degree no longer assured employment. There was also a decline in the differential between the incomes of college graduates and nongraduates. More recently, from 1979 to 1983, the earnings gap between college and high school graduates has increased, with college graduates earning on the average about 40 percent more in annual income. Consequently, many factors can influence an individual's choice about going to college or not. The cartoons that follow reflect different aspects of this decision. And the following article from the *New York Times*, July 20, 1977, suggests that going to college, on the average, is a rational economic decision.

DOONESBURY by Garry Trudeau

Copyright © 1973, G. B. Trudeau/Distributed by Universal Press Syndicate.

Copyright © 1973, G. B. Trudeau/Distributed by Universal Press Syndicate.

A COLLEGE DEGREE STILL MAINTAINS ITS AURA

Edward B. Fiske

Despite published research and widespread anecdotal evidence to the contrary, a college degree is still a solid economic investment, according to a new study by the Conference Board.

The analysis, based on Federal labor and census figures, acknowledges that the income advantages of recent college graduates over their noncollege peers has been blunted in recent years. It argues, however, that figures shaped by "the recession experience of the past 10 years" should not be used as a basis for longterm projections.

"Measured by the likelihood of becoming unemployed, by earnings, or by the increases in earning with age and experience," it concludes, "college graduates continue to make up an economically favored group."

The Conference Board is a nonprofit, Manhattan-based organization that conducts research in the areas of economics and management. The analysis published in its monthly magazine, *Across the Board,* was written by Leonard A. Lecht, director of special projects research.

JOBLESS GRADUATES

Questions about whether a college education is worth the investment of time and money have frequently been raised in the wake of stories of college graduates who cannot find jobs or who have been forced to accept blue-collar jobs that do not make use of their education. . . .

In the Conference Board study, Mr. Lecht acknowledged the decline in income differentials for college graduates. "Males age 25 and over with four or more years of college who worked a full year in 1969 received, on an average, 46 percent more income than their high school counterparts," he said. "By 1974 the differentials had shrunk to something more than a third, 36 percent."

BASED ON UNIQUE PERIOD

The "pessimistic analysis of the status of college graduates in the labor market," he said, is based on a unique period in which the proportion of young people in the population was high and the supply of graduates substantially outstripped the growth of new jobs. . . .

Mr. Lecht suggested that the supply side of the job squeeze is likely to ease up in the coming years for several reasons. For one thing, fewer people will be entering the labor market because of declining birth rates. For another, the growth in college enrollment is slowing down. "As a con-

(continued)

sequence," he said, "there will be fewer people, college-educated or otherwise, competing for entry-level jobs in the next decade."

Another change that is likely to give an economic advantage to the college graduate, said the Conference Board report, is a broadening of the definition of "white-collar" occupations. "The graduate who becomes a management trainee rather than a professor, the engineering student who enters technical sales work, or the would-be elementary school teacher who becomes an administrative assistant are more typical than those who have become unemployed or have turned to unskilled work," he stated.

Mr. Lecht estimated that from 1974 to 1985 approximately 2.1 million jobs will have opened up for college graduates because of "educational upgrading" in fields such as physician's assistant and legal paraprofessional. In addition, he said, traditional professional and technical employment is expected to continue to grow more rapidly than total employment.

The report said that any consideration of the value of an investment in a college education must also take into account the facts that college graduates are three times less likely than noncollege graduates to become unemployed and that "income progression" is greater for men with a college diploma. Whereas the income of male college graduates 45 to 54 years old was 133 percent more than that of 18- to 24-year-olds with college degrees, the income of older high school graduates was only 83 percent above their younger counterparts.

The author also argued that, while comprehensive figures are not available, "it is likely that they would show that the college group was also less exposed to occupational accidents and illnesses, and that graduates were typically employed in positions involving more generous fringe benefits—such as paid vacations or retirement benefits—than were generally available."

The Conference Board study also noted that the available data "refers exclusively to males" and that differentials between college and high school educated women have narrowed at only half the rate for men.

"Recent graduates, at least for the next few years, will probably face more difficult problems in finding suitable jobs than their predecessors in the 'golden age' for graduates in the 1960s," Mr. Lecht concluded. "But the evidence also underscores a continuing and substantial economic advantage from attending college. It does, for most people, literally pay off."

12. What are the benefits of going to college?

13. What are the costs (and opportunity costs) of going to college?

14. Did you make the right decision about going to college? Why or why not?

**I shall be telling this with a sigh
Somewhere ages and ages hence:
Two roads diverged in a wood, and I—
I took the one less traveled by,
And that has made all
the difference.**

—Robert Frost, "The Road Not Taken"

CONCLUSION

Scarcity requires choices in both public and private matters. This fundamental economic fact requires societies and individuals to develop institutions and procedures for making hard decisions. Most individuals don't have enough income to buy everything they might want. Governments don't have enough tax money to do everything that their constituents would like them to do. In addition, sometimes decisions mean that someone or some group will benefit, while others suffer losses. The costs and benefits must be weighed in reaching decisions that maximize the use of scarce resources.

One of the most important institutions in a private economy for facilitating such decisions is the market. Markets determine **prices** for goods and resources. With this information, economic agents can make decisions comparing alternative courses of action. Producers can decide what to produce and what resources to use. Consumers can decide what goods to purchase. (Oftentimes government decisions operate "outside" of market forces because there is no profit objective; nevertheless government cost–benefit studies of alternatives must use price data for the resources involved.)

In the next chapter, we will examine the economic theory of markets—how they operate and how prices are determined.

KEY CONCEPTS

microeconomics	opportunity cost
scarcity	the production possibilities curve
economic decisions (choice)	prices
allocation of resources	efficiency

REVIEW QUESTIONS

1. From your own experiences and lifetime, do you think that scarcity is really a problem for the United States?

2. What is the difference between wants and needs?

3. Are wants and needs really unlimited? If they are, why?

4. How does the concept of opportunity cost help societies and individuals to make choices?

5. Why do economic choices have to be made?

6. Think of examples from your own life when the concepts of scarcity and opportunity cost have influenced your decisions.

7. Why don't the advances of science, technology, and exploration eliminate the problem of scarcity?

8. Why, at the beginning of World War II, could the United States increase its military output without sacrificing the production of civilian goods and services? Answer using a production possibilities curve.

SUGGESTED READINGS

The daily newspaper for innumerable examples of choices on private and public issues!

Caroline Bird, 1975. *The Case against College*, D. McKay. On why you made a mistake by going to college!

Robert W. DeGrasse, Jr., 1983. *Military Expansion, Economic Decline*, M. E. Sharpe, Inc. A recent study of the expansion of U.S. military spending and the negative economic consequences.

William Hartung, 1984. *The Economic Consequences of the Nuclear Freeze*, The Council on Economic Priorities. This report published by a New York City research group identifies the opportunity costs of a nuclear freeze and suggests the economic benefits (in addition to the noneconomic benefits) that could be derived from reduced military spending for nuclear arms.

Robert Heilbroner, 1974. *An Inquiry into the Human Prospect*, Norton. One view of possible global scarcity and the results.

Seymour Melman, 1976. *The Permanent War Economy*, Simon and Schuster. On the adverse economic effects (the opportunity costs) of massive military spending since World War II in the United States.

10

Chapter

The Theory of Markets

INTRODUCTION

We intimated in Chapter 9 that markets guide decisions about resource allocation—that is, how society decides to use its scarce resources. How exactly do markets accomplish this? The purpose of this chapter is to develop the economic analysis of markets so that we may begin to get some insight into the relationship between markets and resource allocation.

As we saw in Part I, markets emerged as one of the first and most fundamental institutions of capitalism. Markets replaced tradition and feudal authority as the principal organizers of economic activity. Markets exist in capitalism for all consumer goods and productive resources. **Markets** are the places in which buyers and sellers exchange goods and services. Usually, in our economy, goods and services are exchanged for money. All goods and services, then, must have prices that reflect their values and that govern their exchange. It is these **prices** that end up guiding production and resource allocation. Producers and consumers use prices as basic information in making decisions about which resources to use and which products to purchase. Consequently, to see how markets allocate scarce resources, it is essential to understand *how markets determine prices*.

MARKETS AND PRICE DETERMINATION:
SUPPLY-AND-DEMAND ANALYSIS

In order to highlight the economic analysis of markets, we will use as an example the market for college education in the United States. In the last chapter, we examined the decision about going to college as an example of a personal choice about the use of scarce resources. How much does it cost? What else could one do with the money? Why should (or why shouldn't) one go to college? What does one sacrifice by going to college for four years? Does it make more sense to enter the labor force right after high school? What are the benefits of a college education? Obviously, one crucial element in making such an important decision is the dollar cost of going to college.

In the following analysis, we will try to isolate the factors that determine the price of a college education. We hope the analysis will help us to gain some insights into and understanding of how this market operates—how its price is determined and what implications there are for resource allocation. We will develop a method of analysis, *the theory of supply and demand*, that should assist us in understanding generally the functioning of markets in our capitalist economy.

Before we begin our analysis, however, as in all economic theory, we will have to make some assumptions to simplify our model of the market. Despite these

An example of a market. (Photograph by Bill Weibel.)

simplifying assumptions, our theory should provide us with some tools for understanding the functioning of real markets in the economy. It should also help us to understand why market prices change over time. And it might also help us to develop some possible solutions to economic problems.

> **1. During the 1970s, the cost of a year at college for tuition, room and board, and fees almost doubled. However, the rise in costs was slightly less than the overall rate of inflation for the same period. Why has the price of a college education been continually increasing? What can be done about this problem?**

Now for the assumptions. We will begin with one fundamental assumption of microeconomics: that economic agents are rational calculators and are motivated by self-interest. We assume that consumers are rational with respect to their purchases and that they try to maximize their own welfare through consumption, given their available spending power (that, through calculations and trial and error, consumers seek to maximize their satisfaction). Generally, we assume that producers calculate costs and revenues and try to maximize their profits from production. Markets exist whenever and wherever commodities are exchanged by buyers and sellers. Usually a buyer exchanges money for the good or service, and vice versa, for the seller.

For our particular example of the market for a college education, there are some additional assumptions and qualifications that we should make clear at the outset. First, we will assume that there is, in some sense, a homogeneous product. In other words, we will concentrate on *a* college education as a good that is exchanged in a market of buyers and sellers. That is, we will assume away the differences between a Smith education and a Bucknell education or between a private university and a public university. Obviously, these differences do exist, and they will account in part for the differences in cost among these different possibilities. For the moment, however, we wish to simplify and to concentrate on *one* price for a college education. Once the model of supply and demand is developed, we should be able to use it to account for differences in cost at different institutions of higher learning. We will also assume away the admissions problem (the product is not necessarily available to any buyer who might wish to purchase it) and the graduation problem (actually getting the product in hand is not merely a matter of paying the costs to the cashier). Finally, in this case, the producer of the product is not (presumably) a profit-making institution. However, colleges and universities must take their costs and revenues into account, utilize scarce resources efficiently, and charge prices that reflect their costs.

We will begin by examining each side of this market in isolation from the other. For the buyer's side of the market, we will focus on demand; for the seller's side of the market, we will focus on supply. Then we will put supply and demand together to see how the market price is determined.

DEMAND

First of all, let's isolate and examine the buyer's side of the market. We will call this the **demand** for the product. What determines the demand for any product? In our example, there are many factors that would influence the demand for a college education. The essential factor behind the demand for any product obviously is that it is useful to the buyer; it satisfies some want or desire or need. Beyond this, we can list some other influences on the demand for a product.

Tastes and Preferences

Consumers' tastes and preferences guide their demand for different goods. Tastes and preferences are influenced by social, political, and cultural forces, as well as by the physical, psychological, and mental requirements of daily survival in the world. Obviously, over time, in any given society, tastes and preferences will change and will, in turn, influence changing patterns of consumer demand for different goods and services. Tastes and preferences will also be different in different countries.

Throughout the history of the United States, a college education has been a valued "product." Presumably, it helps to prepare people for coping with the world, it broadens people's horizons and perspectives, it prepares people for professional positions in society, and it paves the way for further education. It may even help people gain entry to the labor force.

In recent years, the demand for a college education has been substantial, primarily because people perceive that it is an almost certain necessity for obtaining specific types of employment. Indeed, the realities of the labor market suggest that a college education is extremely valuable in this regard. Consumers' tastes and preferences thus influence the demand for a college education. Throughout the 1960s the percentage of high school graduates who went on to college steadily increased; however, in the 1970s and early 1980s the percentage leveled off.

> 2. Why do you suppose that tastes and preferences have changed to cause a leveling off in the percentage of high school graduates who go on to college? *Did* tastes and preferences change?

Income

How much consumers can demand of the products they prefer depends on their incomes—how much they have to spend. And who consumes what products depends on the distribution of income in the society. Since we have assumed that consumers try to maximize their satisfaction and that they derive it from goods because the goods are useful, we conclude that with more money consumers will purchase larger quantities of goods and services. During the 1960s, the United States experienced one of its longest periods of prosperity. The real income of the average American family increased throughout this period. This increasing income certainly provided the resources for an increasing percentage of American youth to attend college. In the 1970s, however, the increase in average real incomes began to slow down. This, in part, probably accounts for some of the "leveling off" in college attendance. (Here, families with lower real incomes will no longer be able to afford the "good.")

Prices of Related Goods

Consumers are very sensitive to the prices of goods they consider to be substitutes—goods that satisfy the same need. In this case, if some nonprofessional training schools lowered their prices, then that might reduce the demand for college educations, as some people substituted that educational experience for that of college. On the other hand, there may be some goods that are complementary, i.e., go together or are consumed together. For example, if the price of law school increased, that might dissuade some people (who had planned on being or hoped to be lawyers) from going to college. The point is that the demand for a college education may be sensitive to (and influenced by) the prices of related products.

Number of Demanders

The total demand for a product is obviously affected by the number of people who desire to consume it. During the 1960s and 1970s, the number of college-age people in the United States was steadily expanding. In the 1960s, with an increasing percentage of youths attending college, there was a dramatic increase in the total number of "demanders" in the market. Recently, the increase in the numbers has been less dramatic, although older people are now increasing their attendance in college. In the 1980s, on the basis of population projections of fewer college-age people, experts predict that the total number of people who go to college may actually decrease. The number of 18-year-olds in the population will actually decline by about 25 percent between 1979 and 1994. This has serious implications for the market for a college education in the United States. A number of colleges and universities have begun vigorous efforts to recruit older students and foreign students to make up for this reduction in the "number of demanders." Some private colleges are beginning to accept part-time students. Many of these factors have, in fact, already had an effect: Students over 25 now make up one-third of the 12 million enrolled in higher education, and 40 percent of all students are part-time students.

Expectations of Future Prices

If consumers expect the price of a product to change, oftentimes this will affect their demand for that product. For example, if high school graduates expect that the price of attending college is going to continue to increase in the future, this may cause many of them to attend right away rather than wait, or they may decide not to go at all. Price expectations, then, will tend to influence consumers' demands for the product. (Notice the frequent use in economics of the words "tend to." The conclusions of economists tend to be tentative because they are usually based on assumptions and expectations of normal behavior on the part of the economic agents and variables the economists are examining. In your own thinking, try to replicate this word usage; the conclusions of economists are not carved on stone and should not be accepted as gospel. Economic theory deals with assumptions and tendencies; if "this" happens, probably "that" will happen.)

Miscellaneous Factors

Other factors may also influence consumers' demands for products. In the 1960s the federal government and several state governments significantly increased their support of higher education in the United States. This increased concern with the benefits to the country of higher education probably by itself influenced the demand for a college education. In addition, however, this support made it easier for more high school graduates to attend college. It also opened up the college experience to a class of people that historically had not had access to higher education in the United States by significantly expanding public universities and community colleges throughout the country.

3. **What other factor(s) would influence the demand situation for a college education?** *Remember,* **we are considering so far** *only* **the demand side of the market.**

CETERIS PARIBUS AND THE DEMAND CURVE

If you answered "the *price* of a college education" to the question above, you are on your way to becoming an economist (for what that's worth). Economists attempt to isolate the effect of *price* on the quantity demanded for a product. In analyzing the demand for a product, they acknowledge that all of the factors above do influence demand. But sometimes simplification helps analysis. Therefore economists concentrate on the relationship between price and the quantity demanded of a good. To do this, they assume that at one moment of time all of the other factors are given; then only price will affect the quantity demanded. The other factors are considered to be in a *ceteris paribus* category—all other things being equal. *Demand is concerned with the relationship between price and quantity demanded, all other things constant.*

So let's make that rather large assumption and see what happens. What *is* the effect of price on the *quantity demanded* of a college education? At one moment in time, assuming (again) that there is some one average type of college education, there is only one price for this product. For 1984, the National Center for Educational Statistics estimated that the average cost for tuition, room and board, and required fees at private universities was $9300. For public schools the average cost was just under $4000. So $6600 was about the average cost for the nation as a whole for a year of college.*

*For 1986–1987, tuition, room and board, and fees at Harvard and MIT were in excess of $16,000.

However, we can hypothesize about what would happen to the quantity demanded if the price were different, higher or lower. In fact, we would guess that *if* the price were lower, people would consume more—the quantity demanded would increase—and that *if* the price were higher, people would consume less—the quantity demanded would decrease. This is true for almost all goods and services: If the price is lowered, the quantity demanded will increase, and if the price is increased, the quantity demanded will decrease. Price and *quantity demanded* are inversely related. When the price changes, there is a **change in the quantity demanded**—in the opposite direction.

Well, we've done it in words. Now how about numbers? A demand equation, generally, would show that the quantity of college education demanded, Q_d, is a function of the price of a college education, P_c, *given* all of the *ceteris paribus* conditions. Or $Q_d = f(P_c)$, *ceteris paribus*. We can construct a hypothetical **demand schedule** (Table 10.1) showing different possible prices and the quantities demanded at those prices. Let's hypothesize about the national market for college educations for a year (again assuming that there is some average education).

If the price was $6600 (which is about what the national average cost was in 1984), then about 12 million people would be enrolled in the nation's colleges and universities as full-time students. *If*, however, the cost went up to $9800 per year, then the quantity demanded would be cut back to 6 million. What are the other possibilities?

Not surprisingly, we can also describe the relationship between price and quantity demanded graphically. We will call this a **demand curve.** On the vertical scale we will measure price, and on the horizontal scale we will measure quantity demanded. Any point on the graph then represents a certain price–quantity demanded combination. Let's take the information from our demand schedule and transfer it to the graph. At a price of $5000, the quantity demanded will be 15 million. At $6600, it will be 12 million. And so on. See Fig. 10.1.

If we connect all the price–quantity demanded points, we get our demand curve for a college education during one year in the United States. It shows, hypothetically, all of the possible prices for a college education and the respective quantities demanded. It has a negative slope, reflecting the inverse relationship between price and quantity demanded. At lower prices the quantity demanded is greater, and at higher prices the quantity demanded is lower. Normally, for con-

Table 10.1 THE DEMAND SCHEDULE

P_c (COST PER YEAR, TUITION, ROOM AND BOARD, AND FEES)	Q_d (NUMBER OF STUDENTS, IN MILLIONS)
$11,400	3
9,800	6
8,200	9
6,600	12
5,000	15

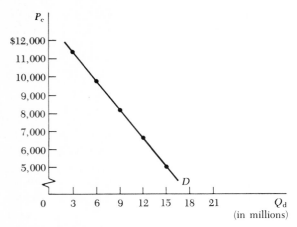

Figure 10.1 Demand curve.

venience, we draw demand curves as straight lines. The graphs of supply and demand curves are very important tools in economics. Make sure you understand how Fig. 10.1 was constructed and what it shows.

The demand curve illustrates the buyers' side of the market. Now let's turn our attention to the sellers' side of the market and consider it in isolation. After that, we will put the two sides of the market together in our model and get a market price for a college education.

SUPPLY

Here we will focus on the sellers' side of the market. What influences the quantity supplied of a product? What factors determine the number of students that colleges and universities can allow to enroll? Obviously the price that they can get from students has a lot to do with it. But for the moment, let's try to list other influences.

Resource Prices

The costs of producing goods and services weigh heavily on the ability of sellers to supply to the market. Thus resource prices will help determine the supply of any product offered for sale. In the supply of college educations, if the salaries of professors and other staff increase, it will tend to reduce the supply offered or to make a college education more expensive. With the inflation of the late 1960s and the 1970s, the labor resource costs of running universities have skyrocketed as employees have demanded commensurate increases in their incomes. Despite the fact that dollar labor costs have increased at colleges, in real terms there was a 20 percent drop in faculty incomes during the 1970s due to inflation. This has prompted many faculties to form labor unions; there are more than 200 at four-year colleges and almost 400 at two-year colleges. Physical plant workers, cafeteria personnel, and office workers are also often in unions on campuses around the country. Increasing food, equipment, maintenance, construction, and energy prices have also increased costs significantly. As a result, the cost of supplying a college education has also increased.

Technology

The techniques of production influence supply. If computers and television sets were used to teach students, to grade their work, and to write letters of recommendation for students, it would probably allow colleges and universities to greatly increase the numbers of students to whom they could supply a college education. Other ways of changing the techniques of production involve the use of large lecture classes, sometimes even with video lectures, or computer-assisted learning. (Of course, these might make the process of getting an education a little bit less attractive. But that is a *demand* factor.) For the time being, however, the technology of education still relies heavily on human beings and, in some places, on relatively small classes.

Prices of Related Goods and Resources

The ability of suppliers to supply any product to the market will also be affected by the prices of other products and resources. If a college or a university could make a better go of it by operating as a summer camp than by offering summer sessions, then maybe it would decide to supply that product instead. In the same way, if resource prices changed, it might influence the decisions of how to provide an education, as well as how much education to offer. For example, if construction costs were to decrease, then a college or a university might be influenced to build some large lecture halls to accommodate more students. Or, if computer companies offered discounts, a college might be influenced to develop its academic program in the direction of increased use of computers.

Sellers' Expectations

Sellers' expectations about the future will condition their supply of a product to the market. If colleges and universities expect lower enrollments in the future, they might be inclined to try to offer more students the chance to go to college now (that is, increase the supply of the product now). They might do this to better prepare themselves for the foreseen lean days ahead. Given the likelihood of continuing high energy prices, some older dormitories might be retired, thus reducing the number of spaces available at some schools.

Numbers of Sellers in the Market

If the number of sellers in the market decreased, it would tend to decrease the supply of the product. And if the number of sellers increased, it would tend to increase the supply. In the late 1970s, a number of colleges and universities in the United States closed their doors. In 1981 there were 3253 institutions of higher learning in the United States; in 1983 there were 3111. The predictions are that this trend will continue into the future.

> 4. Of the five factors above that influence supply, which, in your opinion, is the most influential in determining the supply of a product?
>
> 5. What sorts of factors influence sellers' expectations about their markets?

CETERIS PARIBUS AND THE SUPPLY CURVE

As for the demand curve, we will hold all of these nonprice influences on supply constant. They constitute the *ceteris paribus* conditions for supply. As a result, we will concentrate on the effect of price on the *quantity supplied* of a product. At one moment in time, we assume that all of the *ceteris paribus* factors are given and then consider in isolation the effect of price. **Supply** *is concerned with the relationship between price and quantity supplied, all other things constant*.

Again, there is probably only one price in existence. But we can hypothesize different possible prices and examine the effects on quantity supplied. If the price were higher, we would expect that sellers would increase the quantity supplied. If they are offered a higher price, they will be willing to supply more; if they are offered a lower price, we expect them to reduce the quantity supplied. For supply, price and quantity supplied are directly related. When the price changes, there is a **change in quantity supplied** in the same direction.

In equation form, $Q_s = f(P_c)$, *ceteris paribus*. With all other determinants of supply held constant, the quantity supplied of a college education, Q_s, is a function of the price offered for a college education, P_c. As before for demand, we can construct a hypothetical **supply schedule** (Table 10.2), showing different possible prices and the quantities that would be supplied at those prices. Table 10.2 hypothesizes about the total national supply of a college education.

If the price was only $5000, then colleges and universities would offer places for only 9 million students. *If* the price was $11,400, on the other hand, then colleges and universities would be willing to offer places to 21 million students. What are the other possibilities?

Table 10.2 THE SUPPLY SCHEDULE

P_c ($)	Q_s (IN MILLIONS)
11,400	21
9,800	18
8,200	15
6,600	12
5,000	9

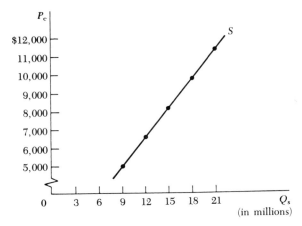

Figure 10.2   Supply curve.

Again, we can show the supply relationship graphically. We measure price on the vertical scale and quantity supplied on the horizontal scale. Each point in Fig. 10.2 then represents a certain price–quantity supplied combination. If we connect the five combinations from the schedule above, then we get a supply curve for a college education. It shows, hypothetically, all the possible prices for a college education and the respective quantities supplied. It has a positive slope showing the direct relationship between price and quantity supplied; at higher prices, greater quantities will be supplied, and at lower prices, lower quantities will be supplied. Usually we draw supply curves as straight lines for convenience.

The supply curve illustrates the sellers' side of the market. The demand curve shows the buyers' side. Let's see what happens when we put them together to look at both sides of the market.

THE MARKET AND EQUILIBRIUM PRICE

First of all, let's put the supply and demand schedules together, as shown in Table 10.3. And then the supply and demand curves together (Fig. 10.3) give us a hypothetical picture of the market. The conclusion of our analysis, when we put supply and demand together, is that the supply and the demand for the product determine a market price. It is an **equilibrium price.** Equilibrium connotes a situation in which the tendency is toward a certain state, and once that state is achieved it will be maintained, in the absence of outside disturbances.

In our example, a price of $6600 is the equilibrium price. At this price, the desires of buyers and sellers are consistent. Buyers want to buy 12 million places at colleges and universities, and sellers are willing to offer 12 million places. The quantity demanded equals the quantity supplied. At $P_c = \$6600$, $Q_s = Q_d$. The equilibrium price and quantity exchanged are the point at which the supply and demand curves intersect. At any other price, Q_s does not equal Q_d; and there will be a tendency for the price to change because buyers' and sellers' desires are *not* consistent.

Table 10.3 THE SUPPLY SCHEDULE COMBINED WITH THE DEMAND SCHEDULE

P_c ($)	Q_d (IN MILLIONS)	Q_s (IN MILLIONS)
11,400	3	21
9,800	6	18
8,200	9	15
6,600	12	12
5,000	15	9

For example, at P_c = $9800, Q_s = 18 million and Q_d = 6 million. *If* the price was $9800, there would be an oversupply, or a **surplus.** That is, 18 million places would be available, but only 6 million students would want to go to college at that price. In this case, sellers would lower their prices to eliminate the excess supply. This has a twofold effect. It reduces the quantity supplied and increases the quantity demanded. We can see this by examining what happens at a price of $8200. At this price, Q_s still exceeds Q_d (15 million > 9 million). Suppliers will then lower prices again. This process will continue until Q_s = Q_d. This occurs at a price of $6600. Thus price changes will eliminate a surplus in the market until the equilibrium price is reached. See Fig. 10.4.

In the same way, *if* the price is below $6600, there will be a tendency to move toward the $6600 price. If the price is $5000, then Q_d = 15 million and Q_s = 9 million. In this case, the quantity demanded exceeds the quantity supplied (15 million > 9 million); and a **shortage** of places at colleges exists. Purchasers, facing a shortage, begin to bid up the price. Again, this causes a twofold effect. It increases the quantity supplied but decreases the quantity demanded. This will continue until the desires of buyers and sellers are consistent at one price where Q_s = Q_d. See Fig. 10.5.

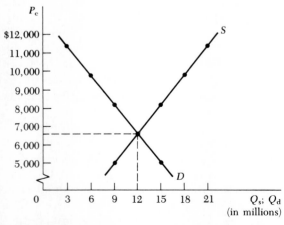

Figure 10.3 The market.

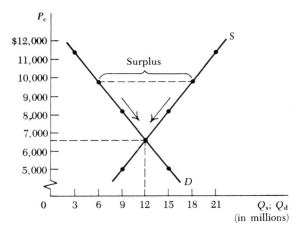

Figure 10.4 Surplus eliminated by price decreases.

Supply-and-demand analysis has shown us how markets determine equilibrium prices! There is a tendency to establish, to move toward, the equilibrium price. And once there, with buyers' and sellers' desires consistent (when the quantity supplied equals the quantity demanded) and no outside disturbances, that price will tend to be maintained.

6. **Why** do sellers lower price when there is a surplus?

7. **Why** do buyers bid up the price when there is a shortage?

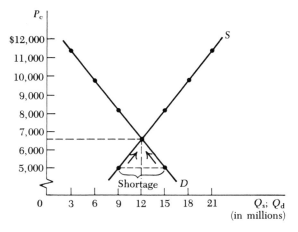

Figure 10.5 Shortage eliminated by price increases.

A TINGE OF REALITY: IT'S NOT A *CETERIS PARIBUS* WORLD

Our supply-and-demand model so far has included the rather strict assumptions involved in our *ceteris paribus* conditions on both sides of the market. However, one of the most beautiful aspects of this model is that we can use it to accommodate changes in the *ceteris paribus* conditions. It is useful because obviously in a changing world these other determinants of supply and demand do change. A couple of examples will suffice to illustrate the richness of this approach and the ability of the supply-and-demand model to explain changes in market conditions and prices.

First, let's take a change in the demand conditions. We will call this a **change in demand,** and it will cause the whole demand curve to shift. Any of the determinants could change, or all of them could change. They could move in the same direction (causing an increase or a decrease in demand), or they could influence demand in opposite directions. Go back and consider the various determinants of demand (or *ceteris paribus* conditions) and consider the complexity of factors that are behind a demand curve.

Let's examine just one possibility. Assume that in the late 1960s and early 1970s, for whatever reasons, a college degree was perceived as being more attractive to students. This represents a change in tastes and preferences. What will it do to demand? What effect will it have on the market for a college education?

First of all, it will cause a shift in the demand curve. It causes an increase in demand; the demand curve will shift to the right. At every possible price, the quantity demanded will have increased, and we thus get a new demand curve. The demand curve for a college education shifts from D_1 to D_2, as shown in Fig. 10.6.

8. **What other changes in demand might cause an increase in demand, a shift of the curve to the right?**

9. **What would cause a shift back to the left, a decrease in demand?**

What happens in the market? Here we must look at supply and demand together, as shown in Fig. 10.7. With the new demand curve, D_2, we get a new equilibrium price, P_2, and a new equilibrium quantity exchanged, Q_2, where $Q_s =$

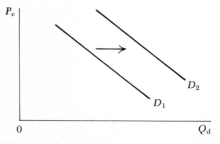

Figure 10.6 Change in demand.

Q_d. With an increase in demand, we get a new higher price in the market. *This analysis suggests to us that one place to look for an explanation of increasing prices in a market is in the dynamic changes in the determinants of demand.* The market price of a college education tended to increase in the late 1960s and early 1970s as the demand for the product increased because of a change in the public's tastes and preferences. Also the amount exchanged by buyers and sellers has increased in our example (from Q_1 to Q_2). A word of caution, however, is in order here. Tastes and preferences were not the only determinants of demand that were changing during this period of time (and, in addition, the determinants of supply were also changing). For example, the increased number of youths in the United States of college age as a result of the postwar baby boom also contributed to the shift in demand. We can conclude, though, that the change in preferences was, in part, responsible for the increase in demand and for the increase in price.

Our final example involves a **change in supply.** Here we allow the determinants of supply to change. Again, any or all could change, in the same direction or opposite directions. Reexamine the determinants of supply (the *ceteris paribus* conditions).

Assume that in the late 1960s and early 1970s the prices of the resources used in providing college educations were increasing. As a result, there would be a change in supply. Suppliers would tend to require higher prices for every different quantity supplied (or they would be willing to offer lower quantities supplied at every possible price). There would be a decrease in supply; the supply curve would shift back to the left. The supply curve for a college education shifts from S_1 to S_2, as shown in Fig. 10.8.

10. What other forces might cause a shift to the left in the supply curve?

11. What would cause a shift to the right in the supply curve?

What will this do in the market? Assume demand conditions are unaltered. Figure 10.9 puts supply and demand together. (We assume that D_1 remains unchanged.) With the new supply curve, S_2, we get a new equilibrium price, P_2, and a new equilibrium quantity exchanged, Q_2, where $Q_s = Q_d$. With this decrease in

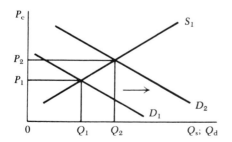

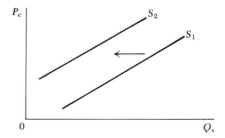

Figure 10.7   Change in demand: the market.   **Figure 10.8**   Change in supply.

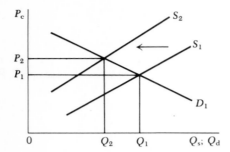

Figure 10.9 Change in supply: the market.

supply we get a new higher market price and a lower quantity exchanged. Again, *this analysis may help us to explain price increases by examining what happens to the determinants of supply*. If forces are creating decreases in supply for a particular product, that will help to explain the emergence of higher prices for it.

12. **What happens if we put both of our examples together, an increase in demand and a decrease in supply? Show this result in your own graphical illustration.**

A WORD OF CAUTION

One aspect of learning economics is identifying and defining economic concepts—and doing so precisely. This involves using words carefully. In some sense, it is like learning a foreign language. Some words that economists use have very specific meanings for particular concepts.

What happens on a demand curve if the price of the product changes? We get a *change in the quantity demanded*. If the price increases, the quantity demanded decreases. And if the price decreases, the quantity demanded increases. This represents a movement along a particular demand curve. What happens if one of the determinants of demand changes? We get a *change in demand*. If income increases, the whole demand curve shifts out to the right for most goods. Whenever there is a change in demand, the whole demand curve shifts. For supply, a change in price causes a *change in quantity supplied*, which is a movement along a supply curve. A change in one of the determinants of supply causes a *change in supply* wherein the whole supply curve shifts.

A higher price causes a decrease in quantity demanded and an increase in quantity supplied. If the income of households decreases, the demand for most goods would decrease (there would be a change in demand). What would happen to the equilibrium price, then, if supply stays the same? Right—price would decrease. And then what happens to quantity demanded and quantity supplied? Right—there are new quantities demanded and supplied at the new equilibrium, lower than the original one. Figure 10.10 shows this result graphically.

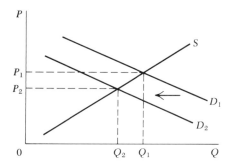

Figure 10.10   A change in demand.

SUPPLY AND DEMAND IN AGRICULTURE

Agricultural prices have always been one of the best applications for supply-and-demand analysis. This is primarily because agriculture is a relatively competitive sector of our economy. There are lots of farmers and lots of consumers of food in the United States. As a result, agriculture is a useful area to try to utilize our supply-and-demand analysis to analyze why prices change and what goes on in markets.

Even if a market is not competitive—and in Chapter 12 we will discover that many markets in the United States are not—supply-and-demand analysis is still very useful because it provides a framework for focusing on key variables and determinants. It also helps us to understand the relationships between the two sides of the market.

Agriculture, as a matter of fact, does have many noncompetitive aspects. Agribusiness, or corporate farming, is on the increase in the United States, especially in California. The small, family farm is an endangered species. There is much economic concentration and power in the intermediary areas between the farmer and the consumer. At the supermarket level there is also a *lack* of competition—in the sense of lots of sellers (we will define competition much more precisely in the next chapter). Nevertheless, agricultural prices are a good example to use in supply-and-demand analysis.

In the early 1980s American agriculture faced a crisis that reminded many of the severe farm depression of the 1920s and 1930s. Farm income, at $19 billion in 1982, was at about the same level in real terms as it was in the 1930s. One-fifth of that income came from federal government support programs, many of which were put in place to supplement farm incomes after the experiences of the 1930s.

In response to increased foreign demand for American grain in the 1970s from sales to the Soviet Union and the People's Republic of China, U.S. farmers had expanded output rapidly. But the 1980 embargo against the Soviet Union and the beginning of the worldwide recession of 1981–1982, plus record harvests in the United States in the early 1980s, produced vast agricultural surpluses. And what happens to prices when there are surpluses? As supply-and-demand analysis suggests, they led to sharply reduced prices for corn, wheat, soybeans, and other agricultural products. These lower prices, plus increased energy costs and interest rates, put a severe squeeze on farm incomes. Farm debt, bankruptcies, and foreclosures began to increase. In 1982, 25 percent of Farmers Home Administration mortgage payments were overdue and almost 800 farm were foreclosed by the FHA, more than twice as many as in 1981.

However, in 1983, several events caused prices to begin moving in the opposite direction. Cold weather conditions in the winter and a summer drought reduced crops. And, in response to the farm crisis, the Reagan Administration began a program to intentionally reduce agricultural harvests. The payment-in-kind program (PIK) gave farmers U.S.–owned surpluses in exchange for leaving land idle. The intention was to reduce surpluses and to stop the downward movement of agricultural prices. The combination of bad weather and the PIK program produced a 48 percent decrease in the corn harvest in 1983, a 33 percent reduction in soybeans, 15 percent in peanuts, and 35 percent in cotton. The result was higher prices, reduced stocks of reserves of all these commodities, and the promise of reduced government expenditures for price supports.

In 1984, an excess of rain in the spring threatened crop output, but with a reduction in the PIK program there was an increase in cultivation over 1983. In addition, due to record crops elsewhere, there was a global wheat glut. Examine a recent newspaper to see what's happening to agricultural prices now. From even this short exploration, though, you should see that agricultural prices are easily influenced by changes in supply and demand. They are quite volatile, they depend very much on the weather, and they go through periods of increase and decrease.

13. Show the effect of increased exports to the Soviet Union on the wheat market in the United States. What happens to price? To quantity supplied?

14. What effect will an embargo and record harvests have on agricultural prices? Show with supply and demand curves. Show the effect of a worldwide recession, too.

15. Using supply and demand curves, show the effects of the PIK program. What effect do higher prices have on quantities supplied next year?

ELASTICITY

Thus far, we have concentrated on the relationship between prices and quantities supplied and demanded. But if a price changes, *how much* does the quantity demanded change? Or if the price goes up, *how much* does the quantity supplied increase?

Elasticity is a concept that attempts to illustrate the sensitivity of the demand (supply) situation for a product to changes in its price. It is concerned with the relationship between the quantity demanded and the price of a particular good or service. For example, we know that, all other things given, if the price of a college education goes up, the quantity demanded will go down. But how much will the quantity demanded be reduced in comparison with the price increase? The **price elasticity of demand** is a measurement of the sensitivity of changes in quantity demanded to changes in price. It measures the responsiveness of the amount demanded to price changes. How elastic is the demand when price changes? (Note that we are using terminology that is associated with the movements along a single demand curve. With all of the determinants of demand fixed at one point in time, we focus on the impact of a price change on the quantity demanded.)

The following is an equation for measuring the price elasticity of demand:

$$E_d = \frac{\text{percentage change in quantity demanded}}{\text{percentage change in price}} = \frac{\Delta Q_d/Q_d}{\Delta P/P}.$$

NbT CHANGING DEMAND CURVE

The percentage change in price is associated with a certain percentage change in the quantity demanded. In calculating elasticity, we ignore the direction of change of each variable and concentrate on the relative relationship between the percentage changes.

If the percentage change in quantity demanded is larger than the percentage change in price, then $E_d > 1$, and we say that the demand for the good is *elastic* with respect to price. If the price of 35mm cameras is reduced by 20 percent and the quantity demanded increases by 30 percent, then $E_d = 1.5$. In this case, the demand for the cameras is relatively sensitive to price changes. On the other hand, if the price of milk (or beer) increases by 10 percent but the quantity demanded decreases by only 5 percent, then elasticity is 0.5. In this case, we say that the demand for milk (or beer) is *inelastic* since the percentage change in quantity demanded is less than the percentage change in price ($E_d < 1$).

For example, let's assume a computer store reduced the price of a personal computer model from $3000 to $2500 and the number of units it sold in a six-month period increased from 100 to 150. That is,

PRICE	QUANTITY SOLD
$3000	100
2500	150

What is the elasticity of demand? The price decreased by $500 or about 16 percent:

$$\frac{3000 - 2500}{3000} = \frac{500}{3000} = \frac{1}{6} = 16\tfrac{2}{3} \text{ percent.}$$

$\frac{\Delta P}{P} = 16^{2}/3 \%$

The quantity demanded increased by 50 units, or 50 percent:

$$\frac{150 - 100}{100} = \frac{50}{100} = 50 \text{ percent.}$$

$\frac{\Delta Q_D}{Q_D} = 50\%$

$E = \frac{50\%}{16^{2}/3} = 3$ $\therefore$ *elastic*

So, the elasticity of demand equals

$$E_d = \frac{\text{percentage change in quantity demanded}}{\text{percentage change in price}}$$

$$= \frac{50}{16\frac{2}{3}} = 3.^*$$

Consequently, the demand for computers is fairly sensitive to price changes; the relative change in quantity demanded is three times the relative change in the price.

Elasticity Graphically

Figure 10.11 shows a typical demand curve. On the upper portion of the curve, the price elasticity of demand is elastic; and on the lower portion, it is inelastic. Elasticity changes along the demand curve. And the elasticity of a demand curve does not equal its slope. The slope of the demand curve is the change in the price over the change in the quantity demanded between any two points (the height over the base, the rise over the run, etc.). The slope equals $\Delta P/\Delta Q$. Elasticity, on the other hand, is equal to

$$\frac{\text{percentage } \Delta \text{ in quantity demanded}}{\text{percentage } \Delta \text{ in price}}.$$

We can rearrange the formula for elasticity as:

$$\frac{\Delta Q/Q}{\Delta P/P} = \frac{\Delta Q}{\Delta P} \cdot \frac{P}{Q}.$$

This obviously makes elasticity unequal to the slope of the demand curve.

Also, on the left portion of the demand curve, any percentage change in quantity demanded will be relatively large (since quantity is at low levels) and the percentage change in price will be relatively small. Consequently, elasticity will be

---

*Notice that there is another way we could have calculated the elasticity. We used the original price and quantity as the denominator in our calculations of the percentage changes in quantity and price. If we used the new price and quantity, we'd get:

percentage change in price = 500/2500 = 20 percent,

percentage change in quantity demanded = 50/150 = 33⅓ percent,

and then elasticity of demand = 1.6.

There is a way to resolve this difference in the calculated elasticity of demand by taking the average of the old and new prices and quantities. This is often called the mid-points formula:

$$E_d = \frac{\Delta Q/[(Q_1 + Q_2)/2]}{\Delta P/[(P_1 + P_2)/2]} = \frac{50/125}{500/2750} = \frac{40 \text{ percent}}{18 \text{ percent}} = 2.2.$$

The important point, though, is that the elasticity of demand measures the *relative* change in quantity demanded due to the *relative* change in price, to see how sensitive quantity demanded is to price changes.

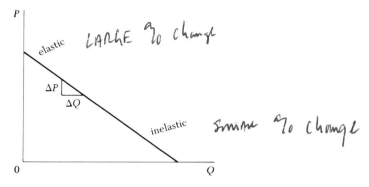

Figure 10.11   Elasticity along a demand curve.

greater than one. On the right portion, percentage changes in quantity will be relatively small and percentage changes in price will be relatively large. And, then, elasticity will be less than one. Moving along the demand curve to the right will reduce elasticity or increase inelasticity.

The Determinants of Elasticity

What determines elasticity; or how sensitive to changes in its price is the demand for a product? Can you think of goods you demand regardless of price? Others to whose price you are very sensitive? Generally, whenever there are substitutes for a good, your demand tends to be elastic. The more substitutes, the more elastic the demand. For example, if the price of green beans increases, people will substitute other green vegetables. When the price goes up, people will reduce their consumption of green beans by relatively more—that is, we'd expect the price elasticity of demand for green beans to be above one. On the other hand, if you heat your house with oil and oil prices increase, you may decrease your use of oil but not by much. The relative increase in price will outweigh the relative decline in the amount demanded; demand is thus relatively inelastic because there are no substitutes for oil to run your furnace. Goods that are necessities tend to have inelastic demands. For example, in a household with young children, the demand for milk is likely to be relatively inelastic. As a student, you have a relatively inelastic demand for books! For these items, the demand is not going to be very sensitive to price changes. The demand for luxuries, however, tends to be elastic. You, and others, are likely to be very sensitive to price changes for records, stereos, cameras, expensive clothes, automobiles, etc. For the most part, the relative importance of an item in a household's budget also influences elasticity. High-priced items have elastic demands, and the demand for low-priced items is usually inelastic.

Finally, time influences elasticity. The more time there is for consumers to adjust to price changes, the more elastic their demand for certain products is likely to be. For example, many people in the United States have adjusted their usage of energy as a result of higher prices throughout the 1970s and 1980s—cars are smaller and more fuel efficient, people are burning more wood as a source of heat, bicycles are used for transportation, and solar energy is being developed. Taking another example, for many urban households, block ice may have been a necessity in the early 1900s, but it isn't anymore.

Elasticity also holds implications for a firm's revenues or a household's expenditures when the price of a product changes. If the demand for a firm's product is elastic and its price decreases, then the percentage change in quantity demanded in the market will be relatively larger than the price change (e.g., records or movies). The firm's revenues would then increase. The firm's revenues are the quantity sold times the price of the product. If the relative increase in quantity is in excess of the relative decline in price, then revenues go up. If a household's demand for a product is inelastic and its price increases, it will decrease its purchases by a relatively lower amount. Consequently, its total expenditures, quantity times price, will increase. The following table summarizes the possibilities (TR stands for total revenue). When demand is elastic, the quantity change is relatively larger. When the demand is inelastic, the price change is relatively larger.

$R = Q_s \times P$

If $E_d < 1$, then percentage Δ in Q_d < percentage Δ in P			If $E_d > 1$, then percentage Δ in Q_d > percentage Δ in P		
$P \uparrow$	$Q_d \downarrow$	TR $\uparrow$	$P \uparrow$	$Q_d \downarrow$	TR $\downarrow$
$P \downarrow$	$Q_d \uparrow$	TR $\downarrow$	$P \downarrow$	$Q_d \uparrow$	TR $\uparrow$

The Price Elasticity of Supply

We can also identify the **price elasticity of supply.** Here, we measure the sensitivity of amounts supplied to price changes.

$$E_s = \frac{\Delta Q_s / Q_s}{\Delta P / P} \qquad \text{Elasticity of supply} = \frac{\text{percentage change in quantity supplied}}{\text{percentage change in price}}.$$

If the elasticity of supply is less than one, the supply of the product is inelastic—that is, the amount supplied is not very sensitive to price changes. If the elasticity of supply is greater than one, then the amount supplied of the good is sensitive to price changes.

Several factors can influence the elasticity of supply. If storage is not possible, then supply will be insensitive to price changes. If you have ten bunches of bananas in your store and the price goes up by 50 percent tomorrow there's not much you can do to increase the amount of bananas that you have for sale. If you can put an item in inventory, the amount that you have available for sale will be sensitive to price. If the price goes down for pencils, for example, you can store them and reduce the amount you have out for sale. On the other hand, if the price goes up, you could significantly increase the amount you have out for sale by taking the pencils out of your inventory.

The length of the production process matters as well. The longer the production period, the lower the elasticity of supply. In 1984 there was a Trivial Pursuits craze in the United States. In the short run, the supply was inelastic; consequently, there was a shortage. What happened to price? And then with higher prices, in the longer run, the supply became more elastic. If it is possible to substitute resources in production, then supply is likely to be more elastic. For example, in the fast foods industry, there are numerous sources of unskilled labor, many sources of hamburger meat, buns, etc., and consequently the supply of fast foods is likely to be relatively sensitive to increased prices.

Income Elasticity

We can also identify the **income elasticity of demand.** This measures how much the demand for a product changes when income changes.

$$\text{Income elasticity of demand} = \frac{\text{percentage change in quantity demanded}}{\text{percentage change in income}}.$$

When income changes, we know that one of the determinants of demand has changed. Consequently, the entire demand curve will shift. For most goods, if income increases, the demand curve shifts out to the right. The income elasticity of demand, in essence, measures the relative change in the demand curve. For most goods, the income elasticity will be positive. Only inferior goods have a negative income elasticity of demand. For example, you might decrease your consumption of cheap meats if your income increased. For some goods we increase our consumption, but only by a little bit, when our incomes go up. Food products in general fit into this category. The relative increase in the quantity demanded of food will be less than the relative increase in income. For goods like these, the income elasticity of demand is relatively low. For other goods, we increase our consumption a great deal when our incomes go up. Then the relative change in quantity demanded will be larger than the percentage change in income, and the income elasticity of demand will be greater than one. The demand for "luxuries" is elastic with respect to income.

Agriculture is a good example to illustrate the importance of the concept of elasticity. In the long run, as a result of technological advances, American agriculture has been incredibly productive. In the late 19th century, more than half the population lived in rural areas and almost 40 percent of the population was involved in agricultural production. Today, less than 5 percent of the population produces all of our food plus all that we export. Over time, the total supply of agricultural goods that the country can produce in a year has increased rapidly. However, the income elasticity of demand for agricultural goods is relatively low. The demand for food doesn't grow as fast as income does. Consequently, over the long run, there will be a tendency for the supply of agricultural goods to outpace the growth of the demand for them. What will this tend to do to long-run prices? Right—they will tend to fall. That is one of the reasons for having governmental price-support programs and other efforts to boost farmers' incomes.

In addition, in the short run, the price elasticity of supply for many agricultural products is low. That means that if there is a bumper crop then prices will go down, but that the supply available can't be reduced. Or, if there is a crop failure the supply can't adjust rapidly and prices will rise quickly. Consequently, in the short run, there is great volatility in agricultural prices. Furthermore, because the demand for agricultural products as a whole is relatively inelastic, farmers' incomes vary with price fluctuations. When prices plummet, because of the inelasticity of demand, farmers' total revenues decrease. The increase in amounts demanded is less than the reduction in price. On the other hand, when prices go up, farmers' incomes also tend to go up.

16. Do you think that the price elasticity of demand for a college education is greater or less than one? Why?

17. For what kinds of goods and services will quantity demanded be relatively insensitive to price changes (i.e., inelastic)? Give some examples.

18. For what kinds of goods and services will quantity demanded be relatively sensitive to price changes (i.e., elastic)? Give some examples.

19. List some goods for which your income elasticity of demand is greater than one.

In this chapter we have developed a theoretical model of markets to explain how markets determine prices. We have focused on demand and supply, how they are determined, and how they interact in markets. In the next chapter, we will explore the theoretical implications that this has for resource allocation.

KEY CONCEPTS

markets
prices
demand (schedule, curve)
change in quantity demanded
supply (schedule, curve)
change in quantity supplied
equilibrium price

surplus
shortage
change in demand
change in supply
price elasticity of demand
price elasticity of supply
income elasticity of demand

REVIEW QUESTIONS

1. Use supply-and-demand analysis to explain why your school's tuition and overall charges have been continually increasing the past few years. Address yourself to demand factors first and supply factors second; then put them together.

2. How are tastes and preferences for goods and services determined in the United States?

3. Markets and prices for different products are interrelated. Why? Can you give some examples?

4. Examine recent issues of newspapers to see how prices of certain products are changing. Use supply-and-demand analysis to explain these changes.

5. *How* do prices influence resource allocation? Use examples.

6. Assume that the price elasticity of demand for gasoline in the United States is 0.3. If the President wanted to reduce gasoline consumption in the United States by 30 percent, by how much would prices have to be increased?

7. Many people in the oil industry have argued that one way to solve the energy crisis is to increase the supplies of energy available. They further argued at the beginning of the 1980s that the removal of energy price controls would tremendously stimulate domestic production of oil and natural gas. What does this argument implicitly assume about the price elasticity of supply for oil and natural gas?

SUGGESTED READINGS

Other introductory textbooks also provide treatment of the supply-and-demand model. Try Paul Samuelson's *Economics* (McGraw-Hill), Campbell R. McConnell's *Economics* (McGraw-Hill), or Daniel Fusfeld's *Economics* (D. C. Heath).

Samuel Bowles and Herbert Gintis, 1977. *Schooling in Capitalist America*, Harper Colophon Books. A political economic analysis of education in the United States that goes beyond (and behind) supply-and-demand analysis of the market for a college education.

Douglass C. North and Roger Leroy Miller, 1983. *The Economics of Public Issues*, Harper & Row. The model applied to several issues, e.g., marijuana.

Wherein Profit Maximization and Perfect Competition Produce Consumer Sovereignty, Efficiency, and the "Invisible Hand"

INTRODUCTION

Microeconomics assumes that consumers, in demanding goods, attempt to maximize their satisfaction. Firms, furthermore, are assumed, in supplying goods, to be concerned with **profit maximization.** In Chapter 10 we saw how supply and demand for a good will determine a market price, *given* certain conditions (i.e., *a* supply curve and *a* demand curve). If either the demand curve or the supply curve shifts, or if both shift, we will tend to get a new equilibrium price in that market.

In this chapter we will examine how profit maximization *and* competition, using supply-and-demand analysis and some new tools of economics, theoretically produce Adam Smith's "invisible hand" and *consumer sovereignty*. That is, we will discover how competitive markets operate to allocate resources *efficiently*.

PROFIT MAXIMIZATION AND THE COMPETITIVE FIRM

In the following we will examine a particular market and what happens in it over time; we will concentrate our attention on the *firm*. This is a theoretical market, so

I'm pleased to tell you, gentlemen, that in addition to serving the public, helping find the answers to some of the world's problems, improving the quality of life in America, and providing new and better products for the consumer, this quarter we made a *bundle!*

Reproduced by permission; copyright © James Stevenson. Originally in *Saturday Review.*

we will state some definitions and make some assumptions. Our market will be the national market for pocket calculators.

The *consumer* is the economic unit that demands goods and/or services because they serve some purpose and give the consumer some satisfaction. Our consumers in this example include accountants, homemakers, elementary school students, college students, and so on, who have a particular need for instant calculation. In the United States, with the recent invention and development of transistors and miniaturized circuits, there has been a boom in the market for pocket calculators. There is a wide variety of calculators designed to accomplish a whole range of mathematical and statistical operations. In our example, we will assume that there is some average type of calculator and concentrate our attention on that market.

The *firm* is the economic unit that brings goods to the market. It takes raw materials and other resources and transforms them into final consumer goods. Its motivation, or goal, is to maximize its profits. In our example, the firm would be any company that produces and sells pocket calculators.

If we put the firms and the consumers (sellers and buyers) together, we have a market for pocket calculators. We will assume that this is a competitive market, that is, one characterized by perfect **competition.** This means that:

1. The product is homogeneous.

2. There is a large number of buyers and sellers in the market.

3. No *one* buyer or seller can influence the price of the product (a seller can't raise his or her price, because buyers can go to a competitor and buy).

4. There is free entry into the market (anyone can be a buyer or seller).

In competition, firms don't need to advertise. (Photograph by John Herrlin.)

5. There is no need for advertising (since every seller has the same product and charges the same price).

Thus there is a *market equilibrium* price. Can you illustrate this market graphically?

1. Are any of these theoretical characteristics absent in our real-world example of the market for pocket calculators in the United States? Why?

Let's return to the firm. The firm raises **revenues** by selling its product. The more it sells, the greater are its revenues. The greater the number of pocket calculators the firm sells, the more money it receives. In producing calculators and bringing them to market, the firm also has certain costs—labor, raw materials, depreciation, rent, interest payments on loans, and the firm's *opportunity cost*. We define the firm's opportunity cost as being the amount of money that the firm could earn by using its facilities and its resources to produce something else (such as fire alarms or CB radios, etc.). The firm has some expectation of a "normal profit" from doing business. Therefore the firm has as one of its **costs** of doing business that opportunity cost. Stated slightly differently, the producer of pocket calculators must earn at least its opportunity cost (a normal profit) to stay in the business of making

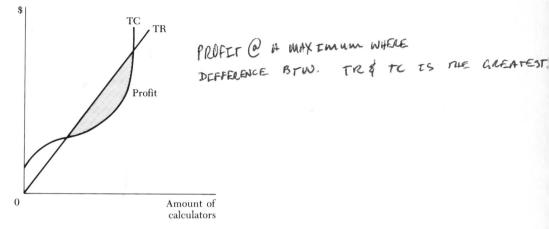

Figure 11.1   Total revenue and total cost.

calculators. Anything above that is **economic profit.** Profit equals the difference between the firm's total revenues and its total costs. Or profit equals TR − TC, where TR equals **total revenues** and TC equals **total costs.** If the firm's revenues are just sufficient to cover all of its costs for raw materials, labor, etc., *and* its opportunity cost, then the firm will earn no economic profits. If revenues exceed costs, then there will be economic profits. That is, the firm will earn a return over and above its opportunity cost.

On the basis of these definitions and assumptions, we will now proceed to examine the behavior of the firm in a competitive market. Profits, revenues, and costs for the firm will vary with the amounts of calculators produced and sold. Total revenue is equal to the quantity sold times the price of the product; or, TR = $P \times Q$. For a firm in a competitive market, the price is determined by the market and will not vary with the number of units that the firm sells (see the third characteristic of a competitive market above). Consequently, total revenue increases at a constant rate as more pocket calculators are sold. Total cost also increases as more calculators are produced. It costs more to produce more. Total cost is usually considered to increase at a decreasing rate and then, beyond some level of output, to increase at an increasing rate. (We will explore the reasons for this in a moment.) In Fig. 11.1, *profit* (the shaded area) is the difference between TR and TC. We measure amounts of calculators on the horizontal axis and money (costs and revenues) on the vertical axis. Profit is at a maximum when the difference between TR and TC is greatest.

A DIGRESSION ON TOTAL COST AND THE LAW OF DIMINISHING RETURNS

Before we proceed with our analysis, it is useful to pause for a bit to explain the shape of the total cost curve. The total cost curve increases slowly at first with increasing output; but then, beyond some point, as output increases, total costs increase by greater and greater amounts. The reason for this is the **law of diminishing returns.**

Output requires the use of inputs. In production, there are certain physical relationships between these inputs and the output. Let's construct a simplified example to illustrate the law of diminishing returns. Assume that a farmer has one acre of land on which to grow wheat. We will hold constant the land used as an input, the amount of seed used, and the level of technology available. The only variable resource, then, will be the amount of labor that the farmer uses as an input to produce wheat. At first, with increasing amounts of labor, the farmer will be able to produce increasing amounts of wheat. With each additional worker the farmer is able to add larger and larger amounts of wheat. Each worker adds more to total output than the last worker. However, beyond some point, when the farmer adds more workers, although they may continue to add to output, the marginal contributions of the last workers are less than the contributions of the previously added workers. The problem is essentially that there is not enough space for all the workers to work together well. They get in each other's way, etc. In fact, the farmer might add so many workers to the land that the marginal contributions of the last added worker to total output might be negative; that is, the last worker added might cause total output to decrease. (See the boxed material.) This simplified example is intended by economists to describe what happens in any productive activity in which there are fixed and variable resources. In the case of a calculator producer, the fixed resources would be the plant and the equipment used in production, and the variable resources would be the raw materials and the labor utilized.

The Law of Diminishing Returns

For those who like numbers:

Input of Land	Input of Labor	Total Output	Marginal Contribution of Last Unit of Labor
1	1	100	
1	2	110	10
1	3	130	20
1	4	160	30
1	5	180	20
1	6	190	10
1	7	185	−5

We have just illustrated **the law of diminishing returns**! As more and more of the variable resource is added to the production process, given fixed amounts of other resources, the marginal contribution of the variable resource will eventually diminish. Total output would continue to increase but by a smaller and smaller amount as more of the variable resource is added. In our example, as we added more labor, eventually the continued use of labor resulted in diminishing returns in terms

AS ADD MORE VARIABLE RESOURCES TO FIXED RESOURCES, THE MARGINAL ~~PRODUCT~~ CONTRIBUTION OF VARIABLE WILL GO ↓. TOTAL OUTPUT ↑, BUT BY SMALLER AMOUNTS.

of output. So much of a variable resource can be added that the marginal contribution of the last unit may be negative. That is, with the addition of one more unit of a resource, total output actually decreases.

So now that we know what the law of diminishing returns is, what does it have to do with the shape of the total cost curve? The cost curve compares total costs with increasing output. If we assume that the law of diminishing returns holds for *all* variable resources, it follows that there will be some point in increasing output at which costs will begin to increase at an increasing rate. If resources have diminishing returns, then more and more resources must be added to get equivalent increases in output. But to use more resources costs more. And when diminishing returns set in, the total costs will increase at an increasing rate. To produce an additional unit of output will cost more than the last additional unit of output because more resources will be required. Because of the law of diminishing returns, the total cost curve, beyond some level of output, will increase at an increasing rate.

> **2. Why does the total cost curve increase at a *decreasing* rate at relatively low levels of output?**

PROFIT MAXIMIZATION IN THE SHORT RUN

Let's return to Fig. 11.1 on total costs and revenue. This illustration shows us a very important relationship. As the amount of pocket calculators brought to the market and sold changes, so do costs and revenues. In fact, as output increases, costs increase; and as sales increase, revenues increase. Both costs and revenues are a function of output:

$$TC = f(Q), \quad \text{and} \quad TR = f(Q).$$

Before we explain the theory of profit maximization for the firm in the short run, we need to examine more fully the costs and revenues of the firm. Profits are determined by the relationship between costs and revenues:

$$\text{Profit} = TR - TC.$$

The Firm's Costs

The costs of production result from the very act of production. In order to produce any good or service, resources must be used—raw materials, mental and physical labor, machinery, energy, etc. In order to secure the various factors of production, resources must be purchased in markets; they must be paid their opportunity costs. Hence the costs of production are determined by the prices of resources in resource markets.

In the **short run,** a firm has a fixed-size plant or operation. The scale of its productive activities has been determined by decisions it has made about its physical

 MARGINAL PRODUCT DECREASES AS ADD MORE VARIABLES

location, the buildings it will use, the machinery and equipment it has purchased, and its management team. Let's take a simple example of a small firm engaged in the production of pocket calculators. It is run by one individual, it leases a factory building in Chicago, and it owns all of the machinery and equipment in the factory. It has borrowed money from the Continental Illinois Bank of Chicago to finance its business. In this sense, then, it has a certain size of operation for its short-run production expectations. Within this fixed plant size, it can expand its output of pocket calculators by using more variable resources—i.e., more raw materials and more labor. These variable resources can use the fixed plant more or less intensively to produce more or less output. (In the long run, as we will see shortly, all of the resources that the firm uses in production can be expanded or contracted. That is, the firm can change the size of its operation.)

In the short run, then, for the firm, there are two types of costs—fixed and variable costs. **Total fixed costs** are the costs that must be paid to the fixed resources of production involved in the firm's particular short-run plant size. These costs do not vary with the rate of output that the firm produces. They are fixed. The firm has a monthly mortgage payment that it gives to the bank to repay the loan it used to purchase its equipment for producing pocket calculators. The owners of the firm also have an opportunity cost for their involvement in the firm's activities. In other words, the owners will get salaries based on what they could earn in some other activity. If these salaries weren't paid, the owners would pursue some other activity in which they could earn their opportunity cost (e.g., as computer programmers). All of these costs are fixed costs; they are incurred by the firm regardless of the level of output in any particular month. They are invariant with respect to the level of output. Even if output is zero in the short run, fixed costs are still positive.

Let's assume that the monthly fixed costs of a pocket calculator firm are $10,000. Figure 11.2 illustrates total fixed costs (TFC). It shows that as output (measured on the horizontal axis) increases, total fixed costs remain constant.

Total variable costs are the expenses for using varying amounts of raw materials and labor to expand output within a fixed-size plant (in the short run). To get greater amounts of output requires the use of more and more variable resources; consequently, total variable costs increase as output increases. However, given the law of diminishing returns, we know that at first, relatively few added resources will achieve expanded output, and that later, greater amounts of resources will have to be added to get equivalent additions to output. Therefore, total variable costs will increase first at a decreasing rate and then, when diminishing returns set in, at an increasing rate. Figure 11.3 illustrates total variable costs (TVC). It shows what happens to total variable costs, measured on the vertical axis, as output increases. At rates of output below Q_1, total variable costs increase at a decreasing rate, and at rates of output greater than Q_1, diminishing returns to the use of variable resources set in and total variable costs increase at an increasing rate. Notice that total variable costs at a rate of output of zero are zero.

If we add total fixed costs and total variable costs together, we get the **total costs** (TC) of production:

$$TC = TFC + TVC.$$

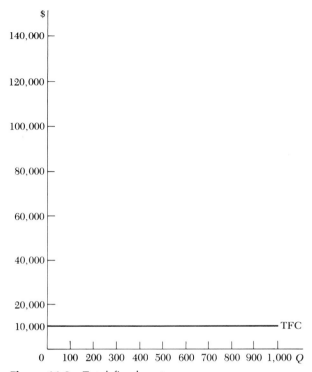

Figure 11.2 Total fixed costs.

Table 11.1 presents information for different possible levels of output during a one-month period for our calculator firm and the total fixed costs, total variable costs, and total costs of each of those levels of output. In Fig. 11.4 total costs are illustrated with costs measured on the vertical axis and output measured on the horizontal axis. Notice that when output is zero, total costs equal total fixed costs.

We can also use the cost information that we have developed thus far to derive average and marginal costs. This will prove useful in analyzing the profit maximization decisions of the firm. Average cost takes the various total costs of production and averages them over each unit of output. For example, at 100 units of output, total fixed costs are $10,000. The average fixed cost for each unit of output is $100. For each different level of output, then, **average fixed cost** is

$$AFC = TFC/Q.$$

In the same way, **average variable cost** is

$$AVC = TVC/Q,$$

and **average cost** is

$$AC = TC/Q.$$

Since TC = TFC + TVC, then AC = AFC + AVC.

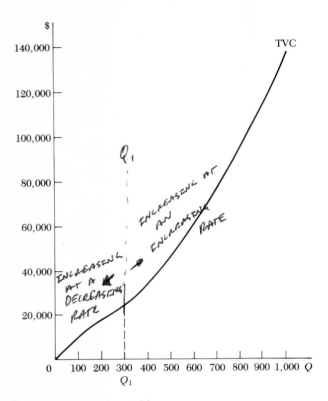

Figure 11.3 Total variable costs.

Table 11.1 TOTAL FIXED COSTS, TOTAL VARIABLE COSTS, AND TOTAL COSTS

LEVEL OF OUTPUT	TOTAL FIXED COSTS	TOTAL VARIABLE COSTS	TOTAL COSTS
0	$10,000	0	$ 10,000
100	10,000	$ 10,000	20,000
200	10,000	18,000	28,000
→ 300	10,000	24,000	34,000
400	10,000	34,000	44,000
500	10,000	46,000	56,000
600	10,000	60,000	70,000
700	10,000	76,000	86,000
800	10,000	94,000	104,000
900	10,000	114,000	124,000
1,000	10,000	136,000	146,000

$$TFC + TVC = TC$$

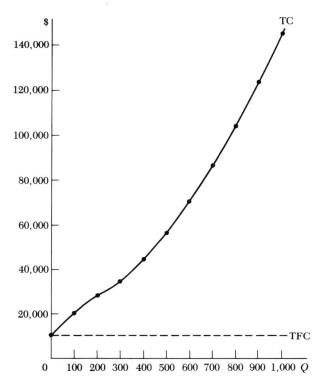

Figure 11.4   Total costs.

Marginal costs are the additional costs of producing one additional unit of output. It's how much total costs change as a result of additional output. That is,

$$MC = \frac{\text{change in TC}}{\text{change in } Q} \text{ or } \boxed{\frac{\Delta TC}{\Delta Q}}.$$

Since fixed costs don't change with the level of output, marginal costs could also be defined as the change in total variable costs as output changes. For example, when the firm moves from producing 100 units of output to 200 units of output, total costs increase from $20,000 to $28,000 (and total variable costs increase from $10,000 to $18,000). Consequently,

$$MC = \frac{28,000 - 20,000}{200 - 100} = \frac{8,000}{100} = 80.$$

$$\frac{\Delta TVC}{\Delta Q} = MC$$

The marginal cost of producing 100 more pocket calculators is $8,000, or $80 for each one. In essence, marginal costs are equal to the slope of the total costs (or total variable costs) curve. Since total costs increase at a decreasing rate and then begin increasing at an increasing rate, MC will first decrease and then begin increasing. Table 11.2 presents data on average fixed costs, average variable costs, average costs,

MC CURVE WILL BE U-SHAPED by B/C OF LAW OF DIMINISHING RETURNS.

(ALL COST CURVES?)

Table 11.2 AVERAGE AND MARGINAL COSTS

OUTPUT	AFC	AVC	AC	MC
0				
100	$100	$100	$200	$100
200	50	90	140	80
300	33	80	113	60
400	25	85	110	100
500	20	92	112	120
600	17	100	117	140
700	14	109	123	160
800	12	117	129	180
900	11	127	138	200
1,000	10	146	156	220

and marginal costs derived from the information in Table 11.1. Figure 11.5 illustrates AFC, AVC, AC, and MC.

AFC, AVC, AC, and MC all vary with the rate of output. In each case, costs are measured in per-unit or marginal terms. The horizontal axis always measures output and the vertical axis measures average or marginal costs. Average fixed cost in Fig. 11.5(a) constantly decreases since it is total fixed cost divided by increasing rates of output. Average variable costs (Fig. 11.5b) will generally be U-shaped, reflecting the law of diminishing returns. At first, over a range of output, AVC decreases; then it reaches a minimum, at Q_1, and begins to increase for greater levels of output. At first, when there are increasing returns to the use of variable resources, the per-unit cost of production will decrease as output increases. The per-unit amount of resources needed to produce increasing amounts of output decreases. However, beyond Q_1, AVC begins to increase as each unit of output requires the use of increasing amounts of variable resources. This, again, is the result of diminishing returns to the use of variable resources.

Average costs (also Fig. 11.5b) are also U-shaped because of the law of diminishing returns. AC is the sum of AFC and AVC. Since AFC is positive and constantly decreasing, AC will be above AVC but the difference between them will be constantly decreasing. AC will reach a minimum at the rate of output of Q_2. This is a slightly higher rate of output than Q_1. AVC is increasing, but because AFC is constantly decreasing, it takes a higher level of output for AC to begin increasing (where the effects of increasing AVC begin to outweigh the effects of decreasing AFC).

Marginal costs (Fig. 11.5c) are also U-shaped due to the law of diminishing returns. Since marginal costs register the *additional* costs of producing greater rates of output, rather than the per-unit costs, marginal costs will more dramatically illustrate the effects first of increasing returns and then of decreasing returns to the use of variable resources. It is also useful to know the exact relationship of the MC curve to the AVC and AC curves.

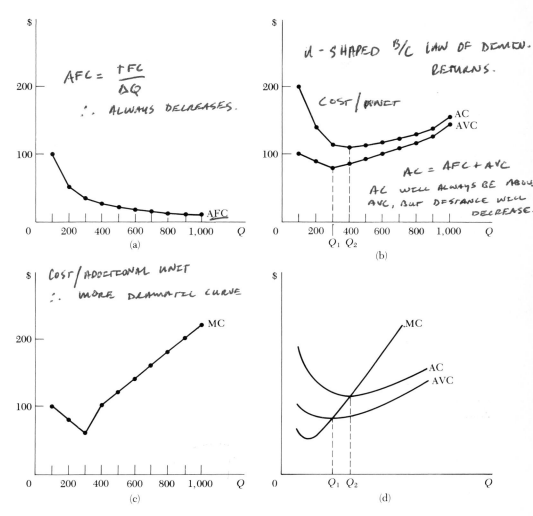

Figure 11.5 Average fixed costs, average variable costs, average costs, and marginal costs.

Figure 11.5(d) relates marginal costs to both average variable costs and average costs. Marginal cost, average variable cost, and average cost curves are usually represented by smooth, curved lines; in Fig. 11.5(d) we have transformed the curves of Fig. 11.5(b) and (c) so that they are smooth. The MC curve cuts through the minimum point of both the AVC and AC curves. We will not go into a lengthy proof of these relationships. Suffice it to say that if MC is below AVC or AC, then AVC or AC must be decreasing. If the cost of producing the last unit of added output is below per-unit cost, then per-unit cost has to decrease. From output levels 0 to Q_1, MC is below AVC, and AVC is decreasing. From output levels 0 to Q_2, MC is below AC, and AC is decreasing. If, on the other hand, MC is above AVC or AC, then AVC or

AC must be increasing. (Why?) Beyond Q_1, AVC is increasing and beyond Q_2, AC is increasing. Then, at output Q_1, where AVC is at a minimum, MC = AVC. And, at output Q_2, where AC is at a minimum, MC = AC.

The significance of the point where average costs are at a minimum is worth further comment. The level of output that minimizes the average cost of output is the *most efficient rate of output* because it means that society is minimizing the cost of using its resources with respect to the production of a good. Q_2 in Fig. 11.5 represents an *optimum level of output* because it minimizes the per-unit cost of producing that good. Raising or lowering output would increase average costs.

3. *Explain* how the law of diminishing returns will cause the MC curve to be increasing.

4. Why are marginal costs equal to the slope of the total costs curve? What is the slope of the total costs curve?

5. If the Los Angeles Dodgers have a team batting average of .275 (that is, on the average they get 275 hits every 1000 times they come to bat) and they acquire a new outfielder whose batting average is .298, what happens to the team batting average? What if they trade away two players with averages of .260 and .274 for one player with an average of .278?

6. *Explain* why the minimum point on the AC curve represents an optimum rate of output.

The Firm's Revenues

The firm's revenues come from producing pocket calculators and actually selling them to consumers. **Total revenues,** in fact, equal the price of the pocket calculators multiplied by the number of units sold, or

$$TR = P \times Q.$$

We can also define average revenues and marginal revenues for the firm. **Average revenues** are revenues per unit, or

$$AR = \frac{TR}{Q}.$$

Marginal revenues are the change in total revenues from producing and selling an additional unit of output, or

$$MR = \frac{\text{change in TR}}{\text{change in } Q} \text{ or } \frac{\Delta TR}{\Delta Q}.$$

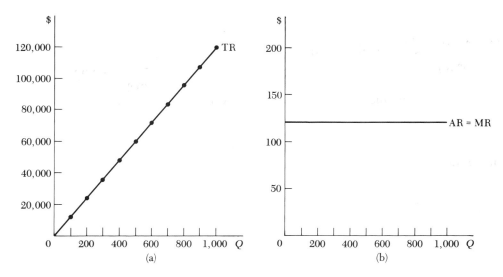

Figure 11.6   Total revenues, average revenues, and marginal revenues.

For a firm in a perfectly competitive market, the price is determined in the market by the forces of supply and demand. Remember, we have assumed in a perfectly competitive market that no one producer can affect the market price. Consequently, the firm gets the price of the product for every unit that it sells, and then $P = \text{MR} = \text{AR}$. If the price is \$120 for a fancy pocket calculator that does a full range of mathematical and statistical operations, then the firm's revenues per unit are \$120 and its marginal revenues are also \$120. Figure 11.6(a) illustrates total revenues and Fig. 11.6(b) marginal and average revenues. These show what happens to revenues, measured on the vertical axis, as output expands. We are now ready to put the cost information and the revenue information together to describe the profit maximization decision of the pocket calculator firm.

Profit Maximization

Table 11.3 and Fig. 11.7 provide information and an illustration of the firm's profit maximization decision. What level of output could the firm produce to get the maximum level of profits? We have assumed that the firm's objective is to maximize its profits, that in the short run it has a fixed-size plant, that it has access to certain production techniques, and that it can buy resources in markets for certain prices. (In the long run, some of these assumptions can be altered.) The answer to the question above is that the pocket calculator firm will produce that rate of output at which the difference between TR and TC is greatest. This also happens to be the rate of output at which MC and MR are equal. *When the marginal cost of producing one more unit of output is just equal to the marginal revenue from selling one more unit, profits for the firm are maximized.* This occurs at Q_e in Fig. 11.7. By referring to this illustration

$MC = MR$

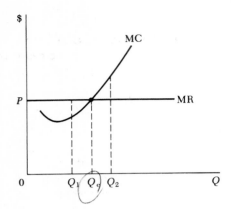

Figure 11.7   MR, MC, and profit maximization.

Table 11.3 PROFIT MAXIMIZATION

OUTPUT	TC	MC	TR	MR (AND AR)	PROFIT (OR LOSS)
0	$ 10,000	—	0	0	$(−10,000)
100	20,000	$100	$ 12,000	$120	(− 8,000)
200	28,000	80	24,000	120	(− 4,000)
300	34,000	60	36,000	120	2,000
400	44,000	100	48,000	120	4,000
500	56,000	120	60,000	120	4,000
600	70,000	140	72,000	120	2,000
700	86,000	160	84,000	120	(− 2,000)
800	104,000	180	96,000	120	(− 8,000)
900	124,000	200	108,000	120	(−16,000)
1,000	146,000	220	120,000	120	(−26,000)

and the information in Table 11.3 perhaps we can see why this level of output will maximize profits. (Remember: Profit = TR − TC.)

If the producer were to bring Q_1 to market, the MR of the last unit sold would be above the MC of producing it. In this case, the addition to revenues from selling the last calculator is greater than the addition to costs, on the margin. As a result, total revenue will have increased more than total costs (since MR > MC); thus profits will go up. The addition to revenue was greater than the addition to cost from producing and selling the last calculator, and so profits will increase. In fact, as long as MR is greater than MC, the producer will increase profits by bringing additional amounts to market (the marginal revenues from doing so exceed the marginal costs). These marginal additions to profit stop when the producer reaches that level of output at which MC = MR. If additional amounts of calculators are brought to market, the MC of doing so will exceed the corresponding MR. As a result, additional costs will exceed additional revenues, and profits will decrease. For example, at Q_2 marginal cost is greater than marginal revenue: The addition to total costs from producing the last unit of output to get to Q_2 is greater than the added revenue from doing so. As a result, profits will be decreased. Profits would be increased by moving to lower levels of production. Profits are at a maximum at Q_e, where MC = MR.

As we can see from Table 11.3, MC is equal to MR at 500 units of output. It is also at this rate of output that total profits are at a maximum. At higher rates of output, marginal costs are larger than marginal revenues, and profits decrease. At lower rates of output, marginal revenues are in excess of marginal costs, and the firm can increase its profits by producing and selling larger levels of output.

Figure 11.8 adds average costs to the picture. This provides some useful information about profit maximization. The firm will choose to produce a rate of *AC* output of Q_e, since this is where MC equals MR and profits are maximized. At this rate of output, we should also notice that the price of the calculators is greater than the average cost of producing each unit. That is, for each unit, the revenue that the firm takes in is in excess of its cost. This is, in fact, profit per unit, since

profit = TR − TC.

Dividing both sides of this equation by the rate of output, we get

$$\frac{\text{profit}}{Q} = \frac{\text{TR}}{Q} - \frac{\text{TC}}{Q},$$

or

profit per unit = P − AC. $P > AC$
                                $TP = Q(P - AC)$

As long as price is in excess of AC, the firm will earn profits. And total profits will equal $Q(P − AC)$. Total profits are equal to the area of the shaded rectangle in Fig. 11.8. If price is below AC, however, the firm will experience losses. Does this check out with the information in Tables 11.2 and 11.3?

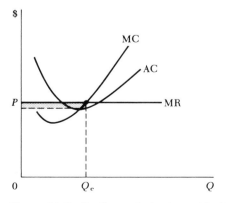

Figure 11.8 Profit maximization with AC.

What we have just shown summarizes one of the most important results of the economic theory of the firm. A firm will maximize its profits when it produces a rate of output at which its marginal revenues are equal to its marginal costs. This is its equilibrium rate of output. Notice that this is a rather compelling result. If a firm expands its output to a point at which MC exceeds MR, what will happen? Its profits will decrease. What will it do in response? It will probably reduce its rate of output. The theoretical conclusion would seem to be borne out by what we expect firms in the real world to do. They will tend to produce that rate of output at which MC = MR.

7. **For our pocket calculator firm, what happens to its profits if it reduces output from 500 to 300? What's the relationship between *P* and AC at this rate of output? What's the relationship between MC and MR?**

8. **For Fig. 11.7, explain why profits will increase by moving to lower levels of output from Q_2.**

9. **Construct an AC curve with its own MC curve. What would the firm do if the price of its product passed through the point at which MC = AC? What level of output would it produce? What would its profits be? Would this firm be getting its opportunity costs?**

10. **From Table 11.3, if the firm produces 800 units of output, what are its profits? What's the relationship between *P* and AC? Between MR and MC?**

THE FIRM IN THE LONG RUN

In the long run, the firm always has more options open to it. It can alter the size of its plant. It can change the technological approach to the production of its good or service. For our pocket calculator firm, if the market for the product expands or the firm thinks that it will, it can seek a larger factory building to rent, it can borrow more money so that it can purchase more machinery and equipment, or it can take on partners to expand the size of its operation. In the **long run,** the firm can vary all of the resources that can be used in production. In the long run, there are no fixed resources. The long run is no specific period of time; rather, it refers to that time frame in which people make decisions based on the future. If a pocket calculator firm expects the market to expand in the future, it will adjust for the long run. Or if it expects the market to begin to contract it can make a different long-run adjustment. In addition, in the long run, firms can enter or leave the pocket calculator industry. The decision to enter or leave is a long-run investment decision for individuals and firms.

In essence, the firm can pick an infinite number of different possible short-run plant sizes in the long run. At any moment in time, the firm will be in the short run, will have a fixed-size plant with fixed resources, and will have a corresponding short-run average cost curve. Given the long-run option of different possible plant sizes, the firm will obviously pick that plant size that minimizes the average cost of producing every different possible level of output. For example, in Fig. 11.9, there are three different short-run average cost curves representing different possible plant sizes for different ranges of output. AC_1 represents the first size plant, AC_2 the second size plant, and AC_3 the third size plant. For Q_1, AC_1 minimizes the AC of production. So if the firm wanted to produce Q_1, it would pick plant size 1. But if the firm wanted to produce Q_2, it would pick plant size 2 since this minimizes the AC of that rate of output. Similarly, if it wanted to produce an even larger rate of output, say Q_3, it would pick plant size 3. Notice that this represents a long-run decision. The firm makes a choice of a plant size based on its expectations of or experiences with the market. It's a decision that requires the time to make arrangements for physical facilities, new and larger equipment, borrowing, etc. The long-run average cost curve is generated by picking the plant size that minimizes the cost of producing every possible rate of output. It is the darkened line in Fig. 11.9.

Figure 11.10 represents a typical long-run average curve when we assume that there are an infinite number of possible plant sizes for the firm to choose from. It is U-shaped just like the short-run AC curve (and has its own long-run marginal cost curve, LMC), but for different reasons. The short-run curve was U-shaped because of the law of diminishing returns, which assumed that output was increased by applying variable resources to fixed resources. But, in the long run, there are no fixed resources; output is expanded by using more of all resources. If that is the case, then why would long-run average costs (LAC) decrease over a range of output, reach a minimum at Q_0, and then begin to increase?

Economists explain the shape of the LAC curve through reference to economies and diseconomies of scale. As the firm adjusts its plant size, it alters the scale of its operations. At first, as the firm expands at relatively low levels of output, by building a larger plant, it can take advantage of specialization, division of labor, and more advanced technology. The result is lower average costs. The firm experiences **economies of scale.** However, beyond some rate of output (Q_0 in Fig. 11.10), the firm

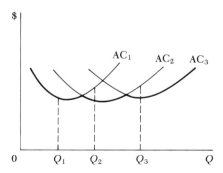

Figure 11.9 Long-run average costs.

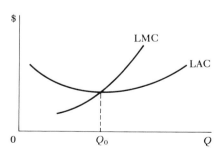

Figure 11.10 A typical long-run average costs curve.

SEE
P. 592–
93

begins to experience difficulties in organizing the now larger-size operation— coordination and communication make efficient production more difficult. Average costs begin to increase; it costs more to produce each unit of output. **Diseconomies of scale** have set in. As in the short run, the long-run marginal cost curve in Fig. 11.10 is below LAC while it is decreasing and above it while it is increasing.

The shape of the long-run average cost curve defines an optimum size of plant. At the rate of output at which LACs are at a minimum, the firm will pick the plant size that produces that rate of output at lowest average cost. The firm expands output and plant size throughout the range of economies of scale. At higher rates of output, LACs begin to increase because of diseconomies of scale. At Q_0, the firm produces a rate of output that minimizes the per-unit cost of production.

In fact, in the long run, in competitive industries, firms will tend to produce a rate of output that minimizes long-run average costs. Competition forces them to do so.

11. **If a firm experienced economies of scale over some range of output and then LACs were constant, what would its LAC curve look like? Does it seem reasonable to you that a firm could keep expanding and not encounter diseconomies of scale? If this happened, what would the optimum size plant be?**

12. **In Fig. 11.10, Q_0 represents the optimum rate of output and the optimum size plant. Does the firm earn its opportunity costs if it gets a price equal to this level of average costs?**

PERFECT COMPETITION IN THE LONG RUN: EFFICIENCY, THE "INVISIBLE HAND," AND CONSUMER SOVEREIGNTY

In this section, we will develop a general model of the behavior of a competitive market. The analysis focuses on the long-run equilibrium for the firms in the industry and for the entire industry. Although we have concentrated on a single example, the model of a competitive market is intended to be generalizable to all competitive markets or to an entire economy that is competitive. We will also interpret the results of the long-run equilibrium for competitive markets.

In Fig. 11.11, with a price of P_1, the firm will produce Q_1, since it is at this rate of output that MR = MC. The price is determined in the competitive market for the firm's product. This price is constant and the firm has no effect on it. Hence, P = MR = AR, and the firm can produce as much as it wants at that price. The firm, of course, will produce Q_1 since that is where its profits are maximized. At Q_1, price exceeds AC, so we know that the firm is earning economic profits. But in the long run, *if resources can earn above their opportunity costs, new firms will enter the industry* so that they can earn economic profits, too. In other words, the existence of economic profits provides an incentive for other firms to enter the industry. If economic profits

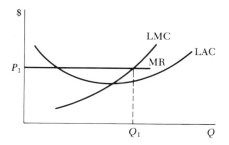

Figure 11.11   The firm in the long run.

can be made, given the price in the market for pocket calculators and the average costs of production, new firms will enter that market and begin to produce and market them.

As new firms enter the market, however, the market supply curve will shift out to the right. There is an increase in supply—one of the determinants of supply has changed. This increase in supply, assuming that the demand doesn't change, produces a lower price for pocket calculators, say P_2 (see Fig. 11.12). At P_2, the firm will pick a new rate of output, Q_2, at which MR = MC. But P still exceeds AC, firms will make economic profits, and other new firms will enter the market. This further drives down the price of the product. This process will continue until economic profits no longer exist to provide an incentive for new firms to enter the industry. This occurs at a price of P_3 in Fig. 11.13.

At this price, the firm picks Q_3 since that's where MR = MC. At this rate of output P = AC, so there are no economic profits. The firm is in equilibrium because it's producing that rate of output that maximizes its profits—even though this means zero economic profits. But the firm does earn what we called, at the beginning of this chapter, normal profits—that is, all of its opportunity costs are covered. The firm collects enough revenues to pay opportunity costs to all of its variable and fixed

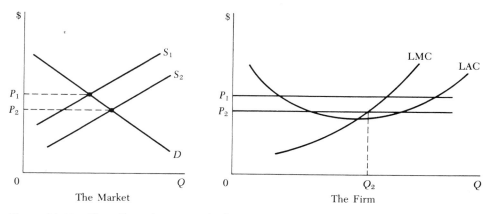

Figure 11.12   The effect of entry in the long run.

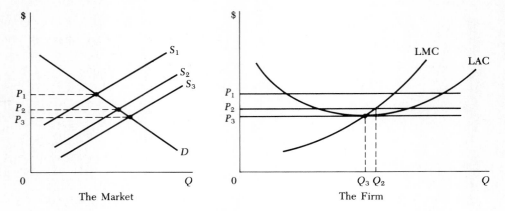

Figure 11.13 Long-run equilibrium in competition.

resources including a return to the owners of the business equivalent to their opportunity costs. The firm earns as much from its involvement in this activity as it could earn doing anything else. If a firm cannot earn normal profits in the long run, it will exit from that market.

Competition and Efficiency

The existence of economic profits encourages new firms to enter the industry in our example. This process continues until economic profits are eliminated. Firms choose a rate of output that maximizes their profits, which in long-run equilibrium equals zero economic profits, or normal profits. The industry is in equilibrium because there is no incentive for firms to enter or to exit from the industry. This result also produces efficiency in production and resource allocation.

   Efficiency in production occurs when the per-unit cost of production is minimized. The firm produces at that rate of output that minimizes AC. This means that the amount of resources used to produce each unit of output is minimized. Given resource scarcity this is an attractive result of the operation of competitive markets. But note how this has happened. Because of competition and free entry, the firm has been forced to produce at that level of output that minimizes average cost! Competition, consequently, through the forces that we have analyzed, *tends over time* to result in efficient production. Firms tend to produce at the optimum level of output, minimizing the per-unit cost of production. So competition tends to produce *efficiency*.

   What assumptions have we made? We assumed that D stayed constant. And we assumed that the cost curves did not change. With these simplifying assumptions, our analysis showed the tendency toward efficiency. Obviously, the real world would involve more change that would make our analysis a bit more complicated, but the essential conclusion remains: Competitive markets tend to result in efficiency in the use of scarce resources.

13. **Explain and show in an illustration what happens in our competitive market when market price goes below P_3. What happens to profits? What do the firms in the industry do? What happens to market supply? Market price? What is the new equilibrium?**

14. **Do you think that the model of long-run equilibrium—wherein profits attract entry, prices fluctuate, exit of firms is possible, and there is a tendency toward efficiency in production—is applicable to the example we have been using, the market for pocket calculators? Why or why not? Can you think of some other markets that have demonstrated some of these same characteristics in recent years?**

There is another sense in which the long-run equilibrium result in competitive markets produces efficiency. We can call this **efficiency in resource allocation.** At the long-run equilibrium result in Fig. 11.13, we have already noted that P_3 equals minimum AC. But P_3 also equals MC at the equilibrium rate of output, Q_3. This is an important result. The price of a product measures the amount of money that people are just willing to spend to purchase one more unit of that good. In other words, the price provides a measure of the marginal benefit that people derive from purchasing a unit of the good or service. The MC of the good (shown by the LMC curve) measures the cost to society of getting additional units of the good. In order to get one more unit, resources must be paid their opportunity costs. A rate of output that equalizes the marginal cost to society of getting one more unit of a good with the marginal benefit that people get from consuming one more unit maximizes social welfare (with respect to the production of that good). It also implies that resources have been allocated in an efficient manner given the opportunity costs of resources and given consumers' valuations of goods shown by their prices.

To demonstrate this, let's consider different rates of output in Fig. 11.13. First, take any rate of output lower than Q_3. At all rates of output lower than Q_3, the price of the product is in excess of LMC. This means that by expanding output the marginal benefit from getting one more unit of the good is larger than the marginal cost to society of producing it. Expanding output, then, will make a positive contribution to the society's welfare. The additional benefit exceeds the additional cost, so social welfare increases. More resources should be allocated to producing the good.

On the other hand, any rate of output greater than Q_3 results in MC being in excess of P. The additional cost of producing one more unit is larger than the extra benefit from getting one more unit for consumers. Consequently, at rates of output above Q_3, social welfare will decrease. To increase social welfare would require reducing the rate of output and allocating fewer resources to its production. Therefore, social welfare is maximized at a rate of output of Q_3 at which $P = $ MC. This represents efficiency in resource allocation. And the long-run equilibrium tendency of competitive markets is to produce exactly this result! Competitive markets tend to produce efficiency in resource allocation.

Zero economic profits, production at lowest AC, and efficiency in resource allocation are all theoretical results of the operation of competition. These results are brought about by the pursuit of profit by firms within the market and by the force of competition itself—the free entry and exit of firms to and from the market and in competition with one another for consumers.

Notice that we have again been using the term *tends to* in our analysis of the long-run equilibrium for a competitive market. We have been constructing a model of competition, a theory about how competitive markets work. Given the assumptions that we have made and the concepts that we have defined, we have determined the equilibrium result for competition. This does not mean that such equilibrium exists all the time for every competitive market, or that there won't ever be any economic profits in competitive markets. What it does suggest, though, is that without disturbances (given our assumptions) there are some general tendencies in the operation of competition. The system tends toward equilibrium. And even if it is disturbed—for example, by a change in consumers' incomes or tastes and preferences, or in resource prices, or in technological advances, etc.—the model that we have developed will allow us to follow through the effects to determine what the new equilibrium will be. In fact, competition encourages adaptability and responsiveness to changes in consumers' behavior.

THE "INVISIBLE HAND" AND CONSUMER SOVEREIGNTY

What does all this have to do with the **"invisible hand"** and **consumer sovereignty**? Markets and prices indicate to potential producers where profits can be made in the economy. If producers can produce a product at a lower average cost than the price at which they can sell it, then a profit can be earned. In addition, producers will attempt to maximize their profits. We can immediately see, then, that producers will probably try to lower their costs—because that will increase their profits. Consumers will also benefit from this because the price of the product will eventually be lowered because of the cost reduction. This may not be intuitively obvious, so let's examine this theoretical conclusion in more detail.

Say we have a calculator producer who has an MC and MR graph that looks like Fig. 11.14. MC_1 represents the firm's costs, and MR is determined by the market price for calculators. This firm then discovers a new and cheaper method of making its calculators. As a result, MC falls from MC_1 to MC_2 (each successive calculator can now be brought to market for a lower marginal cost).

With the change in costs, the firm makes a new decision about the level of output to produce. Originally, profits were maximized at Q_1; with the new marginal cost curve, the profit-maximizing level of production increases to Q_2. (Since average costs also decrease, the firm also will make larger profits since price is still the same and the firm is now producing more.) At first, the price stays the same; the firm is so small in relation to the market that the additional amount brought to market is not

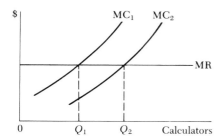

Figure 11.14 Change in cost.

noticeable and has no effect on market price. However, the firm does have larger profits.

Eventually, other participants in the market notice the improvement made by this firm and the extra profits that are being earned as a result. These other suppliers begin to attempt to utilize the same or similar cost-reducing methods of production. In addition, the lure of economic profits (a return to the firm over and above opportunity costs, remember) may induce some new firms to enter the market as sellers. (Again, a characteristic of a competitive market is free entry.) What does this do to market supply? It increases it; more calculators will be brought to market. Graphically, in Fig. 11.15, we get a new supply curve, S_2; more pocket calculators are brought to market at each possible price.

Consequently (*note* we have assumed that D stays the same), the market price will decrease from P_1 to P_2. The cost reduction ended up also reducing the market price! This was brought about through the market and by competition. The market showed that profits could be made, and competition allowed new firms to enter the market. (Note that each producer's profits are lowered because of the price decrease, although each producer will still bring to market that amount that maximizes its profits. *Show this using MR, MC, and AC curves.*)

Despite the fact that each producer (firm) is out to maximize its own profits, the market and competition have brought about a situation in which there is an incentive to lower costs and whereby prices are reduced also when costs are. Consumers

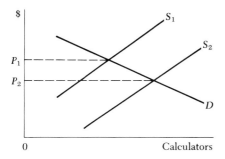

Figure 11.15 Change in supply.

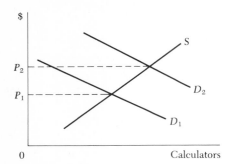

Figure 11.16   Change in demand.

benefit as a result; they get their product for a lower price. The "invisible hand" lives (at least theoretically)! (Go back to Chapters 4 and 6 and read what Adam Smith had to say about the "invisible hand.")

In addition, the market will respond to consumers' demands. This is referred to as **consumer sovereignty.** For example, let's assume that calculators become regarded as necessities by college students, accounting majors, engineers, even economics students! This change in tastes and preferences will tend to increase the demand for pocket calculators. What effect will this tend to have on the market price for calculators? Figure 11.16 shows that the price of calculators will tend to increase. What assumption did we make?

With this increased price, the profits of calculator producers should increase, and they will produce increasing amounts of calculators. Consequently, the desires of consumers show up in the market and indicate to producers what to do with respect to production. If consumers want more calculators, the market will indicate that and the producers will respond by producing more. This is **consumer sovereignty.** By extension, this process also has implications for resource use in the economy. When production of any good or service is expanded or contracted, the use of resources for that purpose will also increase or decrease.

15. **If a technological breakthrough allowed a pocket calculator firm to lower its long-run average costs, show what the new long-run equilibrium would be for the firm and for the industry.**

CONCLUSION

The competitive market model has some attractive results. Firms earn normal profits. There is a tendency toward an equilibrium at which entry and exit cease. The firms in the market produce a rate of output at which average costs are minimized; there is efficiency in production. Output takes place at a rate that maximizes social welfare; when $P = MC$ there is efficiency in resource allocation. If products are homogeneous, then there is no need to allocate resources to advertising. Competitive markets are adaptable. Whenever costs change, or supply and demand conditions change, these changes are registered and are taken into account in the decisions that firms make in pursuit of maximizing their own profits. Since technological change can lower the firm's costs, there is always an incentive for the firm to try to lower costs because profits will increase (at least for a while). Competitive markets register the desires of consumers, and those desires guide production and the allocation of resources. The invisible hand will bring about cost and price reductions for consumers.

The competitive market system also links the interdependence of all economic agents in the whole economy. Markets for resources and products provide prices that are used as information in all of the decisions that people make about what work they will do, what goods and services they will consume, what business activities they will pursue, and what resources firms will use. The result of all of these decisions linked by the operation of markets is the allocation of the scarce resources of society to meet the needs of people in that society. The competitive market system thus operates to solve the question of what to produce, how to produce it, and how to distribute it. All of this occurs because of the existence of markets and of competition. Competition and markets guide resource allocation. *If* every market were competitive (remember our definition of what that means), then the whole economy would be characterized by efficiency, the invisible hand, and consumer sovereignty. Stated differently, the *theory* of the competitive market model produces efficiency, consumer sovereignty, and the invisible hand. As a result, there is no need for the government to be involved in the economy (except for the purposes outlined by Adam Smith). If the competitive markets are allowed to operate freely and individuals are allowed to follow their maximizing opportunities, the best economic results are achieved. The competitive model, then, justifies a policy of *laissez-faire*.

Unfortunately, however, the model of competitive markets is not exactly the same thing as the real economy. The theoretical results of the model of competition that we have developed are certainly attractive. In fact, this theory is the basis of the argument that the free enterprise system is the best economic system possible. It can be seen in innumerable advertisements from corporate America as well as the ideas of the Chamber of Commerce or the National Association of Manufacturers. The argument is also often used by politicians to demonstrate their own patriotism in search of support and votes. But the real world doesn't always exactly duplicate theory, and the results of the model cannot uncritically or without qualification be ascribed to the real world.

It is important to recognize the various ways in which the operation of the real economy departs from the model of competitive markets. Not all markets are, in fact, competitive. Corporations and labor unions, for example, have market power, can influence prices, and have been able to limit the effects of competition. Sometimes markets don't work at all because no one can make profits putting up street signs, for example. In the calculation of profits by the firm, the external costs of production (such as pollution) aren't taken into account and can as a consequence interfere with efficient resource allocation. The operation of resource markets can result in a distribution of income that is unfair. All of these results of the operation of the real economy limit the extent to which it produces the attractive results of the theoretical model of competition.

In the next four chapters, we will develop some economic theory that analyzes these problems in the operation of the real market system. And we will also explore the response of public policy to the existence of these problems connected with the operation of the economy. In the next chapter, we will concentrate on the structure and results of markets that are not competitive—monopoly, oligopoly, and monopolistic competition. Given the existence of these market structures in the real economy, we are less likely to get the operation of the invisible hand and consumer sovereignty, as described in the competitive market model.

KEY CONCEPTS

profit maximization	average variable cost
competition, perfect	average cost
revenues	marginal costs
costs	average revenues
economic profit	marginal revenues
total revenues	long run
total costs	economies of scale
law of diminishing returns	diseconomies of scale
short run	efficiency in production
total fixed costs	efficiency in resource allocation
total variable costs	invisible hand
average fixed cost	consumer sovereignty

REVIEW QUESTIONS

1. How accurate is this competitive model with respect to the current U.S. economy? Are its conclusions applicable to our economy?

2. Why are profits maximized when MR = MC? Can you explain this logically?

3. Do you think firms really *do* try to maximize their profits? Do they have other goals? Which is most important?

4. Give some examples of the law of diminishing returns in production. Specify which resource is variable and which ones are fixed.

5. Explain why economic profits cease to exist in competition (as a tendency). What is the implication of this? Why do firms stay in a market in which there are no profits?

SUGGESTED READINGS

Any of the introductory books suggested in Chapter 10 will provide a detailed treatment of this theory.

Adam Smith, *The Wealth of Nations*, represents an even fuller treatment—the classic treatment—of these theories expanded to almost 1000 pages! (Especially see Book I, Chapters 5–7.)

Wherein Noncompetitive Market Structures Disturb Adam Smith's Perfect World

INTRODUCTION

One of the things we have learned so far in this part is that, according to neoclassical theory, competitive markets tend to produce consumer sovereignty, to provide for the operation of the invisible hand, and to lead to economic efficiency. However, if markets are *not* competitive—i.e., do not have all of the characteristics of competition—then these results are less likely. In fact, in noncompetitive markets there is likely to be some amount of *producer sovereignty*, the existence of "monopoly" profits (i.e., economic profits will not be reduced by competition), and some amount of inefficiency. In this chapter, we will define some other models of market structure and examine their results.

NONCOMPETITIVE MARKET STRUCTURES

The competitive market model gives us a standard by which to judge *real* economic markets and other models of market structures. Chapter 11 defined a competitive market and examined its workings and results. In what follows, we will define some other models of market structures and examine their workings and results. With these additional models we will have a more complete theoretical system for understanding the behavior of firms in the economy and for evaluating their performance.

Before we examine monopoly, oligopoly, and monopolistic competition, we ought to point out that the competitive model is a *model*, and that it roughly describes only about 10 percent of the total private economic activity in the United States. The best examples of competitive markets are those of raw agricultural products—which are homogeneous, are not advertised, have large numbers of buyers and sellers, and can be entered by almost anyone. In the rest of the economy, there are firms and markets from which some or all of these characteristics are missing. There may be very few firms in an industry, and they may have the market power to control their prices. Products may be differentiated rather than homogeneous. Advertising obviously occurs beyond the simple level of informing consumers about products. And entry into markets isn't always "free" or easy. In fact, the existence and the emergence of noncompetitive market structures should not be too surprising. As we have demonstrated in Chapter 11, the long-run tendency of competition is to eliminate economic profits. One effective way to ensure long-run economic profits for a firm is to limit the effects of competition, which may involve the elimination of competition.

MONOPOLY

Monopoly is a market structure in which there is only *one seller* of a good or service. The firm is the industry. Many monopolies are legalized because of the confusion that competition would create. At the same time, their prices are usually regulated by public authority. Examples of legal monopolies are local gas, electric, telephone, and water companies. Professional sports teams in the United States have regional monopolies. F. M. Scherer, an industrial economist, has estimated that about 6 to 7 percent of private economic output originates in monopolies.

The characteristics of monopoly markets include the following:

1. There is one seller of a good or service.

2. The product is unique, and there are no close substitutes; buyers must buy the good or service from the monopolist.

3. The monopoly can exercise control over the price of the good/service, since it supplies the total quantity of the good/service. The firm has **market power.** This is opposed to the competitive firm, whose price is determined by the market; the competitor has no influence on the price of its product.

4. Monopolies usually exist because there are absolute **barriers to entry** into the market; no other firm can supply the product because of legal, technological, or geographical barriers.

5. The monopoly may or may not advertise.

The theoretical results of monopoly markets are that producers tend to restrict output and tend to charge higher prices than they could if there were competition in the market for that monopoly's product. As a result, monopoly markets are less beneficial to consumers, who would prefer to have more of the product at a lower price. As a result, monopolies also interfere with efficient resource allocation. Monopoly power allows a firm to remain immune from competition and to retain monopoly profits. (For these reasons, most monopolies in the United States are regulated.) Monopoly thus is less desirable than competition. The theoretical analysis that demonstrates these results is not too terribly complicated, so let's try to follow it through.

The monopolist faces the entire demand curve for a product, since there are no competitors. Thus to sell more, the monopolist must lower price. Or if the monopolist raises prices, less will be demanded. As a result, the monopolist's marginal revenue curve will be below the demand curve. Since price must be lowered to sell more, the marginal addition to revenue will always be below the price. This is demonstrated in Table 12.1 and illustrated in Fig. 12.1. This information shows the revenue situation for the typical monopoly firm, with a downward-sloping demand curve and a marginal revenue curve below it. If we assume that the monopoly buys

Table 12.1 MONOPOLY PRICE AND MARGINAL REVENUE

OUTPUT	PRICE	TOTAL REVENUE	MARGINAL REVENUE
1	10	10	—
2	9	18	8
3	8	24	6
4	7	28	4

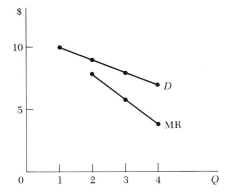

Figure 12.1 Monopoly demand and marginal revenue.

its resources in competitive markets, its MC and AC curves will look like the ones we derived in Chapter 11. Figure 12.2 illustrates the cost situation for the monopolist.

Figure 12.3 puts the revenue and the cost information together to demonstrate the equilibrium result for a typical monopoly firm.

What level of output will the monopoly choose to produce? It will produce Q_m, where MC = MR, because that level of output maximizes its profits. It will charge a price of P_m for that amount of output, because that is the price the market is willing to pay for that quantity. The monopoly is earning profits since P is well above AC. And the monopoly is producing at a rate of output that does not minimize average costs (Q_0 is where AC is at a minimum).

This illustrates the short-run equilibrium for a monopoly. In this case, the monopolist earns economic profits. However, there is no assurance that even monopolies will always earn profits. If costs are too high or there is no demand for the monopolist's product, a monopoly could suffer economic losses. For example, there is no major league baseball team in Washington, D.C.

What happens in a monopoly in the long run? Figure 12.4 shows the long-run cost and revenue curves for a monopolist (assuming economies and diseconomies of scale). In the long run, the monopolist has the option of building different size plants and the demand curve for the product could change. Given the cost and revenue curves in Fig. 12.4, the monopolist produces at Q_{mlr}, the rate of output at which MC = MR, and charges a price of P_{mlr} (from the demand curve). P is above AC, so the monopolist earns economic profits. The monopolist is in long-run equilibrium. But in a pure monopoly, even with the existence of economic profits, there is no entry into the market; this firm has a monopoly. Therefore, Fig. 12.4 shows the long-run equilibrium result for a typical monopoly market. As long as cost and demand conditions remain the same, the monopoly firm produces Q_{mlr}, charges a price of P_{mlr}, and earns economic profits.

What conclusions can we draw about the theoretical results of monopoly? Economic profits may exist, but because of the monopoly no entry occurs to seek those extra returns above opportunity costs. The monopolist will not produce at a rate of output that minimizes average cost (Q_0); nothing forces the monopolist to produce at the most efficient rate of output. In monopoly, then, there tends to be

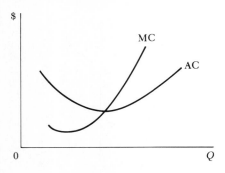

Figure 12.2   The monopolist's cost curves.

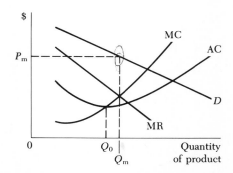

Figure 12.3   Equilibrium for the monopoly firm.

PRODUCE @ MC = MR
Pm = B/c MARKET WILL PAY.

inefficiency in production (at least from the perspective of the society). The monopoly firm produces the rate of output that maximizes its profits—that's its goal. Moreover, at that rate of output, price exceeds marginal costs. Society values an additional unit of the good or service more than it costs to produce an additional unit. From a social perspective, then, it would be preferable if more resources were allocated to increased production of the commodity. Monopoly thus tends to result in inefficiency in resource allocation. Because monopolies get economic profits, some resources earn over and above their opportunity costs. Finally, some monopolists may engage in advertising, which requires the use of scarce resources. (In 1983, American businesses spent over $75 billion on advertising.) Consequently, we can see that the long-run equilibrium result of monopoly is significantly inferior to the long-run result of competition. The pursuit of profit, in this case, doesn't maximize social welfare.

We can also examine the theoretical results of monopoly by focusing on the market, shown in Fig. 12.5.

If there were competition in the market, new firms would enter, market supply would increase to S_c, and market price would decrease to P_c. Thus monopoly restricts output, since $Q_m < Q_c$. And monopoly charges higher prices, since $P_m > P_c$. Finally, monopolies earn monopoly profits.

An important conclusion that can be drawn from the monopoly model is that the existence of market power (ability to control supply and price) tends to prevent the occurrence of consumer sovereignty, the attainment of economic efficiency, and the operation of the invisible hand. The monopoly benefits at the expense of the society. This says nothing at all about the further problem of the relationship of economic power to political power. Monopolies, through their economic power and resources, may come to wield undue political power. Monopolies, as a result, may also tend to disrupt democracy. As Henry Simons, an economist who taught at the University of Chicago, noted "political liberty can survive only within the effectively competitive economic system. Thus, the great enemy of democracy is monopoly." Any economic unit tending toward monopoly power, consequently, tends toward these same results.

As a result of these adverse effects of monopoly, the public sector has frequently been involved in regulating the operations and/or the prices of monopolies. Many

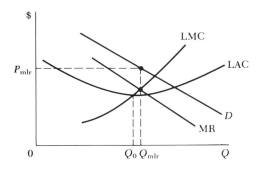

Figure 12.4 Long-run equilibrium for the monopolist.

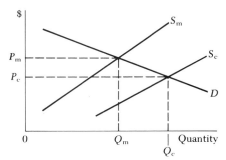

Figure 12.5 Monopoly—output restriction and high price.

times, the public regulation is in return for the governmental granting of a legal monopoly, as is the case with local telephone service, for example. The goal of the public oversight is usually to increase monopoly output, lower monopoly prices, or reduce monopoly profits. (In Chapter 15, we will go into the regulation of monopoly in more detail.)

Occasionally the operation of the profit motive itself can limit the existence of a continuing monopoly. For example, a monopoly might produce a good or service for which a close substitute could be developed. Or the monopolist might have some technical advantage that can be duplicated. The very existence of monopoly profits gives other firms an incentive to try to "break" the monopoly. For example, Kodak until 1986 produced an instant camera to rival Polaroid's. Polaroid had a monopoly for almost two decades, but Kodak had the incentive to develop its own instant camera so that it could share the profits in this market. Polaroid, however, restored its monopoly by filing a suit charging patent violations against Kodak. In a 1985 court decision, Kodak was ordered to stop producing instant cameras. Xerox developed the technique and the machinery for instant photocopying. Given the lucrative results from the monopoly on their technique, other firms developed substitutes and entered the market. Similarly, Trivial Pursuit spurred the entry of a number of close substitutes to limit its monopoly over a segment of the board-game market. The extent to which other firms challenge a monopoly may reduce the adverse theoretical consequences of monopoly.

1. What's so bad about monopolies? What can we do if they exist?

2. Analyze Henry Simons's comment above. Do you agree or disagree? Why?

3. Local phone companies often have a monopoly, but advertise. Why?

4. In Fig. 12.3, explain what would happen to the firm's profits if it produced at Q_0.

5. "Some resources in monopoly earn over and above their opportunity costs." Can you think of any examples?

MONOPOLISTIC COMPETITION AND OLIGOPOLY

Monopolistic competition and oligopoly are the other two major market structure models that economists have developed to approximate economic reality. Somewhere around 80 percent of private economic production comes from firms with monopolistic competition or oligopoly elements. (In *Economics and the Public Purpose*, John Kenneth Galbraith estimated that about 50 percent of private production originates in industries that are competitive or monopolistically competitive, and the remainder comes from firms that are monopolies or oligopolies.)

Monopolistic Competition

The model of monopolistic competition was developed in the 1930s by E. H. Chamberlin and Joan Robinson. It is used to describe industries that are close to competitive but have some elements of monopoly. The following are the major characteristics of **monopolistic competition:**

1. There are large numbers of buyers and sellers in the market. The firms are all relatively small with respect to the total size of the industry.

2. The products in monopolistically competitive industries are **differentiated** by quality and design differences, advertising, and psychological appeal. Each firm attempts to distinguish its products from those of its competitors. The products are all very close substitutes for one another, but each firm tries to create a "monopoly" for its product. A strong stimulus for the emergence of this primary characteristic of monopolistic competition is the tendency in competitive industries with homogeneous products for the elimination of profits.

3. Firms have limited control over the prices of their products. The firms are small in relation to the market, but they sell a differentiated product. Some consumers are loyal to the unique brands of individual firms, even though there are close substitutes. It is because of this "monopoly" element that firms have some control over their prices.

4. Entry into the market is relatively easy, although the costs of differentiation can be large for advertising, etc. Since the firms are small, relatively small initial investments make entry feasible.

5. As distinct from competition, there is an abundance of advertising in monopolistic competition. The products are not homogeneous, and advertising exists to convince and persuade consumers about the differences. (As mentioned earlier, in 1983, U.S. businesses spent over $75 billion on advertising.)

Some examples of monopolistically competitive industries are retail sales in urban communities, fast food establishments in any particular area, computer software, processed chicken for retail sales, and clothing. Toothpaste, cigarettes, and breakfast cereals are monopolistically competitive if we look only at the competition among brand names.

Now that we have some sense of what the characteristics of monopolistic competition are and how it is different from both competition and monopoly, we will develop the model of what happens in this type of market structure. First of all, let's examine the firm's output and pricing decision in the short run. Since the objective of a firm in monopolistic competition is the same as that of any other firm, this decision will be a function of the firm's cost and revenue conditions.

Because the firm has some control over the price that it charges for its differentiated product, it will face a downward-sloping demand curve. It can raise its price and not lose all of its sales, which is what would happen in perfect competition because consumers will just go to the firm's competitors if it raises its prices. In monopolistic competition, some consumers will remain loyal to the firm's product and continue to purchase it even though the price has gone up and there are close substitutes. Even so, when the firm raises its price, it will experience a decrease in its sales because there are substitutes. The firm can also lower its price and expect to get a significant increase in its sales because its loyal customers will consume more and because it may also steal business from its competitors. In other words, the demand curve for a monopolistic competitor is downward sloping and relatively elastic. Because the demand curve is downward sloping, the firm's marginal revenue curve will also be downward sloping and below the demand curve. See Fig. 12.6 for typical demand and marginal revenue curves for a firm in monopolistic competition.

Since monopolistically competitive firms buy their resources in the same markets as do all other firms, their cost curves will be the same. The typical short-run average cost and marginal cost curves, reflecting the law of diminishing returns, are shown in Fig. 12.7.

Figure 12.7 gives us the information that we need to describe the output and price decision of the monopolistic competitor in the short run. Given these cost and demand conditions, the firm produces at Q_{mc} since that's the rate of output at which MC = MR. And the firm will charge a price of P_{mc} since the market will be willing to pay that price for the amount produced and offered for sale. The firm is earning economic profits because P is greater than AC. This is the firm's short-run equilibrium position.

What happens in the long run in a monopolistically competitive industry? In Fig. 12.7, the firm is earning economic profits. Since entry is relatively easy, other firms will enter the market in search of returns above opportunity costs. The entry of new firms will tend to reduce the share of every firm already in the industry (here, we are assuming that the size of the market is "constant"). This will have the effect of shifting every firm's individual demand curve back to the left. For example, let's say that entry has occurred and Fig. 12.8 illustrates the effect that this has on the firm's demand curve. It also reflects the firm's long-run plant-size choices with an LAC curve. What's the new output–price decision by our typical firm?

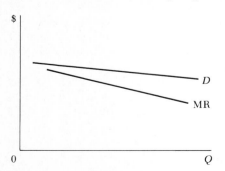

Figure 12.6   Demand and marginal revenue curves for a firm in monopolistic competition.

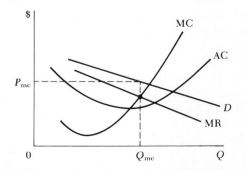

Figure 12.7   Short-run equilibrium for the firm in monopolistic competition.

The firm will pick Q_2 as its rate of output and charge a price of P_2. P is still above AC, however, so the firm earns economic profits. The continued existence of economic profits still offers an incentive for firms to enter the market. As long as profits exist, entry will continue. Entry will cease and the industry will achieve long-run equilibrium when economic profits no longer exist. This result is shown in Fig. 12.9. The firm produces at Q_{mcl} and charges a price of P_{mcl}. Since $P = AC$, the firm does not earn any economic profits. New firms will stop entering the market. And *the firm* is in equilibrium as well, earning zero economic profits.

What are the implications of this long-run equilibrium result for monopolistic competition? $P = AC$ so there are no economic profits. However, P does not equal minimum average cost (at Q_0). The long-run equilibrium in monopolistic competition does not result in efficiency of production, then. In addition, P exceeds MC, which means that there is inefficiency in resource allocation. From the perspective of social welfare, monopolistic competition results in an underallocation of resources to the production of its goods and services. Since one of the primary characteristics of this market structure is product differentiation, resources also get used up in the advertising and promotion of one product over another. From the perspective of the efficient use of resources by the society, this represents a waste. Compared with the model of competition, then, monopolistic competition falls short of a social welfare maximization.

On the other hand, there are some positive attributes of the functioning of monopolistically competitive markets. Relatively free entry by firms when economic profits exist promotes adaptability; resources are reallocated in response to market conditions. Entry also puts downward pressures on prices, as in competitive markets. Product differentiation contributes to one of the wonders of American civilization and freedom—variety and choice. When efforts to differentiate products lead to quality improvements, consumers benefit, and firms must be sensitive to consumers desires. There is also the possibility, however, that product differentiation may not lead to real improvements or that too much choice will only confuse consumer's informed decisions. Finally, in monopolistic competition, entry and limited competition does force firms to produce as efficiently as possible. If firms don't match the costs of other firms, they are in danger of being eliminated from the market by economic losses.

Given the tendency of monopolistic competition to eliminate economic profits in the long run, occasionally the firms in such an industry will engage in efforts to

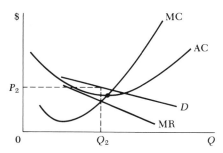

Figure 12.8 Equilibrium in monopolistic competition after entry.

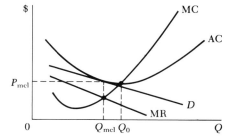

Figure 12.9 Long-run equilibrium in monopolistic competition.

prevent the disappearance of long-run economic profits. A favorite tactic is to stay ahead of the effects of entry by continued differentiation and advertising. By improving the quality, design, or even advertising of a product, a firm may be able to continue to earn economic profits in the long run. In addition, monopolistically competitive firms might be able to get legislative protection that controls the entry of firms into the industry. For example, beauty parlors and barber shops must have licenses from the state in order to operate. The requirement of the license restricts entry into the market, and it serves to preserve some economic profits for existing firms.

6. In Fig. 12.9, show and explain what would happen if the demand for the firm's product (and its close substitutes) increased (e.g., from a change in consumers tastes and preferences).

7. In Fig. 12.9, show and explain what would happen if the costs of production were decreased as a result of a technological breakthrough.

8. For the long-run equilibrium result of monopolistic competition, show the effect of an improvement in quality, design, or advertising on the part of one firm attempting to maintain long-run economic profits.

9. Why is the market for processed chicken sold in grocery stores an example of monopolistic competition?

MONOPOLISTIC COMPETITION IN FAST FOODS

It used to be hamburgers, french fries, milk shakes, and soft drinks—and that was it. Now it's all of that plus breakfasts, chicken nuggets, salad bars, stuffed potatoes, and more. The fast food industry in the United States is a good example of a monopolistically competitive industry. Although McDonald's, Burger King, and Wendy's account for 67 percent of the national hamburger fast food market, the market is broader than that.

The fast food market did more than $40 billion worth of business in 1983. It consists of hamburger, pizza, chicken, taco, and other establishments. And, while McDonald's and "friends" dominate the national markets for fast foods, in area markets there is stiffer competition, with local and regional firms competing for customers' stomachs and dollars. Also, the fast food firms must compete in the broader category of commercial dining, which was a $120 billion industry in 1983. The market itself has expanded tremendously in the post–World War II period, with mobility and changing life styles. The late Ray Kroc took over two ham-

(continued)

Nicole Hollander, *Hi, This Is Sylvia,* St. Martin's Press, Inc., New York. © 1982 by Field Enterprises and Nicole Hollander.

burger stands run by the McDonald brothers in 1955, and McDonald's hasn't stopped expanding since then. There are now well over 7000 Mc-Donald's—6000 in the United States and about 1500 abroad. Burger King has about half that number of outlets.

What characteristics of monopolistic competition are demonstrated by the fast foods industry? In regional markets, there are a large number of competitors, and entry is relatively easy. You don't have to rival the size or sophistication of McDonald's in order to start a hamburger or pizza joint. There is also a high rate of failure in the market, with thousands of restaurants going bankrupt every year. There is obvious and substantial product differentiation. Pizza is not chicken, and hamburgers are not salad. Some hamburgers are frozen and some aren't. Some are fried while others are grilled. French fries are notoriously nonstandardized. You can't get a hot dog everywhere. Pizza comes in infinite styles and qualities. The decors of different places distinguish them from one another. Quality is an issue among the various choices. And, recently, the fast food industry has become concerned about its junk-food image and some firms have begun to offer more nutritional food items. Finally, since McDonald's first started in 1966, television advertising has become a necessary aspect of the competition for the national fast food industry. The name of the game is diversification, differentiation, aggressive advertising and marketing, and broad appeal. So, where's the fast food?

Oligopoly

Oligopolistic industries are those that are dominated by large firms. They are not like small competitive firms, but they are also not monopolists. There is great variety in oligopolistic industries, so economists have developed a number of different models of oligopoly to describe their behavior and results. The following are the major characteristics of **oligopoly:**

OLIGOPOLIES

(handwritten in left margin: AUTO MAKERS STEEL PRODUCERS)

1. A few firms produce most of the output in an industry. These firms are thus usually large with respect to the market, and dominate its activities. Examples include automobiles, computers, steel, aluminum, cigarettes, and chewing gum. In some cases, there may be fewer than ten firms in the entire industry. In others, there may be hundreds of companies, but four or five firms dominate.

2. The product of an oligopoly may be homogeneous or differentiated. If it is a consumer good, it's usually differentiated to gain consumers' attention and loyalty (e.g., automobiles). And, if it's a raw material sold to other firms, it's usually homogeneous (e.g., steel, copper, or aluminum).

3. There may be technological reasons for domination of an industry by a few firms. Costs may be reduced in large-scale operations. Economies of scale may allow for only a few firms to constitute the entire industry, given the size of the market. Firms may also have grown large due to mergers. As a result, entry into such markets is difficult. A firm must be large to enter. How many firms have entered the automobile industry recently and been competitive with the Big Three?

4. The firms in an oligopolistic industry are **interdependent.** Their pricing and output decisions all affect the other firms in the industry. They all must pay attention to the actions of their rivals. This creates a constant possibility for **price wars** among oligopolists, or collusion to avoid those price wars. It can also lead to price leadership or a reluctance to alter price. Despite this interdependence, oligopolies do have some control over their prices.

5. Oligopolies usually have a significant amount of nonprice competition, i.e., product differentiation and advertising.

Because of the interdependence of oligipoly firms, it is difficult to develop one model of what happens in an oligopolistic industry. Depending on the reactions of rivals to price and output decisions, there are a variety of different possibilities, including price wars, collusion, price leadership, and stable prices. We will now briefly develop some of these models.

Figure 12.10 illustrates a general possibility for an oligopolist. Because the firm has some control over the price of its product, it has a downward-sloping demand curve and a marginal revenue curve that lies below it. Many oligopolies experience economies of scale. The long-run average cost curve in Fig. 12.10 reflects economies of scale that are reached at relatively low rates of output and thereafter average costs remain constant. That is, the firm does not encounter diseconomies of scale; there is no limit to the firm's expansion as a result. If LAC's are constant, then, for that range of output, AC = MC. Given these demand and cost conditions, the firm will pick Q_o as the rate of output that maximizes its profits (since that's where MC = MR). The price will come off of the firm's demand curve, at P_{oc}. At this price–output combination, the firm earns economic profits since P is above AC. Since entry is very difficult in oligopoly, these long-run profits are relatively secure. However, in oligopoly there is always the possibility of price cutting by rivals. Other firms might try to steal away customers by lowering their prices; this action could spark retaliation. Theoretically, firms could lower prices all the way down to P_{o2} before losses would be encountered. As prices were decreased, the oligopolists' profits would be reduced. One of the things that oligopolists might do in response to this threat of price wars and the possibility of losing all of their economic profits is to collude to avoid price competition among themselves.

Collusion to avoid competition and/or to set prices is illegal in the United States. However, light bulb manufacturers, paperboard companies, and others have been found guilty of price fixing. And there may be indirect ways of setting prices to avoid price wars, such as trade associations, industry meetings, governmental standardization of technical materials, or informal tacit agreements. Given the illustration in Fig. 12.10, the firms could simply attempt to set prices at close to the P_{oc} level as possible. This would maximize their economic profits.

In international markets and in some European countries, **cartels** are legal and are allowed to set prices for their products. One example of a cartel is the Organization of Petroleum Exporting Countries. OPEC consists of 13 oil-producing countries that operate government-owned petroleum industries and sell oil in international markets. OPEC functions as a cartel that sets production quotas and prices for its members. The intention of the cartel is to control the world's supply of oil, to avoid price wars among the members, and, consequently, to maximize their joint profits. The members of OPEC in the 1970s and early 1980s had a dominant position in the international oil market, and they used this position and their cooperation to control the international price of oil. With the development of non-OPEC sources of oil (e.g., Mexico and Great Britain), OPEC's ability to maintain high prices has been reduced. In essence, what a cartel can accomplish is a result similar to that of monopoly. For example, Fig. 12.11 shows the combined cost and revenue conditions for a cartel as a whole.

The cartel then decides to produce a combined output of Q_{oc} and to charge a price of P_{oc}. As in monopoly, output is restricted and the price is higher than it would be if there were competition. Economic profits exist for the cartel as a whole. The members of the cartel then agree among themselves how to split up the production

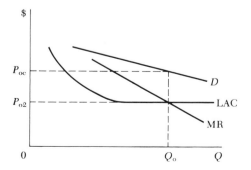

Figure 12.10 Oligopoly pricing and output.

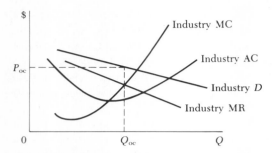

Figure 12.11   A cartel to ensure oligopoly profits.

goal and profits based on their different cost functions, reserves, and negotiating skills.

Whether collusion is formal, as in a cartel, or informal, it is often difficult for its members to maintain it—even though the reward for doing so is the avoidance of price wars and the accumulation of continued long-run economic profits. If the cartel consists of a large number of countries or firms, it is more difficult to reach and to maintain agreement on production quotas and price levels. If the products of the cartel are differentiated (e.g., quality of oil), it is more difficult to establish consistent price schedules for the varieties of the commodity. If the members of a cartel have different cost conditions in their productive operations, it will be more difficult for them to agree on price levels. Those with relatively high costs will want higher prices, or they will experience lower profits. In the same way, the size of the firm or country in the market will influence its bargaining power in the cartel—that is, different members will have different negotiating power when it comes to setting production quotas and prices.

The characteristic of cartels that most demonstrates their fragility is their tendency toward *price breaks*. Given the controlled price of the cartel, which will always be higher than the price that might prevail without the cartel, there is always a temptation for an individual member to offer lower prices to attract its rivals' customers. If it can get away with secret price breaks, it can increase its sales and its profits. The problem is that once one member does it, others are likely to do the same, and then the cartel is faced with a price war and reduced profits for all its members. The other difficulty with cartels in the United States is that they are illegal! For all these reasons, collusive behavior and its ultimate form—the cartel—are difficult to establish and to maintain.

10. **Ever since OPEC raised its oil prices in 1974, many U.S. analysts have argued that it would be difficult for OPEC to maintain its cartel. With the passage of time, they suggested, oil prices would fall as OPEC dissolved. What was the basis of their argument? Why has OPEC recently lost its ability to control world oil prices?**

Another tactic that oligopolistic industries use to avoid price wars involves simply keeping prices stable. If all of the firms in the industry maintain their prices over some period of time, they will avoid the tendency of interdependent firms toward self-destructive price competition.

When oligopolists do, in fact, change their prices occasionally, there is one other tactic that they have developed to avoid price wars. It is called **price leadership**—the practice of a single firm in an industry announcing a price change and then having most if not all of the other firms follow that lead. In some industries the same firm is consistently the leader. General Motors, for example, is traditionally the first to announce its new model prices every fall. Ford, Chrysler, and American Motors usually follow. For the most part, automobile prices have also been very stable over annual periods. In other industries, the leader may change; it may be one of the giants in the field or it could be one of the smaller firms. The leader of changes in the prime rate, the rate that banks charge their best borrowers, is not always one of the big New York City banks. In addition to this form of price leadership, uniformity in prices that avoids the danger of price wars can also be achieved through the sharing of information in informal contacts (at lunch, golfing, etc.) among the firms in an industry or through more formal meetings in conferences and trade associations. The primary goal is the same, though—the protection of oligopoly profits.

What are the theoretical results of oligopoly? There is no one model of oligopoly, as we have seen. But, in general, oligopolies are protected from the results of competition because entry is difficult. Oligopolies have market power over their output and prices, they tend to earn oligopoly profits, and they are somewhat insulated from the dictates of market forces. The force of competition does not require them to produce at the most efficient rate of output. And, because they, like other noncompetitive firms, face a downward-sloping demand curve, P will always exceed MC; consequently, oligopolies result in inefficiency in resource allocation. Oligopolies that sell differentiated products also engage in advertising and use scarce resources to convince consumers that their products are better than their rivals. Because oligopolies do not face the competition of new entrants into their markets and have market power, some critics suggest that such firms can resist technological change. For example, it might be possible for an automobile company to introduce production and product improvements that would benefit consumers, but, because they have money tied up in current production techniques and product lines, they put off introducing changes.

Large oligopolistic firms have enormous resources at their command; they have economic power over plant location, the pace of investment spending in the economy, and the advance of technology. This concentrated economic power can also be translated into concentrated political power, which can pose some difficulties for the operation of democratic institutions.

On the other hand, the defenders of oligopoly and large firms have argued that the pursuit of profit by such firms has spurred technological advancement and economies of scale in many oligopolistic industries. The history of some of the dominant heavy industries in the United States offers proof that economic concentration has accompanied increased output and efficiency. The steel and automobile industries pioneered large factories and the assembly line. The aircraft industry stimulated other industries and transportation in the post–World War II period. More recently, photocopying and computers have revolutionized information processing. Large firms with their economic profits can also afford to establish research and development labs to discover new processes and products. Finally, it is suggested that the persistence of large corporations lends a certain stability to the operation of the entire economy. Without the rapid entry and exit of competitive markets, oligopolists can plan for the long run and serve the society.

11. Can you think of examples of firms in oligopolistic industries that have not been very sensitive to the wishes of U.S. consumers in recent years?

12. Do you think that large corporations tend to provide a certain dynamism to the economy, or do you think that they obstruct progress?

THE IMPORTANCE OF NONCOMPETITIVE MARKETS IN THE AMERICAN ECONOMY

The models of noncompetitive market structures are helpful in building a theory of the operation of the U.S. economy because of the presence of product differentiation and economic concentration throughout the real economy. The following data on economic concentration are intended to demonstrate the pervasiveness and the importance of concentrated markets in the United States.

In 1963, the 100 largest manufacturing corporations accounted for

25 percent of all domestic manufacturing employees,

32 percent of domestic manufacturing payrolls,

33 percent of value added in manufacturing,

43 percent of after-tax profits in manufacturing,

34 percent of domestic manufacturing sales, and

36 percent of domestic manufacturing assets.

In 1950, the top 200 corporations in the United States controlled 48 percent of all corporate assets; in 1960, they controlled 56 percent; in 1965, it was 57 percent; in 1975, it increased to 58 percent; and it had reached 60 percent by 1981.

In the post–World War II period, the top 50 industrial corporations have accounted for 25 percent annually of value added in manufacturing; the top 100 have accounted for 33 percent; and the share of the top 200 has increased from 30 percent in 1947, to 40 percent in 1962, to 43 percent in 1970, and to 44 percent in 1977.

In 1982, the 500 largest industrial corporations accounted for almost 70 percent of final sales in the manufacturing sector of the economy,

about 40 percent of total profits in the economy, and

about 14 percent of employment in the whole economy.

Furthermore, all of these percentages have been increasing steadily throughout the 20th century. In Chapter 14, we will explore the dimensions and the implications of the corporate sector of the economy in more detail.

Tables 12.2 and 12.3 show the concentration ratios in various American industries. The **concentration ratio** shows what percentage of total sales in an industry is

Table 12.2 SHARE OF VALUE OF SHIPMENTS ACCOUNTED FOR BY THE FOUR, EIGHT, AND TWENTY LARGEST COMPANIES IN SELECTED HIGH-CONCENTRATION MANUFACTURING INDUSTRIES, 1977

	FOUR LARGEST FIRMS	EIGHT LARGEST FIRMS	TWENTY LARGEST FIRMS
Chewing gum	93%	99%	100%
Motor vehicles & car bodies	93	99	99+
Flat glass	90	99	99+
Electric lamps (bulbs)	90	95	98
Cereal breakfast foods	89	98	99
Primary copper	87	100	—
Tanks & tank components	87	97	100
Cigarettes	84*	100	—
Sewing machines	83	91	96
Household refrigerators & freezers	82	98	99
Primary aluminum	76	93	100
Aircraft engines & parts	74	86	93
Photographic equipment & supplies	72	86	90
Carbon black	70	100	—
Tires & inner tubes	70	88	97
Guided missiles & space vehicles	64	94	100
Malt beverages	64	83	98
Roasted coffee	61	73	89
Metal cans	59	74	90
Soap & other detergents	59	71	82
Cookies & crackers	59	68	83
Distilled liquor	52	71	91
Elevators & moving stairways	52	68	82
Radio & TV receiving sets	51	65	81
Phonograph records & prerecorded tapes	48	62	75
Petroleum refining	30	53	81

*1970

Source: Bureau of the Census, *1977 Census of Manufacturers*.

Table 12.3 SHARE OF VALUE OF SHIPMENTS ACCOUNTED FOR BY THE FOUR, EIGHT, AND TWENTY LARGEST COMPANIES IN SELECTED LOW-CONCENTRATION INDUSTRIES, 1977

	FOUR LARGEST FIRMS	EIGHT LARGEST FIRMS	TWENTY LARGEST FIRMS
Concrete blocks & bricks	4%	6%	12%
Ready-mixed concrete	5	8	14
Typesetting	6	9	17
Commercial printing, lithographic	6	10	17
Wood pallets & skids	6	10	18
Signs & advertising displays	6	11	19
Miscellaneous plastic products	7	11	18
Plating & polishing	8	12	18
Women's & misses dresses	8	12	19
Metal doors, sash, & trim	8	15	30
Fur goods	11	19	31
Boat building & repairing	11	19	32
Women's & misses blouses	12	18	30
Wood kitchen cabinets	14	21	33
Women's & misses suits & coats	15	20	31
Bottled & canned soft drinks	15	22	36
Brass, bronze, & copper foundries	16	23	37
Sawmills & planing mills	17	23	36
Men's & boy's dress shirts & nightwear	17	28	48
Fluid milk	18	28	43
Newspapers	19	31	45
Sporting & athletic goods	21	28	41
Men's & boy's suits & coats	21	32	48

Source: Bureau of Census, *1977 Census of Manufacturers*.

accounted for by a specific number of firms. Usually, if the ratio is above 50 percent for the four largest firms in an industry, we say that it is an oligopoly. If one firm had 100 percent of a national market, it would be a monopoly. Some oligopolistic industries are identified in Table 12.2. If the eight largest firms had less than 10 percent of industry sales and there were lots of other firms in the industry, we'd say that it was close to being a competitive market. Table 12.3 lists some markets with relatively low concentration which have some of the characteristics of monopolistic competition. From these two tables, the importance of concentration in the American economy should be apparent. Most of the leading sectors of the U.S. economy are heavily concentrated—and hence the relevance of models of noncompetitive market structures.

13. **Examine Tables 12.2 and 12.3. Are there any industries in these tables that surprise you by their high or low concentration ratios? Do they exhibit the characteristics of monopolistic competition and/or oligopoly?**

14. **Can you offer explanations for why some of the industries in Table 12.2 are oligopolies, and why some of the industries in Table 12.3 are not as concentrated?**

SOURCES OF CONCENTRATION IN THE ECONOMY

The following factors have contributed to increasing concentration and centralization in the economy over the last century.

1. Legislation and government policy have promoted both competition and monopoly. Governments have granted legal monopolies. In addition, the government has provided support and assistance to several industries with a high degree of concentration—e.g., railroads, airlines, defense, automobiles, etc. On the other hand, *antitrust legislation* and some regulatory legislation are designed to promote competition. The goal is to control the adverse results of market power by splitting up companies, preventing mergers, prosecuting price setting and other noncompetitive activities, and regulating monopolies. These laws are based on economic arguments; our theory has demonstrated that competitive markets tend to produce efficiency, consumer sovereignty, and the invisible hand; and that noncompetitive markets, with market power and economic concentration, do not operate as well.

15. **Articulate why the government ought to promote competition and prevent extreme economic concentration and market power.**

One could argue over how well the antitrust laws have been enforced and whether they have prevented the accumulation of economic power by many of our industries and large firms.

2. Business policies and practices, including trusts, pools, holding companies, and mergers, have tended toward the creation of monopolies and/or oligopolies. If competition tends to eliminate economic profits, then one way to ensure long-run profits is to eliminate competition. Many firms have amassed substantial economic power in their markets and in the economy at large. The elimination of cutthroat competition through bankruptcy and merger, etc., has decreased the number of competitors in many industries. The auto industry used to have over 100 companies in the late 1920s. There

have been several merger waves in American economic history that have produced increased economic concentration. Corporate America is currently experiencing a wave of "unfriendly" mergers, wherein a company gets merged with another against its will.

3. Technology has developed in some industries to the extent that large-scale operations are necessary for efficiency. This promotes large firms and oligopoly. Technology allows some firms to outpace their competitors, who then fall by the wayside. An argument in favor of oligopoly, in fact, is that it can use some of its oligopoly profits to finance research to further advance technology (and presumably its own oligopoly power!).

4. Capitalism's economic freedom of enterprise is permissive of the growth of private corporations. With a motive of profit making and a laissez-faire attitude by government, the creation of economic power was tolerated (and even lauded by some) in our economic history.

CONCLUSION

Whatever the reasons for noncompetitive markets, we can still conclude that they are theoretically inferior to competitive markets in terms of consumers' and society's preferences. Resources *are* allocated throughout the noncompetitive sectors of the American economy, but noncompetitive markets and prices do not produce the ideals of the invisible hand, consumer sovereignty, and efficiency, as do competitive markets (theoretically). Adam Smith, where are you?

In the next chapter, we will shift our attention to the operation of resource markets and examine the factors that influence resource prices. One important result of resource markets is that they determine resource owners' incomes. We will also take a look at the distribution of income in the United States.

KEY CONCEPTS

monopoly
oligopoly
monopolistic competition
market power
concentration ratio
price leadership

barriers to entry
product differentiation
interdependence
cartels
collusion
price wars

REVIEW QUESTIONS

1. What are the theoretically adverse results of monopoly markets?

2. What benefits might be derived from oligopoly to offset its inefficiencies and higher prices? Can you give some examples?

3. Why do you think that the automobile industry is not competitive, according to our model of competition? What evidence can you cite to show its noncompetitiveness and inefficiency?

4. Why is local phone service a monopoly? What would happen if it weren't?

5. What would happen to the marijuana "industry" if it were legalized in the United States? What kind of market is it now?

6. If you were the adviser for an OPEC country that had relatively low levels of petroleum reserves, would you advise the setting of high or low prices? Why? What if you were advising a country with lots of reserves?

SUGGESTED READINGS

Walter Adams (ed.), 1982. *The Structure of American Industry* (5th ed.), Macmillan. Case studies of some noncompetitive industries in the United States, e.g., steel, telephone, automobiles, and beer.

John M. Blair, 1972. *Economic Concentration*, Harcourt Brace Jovanovich. A wealth of information on economic concentration, as well as some economic theory explaining it.

Richard Edwards, Michael Reich, and Thomas Weisskopf (eds.), 1978. *The Capitalist System* (2nd ed.), Prentice-Hall. See Chapter 4 on economic concentration.

John Kenneth Galbraith, 1979. *The New Industrial State*, New American Library; and 1973, *Economics and the Public Purpose*, Houghton Mifflin. Two well-written treatments of the sources and implications of economic concentration in the American economy.

Resource Markets and the Distribution of Income

INTRODUCTION

In the last two chapters, we have developed models of competitive and noncompetitive markets for produced goods and services. As we have mentioned previously, there are also markets for the resources that are used by firms in production. (It's actually a bit more complicated than that, since some firms produce raw materials that are used by other firms as factors of production.) In this chapter, we will explore the operation and the significance of resource markets—how resource prices are determined and how resources are allocated throughout the economy. The basic resources of the society are mental and/or physical labor, land and its raw materials, and capital. Resource markets are important for two primary reasons. First of all, resource prices determine costs for firms. Second, since resources are owned by individuals, the operation of resource markets forms the basis of the distribution of income in the society. In this chapter, we will also examine the distribution of income in the United States and attempt to explain why it is relatively unequal.

THE ECONOMICS OF RESOURCE MARKETS

In the following discussion, for the sake of simplicity, we will concentrate on one resource to illustrate the general operation of resource markets. There are markets for all resources because they are productive; they are used to produce goods and services that are sold in markets. The demand for resources is thus a **derived demand.** While we could develop models of the markets for raw materials, land, and capital, we will present a model of the market for unskilled labor. It is one of the broadest of labor markets. The number of people who could work in a McDonald's or do unskilled work in a factory is about equal to the size of the labor force in the United States—now over 110 million people. And there are many businesses that utilize unskilled workers. As in all markets, there is a demand and a supply side to the market. Figure 13.1 illustrates the market for unskilled labor.

On the supply side of the market, there is a positive relationship between wages offered and the amount of unskilled labor supplied by workers. The higher the wage, the greater the amount of labor supplied. On the demand side, there is an inverse relationship between wages and the amount of unskilled labor demanded by employers. The higher the wage, the lower the amount of unskilled labor the employers will want to use. This market, with large numbers of suppliers and demanders, will determine an equilibrium wage and quantity for unskilled workers. That wage influences a firm's potential costs and its decisions about how much of this resource to use (compared with other resources). The wage also determines the decisions that workers make about offering their labor to employers and influences their incomes (compared with other work–leisure possibilities that they have). This model is applicable, in a general way, to other resource markets. Now let's explore both sides of this market in a little more depth.

The Demand for a Resource

The demand for any resource is derived from consumers' demands for goods and services and from producers' "demands" for profitable enterprise. But we can be much more specific about the nature of the firm's demand for a resource.

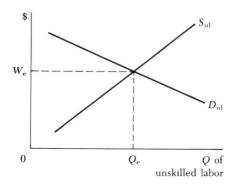

Figure 13.1   The market for unskilled labor.

Remember, the firm's objective is to maximize profits, the difference between total revenues and total costs. Whenever a firm uses a resource, both the firm's costs and its revenues are affected. If a firm uses one unit of a resource, how much will its costs increase? If a McDonald's restaurant hires one more unskilled worker to be a cook, its costs will go up by the worker's wage, i.e., the minimum wage times the number of hours worked. The firm's costs increase by the price of the resource, and that price is determined in a market. The added cost of the resource, or its **marginal factor cost** (MFC), equals its price. Or,

MFC = price of the resource.

In this case,

$MFC_{ul} = P_{ul}$,

where P_{ul} is the wage of unskilled labor. Since it's a relatively competitive market, the firm will be able to use as much of that resource as it wants at that price.

The second effect of using more of a resource is that it adds to the firm's revenues. Why? Because it adds to the firm's output and that output presumably gets sold in a product market. In fact, the addition to the firm's revenues, which we will call the **marginal revenue product** (MRP) of unskilled labor, equals the **marginal physical product** of unskilled labor (MPP_{ul}) times the marginal revenue of the product (MR_x). Or,

$MRP_{ul} = MPP_{ul} \times MR_x$.

The marginal physical product of unskilled labor is the additional output from adding one additional worker to the production process (with other factors held constant). It's the extra output from adding one more unit of a variable resource (does that sound familiar?). Table 13.1 shows the number of Big Macs that can be produced in one hour at a McDonald's as additional cooks are hired. The marginal physical product of each additional worker, then, is the addition to total output. The MPP of the sixth worker is three Big Macs.

Table 13.1 THE MARGINAL PHYSICAL PRODUCT OF UNSKILLED LABOR

NUMBER OF WORKERS	TOTAL OUTPUT OF BIG MACS	MARGINAL PHYSICAL PRODUCT OF UNSKILLED LABOR
1	20	—
2	27	7
3	34	7
4	40	6
5	44	4
6	47	3
7	49	2

And what happens to that extra output? It will be sold for the market price of Big Macs. If we assume, for ease of analysis, that McDonald's is in a competitive market, then the marginal revenue of a Big Mac is equal to the price of a Big Mac (that is, they are both constant). The firm's additional revenue from hiring one more unit of unskilled labor comes from the extra output produced and then sold.

Given that using more of the resource has a marginal effect on the firm's costs and revenues, it should not surprise you that a firm maximizes its profits by using that amount of a resource whose marginal contribution to the firm's revenues is equal to the marginal contribution to the firm's costs. That is, it should use that amount of the resource so that

$$\text{MFC}_{ul} = \text{MRP}_{ul}.$$

This is illustrated in Fig. 13.2. Since the MPP_{ul} is decreasing due to the law of diminishing returns and MR_x is constant if the firm sells its product in a competitive market, MRP_{ul} will be decreasing as we add more unskilled labor (along the horizontal axis). The MFC_{ul} is equal to the prevailing wage for unskilled labor from its market (i.e., the minimum wage).

For profit maximization, this firm would use L_1 of unskilled labor, since that's where $\text{MFC}_{ul} = \text{MRP}_{ul}$. If the firm uses less unskilled labor, the firm's revenues from using one more worker exceed the extra cost of using an additional unit. Therefore, expanding the use of the resource would add to the firm's profits. At levels above L_1, the extra cost for the resource is above what it adds to the firm's revenues. If the firm uses unskilled labor beyond L_1, the firm's profits will decrease. (Notice that we are assuming here that the demand for the product is constant; this shows up in the marginal revenue that the firm receives for selling additional units of output.)

1. **Assume that the minimum wage for unskilled workers is $3 an hour and that the price of a Big Mac is $1. Given the information in Table 13.1, how many workers would McDonald's hire? Why?**

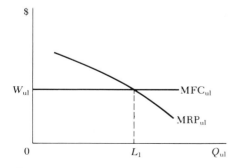

Figure 13.2   The firm's use of a resource.

Profit maximization leads a firm to decide on a specific amount of a resource to use in its productive activities. In addition, the marginal revenue product curve in Fig. 13.2 represents the firm's demand curve for this resource. Remember, a demand curve shows the amounts of a good or service that will be demanded at different possible prices. If the price of unskilled labor were lower, with everything else the same, the firm would hire additional workers; if the price were higher, the firm would hire fewer workers. The MRP_{ul} curve, then, gives us the firm's demand for unskilled labor.

The firm's demand for a resource is thus determined by the productivity of the resource, the importance of that resource in producing the good, and the price of the good itself.

2. **Using Fig. 13.2 explain why a firm would hire fewer workers if the price of the resource were higher.**

3. **Show what would happen to the demand for unskilled labor if there were an increase in the demand for Big Macs.**

The Supply of a Resource

As we pointed out earlier in this chapter, in general the amount supplied of a resource increases as its price increases. If the wage for unskilled work increased, for example, we would expect that the amount of unskilled labor offered would also increase. The wage for labor indicates the opportunity cost of time. An increase in a wage or a salary makes time more valuable and, in most cases, will encourage people to work more. From the perspective of an employer the wage indicates the opportunity cost for the resource; it's what the firm must pay to get that resource to work for it. In a similar manner, buildings and land earn rent, raw materials have prices, capital or money gets interest, and professional workers get salaries.

The sensitivity of a resource to the price offered for its productive services will vary over time. That is, the elasticity of supply of a resource can be different in the short run and in the long run. In the short run, the response of the amount of a resource supplied depends on the mobility of the resource to different possible uses. For example, for unskilled workers, raising the wage at McDonald's would most likely lead to a significant increase in the number of people willing to work there. (Remember, a supply curve is a hypothetical construction; it shows the amounts supplied at different possible prices.) A large number of individuals are available to work for the relatively low wages in fast foods and would be attracted by a higher wage. This means that the supply of unskilled labor is relatively elastic. On the other hand, if wages were increased for nurses, it would presumably require some time for the amount of nurses supplied to increase because of the training necessary. For nurses, then, the supply is somewhat inelastic in the short run. For buildings and machinery, supply is relatively inelastic in the short run due to the time required to construct them or to free existing ones for other uses.

In the short run, then, the supply of a resource can be elastic or inelastic depending on the type of resource. Price increases (or decreases) will produce large or small responses in the quantity supplied depending on the nature and qualities of the resource.

In the long run, the supply of most resources is more elastic. The long-run supply of any resource depends on decisions about the development of resources, which is in turn determined by expected rates of return. People decide to go to college depending on the expected payoff from graduating. That decision consequently influences the supply of professional employees. Decisions about graduate, law, or medical school involve the same calculation, which eventually affects the supply of Ph.D.s, lawyers, and doctors.

These factors determine the supply curves for resources. And, as we suggested at the beginning of this chapter, it is the supply-and-demand conditions for resources, taken together, that produce resource prices. Markets for resources establish resource prices. What other factors influence resource prices? Legislation may affect the wage that can be paid certain types of workers, e.g., the minimum wage. Licensing requirements will affect the supply of barbers, real estate agents, and many professional workers. Unions can control the supply of certain types of workers through apprenticeship programs, seniority systems, and membership dues. Cartels and trade associations can influence resource prices. Finally, the general state of the economy and the level of unemployment have a profound effect on wages and salaries. The larger the level of unemployment, in general, the lower the wages of unskilled and semiskilled workers.

4. **Why would higher rates of unemployment put downward pressure on wages?**

5. **Wages in Alaska are relatively high. Why would the elasticity of supply for labor provide a partial explanation for this?**

THE ECONOMICS OF THE MINIMUM WAGE

Regarding the treatment of unskilled labor in the text, we suggested that the wage for unskilled labor was determined by the supply and demand for that resource (see Fig. 13.1). This is a slight oversimplification. In fact, whenever interstate commerce is involved, employers are required to pay workers at least the minimum wage. This wage is mandated by con-

(continued)

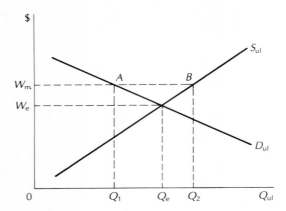

Figure 13.3   The effect of minimum wage laws on the market for unskilled labor.

gressional legislation, and it has progressively increased throughout the post–World War II period. In 1986 it stood at $3.35 an hour. The intent of this legislated minimum wage is to require employers to pay a wage higher than the rate that would be totally determined by the market for unskilled labor. It is meant to support the incomes of people who work in low-wage jobs, and it was motivated by a concern with fairness. Low-wage jobs are usually filled by people with little experience and/or few skills. In other words, they have relatively low marginal productivities. Also, the products they produce may have low market values. Dishwashers get low wages; doctors, lawyers, and engineers don't. In addition, with any amount of un-employment there is ample supply of unskilled workers. These factors pro-duce a market that can be illustrated with the supply and demand curves shown in Fig. 13.3. The equilibrium wage would be at W_e, but legislation mandates a wage above that at W_m.

What are the results of the minimum wage then? At W_m, employers hire Q_1 of unskilled workers. But Q_2 workers are willing to work at W_m. Hence, there is a surplus of unskilled workers—there is unemployment of unskilled workers equal to AB. Those who have jobs have higher incomes than they would have at a wage of W_e. But the minimum wage has cre-ated increased unemployment among unskilled workers.

Some economists, and politicians, have argued that lowering the minimum wage would decrease unemployment. The Reagan Administration has suggested a lower minimum wage for teenage workers several times (actually, one version would have made it applicable during the summer months to workers under the age of 21), but Congress has thus far refused to pass such legislation. The basis of the Administration's argument lies in the above illustration. If the wage were reduced to W_e, there would be an increase in the amount of unskilled labor demanded and a decrease in the amount of unskilled labor supplied. At Q_e, there would an equilibrium

(continued)

amount supplied and demanded—no unemployment in this market! Employers would tend to increase the number of unskilled workers that they used.

But there are several critical questions that can be raised about this analysis of the effects of lowering the minimum wage for some workers. Employers might replace older, higher-paid workers with younger, lower-paid workers, which would only shift the incidence of unemployment and would not necessarily reduce the overall amount of unemployment. And what about the difference between Q_2 and Q_e in terms of the amount of unskilled labor supplied? One effect of lowering the minimum wage would be that some teenagers would prefer to spend their summers doing something other than working for $2.75 an hour. Does that mean that they are not unemployed?

The minimum wage does not create unemployment. To some extent, it may exacerbate unemployment because it does tend to reduce the amount demanded and increase the amount supplied of unskilled labor. But the reasons for unemployment among low-wage, inexperienced, and unskilled workers have more to do with the overall level of economic activity than with the minimum wage. In addition, even though the minimum wage increased from $2.10 in 1975 to $3.35 in 1984 (which has led some people to argue that it has increased unemployment), in real terms (after taking inflation into account) the minimum wage has continually decreased throughout that period. By 1983, the purchasing power of the minimum wage had declined by about 25 percent from what it had been in 1975. Since the "real" minimum wage has decreased, it ought to have produced an increase in the amount of unskilled labor demanded by employers *(ceteris paribus)*. At any rate, over time, numerous other factors have changed that have also had an effect on the supply and demand for unskilled labor. The point here is that the claim that reducing the minimum wage would relieve unemployment is oversimplified.

There are 3.5 million people who work in the fast food industry in the United States. Seventy percent of them are 17 to 20 years old. Given the analysis that we have developed about a firm's demand for a resource, show how lowering the minimum wage would increase the amount of unskilled labor that McDonald's, for example, might hire. Do you think that there should be a lower minimum wage for teenage workers? Explain.

THE DISTRIBUTION OF INCOME

In Chapter 6 we examined how income is divided among the different factors of production in a private, market economy; labor gets wages, landowners get rent, and owners of capital get profits. Adam Smith concluded that any conflict over the distribution of income would be resolved, to the benefit of all, by the operation of the competitive market system. However, there are some other ways of looking at income distribution. A society may decide that the manner in which markets distribute income is undesirable. In a market system, the distribution of income tends to be fairly unequal. Why?

As we have suggested, income is derived from the participation of resources in productive activity. Income is paid to the factors of production for their involvement in the production process. The incomes that individuals earn therefore depend on the resources that they own and the prices that they command in resource markets. Some individuals have only their unskilled labor power to sell; consequently, they tend to have low incomes. On the other hand, people who possess professional skills, work experience, and/or capital resources will have higher incomes. What is the actual distribution of income in the United States?

The Size Distribution of Income

A convenient and instructive method of examining the distribution of income is to group people in families and then rank them by income. This is called the **size distribution of income.** Table 13.2 shows the size distribution of income for the United States in 1984. It covers all before-tax income—including governmental transfer payments such as Social Security and Veteran's benefits, unemployment compensation, and welfare—for the 62.7 million American families in 1984. When all of the families are ranked by income from the highest to the lowest, we take each successive 20 percent (12.5 million) of the families, add up all of their incomes, and take that income as a percentage of total income. For example, the bottom 20 percent of the families received 4.7 percent of total family income in 1984, the middle 20 percent got 17.0 percent of total income, and the top 20 percent got 42.9 percent. The *median family income* (the one in the middle of the entire ranking) for the United States in 1984 was $26,433. Table 13.2 also shows the ranges of income for each

Table 13.2 THE SIZE DISTRIBUTION OF FAMILY INCOME, 1984

QUINTILE	PERCENTAGE OF TOTAL INCOME	INCOME RANGE ($)
Lowest 20%	4.7	0–12,489
Second 20%	11.0	12,490–21,709
Third 20%	17.0	21,710–31,500
Fourth 20%	24.4	31,501–45,300
Highest 20%	42.9	above 45,301
(Top 5%)	(16.0)	(above 73,230)

Source: Statistical Abstract of the United States, 1986.

successive 20 percent. For example, with incomes below $12,490 families found themselves in the bottom 20 percent. If your family's income was $35,000 in 1984, it was in the fourth quintile. To get into the top 5 percent of family income required at least $73,230.

These statistics indicate a relatively unequal distribution of income. The 12.5 million families at the bottom of the income ladder got only 4.7 percent of total family income, while the same number of families at the top got 42.9 percent. The top 5 percent (just over 3 million families with incomes over $73,230) got more than three times as much income as the poorest 20 percent. If income were distributed totally equally, each 20 percent would get 20 percent of total income. No society has a totally equal distribution of income. However, many of the Western European countries and the socialist countries have distributions of income that are significantly less unequal than that in the United States.

A **Lorenz curve** can be used to illustrate the degree of inequality in the distribution of income. A Lorenz curve based on the distribution of income in the United States in 1984 is shown in Fig. 13.4. The horizontal axis measures each 20 percent of the families, and the vertical axis measures their cumulative shares of total income. The bottom 20 percent got 4.7 percent of total income, the lowest 40 percent got 15.7 percent, etc. If income were distributed equally, we would get a straight Lorenz curve at a 45° angle. Instead we get the curved line in Fig. 13.4. The degree of inequality can be measured by taking the area between the straight line and the Lorenz curve (area A) and comparing it to the area below the 45° line (area A plus area B). The technical name for this ratio is the **Gini coefficient.** The lower this ratio is the lower the degree of inequality; the higher the ratio, the greater the degree of inequality. In 1960, the Gini coefficient for the distribution of income in the U.S. was 0.364; in 1970, it was 0.354; and in 1980, it was 0.365.

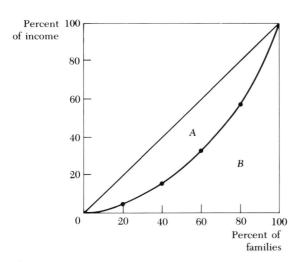

Figure 13.4 A Lorenz curve.

6. Do you think that income should be distributed more equally than it is? Why or why not?

7. According to the Gini coefficient, the distribution of income in the United States became less unequal from 1960 to 1970 and then more unequal from 1970 to 1980. Can you suggest some reasons why this may have happened? What do you suppose has happened to the degree of inequality in income distribution since 1980?

Why is income distributed so unequally in the United States? Fundamentally, it is a function of the ownership of resources and the prices that those resources get. Individuals possess different labor and nonlabor resources, and different resources get different prices. Furthermore, the private market system relies on those very differences to allocate and motivate resources.

The Influence of Property

The U.S. economy is basically a capitalist system with private property as one of its most fundamental characteristics. The ownership of land, money, and capital resources is even more unequally distributed than income. This fact is demonstrated in Tables 13.3 and 13.4. Wealth statistics for the United States are not readily available, but studies done in the mid-1960s and the mid-1970s show that the poorest families have very little in personal assets, such as private homes, real estate, savings accounts, corporate stocks, bonds, etc. Most of these assets are owned by the top 5 percent of the population, in fact. Tables 13.3 and 13.4 both show that income-producing forms of wealth are even more unequally distributed than general forms of wealth.

Table 13.3 THE DISTRIBUTION OF WEALTH, 1962

		WEALTH, %	INCOME-PRODUCING WEALTH, %	CORPORATE STOCK, %
Poorest	20%	0	0	0
Second	20%	2	0	0
Third	20%	6	2	0
Fourth	20%	17	9	4
Richest	20%	75	89	96
Top	5%	50	70	83
Top	1%	31	50	61

Source: D. Projector and G. Weiss, Survey of Financial Characteristics of Consumers, Federal Reserve Board, 1966.

Table 13.4 THE DISTRIBUTION OF PERSONAL WEALTH, 1976

TYPE OF WEALTH	PERCENTAGE SHARE OF TOP 1/2 PERCENT	PERCENTAGE SHARE OF TOP 1 PERCENT
Total assets	13.8	18.3
Real estate	8.6	12.6
Corporate stock	38.3	46.0
Bonds	25.7	29.8
Cash	6.7	10.9
Notes & mortgages	27.2	36.9
Life insurance	4.4	7.1

Source: Statistical Abstract of the United States, 1984.

Table 13.4 shows the shares of different forms of personal wealth owned by the top ½ percent and the top 1 percent of all persons. For example, about 2.2 million individuals hold almost 11 percent of all the cash in the United States, and about 1.1 million individuals hold almost 40 percent of all the corporate stock. This unequal distribution of wealth contributes to the unequal distribution of income in the United States. Based on 1979 data from the Internal Revenue Service, the 81 percent of U.S. families with incomes below $25,000 got 92 percent of their income from wages and salaries, while the significantly less than 1 percent of the families with incomes in excess of $1,000,000 got 20 percent of their incomes from wages and salaries and 80 percent from ownership of property.

A new survey by the federal government conducted in 1984 shows that the top 2 percent of families control 30 percent of all financial assets, 50 percent of all stock in private hands, 20 percent of all real estate, 39 percent of taxable bonds, and 23 percent of individual checking account deposits.

8. Do you or your family members own any income-producing wealth?

The Influence of Labor Incomes

Approximately 80 percent of personal income in the United States comes from wages and salaries. And income from mental and/or physical labor is also unequally distributed. There are a variety of reasons for the different wages and salaries that individuals receive for their contributions to economic activity. First of all, the labor that people perform is not homogeneous, and, second, there are differences in the jobs that people hold.

The capabilities, training, and intelligence of different individuals will have a great deal to do with their respective incomes; consequently, the distribution of these attributes will contribute to an unequal distribution of income. Some people are more productive in certain tasks than others are. For example, someone with physical strength is likely to be able to lift and stack more bales of hay in an hour than someone with less strength, or someone with mathematical aptitude can more quickly and easily balance a firm's books than can someone without such aptitude. Some people, because of their concentration and motivation, actually produce more than other people in specific activities over a given period of time. In general, the higher the level of productivity, or the greater the contribution to economic output, of an individual worker, the higher her or his wages will be. Consequently, differences in productivity among human laborers account for some of the difference in labor incomes.

Different people also have different skills. A large number of people are available for jobs that require minimal skills (e.g., clerks, sales personnel, custodians, etc.). As a result, they will usually command low wages in labor markets. Others, who make up a smaller segment of the population, have professional skills (doctors, lawyers, economists) or possess unique qualities (athletes, entertainers) that earn them higher incomes. The more specialized the skill or the longer the period of training or education necessary to develop a skill, the higher the wages of people with those skills will tend to be. For example, people with college educations, on the average, earn more than people with only high school degrees. For men, a college degree increases potential lifetime earnings by $329,000, according to a 1984 report from the Census Bureau. For women, a college degree increases potential lifetime earnings by $142,000.

Age and experience also contribute to the unequal distribution of income. People who are older and have accumulated work experience tend to be paid more than younger, inexperienced workers. An English professor who has taught for 20 years in a university earns more than a colleague who has taught for only 2 years. Individuals also have different attitudes and preferences about work and income. Some people have a strong preference for work over leisure. Some people have very strong desires to earn high incomes. In fact, capitalism is a system that relies on monetary incentives for productive activity and, as a result, has developed a hierarchy of jobs with different levels of pay. People are motivated to work hard in order to move up the job ladder and to get higher incomes. Racial and sexual differences also have an impact on the unequal distribution of income. As we shall see in some detail in the next section, white males in the United States tend to earn higher incomes than nonwhite males, and males tend to earn more than females.

In addition, differences in the kinds of jobs that people perform contribute to inequality in income distribution. The type of work performed and the conditions surrounding it influence compensation. Dangerous or unpleasant work is often rewarded with premium wages (e.g., coal miners or garbage collectors). Some people, on the other hand, may be willing to give up higher wages in return for significant control over the work that they do. Teachers or people who work for small businesses tend to be paid less than people whose work is more directly controlled by supervisors or institutional demands. The organizational structure of an individual's employment also influences their wages and salaries. People who work for large corporations tend to get paid more. Workers who are members of labor unions usually have higher wages than nonunion workers (see Chapter 14). Finally, the location of a job may influence an individual's remuneration. Someone who works in Idaho with exactly the same job, skills, and experience as a person who works in Los Angeles will tend to be paid less.

9. Why is the "payoff" for a college degree higher for men than for women?

Many factors account for the differences in the wages and salaries that people earn for the work that they do, and these factors help to explain the inequality of income distribution in the United States. It is implicit in most of the explanations above that market forces play an important role in determining the different wages and salaries that individuals receive in our society. The necessity of a medical education, for example, limits the supply of doctors and hence tends to increase their incomes. The widespread demand for the records and other products of Michael Jackson accounts for his astronomical income. On the other hand, there are many nonmarket conditions that also influence people's wages and salaries. The management of households and childcare in the United States is predominantly performed by women, and that activity is unpaid work. People's class backgrounds have an impact on the development of their skills and attitudes toward work. Luck—being in the right place at the right time—can play a role in the jobs and the incomes that people have. Furthermore, labor incomes tend to be positively related to **property income;** that is, those with high labor incomes are also likely to have property income. This further contributes to the unequal distribution of income.

The Influence of Race and Gender

The existence of racism and sexism in our society contributes to income inequality in a number of ways. **Racism** and **sexism** are systems of social, political, cultural, ideological, and economic domination, whereby one group has less power and control over decisions than another group. Instances of both racism and sexism are manifested in numerous noneconomic ways in the day-to-day life of our society. In addition, racial minorities and women in the United States are systematically less well off in economic terms than white males.

The racial and ethnic composition of the U.S. population is quite diverse. Approximately 80 percent of all Americans are white, while 11.5 percent are black, 6.5 percent are Hispanic, 1.6 percent are of Asian origin, and fewer than 1 percent are descended from Native American tribes. Blacks, Native Americans, and Hispanics are more likely to be unemployed than whites. In 1980, the unemployment rate for all white persons over 16 was 5.8 percent; for blacks, it was 11.8 percent; for

Native Americans, it was 13.7 percent; and for Hispanics, it was 8.9 percent. Members of racial minority populations in the United States are less likely to work in professional and white-collar occupations than whites, and more likely to work in the lower-paying blue-collar and service-sector jobs. Fifty-four percent of whites work in white-collar jobs, and 60 percent of blacks and Hispanics work in blue-collar and service jobs. As a consequence of these factors and outright racial discrimination, nonwhites in the United States, on the average, earn less than whites do. Table 13.5 shows data comparing the median income of black families with that of white families for various years from 1955 to 1984. The median income of black families has consistently been significantly below that of white families. Some of the decline since 1975 reflects an increase in black families headed by women, and some of it reflects the impact of the recessions of 1980–1982. Similarly, in 1979, the median income of Hispanic families was 74 percent of the median income of white families, and the corresponding figure for Puerto Rican families was 45 percent.

The incidence of poverty also demonstrates differences among racial groups. In 1980, fewer than 10 percent of whites in the United States were classified by the federal government as being in poverty, while the figure for blacks was almost 30 percent; for Native Americans, 27.5 percent; for Asians, 13.1 percent; and for Hispanics, 23.5 percent.

These data suggest that racial factors have an important impact on the unequal distribution of income in the United States. In a 1982 report to President Reagan, the U.S. Commission on Civil Rights concluded that, despite a generation of civil rights and affirmative action legislation, discrimination persists "virtually everywhere, at every age level, at every educational level, at every skill level."

Similarly, a study in 1981, prepared for the Equal Employment Opportunity Commission by the National Research Council (a branch of the National Academy of

Table 13.5 MEDIAN BLACK FAMILY INCOME AS A PERCENTAGE OF MEDIAN WHITE FAMILY INCOME

YEAR	PERCENTAGE
1955	55
1960	55
1965	55
1970	61
1975	62
1979	57
1982	55
1983	56
1984	56

Source: Statistical Abstract of the United States, 1986.

Sciences) and focusing on the economic position of women, found that "despite the tremendous changes that have occurred in the labor market over the past 20 years, there has been no change in the relative earnings of men and women."

During the 1960s and 1970s, in response to economic and social trends, there was a tremendous increase in the participation of women in the paid labor force. In 1960, about 40 percent of women over 16 were in the labor force (working for wages or looking for paid work); by 1980, women's labor force participation rate was up to 53 percent. Yet women are concentrated in low-paying jobs, tend to work for low-paying concerns, and are "systematically underpaid." Table 13.6 presents information on the incomes of year-round, full-time female workers compared to the incomes of year-round, full-time male workers for various years from 1955 to 1983.

Men and women are often segregated into different occupations, and usually, the women are concentrated in the lower-paying occupations. Seventy percent of the nation's working men and 54 percent of working women are concentrated in jobs done largely by one sex. One-half of the nation's working women are in occupations that are at least 70 percent female, and one-fourth of working women are in occupations that are at least 95 percent female. Women constitute 96 percent of registered nurses, 99 percent of secretaries, 90 percent of bookkeepers and accounting clerks, 90 percent of licensed practical nurses and health aids, 88 percent of waitresses and waiters, and 85 percent of textile machine operators. Men constitute 95 percent of engineers; 99 percent of auto mechanics; 98 percent of carpenters; 95 percent of machinists; 94 percent of heavy equipment operators; 88 percent of guards, police, and firefighters; and 85 percent of economists. For many jobs that require equal educational levels and comparable skills, women are systematically paid less than men. In addition to these income data, poverty in the United States is becoming increasingly feminized. In 1960, 20 percent of all families below the poverty line

Table 13.6 MEDIAN MONEY INCOME OF YEAR-ROUND, FULL-TIME FEMALE WORKERS AS A PERCENTAGE OF MEDIAN MONEY INCOME OF YEAR-ROUND, FULL-TIME MALE WORKERS

YEAR	PERCENTAGE
1955	64
1960	60
1965	60
1970	59
1975	59
1980	60
1981	60
1983	64

Source: Statistical Abstract of the United States, 1986.

Nicole Hollander, *My Weight Is Always Perfect for My Height—Which Varies*, St. Martin's Press, New York. © 1982 by Field Enterprises and Nicole Hollander.

were headed by women with no husband present. By 1981, this figure had increased to 47 percent.

The influence of occupation-linked gender differences and sex discrimination thus also contributes to inequality in the distribution of income in the United States.

10. **Why do economic differences on race and sex lines persist in the United States?**

11. **In recent years, the civil rights and women's movements have challenged racism and sexism. These struggles have led to legislation regarding equal opportunity and affirmative action programs, as well as to some court cases. In a case in Colorado in the late 1970s, a group of nurses sued the city and county of Denver for sex discrimination. Tree trimmers, sign painters, and repairmen were all paid more than the nurses. U.S. District Judge Fred Winner decided against the nurses' claim and concluded that: "This is a case pregnant with the possibility of disrupting the entire economic system of the United States of America. . . . I'm not going to restructure the entire economy of the U.S." What was Winner worried about? Does the operation of the U.S. economy require that women be paid less than men (even for comparable work)? Why/why not?**

CONCLUSION

In this chapter we have briefly considered the operation of resource markets and the distribution of income in the United States. Resource markets, through the forces of supply and demand, determine the costs of production for firms and the incomes of households. Many factors account for the relatively unequal distribution of income in the United States. People own different resources, the jobs they do are different, and race and sex both influence wages and salaries. We conclude this chapter with an article from *Dollars and Sense* assessing recent trends in the distribution of income.

SLIMMER MIDDLE, BIGGER BOTTOM

Reagan Rearranges Income Distribution

Last year, Treasury Secretary Donald Regan opposed a tax increase for people who earn more than $50,000 a year on the grounds that it would "strike squarely at our great middle-income class." But if aimed at our great middle, this pitch was high and outside: 90% of the country earns less than $50,000 a year.

The middle of U.S. income distribution is an elusive target; lately it has been getting thinner and thinner. From the 1950s through the early 1970s, there was a gradual trend toward income equality; more recently this trend has been reversed. In the 1980s, the rich are getting richer, and more people are becoming poor. The Reagan administration bears part of the blame: since the last election, both tax and spending policies have been tilted toward the rich. . . .

WHAT'S A GOVERNMENT TO DO?

The recovery is officially rumored to be going full blast; according to the business press, happy days have been here again for more than a year. Unemployment is now only slightly worse than when Jimmy Carter left office. For Reagan, this is a triumph of sorts—just as spilling a puzzle and then picking up most of the pieces is an accomplishment for a toddler. Inflation is temporarily quite low, which is common after a severe recession. . . . But the pieces of the U.S. economy have been put back in a somewhat different design than before. Some parts of America are back more emphatically than others, as can be seen in the changes in both spending and tax policies.

For all the talk of budget-cutting, Reagan's proposed 1984 budget was about 13% greater than Carter's 1980 budget, corrected for inflation. But some things have grown much faster. The leading growth sector of the federal budget has been interest on the national debt, up a whopping 51% (after inflation) in those four years. In the same years, real military spending jumped 34%. Total benefits paid to individuals rose 15%, as a result of the increased number of people eligible for Social Security and the rise in unemployment. But benefit levels per person failed to keep pace with inflation. Other federal spending, on highways, environmental protection, job training, and all the rest, fell by 35%.

(continued)

Paying interest on the national debt amounts to a transfer of money from all taxpayers to those rich enough to own government bonds. . . . The massive deficits and high interest rates of the past few years have driven up these interest payments, to the delight of bondholders. On the other hand, benefits to individuals, which go largely to the elderly and poor, have been cut back. The combination of these two changes has made federal spending far more favorable to the rich.

The same bias can be seen even more dramatically in taxes. In 1981, Ronald Reagan claimed that his income tax cut was "not merely a shift of wealth between different sets of taxpayers." Indeed, it was no *mere* shift, but a massive one. Much ballyhooed as an equal, across-the-board reduction in everyone's taxes, Reagan's tax cut contained three hidden biases which made it immensely more valuable to the rich.

First, since income taxes are progressive—the higher a person's income, the larger the percentage they pay in taxes—an equal cut in tax *rates* gives a bigger break to those with bigger incomes. . . .

Second, the income tax cut only changed the rates you pay on the portion of your income that is left after deductions and exemptions. Unlike most previous tax cuts, the Reagan cut did not increase the size of the personal exemptions and standard deduction. For poor families, the standard deduction and personal exemptions can amount to a large proportion of family income. Thus this omission was much more important for low-income taxpayers than the change in rates in higher brackets. For high-income taxpayers, the rates in their brackets are crucial, while the exemptions and personal deduction are such a small proportion of their income that they hardly matter.

Finally, the claim that all tax rates were cut equally in 1981 is simply a lie. A careful reading of the 1981 tax cut reveals that on each family's first $86,000 of income, the rates were, indeed, cut by 23%—but over a period of three years. Income from $86,000 to $162,000, however, got its 23% rate reduction all at once, in the first year. And taxes on income beyond $162,000 got cut even more—by 26% or 29%, depending on how much more than $162,000 was earned.

The result of all this generosity can be seen in table 1. It shows the tax burden as a percentage of income at different levels in 1980 and 1984 (assuming in each case that the family's income just kept up with inflation for those four years).

As if it weren't enough to cut a progressive tax, the Reagan administration, with congressional help, also increased a regressive one—the Social Security tax. When the income tax cut and the Social Security tax hike are combined, few people come out ahead. The poorest families saw their tax burdens increase the most; the richest had their taxes cut substantially. The break-even point was at around $35,000, which may sound like the middle—but it's not. Five-sixths of all U.S. families earn less than $35,000 a year.

(continued)

Table 1 THE TAX BURDEN BEFORE AND AFTER REAGAN

FAMILY INCOME 1980	AS A PERCENTAGE OF FAMILY INCOME			
	INCOME TAX ALONE		INCOME AND SOCIAL SECURITY TAXES	
	1980	1984	1980	1984
$10,000	3.7%	5.2%	9.9%	12.2%
$20,000	11.3%	11.1%	17.5%	18.1%
$35,000	18.9%	18.4%	25.0%	25.4%
$50,000	24.2%	22.1%	30.4%	29.1%
$100,000	35.7%	30.8%	38.9%	35.0%
$250,000	49.5%	39.2%	50.8%	40.9%

Source: F. Ackerman, *Hazardous to Our Wealth.*

AFTER EQUALITY

The Reagan administration's tax and budget programs are only part of the problem. They come as a knockout punch to an economy that was already moving towards more inequality because of long-term changes in its industrial structure.

Most people's image of income distribution is that it doesn't change much from year to year. That is to say, the percentage of all personal income received by the poorest 20% of the population, the richest 20%, or any such group, is about the same each year. In fact, this is not quite as true as it used to be, as seen in Table 2. The top line shows the share of all personal income received by the poorest fifth of the population—the families with incomes of less than about $11,000 in 1982. The second line shows the share of the middle three-fifths:—families who earned between $11,000 and $38,000 in 1982. The third line shows the share of the richest fifth.

(continued)

Table 2 DISTRIBUTION OF FAMILY INCOME, 1950–1982

	1950	1960	1970	1979	1982
Poorest 20%	4.5%	4.8%	5.4%	5.2%	4.7%
Middle 60%	52.7%	54.0%	53.6%	53.2%	52.6%
Richest 20%	42.8%	41.3%	40.9%	41.6%	42.7%
Total, all families	100.0%	100.0%	100.0%	100.0%	100.0%

Source: Census Bureau, Current Population Reports, P—60 series, various years. Some columns do not add up to exactly 100.0% because of rounding-off errors.

From the 1950s through the early 1970s, the share of income going to the poorest fifth of the population gradually increased. By 1970, that share was almost a full percentage point higher than it had been twenty years earlier. Creeping progress, but progress nonetheless. But in the late 1970s, the bottom fifth began to lose ground; by 1982, . . . each group's position was almost the same as it had been in 1950.

The amount of money lost by the poorest fifth in recent years—0.5% from 1979 to 1982—sounds small when expressed as a percentage. In fact, it amounts to $8 billion, or more than $600 apiece for each of the roughly 12 million families in the poorest fifth of the population.

Other measures confirm that there was a high point of relative equality in the late 1960s and early 1970s, not equalled before or since. The ratio of black to white income was higher in those years; the number of people falling below the government's official poverty line was lower.

The conscious policies of the Reagan administration have done their bit toward this retreat from equality, but in a capitalist economy, there are always strong pressures towards the concentration of wealth in a few hands. If you have money, you earn interest on it; if you need to borrow money, you have to pay for it. Businesses, seeking to maximize profits, are always looking for ways to replace their most skilled, highly paid workers with unskilled labor or machines. Profits go to pay dividends to those who already have enough wealth to own stocks. Thousands of small businesses are started every year, and most sink quickly. A handful grow rapidly, swallowing less successful businesses along the way, and make their owners rich.

In light of such continual pressures towards *inequality,* it is the periods of progress toward equality, as in the 1950s and 1960s, which appear remarkable. Two major forces raised the incomes of the poor in the post–World War II era: the movement into industrial employment, and the growth of the welfare state.

In 1950, 12% of the labor force worked in agriculture, and 3% worked as servants. While employing only a small portion of the labor force, "private household service," as government statisticians call it, was a major occupation among low-income women, especially black women. Farmworkers and servants have long been some of the worst paid members of the labor force. These were also the years of growth in relatively well-paying industrial jobs in the Midwest and Northeast, and of government employment throughout the country. As millions of people left farms and kitchens for factories and government jobs, the incomes of those at the bottom were pushed up rapidly.

But by the 1980s, only 3% of the labor force still worked in agriculture, and 1% in household service. The long exodus from these low-paying jobs was all but over. Instead, the new migration was *out* of the formerly booming, frequently unionized industries of the 1950s and 1960s, into usually lower paid jobs in the service sector.

(continued)

In 1948, 57% of all jobs were in the service sector; today, 70% are. These new jobs pay lower average wages; they also tend to be more polarized in terms of earnings than are manufacturing jobs. Many service sector jobs are concentrated in low-wage occupations, like department store clerks, food service workers, and clerical workers. On the other end of the spectrum, the service sector also employs many highly paid professional and technical workers, with not too many other jobs in between.

The Bureau of Labor Statistics recently compared the twenty fastest growing industries with the twenty slowest growing ones. The declining industries were primarily in manufacturing; their average weekly wages were $310 a week. The high-growth industries were primarily service-producing; they accounted for 20% of all jobs and paid average weekly wages of $210. Major shifts in patterns of employment, formerly a force for equality, are now a force for inequality.

The changes in government spending in the 1950s and 1960s also promoted equality. Benefits such as Social Security, unemployment compensation, and welfare spread rapidly. Although government benefits provided only 7% of personal income in 1950, they comprised 14% of all personal income by the late 1970s. The growth of the welfare state, particularly the commitment to security for senior citizens, boosted the incomes of those on the bottom. This, too, is in decline; it is here that Reaganomics has collided with former pressures for equality.

Neither the welfare state or high-wage industrial employment fell from the sky; both were the results of political battles of previous generations. Industrial wages were relatively high as a result of the successes of CIO unions in the 1930s and 1940s; the growth of government benefits stemmed from the progressive political consensus and reform movements of the 1930s and 1960s. To stop the new drift into inequality will require similar political changes—a new wave of unionization in today's growing low-wage occupations, and a renewed commitment to social justice in national politics. Otherwise, the ominous direction of the early 1980s— toward greater and greater inequality—will only become worse.

Sources: Ackerman, *Reaganomics, Rhetoric vs. Reality;* Bluestone and Harrison, *The Economic State of the Union in 1984,* unpublished paper; Levy and Michel, *The Way We'll Be in 1984,* Urban Institute discussion paper.

12. **What factors account for the lower share of total income for the bottom 20 percent of families since 1970?**

13. **Should people be concerned with the tendency toward increasing inequality suggested by this article? Why or why not?**

KEY CONCEPTS

derived demand

marginal factor cost

marginal revenue product

marginal physical product

size distribution of income

Lorenz curve

Gini coefficient

property income

sexism

racism

REVIEW QUESTIONS

1. Why is the market for unskilled labor relatively competitive?

2. What influences a firm's *demand* for a particular resource?

3. A firm will tend to use that amount of a resource at which its MRP equals its MFC. Explain why.

4. In the September 17, 1984, issue of *Business Week*, there was an article titled, "The U.S. May Finally Have Too Many Lawyers." Using the economic analysis of resource markets, explain how this could happen.

5. Money is a resource; it can be used to finance capital projects. What influences the demand for credit? What influences the supply of credit? What is the price of credit?

6. In 1984, Michael Jackson and the Jackson Brothers were paid $5 million for two Pepsi television commercials. In that same year, a Louis Harris poll reported that a significant majority of people in the United States thought that star athletes, entertainers, and corporate executives were all overpaid. What do you think? Why?

7. Do you think that the federal government should develop explicit policies to redistribute income to reduce the inequality of the distribution of income? Why or why not?

8. What are the sources of inequality in the distribution of income? Which ones might be reformed to reduce income inequality? What political and/or systemic limits are there on the redistribution of income?

SUGGESTED READINGS

Edmund Blair Bolles, 1984. *Who Owns America?*, Evans. An anecdotal treatment of property ownership in the United States.

Richard Edwards, Michael Reich, and Thomas Weisskopf (eds.), 1978. *The Capitalist System* (2nd ed.), Prentice-Hall. See Chapters 8, 9, and 10 on inequality, sexism, and racism.

Arthur Okun, 1975. *Equality and Efficiency*, Brookings. A classic liberal statement about income redistribution in capitalism.

Lars Osberg, 1984. *Economic Inequality in the United States*, M. E. Sharpe, Inc. Theoretical perspectives on income distribution and data.

Michael Reich, 1981. *Racial Inequality*, Princeton University Press. Data on and analysis of racial inequality in the United States from a leftist perspective.

Stephen J. Rose, 1983. *Social Stratification in the United States* (3rd ed.), Social Graphics Company. An excellent description and analysis of income distribution in the United States, accompanied by a poster showing the relationships among income, race, sex, age, and occupation.

Lester Thurow, 1980. *The Zero-Sum Society*, Basic Books. In Chapter 7, this leading liberal economist focuses on income distribution and redistribution.

Howard P. Tuckman, 1973. *The Economics of the Rich*, Random House. On the production and reproduction of wealth and its relationship to the distribution of income.

Howard Wachtel, 1984. *Labor and the Economy*, Academic Press. See Chapters 8 and 9 on income distribution and Chapter 12 on the economics of discrimination.

14
Chapter

Corporations and Labor Unions

INTRODUCTION

Now that we have examined the economic theory of the competitive and noncompetitive market structures and explored the results of different types of firms, it is worthwhile to take a more "realistic" approach to the *firm*. The corporation, as a productive unit in the American economic system, has become a dominant institution. In Chapter 12 we saw some statistics that showed the impact of the 100 and 500 largest industrial corporations on several economic categories—manufacturing employment, manufacturing assets, etc. American corporations stand out for consideration in any discussion of production and how resources are allocated in the United States. Therefore, this chapter will concentrate on American corporations: a description of what they are, the economic power they have, *and* an analysis of what that power implies.

In Chapter 13 we surveyed the operation of resource markets. We suggested that in addition to the forces of supply and demand, labor unions have an impact on labor markets. Labor unions have also emerged as important institutions in the structure of the U.S. economy. The chapter will conclude with a brief examination of the history and the effects of labor unions in the economy.

THE CORPORATION

Corporations are legal entities that engage in the provision of goods and services for the public. They have legal authority to enter into contracts with other parties. The characteristic of corporations that distinguishes them from other productive units — e.g., partnerships or proprietorships — is that the individuals who own the corporation, the stockholders, have *limited liability*. Stockholders are liable to the corporation's creditors only to the extent of the value of their stock. They cannot be sued by creditors. This differs from other forms of business, in which individuals who operate them *are personally liable* to creditors. This gives the corporation a great advantage in amassing financial resources to underwrite production. Issues of corporate stock can raise capital, and this capital base can be used to raise further capital through bank loans, etc. Corporations have used this ability to form large productive operations — large plants, nationwide productive and distributive facilities, and even worldwide networks. The technological advances of the Industrial Revolution spurred the development of larger and larger corporations, and modern technology continues to do the same.

Through these legal advantages and historical developments, many American corporations have grown to be quite large in terms of assets, profits, employees, and economic (and political) power.

How many corporations are there in the United States? And just how large have they grown? The following tables should help us to answer these questions. Table 14.1 presents information on the types and numbers of business firms in the United States in 1982.

In 1982, there were more than 2.8 million corporations in the United States; they constituted 20 percent of businesses but had 90 percent of all business receipts. So corporations handle the vast majority of business transactions in the United States. They also earn most of the profits in the economy.

Which corporations are the biggest, and how big are they? Table 14.2 shows the 25 largest industrial corporations in the United States in 1984, ranked by sales. It also shows total assets, number of employees, net income for each, and net income as a percentage of stockholders' equity. (Stockholders' equity is the value of the outstanding shares of stock of a corporation.)

Table 14.3 presents data on the 1000 largest industrial, banking, insurance, retailing, transportation, and utility corporations for 1984. Note that these 1000 companies, which constitute less than 1 percent of all corporations, accounted for almost 25 percent of *all* employment in the United States in 1984. Their gross sales were even larger than the value of the gross national product for 1984. And their combined net income was almost 50 percent of all corporate profits for 1984.

Some American corporations have grown very large indeed and dominate certain sectors of our economy. So what? The question is a good one, and the answers to it will differ among those of us in the United States who are affected by corporations. Some will argue that the large size and dominance of corporations is necessary to organize production, to provide employment, and to produce goods and services efficiently. Others might use economic arguments, pointing out that almost all large

Table 14.1 TYPES OF U.S. BUSINESS FIRMS, 1982

TYPES OF BUSINESS ORGANIZATIONS	NUMBERS OF FIRMS		PERCENTAGE OF TOTAL RECEIPTS
	MILLIONS	AS PERCENTAGE OF TOTAL	
Proprietorships	10.1	70	6
Partnerships	1.5	10	4
Corporations	2.9	20	90
Totals	14.5	100	100

Source: *Statistical Abstract of the United States*, 1986.

Table 14.2 THE TOP 25 INDUSTRIAL CORPORATIONS FOR 1984

COMPANY*	SALES ($ BILLIONS)	ASSETS ($ BILLIONS)	NET INCOME ($ MILLIONS)	NET INCOME AS A PERCENTAGE OF STOCKHOLDERS' EQUITY	EMPLOYEES
Exxon	90.9	63.3	5,528	19.2	150,000
General Motors	83.9	52.1	4,516	18.7	748,000
Mobil	56.0	41.9	1,268	9.3	178,900
Ford Motor	52.4	27.5	2,907	29.6	383,700
Texaco	47.3	37.7	306	2.3	68,088
IBM	45.9	42.8	6,582	24.9	394,930
Du Pont	35.9	24.1	1,431	11.7	157,783
AT&T	33.2	39.8	1,370	9.1	365,000
General Electric	27.9	24.7	2,280	18.1	300,000
Standard Oil (Ind.)	26.9	25.7	2,183	17.4	53,581
Chevron	26.8	36.4	1,534	10.4	37,761
Atlantic Richfield	24.7	22.1	567	5.7	39,400
Shell Oil	20.7	23.7	1,772	14.2	34,699
Chrysler	19.6	9.0	2,380	72.0	100,439
U.S. Steel	18.3	19.0	493	8.1	88,753
United Technologies	16.3	9.9	645	15.5	205,500
Phillips Petroleum	15.5	17.0	810	12.2	29,300
Occidental Petroleum	15.4	12.3	569	11.3	40,630
Tenneco	14.8	18.2	631	9.3	98,000
Sun	14.5	12.8	538	10.2	37,000
ITT	14.0	13.3	448	7.4	252,000
Procter & Gamble	12.9	8.9	890	17.5	61,700
R.J. Reynolds Industries	11.9	9.3	1,210	25.8	97,551
Standard Oil (Ohio)	11.7	17.5	1,488	17.7	44,200
Dow Chemical	11.4	11.4	585	11.6	49,800

*Ranked by sales.

Source: Adapted from *Fortune*, April 29, 1985.

Table 14.3 THE ASSETS, SALES, INCOME, AND EMPLOYEES OF THE 1000 LARGEST INDUSTRIALS, BANKS, DIVERSIFIED SERVICE COMPANIES, LIFE INSURANCE COMPANIES, DIVERSIFIED FINANCIAL COMPANIES, RETAILING COMPANIES, TRANSPORTATION COMPANIES, AND UTILITIES, 1984

	ASSETS ($ BILLIONS)	SALES ($ BILLIONS)	NET INCOME ($ BILLIONS)	EMPLOYEES
500 largest industrials	1,409	1,759	86.4	14,195,792
100 largest commercial banks	1,569	1,101*	7.8	895,770
100 largest diversified service companies	208	180	5.5	1,601,878
50 largest life insurance companies	526	76	3.3[†]	435,160
100 largest diversified financial companies	844	171[‡]	4.9	646,440
50 largest retailing companies	297	170	8.2	3,624,016
50 largest transportation companies	118	107[§]	5.9	965,902
50 largest utilities	467	202[§]	22.6	1,282,293
Totals	5,438	3,766	144.6	23,647,251

*Deposits.
[†]Net gain from operations.
[‡]Revenues.
[§]Operating revenues.
Source: Fortune, April 29, 1985, and June 10, 1985.

corporations are in concentrated industries and are thus likely to be theoretically deficient because of their economic power. (If it were a perfectly competitive economy, there would be many more companies, and none would be so dominant.) Others might be less theoretical and say that corporations are only out to make a buck, have too much economic power, and sometimes do things to the detriment of society.

1. How do you feel about corporations?

2. Would you like to work for one? Why or why not?

3. How would you like to work for GM, where you would be one of more than 700,000 employees?

4. Why are some American corporations so big?

5. What company in the top 25 in Table 14.2 had the highest rate of return for 1984 (net income as a percentage of stockholders' equity)? Why?

THE ROLE OF PROFITS IN THE CORPORATE SYSTEM

In 1974, the Chairman of General Motors, Richard C. Gerstenberg, argued in the *New York Times* that "there is no conflict between corporate profits and social progress. Not one of our grand national goals can be accomplished unless business prospers. Profits fuel the growth of our nation, and our future depends on the profitability of free enterprise." At one level, he is correct: Given corporate concentration and economic power, we are dependent on **corporate profitability** for our jobs, our products, capital accumulation, technological change, and so on.

Corporations are in business to earn profits, and in the process of doing so, they do provide jobs, investment, goods and services, and economic growth. If they are profitable, they do pay taxes that help to finance social programs, and they often make contributions to civic and educational endeavors.

However, there are counterarguments that inform public sentiments about corporations and lead to public opinion polls concluding that corporate profits are too high. The following list of complaints of corporate wrongdoing and questionable behavior is a long one and *not* exhaustive: pollution for decades without cost to the corporation, exploitation of workers (minorities, women, children, illegal immigrants, etc.), three-martini lunches charged off as business expenses, corporate bribery of foreign officials, illegal corporate political campaign contributions, high oil-company profits in the midst of gas lines, food additives that destroy our health, disproportionate economic and political power, misleading advertising, and so on—all to make a buck.

Corporations have tended to respond to these criticisms defensively. Gerstenberg charged that "most [Americans] are ill-equipped to recognize the economics in these issues, much less to recommend the economic remedies. This lack of public understanding," he suggested, "seriously threatens the continuation of our competitive private enterprise system."

In 1980 the *Wall Street Journal* and the Gallup Organization polled about 800 chief executives of small, medium, and large companies on their perceptions of the public's opinion of business. Almost two-thirds of the executives from medium and large businesses thought the public's opinion was unfavorable, whereas only 36 percent of the small-business executives thought so. "The public thinks when business reports a profit, it goes right into our pockets. They have to be told the truth," said one business leader.

The business people had plenty of ideas about how to improve the image of business in the country. Small-business leaders suggested the importance of product quality and ethical standards. Many of the executives of the large companies emphasized communication and education, based on the conclusion that the low regard for business comes from a lack of knowledge. Suggested remedies ranged from getting the "media and press on the side of business," increasing corporate involvement in community issues, teaching more courses about **free enterprise** in high schools and colleges, and making advertising better. "We need to start in the elementary schools, with teachers and students both," said one respondent. An energy executive said, "We need to make people realize that it is business and not the government that provides 96 million jobs in this country." And a transportation company official added, "We need to make it clear that business profits are not just arbitrarily squirreled away, but reinvested for the benefit of the company, its workers and the public. If we can get this across, we may be able to change the adverse to at least normal."

6. Is "lack of knowledge" the basis for the public's "low regard" for business? Why are corporate leaders so defensive? Is the public, in fact, ignorant about the role of corporations and the importance of profits to our society?

7. What is your reaction to the recommended courses of action to improve the image of business?

8. Does your school receive contributions from corporations? Why do corporations make such contributions? How do you feel about such contributions?

FREE ENTERPRISE VERSUS THE GOVERNMENT

A perennial issue surrounding corporate power concerns the relationship between corporations and the federal government. Corporate officials constantly complain of **governmental regulation** of and interference with their business, e.g., occupational health and safety legislation, and environmental protection legislation. They argue that this restriction on their business hampers their initiative and independence in bringing the goods to the American consumer. Sometimes they even imply that continued regulation will dry up their profits and hence their corporations. This view sees corporations and the government as adversaries.

Critics of this position argue that, if anything, regulation and governmental controls over business merely increase the costs of business—which the corporations then succeed, through market power, in passing on to consumers. Beyond that, a more fundamental criticism is offered. In most cases, governmental regulation is designed to *protect* corporations from competition. An oft-cited example is the protection the railroad and trucking industries receive from the ICC. The government, rather than being an adversary, is an ally of business. Also, in many cases, the government has provided direct assistance in the form of loans to troubled corporations such as Lockheed, Chrysler, and the Penn Central. This symbiotic relationship has its roots in common goals shared by business and government, such as economic growth, profits, employment, technological advance, and defense. Furthermore, it can be argued, corporations have substantial political power in the government through lobbying, direct campaign contributions, and corporate representatives in all branches of the government.

Two lighthearted but nevertheless serious treatments of this issue follow.

THE *MODERN* LITTLE RED HEN

Once upon a time, there was a little red hen who scratched about the barnyard until she uncovered some grains of wheat. She called her neighbors and said, "If we plant this wheat, we shall have bread to eat. Who will help me plant it?"

"Not I," said the cow.

"Not I," said the duck.

"Not I," said the pig.

"Not I," said the goose.

"Then I will," said the little red hen. And she did. The wheat grew tall and ripened into golden grain. "Who will help me reap my wheat?" asked the little red hen.

"Not I," said the duck.

"Out of my classification," said the pig.

"I'd lose my seniority," said the cow.

"I'd lose my unemployment compensation," said the goose.

"Then I will," said the little red hen, and she did.

At last it came time to bake the bread. "Who will help me bake the bread?" asked the little red hen.

"That would be overtime for me," said the cow.

"I'd lose my welfare benefits," said the duck.

"I'm a dropout and never learned how," said the pig.

"If I'm to be the only helper, that's discrimination," said the goose.

"Then I will," said the little red hen.

She baked five loaves and held them up for her neighbors to see.

They all wanted some and, in fact, demanded a share. But the little red hen said, "No, I can eat the five loaves myself."

"Excess profits!" cried the cow.

"Capitalist leech!" screamed the duck.

"I demand equal rights!" yelled the goose.

(continued)

And the pig just grunted. And they painted "unfair" picket signs and marched round and round the little red hen, shouting obscenities.

When the government agent came, he said to the little red hen, "You must not be greedy."

"But I earned the bread," said the little red hen.

"Exactly," said the agent. "That is the wonderful free enterprise system. Anyone in the barnyard can earn as much as he wants. But under our modern government regulations, the productive workers must divide their product with the idle."

And they lived happily ever after, including the little red hen, who smiled and clucked, "I am grateful. I am grateful."

But her neighbors wondered why she never again baked any more bread.

At the conclusion of the required business of the 1975 Pennwalt Annual Meeting, Chairman and President William P. Drake, commenting on the state of the company in today's economy, read this, his own adaptation of a modern version of the well-known fable of The Little Red Hen.

9. Do you think Mr. Drake has engaged in hyperbole? Why? Why not? What is his point?

THE FABLE, AMENDED

This is what *really* happened to the Little Red Hen

BRUCE R. MOODY

Vice President in Charge of Corporate Mythology
Pennwalt Corporation
Three Parkway
Philadelphia, PA 19102

Dear Sir (or Madam):

The advertisement entitled "The *Modern* Little Red Hen" was most entertaining, but certain documents that have recently come into my possession suggest certain inaccuracies. Just for the record, here's what really happened.

(continued)

Once upon a time there was a little red hen who got a tip from a friendly rat that there was a sizable quantity of wheat in a grain elevator in New Orleans that had been illegally diverted from its rightful owners and thus could be had for a song.

Thanks to a family trust set up by Grandfather rooster, which provided the little red hen with bundles of tax-free income, she was able to take such a flyer with ease, and so she did.

"Now that I own all this grain," she said, "what should I do with it?"

"I happen to know of a bakery that is having tax problems," answered a duck who made a nice living advising the little red hen and other well-to-do animals on such matters. "With a little nudge from my friends in Washington I can see that the IRS puts the screws to them and thus softens them up for a deal."

"Dandy!" cried the little red hen, tossing half a dozen tons of grain to the duck. And half an hour and three phone calls later, the thing was done.

When the grain had been milled and baked into bread, all the animals crowded around to see what it would taste like. The little red hen took the first bite.

"Goodness," she coughed, "this is the strangest-tasting bread I ever ate. What could be wrong with it?"

"It's moldy," said a mouse, who was an expert in such matters. "You got stuck with a shipload of moldy grain."

"But what do I do now?" wailed the little red hen.

Once again, it was the duck who had the answer. "Very simple," he winked, "just dose the next batch with a little diflourinated oxylactidaze. It doesn't exactly stop mold, but it does paralyze the taste buds so the customer doesn't know what he's eating."

Now the cow spoke up for the first time. "But wasn't I reading that diflourinated oxylactidaze makes people's hair fall out?"

"Never mind," said the duck, "leave everything to me."

But for good measure, it was decided to mount a million-dollar advertising campaign pointing out that the new bread was not only tasty and nutritious, but was also an effective depilatory. And the sales curves went off the chart.

Now it so happens that about this time the animals were experiencing great financial distress, largely because of the elaborate and costly missile system that had been set up around the barnyard to guard against chicken hawks. A few of the more intelligent animals had argued that since chicken hawks attack only chickens, it was unfair to make the pigs, cows, and horses pay for this system. But the duck had masterminded an expensive but effective campaign to replace the term "chicken hawk" with the term "animal hawk," a huge and rapacious creature that carried off animals as big as a horse and ate them. This effectively silenced the grum-

(continued)

blers, who no longer dared open their mouths for fear of being called anti-animal.

But the money problem still existed, and was in fact made worse because the little red hen, who had insisted upon the missiles in the first place, did not, as was mentioned earlier, pay any taxes at all.

"I'm getting awfully hungry," said the pig. "Remember how you used to creep into my pen to sleep when you got cold?"

"I'm starved," said the goose. "Remember how I used to sit on your eggs when you went shopping?"

"Me too," said the horse. "Remember how I used to carry you around on my back when you were a little baby chick?"

"Buzz off!" cried the little red hen. "You're not going to sponge off of me! If you want bread, steal your own grain, grab your own bakery, and bribe your own inspectors. You're nothing but a bunch of cheats and parasites!"

And so saying, she sat down to count her bags of grain for the hundredth time, breathing thanks that she still lived under a system in which diligence and enterprise are justly rewarded.

Moral: So bemused and bewildered is the public at large by tax-free corporate advertising, public relations experts, lobbyists, and bought politicians that an accurate account of the facts seems bizarre, tendentious, and even subversive.

You have my permission to make use of the fable as amended in any way you see fit.

Sincerely,
Bruce R. Moody

---

10. Who wins? Mr. Drake or Mr. Moody? What is Moody's point?

11. Should the U.S. government provide assistance to corporations in financial difficulty, as it did for the Chrysler corporation in 1980 and the Continental Illinois Bank in 1984? Why or why not?

This debate about the relationship between corporations and the government is relevant to recent discussions concerning the source of the economic difficulties of the United States in the 1970s and 1980s. The U.S. economy has experienced "waning competitiveness," with lower rates of productivity growth than its trading rivals in the other advanced countries and with several of its leading industries (such as steel, auto, rubber, and machine tools) experiencing hard times and retrenchment. Some, including Ronald Reagan, have charged that the federal government's involvement in the economy—its claim on resources for its programs and its regulation of the private sector—is the principal source of the problem. Others point to labor union demands, the oil crisis, or the decline of the work ethic to explain our economic problems. An alternative account of these trends was offered in the early 1980s by two professors at the Harvard Business School.

Robert Hayes and William Abernathy published an article entitled "Managing Our Way to Economic Decline" in the *Harvard Business Review* in 1980, which laid much of the blame for waning competitiveness on the doorstep of corporate America. Abernathy and Hayes argued that the very approach of corporate managers to their businesses accounted for lower productivity growth and decreased competitiveness in international markets. American managers, they charged, take a technocratic view of production emphasizing technology, internal planning, and computer analysis. But technology and plans don't always work in practice. With more attention to hands-on experience and what's actually happening with the production process on the factory floor, Japanese and European firms have made faster advances in production techniques and quality. In addition, American managers tend to focus on short-run profits through portfolio management, financial oversight, and market control. The stress is always on short-run financial performance. The long-run vision, which would insure the maintenance of competitiveness and technological development, is lacking.

Abernathy and Hayes' analysis argues for a changed outlook, approach, and strategy on the part of American managers. It could also be consistent with another set of suggestions made by a growing body of analysts of American corporations and the economic crisis of the 1970s and 1980s. A number of corporate executives and economists have begun to argue for an American "industrial policy" to resolve the competitive difficulties and the production dilemmas of American corporations. Such a policy would generally call for increased cooperation between the government and the corporate sector over future plans for economic growth and technological development. The intention is to move toward more coordinated and effective efforts to compete with the Japanese and Europeans. We will deal with this policy option in more detail in Chapter 30.

AMERICAN CORPORATIONS GO GLOBAL

No treatment of the modern American corporation would be complete without reference to one of the dominant corporate trends in the post–World War II period. This is the increasing multinationalization of American corporations. We will explore this issue in some more detail in Part V, on international economics.

Multinational corporations are those that have productive facilities, offices, and operations in more than one country. The multinationalization of some American companies goes back to the end of the 19th century. At that time, however, the international activities of most companies involved trade. But in the post–World War II period, American corporations began increasingly to invest in productive facilities in other parts of the world. At first, this process of foreign direct investment was directed toward getting around tariff barriers and other impediments to U.S. exports. Much of this investment took place in Western Europe and Canada. In addition, multinationalization was motivated by efforts at cutting transportation costs for international markets, at taking advantage of various tax incentives offered by many countries, and at cutting production costs with cheaper foreign labor. In the 1950s and 1960s, much of this investment by American corporations took place in the underdeveloped countries of Latin America, Asia, and Africa. By 1983, the book value of U.S. direct investment in foreign countries was over $220 billion. The income that derived from these and other foreign investments amounted to almost $80 billion in 1983.

In the 1970s the pace of U.S. multinational investments in the rest of the world slowed down somewhat for a variety of reasons. The dollar was devalued during the 1970s and made foreign investment more expensive for American corporations. Many Third World nations have become more critical about unconditional multinational investment in their countries. Political instability and the expropriation of corporate assets in some Third World countries led to a deterioration of the investment climate, as perceived by American multinationals. The primary motivation for multinationalization has always been profitability—from cutting transportation and labor costs to access to raw materials and foreign markets. As the potential profitability of foreign investment was reduced or threatened, U.S. corporations have *slowed down* their overseas expansion.

A multitude of issues are raised by the existence and the operation of U.S. multinationals. In some sense, these facilities are of crucial importance to the corporations themselves in their search for profits. By the end of the 1970s, one-third of the profits of the 100 largest industrial companies and banks came from their overseas operations. In 1976, about one-third of U.S. imports came from majority-owned U.S. corporations in foreign countries. In that same year, U.S. exports totaled $115 billion, and exports from U.S.–owned corporations in foreign countries totaled $140 billion. Without these activities, presumably, U.S. corporations would be less profitable than they are.

On the other hand, the importance of these activities places some constraints on the development of American foreign policy. Multinationals are more than happy to operate in those countries that limit the ability of labor unions to organize, and often these policies are followed in countries that are dictatorial and oppressive. Consequently, American foreign policy often ends up supporting these kinds of regimes and opposing national independence movements. Similarly, the Middle East policies of the United States have always been at least partly informed by the importance of that area of the world to U.S. oil companies.

The relationship between multinationals and Third World countries has created a debate about the effects of these corporations on economic development. Some argue that the multinationals bring jobs and technology and stimulate growth. Others have suggested that what they bring is economic dependence; unequal growth, as some prosper while others remain mired in poverty; and exploitation, as the corporations take advantage of cheap labor and raw materials, only to export their profits. (We will return to this issue in Chapter 27.)

A particularly controversial domestic consequence of U.S. multinationals is the movement of productive facilities out of the Northeast and the Midwest, as well as other parts of the country. Corporations often choose to close down old factories and to relocate new facilities in other parts of the United States or the world. This is a fundamental aspect of the free enterprise system. Capital is mobile and corporations make decisions about what to do with their capital based on profitability. "Capital flight" may occur in the search for lower taxes, lower wages, less regulation and unionization, or closer proximity to expanding markets. Unfortunately, along with these "runaway shops" go jobs and, in some cases, the health of local communities. Labor unions and communities have often reacted to threats of corporate capital flight with wage and tax concessions. When corporations actually do close down operations, people lose their jobs, communities lose income and business, and governments lose tax revenues. Occasionally, workers or communities have attempted to take over the ownership and operation of these facilities. Barry Bluestone and Bennett Harrison have suggested that this is part of the "deindustrialization" of the United States and will be a continuing problem in the near future (see Chapter 30).

12. **Why do firms run away? What effects does capital shifting have on workers and communities? What would Adam Smith say about this?**

13. **A number of states have legislation pending that would require pre-notification of shutdowns or assistance to workers who want to restart businesses. Does this seem like a good idea to you? What do you think American multinationals think about these proposals?**

LABOR UNIONS IN THE UNITED STATES

We have referred to the influence of **labor unions** on wage rates and on the decisions that firms make about plant location. In the remainder of this chapter, we will briefly explore the history of labor unions in the United States and the effects they have on the economy. However, we should first know something about the status of labor unions in the United States.

In 1984, labor unions and employee associations represented 18.8 million workers. This amounted to 16.6 percent of the 113.5 million people in the public and private sectors of the labor force. In a 1977 report from the Bureau of Labor Statistics of the Department of Labor, it was also noted that although women were 40.5 percent of the civilian labor force, they accounted for only 27.6 percent of union members. Blacks and other minorities were 11.6 percent of the labor force but 14.2 percent of union members. Unionization is more likely in the North: 35.9 percent of the workers in the Middle Atlantic states were represented by unions, but only 14.9 percent of the workers in the South Central states were. In addition, blue-collar workers (43%) were more likely to be union members than service workers (19%) or white-collar workers (18%). Finally, the report showed that union members earned higher wages than nonunion workers—an average of $262 a week vs. $221.

There are over 200 labor unions across the United States, representing industrial workers, secretaries, teachers, and many other employees. Some of the largest and most powerful unions are well known, such as the United Auto Workers, the Teamsters, and the United Steel Workers. Others are less well known but are growing rapidly, such as the United Food and Commercial Workers and the American Federation of State, County, and Municipal Employees.

Labor unions were formed and exist to promote the interests of their members and other workers. Unions are often charged with responsibility for inflation and with disrupting economic and community life with strikes and other acts of conflict. To address the impacts of labor unions, it is best to start with a brief history.

THE HISTORY OF LABOR UNIONS IN THE UNITED STATES

Labor unions have emerged in capitalism as a response to the lack of bargaining power that individual workers have with their employers over such things as wages, control of work, and working conditions. The employer owns the factory and offers employment. If there are a large number of unemployed people, an individual employee will not be very successful in demanding higher wages or better working conditions. And employers would prefer to pay as low wages as possible. It was in response to this structural reality of capital–labor relations that employees began to form associations of working people. Only through association and unity could they have the power to protect their interests. In the early part of the 19th century, courts held such organizations to be illegal restraints of trade, and thus labor unions were powerless to bargain with employers or to withhold their work in strikes. However, in 1842 the Supreme Court ruled that attempts to organize workers into labor unions were not criminal conspiracies. It was in the period after this that labor unions began to have a national history. It was also during this period that the economy was becoming increasingly industrialized—one of the preconditions for effective labor organization.

Following the Civil War, the National Labor Union attempted to build a social and political movement around a loose federation of trade unions. However, the craft unions left the organization because they were more interested in union recognition by employers, bargaining with employers over wages, and increasing their wages. In the 1870s and the 1880s, the Knights of Labor attempted to unite all workers against monopolies and to promote the interests of working people. The Knights of Labor organized some successful nationwide strikes against the railroads, but the organization was eventually disbanded because of a lack of internal cohesiveness and as a result of Jay Gould's use of strikebreakers in the 1886 railroad strike.

The modern labor movement can be traced back to the formation of the American Federation of Labor in 1886. The American Federation of Labor (AFL), under the leadership of Samuel Gompers, organized in the crafts, accepted capitalism as an economic system, and focused on obtaining higher wages, better working conditions, and shorter hours through collective bargaining, trade agreements, and strikes. It was a confederation of craft unions, each of which was powerful in its own area, that united in conventions and in cooperation in strikes, picketing, and boycotts. The AFL believed firmly in the union shop, requiring all employees in a factory or shop to belong to the union (and this requirement was included in contracts with employers). The AFL also believed firmly in supporting the strike as the ultimate weapon of organized labor in disputes with employers over union recognition, wage settlements, or working conditions.

The AFL shunned direct political activity and also avoided attempting to organize in the emerging industrial sectors of the U.S. economy in the late 19th and early 20th century. Many of these industrial workers were unskilled, and many were immigrants. However, there were other labor organizers throughout the 1920s and 1930s who actively began industrial organizing and eventually formed the Committee for Industrial Organization (CIO). In the 1930s these forces were successful in forming labor organizations that won the right to represent and collectively bargain for the automobile and steel workers. It was also in the 1930s that **the Wagner Act** was passed. This important piece of labor legislation gave labor unions the right to organize and to collectively bargain for their members with employers. Since 1935, labor relations have been overseen by the National Labor Relations Board, which has the authority to spell out the rules of labor organizing for both employers and labor unions.

Since World War II, labor–management relations have seen the emergence of three-year, industrywide contracts negotiated by industry representatives and national labor unions in some cases. In other cases, large corporations and large labor unions have reached settlements that establish a pattern for the rest of the industry. During this period there has also been a tremendous increase in public employees unions for police, firefighters, teachers, etc. The 1950s saw the merger of the AFL and the CIO as a national labor organization to support workers' interests. The Taft-Hartley Act in 1947 allowed states to pass "right-to-work" laws that forbid union shops. Most of the right-to-work states are in the South. The act also allowed the president to order a 90-day injunction against any strike deemed to threaten "national security." Table 14.4 shows the growth in the organized labor force in the United States.

Before we examine some of the effects of the labor unions on the economy, we should emphasize that the history of labor organization in this country has been characterized by conflict and occasionally by violence. There have been clear and opposing interests over such issues as the rights of employees to form labor unions, the level of wages, the length of the working day, and working conditions. Capital owners and corporations have always had the power of ownership, and labor has had the power of numbers, unity, and strikes. The interests have clashed and tempers have flared. Labor organizers were often branded as revolutionaries and Communists. The police force of the state has often been used to break strikes, and working people have often responded with their own weapons. To some extent, the conflict is inherent in the structure of the economy, with private ownership and workers dependent on labor for their incomes. However, one of the great achievements of modern labor legislation has been to mute this conflict and reduce it to legal and institutional forms that are much less likely to break out into violence.

Table 14.4 UNION AND ASSOCIATION MEMBERSHIP IN THE UNITED STATES, 1880–1984

	UNION MEMBERSHIP ONLY			UNION AND ASSOCIATION MEMBERSHIP		
YEAR	TOTAL (IN THOUSANDS)	PERCENTAGE OF LABOR FORCE	PERCENTAGE OF NONAGRICULTURAL EMPLOYMENT	TOTAL (IN THOUSANDS)	PERCENTAGE OF LABOR FORCE	PERCENTAGE NONAGRICULTURAL EMPLOYMENT
1880	200	n.a.	2.3			
1890	372	n.a.	2.7			
1900	791	n.a.	5.2			
1910	2,116	n.a.	9.8			
1920	5,034	n.a.	18.3			
1930	3,401	6.8	11.6			
1940	8,717	15.5	26.9			
1950	14,300	22.3	31.5			
1960	17,049	23.6	31.5			
1970	19,381	22.6	27.3	21,248	24.7	30.0
1978	20,246	19.7	24.0	22,757	22.2	26.2
1980	n.a.	n.a.	n.a.	22,366	20.9	24.7
1982	n.a.	n.a.	n.a.	19,800	17.9	20.5
1983	n.a.	n.a.	n.a.	20,100	18.9	20.6
1984	n.a.	n.a.	n.a.	18,800	16.6	18.5

Source: Robert J. Flanagan, Robert S. Smith, and Ronald G. Ehrenberg, *Labor Economics and Labor Relations*, Scott, Foresman and Company, 1984, p. 334; Associated Press, "Union Membership in Nation Declines Sharply, Survey Shows," *Boston Globe*, September 25, 1984; and *Statistical Abstract of the United States*, 1986.

14. Do any members of your family belong to labor unions? What are their opinions of their unions? What do you think of labor unions? Would you want to be in one? Why or why not?

THE EFFECTS OF LABOR UNIONS ON THE ECONOMY

Labor unions are an important force in the economy and in American society. They affect wages, working conditions, and the lives of union members. They also affect the decisions that are made by businesses throughout the United States about location, numbers of employees, and so on. Unions also affect communities through civic work, political action, and sometimes strikes. In the following discussion we want to concentrate on two of the most significant effects of labor unions on economic conditions.

First of all, what is the general effect of labor unions on wages and employment? Here it will be useful to refer to the supply-and-demand model for a labor market. Assume that there is an organized work force negotiating with an employer over a new contract. The workers are willing to supply their labor power for wages. The higher the wage, the greater the quantity of labor power they will tend to supply. This can be seen in the supply curve, S_L, in Fig. 14.1. The employer has a demand for labor; the higher the wage, the lower the quantity of labor the employer will demand. This can be seen in the demand curve, D_L, in Fig. 14.1. At the point where the two curves intersect are the equilibrium wage rate and the equilibrium quantity of labor that will be supplied and demanded. The labor union is presumably interested in obtaining higher wages for its workers. The power it has to achieve this goal is its ultimate weapon, the strike. The workers can shift their supply curve for labor upward to get higher wages. What this means is that they will supply every different possible quantity of labor power only for higher wages. If the employer is unwilling to meet this request for higher wages, the workers may go on strike. The effect of shifting the supply curve upward, S_{L2}, is to increase the equilibrium wage rate. It also tends to reduce the equilibrium quantity, *if* the demand curve for labor does not change. Consequently, we can conclude that labor unions tend to increase wages for their members. It is usually true that labor union members do get higher wages *and* higher wage increases than nonunion workers. For example, in 1979, wages for union members increased on the average of 9.1 percent, while nonunion workers got increases that averaged 7 percent or less. And we have seen that in 1977, union workers got a wage that was, on the average, about 20 percent higher than that of nonunion workers.

The second significant effect that labor unions have had on the economy concerns the general demands they have made for reforming the institutions and the conditions that surround work in the United States. In their negotiations with employers they have focused on their own wages and their own conditions of employment. In addition, the labor movement has been at the forefront of political efforts to improve the wages and the working conditions for all workers in the

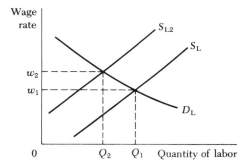

Figure 14.1   The effect of unions on wages and unemployment.

country. This has been accomplished primarily through legislation at both the state and federal level. It includes workmen's compensation, minimum wage laws, the eight-hour day and overtime, the right of workers to form labor organizations and collectively bargain with employers, improved working conditions, and occupational health and safety regulations. Unions have also supported other broad social legislation directed toward improving the lot of working and poor people, including public education, Social Security, Medicare and Medicaid, environmental protection, and the government's income-support programs.

Labor unions have been successful at gaining legitimacy in our society, winning improved wages and working conditions for members, and promoting general labor and social legislation. However, they are not without internal problems and potentially adverse effects on the economy. Some unions have become tremendous bureaucracies that have lost touch with the rank-and-file workers. Some union officials have been found guilty of corruption and illegal activities. And finally, it has been argued that unions contribute to the wage–price spiral that fuels inflation. We will return to this last point in Part IV.

CONCLUSION

In this chapter we have focused on two of the most important economic institutions in the United States. Having stepped outside the realm of pure microeconomic theory, we examined the development, behavior, and importance of corporations and labor unions. In the next chapter, we will explore in some detail the economic role of another major institution in our society—the government.

KEY CONCEPTS

the corporation
corporate profitability
governmental regulation
free enterprise

multinational corporations
labor unions
the Wagner Act

REVIEW QUESTIONS

1. Why is the corporation a dominant institution in the American economic system?

2. Is the relationship between big business and big government adversarial? Or symbiotic?

3. Why have corporations gone global? What are some of the implications of this trend?

4. Why are labor unions a dominant institution in the American economy?

5. Is the relationship between big corporations and big labor unions adversarial? Or symbiotic?

6. Corporations have gone global. Will labor unions, too? Why or why not? Why would they want to?

7. See Table 14.4. Why did union membership decrease by 2.6 million from 1980 to 1982?

8. From June 1985 to June 1986, pay raises for union members increased by an average of 2.5 percent while they increased by 4.1 percent for nonunion workers. The average weekly manufacturing wage for union members ($400) was 15 percent above that for nonunion workers ($347). What accounts for these indications of weakened union strength (see data on page 256)?

SUGGESTED READINGS

Richard Barnet and Ronald Müller, 1976. *Global Reach*, Simon and Schuster. An excellent book on the growth and effects of multinational corporations.

Richard Boyer and Herbert Morais, 1974. *Labor's Untold Story*, United Electrical Workers. A passionate history of the labor movement from the mid-19th century through the 1950s.

Harry Braverman, 1976. *Labor and Monopoly Capital*, Monthly Review Press. A Marxist analysis of the labor process and labor history.

Robert J. Flanagan, Robert S. Smith, and Ronald G. Ehrenberg, 1984. *Labor Economics and Labor Relations*, Scott, Foresman and Company. A textbook on labor economics and relations.

Sheila Harty, 1979. *Hucksters in the Classroom*. Center for the Study of Responsive Law. A treatment of the preparation and use of corporate teaching materials in the schools.

Fletcher Knebel, 1975. *The Bottom Line*, Pocket Books. A novel on the modern corporation.

Morton Mintz and Jerry S. Cohen, 1971. *America, Inc.*, Dell. A critical and fact-filled book on corporate power and abuse in the United States.

Kurt Vonnegut, 1983. *Jailbird*, Dell. In part, a fictionalized history of labor union–corporate relations.

Howard Wachtel, 1984. *Labor and the Economy*, Academic Press. A labor economics text; see Chapters 1, 2, 6, and 7 on labor and labor unions.

The Economic Role of Government

INTRODUCTION

In the previous chapters of Part III, on microeconomics, we have concentrated on the operation of markets and their role in allocating resources. We have also introduced the importance of corporations and labor unions as economic factors in the private sector. But the United States, in fact, has a **mixed economy**—in which business firms and markets in the private sector exist alongside economic institutions in the public sector.

> 1. **Do you think governments should reduce their spending? On which programs? Why or why not?**

The **public sector,** in the form of local, state, and federal governmental offices, organizations, and institutions, performs many important economic functions. Think about your local community. What goods and services are provided by governmental

259

units? It's actually quite a long list, and the activities are of fundamental importance to the ongoing day-to-day economic (as well as noneconomic) operation of a community. Public services also provide for the long-run survival capabilities of a society. Postal service, police and fire protection, road construction and maintenance, street signs, sewers, parks and recreation services, a court system, schools, traffic signals, welfare services, and so on are all provided by local, state, and federal governmental units.

In general, the economic role of government in capitalism results from the failure of markets to allocate resources to certain tasks or from a public conclusion that the results of markets are unacceptable. Consequently, governments have taken responsibility for limiting the practice and the results of economic concentration, for correcting the inequality of the distribution of market-determined incomes, for providing public goods when markets fail to supply them, and for regulating those activities of the private sector that produce external costs to the rest of society. In this chapter, we will explore each of these aspects of governmental economic activity in more detail.

THE ROLE OF GOVERNMENT IN THE ECONOMY

In response to the various failures of the market system, government has developed many different programs. Public regulation of monopolies and antitrust legislation are intended to control economic concentration. The progressive income tax system and income support, job training, equal opportunity, and affirmative action programs exist for the purpose of reducing economic inequality. The public use of resources to provide such socially desirable goods and services as education, parks, police and fire protection, and roads results from the failure of the private sector to adequately supply them. Zoning laws, pollution controls, environmental protection legislation, restrictions on child labor, occupational health and safety regulations, and food and drug inspections are meant to correct some of the abuses resulting from the operation of private markets. These public activities have all been developed throughout the history of American capitalism.

In addition, governments provide an economic framework within which private economic activity takes place. The justice and legal systems, public infrastructure (e.g., transportation and national defense), the monetary and banking systems, and, frequently, public subsidies for private businesses all create an environment in which short-run and long-run economic activity can proceed. Seen in this light, the public sector complements the private sector. Furthermore, local, state, and federal governments have created a taxation and revenue system to finance their activities. Through raising money, governments can make a claim on the resources of the society by purchasing them in markets. (The federal government also uses its spending and taxing power, as well as its influence over the money supply, to limit economic instability. We will explore this function of government in Part IV, on macroeconomics.)

All these governmental activities are intensely political and controversial. The decisions about which programs to pursue, how much money to spend on them, and how to raise the revenues to finance them involve public discussion and debate, legislative resolution, administrative direction, and judicial oversight. People, organizations, politicians, political parties, and even ideas are joined in the political process to decide what governments will do and how they will do it.

Throughout the history of American capitalism there has been debate about the economic role of the government. At times the debate has been quite lively and heated. Almost two hundred years ago, Alexander Hamilton and Thomas Jefferson argued about whether the country should be an agrarian or an industrial society and about what role the federal government ought to play in promoting one or the other. Prior to the Civil War, the South and the North disagreed about the imposition of tariffs by the federal government. Later in the 19th century, the controversial issue was the role of the government in giving land to the railroads and then in regulating their rates. During the Depression, there was vociferous debate about the growing role of the government in regulation, relief, public employment, social spending, labor legislation, and even public ownership. Since that time, along with the growth of government, the issue has continued. With the election of Ronald Reagan to the Presidency in 1980, the debate was revitalized with a renewed attack on the general role of the government in the economy. One of Reagan's primary campaign themes was that the government was interfering too much in the private sector and that its size and its rules were preventing economic growth. Only time will tell if this challenge will successfully reduce the role of the government in the economy. We can be sure that it will be an intensely political process, as the 1984 presidential election demonstrated.

Going back to the writings of Adam Smith, we can see that there has always been a case for some necessary tasks on the part of the state in support of the operation of the economy. Smith suggested that the government needed to protect private property, enforce contracts, provide for a monetary system, supply a defense capability, and provide some public goods, such as education and transportation. Beyond that, the role of the government should be circumscribed. Note, however, that what Smith has delineated is of fundamental importance to the economy and requires a large and powerful government. Smith said that its powers should be limited—never that it should be weak.

Since Smith's time the general discussion about the role of the government has been partly about the scope of its activities and partly about its limitations within the kind of economic system that we have. Here it is useful to use the liberal, conservative, and radical categories to review the debate. Conservatives would argue that the state's involvement in the economy limits personal freedoms, and that markets, if left alone, will produce economic growth and social welfare. This follows the lines of Smith's arguments in *The Wealth of Nations*. Conservatives, consequently, tend to oppose efforts to break up big corporations, to redistribute income, and to regulate directly the externalities of the private sector. It is largely the conservatives who have mounted the New Right attack on the government's role

CONSERVATIVES: LIMIT GOV'T

LIBERALS: GOV'T NECESSARY TO CORRECT FAILURES OF MARKET.

in the economy. (Part of their critique also deals with Keynesian fiscal and monetary policy, which we will deal with in Part IV.)

The liberal position suggests that the operation of the market economy in capitalism tends to produce economic growth and efficiency, along with an emphasis on individual economic freedom. However, liberals acknowledge some of the problems that the development of the economy produces, e.g., economic concentration, income inequality, and externalities. Consequently, they think that it is entirely appropriate for the governments to attempt to correct and address some of those problems. They also argue that such government intervention can, in fact, improve the allocation of resources in society. It is largely this position that has won out in the public debate in the 20th century concerning the role of government.

The radical position begins with the assertion that the government plays a ~~RADICAL~~ particularly important role in the operation and maintenance of capitalism as an economic system. For example, the state protects private property and the rights of owners to pursue their economic freedom. However, it does not offer the same kind of freedom or protection to poor people. Another way of saying this is that the state's role is constrained by its relationship to capitalism as a particular type of economic system. This point is the basis of the radical critique of liberal policies of government involvement in the economy. There is a limit on the extent of government involvement in the private sector as to redistributing income, regulating externalities, or enforcing antitrust laws. The limit is the requirement of capital accumulation for the growth of capitalism. Without capital accumulation, the economy will stagnate. If state policies interfere with profits or profit expectations of corporations, capital accumulation can be endangered. In other words, if state intervention proceeds too far, it may interfere with capital accumulation, and government policies will have to retreat somewhat. On the other hand, radicals recognize that the political response to the abuses and inequities of capitalism has required and led to governmental programs that address these problems.

The three positions, as well as others that are directly concerned with specific issues of any particular government policy, inform the general debate and political developments about the role of government in the economy.

Nicole Hollander, *My Weight Is Always Perfect for My Height — Which Varies,* St. Martin's Press. © 1982 by Field Enterprises and Nicole Hollander.

> 2. **Does welfare spending hinder the operation of capitalism? What programs are included in "welfare spending"? How would you find out if you are right (or if you don't know)? Why does welfare spending take place? What would a conservative say? A liberal? A radical?**
>
> 3. **Which position best describes your attitudes toward government spending in general? Why? How do you feel about government spending for defense?**

THE GROWTH OF GOVERNMENT'S ROLE

The public sector has significantly expanded its role in the economy during the 20th century. This can be seen in a variety of ways.

Through the political process, governmental institutions make decisions about pursuing particular programs. Table 15.1 presents information on the range of spending programs and the relative priorities of state, local, and federal governments in the early 1980s. Education is by far the most important category for state and local governments; it accounted for 35 percent of state and local government spending in 1983–1984. In the federal government's budget for fiscal year 1985 (October 1, 1984, to September 30, 1985), national defense, income security, Social Security, and interest on the debt were the four largest spending categories; they accounted for more than 70 percent of total federal spending.

Table 15.2 presents information on public sector taxes and receipts for federal, state, and local governments for various years from 1929 to 1985. The table includes data on the total amount of governmental revenues as well as their percentage share of gross national product (GNP, the total value of output for each year). For example, in 1929, total governmental revenues were $11.3 billion, which amounted to 10.9 percent of GNP. From even a quick look at this table, we can see that the relative importance of government in the economy has increased significantly over the past half-century. Revenues in 1985 amounted to more than $1.2 trillion. Looking only at the amount of money collected, we could state that governmental revenues have increased by almost a thousandfold since 1929! However, the most useful way to gauge the relative position of any economic variable is to compare it to GNP. Revenues in 1985 were more than 30 percent of GNP. This threefold increase in government's share since 1929 represents a shift in the role of government in the economy.

From 1929 to 1940, total revenues increased from 10.9 percent to 17.7 percent of GNP. Most of this increase occurred in the federal sector in response to the Great Depression. (The increase in the share of governmental revenues in GNP resulted from an increase in those revenues as well as from the slow growth of GNP due to the effects of the Depression. See Chapter 17 for more on the Great Depression.) The increase in the share of total revenues from 1940 to 1950 from 17.7 to 24.1 percent

Table 15.1 STATE–LOCAL AND FEDERAL GOVERNMENT SPENDING

STATE AND LOCAL GOVERNMENT SPENDING, 1983–1984 ($ BILLIONS)	
Education	176.1
Highways	39.5
Public welfare	66.4
All other*	223.0
Total	505.0

FEDERAL BUDGET OUTLAYS, FISCAL YEAR 1985 ($ BILLIONS)	
National defense	252.7
International affairs	16.2
General science, space & technology	8.6
Energy	5.7
National resources & environment	13.4
Agriculture	25.6
Commerce & housing credit	4.2
Transportation	25.8
Community & regional development	7.7
Education, training, employment, & social services	29.3
Health	33.5
Medicare	65.8
Income security	128.2
Social Security	188.6
Veterans benefits & services	26.4
Administration of justice	6.3
General government	5.2
General purpose fiscal assistance	6.3
Net interest	129.4
Offsetting receipts	−32.7
Total	946.3

*Includes health and hospitals, police and fire protection, correction, interest on debt, parks and recreation, sanitation, administration, housing and urban renewal, protective inspection and regulation, etc.

Source: Economic Report of the President, 1986.

resulted from the expansion of the federal government and the retrenchment of state and local governments during World War II. From 1950 to 1970, there was continued expansion in the public sector, and revenues increased to 30 percent of GNP. During this period, federal revenues increased their share by about 11 percent while the share of state–local revenues expanded by almost 70 percent. More recently, the relative share of governmental revenues in GNP has stabilized. Total revenues have

Table 15.2 PUBLIC SECTOR TAXES AND RECEIPTS, FROM OWN SOURCES

YEAR	TOTAL GOVERNMENT ($ BILLIONS)	PERCENTAGE OF GNP	STATE–LOCAL GOVERNMENTS ($ BILLIONS)	PERCENTAGE OF GNP	FEDERAL GOVERNMENT ($ BILLIONS)	PERCENTAGE OF GNP
1929	11.3	10.9	7.5	7.3	3.8	3.6
1940	17.7	17.7	9.1	9.1	8.6	8.6
1950	69.0	24.1	19.0	6.7	50.0	17.4
1960	139.5	27.5	43.4	8.5	96.1	19.0
1970	302.8	30.5	110.9	11.2	191.9	19.3
1980	838.3	31.8	297.4	11.3	540.9	20.5
1983	1059.6	31.1	401.5	11.8	658.1	19.3
1985*	1262.2	31.6	476.5	11.9	785.7	19.7

*Preliminary figures.

Source: *Economic Report of the President*, 1984 and 1986.

remained at just over 30 percent of GNP, federal revenues are just under 20 percent, and state–local revenues have been about 11 percent of GNP since 1970.

4. **Look at the figures for federal revenues from 1970 to 1983. When Ronald Reagan ran for the Presidency in 1980, he argued that the growth of government was a primary reason for the economic difficulties of the 1970s. Was this an exaggerated claim? What happened from 1980 to 1983?**

For comparative purposes, Table 15.3 shows the relative importance of government in several other economically advanced countries. Expenditures as a percentage of gross domestic product are higher in Sweden, France, West Germany, Great Britain, Canada, Denmark, and Italy than they are in the United States.

Table 15.4 contains data on governmental expenditures in the United States from 1929 to 1985. In 1929, all levels of government spent $10.3 billion, which was 10.0 percent of GNP. By 1985, total governmental spending was over $1.4 trillion and amounted to 35.1 percent of GNP. In this period, there has been a more than threefold increase in the relative importance of the governmental sector in the economy. The relative share of state and local government spending has almost doubled, while the share of the federal government has increased almost ten times. From 1929 to 1940, most of the growth was in the federal sector as a result of New Deal programs to cope with the effects of the Great Depression. From 1940 to 1970, there was growth in the federal share as a result of defense spending and expanding social spending. There was also an expansion of federal grants to state and local governments, which contributed to their increasing share. From 1970 to 1980, the

Table 15.3 THE PUBLIC SECTOR IN OTHER ADVANCED COUNTRIES, 1982

GOVERNMENT SPENDING AS A PERCENTAGE OF TOTAL OUTPUT

Canada	45.8
Denmark	60.7
France	50.7
Germany	49.4
Italy	53.7
Japan	34.2
Sweden	67.3
United Kingdom	47.4
United States	37.6

Source: Peter Saunders and Friedrich Klau, *The Role of the Public Sector,*
OECD Economic Studies, No. 4, Spring 1985.

Table 15.4 GOVERNMENTAL EXPENDITURES, COUNTED BY SPENDING SOURCE*

YEAR	TOTAL GOVERNMENT ($ BILLIONS)	PERCENTAGE OF GNP	STATE–LOCAL GOVERNMENTS ($ BILLIONS)	PERCENTAGE OF GNP	FEDERAL GOVERNMENT ($ BILLIONS)	PERCENTAGE OF GNP
1929	10.3	10.0	7.7	7.4	2.6	2.5
1940	18.4	18.4	9.3	9.3	9.1	9.1
1950	61.0	21.3	22.5	7.9	38.5	13.4
1960	136.4	26.9	49.8	9.8	86.6	17.1
1970	313.4	31.6	133.5	13.5	179.9	18.1
1980	869.0	33.0	355.5	13.5	513.5	19.5
1983	1190.4	35.0	439.1	12.9	751.3	22.1
1985[†]	1401.2	35.1	517.1	13.0	884.1	22.1

*Intergovernmental grants are counted by the spending source.

[†]Preliminary figures.

Source: Economic Report of the President, 1984 and 1986.

share of state and local spending stabilized, and the share of the federal government increased slightly, reflecting continued growth of social spending in the 1970s. From 1980 to 1985, the share of state–local governments decreased due to the recession and cutbacks by the Reagan Administration in intergovernmental grants. Despite the efforts of the Reagan team to reduce the role of the federal government in the economy, the federal share increased from 19.5 percent to 22.1 percent. This resulted from increased defense spending, increased unemployment compensation due to the 1980–1983 recessions, and increased interest payments on the federal debt.

Table 15.4 compiles all government spending, including transfer payments. **Transfer payments** are governmental programs that transfer spending power from one group to another group. Examples include veterans' benefits, unemployment compensation, Medicaid, food stamps, Social Security benefits, and Aid to Families with Dependent Children. Consequently, total government spending overestimates the claim of government programs on the society's resources. The government does, in fact, for example, collect Social Security taxes from people's wages and salaries, and then it pays benefits to people who are retired and eligible for Social Security. But the claim on the society's resources is transferred through this program from one set of people (those working now) to another (those retired). People who pay taxes have their spending power reduced, and people who receive benefits have their spending power increased. The money flows through the Social Security Administration, but the federal government makes no direct claim on resources in this transfer program (except for the costs of administering the program). Much of the growth in federal government expenditures as a percentage of GNP since 1929 has come as a result of the expansion of federal transfer programs.

This conclusion is reinforced by examining the information in Table 15.5 on governmental purchases of goods and services. Governmental purchases of goods and services represent **exhaustive spending.** Exhaustive spending means that the governments are making claims on society's resources in the pursuit of their priorities. It includes the purchase of weapons, pencils, government employees' labor, road construction materials, typewriters, police and fire vehicles, etc. By spending on public programs, governments demand the use of resources. This is different from a governmental program that transfers spending power from one group to another.

From 1929 to 1940, total governmental purchases almost doubled their share of GNP, with almost all of the growth in spending coming from the federal government. From 1940 to 1960, total purchases increased their share from 14.2 percent to 19.8 percent. Most of this growth occurred in the federal government sector, with the lion's share being accounted for by purchases of goods and services for national defense, although from 1950 to 1960, there was also a significant postwar expansion in state and local spending, especially for roads and schools. Since 1960, the overall level of governmental purchases has stabilized at about 20 percent of GNP. Government, consequently, makes a direct claim on about one-fifth of the society's output every year.

Figure 15.1 illustrates the growth of the government in the economy from 1929 to 1983. It also contrasts the growth of total government spending with purchases of goods and services. Since 1960, total governmental exhaustive spending has stabilized as a proportion of GNP. During the same time, transfer programs have continued to expand, thereby increasing the share of total governmental spending as a percentage of GNP.

One last statistic demonstrates the growth of government in the 20th century in the United States. Figure 15.2 illustrates the increase in public sector employment

Table 15.5 GOVERNMENTAL PURCHASES OF GOODS AND SERVICES

YEAR	TOTAL GOVERNMENT ($ BILLIONS)	PERCENTAGE OF GNP	STATE–LOCAL GOVERNMENTS ($ BILLIONS)	PERCENTAGE OF GNP	FEDERAL GOVERNMENT ($ BILLIONS) (DEFENSE)	PERCENTAGE OF GNP (DEFENSE)
1929	8.8	8.5	7.4	7.2	1.4	1.3
1940	14.2	14.2	8.1	8.1	6.1 (2.2)	6.1 (2.2)
1950	38.5	13.4	19.8	6.9	18.7 (14.0)	6.5 (4.9)
1960	100.3	19.8	46.5	9.2	53.7 (44.5)	10.6 (8.8)
1970	220.1	22.2	124.4	12.5	95.7 (73.6)	9.6 (7.4)
1980	537.8	20.4	340.8	12.9	197.0 (131.2)	7.5 (5.0)
1983	675.7	19.9	390.9	11.5	284.8 (215.7)	8.4 (6.3)
1985*	814.6	20.4	460.7	11.5	353.9 (262.0)	8.9 (6.6)

*Preliminary figures.

Source: *Economic Report of the President,* 1984 and 1986.

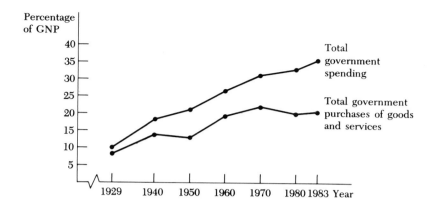

Figure 15.1 The expansion of government.

since 1929. In 1929, public sector employees were about 6 percent of the total labor force in the country; by 1984 this figure had increased to about 14 percent. In 1984, there were over 16 million people employed by the federal, state, and local governments: over 9 million worked for local governments, state governments employed almost 4 million people, and the federal government had 2.9 million civilian employees. As is clear from Fig. 15.2, the vast majority of the growth in public sector employment since 1950 has come in state and local government. In 1983, 5.3 million state and local employees worked in education, 1 million in hospitals, 600 thousand

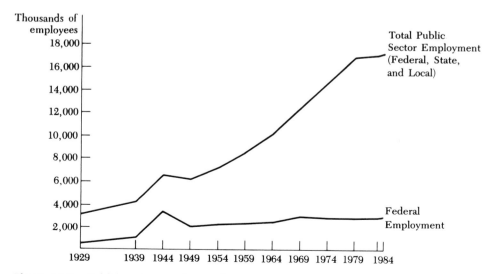

Figure 15.2 Public sector employment.

(*Sources:* Advisory Commission on Intergovernmental Relations, *Significant Features of Fiscal Federalism* (1984 edition), Washington, D.C., 1985; and U.S. Department of Commerce, Bureau of the Census, *Statistical Abstract of the United States, 1986, #482,* p. 294.)

in law enforcement, 500 thousand on highway work, and 400 thousand in general governmental administration.

---

5. Why has the relative importance of government increased in the past 50 years?

MARKET FAILURE, PUBLIC GOODS, AND EXTERNALITIES

In Chapter 11, we demonstrated that competitive markets operate in a manner that produces efficiency in resource allocation and a maximization of social welfare. The theoretical model of perfect competition proves Adam Smith's contention about the invisible hand in a private market economy—it promotes growth, efficiency, and consumer sovereignty. However, there are some aspects of economic reality that interfere with the attractive theoretical results of competitive markets in the allocation of resources.

We have already examined one instance when markets fail to produce an efficient allocation of resources. In Chapter 12, we showed that whenever there is imperfect competition in a market there is also inefficiency in resource allocation. In perfect competition, allocative efficiency occurs because firms in the long run produce at the rate of output where $P = MC$. In oligopoly, monopoly, and monopolistic competition, firms tend to produce a rate of output in the long run at which P is greater than MC. Because P indicates the extra benefit that consumers derive from one more unit of a good and MC indicates the extra cost of one more unit of the good, society would prefer to have more of that good produced. That is, there is a restriction of output, or an underallocation of resources to the production of that good. Whenever markets are imperfectly competitive, the operation of markets fails to maximize social welfare.

In Chapter 13, we also learned that the distribution of market-determined incomes might fail to satisfy society's concerns with fairness. Consequently, the public sector might decide to redistribute income through taxing and spending programs.

But there are other instances in which markets fail. Private markets organize the exchanges of goods and services between suppliers and purchasers. These exchanges between willing participants are based on the costs to producers and the benefits to consumers of the relevant commodities. The price indicates how much money someone is willing to give up in order to possess something, and it also registers the amount of money a seller must get to turn that something over to someone else. However, this exchange can miss a proper evaluation of the true social benefits and costs of the production and consumption of some goods and services. Whenever there are **externalities** present, the operation of markets does not assure an efficient allocation of resources. Externalities are social benefits or costs that occur outside of the exchange of a good or a service between a buyer and a seller. For example, someone buys a pack of cigarettes based on that person's demand for them and the costs of production for the producer. But there are external effects outside of this exchange—other people are affected by cigarette smoke and even the smoker may develop medical problems associated with smoking (which may not have been part of the original demand). These are **external costs** connected with this one good. In a similar fashion, if someone who lives next to you purchases a record and plays it so loud that you can hear it, and you like it, then you derive an **external benefit** from that exchange. In both cases, the external results are not taken into account in the transaction between the buyer and the seller of the commodity. The existence of externalities can interfere with the efficient allocation of resources.

In all of these instances of **market failure,** it is appropriate for the public sector to attempt to improve the allocation of resources. That is, governmental programs to limit the effects of economic concentration and to account for external benefits and costs can improve the allocation of resources and increase social welfare.

6. **Identify at least one other external cost of a specific exchange. Also, identify one other example of an external benefit.**

7. **What external costs might be associated with a cigarette smoker's eventual medical bills?**

Public Goods

Public goods are services or activities provided or subsidized by the public sector. In some cases, the operation of markets will either fail to provide any of a good or will underallocate resources to it. Street signs are a good example. Without street signs, businesses wouldn't be able to deliver products, people couldn't find each other's homes, and general confusion would reign. But street signs aren't provided by markets—why not? Private markets require suppliers to be able to charge people for the right to possess or consume a commodity. There is property ownership in a private exchange. Someone who owns a bicycle can prevent other people from using it. With street signs, however, there is no ownership and people cannot be excluded from using them. In this case, no private firm would provide them because there would be no way to force people to pay for them. Some people might be willing to pay for them, but not everyone would. Consequently, communities have used governmental institutions to create public provision of street signs, and citizens are compelled to pay for them through taxation. If the society relied only on markets to allocate resources to important activities, some things might not get done (i.e., there would be inefficiency in resource allocation).

In the same way, even when private markets do work to provide a certain good or service, if external benefits aren't taken into account there could be an underallocation of resources to that activity. A good example here would be education. Figure 15.3 shows the demand for education based on the collected individual preferences of people for their own education and the supply of education based on the resources necessary and their costs. The equilibrium is at P_e and Q_e.

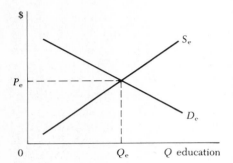

Figure 15.3   The supply and demand for education.

But there are external benefits to education that accrue to the whole society. Literacy, the advance of science and technology, culture, and economic intercourse require and benefit from having an educated population. The total social benefits from education, then, would include the private benefits to individuals and the external benefits to society. In Fig. 15.4, D_s is a "social demand curve" that includes both the private and the external benefits of education.

If the external benefits are not taken into account, there will be an underalloca-tion of resources to education. At Q_e, the social benefit of education, at P_1, is in excess of its MC at P_e (off the supply curve). Society would benefit from increased output of education. In fact, social welfare maximization would occur at Q_2, where the marginal social benefit of additional education is equal to the marginal cost of education (where the supply and demand curves intersect). The public sector in the United States, for more than a century now, has responded to this situation by providing various forms of assistance to education—the provision of public schools, scholarship assistance, tax exemptions to private educational institutions, funds for teacher training and educational development, and others. When external benefits are present, markets will tend to underallocate resources. Public sector provision of the good or service, or subsidization, can therefore improve social welfare by encouraging the increased allocation of resources to the activity.

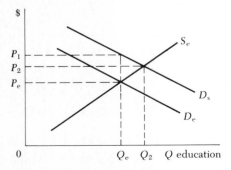

Figure 15.4   External benefits from education.

8. Dr. Benjamin Spock, the famous pediatrician, in an interview in the October 1984 *Redbook,* argued that "the family was the most important thing in life" and that "fathers have just as much responsibility as mothers for caring for their children or deciding who will care for them." Spock went on to suggest that the United States needs more quality day-care centers and that there should be subsidies for parents who prefer to stay home with young children. What are the external benefits from good parenting that might justify the use of public resources for child-care or home-parenting subsidies? Would you favor such programs? Why or why not?

Externalities (External Costs)   V₅ INTERNAL COSTS   SOCIAL COSTS - POLLUTION

In Chapter 11 we developed the cost curves that the firm faces in making decisions about what level of output to produce (the one that maximizes profits). We also saw how the competitive market operates to encourage firms to produce at the lowest average cost—that is, the rate of output that minimizes the per-unit use of scarce resources. However, there is one large problem in this characterization of the behavior of the competitive firm. (It must be emphasized that this problem also occurs in noncompetitive markets and further reduces their efficiency.)

When firms make decisions about the use of resources and the rate of output, the cost information they take into account concerns their own out-of-pocket, internal costs. But there may be some other costs of production that are external to the firm. These are costs of productive activity that the firm is not forced to bear. Economists call them **externalities.** For example, a paper company may produce air and water pollution in the process of making its paper. The costs are borne by the public at large that must breathe and smell the befouled air and by the potential downstream users of the dirtied water. These are social costs of production that are external to the firm. It does not have to pay a price for the use of these resources. Because these costs do not enter into the calculations of the firm, these resources will tend to be overused, and there will be an inefficient use of resources. In other words, the conclusion that competitive markets tend to produce resource efficiency is true only if there are no externalities in the production process.

POLLUTION — OVERUSE OF A RESOURCE

9. **What other social costs of production, besides pollution, can you identify?**

We can illustrate this point graphically. In Fig. 15.5 MR $= P$ is the price for the firm's product. MC represents the marginal private costs that face the firm at different levels of output, and MSC represents the marginal social costs of production at different levels of output. Included in MSC are the private, internal costs to the

SOCIAL COSTS PUSH COSTS UP

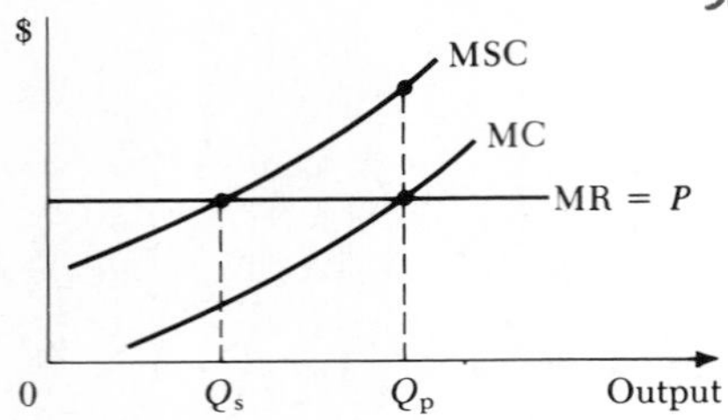

Figure 15.5   Marginal social costs.

firm from using resources that it buys on markets *and* the social costs that are external to the firm. That is, MSC = MPC + MEC, where MSC = marginal social cost, MPC = marginal private cost, and MEC = marginal external cost. The firm, in attempting to maximize its profits, will produce output Q_p. However, from a social perspective. MSC = P at output Q_s. With social costs taken into consideration, there would be a tendency toward lower rates of output. Alternatively, if the external costs were taken into consideration and if the firm were to maintain its rate of output at Q_p, the price for the product would have to be higher.

> **10.'Would an individual firm be willing to take any or all of its social, external costs of production into account? Why or why not?**

The existence of externalities in capitalist production has produced the necessity of outside intervention on the part of the state, local, and federal governments to force firms to take externalities into consideration. Because the elimination of such externalities as pollution requires costs, firms will avoid incurring them—because they reduce profits and because the firm faces competition. Consequently, government control is necessary to force firms to take the externalities into account. Areas where governmental regulation has emerged include occupational health and safety, strip-mining land reclamation, air and water pollution, the operation of nuclear power plants and the disposal of their wastes, noise pollution, and hazardous wastes. In each of these cases, the government has made private firms accountable for these external costs.

For example, each year billions of pounds of hazardous wastes—acids, strong bases and chlorinated hydrocarbons—are produced in the United States. In the past, most of these found their way to illegal waste dumps. There they pose severe potential health problems for local communities. Douglas Costle, administrator of the Environmental Protection Agency, noted the dangers in 1980: "These sites with their contents of long-lasting chemicals now represent time capsules releasing their toxic contents into the surface waters, into our groundwaters and seriously degrading our landscapes and our water supply." The Hooker Chemical Company dump at Love Canal in Niagara Falls, New York, is only the most widely publicized of these;

Hazardous wastes. (Photograph by Paul Bush.)

some experts have estimated that there are more than 55,000 illegal waste dumps in the country. As a result of rules established by the Environmental Protection Agency in 1980, companies are now responsible for keeping track of their hazardous wastes and ensuring that these are properly disposed of. They must take some of the cost into consideration and will not be able to pass all of it along to the public at large.

In the early 1980s, Congress passed legislation that gave $1.6 billion to the Environmental Protection Agency to set up a "Superfund" for the cleanup of abandoned hazardous waste dumps all over the country. By the end of 1984, there were nearly 800 locations where the EPA had identified a "significant long-term threat to human health and the environment." The list is expected to grow to include somewhere between 1400 and 2200 sites eventually. Toxic chemicals have a linkage to higher incidences of cancer among workers and residents of areas where such chemicals have been produced in the past. Toxic wastes are considered to be the third-largest environmental cause of cancer. The high-tech industry, one of the most rapidly expanding sectors of the U.S. economy in the 1980s, relies heavily on the use of many chemicals (arsenic, strong acids, and solvents) that are poisonous or carcinogenic. Thus, as we near the end of the 20th century, workers and communities across the United States are faced with a major, continuing environmental hazard in coping with the production, usage, and storage of toxic chemicals.

How much of our resources should we devote to dealing with this problem? In 1984, environmentalists wanted the Superfund increased to $9 billion, but the Reagan Administration wanted it kept at $1.6 billion. Who is responsible for the dangerous waste sites already in existence? Who should have to pay for their cleanup? How long will it take? Who will be liable for the health effects of toxic wastes, which may not appear for over two decades? The externalities associated with one of the most dynamic and important sectors of our economy in the post–World War II period obviously raise some fundamental economic and political questions.

11. *Explain* why no one firm would be likely, *on its own,* to reduce the air pollution or to keep track of and clean up the toxic wastes from its production process.

12. In recent years, there has been intense controversy over acid rain. Many residents of Canada and the northeastern United States, as well as scientific studies, blame pollution from coal-burning electricity-generating plants and other factories in the Midwest for higher acidity in lakes and rivers. The higher acidity, in turn, has threatened the ecology; in fact, many lakes no longer can support fish life. The Reagan Administration throughout its first term resisted efforts to institute stricter controls on sulfur-dioxide emissions on the grounds that not enough information existed to place the blame for acid rain on air pollution. Explain why acid rain is or is not an externality. What should be done about it? By whom? What difference does it make?

THE REGULATION OF ECONOMIC CONCENTRATION

In Chapters 11 and 12, we demonstrated that the theoretical results of competitive markets are superior to those of all forms of imperfect competition. This conclusion suggests that an appropriate response by the public sector would involve attempting to control the effects of imperfect competition and to encourage competition. The regulation of monopoly prices and antitrust policy are both informed by this approach.

Regulating Monopolies

If a monopoly exists, the government has several options. The monopoly can be left alone with the notion that in the long run monopoly profits will provide an incentive for some competition. The government can take over the operation of the activity itself, e.g., the postal service. It can break up the monopoly so that it has less economic power, e.g., the recent reorganization of AT&T. On the other hand, oftentimes governmental units acknowledge the existence of a monopoly, give it legal sanction, and then regulate its prices.

Figure 15.6 illustrates the demand and cost conditions for a monopolist. With the goal of profit maximization and its monopoly, the firm would produce at Q_m and charge a price of P_m. Since P is greater than MC at Q_m, we know that output is restricted. Society would be better off if the monopolist could be forced to produce a greater rate of output and charge a lower price. **Price regulation** can accomplish this goal. If the government regulates the price of the monopolist at P_{reg}, the monopolist may not charge a higher price. From rates of output 0 to Q_{reg}, the firm's demand curve becomes P_{reg}, and MR equals P_{reg}. Profit maximization then would require the firm to produce Q_{reg} and to charge a price of P_{reg}. The effect of the price regulation is that the firm is forced to charge a lower price and to produce at a higher rate of output. At Q_{reg}, P equals MC, and there is efficiency in resource allocation, *ceteris paribus*. At Q_{reg}, P is still above AC, so the monopolist still earns economic profits, but they are less than they would be at Q_m.

Governmental price regulation, therefore, can improve the economic results of monopoly. However, the actual process of price regulation is not quite as easy as Fig. 15.6 suggests. Governmental regulators need to have information on the monopoly's costs, its capital assets, and the demand for its products. They cannot regulate the

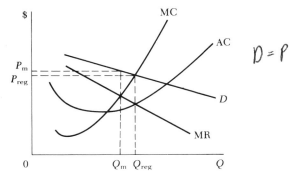

Figure 15.6   Monopoly price regulation.

$Q_m : MR = MC$

$Q_{REG} : D = MC$
$D = P$

quality of the service provided. And there are also problems of the relationships between regulators and the regulated. The Federal Communications Commission's regulation of AT&T offers some examples. The FCC begins with a decision to provide AT&T with a certain rate of return based on the value of its capital assets. Prices are then set so that the excess of revenues over costs produces the determined rate of return. AT&T then has an incentive to exaggerate its capital base as well as its costs so as to increase its profits. The FCC already must collect a great deal of information, plus it needs to keep tabs on AT&T's capital and cost estimates. Given the specialized knowledge required to regulate AT&T's business, the regulators are often people who are familiar with the industry, perhaps through past involvement in it. Despite these potential difficulties, price regulation of utility rates throughout the United States does succeed in limiting monopoly pricing power and in requiring monopolies to submit to some degree of public accountability.

Antitrust and Economic Concentration

Antitrust policy in the United States has always been controversial. Its roots lie in the theoretical economic argument that competition produces a maximization of social welfare and that imperfect competition, in the form of economic concentration, interferes with an efficient allocation of resources. The first national antitrust legislation was the Sherman Antitrust Act passed by Congress in 1890. Political support for the act was based on a reaction to and antipathy for large and rapacious trusts at the end of the 19th century. Farmers, workers, consumers, and small businesses all were, or felt they were, victimized by the railroad, steel, sugar, and other trusts. The act prohibited combinations in "restraint of trade" and price-fixing. Most national corporations and the trusts themselves, however, were not enthusiastic about the new legislation. And, in fact, the Sherman Antitrust Act was first applied to labor unions as conspiracies in restraint of trade! Since that time, the act has been used to break up some large companies (e.g., the Standard Oil Company), and it has been supplemented by other legislation aimed at preventing mergers that would limit competition or move industries toward "too much" concentration.

In recent years, the antitrust debate has shifted ground to some extent. During the early 1980s, a merger wave swept the U.S. economy. Mergers occur when one company purchases the stock of another company. In a **horizontal merger,** companies in the same industry are merged, e.g., Texaco Oil's purchase of Getty Oil in 1984. In a **vertical merger,** the merged companies are in different production stages of a particular product, e.g., the large oil companies that have merged the production, refining, and distribution systems of petroleum products. A **conglomerate merger** takes place when the merging companies don't have similar or related businesses, e.g., ITT, which is composed of a large number of previously independent companies producing many different goods and services. Antitrust policy has historically been concerned with mergers because they tend to limit competition and to increase economic concentration—with the possible consequence of raising prices, leading to monopolization, and causing economic inefficiency. In addition, increased economic concentration has always been accompanied by a fear that individual firms will wield increased economic and political power.

Problems w/ anti-trust legislation

The number of mergers valued at $1 million or more increased every year from 1975 through 1984. In the first four months of 1984, there were 32 deals involving sums in excess of $200 million each; this compared with 42 such deals in all of 1983. Those 32 mergers in 1984 involved $15 billion more than the 42 in 1983. Included in the 1984 deals were the $10 billion takeover of Getty by Texaco, the $13 billion purchase of Gulf Oil by Standard Oil of California, and the "modest" $3 billion merger of Carnation with Nestlé. Some economists have charged that this activity has increased corporate borrowing and has contributed to higher interest rates in the early 1980s. Others are concerned about the implications for the concentration of economic and political power if this trend is not checked. Many liberal economists would like to see the antitrust laws enforced more vigorously, and many anti-corporate radicals would even like to see some of the larger corporations broken up.

On the other hand, some liberal economists and most conservative economists would prefer to follow a policy of "benign neglect" toward merger activity and large corporations. They do not see bigness per se as a problem. Large firms must still be sensitive to the market, they argue; if the demand for a product shifts, the firms will respond. Large firms still have an incentive to innovate, because it might increase their profits. Large firms can take advantage of economies of scale, thereby increasing the efficiency of production. Antitrust enforcement, they charge, can limit the ability of American firms to compete with overseas companies, or it can prevent a healthy company from swallowing up an unhealthy one—which might have improved the overall operation of the merged entity. Furthermore, antitrust litigation costs corporations, and ultimately consumers, billions of dollars in court and legal fees.

13. **Is there a difference between a "bad merger" and a "good" merger? Are the mergers between Gulf–Standard Oil and Texaco–Getty good or bad? Do you think that antitrust policy should be vigorously enforced? Why?**

14. **In Chapter 3 we encountered the example of the public (and political) definition of property in Hawaii, where land was taken by the state to reduce economic concentration. In writing the majority opinion for the Supreme Court, Justice Sandra Day O'Connor concluded, "Regulating oligopoly and the evils associated with it is a classic example of a state's police powers. We cannot disapprove of Hawaii's exercise of that power. . . . [It is] a comprehensive and rational approach to identifying and correcting market failure." What's the "market failure," and is it appropriate for the state to correct it?**

POVERTY AND INCOME REDISTRIBUTION

In Chapter 13 we examined the size distribution of income in the United States and we explored why it is distributed relatively unequally. One aspect of income inequality is the existence of poverty. Poverty can be both an absolute and a relative concept. In an absolute sense, poverty might refer to a society or individuals within it that cannot easily meet the day-to-day requirements for continued survival. For example, street beggars in an underdeveloped country or homeless people in the United States are poor. But poverty can also have a relative meaning. Even those families in the United States with the lowest incomes are probably better off materially than many families were in the latter half of the 19th century. Nevertheless, given the standard of living and the operation of markets in our economy, it is clear that some people and some families are demonstrably much less well off than most and that survival and development are very difficult for them.

The federal government estimates a level of income called the **poverty line.** For different family sizes and locations in the country, the poverty line is meant to measure the amount of income necessary to purchase the basic necessities of life—food, clothing, and shelter. For an urban family of four in 1984, the poverty line was $10,609. All urban families of four with incomes less than this for 1984 are then classified as being poor. (Only cash income from work or from assistance is counted.) Given this standard, then, the federal government estimates the number and percentage of people below the poverty line every year. Table 15.6 gives the number of persons below the poverty line and their percentage of the total population for various years from 1960 to 1984.

In the early 1960s, almost 40 million Americans, or more than one-fifth of the nation's citizens, were classified as being poor. In 1973, the number and the percentage reached their lowest levels—23 million people and 11.1 percent of the population. Since then, both the number and the percentage in poverty has been increasing. In part, the general health of the economy in the 1960s and early 1970s and the crisis in the economy since the mid-1970s accounts for this movement in the country's poverty population. But the response of the public sector has also had an impact on the incidence of poverty.

The case for income redistribution to correct for the inequality of market-determined incomes is at its strongest when directed toward attempts to limit poverty. At the height of its post-war prosperity in the early 1960s, the United States recognized the extent of the poverty in its midst and developed public policies to try

Table 15.6 PERSONS BELOW THE POVERTY LINE

YEAR	NUMBER OF PERSONS (IN MILLIONS)	PERCENTAGE OF POPULATION
1960	39.9	22.2
1965	33.2	17.3
1970	25.4	12.6
1975	25.9	12.3
1980	29.3	13.0
1982	34.4	15.0
1983	35.5	15.3
1984	33.7	14.4

Source: Statistical Abstract of the United States, 1986.

to eradicate it. A young Catholic priest, Michael Harrington, wrote *The Other America*, identifying the extent and incidence of poverty in the country; and another Catholic, John F. Kennedy, took up the political challenge of persuading the country to develop federal programs to give relief and promise to its poor. In 1980, the National Advisory Council on Economic Opportunity in its 12th annual report on poverty concluded that the progress in reducing the ranks of the poor between the mid-1960s and 1980 was almost totally the result of federal income assistance and antipoverty programs. During the 1970s, they noted that the number of poor people stayed fairly constant, at about 25 million, and that the growth of the economy did not contribute much to the access of poor people as a whole to adequate jobs and earnings. And, while the total number of poor remained stable, the composition of the poverty population became increasingly concentrated among women, the very young, and minorities. They also predicted that if federal programs for the poor were cut back the poverty rate would increase.

Their prediction has been borne out. The Reagan Administration, as part of its overall economic program, has cut back on the growth of many federal programs directed at the poor, including cash transfer programs such as Aid to Families with Dependent Children and noncash programs such as food stamps, housing assistance, Medicaid, and school lunch subsidies. As a result of these cutbacks and the worst recession since the Depression (in 1981–1983), the poverty rate has indeed increased. In 1983, more than 35 million people were classified as being poor—15.3 percent of the country's population.

15. Do you think that the federal government should contribute income to poor families? Noncash assistance such as food stamps? Training programs for disadvantaged youth? Why or why not? Do we have a public responsibility to eliminate poverty? What external costs are there to poverty?

16. In 1984 the Census Bureau reported that 29.6 percent of all nonfarm Americans received at least one form of federal assistance ranging from Social Security to unemployment compensation to Medicare. Further, 18.8 percent of the population received benefits based on need, such as Medicaid, food stamps, public housing, or Aid to Families with Dependent Children. Why is the impact of the federal government on people's incomes and economic status so widespread? Is it too widespread?

THE LIMITS OF GOVERNMENT'S ROLE

In this chapter, we have focused on the expanding role of government in the economy and the economic arguments that can be and have been made to justify that expansion. During the 20th century, it is largely the liberal view of the state that has won the debate and informed public choices about antitrust policy, the provision of public goods, the regulation of externalities in the private sector, and income redistribution programs. However, there are some criticisms that can be made of government's economic role, as well as some inherent limitations on its ability to pursue its objectives efficiently.

As conservatives point out, governmental programs often limit the pursuit of individual freedom in a democratic society. Public provision of goods and services, taxation to finance governmental activities, and regulation all require compulsion. Young children must go to school, property owners must pay taxes, factories must clean up their pollution, etc. It is the nature of political decisions in a democracy that individuals have some limitations placed on them in the interests of the general welfare. The trade-off, which is often only implicit, is a collective good for individual sacrifice. In return for paying taxes, we get schools, parks, national defense, welfare, and so on. As individuals, we might not choose all of the things we get, but as members of local, state, and national communities, we participate in the political decision-making process (to a greater or a lesser extent) and must live with the results. Freedom is not an unqualified right. Nevertheless, there is fervent debate about the appropriate degree of limitation on individual freedom.

In order to facilitate the legislative process and to administer public programs, public institutions have been created. Office buildings, legislatures, and other public edifices are physical evidence of the public sector, and the bureaucracies that they contain are living and continuing proof of its vitality. In order to accomplish public objectives, bureaucracies are necessary, but the operation of them can produce some problems. If there is no measurable output sold in markets (as in the private sector), there is no way to calculate success in economic terms. Without profits as an indicator, bureaucracies may have difficulty maintaining efficiency. Roads obviously provide an important public service, but how do we know whether road crews are performing at top efficiency? In the private sector, the market weeds out inefficiency. In the public sector, patronage and/or a civil service system might limit the ability of supervisors to fire employees (justly or unjustly). Finally, bureaucracies develop vested interests in their own programs. Consequently, inertia may affect the decisions that are made about the allocation of resources to public programs—rather than having the decision based on the maximization of social benefit compared with the social costs incurred in the use of scarce resources.

The decision-making process in the public sector is not perfect. When it is suggested that public involvement in the economy might improve the overall allocation of resources or correct some of the problems of the private sector, we are implicitly assuming that the decision-making process is rational. Through reasoned debate, research on the effects of different programs, cost–benefit analysis, a free press, and democratic procedures and institutions, we may approach rationality. However, the practice of democracy may also veer off from the ideal. Voters and the voting process often emphasize the people, personalities, and parties involved rather than an unemotional, reasoned consideration of the issues. Modern media certainly reinforce the tendency toward superficiality. Special interests always have the edge in the political process. Their interests are well defined, their numbers are organizable, and they often have access to significant amounts of money. They lobby, they advertise, they persuade, and they are effective in influencing the course of legislating and administering public policies.

As was emphasized at the beginning of this chapter, the role of the government in the economy is an issue that is rich with controversy. In addition, the interpretations of its actual operations and institutions are varied, depending in part on the ideological predispositions of the analysts.

CONCLUSION

Much of the analysis in Part III on microeconomics is directly derived from classical and neoclassical economics. In the realm of the market and the firm, the analysis of those theories is helpful, although slightly qualified by the historical emergence of noncompetitive market structures and the corporation. We are no longer in the ideal and competitive world of Adam Smith. However, supply-and-demand analysis can still help us in understanding how markets work to determine prices and allocate resources. And the focus of microeconomics on the firm has caused economists to pay increasing attention to the modern corporation and to labor unions. The existence of various market failures, ranging from external costs and benefits to the distribution of income to economic concentration, has also led to the continued development of the role of the public sector in the economy.

In the realm of the total economy, though, classical theory has had more severe problems. It contended that the market system would produce growth and full employment. However, this theoretical result conflicted with historical experience. As a result, Keynesian theory emerged to provide an alternative understanding of the macroeconomy. It is this theory that we will explore in Part IV on macroeconomics.

KEY CONCEPTS

mixed economy
public sector
transfer payments
exhaustive spending
market failure
externalities
external costs

external benefits
public goods
price regulation
antitrust policy
mergers, horizontal, vertical,
   and conglomerate
the poverty line

REVIEW QUESTIONS

1. What is the appropriate role for the government in the economy? What functions should it be responsible for performing?

2. Is it proper for the government to regulate the prices of monopolies? Why or why not?

3. The federal government, in particular, has a number of programs intended to reduce poverty in the United States. Should the government be responsible for this effort? What other possible solutions are there to the problem of poverty? Or is there nothing that can be done about it?

4. Traffic accidents as a result of intoxication are an external cost of the consumption of alcohol. Is this true? Why or why not? If yes, specify what the external costs are. If not, explain. What private and public efforts might contribute to a reduction of this problem?

5. The postal service provides a public good. (Before you start thinking of all kinds of nasty jokes and comments about the post office, consider what has to happen in order for a letter that you put in a box somewhere to get to whomever you send it to, say all the way across the country.) What's the *external* benefit from postal service? Could the same service be provided by the private sector? Who would object to the private provision of postal service?

SUGGESTED READINGS

Martin Carnoy, Derek Shearer, and Russell Rumberger, 1983. *A New Social Contract: The Economy and the Government After Reagan*, Harper and Row. A leftist liberal consideration of the role of the government in the economy, a critique of Reaganomics, and a progressive alternative.

Milton and Rose Friedman, 1980. *Free to Choose*, Harcourt Brace Jovanovich. A classic conservative treatise on the limits of government activity in the economy.

Arthur B. Laffer and Jan P. Seymour (eds.), 1979. *The Economics of the Tax Revolt*, Harcourt Brace Jovanovich. Articles on the role of government in the economy, especially on taxes, with a focus on the supply-side case against the government and a critique of that position.

Charles Schultze, 1977. *The Public Use of the Private Interest*, Brookings. A leading liberal economist rethinks the liberal position about the role of the government in the economy.

Thomas R. Swartz and Frank J. Bonello (eds.), 1984. *Taking Sides: Clashing Views on Controversial Economic Issues* (2nd ed.), Dushkin Publishing Group. Radical, liberal, and conservative views of several issues around the government's role in the economy, including antitrust policy, regulation of business, antipoverty programs, and the size of the government.

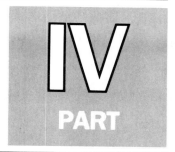

MACROECONOMICS

As we learned in Part III, *microeconomics* analyzes the behavior of consumers and firms in our economic system. We focused on topics such as consumer behavior, the behavior of markets, the different types of market structures, efficiency, scarcity, the nature of the modern corporation and labor unions, and the role of the government.

We will now supplement this microeconomic theory with macroeconomic theory and policy. What is macroeconomics, and what does it attempt to explain? **Macroeconomics** is the body of economic theory that attempts to analyze the behavior and performance of the whole economy. It describes and explains the dynamics of the institutional and governmental framework of our economic system by focusing on *the total or aggregate performance* of the economy. This usually begins with an exposition of income-expenditures theory, which explains the performance of the economy in terms of *employment, income, output,* and *price levels.* A macroeconomic perspective further requires that we explore the relationship between the monetary system and the aggregate performance of the whole economy. We can then utilize our understanding of *monetary theory and policy* and the role of governmental *fiscal policy* (government spending and taxation) to focus on how best to achieve the major macroeconomic goals of *full employment, economic growth,* and *price stability.*

Chapter 16 identifies and describes some of our most important macroeconomic goals and problems. The measuring tools of the National Income Accounts are developed, with an expanded treatment of the accounts in an appendix. Chapter 17 explores the theoretical roots of modern macroeconomics. Chapter 18 describes the Keynesian model, using graphical analysis and simple algebraic formulas, while Chapter 19 focuses on the role of government in making fiscal policy. Chapter 20 introduces the concept of money, its role, and its institutions, in the macroeconomy; and Chapter 21 deals with monetary policy. Chapter 22 turns to an examination of aggregate supply theory. And finally, Chapter 23 explores the major macro problems we face today—unemployment, inflation, and slower economic growth. This last chapter also integrates, summarizes, and critically reflects on the past and present efficacy of contemporary macroeconomic policy in the United States.

16 Chapter

Macroeconomics: Issues and Problems

Macroeconomics examines the economy as a whole. We will no longer look at individual parts of the economy, such as firms or labor unions, or at concepts such as property and value. Our attention now turns to entire sectors that make up our national and international economic system and to aggregate concepts and problems, such as unemployment, inflation, interest rates, deficits, and tax schemes. These are concerns that affect each and every one of us. While this agenda may sound grand and complex, the basic underpinnings of macroeconomic theory are to be found in the circular flow model we will examine in Chapters 17 and 18. National income and thus the wealth of the nation, to use Adam Smith's words, are determined by the actions of and interactions among four basic sectors of the economy—consumption, investment, government spending, and international activity.

In this chapter we shall examine the goals of macroeconomics, review postwar U.S. macroeconomic trends, and develop several tools that will aid our understanding of macroeconomic theory and aspects of macroeconomic policy. We shall, however, begin with a consideration of the importance of macro theory and some of the ways that macroeconomic policy can be used to alleviate economic problems.

GOALS OF THE UNITED STATES ECONOMY

In the early 1950s the U.S. government accepted as its responsibility three basic **macroeconomic goals.** These were (1) maximum employment, (2) economic growth, and (3) price stability. These goals meant that the government accepted as its responsibility the quest for policies that would ensure some recognition of these goals. We will discover later that these goals are not necessarily compatible. That is, one might have to trade some price stability for a greater number of jobs in the economy. And economic growth might mean increasing prices, so that growth must be contained to ensure economic progress without rapidly increasing prices. Despite conflicts among these goals, most of us would agree that full employment, economic growth, and price stability are rational goals. We all want people to be employed. Stable prices are good for most of us. And economic growth has become synonymous with economic progress.

Economic Growth

One of the primary features of the Keynesian macro model we shall examine is the emphasis on **economic growth.** We have adopted a general attitude as a nation that economic growth is not only necessary and good but that more growth is better. Economic growth, after all, creates employment, income, and greater output of goods and services. In our preoccupation with economic growth we have developed very sophisticated tools by which we measure the performance of the economy and its annual rate of real economic growth. By using a method of National Income Accounting (explained in this chapter's Appendix) we have been able to calculate and monitor the rates of growth of **gross national product**—the total dollar value of all goods and services produced in a given year. Our obsession with economic growth is somewhat symbolized by a "GNP clock," built by the Nixon Administration in the early 1970s at a cost of $1 million. In 1978 it ticked off a GNP of $2 trillion and in 1982 recorded a GNP of $3 trillion. It reached $4 trillion in 1985, officially registering the fact that the United States continues to have the world's largest GNP.

During the 1960s and early 1970s the basic assumptions concerning economic growth were challenged by critics who argued that more growth does not necessarily mean that our standard of living has improved. Others now charge that the GNP is becoming a meaningless statistical measurement. It can quantify the performance of the economy, but it does not reflect or include the "qualitative" dimension that considers the question "What is the real societal value and/or cost of increased GNP growth?" Much of this critique stems from a consideration of the environmental aspects of increasing economic growth. Human health and well-being are endangered by toxic wastes and air and water pollution, while acid rain threatens the quality of our food supply. Growing ecological awareness in the context of energy and environmental crises has made us examine our values, attitudes, goals, and economic assumptions more intensely. The economic growth controversy has also raised the critical issue of income distribution in the United States. If economic growth increases from year to year, does this mean that the increased output is being distributed more equitably? Empirical data support the claim that despite the tremendous increases in GNP since World War II, the distribution of income in the United States has not changed significantly, and may have become less equal in the past five years. In addition, economic growth has not evolved in a stable pattern. We have experienced eight major recessions since World War II. The instability characterized by the fluctuations of the business cycle has been a primary feature of the post war era (Table 16.1).

Table 16.1 ANNUAL RATES OF GROWTH, UNEMPLOYMENT, AND INFLATION, BY DECADE

	1950s	1960s	1970s	1980s
Real Growth Rate	2.97	2.91	1.37	
(Nominal Growth Rate)*	(6.63)	(6.77)	(9.73)	(1.0)
Unemployment	4.07	4.78	6.19	8.70
Inflation	2.23	2.33	7.11	7.45

*Not adjusted for inflation.

Source: Economic Report of the President, 1981, 1984.

Full Employment

The attainment of high levels of employment has been one of our nation's macro goals since the **Employment Act of 1946.** It was reaffirmed by Congress in the Full Employment and Balanced Growth Act of 1978, which set goals of a 3-percent rate of inflation and a 4-percent level of unemployment and directed the president to take steps consistent with these goals. Thus far, however, we have come close to the objective of full employment only during times of war. We have not been able to achieve full employment in peacetime. One great problem associated with **unemployment** is the economic (opportunity) cost. In 1984, for every 1 percent of the labor force unemployed, we lost about $60 billion in potential GNP. That amounts to a $420-billion loss in GNP at a 7-percent level of unemployment. In addition, we are learning more about the social and psychological costs associated with unemployment—crime, family disintegration, and increasing mental health problems, to name a few. An examination of the nature of unemployment in the United States also reveals an indentifiable institutionalized process of discrimination according to race, sex, and age. This became increasingly evident as unprecedented numbers of minorities, women, and teenagers entered the labor force in the past decade. When we see a national unemployment rate averaging 8 percent over the last several years, a 14 percent unemployment rate for minorities, 8.5 percent for women, and 40 percent for black teenagers, the charges of discrimination have more validity. Critics also claim that the national measures of unemployment actually understate the real rate of unemployment. They argue that a different definition and measurement technique would reveal a national *underemployment* rate of 14 to 17 percent.

A last consideration related to unemployment is poverty and welfare. Almost 10 million Americans who work full-time or part-time are earning less than the U.S. government's poverty level of income of $10,166 (1983) for an urban family of four. For U.S. citizens who are neither employed nor receiving any form of income from unemployment compensation, Social Security, or disability, being on welfare is the only choice in terms of survival needs. Welfare has become a very costly, cumbersome, degrading, inefficient, and unmanageable government program, and it is currently in need of drastic reform. Nevertheless, its necessity is a function of the absence of full employment.

Price Stability

Perhaps the one thing that most of us have in common is our aversion to increasing **inflation**. We complain when we see the increases in tuition each year as well as the higher price of textbooks, food, and clothing. Our parents are appalled by inflated prices of homes and the interest rates required to finance them. We all have a greater sense of well-being when prices are stable. We don't have to worry (as much) if our seemingly meager savings will suffice to send our children to college or help us maintain our standard of living after we retire. We do know, however, that inflation is not a problem for those of us who correctly anticipate it and can take appropriate precautions. Suppose prices rise by 7 percent and I expect that. If I demand at least a 7 percent wage increase and put my savings into an asset that will yield at least 7 percent, I will not be hurt by inflation. If my wages rise by only 4 percent, I will be losing purchasing power of 3 percent.

Those hurt by inflation include people on fixed incomes, usually the elderly; those working under fixed cost or fixed wage contracts; and individuals or institutions who have lent money at an interest rate less than the current rate of inflation. Fortunately, many contracts now allow for price fluctuations and many pensions are adjusted for inflation. Financial institutions have reacted to inflationary pressures by charging higher interest rates, or even variable rates pegged to inflation. Still, we all prefer price stability so that we may avoid the necessity of forecasting correctly and adjusting our behavior to that forecast.

1. **Which of these three goals is the most important to you? Why?**

2. **If you could add another goal to this list, what would it be? Explain.**

With these three goals in mind then, the government was and is expected to utilize economic theory to analyze the economy and to apply macroeconomic policy to produce the desired results. The primary macro tools are monetary and fiscal policy. Let's briefly define each of these and see how they are used.

MACROECONOMIC TOOLS

Through the Federal Reserve System the government manages, coordinates, and controls the monetary system of the U.S. economy. Proper management of this system makes available the quantity of money necessary for desired economic growth at interest rates capable of inducing the desired levels of investment and spending. **Monetary policy** tools are administered by the Federal Reserve System to achieve and promote economic growth, maximum employment, and price stability.

Fiscal policy is administered by the executive and legislative branches of the government and is coordinated with monetary policy to achieve the desired objectives. With fiscal policy, the government manipulates government expenditures and taxation to attain the basic macroeconomic objectives.

This briefly is the essence of contemporary macroeconomic policy as it has developed over the last two-score years. There are several important issues and problems associated with this theory and policy. We shall examine a few of these in the context of the economic history of the post-war period, the period when monetary and fiscal policy became mainstays in the American economy, trying to achieve the current goals of growth, high employment, and price stability.

THE RISE AND FALL OF PAX AMERICANA

Just as the late 19th century, the Victorian period, was dubbed "Pax Britannia," the period after World War II until the middle to late 1960s has recently been called Pax Americana. The world seemed ripe for economic quests and success by the United States. In the last decade and a half, however, we have become acutely aware of the lack of U.S. powers in the economic world and are often uncomfortable with our new position. Many predict that position will worsen unless new conditions can be generated to take advantage of economic growth and improvement in levels of employment. During this entire period many important characteristics of the U.S. economy were already in place. Monopolies and large corporations had been present since the turn of the century, and the 1930s brought increasing levels of government intervention in the economy.

The setting was ripe for the United States to push ahead and prosper. The 1930s brought prolonged recession and depression. The 1940s brought war. The 1950s arrived with abundant potential and opportunity; Europe and Japan lay in devastation, and the United States possessed the only industrial capacity not debilitated by the war. Our productive capacity was immediately called on to rebuild Europe and Japan, as well as to meet the increased demands for consumer goods and services that had developed in the United States during the war. In the decade following the war, economic growth skyrocketed. Real weekly earnings increased on the average of 2.3 percent per year. Productivity increases averaged a steady 3.2 percent, with GNP growing at about 4 percent. Unemployment averaged only 4 percent. When unemployment rose to 5.5 percent in the recessions of 1949, 1954, 1958, and 1960, inflation was slowed to a now astoundingly low level of 2 percent (or less).

As the prosperity of the 1950s passed into the 1960s, the government began to actively participate in the growth that had been dominated by the private sector. A new federal highway system was the highlight of federal expenditures of the 1950s. These expenditures continued into the 1960s and were joined by a federal Model Cities program that contributed to the U.S. urban infrastructure. A tax cut specifically designed to increase income was passed in 1964—the first planned policy action of its type. Later in the 1960s the Great Society Program worked to reduce poverty. Only now do we realize the great success of these programs as well as some of their shortcomings. The 1960s also brought a new war and again a demand for more federal expenditures to finance it. Yet, during the 1960s, many nations of Western Europe had rebuilt their ruined plants and their economies were again strengthened. Increased foreign production once again challenged U.S. goods in world markets, and U.S. economic growth slowed to 2.9 percent, with average real weekly earnings growing at a more moderate 1.2 percent. Inflation took off as a result of increased federal expenditures for domestic and military purposes. Meanwhile, in the international sphere, the dollar, which served as the "key currency" in all international transactions, was coming under increasing economic attack as other nations regained their prewar economic positions. This eventually led to devaluation of the dollar and a new system of international exchange rates.

The decade of the 1970s was to bring even more distressing news on the economic front. U.S. economic growth and strength were challenged from several sides. The oil embargo of 1973 coupled with agricultural shortages showed just how vulnerable our economy (and others as well) was to supply shocks on a world level. Budget deficits and the continued declining international position of the United States contributed to the inflationary character of the early 1970s. President Nixon's imposition of wage and price controls simply delayed price increases at the time. A severe recession occurred in 1974, and business investment declined. At its peak in 1975, unemployment reached 9 percent. Inflation fell from 8.8 percent in 1973 and 12 percent in 1974 to 4.8 percent by 1976. As the economy began to recover in 1977 and 1978, inflation skyrocketed to 13.3 percent in 1979. In the last half of 1979, President Carter put in motion a series of credit restraints that sent the economy plummeting into yet another recession. Both fiscal and monetary policies were used to try to stabilize the economy, with little apparent success. Economic growth slowed to 1.4 percent and average weekly income increased by a paltry 0.6 percent, in real terms, during the decade. The trade-off between inflation and unemployment had increased as economic growth waned. Growth during this decade was due almost entirely to growth of employment and not growth of productivity or growth in the economy. This employment growth was dominated by the service sector, where many dead-end, low-paying jobs provided entry for an expanding labor force.

While the decade of the 1970s presented us with record levels of inflation, the 1980s have given us the highest levels of unemployment. In 1981 the economy experienced a recession and modest recovery and then plunged into the largest recession (depression) since the Great Depression of the 1930s. Over 10 million people were out of work, with additional numbers uncounted who tired of looking for jobs and others who simply chose not to enter the labor force at this inopportune time. This deep recession can be easily explained by actions of the Federal Reserve, which was using monetary policy to actively restrict the supply of money between late 1979 and 1982. The Fed hoped to curb the inflationary pressures of the 1970s (and to protect the dollar). This monetary policy succeeded temporarily, though many wonder if it was worth the high price of unemployment and lost production.

Monetary ease and historically high government expenditures and tax cuts combined to generate the recovery of 1983–1984. Unemployment fell to 7.1 percent while economic growth averaged an astounding 6 percent as workers headed back to the once-idle factories. Inflation remained at a stable 3 percent, but increases in real weekly earnings averaged only 0.3 percent. The economy, however, had been left with very high rates of interest, resulting at least partially from large government expenditures and tax cuts. High interest rates hurt the economy by hindering investment and job creation in new plants, equipment, and housing. In addition, foreign money is attracted into the United States in order to earn high rates of return, which keeps the value of the dollar high and thus promotes the importing of relatively cheap foreign goods. This hurts U.S. producers, who lose out in two ways. Not only are more foreign goods purchased in the United States, but fewer U.S. products are exported to the rest of the world. High interest rates also affect developing nations, who must pay even larger amounts on their debts with each rise in the U.S. rate of interest.

3. **Why do you think inflation is usually high when unemployment is low? Explain.**

4. **What is debt? How does it arise? Do you worry about going into debt? Why?**

During 1985 and 1986 economic growth continued, averaging just over 2.5 percent for 1985, as the Federal Reserve continued to increase the money supply and interest rates fell. This fall in interest rates, coupled with an agreement by the United States, the United Kingdom, Japan, France and West Germany to work toward a realignment of exchange rates which caused reductions in the value of the dollar, had the effect of slightly decreasing U.S. imports and increasing some exports. The housing and the construction industries responded to these lower rates by accelerating production. Inflation, prompted mainly by plummeting oil prices, continued to remain under control.

5. **Since mid-1986, what has happened to economic growth? What has stimulated the rapid or slow growth? Which industries responded to the lower interest rates of 1986 in the following year? Why?**

Table 16.2 SCORECARD FOR ECONOMIC GOALS, 1980–1988

| | 1980 | | 1984 | | 1985 | | 1986 | | 1987 | | 1988 | |
	TARGET	ACTUAL	TARGET	ACTUAL	TARGET	ACTUAL	TARGET	ACTUAL	TARGET	ACTUAL	TARGET	ACTUAL
Unemployment rate (percent) fourth quarter level*	7.5	7.2	7.5	7.4	7.6	7.1	7.5		6.8		6.1	
	Percent change, fourth quarter to fourth quarter											
Consumer prices	10.7	13.4	4.4	4.2	4.6	3.6	4.5		4.2		3.9	
Real GNP	−1.0	−1.0	5.3	6.5	4.1	2.3	4.0		4.0		4.0	
Real disposable income	0.5	−2.4	0.5	1.0	1.3	1.0	1.5		1.9		1.9	
Productivity†	−0.3	−0.5	1.9	2.1	2.1	0.3	1.8		1.5		1.0	

*Seasonally adjusted

†Based on real GNP per hour worked

Source: Economic Report of the President, 1985, pp. 283, 293, 303, and 320.

Economic Goals for the 1980s

Each annual *Economic Report of the President* contains projections about the economic future of the country using administration assumptions about future growth rates and trends (see Table 16.2). Generally, the president, Congress, and the Federal Reserve will use both monetary and fiscal policy in attempting to achieve these targeted levels. It is always interesting not only to see how well they do but also to observe the political and economic side effects of these policies. In addition, we know that external events and international factors also play a considerable role in economic policy decisions.

As we chart these goals through the next few years it is important that we understand just what these concepts mean and where the measures come from. The scheme of National Income Accounting developed in the Appendix puts these measures into perspective, gives us working definitions for the activities of the three major macroeconomic actors (consumers, businesses, and governments), and shows how they interact to generate production, consumption, and investment.

ECONOMIC THEORY VERSUS ECONOMIC REALITY: THE FUTURE?

This brief overview of macroeconomic problems and issues and of aggregate economic measurements provides us with a conceptual framework for describing relationships among important economic variables. While it is clear that recent trends in the U.S. economy have left us with many questions concerning future directions, we need to ask ourselves this: To what extent does contemporary macroeconomic theory adequately explain our current economic reality? We will attempt to provide satisfactory answers for this question and gain an understanding of macroeconomic theory and policy in this section. So let us embark upon this voyage through macroeconomics by first learning what the theory is in the context of its historical roots.

KEY CONCEPTS

macroeconomics	unemployment
macroeconomic goals	inflation
economic growth	monetary policy
gross national product (GNP)	fiscal policy
Employment Act of 1946	

REVIEW QUESTIONS

1. Why were full employment, economic growth, and price stability selected as the basic macroeconomic goals in the United States?

2. The three goals are often at odds with each other. Has the relative emphasis of these different goals changed over time? Why?

3. What do you see as some of the costs associated with unemployment?

4.   Do events elsewhere in the world have an effect on the U.S. economy? Give some examples.

5.   Is it possible to establish an effective body of macroeconomic policy using only fiscal tools or monetary tools? Why are both fiscal and monetary policy necessary?

6.   Do policy measures aimed at alleviating one set of economic problems sometimes make others worse? Should a policy action be undertaken to aid one aspect of the macroeconomy to the detriment of another?

7.   Examine a daily newspaper (e.g., *The New York Times*) for a few days and see how many articles address macroeconomic issues and problems. Make a list of the macroeconomic terms, concepts, and issues that you find.

SUGGESTED READINGS

Michael Best and William Connolly, 1976. *The Politicized Economy*, D. C. Heath. See Chapters 1, 2, and 3 for an excellent introduction to our major macroeconomic issues and problems.

Peter Duignan and W. Glenn Campbell (Eds.), 1980. *The United States in the 1980s*, The Hoover Institution. This book of essays provides a review and analysis of major domestic and international economic issues that will face the United States in this decade. This is a well-written, well-researched group of essays that should be considered as some of the best of conservative economic thought.

Robert Lekachman, 1973. *Inflation: The Permanent Problem of Boom and Bust*, Vintage. A good primer on the modern sources of inflation and on the economic problems of economic growth, unemployment, and economic instability.

Lester Thurow, 1980. *The Zero-Sum Society*, Basic Books. Chapters 1, 3, and 7 deal with many of the economic issues mentioned in this chapter.

APPENDIX 16A
Measuring GNP

GNP, NNP, PI, DI, . . .

People—and economists are no exception—have been measuring things, or at least trying to, since the beginning of time. Although many of us are still not convinced that metrics is magnificent or any better than our conventional foot, we nonetheless will measure with it—to compare the size or the value of things. When one speaks of the product of a nation, one speaks in terms of GNP, or gross national product. This mystical number for the United States is given to us in quarterly reports issued by the Department of Commerce. Wily reporters seemingly hover over the Commerce Department for days and then give us the verdict as to whether GNP is up or down. Then one finds that the results are most often qualified—GNP was up 3 percent over last quarter, *but* the rate of inflation has been increasing at 4 percent at the same time.

Perhaps we *should* spend an appendix looking at the ins and outs (or rather the ups and downs) of the GNP, an area better known in economics jargon as the *National Income Accounts*.

There are two basic ways of arriving at final figures for the various accounts. There is the **goods-flow** approach and the **income-flow** approach. These may be seen in the circular flow diagram in Fig. 16A.1. One can measure either the top or the bottom of the circular flow and measure national income.

The definitions, relations, and data in Tables 16A.1 and 16A.2 show the derivation of GNP. If you start from the top, you quickly arrive at

$$GNP = C + I + G + (X - M)$$

via the goods flow. Starting from the bottom takes longer, but you will eventually arrive at GNP via the income-flow approach as well.

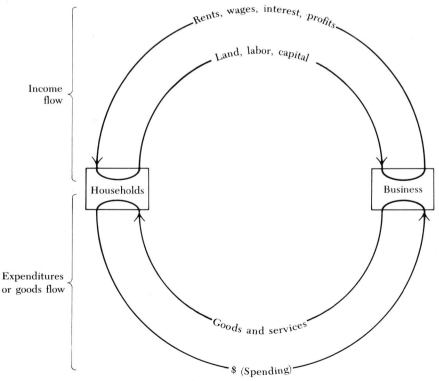

Figure 16A.1   The income and spending flows.

$C = $ consumer spending
$I = $ investment
$G = $ gov't spending
$(X - M) = $ foreign investment

Table 16A.1 RELATION OF GROSS NATIONAL PRODUCT, NET NATIONAL PRODUCT,

		1973	1976	1978
	The sum of			
	Personal consumption expenditures (C)	809.9	1094.0	1350.8
Expenditure flow	Gross private domestic investment (I_d)	213.0	243.3	351.5
	Government purchases of goods and services (G)	269.5	361.4	435.6
	Net exports of goods and services (X – M)	7.1	7.8	–10.3
	Equals: Gross national product (GNP)	1306.6	1706.5	2127.6
	Less: Capital consumption allowances with capital consumption adjustment	117.7	179.0	216.9
	Equals: Net national product (NNP)	1189.0	1527.4	1910.7
	Less: Indirect business tax and nontax liability	120.2	150.5	178.1
	Business transfer payments	5.4	8.1	9.2
	Statistical discrepancy	2.6	5.5	3.3
	Plus: Subsidies less current surplus of government enterprises	3.9	0.8	4.2
	Equals: National income (NI)	1064.6	1364.1	1724.3
Income flow†	Less: Corporate profits with inventory valuation and capital consumption adjustments	99.1	128.1	167.7
	Net interest	52.3	88.4	109.5
	Contributions for social insurance	91.5	123.8	164.1
	Wage accruals less disbursements	–0.1	0	0.2
	Plus: Government transfer payments to persons	113.5	184.7	214.9
	Personal interest income	84.1	130.3	163.3
	Dividends	27.8	35.8	47.2
	Business transfer payments	5.4	8.1	9.2
	Equals: Personal income (PI)	1052.4	1382.7	1717.4
	Less: Personal tax payments	150.7	196.9	328.6
	Equals: Disposable personal income (DPI)	901.7	1185.8	1458.4
	Less: Personal outlays	831.3	1119.9	1386.4
	Personal consumption expenditures (C)	809.9	1094.0	1350.8
	Interest paid by consumers	20.2	25.0	34.8
	Personal transfer payments to foreigners	1.3	0.9	0.8
	Equals: Personal saving (S_p)	70.3	65.9	72.0

*Numbers may not add up to totals shown because of adjustments or inclusion of minor categories.

†Note that indirect business taxes and business transfers and capital consumption allowances must be added to national income to arrive at GNP via the income-flow approach.

Source: Survey of Current Business, July 1977, July 1979, June 1980, March 1986.

NATIONAL INCOME, PERSONAL INCOME, AND DISPOSABLE INCOME ($ BILLIONS)*

1979	1980	1981	1982	1983	1984	1985
1509.8	2668.1	1857.2	2050.7	2229.3	2423.0	2582.3
387.2	401.9	474.9	447.3	501.9	674.0	669.3
476.4	537.8	595.7	641.7	675.7	736.8	815.4
−4.6	23.9	26.3	26.3	−5.3	−59.2	−78.5
2368.8	2631.7	2954.1	3166.0	3401.6	3774.7	3988.5
243.0	293.2	329.5	383.2	399.6	418.9	438.4
2125.8	2338.5	2624.6	2782.8	3002.0	3355.8	3550.1
189.5	213.4	250.0	258.8	282.5	310.6	328.4
10.2	11.7	12.9	14.3	15.6	17.3	19.3
3.7	2.3	−4.9	−0.1	−0.6	−1.5	−0.9
2.3	5.5	6.4	8.7	13.9	10.1	9.5
1924.8	2116.6	2373.0	2518.4	2718.3	3039.3	3212.8
178.2	175.4	192.3	150.0	213.8	273.3	297.0
129.7	192.6	249.9	272.3	273.6	300.2	287.4
189.8	203.7	237.0	269.6	290.8	325.2	354.9
−0.2	—	0.1	—	−0.4	0.2	−0.2
241.9	285.9	324.3	396.2	426.6	437.4	465.2
192.1	266.0	341.3	369.7	385.7	442.2	456.3
52.7	56.8	62.8	63.9	68.0	74.6	78.9
10.2	11.7	12.9	14.3	15.6	17.3	19.3
1924.2	2165.3	2435.0	2670.8	2836.4	3111.9	3293.5
380.6	336.5	387.4	409.3	411.1	441.8	492.7
1624.3	1828.9	2047.6	2261.4	2425.4	2670.2	2800.8
1550.5	1718.7	1912.4	2107.5	2292.2	2497.7	2671.8
1509.8	1668.1	1857.2	2050.7	2229.3	2423.0	2582.3
39.6	49.6	54.3	55.5	61.8	73.3	87.4
1.1	1.1	0.9	1.3	1.0	1.3	2.1
73.8	110.2	135.3	153.9	133.2	172.5	155.0

Table 16A.2 DEFINITIONS

The sum of:

1. *Personal consumption expenditures (C)* consists of the market value of purchases of goods and services by individuals and nonprofit institutions and the value of food, clothing, housing, and financial services received by them as income in kind.

2. *Gross private domestic investment (I)* consists of acquisitions of newly produced capital goods by private business and nonprofit institutions and of the value of the change in the volume of inventories held by business. It covers all private new dwellings.

3. *Government purchases of goods and services (G)* consists of government expenditures for compensation of employees, purchases from business, net foreign purchases and contributions, and the gross investment of government enterprises. It excludes transfer payments, government interest, and subsidies.

4. *Net foreign investment (X–M)* measures the excess of (1) domestic output sold abroad over purchases of foreign output, (2) production abroad credited to U.S.–owned resources over production at home credited to foreign-owned resources, and (3) cash gifts and contributions received from abroad over cash gifts and contributions to foreigners.

Equals

5. *Gross national product (GNP)* = the market value of the newly produced goods and services that are not resold in any form during the accounting period (usually one year).

Less

6. *Capital consumption allowances* is an allowance for capital goods that have been consumed in the process of producing this year's GNP. Consists of depreciation, capital outlays charged to current expense, and accidental damage.

Equals

7. **Net national product (NNP)** is the net creation of new wealth resulting from the productive activity of the economy during the accounting period.

Less

8. *Indirect business tax* consists primarily of sales and excise taxes, customs duties on imported goods, and business property taxes. These taxes are collected from business and are chargeable to their current costs.

Equals

9. **National income (NI)** = the total income of factors from participation in the current productive process.

Less

10. *Social Security contributions* consist of payments by both employees and the self-employed.

11. *Corporate income taxes* comprise federal and state taxes levied on corporate earnings.

12. *Undistributed corporate profits* are what remains of corporate profits after both corporate income taxes and dividends have been paid.

Table 16A.2 (*Cont.*)

Plus

13. **Transfer payments** (government and business) consist of monetary income receipts of individuals from government and business (other than government interest) for which no services are rendered currently.

Equals

14. **Personal income (PI)** = income received by households, as opposed to income earned by households.

Less

15. *Personal taxes* consist of the taxes levied against individuals, their income, and their property that are not deductible as expenses of business operations.

Equals

16. **Disposable income (DI)** is the income remaining to persons after deduction of personal tax and nontax payments to general government.

Less

17. *Personal consumption expenditures (C)*—same as (1).

Equals

18. **Personal saving (S)** may be in such forms as changes in cash and deposits, security holdings, and private pension, health, welfare, and trust funds.

PROBLEMS WITH NATIONAL INCOME ACCOUNTING

In these definitional relationships, many difficult and rather perplexing problems are ignored. First, there is the problem of the yardstick, money—and a very flexible yardstick it is, too, dollars being worth more or less as time passes (usually less). In order to solve the flexibility dilemma, index numbers are used in which "market baskets" of goods and services in one accounting period are compared with a similar basket in some base accounting period. Thus statisticians can avoid the perils of price instability by inflating or deflating accordingly. This device allows us to remove the effects of price changes from GNP, so that we can measure the changes in *real* output, the actual physical volume. The GNP deflator is a systematized equation that has been shown to be a "reasonable" indicator of how much the national product has gained or lost due to recession or inflation. For example, in 1979 GNP went up by 12 percent, but prices went up by 11.3 percent, so **real GNP** increased by only 0.7 percent. Figure 16A.2 shows what has happened to the GNP since 1950 in both current dollars and "real" 1972 dollars.

A second problem in the national income accounts is the actual counting process. One can either count the final products produced or sum each of the values added by each phase of the production process. Both methods should yield the same result, but there is often a chance of double counting in the final product method.

The most recent criticism involves the significance of the accounts, or the lack of it. Many market transactions are excluded from the accounts (an estimated $80 billion of Mafia money, for example) as well as capital gains and losses, and many

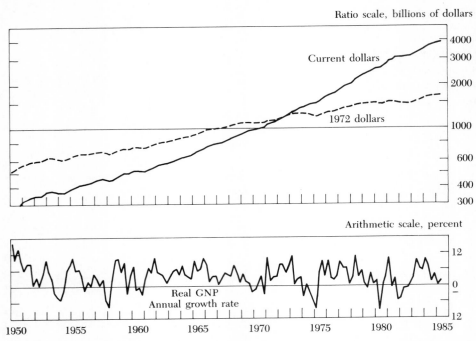

Figure 16A.2 Gross national product (GNP), seasonally adjusted annual rates, quarterly.

nonmarket transactions are included. Imputed values are added for owner-occupied homes, room and board for services exchanged, etc. And imagine what would happen to the accounts if homemakers simply traded homes with their neighbors each day and paid one another $48 a day (the estimated market worth of homemakers' services.) These activities are productive; they are services, but they are not included in the national income accounts.

Another misleading characteristic of the national income accounts involves the social costs that, rather than being subtracted from, are added to the GNP. As we spend more and more to clean up pollution, the spending *adds* to our national product. As cigarette sales increase, GNP increases. As hospital costs for increased numbers of cases of lung cancer and emphysema occur, the GNP increases. GNP, in other words, is not a measure of overall welfare. Recently economists and other social scientists have been attempting to gather together a qualitative index that measures social welfare. Thus far the index is quite crude, but it shows significantly that nations with the highest GNP don't necessarily have the highest social welfare ratings, while a few countries with extremely low GNPs have *relatively* high standings on the social welfare index.

1. **Why is it important to collect data on all of these different macroeconomic variables?**

KEY CONCEPTS

goods-flow approach
income-flow approach
net national product (NNP)
national income (NI)
transfer payments

personal income (PI)
disposable income (DI)
personal savings
real GNP

17

Chapter

The Classical and Keynesian Models and the Great Depression

INTRODUCTION

The tenets of classical macroeconomic theory, formed by Adam Smith, David Ricardo, John S. Mill, and others, were carried pretty much intact through the 19th century. Economists in the latter part of that era concentrated more on the microeconomic elements of utility and production than on the total economy. This chapter will sort out three major parts of the classical doctrine, illustrate their use, and then examine the Keynesian critique of classical macro theory and its inability to deal with high unemployment in the depression-plagued world of the 1930s. The logic of the Keynesian argument will then be formulated.

Keynes's theory challenged the longstanding economic traditions, and his efforts were criticized as heresy before he was knighted for his genius. Some view the Keynesian contribution as a new paradigm, while others view it as simply a major revision of classical theory. It might be noted that the classical model discussed here was never formally set up as such by any of the classical economists. Rather, Keynes drew together the foundations from the writings of the classical economists and constructed the model primarily as a "strawman." He then proceeded to break the model down, a part at a time, in *The General Theory of Employment, Interest, and Money*.

THE CLASSICAL SYSTEM

MV = PQ or the Quantity Theory of Money

One of the major tenets of classical economic theory was the **Quantity Theory of Money.** Most often this is expressed by the "**equation of exchange,**"

$$MV = PQ,$$

where M is the money stock in the economy, V is the income **velocity of money** or the rate of turnover of money, P is the price level, and Q is the level of real national income. This equation appears simple enough—perhaps too simple, for when it is examined carefully it becomes an obvious tautology. It is true because it is by definition true. It is redundant because of the definition of velocity—the rate at which money moves through the economy during a given period, or the number of times a piece of money gets spent:

$$V = \frac{P \times Q}{M}.$$

Since national income is a measure of all output (Q) in a country for a year multiplied by the price (P) of each good or service, V is equal in effect to national income in a given year divided by the total amount of money available (on the average) during that year.

The classical economists elaborated further on each of the variables in the "equation of exchange." They expressed the belief that each of the variables in the equation was affected by a variety of external and internal forces. Q, or national output, was determined primarily by real factors that changed slowly over time, such as capital, technology, resource availability, and labor. The quantity of money (M) would not influence these variables in any significant way. The classical economists argued that the income velocity of money (V), on the other hand, was determined by institutional factors that were also independent of any change in the money stock (M). Some of these institutional factors accounting for changes in V or payment habits of the public were population density, custom, transportation factors, the state of the art of banking, wage payments and practices, and so on. With Q and V unaffected by changes in the supply of money, the level of prices, P, is left to have some connection with changes in the quantity of money (M).

According to the classical economists, only the price level was determined in the money market. Since Q and V were defined as relatively constant, this meant that changes in the quantity of money produced nearly proportional changes in the price level. Thus, if the quantity of money in the economy is doubled, the price level is likely to double as well. In terms, then, of output and employment in the economy, money didn't matter very much; in terms of wages and prices, however, it mattered a great deal. The following equations show this:

$$M\bar{V} = P\bar{Q}, \qquad \Delta M = \Delta P.$$

Since $\bar{V}$ and $\bar{Q}$ are constant at a point in time, changes in the quantity of money lead to changes in prices.

In the world of the classical economists, **money** was considered to be **neutral** in that it satisfied no direct utility or want. It merely reflected real activity in the economy. It served as a veil behind which the real action of economic forces, such as the growth of the national product and employment, were concealed. Yet money was viewed as a lubricant for the economy, keeping it well oiled and enabling it to run smoothly and effectively.

The Goods Market in Classical Economics

A second major scheme of the classical model centered on the production of goods, or real output. Equilibrium output was determined by the demand for and the supply of labor. Increases in the demand for labor increased output (Q), and decreases in the supply of labor decreased output. The level of output was determined by the full-employment level in the classical system. The equilibrium real wage defined the level of full employment in the labor force. Anyone willing to work at the prevailing equilibrium wage would be employed—the quantity supplied of labor would equal the quantity demanded of labor. Anyone unwilling to work at that wage was regarded as not desiring to work (i.e., was not classified as unemployed). As long as wages were flexible (both upward and downward) in the classical world, no conflict arose. Full employment, as they defined it, was the norm.

Say's Law

A third major foundation of classical macroeconomic theory was **Say's law,** named for the French economist Jean Baptiste Say (1767–1832), who popularized the principle. In its oversimplified form, the "law" states that *supply creates its own demand*. In other words, no matter what the level of output (supply), the income created in the process of its production must create an amount of spending sufficient to purchase those goods and services produced. For every dollar of product produced, there is a dollar of income created and spent.

Say's law gives rise to the **circular flow** diagram, shown in Fig. 17.1, that is very important to the discussion of both the Keynesian and classical models. The crude circular flow of the classics shows (1) the movement of goods from the business sector of the economy to the household sector in return for spent income; *and* (2) the transfer of the services of land, labor, and capital from households to business for use in the production of goods and services in exchange for rents, wages, and interest.

The **aggregate supply,** or output, that "creates its own demand" is the goods and services that are produced by the firms or businesses. The factors of production (land, labor, and capital) receive returns of rents, wages and salaries, and interest and profits for their part in the production process. Higher income levels in the household sector create more demand for goods and services; thus **aggregate demand**

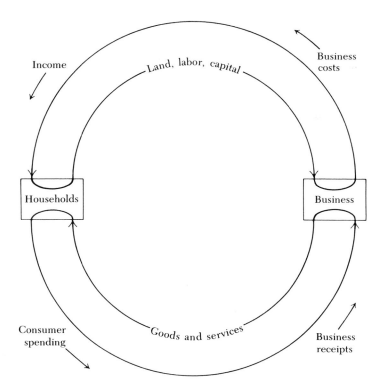

Figure 17.1 The circular flow.

increases. This income in the household sector is then spent on the goods and services that have been produced; this creates an income stream, through spending, for the business sector. The result is that the aggregate demand for goods and services of the household sector will equal the aggregate supply of those goods and services produced by the business sector. Equilibrium, then, occurs when aggregate supply or income equals aggregate demand or spending.

THE FLAWS IN THE CLASSICAL SYSTEM

Between 1860 and 1929 the U.S. economy was growing rapidly. The phases of growth tended to be cyclical, with upswings in economic activity accompanied by downswings, but with an overall upward secular trend in economic activity *averaging* about 2 percent per year. Figure 17.2 shows a hypothetical series of business cycles. Note that periods of growth peaks are followed by periods of slump and a trough.

1. **If you were to extend Fig. 17.2 to include this year, where would the economy be? In an upswing? A downswing? A peak or a trough? Why?**

Figure 17.2   Business cycles.

Many explanations were offered to account for the waves in the **business cycle** (Fig. 17.2). These ranged from increases in sunspot activity to overconsumption/ underinvestment, monetary expansion and contraction, and innovation. Indeed, compelling arguments have been made for each of these in explaining the pattern of growth.

> **2. What argument might you use to convince your roommate that the level of business cycles might be the result of sunspots? Of underconsumption followed by overinvestment?**

When economic conditions were in the downswing or trough of the cycle, as in the 1930s, classical economic theory explained the resulting levels of unemployment by insisting that those out of work were simply voluntarily or temporarily un- employed. They believed that more employment opportunities could be made by reducing the prevailing wage rate. As wages fell, there would be an increase in the demand for labor. According to classical theory, these unemployed workers would be more than happy to work as long as their wages were above zero. However, during the Great Depression, as wages dropped lower, even more people were out of work—not fewer.

THE GREAT DEPRESSION

The Great Depression was a result of many different phenomena that seemed to culminate all at once. Some people who are interested in business cycles believe that short-, medium-, and long-run cycles all reached bottom at the same time. Nonethe- less, we should explore some of the causes of this depression that lasted for ten years and left enduring imprints on millions of Americans.

It took more than just the 1929 stock market crash to sustain the Depression for such a long period. Despite the robustness of the stock market before its fall, several sectors of the economy were essentially weak. Agriculture and manufacturing were perhaps the most important sectors contributing to the duration of the Depression.

As the country had grown in the first few decades of the century, the agricul- ture sector had dwindled. Hurt by the exploitation of the rail and storage bosses, and burned by their own speculative activities in land, more and more farmers were leaving or selling out to join the urban migration or to become tenants. The number of independent farms had dropped by 40 percent during the 1920s. Output, however, was increasing, and the inelastic demand for farm production did little to help the agriculture sector. Unlike the other sectors of the economy, in which greater supplies meant lower prices and increased demand, demand was not forthcoming to the lower-priced agricultural products. In addition, the European export market was lost as European agricultural production was restored following World War I.

In manufacturing concerns, conditions were mixed. Many people in business foresaw a time of weakness ahead, and although sales, prices, and output were at an all-time high, employment had been cut back substantially, especially in the mines and mills. Only in the service and construction industry did employment levels hold their own—for this was an area in which men and women could not yet be displaced by technology. Prosperity increased throughout the 1920s. But workers were no better off than before. Wages and employment levels simply did not increase. Profits, on the other hand, swelled rapidly, as did the concentration of economic power in the hands of a few wealthy individuals. Profits in 1929 were three times those of 1920. But firms were not reinvesting. This was partially due to the fact that demand was unable to keep up with supply.

The weaknesses in these two sectors are directly linked to other causes of the Depression: the lopsided distribution of income, with 5 percent of the population receiving about 30 percent of all income, and the lack of new investments by the business sector. In addition, the existing banking system was such that runs on poorly managed banks created a fear among depositors, so that even economically sound banks were subjected to "runs" and potential failure. Some 5000 of the nation's banks failed during the Great Depression. Other factors added to the instability: Several European governments defaulted on U.S. loans, and in the United States, Congress adopted a "balanced budget" philosophy that, by increasing taxes and reducing government expenditures, helped to make a bad situation even worse.

All of this suggests that the U.S. economy was fundamentally unsound at the time of the stock market crash. From the widespread prosperity of the early 1920s, the late 1920s saw a lack of capital formation, overproduction of goods and services, and an agricultural glut, in addition to international disequilibrium and deep-seated psychological effects from the crash. All these led to prolonged instability, which in turn led to the devastation of many businesses, organizations, and institutions and brought havoc to the lives of most people. Between 1929 and 1932, 85,000 businesses failed, and stock values decreased from $87 billion to $19 billion. Manufacturing and farm income decreased by 50 percent. By 1933, the GNP had declined from $104 billion in 1929 to $56 billion, and unemployment stood firmly at 25 percent, with 12 million people unemployed.

The Depression in Human Terms

The Depression of the 1930s is the example most people reflect upon as a time of severe unemployment and poverty for the men, women, and children who suffered and endured through it. Ask your grandparents about the era sometime. Over one-third of the nation was unemployed or living in poverty. And conditions were abysmal for all but a few of the well-to-do. The middle class suffered, and the poor starved. The following excerpt illustrates the reality of the Depression.

> When the breadwinner is out of a job he usually exhausts his savings if he has any. Then, if he has an insurance policy, he probably borrows to the limit of its cash value. He borrows from his friends and from his relatives until they can stand the burden no longer. He gets credit from the corner grocery store and the butcher shop, and the landlord forgoes collecting the rent until interest and taxes have to be paid and something has to be done. All of these resources are finally exhausted over a period of time, and it becomes necessary for these people, who have never before been in want, to ask for assistance. The specter of starvation faces millions of people who have never before known what it was to be out of a job for any considerable period of time and who certainly have never known what it was to be absolutely up against it.
>
> Lester V. Chandler, *America's Greatest Depression.* New York: Harper & Row, 1970, pp. 41–42.

ENTER JOHN MAYNARD KEYNES

John Maynard Keynes (1883–1946) was born into a prosperous Victorian family. He watched the economic importance of his native Britain wane with the rapid growth of the United States and continental Western Europe.

Certainly one of the most illustrious and eccentric of all economists, Keynes's interests were centered in the "Bloomsbury Group," comprising such people as Leonard and Virginia Woolf, Clive Bell, and Sidney and Beatrice Webb, who, along with the brightest economists of Cambridge, served as the sounding board for all of Keynes's work.

Keynes's ideas and his critique of the classical model were developed slowly and over a rather lengthy period of time. Much of his writing was highly critical of the British authorities. He was one of the first to recognize the implausibility of the British attachment to the gold standard and to object to the Versailles Peace Treaty. (He felt that it would be impossible for Germany to meet the reparations called for by the treaty.) His work came at a time when the classical model was most under fire because of its inability to account for continued and worldwide depression and the masses of unemployed in the 1930s.

The major question being asked in each world capital was what to do? According to the classical doctrine, the simple remedy was a wage reduction. But wages *were* falling, and more unemployment resulted, not less. Say's law was being violated. Supply was not creating its own demand. The circular flow was not working right. Classical theory and classical economists were in a quandary. By focusing on the question of unemployment and arguing that "the postulates of the classical theory are applicable only to a special case and not the general case . . . and not . . . those of the economic society in which we actually live," Keynes proceeded to illustrate the futility of the classical scheme, particularly Say's law and the limited circular flow.

KEYNES TO THE RESCUE

Keynes and some contemporary economists recognized that there were leakages from the income and spending flows as well as injections to them. **Leakages** included savings, taxes, and the purchases of goods and services from foreign nations (imports). With each of these actions, income would flow out of the circle in the circular flow diagram of the classical economists. Saving and hoards remove money from the spending stream and occur when households, deciding that future consumption is better than present consumption, put their money into savings and time accounts at financial intermediaries, into the stock market, or under their mattresses. Taxes leave the spending stream of the household and business sectors and are turned over to the government. Imported goods and services from other nations increase the goods and services received by households but reduce the total domestic spending since these dollars now go abroad to pay for the goods and services received.

On the other hand, Keynes noted that there were **injections** that could be and were made to the income and spending stream. Government spending, investment, and the purchase of goods by foreign nations (exports) added to the flow. Government spending, like consumer spending, increases the income received by the business sector, since purchases are made of business products. Government spending may also go directly to the household sector in the form of transfer payments or income supplements, which in turn will increase spending as well. Investment occurs when the business sector creates new capital in the form of new plants, or additions to equipment or the buildup of existing inventories—or stocks of goods and services that are in their warehouses. Investment is, in effect, business spending. Exports create an injection into the income stream since businesses have a new market for their products and receive income in return. (Figure 17.3 illustrates the dynamics of these flows.)

3. **Trace each of the injections—government spending, investment, and exports—in Fig. 17.3. Trace each leakage—saving, taxes, and imports—in Fig. 17.3.**

For the economy to be in equilibrium, then, the injections have to equal the leakages. As a result, aggregate demand for goods and services in the economy would be equal to the aggregate supply. This would establish an equilibrium level of income and output that might or might not be at full employment. According to Keynes, an infinite number of equilibrium positions could exist in an economy, one of which is at full employment. The classical economists, however, saw one and only one equilibrium—the one that existed at full employment.

According to the Keynesian theory, equilibrium would be inevitable since self-adjusting mechanisms would be at work within the economy to restore equilibrium. In the following, we will abstract and concentrate on the savings leakage and the investment injection, ignoring for the moment taxes, government spending, and

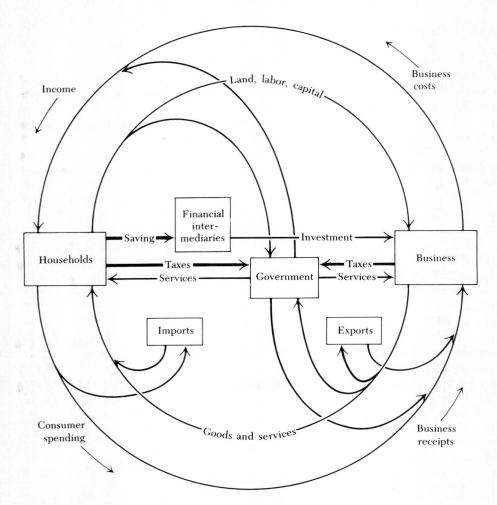

Figure 17.3 The circular flow with leakages and injections.

imports and exports. If a situation of disequilibrium existed where injections were not equal to leakages, there would be a "natural" tendency for readjustment.

As the economy grew, each increase in investment would lead to even higher levels of income in the economy through a multiplier effect. Keynes predicted that as incomes increased, **savings** would increase since individuals with higher incomes saved proportionally more (and consumed proportionally less) than individuals with low incomes. For the economy to continue to grow and for business to expand profits, **investment** must increase over time. Investment funds could be borrowed from households' savings funds. This most likely was facilitated by some financial intermediary, such as a commercial bank.

If the planned savings of the household sector exceeded the investment levels planned by the business sector, a disequilibrium would result. With planned savings greater than planned investment, consumers simply would not be purchasing sufficient goods and services to keep pace with investment. The leakage from the spending flow would cause **inventories** to build up. Aggregate supply of goods and services would exceed aggregate demand for these goods and services, and producers would alter their investment decisions. As inventories accumulated in the warehouses, businesses would begin to cut back on output, and these actions could decrease the level of production, income, and, finally, saving. At some point, reduced planned saving would equal planned investment.

4. What would happen if planned investment was greater than planned saving?

In the case of a depression, this circle of causation simply feeds on itself. As a firm sees income decreasing, it becomes more myopic, planning even lower levels of investment. Again, with saving greater than investment, consumption falls lower and inventories increase more, so the cutback of firms is even greater, resulting in more unemployment and incomes lower than ever. (Note, however, that the economy is still in equilibrium since as income drops, savings will drop to the level at which $S = I$.) How is it possible to end this recessionary process?

As we've stated before, the classical economists believed that wages simply weren't low enough. Keynes, on the other hand, viewed wages as moving inflexibly downward and saw relief from the downward spiral with new injections into the economy in the form of increases in government spending, rather than through the normal investment channels that could not be relied on when business expenditures were low. With the government employing people in public works, social services, the military complex, or whatever, the cycle could be broken and full employment restored. Keynes was only partially concerned about the form this spending took, as we see in this passage from *The General Theory*.

> If the Treasury were to fill old bottles with banknotes, bury them at suitable depths in disused coalmines which are then filled up to the surface with town rubbish, and leave it to private enterprise on well-tried principles of *laissez-faire* to dig the notes up again (the right to do so being obtained, of course, by tendering for leases of the note-bearing territory), there need be no more unemployment and, with the help of the repercussions, the real income of the community, and its capital wealth also, would probably become a good deal greater than it actually is. It would, indeed, be more sensible to build houses and the like; but if there are political and practical difficulties in the way of this, the above would be better than nothing.

Excerpted from *The General Theory of Employment, Interest, and Money,* by John Maynard Keynes, 1936. Reprinted by permission of Harcourt Brace Jovanovich, Inc.

5. Does it make any difference what the government might spend money on? Why or why not?

And so it was that the Keynesian solution and analysis eventually captured the minds and hearts of economists throughout the world—and how very simple that solution was. Increased government spending would increase the levels of income, employment, and output. If government spending policies were used to operate counter to the business cycle, a full range of economic maladies could be cured.

KEY CONCEPTS

equation of exchange
  (*MV* = *PQ*)
quantity theory of money
velocity of money
money as neutral
Say's law
circular flow
aggregate supply

aggregate demand
business cycle
John Maynard Keynes
leakages
injections
savings
investment
inventories

REVIEW QUESTIONS

1. What phenomena caused the Great Depression to be as long and as deep as it was?

2. Why might Keynes's theory be called a "depression theory"? Can you make a few arguments as to why it might command a more general use?

3. Why would the classical economists distinguish among the variables in the equation of exchange being determined by real factors or monetary factors? What is the implication of prices increasing as the quantity of money increases?

4. What is the logical flaw in Say's law?

5. What were Keynes's major criticisms of the classical theory?

6. Why must leakages equal injections in the Keynesian world for an equilibrium level of income to exist?

7. Look at the Keynesian circular flow diagram (Fig. 17.3). Do leakages and injections ever leave the economy permanently? How are they fed back into the economy?

8. If depressions become self-fulfilling prophecy, can inflationary periods also be self-fulfilling? What would you expect the Keynesian prescription to recommend in such a case?

9. In your experience, are wages "sticky" (inflexible) in a downward direction? Was Keynes "right" in assuming this inflexibility? How sticky are wages when they are going up?

SUGGESTED READINGS

Frederick Lewis Allen, 1931 and 1939. *Only Yesterday* and *Since Yesterday*, Harper & Row. *Only Yesterday* gives a highly readable account of the 1920s, including discussions of the big bull market and the crash. *Since Yesterday* begins in 1929 and ends in 1939, with an account of the Depression and the recovery process.

Business Week, September 3, 1979. This 50th-anniversary issue contains a number of articles dealing with the causes of the Depression and its economic legacy.

John Kenneth Galbraith, 1954. *The Great Crash, 1929*, Houghton Mifflin. An interesting and readable account of the Depression.

Robert L. Heilbroner, 1980. *The Worldly Philosophers*, Simon and Schuster. A well-written and humorous account of the lives of classical economists through Keynes—and then some.

Robert Lekachman, 1966. *The Age of Keynes*, Random House. This work provides an interesting biography of Keynes and an analysis of his work.

Joan Robinson, 1962. *Economic Philosophy*, Aldine. The second chapter gives a good summary of the work of the classical economists. Chapter 4 is devoted to Keynes.

David A. Shannon, 1960. *The Great Depression*, Prentice-Hall. This little book examines the impact of the Depression on the lives of the people in the United States.

Time, "We are all Keynesians now," December 31, 1965. A short, readable essay on the Keynesian influence.

18

Chapter

Keynes in Words and Pictures

INTRODUCTION

The Keynesian model has remained the prevailing economic paradigm for the past 45 years. Originating in the depression-plagued world of the 1930s, Keynesian economic theory has persisted through the slow-moving 1950s, the inflationary 1960s, the unstable 1970s, and the short-run busts and booms of the 1980s. It has not always been successful, as economists have bent its rules and principles and redefined the priorities to fit the current circumstance; but despite the recent supply-side challenges it still solidly forms the basis for the macroeconomic theory of the age. Monetarist Milton Friedman perhaps stated it best when he said, "We are all Keynesians now." This chapter will describe and explore in detail the assumptions, methods, and the implications of the full Keynesian *model*. Both verbal and graphical analyses will be used to illustrate the theory since, to many, a picture is indeed worth a thousand words. Several examples will follow illustrating the use of Keynesian theory.

CONSUMPTION

The very best place to start is, of course, the beginning, and though it is sometimes difficult to distinguish the beginning from the middle or the end in Keynesian theory, this examination will start with the consumption function and the assumptions and hypotheses that underlie one of America's favorite pastimes. **Consumption** is the purchasing of goods and services, the spending of income for necessities and luxuries. It is perhaps intuitive that consumption depends on many things. Some of these are income, interest rates, price levels, and expectations, along with the other financial assets the consumer might possess. But as one might well expect, consumption is primarily a function of income. This can be expressed

$$C = f(Y),$$

where C is the consumption of individuals over some period of time, Y is income, and f is a functional notation.* Keynes in his "fundamental psychological law" states: "Men are disposed, as a rule and on the average, to increase their consumption as their income increases." In other words, as your income increases (perhaps upon graduation and securing a job), your expenditures will rise as well—but, says Keynes, not by as much. This relationship may be expressed graphically with consumption (C) on the vertical axis and income (Y) on the horizontal axis. Since consumption is an increasing function of income (Y), as Y increases, C will also increase (Fig. 18.1).

What will be done with the income *not* spent on consumption? Simple! It will be saved. Saving is any part of income that is not spent on consumption. There is nothing left to do with it. (Burning it isn't rational—and Keynes assumes that we are all rational.) In equations, our relationship is

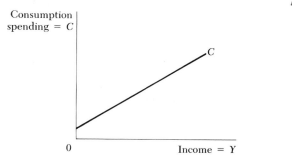

AS INCOME RISES,

CONSUMPTION RISES

$$y = C + S$$

Consumption spending = C

0   Income = Y

Figure 18.1 The consumption function.

---

*Studies have shown consumption to be a linear function of income, or $C = a + bY$, where C is the consumption of individuals over time; a is the intercept of the consumption function, or C where $Y = 0$. Since a is positive, it indicates that individuals must consume some amount of food, clothing, and shelter even if they have no income; b is the slope of the function; Y is disposable income; that is GNP – depreciation – taxes – retained earnings + transfer payments. Y, then, is the income that a household has available to it for consumption purposes.

$$Y = C + S.$$

Again, Y is income, C is personal consumption expenditures, and S is personal saving. Saving is, in effect, a residual of consumption. Saving occurs when individuals defer present consumption or spending and keep the funds for future use. People save for many different reasons. It may be for precaution or fear of what might lie ahead. It may be for a desire to become "financially independent" sometime in the future. Or it may be for pride or avarice. For whatever reasons, saving does occur; and, like consumption, it is also a function of income [$S = f(Y)$].

Before we proceed further in the analysis of consumption and saving, it is important to establish a reference position (or helping line) so that the relation of the level of consumption to the level of income may be more easily discussed. This helping line is a 45° line from the origin of the consumption–income axis (see Fig. 18.2). This line may be thought of as the aggregate supply curve of producers when prices are constant. This aggregate supply curve shows the dollar amount firms expect to receive if they supply a particular level of output (Y). If firms supply $1.5-trillion worth of goods and services, they must expect to receive $1.5 trillion in receipts in order to maintain that level of production. They are paying $1.5 trillion to the factors of production to produce this output, and therefore must expect to receive $1.5 trillion. If the firm increases production to $2 trillion, then $2 trillion is expected from sales. If production decreases to $1 trillion, $1 trillion is expected. At each level of income (Y), firms desire to sell a maximum amount of their products. Each of these points is on the 45° line, which bisects the origin and represents a level of business receipts (consumer spending) just equal to the corresponding level of income (Y). Thus, points on the 45° line form the desired aggregate supply curve for firms. Note that prices are constant here and throughout the Keynesian analysis.

We can now utilize this relationship in examining consumption. Since the 45° line bisects the 90° angle, at any point on the line, income will equal consumption. For example, at point A, both Y and C are equal to $1.5 trillion; at point B, $Y = C = $2.0 trillion. If the consumption curve is now superimposed on this 45° line, it will allow an examination of the relationship of consumption to the actual level of income in the economy.

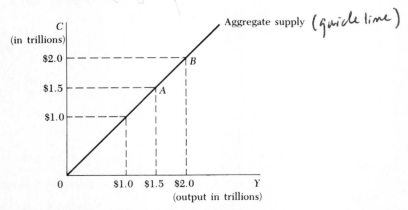

Figure 18.2   The 45° line (aggregate supply).

In Fig. 18.3 at point A, consumption and income are equal since the consumption curve passes through the 45° line at that point. Point A is called the **break-even level of income** as $Y = C = \$1.5$ trillion. **Saving** equals zero. At point D, however, consumption is less than income, indicating that some amount of saving must be taking place. Since income is \$2.0 trillion and consumption is only \$1.75 trillion, \$.25 trillion must be saved. At point B, consumption is greater than income: Income is \$1.0 trillion, but consumption spending is \$1.25 trillion. **Dissaving** is taking place to allow the desired level of consumption to occur. Dissaving consists of borrowing or drawing down other financial assets in order to purchase products for consumption purposes. Individuals on low fixed incomes frequently dissave. So do young people starting families or households. (Note that even when income is zero, there is some amount of consumption spending.)

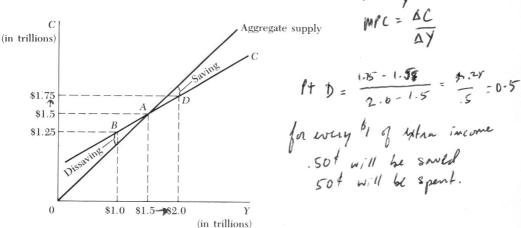

$APC = \dfrac{C}{Y}$

$MPC = \dfrac{\Delta C}{\Delta Y}$

$Pt\ D = \dfrac{1.75 - 1.5\!\!\!/8}{2.0 - 1.5} = \dfrac{\$.25}{.5} = 0.5$

for every $1 of extra income
.50¢ will be saved
50¢ will be spent.

Figure 18.3   The consumption function and the 45° line.

1. **Do you dissave now? Do you expect to dissave in the next year or two? Draw a curve on the graph in Fig. 18.4 indicating what you expect your consumption pattern to look like for the rest of your life. At what periods do you think you might be dissaving?**

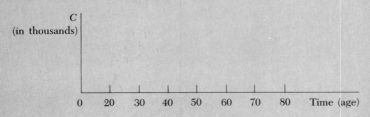

Figure 18.4   Your consumption pattern.

Average and Marginal Propensity to Consume

The average consumption–income ratio can be determined by the information given thus far. This ratio is simply C/Y. At point A in Fig. 18.3, the average consumption–income ratio, the **average propensity to consume** or the **APC**, is C/Y = $1.5 trillion/$1.5 trillion, or 1. At point D, it is C/Y = $1.75 trillion/$2.0 trillion = 0.875; at point B, APC = C/Y = $1.25 trillion/$1.0 trillion = 1.25. The APC is one of the two fundamental ratios that are derived from the consumption function. The second of these ratios, and perhaps the more important, is the **marginal propensity to consume,** or the **MPC.** The MPC is the ratio between the *change* that occurs in consumption with some given change in income. This may be expressed as $\Delta C/\Delta Y$, where Δ is a symbol for change, C is consumption, and Y is income. If income increases from $1.5 trillion to $2.0 trillion, we find consumption increases from $1.5 trillion to $1.75 trillion. The change in income is $2.0 trillion – $1.5 trillion, or $.5 trillion; the change in consumption is $1.75 trillion – $1.5 trillion, or $.25 trillion. The MPC, then, is $\Delta C/\Delta Y$ = $.25 trillion/$.5 trillion, or 0.5. This means that for every additional dollar of income, $.50 will be used for consumption and the remaining $.50 will be saved.

2. What is the MPC when we move from point B to point A in Fig. 18.3?

The MPC or $\Delta C/\Delta Y$ relationship is also the slope of the consumption function.* (See Fig. 18.5.) Note that the consumption function will be a straight line only when the MPC is constant at all levels of income. This will seldom occur since each

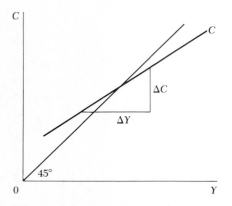

Figure 18.5   The marginal propensity to consume.

*MPC is the slope of the consumption function, or b in $C = a + bY$.

individual as well as each income-earning group reacts differently to changes in income. However, for ease of analysis, in most cases we will assume a constant MPC (and thus a straight-line consumption function).

> **3. How might your reaction to a change in income be different from that of David Rockefeller? From that of a poor person?**

Table 18.1 summarizes our data thus far.

Table 18.1

Y	C	APC	MPC
(1) $1.0T	$1.25T	1.25	
			0.5
(2) 1.5T	1.5 T	1.00	
			0.5
2.0T	1.75T	0.875	

$$MPC = \frac{\Delta C}{\Delta Y} = \frac{1.5 - 1.25}{1.5 - 1.00} = \frac{.25}{.50} = \boxed{.5}$$

SAVING

Earlier we established that the saving function is a residual of consumption. Whatever income is not spent for consumption purposes is saved. $(Y = C + S$, so $S = Y - C.)$ An analysis similar to the one developed for the consumption function can be developed for the saving function. Data for a saving function are derived in Table 18.2.

Table 18.2

Y	C	S = Y − C
$1.0T	$1.25T	$−.25T
1.5T	1.5 T	.00T
2.0T	1.75T	.25T

This information also can be expressed graphically, as in Fig. 18.6.

The Average and Marginal Propensity to Save

The ratio of saving to income, S/Y, or the **average propensity to save (APS)**, can also be found, as can the **marginal propensity to save (MPS)**, which is the ratio of the

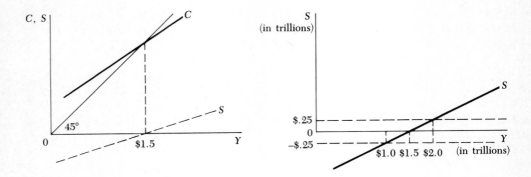

Figure 18.6 The saving function.

change in saving to any change in income, $\Delta S/\Delta Y$. Our information thus far is summarized in Table 18.3.

Table 18.3

Y	C	—	S	APS = S/Y	MPS = $\Delta S/\Delta Y$
$1.0T	$1.25T		$-.25T	-0.25	
					0.5
1.5T	1.5 T		.00T	0.00	
					0.5
2.0T	1.75T		.25T	0.125	

It might be noted that MPS + MPC = 1. This must be true since the change in C and the change in S must add to the whole of every new dollar of income.*

INVESTMENT AND THE TWO-SECTOR MODEL

The simplest Keynesian model consists of an analysis of two sectors in the economy. The household and business sectors will be examined first, in a model that has no government and no foreign sectors. Total income from these two sectors in the economy then must be

$$Y = C + I,$$

where Y is income, C is consumption, and I is investment. This relationship is derived from the national income accounts that we examined in the Chapter 16

---

*$Y = C + S$,
$\Delta Y = \Delta C + \Delta S$,
$\Delta Y/\Delta Y = \Delta C/\Delta Y + \Delta S/\Delta Y$, and 1 = MPC + MPS.

Appendix, as well as from the circular flow diagram, where Y comes from the production of goods and services (aggregate supply). Consumption represents spending by households on consumer goods and services. Investment is the spending by businesses for inventories and capital goods. Together they make up the aggregate demand for goods and services produced. From the preceding section we know that $C = f(Y)$. But we know little about investment. **Investment** consists of additions to plant, equipment, and inventories in the business sector. Inventories may be goods of any type, from raw material inputs to intermediate and finished products. In this simple two-sector model, we will assume that investment is an exogenous variable determined outside the model itself. For example, if General Motors decides to invest $1000, it is a decision made without considering the variables included in this model. Expected profits, interest costs, or business confidence might be more important to investment decisions than income and consumption levels.* Graphically, then, investment would be constant at all levels of income, as in Fig. 18.7.

In the two-sector model, it is known that

$$Y = C + I,$$

and that

$$Y = C + S.$$

Putting these two equations together tells us that in the two-sector Keynesian model the only leakage from the system, saving, must be equal to the only injection, investment. This describes the equilibrium condition for the model; when aggregate supply $(Y = C + S)$ equals aggregate demand $(Y = C + I)$, then $S = I$.

$$C + S = C + I,$$
$$S = I.$$

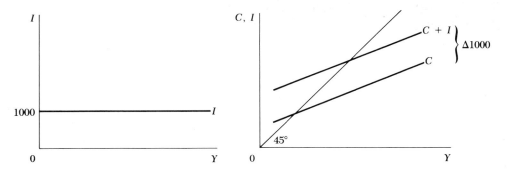

Figure 18.7 The investment function.

*Investment in a more sophisticated model is a function of income, since as income in the economy increases, businesses will more than likely increase their level of investment. For simplicity, however, we will use the less complex model and assume that investment decisions are exogenous to the system.

Several important factors should be noted in the $S = I$ relationship. First, saving and investment are done by two different groups of people for totally different reasons. The second point is that realized, or actual, savings must equal realized, or actual, investment. There is no guarantee that the dollar amount of investment *planned* by the business sector will be the same as the savings planned in the household sector. Using the data in Table 18.4 with planned investment spending of $.25 trillion, we can graphically and logically view the following problem. I_p equals planned investment and I_a equals actual investment.

Table 18.4

Y	C	S	I_p	I_a
$2.0T	$1.75T	$.25T	$.25T	$.25T
2.5T	2.0 T	.5 T	.25T	.5 T

Figure 18.8 shows that the equilibrium income level of the two-sector model is at point A, where the $C + I$ line intersects the 45° reference line. This point is sometimes referred to as the "Keynesian cross." Here $Y = C + I$; $Y = \$2.0$ trillion, $C = \$1.75$ trillion, and $I = \$.25$ trillion. All higher and lower levels of income are not at equilibrium. At those points, $S \neq I$ and aggregate demand $\neq$ aggregate supply. At $Y = \$2.0$ trillion, $C + I = C + S$, and aggregate demand equals aggregate supply. Only when income and output are at $2.0 trillion does **planned** $I =$ **actual** I.

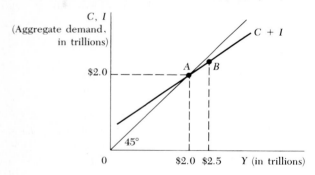

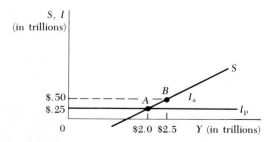

Figure 18.8   The equilibrium level of income.

One can examine the disequilibrium position B, where $C = \$2.0$ trillion, $S = \$.5$ trillion, and $Y = \$2.5$ trillion. Here, intended savings are greater than intended investment since savings are $\$.50$ trillion and investment is only $\$.25$ trillion. With planned I at $\$.25$ trillion, there will be an unplanned increase in inventories since some of the goods produced will not be sold because consumers desire to increase their savings balances. At $Y = \$2.5$ trillion, $C + I = $ (only) $\$2.25$ trillion (and $C + S = \$2.5$ trillion). Aggregate supply is greater than aggregate demand. Total output is $\$2.5$ trillion, but total spending is only $\$2.25$ trillion. Therefore, inventories increase by $\$.25$ trillion. Since the increase in inventories is counted as investment, actual I will increase to $\$.5$ trillion. **Actual savings** equal actual investment.

4. **In the next time period with an increased supply of inventories already accumulated, what do you expect the planned I response of business would be? What would this do to the equilibrium level of income?**

However, since **planned** S is greater than planned I, this is not an equilibrium position. With increased inventories, *which* were unplanned, producers will cut back production and as output is cut, income will also be reduced. This movement will continue until an equilibrium is reached where aggregate demand equals aggregate supply. This occurs at point A, where $C + S = C + I$, and where planned S of $\$.25$ trillion equals planned I of $\$.25$ trillion. This equilibrium may be or may not be at full employment. Unlike the classical model, the Keynesian model may have equilibrium conditions at greater than, at less than, or at full employment.

CHANGES IN INVESTMENT AND THE KEYNESIAN MULTIPLIER

Once equilibrium has been reached in the two-sector model, there will be no tendency for the system to change until some exogenous disturbance occurs, such as a change in the level of investment. Suppose investment increases from $\$.25$ trillion to $\$.45$ trillion for a *change* of $\$.2$ trillion. This is represented graphically in Fig. 18.9.

How much will income increase as a result of this $\$.2$ trillion increase in investment? What is the new equilibrium level of income? It is here that the **Keynesian multiplier** (k) has its effect. When additional investment enters into the model, a response occurs that increases the equilibrium level of income by some multiple of the change in investment. This multiple (called the Keynesian multiplier) is equal to $1/(1 - \text{MPC})$ and is equal to the ratio between the change in income and the change in investment, or $\Delta Y/\Delta I$.

As an example of this multipler process, consider a nursery that decides to expand by adding a greenhouse costing $\$200,000$. The first round of spending, then, is $\$200,000$, which is added to the income stream. The contractor who built the greenhouse now has the $\$200,000$ (as income) and will respend it according to the MPC formulation. If the MPC is ½, or 0.5, the contractor will spend $\$100,000$

$$k = \frac{1}{1 - \text{MPC}} = \frac{\Delta Y}{\Delta I}$$

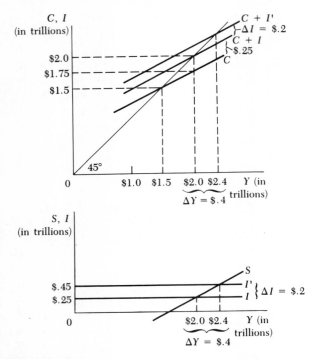

Figure 18.9   An increase in investment spending.

(perhaps on sand, gravel, and a CB for the rig) and save the remaining $100,000. The $100,000 then enters the income stream (as other people's income), and one-half of that will be spent and one-half saved in the third round. Table 18.5 illustrates this process.

Table 18.5

EXPENDITURE			ΔY	$\Delta C = \frac{1}{2}Y$	$\Delta S = \frac{1}{2}Y$
Greenhouse	= round 1		$200,000	$100,000	$100,000
Sand & sound	= round 2		100,000	50,000	50,000
	round 3		50,000	25,000	25,000
	round 4		25,000	12,500	12,500
	round 5		12,500	6,250	6,250
	round 6		6,250	3,125	3,125
	etc.				
Total*			$400,000	$200,000	$200,000

*Until $200,000 [1/(1 − 0.5)] = $200,000 × 2 = $400,000 is generated in new income. The initial increase in spending is multiplied through the economy.

A SIMPLE DERIVATION OF THE MULTIPLIER

We know that in the Keynesian system $\Delta I = \Delta S$. If both sides of this identity are divided by ΔY, the right side of the equation becomes the MPS:

$$\frac{\Delta I}{\Delta Y} = \frac{\Delta S}{\Delta Y} = \text{MPS} = \frac{1}{\text{the multiplier}}.$$

If we invert the equation we get

$$k = \text{the multiplier} = \frac{\Delta Y}{\Delta I} = \frac{\Delta Y}{\Delta S} = \frac{1}{\text{MPS}}.$$

Since MPC + MPS = 1,

$$\frac{\Delta Y}{\Delta I} = \frac{1}{1 - \text{MPC}} = \text{the multiplier} = k.$$

Example: Given MPC = 0.75,

$$k = \frac{\Delta Y}{\Delta I} = \frac{1}{1 - 0.75} = \frac{1}{0.25} = 4.0,$$

so for each ΔI, income will increase by $4 \times \Delta I$.

Thus $400,000 of new income will be generated by the $200,000 increase in investment, given an MPS of 0.5 (which yields a multiplier of 2). We are assuming that one can "generalize" an MPC for the whole economy at some point in time in consistently using MPC = 0.5.

In Fig. 18.9, an increase in I of $.2 trillion will produce a new equilibrium level of $Y = \$2.4$ trillion (with an additional "multiplied" increase in Y of $.4 trillion).

5. **What is the new level of consumption in Fig. 18.9 at $Y = \$2.4$ trillion? What is the level of saving?**

THE THREE-SECTOR MODEL

To add a bit more realism to the model, the government sector will now be added to the simple two-sector Keynesian model. The government enters into this analysis, like investment, as an exogenous variable,

$$G = G_0.$$

Believe me, the whole economy profits. We rob somebody of five grand. Then we buy some stuff from a fence. He gives his cut to the mob. They pay off the cops. . . .

"From the Wall Street Journal—Permission, Cartoon Features Syndicate."

This indicates that there will be a given level of **government spending** for goods and services at all levels of income, as shown in Fig. 18.10.

Figure 18.10 The government spending function.

Once government spending is added to the two-sector model, the income identity, or aggregate demand, becomes that shown in Fig. 18.11. The aggregate supply or aggregate income line is again represented by the 45° line. Expenditures are now made by consumers, investors, and the government, creating the aggregate demand curve for the economy. The equilibrium level of income is Y_e, and $Y_e = C + I + G$. At any other level of income, $Y \neq C + I + G$.

Government expenditures are purchases of goods and services during a given period. They include state and local government expenditures as well as federal government expenditures. Currently, between 19 and 20 percent of the GNP is made up of purchases by the government. As you might imagine, the government is the consumer of many different types of goods and services, ranging from typewriter ribbons to F14 fighters and M16 rifles. These expenditures may be part of the course of operating the government, or may be specially designed to stimulate the economy to remedy times of economic decline, as Keynes suggested in his *General Theory*. Be aware that transfer payments from the government are not included as part of these government purchases. The effect of transfers will be examined in the next chapter.

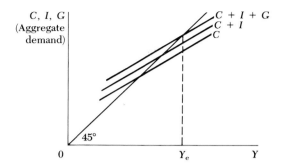

Figure 18.11 The Keynesian model with *C, I,* and *G* spending.

Shifts may also occur in government expenditures. Indeed, the government may make decisions that will affect the level of income in the economy. These expenditures are often aimed at *directly* changing the level of income—perhaps a level of income *not* at full employment to a new equilibrium level of income *at* full employment. Government expenditures for goods and services work through the Keynesian multiplier process just as investments do. Government spending becomes income that enters the spending flow as recipients consume and save at levels reflected by their MPC and MPS. Any increase in *G* will increase *Y* by an amount equal to $\Delta G \times 1/(1 - \text{MPC})$.

The results of government spending may be analyzed if we look at a purchase of 750,000 typewriter ribbons by the Government Services Administration (GSA) at a total cost of $500,000. Graphically in Fig. 18.12 we see that aggregate demand has increased from its equilibrium position at $10 million (where $Y = C + I + G$). If the marginal propensity to consume remains at 0.5, the multiplier is 2. The increase in

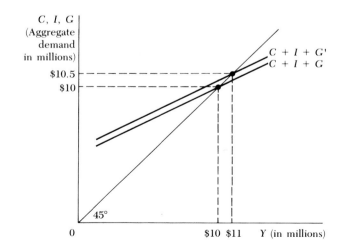

Figure 18.12 The effects of increased government spending on the equilibrium level of income.

income that results from the purchase of typewriter ribbons is $2 \times \$500,000$ ($k \times \Delta G$), or \$1 million. The new equilibrium level of income is \$11 million (\$10 million + \$1 million).

An increase in defense spending by the government will have the effect of stimulating the economies of Wichita, Seattle, and Los Angeles, and more research money spent for the space program will boost the economies of Huntsville, Houston, and Cape Canaveral as well as increasing the enrollments in aerospace engineering next year.

> **6. What kinds of government spending programs would stimulate growth in your area? What are a few government spending programs that would help us all?**

THE FOUR-SECTOR MODEL

Thus far we have extended our economic model by adding *injections* of investment expenditures and government purchases of goods and services into the spending flow and observing (deducing) how the Keynesian multiplier affected each of them. There is, of course one more injection into the spending stream, and that comes from the foreign sector. Whenever goods and services are exported to other nations, dollars flow into our economy in payment for these exported goods. These dollars then enter the spending stream as injections. On the other hand, imports take money out of the income flow, since goods and services come into the country in return for dollars that flow out of the U.S. income stream and into the income stream of the exporting nation. In dealing with both of these flows, we use the quantity *net exports*, which is simply the $(X - M)$, where X represents exports and M accounts for goods imported into the nation. If $(X - M)$ is positive, then money is flowing into the U.S. income stream. If $(X - M)$ is negative, then money is flowing out of the U.S. income stream as imported goods and services flow in. A positive net export figure $(X - M > 0)$ will mean additional income, as Y expands by the multiplier times the quantity $(X - M)$. If net exports are negative $(X - M < 0)$, income (Y) will fall by the amount $k(X - M)$.

The equilibrium level of income would be at the point in which this expanded aggregate demand intersects the aggregate supply or income line. When the United States has a balance of trade deficit, imports are greater than exports, so more goods are coming into the country and more income (money) is going out of the country. Net exports are negative. There will be a lower equilibrium level of income.

CONCLUSION

We have examined the impact of the Keynesian multiplier on several sectors of the economy, and noted that income (output) expands by the value of the multiplier times the value of the injection. Prices do not change in the Keynesian model as a result of changes in aggregate demand. In this chapter we have examined *only* the effect of changes in injections on income. We will explore the effect of changes in *leakages*, saving, and transfers in the next chapter, and will explore price changes in Chapter 22. We have made many assumptions about investment and spending decisions and realize that while the economy is somewhat more complex than our model, the model is nonetheless a beginning to our understanding of how the macroeconomy functions.

The Keynesian model gives us a theoretical framework within which to analyze how the aggregate economy operates and to examine the sorts of macroeconomic problems one might expect to encounter. If aggregate supply is greater than aggregate demand, we can expect a lower level of national income. On the other hand, if aggregate demand is greater than aggregate supply, we would expect an expansion of economic activity and a higher equilibrium level of national income. An equilibrium level is where aggregate supply (Y) equals aggregate demand $(C + I + G)$.

KEY CONCEPTS

consumption
break-even level of income
saving
dissaving
average propensity to consume
   (APC)
marginal propensity to consume
   (MPC)
average propensity to save (APS)

marginal propensity to save
   (MPS)
investment
two-sector model
planned investment
actual investment
actual savings
planned savings
Keynesian multiplier (k)
government spending

REVIEW QUESTIONS

Use the information in Fig. 18.13 to answer the following.

1. Explain in words why the equilibrium level of income would be 400 if there were no saving or investment. What would be the level of output at this income level?

2. Why would the consumption function (if extended) intersect the spending axis at a positive value? What does this mean? Is it realistic?

3. The slope of the consumption function tells us that as income increases, consumption (increases/decreases) but at a (slower/faster) rate. Is this realistic?

4. What assumptions are required to draw an investment function parallel to the consumption function? How realistic are these assumptions? What is the amount of desired investment in Fig. 18.13?

5. What is the level of saving at income of 600? What is the level of desired investment at income of 600? Why is income of 600 an equilibrium level of income (with $C + I$)?

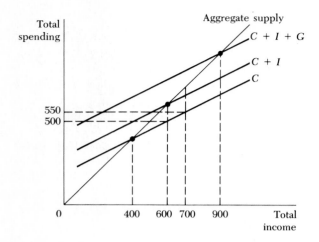

Figure 18.13 A problem on the Keynesian model. The intersection of aggregate supply and $C + I + G = 900$.

6. What would be the level of saving if the income were at 700? What is the level of desired investment at this income level? What forces are at work at an income of 700? What will be the equilibrium level of income?

7. What is the MPC in Fig. 18.13?

8. Assume that income is at 600, but that it takes an income of 900 to generate enough jobs for full employment. What level of government spending will be necessary to achieve full employment?

9. Why is there a multiplier effect for injections into the U.S. economy? Are there different multipliers for different economies? What determines the multiplier?

SUGGESTED READINGS

Gardner Ackley, 1978. *Macroeconomics: Theory and Policy,* Macmillan. This is a major restatement of Keynes. Graph upon graph of Cs, Is, and Gs, as well as policy analysis.

John Kenneth Galbraith, 1958, 1984. *The Affluent Society,* Houghton Mifflin. Gives a good view of the consumer and the consumption ethic in a growing affluent society.

Alvin Hansen, 1953. *A Guide to Keynes,* McGraw-Hill. More graphs and an explanation of the Keynesian system. Hansen's book helped popularize Keynesian economics in the United States in the postwar period.

E. K. Hunt, 1975. *Property and Prophets* (2nd ed.), Harper & Row. Chapter 10 has a simple verbal description of Keynes's economics.

John Maynard Keynes, 1936. *The General Theory of Employment, Interest, and Money,* Harcourt, Brace and World. The Original! Probably a bit over the heads of most "intro students," but after this course—have at it!

Fiscal Policy: Government Spending and Taxation

INTRODUCTION

The federal government has been officially committed to maintaining employment, price stability, and output since the passage of the **Employment Act of 1946.** This act states:

> The Congress hereby declares that it is the continuing policy and responsibility of the Federal Government to use all practicable means consistent with its needs and obligations and other essential considerations of national policy, with assistance and cooperation of industry, agriculture, labor and state and local governments, to coordinate and utilize all its plans, functions, and resources for the purpose of creating and maintaining, in a manner calculated to foster and promote free competitive enterprise and the general welfare, conditions under which there will be afforded useful employment opportunities, including self-employment, for those able, willing, and seeking to work and to promote maximum employment, production, and purchasing power.

It is within the framework of these economic objectives that government **fiscal policy** tries to operate, but that policy is also subject to the constraints of the political process.

According to Keynesian theory, when the economy gets out of kilter for any one of a variety of reasons, governments possess an arsenal of tools with which to fight the economic enemies—inflation and unemployment. While normally we think of the federal government as the major spending and taxing authority, state and local governments are very active in the process as well. In some cases, however, we find that state and local governments actually exacerbate economic problems (pursuing **procyclical** rather than **countercyclical** measures).

In addition to governments, at the state and local as well as at the federal level, many groups and organizations within these governmental organizations are involved in the making of fiscal policy.

The president receives advice on fiscal policy from his **Council of Economic Advisors** (CEA). Some of the advice is accepted and successfully makes its way through the bureaucratic channels. But other advice does not. In addition to advice from the CEA, the president receives advice from the Office of Management and Budget. Meanwhile, Congress has its own Joint Economic Committee and Congressional Budget Office to assist in legislative decisions on government spending and taxation. Policy studies in all these bodies are constantly ongoing. Often the dynamics of these public offices, plus the host of private organizations engaged in economic research, lead to a profusion of mixed analysis and advice. Since each advisory body has its own priorities and operates under its own assumptions about economic growth, policy recommendations vary widely.

When poverty and unemployment arise or inflation rages, the government has tools to deal with each condition. The existence of unemployment and poverty suggests that government spending and/or transfers are necessary. These may take the form of unemployment and welfare benefits, food stamps, Medicaid, or a variety of other payments, or they may be purchases of goods and services. Other remedies that might be suggested are increases in employment opportunities and decreased tax levels. The government may try to stimulate employment by directly adding programs that put people back to work. This may be done through a series of tax credits or advantages for those firms increasing employment and investment.

To combat inflation, fiscal policy requires spending reductions or tax increases. Cutbacks of all types and tax increases restrict household and business spending. Fiscal policy can also be used to affect aggregate supply; for example, a tax cut might be designed to stimulate investment.

This chapter will explore how each type of fiscal action works. We will deal with the shortcomings as well as the advantages of using fiscal policy to deal with economic problems.

FISCAL POLICY

Fiscal policy concerns actions of taxation or government spending that are designed to change the level of income. These actions may be made with respect to a *particular* situation, or they may occur automatically with a given change in economic conditions. The former are **discretionary,** and the latter are automatic. These automatic actions are known as **nondiscretionary** forms of fiscal policy or **built-in**

Congress plays a role in determining the macroeconomic performance of the United States. (Photograph by Tom Riddell.)

stabilizers. Examples of built-in stabilizers include the progressive income tax system, unemployment insurance, and all other compensatory programs that come into effect when income levels are low and that are shut off when income levels are high. As economic activity decreases during a recession, income is lost. This threatens additional decreases in economic activity. However, as unemployment increases, unemployment compensation *automatically* "increases" income and spending to prevent a cumulative decrease in economic activity. Additionally, during a recession, people find themselves in lower tax brackets, which reduces the tax bite on individuals as their incomes fall.

> 1. **If income is increasing at a highly inflationary rate, how do income taxes help to stabilize the economy automatically?**

Government Spending

Policy positions are often taken when employment levels are not deemed adequate by politicians and public opinion—for example, if the full-employment level of income is thought to be at $3.7 trillion and income is currently $3.1 trillion. In this situation, there will probably be a substantial amount of unemployment, and the government can opt for fiscal action that will increase the level of employment and the level of income by $.6 trillion ($3.7 trillion–$3.1 trillion).* In its arsenal of policies are spending, taxing authority, and the ability to issue transfer payments. Transfer payments are income supplements paid to individuals. These payments are not for current productive services and thus are not included in the yearly national product accounts. In some sense, they were "earned" previously. Transfers include Social Security, welfare, and veterans' benefits among others, and are a part of the personal income tally. (Thus they enter the income-spending flow.)

Government spending (on defense, on space, on buildings, etc.) will have the largest expansionary impact on income in the economy *since the full amount of spending enters the economy in the first round*. In the case of transfer payments and tax reductions, some of the impact in the first round is "leaked" into savings (see Table 19.1).

If the MPC in the economy is ⅔, we can easily find that the multiplier is 3, given the formula $k = 1/(1 - MPC)$.† To discover the amount of government spending that is necessary to increase the level of income by $.6 trillion, one need only know these two variables, since $\Delta Y = k \times \Delta G$. We know the desired ΔY to be $.6 trillion and k to be 3, so $.6 trillion $= 3 \times \Delta G$, and $\Delta G = $.2 trillion.

---

*Conversely, we could establish an example in which inflation was the primary problem, with income being above the full employment level. For example, income could be at $3.7 trillion with the full employment level at $3.1 trillion. In that case, the policy measures would be the opposite of those we discuss in the following sections.

$$^\dagger k = \frac{1}{1 - MPC} = \frac{1}{1 - \frac{2}{3}} = \frac{1}{\frac{1}{3}} = 3.$$

Table 19.1 THE MULTIPLIER EFFECT OF GOVERNMENT EXPENDITURES AND TAX CUTS ON INCOME

ΔG = $.2 TRILLION		ΔTx = $.3 TRILLION	
SPENDING SEQUENCE			
Round 1 (direct expenditure;	$\Delta G = \Delta Y = \$.2T$	(indirect expenditure; $\Delta \text{Tx} \times \text{MPC} = \Delta Y =$	$\$.3T \times \frac{2}{3} = \$.2T$
Round 2 $\Delta Y \times \text{MPC}$ =	$\$.2T \times \frac{2}{3} = \$.133T$	($\Delta Y \times \text{MPC}$) =	$\$.2T \times \frac{2}{3} = \$.133T$
Round 3	$.133T \times \frac{2}{3} = \$.09T$		$\$.133T \times \frac{2}{3} = \$.09T$
Round 4	$.09T \times \frac{2}{3} = \$.06T$		$.09T \times \frac{2}{3} = \$.06T$
Round 5	$.06T \times \frac{2}{3} = \$.04T$		$.06T \times \frac{2}{3} = \$.04T$
Round 6	$.04T \times \frac{2}{3} = \$.027T$		$.04T \times \frac{2}{3} = \$.02T$
Round 7	$.027T \times \frac{2}{3} = \$.018T$		$.027T \times \frac{2}{3} = \$.018T$
Round 8	$.018T \times \frac{2}{3} = \$.012T$		$.018T \times \frac{2}{3} = \$.012T$
	$.012T \times \frac{2}{3} = \$.008T$		$.012T \times \frac{2}{3} = \$.008T$
Total	$\$.588T$	Total	$\$.588T$
or approximately $.6T		or approximately $.6T	

Our policy recommendation, then, is that the government build a (big) dam at a price of $.2 trillion to increase income by $.6 trillion to $3.7 trillion (the full-employment level of income). Graphically, this is shown in Fig. 19.1.

Although we can see in the example above that the needed increase in income is $.6 trillion, policy decisions certainly aren't made by such quick calculations. Partisan politics and economic philosophies play a crucial role in these decisions. We might recommend the construction of a dam, but each of the 400-plus representatives and 100 senators has his or her own plan which usually involves a particular congressional district or state. What we are describing in this and the following examples are fast technical economic "solutions" to extremely complex economic, political, and social problems.

2. **What do you suspect *really* goes on in economic policy debates? Clip a recent newspaper article on some federal, state, or local economic issue as illustration.**

3. **Are the various positions based on ideology, theory, or rhetoric?**

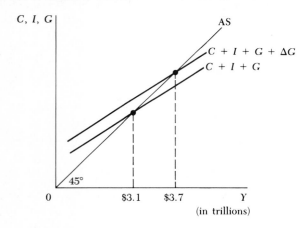

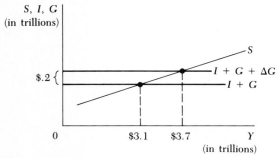

Figure 19.1 The effect of increased government spending.

Tax Policy and Income Effects

If the government decides that the way to accomplish the desired increase in Y of $.6 trillion is a cut in taxes, the same question is raised. How much of a tax reduction is needed to generate new increases in income equal to the $.6 trillion?

The answer is not as easily found as before, since tax cuts work through a different channel in their progression through the economy. Earlier we examined the effect of injections to spending flows; now we must address the behavior of leakages. The crucial difference between the effect of leakages and that of injections occurs during the first round of spending. Instead of $.2 trillion being directly spent on our dam, the $.2 trillion in tax cuts goes into the pocketbooks and bank accounts of the taxpayers. According to our marginal propensities, we will save part of the $.2 trillion and spend the remainder. Again, with an MPC of ⅔ and a tax cut equal to $.2 trillion or $200 billion, the first action is to consume ⅔ of $200 billion or $133 billion and save $66 billion. In the initial round of spending, therefore, only $133 billion enters the total income stream instead of the $200 billion (or $.2 trillion) that entered in the case of government spending. Table 19.1 illustrates the difference between the impacts of taxes and government expenditures.

The **tax multiplier** is thus less than the *spending multiplier*—in fact, one less: $k - 1 = k_{tx}$, or $k_{tx} = -MPC/(1 - MPC)$.* (Note the minus sign, since a tax *cut* will increase income). Using our previous example, to get an increase in income of $.6 trillion with a tax multiplier of 2, $(3 - 1 = 2)$, the decrease in taxes which must occur is

$$\Delta Y = k_{tx} \times \Delta Tx,$$

$$\$.6T = 2 \times \Delta Tx,$$

$$\Delta Tx = \$.3T.$$

Or taxes must be reduced by $.3 trillion to increase Y by $.6 trillion.

The Impact of a Tax Leakage on Equilibrium Income

Thus far we have dealt only with the effect of government spending, investment, and net exports, or injections, on equilibrium income. It is time now to turn our attention to the effect of leakages or withdrawals in our Keynesian model. We will focus specifically on exogeneous, or lump-sum taxation, although the analysis is similar for other withdrawals, including exports and transfers. In our two-sector model the only leakage we encountered was saving. When saving increases and consumption decreases, the saving schedule shifts up and to the left, while the consumption schedule

*This can be derived as follows:
$$-k_{tx} = \frac{1}{1 - MPC} - 1$$
$$= \frac{1}{1 - MPC} - \frac{1 - MPC}{1 - MPC} = \frac{MPC}{1 - MPC},$$
$$k_{tx} = -\frac{MPC}{1 - MPC}.$$

shifts down and to the right (see Fig. 19.2). Just as all injections, C, I, G, and $X - M$, are components of aggregate demand and are graphically represented as part of the aggregate demand function, all leakages or withdrawals are represented on an aggregate leakage curve. As we expand our model from two to three sectors we will add the taxation leakage to the saving schedule. Our exogenous tax leakage then is part and parcel of our residual savings function, which in this analysis gives the leakage function its slope (MPS), just as the consumption function gives the injection function or aggregate demand curve its slope (MPC). The leakage curve represents positive and negative tax and saving changes. (A tax increase would represent a positive leakage, a tax decrease would represent a negative leakage.) An increase in saving or taxes will shift the leakage curve up and to the left. A decrease in saving or taxes will shift the curve down and to the right; thus at every level of income, leakages are lower.

In continuing our example of a $.3-trillion tax cut, we arrive at the new equilibrium income after a series of three steps (see Fig. 19.3). (These three steps occur simultaneously. We are breaking the analysis into a series so you can see clearly each part of the adjustment process.) We must ask ourselves how people respond to a cut in taxes. We know that the cut will bring an increase in income, but we must ask how that increase is allocated. Our answer conforms to what we learned in Chapter 18. Part of the $.3 trillion will be consumed and part will be saved, and

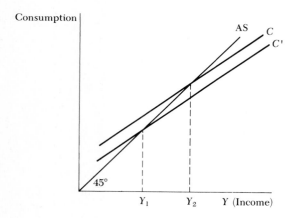

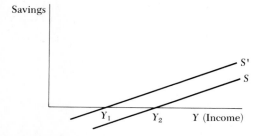

Figure 19.2   Decrease in consumption; increase in saving.

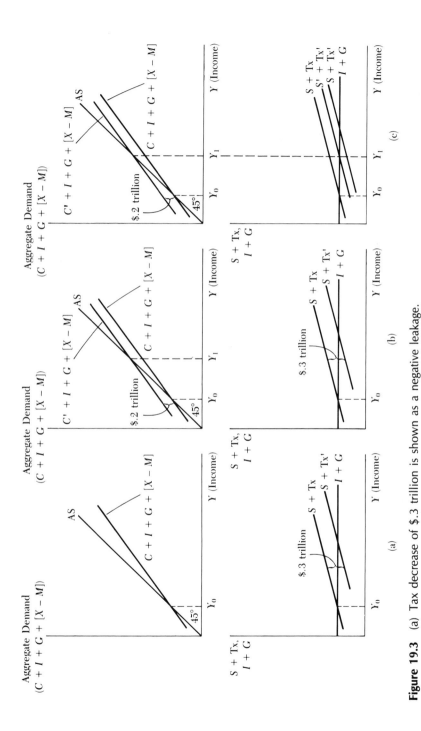

Figure 19.3 (a) Tax decrease of $.3 trillion is shown as a negative leakage. (b) Consumption increases as a result of the addition to income from the tax cut (TC = ⅔ × $.3 trillion = $.2 trillion). (c) Saving increases as a result of the addition to income resulting from the tax cut (↑ S = ⅓ × $.3 trillion = $.1 trillion).

the MPC and MPS tell us how consumption and saving are allocated. In the first step, Fig. 19.3(a), the saving–tax leakage curve shifts down by $.3 trillion, as taxes are cut by the $.3 trillion. Second, since income initially rises by the amount of the tax cut, individuals will boost their consumption by the MPC times the tax reduction or ($\frac{2}{3}$ × $.3 trillion = $.2 trillion). In Fig. 19.3(b), we see the effect of this increase in consumption as the aggregate demand curve shifts up by $.2 trillion. At this point there is an equilibrium level of income in the upper or aggregate demand graph, but not in the lower, leakage graph. To arrive at equilibrium in both the upper and lower graphs we must complete the final step in our logical process. Just as individuals increase consumption by the MPC times the tax reduction, we know that they will increase their saving by the MPS times the tax reduction, or ($\frac{1}{3}$ × $.3 trillion = $.1 trillion). Thus, the saving–tax leakage curve now shifts up and to the left by $.1 trillion (see Fig. 19.3c). In the final analysis, then, we find that income increases from Y_0 to Y_1, or by $.6 trillion. (This result is obtained from multiplying the tax multiplier [see previous section] by the change in taxes: $k_{tx} \times \Delta \text{Tx} = \Delta Y$, or 2 × $.3 trillion = $.6 trillion.)

4. **Create a set of graphs for a $.3-trillion tax increase. Trace through the steps in Fig. 19.3. How much will income increase?**

Transfer Payments

Transfer payments work in essentially the same way as tax cuts. Looking at their impact on the economy we find that the income of households will increase in the first round. This means that the change in income during the first round will be $\frac{2}{3}$ of $.3-trillion since part of the transfer will be consumed and the remainder will be saved. The **transfer multiplier,** like the tax multiplier, is $k - 1 = k_{tr}$ (only it is positive, since an increase in transfers increases income). Transfer expenditures worth $.3 trillion would be necessary to raise income by $.6 trillion.

5. **If there were an increase in Social Security transfers of $4 billion and if the MPC were 0.9, how much of an impact would this transfer package have on the economy?**

The government, of course, might choose one or any combination of tax, spending, or transfer alternatives. It also might decide to pass legislation to encourage new consumer and/or investment spending. Tax credits and incentives have been utilized in recent years to stimulate certain industries that might be suffering more than others in the economy. The 5-percent housing tax credit of 1974 was a fine example of such a policy. Many newly constructed homes provided a 5-percent credit on the purchaser's income taxes. The measure was designed to pick up a depressed housing industry, as well as to stimulate economic activity in general. More recently, the Accelerated Cost Recovery System, a part of the 1981 tax package, was designed to shorten the period in which businesses could write off equipment and building costs in their tax returns. While much of this program was negated by the Tax Act of 1982, the desired effect was to reduce the cost and thus encourage investment.

PROBLEMS WITH FISCAL POLICY

With these mechanical fiscal fixes firmly in mind, it is well to remember that problems are likely to be encountered in the determination of fiscal policy. The political machinery involved in fiscal decisions is often slow, the product of many **lags.** Additionally, state and local governments offer their own brand of fiscal policy, which more often than not is ill timed for national objectives because of interest costs and political considerations. These difficulties must be considered in our understanding of fiscal decisions.

Lags, Lags, and More Lags

From the discussion thus far, it seems that all that is needed for full employment in the economy is a mighty snap of the government purse strings. Several rather sticky problems emerge in the deployment of these strings, however. One problem encountered early on is the one of simple recognition of the fact that a problem exists—in effect a *recognition lag*. Another is trying to estimate the MPC and thus the multiplier effect that each expenditure might have on the economy. Some types of spending tend to generate larger stimulative and investment effects than others. For example, estimates have placed the defense spending multiplier somewhat lower than that of other forms of government spending.

6. Why might defense spending have a smaller multiplier?

Another problem with government spending is that it tends to be lumpy. Projects are normally large and are generally confined to a reasonably small geographical area. A floodwall in Lewisburg, Pa., will hardly help alleviate unemployment in Dubuque or Detroit. (Perhaps that's why the Army Corps of Engineers wants to build a dam on every square inch of the earth—to spread the impact of the dollar as well as of the water.)

Next, log rolling, a delightful game perfected by politicians, is played after the corps is convinced that a dam is desperately needed for a congressional area. "I'll most certainly vote for a dam in your district if you'll vote for a highway in mine," the dialogue goes. As these games continue, unemployment levels may be skyrocketing.

Legislation tends to move slowly through Congress. By the time funds are allocated, new and different problems might emerge, such as inflation, and the expenditure of government funds would only add fuel to the flames of the problem.

DOONESBURY   **by Garry Trudeau**

Although tax policies affect every individual in the nation, they also take time before enactment. The favorite example of economists is the 1964 tax cut, an example of Keynesian economics well thought out and used. The cut was proposed in 1963 and, after more than a year of hearings, was finally approved. (Our loyal members of Congress were unconvinced that the cut would be remembered by their constituents, but they were sure that a tax increase would be necessary at some later point in time—so why bother to cut taxes now?) Oftentimes it is a conflict between the President and the Congress that leads to bitter policy debates. These problems are often referred to as the *legislative lag*.

Execution presents another delay in transferring the legislation into action. Tax policies tend to be faster and more efficient after passage, but spending packages may be hung up in a bidding and allocation process for months. This has been called the *implementation lag*.

Yet, once the legislation for government spending is enacted and executed, it is effective. Empirical results from the Federal Reserve-M.I.T.-Penn (FMP) econometric model show that one year after a government expenditure of $1 billion has taken place, GNP increases by about $3 billion. (The monetarist's model at the St. Louis Fed estimates that there is no effect after one year—but we'll discuss the implications of this model in the chapter on monetary policy.)

Counter-countercyclical Policy

In the introduction to this chapter we suggested that state and local governments have their own fiscal policy. They are active in spending and taxing as well as in issuing transfers. Often, however, these tools are used at the "wrong time." Fiscal policy is designed to counter inflationary and recessionary trends in economic activity. Yet local spending is often done when "good times" prevail. It is much easier to get a school or a library or a park issue through the polls in boom periods, and so construction projects add to the boom.

7. **What does Keynesian theory tell you about this kind of policy? What would be the economic effects?**

8. **Is there any salvation to the procyclical policies of state and local governments? (What happens when bond issues are passed?)**

In the same vein, when times are hard, it is often difficult for state and local governments to finance new spending projects that might stimulate the economy, thus reinforcing a recession.

THE FEDERAL BUDGET: DEFICITS AND OTHER DELIGHTS

The federal budget has gained increasing attention during the past decade. Everyone from Senator William Proxmire, who disapproves of $395 hammers, to political candidates who object to the size of the federal government complains about the size of the budget deficit and its effects. Deficit watchers have always been among us, crying with alarm at prospects of deficits and their implications. Louder cries are being heard as deficits are projected to continue to soar throughout the decade. (The Congressional Budget Office estimates a budget deficit of $270 billion by 1989.) In this section we will review the budget process and examine the history of budget deficits and the federal debt. We will also look at the impact of the federal debt on the economy and the notion of balanced budgets. In addition, we will learn about the concepts of the structural and cyclical deficits.

The Budget and the Economy

Just as the budget of a family or business determines the direction, priorities, and obligations of that unit, so the federal budget determines the direction, priorities, and obligations assumed by our nation. The federal budget is made up of expenditures and receipts. We have seen how some expenditures are incurred by direct purchases of goods and services. Elements of fiscal policy are directly reflected in the annual federal budget, which not only indicates a president's view about fiscal and social policy, but also reflects electoral policies and the process of government. What a President proposes and Congress passes, in what is now a year-long process, reflects what will happen and what priorities are to be set. As with a family budget, receipts are balanced against expenditures; if receipts are greater than expenditures, a surplus results, and if expenditures are greater than receipts, there is a deficit.

Tax receipts are the most obvious source of federal government revenue, with individual income taxes providing 48.1 percent of the total, which was just under $700 billion in 1983. Table 19.2 shows how the importance of individual income taxes has steadily grown since the 1940s. While Social Security taxes now provide the next largest single receipt, increasing from only 11 percent in 1950 to 35 percent in 1983, we must remember that these funds are paid out almost immediately to those now

Table 19.2 TAX TYPE AS A PERCENTAGE OF GOVERNMENT REVENUE, 1940–1985

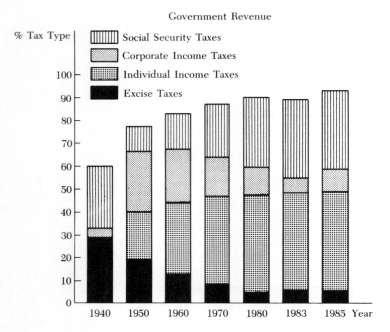

receiving Social Security benefits. Corporate income taxes provided a substantial portion of federal receipts during the 1950s and 1960s, but as a result of the Reagan tax cut package of 1981, the corporate share of the total tax burden was reduced to 6.2 percent in 1983. When the Economic Recovery Tax Act was passed by Congress in 1981, personal income tax rates were cut by 23 percent over the following three years. The measure also accelerated the rate at which businesses could take depreciation deductions, and gave other deductions and additional "loopholes" to individuals and businesses alike. As a result of this legislation, tax receipts were cut by an estimated $38 billion in 1982. This rose to an estimated $93 billion in 1984, and even with passage of the Tax Equity and Fiscal Responsibility Act of 1982, if additional taxes are not levied, the governments tax revenue losses are expected to increase to $211 billion in 1988. Congress passed the Gramm-Rudman-Hollings Balanced Budget Act in late 1985 in an attempt to deal with these large actual and projected deficits. Gramm-Rudman-Hollings mandates a balanced budget by 1991 and divides automatic spending cuts between defense and nondefense expenditures if Congress and the President fail to meet annual deficit targets in the federal budget. If the courts uphold Gramm-Rudman-Hollings, significant changes will be made in the budget process.

Next, of course, we must examine trends in expenditures. Table 19.3 shows the proportion of the budget going to selected areas and as a percentage of GNP for selected years. Defense expenditures, while not changing dramatically as a percent-

Table 19.3 GOVERNMENT EXPENDITURES AS A PERCENTAGE OF BUDGET OUTLAYS AND GNP, 1975–1985 (SELECTED CATEGORIES)

EXPENDITURE	1975 % BUDGET OUTLAY	1975 % GNP	1979 % BUDGET OUTLAY	1979 % GNP	1983 % BUDGET OUTLAY	1983 % GNP	1985 % BUDGET OUTLAY	1985 % GNP
Defense	26.6	5.6	23.1	4.6	26.0	6.2	26.7	6.3
Education/Health	8.7	3.2	10.0	1.8	6.8	1.3	6.8	1.6
Social Security (includes Medicare)	23.9	6.8	25.3	5.1	27.6	6.6	27.2	6.4
Income Security	15.4	4.3	13.2	2.6	15.2	3.6	13.5	3.2
Interest (on debt)	7.1	0.5	8.5	1.7	10.9	2.6	13.7	3.2
Agriculture	0.5	0.1	2.2	0.5	2.8	0.7	2.7	0.6
Total Budget		21.3		20.1		23.8		23.7
Deficit		1.8		1.6		6.1		5.3

Source: Derived from the 1984 and 1986 *Economic Report of the President*, pp. 304 and 340 and 341.

age of the federal budget have increased dramatically as a percentage of GNP. In 1985 total defense expenditures were $253 billion or 6.3 percent of the GNP (see Table 19.3). Social Security, agricultural program expenditures, and interest payments on the federal debt are other areas where substantial increases have occurred. Most budgeted programs have, in fact, been cut as part of the Reagan program to enhance the role of the private sector while reducing the role of government. However, since defense, agriculture, Social Security, and interest expenditures increased by such a significant amount, Reagan was unable to keep his campaign promise of reducing the role of government. Under his administration, expenditures rose to a historical record 23.8 percent of GNP in 1983.

The combination of tax reductions and expenditures increases led to a record budget **deficit.** And while we have seen deficits larger than this when measured as a percentage of GNP, they have seldom been recorded during a time of peace, or a time of economic growth.

Federal Deficits: So What's the Problem?

Continued deficits in the federal budget give rise to the national **debt.** The national debt is the debt or obligation of the federal government, and is the accumulation of annual budget deficits. These deficits are financed by borrowing from the public through the sale of Treasury bills and bonds and savings bonds. Bonds are debt issues of the government that guarantee the repayment of the original investment plus a specified rate or amount of interest, and are sold to the public and to institutional investors. The national debt has always been, and now is even more so, one of the great conversation topics of Americans. Our citizens have always been concerned with both the growth and the size of the national debt. If we look at the historical record, we find that all forms of debt have increased dramatically since World War II. During this period corporate debt and state and local government debt have increased by more than 2000 percent, while consumer debt has increased by 3000 percent! During this period the debt of the federal government has increased by "only" 1500 percent. In the 1960s the total federal debt was $300 billion, while in the mid-1980s it has reached $1.8 trillion, almost $1.5 trillion more than it was at the end of 1965.

We might ask ourselves why the debt is so worrisome to citizens, as well as economists and policymakers. The debt could be eliminated quite simply by assessing every man, woman, and child in the country $7800 (1985) in new taxes, their per capita share of the national debt. But, there are more important facets of the debt that need to be examined. We must also be aware that the federal debt did not concern the majority of economists of the country until this decade. We need to examine the difference in the debt accumulated during other decades and the decade of the 1980s in order to understand why such an issue is being made of the debt.

Most of the national debt was accumulated during war years, especially during World War II and the Vietnam War. Until early 1982 the debt as a percentage of our national income had continued to fall. As long as GNP was rising faster than the deficit each year, there were only three major concerns: (1) Who owns the debt? (2)

Who pays the interest? and (3) Does the debt compete with other uses of credit? Let's discuss these three problems before examining the problems of the debt that has accumulated during this decade.

The obvious concern over who owns the debt arises when the thought of repayment occurs. It is one thing to pay the interest to ourselves and quite another to owe it to someone else. In 1985, about 11.5 percent of the debt was owned by foreign individuals and governments. This has increased by about 4 percentage points in the last seven years. As one might expect, the share of debt held by the foreign sector rose considerably during the 1972–1985 period.

> **9. Why has the foreign-held debt increased? Will it continue to do so?**

It would be naïve to assume that of the $1.8 trillion of debt (government bonds) held by the U.S. public, all of us own some. Obviously some of us own much more of the debt than others, and the richer we are, the more debt we are likely to own (or bonds we hold); the poorer among us hold few if any bonds. Both institutions and middle- and upper-income groups use government bonds as a safe and profitable way to hold their savings. Lower-income groups tend not to have substantial savings, since they consume most if not all of their income.

This brings us to the second problem of the interest payments on the debt. In 1980 our $900 billion debt cost us $52 billion in interest payments. Our $1.8 trillion of debt in 1985 cost us $129 billion in interest payments. Since the interest payments come from budget receipts, and budget receipts come from taxation, you can see how this interest payment/ownership phenomenon leads to a redistribution of income in the economy, from bottom to top. Everyone pays taxes, some of which are used to pay the interest on the debt. But only individuals with higher incomes receive these interest payments, since they are the ones who own government bonds. This is a cause of concern for many economists and politicians.

> **10. Does the ownership of the debt concern you? Why or why not?**
>
> **11. Do the redistributive effects of the debt concern you? Why or why not?**

The final area of concern with the debt lies in the realm of alternative sources for the financing of government expenditures, particularly when the economy is operating at close to full employment. The government can increase taxes or borrow. In either case, spending potential of another sector is reduced. In the case of tax increases, the spending power of the consumer and/or businesses is reduced. Borrowing, or creating a larger debt, may force interest rates up because the government bond issues will have to be offered at a higher yield. Most of these bond issues will be sold to financial intermediaries and corporations, etc., so that government spending will tend to take place at the expense of investment (instead of consumption), since the financial intermediaries would normally lend to corporations for investment purposes rather than buying bonds. This crowding out of private investment occurs when the economy is expanding. If there were severe levels of unemployment and excess capacity, it would probably be unnecessary for interest rates to rise with the new bond issues, and in times of recession, businesses are reluctant to invest anyway, no matter how low the interest rate may fall.

More recently, the large budget deficits have caused immense concern for future levels of economic growth. While there are many uses for funds made available by businesses and household saving, there is a limit to that saving. Given their known size, current government deficits will consume most of the resources that must be parceled out among a variety of credit demands. Interest costs do nothing but rise. These higher costs have detrimental effects on housing and other investment markets. Many economists believe that both deficits and the national debt must be lowered if long-term prosperity is to be achieved.

Historically, the debt has financed wars, higher levels of employment and income, and inflation. Today, it finances additional defense and Social Security expenditures and lower taxes. Some, however, argue that the results are a bargain at $7800 per person.

The Budget Deficit

The Keynesian philosophy toward budgets was that deficits should accumulate during recessions when additional government expenditures were necessary to boost the economy by stimulating aggregate demand. He believed (much to the surprise of many) that governments should accumulate surpluses during times of prosperity. There would then be a cyclically balanced budget. Granted, the amounts spent during the recessions might not equal the amounts accumulated during prosperity, but on the whole it would more or less even out. In the United States, however, during the 88 quarters between 1960 and 1981, only four surpluses were recorded.

When deficits are accumulated as a result of economic downturns they are called **cyclical deficits,** measured by the economic cost of the recession in terms of added expenditures due to unemployment and lost tax receipts. Deficits that accrue during times of prosperity or high employment are called **structural deficits.** They result from the structure of federal receipts and expenditures, regardless of the level of economic activity. Over the past two decades these structural deficits have averaged below 2 percent of GNP, until 1983 when they reached 2.9 percent of GNP. Estimates are for these structural deficits to rise to 5.0 percent of GNP unless government revenues are increased or expenditures are cut. Below, President Reagan's Council of Economic Advisors set forth their views on the deficit, projected deficits, and problems associated with deficits. This excerpt is from the 1984 *Economic Report of the President*.

REDUCING THE BUDGET DEFICIT

Despite the dramatic reduction in the share of national income taken by government domestic spending and the fundamental improvement in the character of our tax system, the Nation still faces the serious potential problem of a long string of huge budget deficits. Vigorous economic growth can eliminate the cyclical component of the deficit. But without legislative action, the structural component is likely to grow just as fast as the cyclical one shrinks. The Administration's economic projections imply that the budget deficit will remain roughly $200 billion a year—or about 5 percent of GNP—for the rest of the decade unless there is legislative action to reduce spending or raise revenue. Deficits of that size would represent a serious potential threat to the health of the American economy in the second half of this decade and in the more distant future.

DEFICIT PROJECTION

The cyclical component of the budget deficit is the part of the deficit that occurs because the unemployment rate exceeds the inflation threshold level of unemployment, i.e., the minimum level of unemployment that can be sustained without raising the rate of inflation. This excess unemployment raises the deficit by depressing tax revenues and by increasing outlays on unemployment benefits and other cyclically sensitive programs.

The remaining part of the budget deficit, known as the structural component, is the amount of the deficit that would remain even if the unemployment rate were at the inflation threshold level. The Administration estimates that the inflation threshold level of unemployment is now 6.5 percent and will decline in the coming years as the relative number of inexperienced workers declines and as the Administration's employment policies are enacted and take effect.

Table 1-2 presents the cyclical and structural components of the budget deficit for 1980 through 1989. The 1983 deficit of $195 billion was divided about evenly between the cyclical and structural components. Because of the lower level of unemployment projected for 1984, a much larger share of the current year's deficit is structural. The projected deficit of $187 billion includes a cyclical component of $49 billion and a structural component of $138 billion. By 1989, the entire projected budget deficit is structural.

A rate of economic growth for the next 5 years that is sufficiently greater than the growth forecast by the Administration and by virtually all

(continued)

Reprinted from *Economic Report of the President,* 1984.

Table 1-2 CYCLICAL AND STRUCTURAL COMPONENTS OF THE DEFICIT, FISCAL YEARS 1980–89 [BILLIONS OF DOLLARS]

FISCAL YEAR	TOTAL	CYCLICAL	STRUCTURAL
Actual:			
1980	60	4	55
1981	58	19	39
1982	111	62	48
1983	195	95	101
Estimates (current services):			
1984	187	49	138
1985	208	44	163
1986	216	45	171
1987	220	34	187
1988	203	16	187
1989	193	−4	197

Sources: Budget of the United States Government Fiscal Year 1985 and Council of Economic Advisors.

private forecasters could in principle eliminate the deficit without legislative action. However, a 1 percent increase in the current level of real GNP would reduce the budget deficit by only about $12 billion. It would require an increase of 40 percent in the projected growth rates over the next 6 years to eliminate the budget deficit by the end of the decade without a change in spending or tax rules. It would clearly be unwise to rely on such an unprecedented and improbably fast rate of growth. A prudent policy at this point must assume that economic growth alone will not eliminate these deficits.

The economic assumptions that are used to project the budget outlays and receipts are based on the premise that there will be a sound monetary policy and that future legislative changes will reduce budget deficits sharply in the years ahead. In the absence of legislative changes to reduce deficits substantially in future years, interest rates will be higher than projected and the real growth rate will probably be lower than projected. The budget calculations assume that real GNP grows at an average annual rate of 4.3 percent from 1983 to 1989. The calculations also assume that the Treasury bill rate will fall from the current 8.9 percent to 5.0 percent by 1989. These assumptions are reasonable if the budget deficit in that year is about 1.5 percent of GNP and is moving toward complete balance. But if legislative changes to reduce outlays and increase receipts are not enacted and the Treasury bill rate remains at its current level, the higher interest payments on the national debt will raise the 1989 deficit by about $60 billion,

(continued)

bringing the total deficit in that year to approximately $250 billion. Growth rates of real income slower than those assumed in the budget calculations would raise the deficit even more.

LONG-TERM CONSEQUENCES

The projected budget deficits would directly and substantially increase the future size of the national debt. If legislative action is not taken, the cumulative budget deficit would be more than $1,100 billion over the next 6 years. The annual interest on this extra debt alone would represent a permanent cost of about $60 billion in 1989, if interest rates fall as assumed, or at least $100 billion a year if the interest rates remain at their present level. These amounts are equivalent to between 10 percent and 17 percent of the personal and corporate income tax revenue now projected for 1989.

This growth of the national debt and the interest on the national debt shows that budget deficits do not eliminate the need for spending cuts or tax increases, but just postpone the time when extra spending cuts or larger tax increases must take effect to pay for current deficits.

The most important long-term economic effect of the prospective budget deficits would be to absorb a large fraction of domestic saving, and thereby reduce the rate of capital formation and slow the potential long-term growth of the economy. Federal borrowing to finance a budget deficit of 5 percent of GNP would absorb about two-thirds of all the net domestic saving that would otherwise be available to finance investment in plant and equipment and in housing.

The reduced availability of investable funds means that the real rate of interest must rise until the demand for funds for private investment is reduced to the available supply. Stated more generally, the real net-of-tax cost of capital must increase relative to the real net-of-tax return on capital until the demand for funds is reduced to the available supply.

Although the 1981 tax changes and the reduced rate of inflation will direct a higher share of the remaining capital formation to business investment and away from owner-occupied housing, the effect of the budget deficits nevertheless would be a lower rate of investment in business plant and equipment as well as in housing. . . .

The current situation also shows how the extent of the crowding out of capital formation in the United States can be temporarily reduced by an inflow of foreign funds that are attracted to the United States by the rise in our real interest rate and increased real after-tax return on equity investments. This capital inflow usually begins after a lag, rises to a peak, and eventually shrinks. Even if the budget deficit remains at a high level, the inflow of capital from abroad eventually contracts as foreigners

(continued)

become increasingly unwilling to hold even more U.S. assets in their portfolios.

If the current services budget deficits that are currently projected were actually to occur, the likely result would be to reduce net investment in plant and equipment to a substantially lower share of GNP than prevailed in the 1960s and 1970s. Net private investment has fallen from 6.7 percent of GNP in the three-decade period through 1979 to only 3.2 percent of GNP in the past 3 years. Much of this decline is attributable to the stage of the business cycle. The 1983 deficit strengthened the recovery and thereby boosted business fixed investment, although the government's competition for funds to finance the structural deficit also depressed the level of investment below what it would otherwise have been.

DEFICITS AND THE RECOVERY

The deficits will have effects on the economic recovery as well as on the capital stock and on long-term economic growth. To understand the effect of budget deficits on the economic recovery, it is important to distinguish the deficits in the early years of the recovery from the deficits that are projected for subsequent years. Although the projected future deficit would be likely to have serious adverse consequences on the character and possibly the duration of the recovery, the near-term deficits probably have a positive impact on the pace of recovery in 1983 and 1984. The tax cuts in 1982 and 1983 raised after-tax incomes and therefore contributed to the rise in consumer spending that has been responsible for so much of the recovery. Similarly, the direct fiscal stimulus of the large 1984 deficit will do more to raise demand in 1984 than the increased real interest rates that result from the 1984 deficit will do to depress demand. . . .

If the deficits persist, the crowding out would also persist but the pattern of crowding out would change over time. As the value of the dollar declines, the merchandise trade deficit is likely to shrink, focusing more of the crowding out on the domestic capital market. The current rise in profits and retained earnings that result from the cyclical upturn and from the 1981 tax changes temporarily protects business investment and concentrates more of the domestic crowding out on residential construction. This too will change with time, placing more of the burden of future crowding out on business investment in plant and equipment.

No one can be sure of exactly how the pattern of crowding out would evolve through time. It is clear however that the persistence of large structural budget deficits would contribute to producing a lopsided recovery. The recovery would not be shared fully by the export industries and by those firms that compete with imports from abroad. Nor would the construction industry and those industries that are directly involved in the production of capital goods and consumer durables be likely to keep pace with overall economic activity.

(continued)

As a result, employment and economic activity would shift from these contracting interest-sensitive sectors to the areas of expanding demand in the services and nondurable goods industries and in the defense-related industries. If this shift of demand proceeds smoothly enough, the overall recovery would continue at a satisfactory pace with declining total unemployment. It is quite possible, however, that the additional demand would concentrate in sectors that are operating close to capacity while the crowding out withdraws demand from industries where a great deal of excess capacity exists. If so, much of the additional demand might be absorbed in price increases while the crowding out adds to unemployment. If this occurs, the resulting recovery would be slower paced, more fragile, and more inflationary than a more balanced recovery.

No one can predict in detail the effects of a continuing series of such large deficits. The economy could continue to experience a satisfactory overall pace of recovery for several years with declining rates of unemployment and inflation. But deficits of this magnitude could lead instead to imbalances within the economy that cause the recovery to lose momentum. There is also the risk that the persistent deficits could lead to inappropriate economic policies in the future. An overly expansionary monetary policy would cause increased inflation while a sudden large fiscal contraction could depress economic activity. Although no one can be sure just how the economy would behave in the face of such unprecedented deficits, the longer the deficits are allowed to persist, the greater are the risks to our economic future.

BUDGET STRATEGY

A major reduction in the structural budget deficit must therefore be achieved over the next several years. This must be done without causing a contraction of economic activity. Because the direct effect of reducing the budget deficit is to reduce government spending and private consumption, there must be an increase in investment and net exports if real incomes and economic activity are to remain at high levels.

A reduction in the level of the current or future budget deficits automatically stimulates investment and net exports by lowering the real rate of interest and the exchange value of the dollar. However, experience shows that the rise in investment and in exports follows the fall in interest rates and the exchange rate only with a substantial lag. . . . Legislation to reduce the deficit by about $100 billion during the next 3 fiscal years would make a significant contribution to reducing deficits and the future national debt. It could also give increased confidence to the financial markets, business investors, and consumers that the projected deficits can be controlled and eventually eliminated. . . .

12. Do you believe that it is possible to cut federal expenditures any more? Why?

13. Have any tax increases been passed since January 1985? Have new or different types of taxes been proposed? What are they?

14. How large was the federal deficit last year? How large is the federal debt?

Balanced Budgets and the Balanced Budget Multiplier

Often we hear of balanced budgets from politicians. In the campaign of 1980 both candidates Carter and Reagan called for a balanced budget by 1985, and in his second inaugural address Reagan called for a Constitutional amendment mandating a balanced budget. The notion of a balanced budget has long been an exceedingly popular campaign device and easily gains a large public following (despite Keynes's put-down). Logically, if family budgets should balance (before creditors start beating at the door), why shouldn't the federal government balance its budget? Balancing the budget means essentially taking in amounts equal to those spent. For example, if the government decides to spend some $.3 trillion, it should collect $.3 trillion in additional taxes so that the budget will balance. Exactly what are the implications of this? Again, using the Keynesian multiplier analysis (given an MPC = ⅔ so that $k = 3$ and $-k_{tx} = 2$), the $.3-trillion increase in government spending would increase income by $.9 trillion ($\Delta Y = k \times \Delta G$, or $3 \times \$.3$ trillion $= \$.9$ trillion); whereas the $.3-trillion *increase* in taxes would decrease income by $.6 trillion ($\Delta Y = -k_{tx} \times \Delta Tx = -2 \times \$.3$ trillion $= -\$.6$ trillion). The *net* result of a balanced budget in this case is an *increase* in income of $.3 trillion. In case you hadn't noticed, the **balanced-budget multiplier** is 1:

$$\Delta Y = k_{BB} \times \text{Budget}, \quad k_{BB} = \frac{\Delta Y}{\Delta \text{Budget}} = \frac{\$.3 \text{ trillion}}{\$.3 \text{ trillion}} = 1.$$

15. What would be the effect on income of a decrease in government spending of $.3 trillion and a tax cut of $.3 trillion? Is this a balanced budget?

16. Given the $180-billion deficit of 1985, what could have been done to balance the budget?

CONCLUSION

This chapter has highlighted the process and ways in which fiscal policy works through the tax, transfer, and spending multipliers. We've noted that fiscal policy isn't always efficient for a wide variety of reasons, but it is most often effective—at least when estimated by Keynesian models. We have seen the growing concern with budget deficits and the desire to balance receipts against expenditures in periods of economic growth. Chapter 20 then introduces money into the Keynesian economy, which gives us yet another set of tools to use to achieve our policy objectives.

KEY CONCEPTS

fiscal policy	transfer multiplier
procyclical policy	lags in fiscal policy
countercyclical policy	deficit
Council of Economic Advisors	debt
discretionary policy	cyclical deficits
nondiscretionary policy	structural deficits
built-in stabilizers	balanced-budget multiplier
tax multiplier	

REVIEW QUESTIONS

1. Most of the examples in this chapter have dealt with policy designed to combat unemployment and recession. What fiscal measures would you recommend if the economy was in the midst of a prolonged period of inflation? (Use an MPC = 0.8 for the economy as a whole.)

2. Do you favor a taxing policy over a curb in government spending? Why?

3. What might be the end result of your policy? How long do you expect the lags to last before it will be enacted?

4. What are the differences between automatic stabilizers and discretionary fiscal policy?

5. Would you ever recommend a balanced budget for the federal government? Why? If so, when?

6. How can deficits be beneficial to the economy?

7. How do deficits limit the productive potential of the economy?

8. Why are structural deficits more cause for concern than cyclical deficits?

9. Would you make any recommendations to alleviate some of the lags involved with fiscal actions? Are these delays "healthy"?

10. If the MPC = 0.8, what would be the effect of a $10-million tax cut and a $6-million increase in government purchases?

SUGGESTED READINGS

E. Ray Canterbery, 1968. *Economics on a New Frontier*, Wadsworth. This interesting and readable account details the first presidential administration employing Keynesian theory in the deployment of fiscal policy.

Milton Friedman, 1972. *An Economist's Protest*, Thomas Horton. See Chapter 4, in which the leading monetarist criticizes fiscal policy during the Nixon era.

Walter W. Heller, 1966. *New Dimensions of Political Economy*, Harvard University Press, The CEA Chairman under Kennedy and Johnson recounts the changes taking place in economic policy.

Walter W. Heller, 1976. *The Economy, Old Myths, and New Realities*, W. W. Norton. Heller focuses on the economic problems that occurred in the mid-1970s and the effect of many of the fiscal measures in this period of instability.

Business Week, "How to cut the deficit," March 26, 1984. This special report gives a detailed set of proposals to cut costs in the Reagan budget.

Gregory B. Mills and John C. Palmer, 1984. *The Deficit Dilemma*, The Urban Institute. This short book sets forth President Reagan's budget objectives and their consequences. There is a good discussion of problems of the structural deficit.

Business Week, "The new debt economy," October 16, 1978. An early analysis of the total debt structure in the United States and its implications.

Joseph A. Pechman, 1983. *Setting National Priorities, The 1984 Budget*, The Brookings Institution. Published yearly, this volume details the proposals for expenditures and receipts and assesses the economic reality of what is often political expedience.

George P. Schultz and Kenneth W. Dam, 1977. *Economic Policy beyond the Headlines*, W. W. Norton. A behind-the-scenes view of fiscal policy in the works—the pressures, demands, and formal and informal promises that lie at the heart of policymaking.

Leonard Silk, 1972. *Nixonomics*, Praeger. A play-by-play of Nixon's economic policies by the economics editor of the *New York Times*.

20

Chapter

The Role of Money and Financial Intermediaries

INTRODUCTION

Money, together with its role in the economy, has been one of the most debated issues among the last generation of economists. Obviously everyone knows all there is to know about money. We need more and we want more of it. Money is a growth industry. **Financial intermediaries** (FIs) have developed as the country has grown, providing the services that are demanded by the consumers in a changing society. Commercial banks are the oldest and still the most important of all FIs. The late 1800s saw the rise of savings banks and insurance companies, and the 20th century has given us credit unions, real estate trusts, investment banks, bank holding companies, and finance companies. The 1980s alone have given us more innovation in financial institutions than we have seen in the past century. We can expect continued changes in these institutions as the deregulation of financial markets proceeds. Financial intermediaries all facilitate the exchange of money. Unlike other FIs, commercial banks have the power to "create money," but other financial intermediaries are having an impact on the **money supply** similar to that of commercial banks.

We shall first look at the utility of money and the demand for it in our examination of money and FIs. Then we shall turn our attention to the mystique of the money supply, examining how money is "created" and what it really is. Finally, we shall examine money in the Keynesian model.

THE USES OF MONEY

Why is money so important? Because of its uses. Money is as money does. Few individuals hold dollars for the sheer joy of counting and stacking them. Money is valued for the goods and services that it buys—for its use as a *medium of exchange*. It is commonly accepted in payment for goods and services. Before money was institutionalized, barter was the rule of the day; one simply exchanged goods and services. Of course, problems would arise when one couldn't agree upon objects to trade—or there was no double coincidence of wants. Perhaps one trader desired shoes and had only nuts to offer while the shoemaker wanted only leather in exchange for shoes. Larger problems would arise if one was trading a horse.

A second use for money, implicit in its medium-of-exchange function, is as a measuring rod for the value of each good or service. It is, in essence, a *unit of account*. A pound of nuts may be valued at $3.69, a pair of shoes at $60.98, and a horse and buggy at $5753. Since all goods are measured by a dollar amount, this accounting function has become extremely important for measuring the national income accounts of GNP and NNP, as well as accounting for the flow of goods and services in an individual firm. Only money fills the medium-of-exchange and unit-of-account functions.

These, however, are not the only two uses of money. Money may serve as a *store of value* and as a *standard of deferred payment*. To be a store of value, an asset must hold its value into the future. Other assets that serve this function are stocks and bonds and diamonds and property. To be a standard of deferred payment, an asset must be accepted by others for future payment. Again, assets other than money adequately serve this function.

1. What assets would you be willing to accept in the future?

DEMANDS FOR MONEY

These four uses are associated with the three demands people have for money. The classical economists recognized only the **transactions demand** (similar to the medium-of-exchange function), which indicates the amount of money balances that individuals desire for transactions (purchasing) purposes. Most often this demand will be constant, given a level of income and a pattern of consumption expenditures.

A second demand for money balances is the **precautionary demand.** This demand was first separated into a category of its own by John Maynard Keynes in *The*

General Theory. Given the rule that it never rains but it pours, one has a propensity to save—to accumulate a nest egg while waiting for the next unfortunate event or cycle. (The car breaks down the week the kids are sick, the dog bites the mail carrier, and the washing machine floods the basement, etc.)

2. Divide your demands for money into transactions and precautionary balances. What percentage of your money balances do you hold for each?

As with the transactions demand, people at certain income levels will tend to save or keep a relatively fixed proportion of their income for precautionary purposes. A demand curve for the transactions and precautionary balances is plotted on a price–quantity axis in Fig. 20.1 to further illustrate (and to add money to the array of goods and services for which there is a demand—and later, of course, a supply). The quantity of money (M) is on the horizontal axis, and the price of money, represented by the interest rate (r),* is on the vertical axis. The vertical line M_d in Fig. 20.1 indicates that at all rates of interest the precautionary and transactions demand will be constant for a given individual at a given income level.

The third demand for money recognized by Keynes is the **speculative demand,** or as he called it, the **liquidity preference.**† This demand rises from the desire of people to maximize their returns on the funds left over after their transactions and precautionary demands have been satisfied. The speculative demand for funds is inversely related to the rate of interest in the economy. If the rate of interest is high, people will hold relatively few speculative or liquid balances. They will be holding stocks and bonds or goods instead of money balances. If, on the other hand, the rate of interest is low, individuals may decide to simply "wait and see" what happens to the interest rates in the future. If interest rates rise, people want to avoid being "locked in" to low-yielding assets—thus they prefer to hold (speculative) cash or money balances. One may plot the speculative demand for money with respect to interest and the quantity of money, since $M_{spec} = f(r)$, as shown in Fig. 20.2.

At extremely high rates of interest, the speculative demand for money balances approaches zero, whereas at very low rates of interest, people will desire to hold only money balances. This low-interest range in which the demand for money is perfectly elastic has been dubbed the Keynesian **liquidity trap.** Keynes pointed out that at

---

*The price of money is the rate of interest, since when one buys or borrows money, one pays for it at the prevailing rate of interest. It should be recognized that there is a wide array of interest rates in the economy at any one time, depending on such factors as risk and time to maturity of the asset. We will, however, focus on *an* interest rate—assuming that all of them will behave in a similar manner.
†Liquidity is the degree of "moneyness." One-hundred percent liquid suggests that all of one's assets are in cash and/or demand deposits. Stocks and bonds and property are assets of somewhat lesser levels of liquidity.

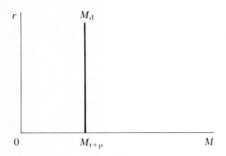

Figure 20.1 The transactions demand for money.

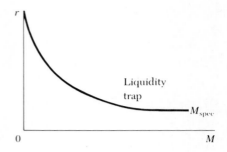

Figure 20.2 The speculative demand for money.

extremely low rates of interest people feel that interest rates can go no lower and can only rise. To buy bonds would be courting disaster, so people hold on to their cash. This trap area becomes important in discussing various aspects of monetary policy, and it will be taken up later in the chapter.

If all three demands for money are combined, the curve for the total demand for money can be plotted as in Fig. 20.3

This demand curve for money indicates that, like all demand curves, the quantity demanded varies inversely with price. It also indicates that as the interest rate rises, fewer money balances will be held—though enough will always be held to meet transactions and precautionary demands.

Changes in the Demand for Money

Like other demand curves, the demand-for-money curve can shift. Shifts or changes in demand are primarily caused by a change in the level of income. For example, if an individual's income increases from $20,000 a year to $25,000 a year, there will more than likely be an increase in that person's demand for money. This is explained by the increase in the demand for precautionary and transactions balances as income increases. Changes in income, as they affect the demand for money, are shown in Fig. 20.4.

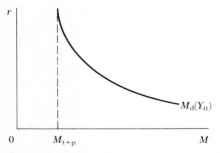

Figure 20.3 The demand for money.

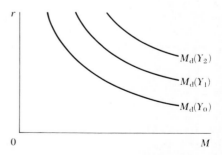

Figure 20.4 The effect of changes in income on the demand for money.

SUPPLY OF MONEY

Unlike the supply of most goods and services, the total supply of money is controlled not by individual firms as such but by the Federal Reserve System, more commonly and affectionately known as the Fed.

The Fed

The **Federal Reserve System** was established by the Federal Reserve Act of 1913 to help mend an ailing National Banking System. The Fed is an *independent* agency of the government established by an act of Congress to centralize control over the banking system and the money supply. The "basic" structure of the Federal Reserve System may be seen in Fig. 20.5.

The members of the Board of Governors of the Federal Reserve System are appointed by the president with congressional approval to coordinate and regulate the money supply in the United States. The chair of the Board of Governors acts as spokesperson for the entire system. The Federal Open Market Committee directs Fed Bond sales and purchases in their directives, and the Federal Advisory Council exists mostly for show.

The 12 regional Federal Reserve Banks and their 24 branches are scattered throughout the country and oversee operations of the member commercial banks in their districts. The locations of these can be seen in Fig. 20.6.

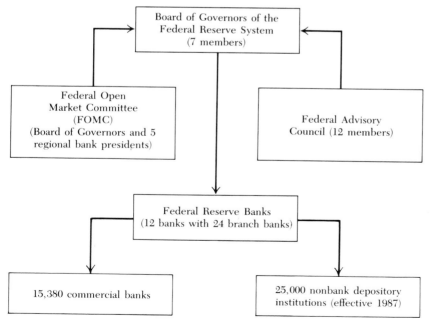

Figure 20.5 Elements of the Federal Reserve System.

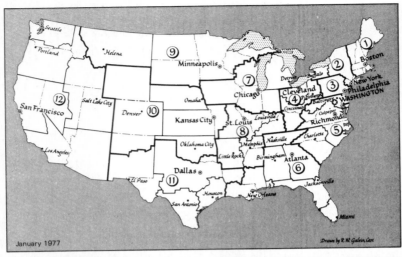

LEGEND

— Boundaries of Federal Reserve Districts   ⊙ Federal Reserve Bank Cities

— Boundaries of Federal Reserve Branch   • Federal Reserve Branch Cities
Territories   · Federal Reserve Bank Facility

✪ Board of Governors of the Federal
Reserve System

Figure 20.6 The Federal Reserve System—boundaries of Federal Reserve Districts, and their branch territories.

Although there are more than 15,000 commercial banks in the country, only 5700 were members of the Federal Reserve System in 1979. Banks had often left the system because of the high cost of membership, yet control over the money supply was maintained because the member banks (40 percent of the total) controlled the majority of deposits in the nation (75 percent). The **Monetary Control Act** of 1980, however, stipulated that the Federal Reserve can require that reserves be held by *all* banks and depository institutions in the country, thereby gaining control of all money held in commercial banks, savings banks, savings and loan associations, and other financial institutions. The period for phasing in these new institutions will end July 1, 1987.

3. **Why was the Federal Reserve established by Congress as an independent agency of the federal government (that is, outside the operational control of the Congress and the President)?**
4. **Who is the current chair of the Fed?**

The Regulation of Financial Markets

The history of financial market regulation has been a stormy one. Financial institutions have seen periods of total control and regulation as well as total banking anarchy, when almost anyone could start a bank—and the bank could then begin printing money. The current period of financial market regulation resulted from controls instituted after the Great Depression in the 1930s. No one wanted widespread banking failures to occur again. Investors as well as depositors wanted protection from financial market failure. As a result many regulations were established to assure the safety of the financial system. In addition to regulations on charters and the geographical location of financial institutions imposed by states, federal deposit insurance agencies began insuring a variety of deposits. The kind of loans and assets each type of financial institution could issue and possess was codified so that, for the most part, the financial industry was segmented into different types of institutions with little competition between them. Commercial banks, for example, specialized in commercial loans to firms, while savings and loans generated home mortgages. Indeed, savings banks were started by builders in the 1870s to make money available so the builders' products could be purchased. Perhaps the most onerous of the regulations to financial institutions was the interest rate ceiling on time and saving deposit accounts initiated in the 1930s legislation. Interest ceilings were instituted to "restrain excessive price competition," which was thought to be a cause of the 1933 banking collapse. This ceiling was known as Regulation Q. The interest ceiling was above the market rate of interest until the mid-1960s and until then caused no concern. After 1966 market rates rose above the interest ceiling on several occasions. This effectively meant that financial intermediaries could not attract money and then lend it. Instead of financial intermediation there was disintermediation. (People took their dollars out of banks and put them into money market funds to get higher rates of interest.) Financial intermediaries began creating new financial instruments to avoid interest ceilings, since only time and saving deposit accounts were then subject to Regulation Q. But the Federal Reserve was not to be caught short. While only two types of accounts were covered by Regulation Q in 1965, 24 types of accounts were covered by 1979. Money market mutual funds became the first "ceiling-free" instrument, and increasing pressure was placed on Congress to begin deregulating financial markets. The regulation of the 1930s had meant less competition and an inability to work within the market system to bid for funds.

During the 1970s lip service was paid to financial market deregulation as financial intermediaries continued innovating—always creating a new instrument to avoid the controls, and seeing the regulators move just as quickly to extend the regulations. By the end of the 1970s the mood toward regulation had substantially changed. The 1984 *Economic Report of the President* characterized this change.

In the 1930s, financial instability was widely attributed to the natural operation of competitive markets, and this view supported a very substantial extension of regulatory controls over financial markets. More recently, however, a renewed respect for the efficiency of competitive markets has developed, as well as increased recognition of the costs of regulation. Regulation tends to spread in unproductive directions and often causes industries to evolve less efficiently than they otherwise would. For these reasons, the promotion of efficiency by furthering competition is also an important regulatory goal. The purpose of regulation should not be to protect poorly managed individual firms from failure, but rather to prevent such failures from shaking the stability of the financial system as a whole. Regulation should be designed to achieve stability of the system, while individual firms are afforded the maximum possible freedom to compete and innovate.

Deregulation has meant that the rules of the game in the financial markets have been significantly changed. At the moment no one is quite sure of the implications.

There Goes One! Is It a Bank?

Between 1980 and 1984 most interest rates on federally insured deposits were deregulated. As a consequence banks and thrift institutions could freely determine the rate of interest they paid on most types of deposits. This has obviously added a great deal of competition and uncertainty to a vast financial system. All of this was brought about as part of the wave of deregulation activity that swept the country in the late 1970s and early 1980s. Financial deregulation is continuing as "nonbanks" try to gain a foothold in the banking industry and large banks try to maneuver their way through loopholes and engage in interstate banking—in effect opening up a truly "national" bank. (Many look to Sears to provide us soon with this nationwide system of complete financial services as well as blue jeans, toasters, tires, and Allstate insurance.)

All of this deregulatory activity was started by the Monetary Control Act of 1980 and extended by the Garn-St Germain Depository Institutions Act of 1982. The Monetary Control Act set lower reserve requirements for all nonmember depository intermediaries and established the Fed as the lender of the last resort for the nearly 40,000 depository institutions. The Garn-St Germain Act authorized all financial institutions to offer interest-bearing checking accounts and permitted some new lending and investing powers.

Many have questioned the wisdom of financial deregulation, particularly in light of the failure of Continental Illinois, a major U.S. national bank. Unable to arrange a merger for this giant, whose net worth totaled $2.3 billion, the Federal Deposit Insurance Corporation (FDIC), which insures deposits of most banks, took over operations. Below, Jeffrey E. Garten, a vice president at Shearson Lehman/

American Express (a financial giant in its own right), comments on Continental in the broad spectrum of financial deregulation. Next, FDIC Chair William M. Isaac, after explaining the role of the FDIC in the Continental case, sets forth his own thoughts about financial deregulation.

DEALING WITH A CHANGED BANKING SYSTEM

Chaos, Not Confidence, Reigns; Congress Must Restore Order

Jeffrey E. Garten

Well before the bubble burst at Continental Illinois National Bank & Trust Co., the push for financial deregulation had gone too far. It is time now for Congress to rein in the banks.

Banks, like any other aggressive business, have been pressing the law to the limits in an relentless drive to peddle new services and to extend their geographical reach. Meanwhile, Congress has been deliberating and pontificating while failing to establish a legal framework within which banks should operate. Paul Volcker is right. "We need assurance that the powerful forces of change are channeled in a manner consistent with the public interest," he said. "The single fact is that assurance is lacking."

Chaos is rampant. Washington prohibits interstate banking, yet Citibank, Mellon, Chase and 28 other bank holding companies have applied to establish some 200 offices across state lines. Our laws mandate a separation between commercial banking and securities underwriting, yet you can write checks and borrow money from firms like Merrill Lynch, and J.C. Penney owns a bank in Delaware.

Last month the Federal Reserve moved to halt a proposed interstate merger between Mellon National Corp. and Heritage Bank of New Jersey, despite the fact that the Comptroller had just granted approval. The FDIC wants state-chartered banks that are not members of the Federal Reserve System to be able to underwrite corporate securities; the Fed disagrees.

Washington and state governments are at war. Against the spirit of federal law, California permits savings and loan institutions that are chartered under state law to take heavy participation in real estate. South Dakota has authorized state-chartered banks to engage in insurance-related activities in 49 states.

Now legal challenges are mushrooming. The Florida banking association is suing to reverse a Federal Reserve Board decision to allow New

(continued)

York's U.S. Trust to do banking in Florida. Citibank is using the courts to stop mergers among regional banks in New England, from which it would be excluded.

Remember, banks are special. They stand guard over most of the nation's savings. They supply most of the credit to families and businesses. They are the Fed's conduit to control money supply and interest rates.

LAWS DELIBERATELY CHANGED

Banks also have unique privileges. They alone can borrow from the Fed. They get special tax breaks on reserves. Uncle Sam insures their deposits. In the wake of Continental, it's a safe bet that banks—big ones anyway—are fail-proof.

Moreover, the deregulation of other industries was sanctioned by Congress; laws were deliberately changed by vote of both Houses. On such issues as interstate banking or the ability of banks to do certain non-bank business, there has been no such public endorsement. In fact, banks, securities houses, thrifts, and savings and loans have thrived by exploiting legal loopholes.

Since the National Banking Act of 1864, which restricted the securities activities of national banks, Congress and the public have worried about confidence, stability, conflict of interest, economic and political concentration. Widespread banking failures in the 1930s—when banks had bought and sold securities, involved themselves in real estate and otherwise engaged in speculative businesses—only heightened these concerns.

New Deal legislation aimed at restoring public confidence. Banks were to remain distinct from other businesses, financial or otherwise. The SEC was created. The Fed was revamped. Deposits were to be federally insured.

It is tempting to say that the concerns of the 1930s are no longer relevant. Don't believe it. Modern banking has become riskier than ever.

Advances in communication and information gathering have not prevented major lending debacles in such areas as energy, real estate and sovereign lending. Spurred by competition from nonbank financial institutions such as Sears or Merrill Lynch, banks are attempting to move into risky new businesses such as insurance and real estate where they have little solid experience. Even in straight lending they are testing fate by throwing good money after bad in Latin America, encouraging easy personal borrowing against home equity with only lax credit analysis and gambling large sums on leveraged buyouts.

The FDIC recently had 650 banks on its problem list, for example, twice the number of 1982. Last year a record 48 banks collapsed; the failures have already reached 33 this year. If the economy turns down now,

(continued)

or interest rates shoot up, or both happen together, or, if for some other reason, a break in confidence occurs—as happened rather mysteriously in the case of Continental—we could have a full-blown banking crisis.

Of course the Federal commitment to bank solvency is stronger than ever. Recall Washington's unprecedented blank check for Continental's depositors. But the public usually pays whenever the safety net is used.

We all pay for bad banking that pushes loans to unworthy customers, thereby denying credit to those who could make better use of it. In the cases of Continental, Penn Square, Seafirst and banks that gorged themselves on Latin American debt, the U.S. has already lost big.

We all pay when a big bank goes bust and the cost of funds for the banking system generally increases, thereby driving up interest rates.

We all pay when financial uncertainty pervades the economy, thereby causing would-be investors in plant and equipment to hold back.

And if the federal bailout is large enough, we'll pay in two more ways: through inflation, as the Fed pours too much money into the system, and through taxes, as the FDIC reaches into the public purse.

Congress has a herculean task. The safety and soundness of the banking system comes first, of course. But in protecting the banks, our legislature has the obligation to ensure that supervision of banks' activities is tight, lest lenders reap the gains of deregulation while the public pays for the losses. And all the while, banks should not be put at a debilitating disadvantage vis-a-vis their nonbank competitors.

Congressional action should now focus on several issues.

We need tougher standards for disclosure, capital adequacy and reserves for bad loans. Latin American debt would be a good place to start.

The separation between banking and other businesses such as securities and insurance underwriting should be reaffirmed and enforced.

Depositors in nonbank money-market funds that are uninsured should be warned about the risks. Federal supervisory oversight to ensure reasonably sound management of these "nonbank" banks is essential.

The FDIC should increase premiums for riskier portfolios. When this happens, depositors should be alerted.

The Fed should be instructed to reexamine the international arrangements now in place to prevent an uncontrollable, cross-border banking crisis. In closed hearings, congressional experts should be satisfied with the global safety net.

Finally, the regulatory authorities should be instructed to hold back approvals of all new banking combinations—nonbank acquisition, expansion into interstate banking, etc.—until Congress can develop broader law. Make it a one-year moratorium. During this time additional issues could be decided, such as the proper structure for regulatory reform.

Much has happened in the absence of a decent legal framework. Nevertheless, Congress should not sit back and accept a *fait accompli*. It

(continued)

will be tough to make the cat walk back. But it would be reckless to let it run wild.

Continental Case Was Handled Well but Shows Need to Push Deregulation

William M. Isaac

The Federal Deposit Insurance Corp., in conjunction with the Federal Reserve, the Comptroller of the Currency and leading banks from around the nation have acted to calm the crisis atmosphere surrounding Continental Illinois National Bank. The FDIC and the banks provided an interim $2 billion infusion of subordinated debt, the banks increased their credit line to Continental and the Federal Reserve reaffirmed the availability of the "discount window."

Never before have the regulators and leading banks responded so swiftly and harmoniously to a situation of this type. Our actions demonstrated both our commitment and our capacity to maintain stability in the financial system. . . .

It's ironic that foes of deregulation are attempting to use this episode to bolster their case. In my judgment, the situation at Continental simply demonstrates that the policies of the past must be altered. The fact is that we do not currently have meaningful deregulation.

The only deregulation in place is on the liability side of bank balance sheets. Banks have been forced to pay more for their deposits but have not been given the opportunity to make up the lost income of the asset side. Rather than permitting banks to invest sensibly in domestic financial-services ventures, public policy has tempted some of them to take higher credit risks to offset their liability costs. When banks try to raise service charges to help cover their increased expenses, they are roundly criticized. Banks like Continental are hemmed in by branching restrictions, which preclude the development of a strong core deposit base and lead to excessive reliance on volatile funding. Even now, in its current plight, Continental's choices of partners for a voluntary merger are severely limited by restrictive laws.

NOT MANY ALTERNATIVES

This is not to argue that Continental would not have gotten into difficulty had the regulatory climate been more benign. Continental's management made serious mistakes and has no one to blame but itself. But the regulatory environment did not give the bank very many attractive alternatives to following the high-risk path it chose.

The Reagan administration has been attempting, with the support of Sen. Jake Garn (R., Utah) and others, for more than two years to get Con-

(continued)

gress to enact a sensible banking-deregulation package. The proposals would greatly strengthen our nation's financial system, while offering the American public a broader range of convenient financial services at more competitive prices. The FDIC has been urging Congress to include in the package some long-overdue and essential reforms to the deposit insurance system, such as risk-related premiums, stronger enforcement tools and a limitation on the deposit-insurance protection made available to sophisticated creditors.

We have maintained from the beginning that, in view of marketplace developments, the choice is not between deregulation and regulation. Liability-side deregulation is an accomplished fact—it cannot be reversed. The only choice is between orderly deregulation and unplanned, helter-skelter deregulation. We are getting a good dose of the latter and I, for one, don't like what I see. Congress should seize this unique opportunity to take control by enacting much needed reforms.

5. **Have any more large banks failed since 1984?**

6. **Should financial institutions continue to be deregulated? What are the costs (risks)? What are the benefits?**

7. **Are the concerns of the 1930s still relevant, as Mr. Garten suggests? Explain.**

The Suppliers of Money

The Fed controls the amount of credit in the banking system. One is always tempted to say the Fed controls the money supply—but then the question "What is the money supply?" is sure to arise. This is a question to which each economist has a different answer. Generally, in economics texts we define the money supply as being coin and currency plus demand deposits held by the public, or M_1 in economics jargon. In 1983, currency and coins accounted for about 35 percent of the money supply (M_1), and demand deposits (which are checking accounts) for 65 percent. The total money supply stood at $626.3 billion at the end of 1985, and it tends to grow at an annual rate of around 5 or 6 percent, although it has averaged over 10 percent during 1984 and 1985. On November 1, 1980, **NOW accounts** became legal throughout the country. These Negotiable Order of Withdrawal accounts are interest-bearing checking accounts. The initial maximum interest placed on these accounts was 5¼ percent. NOW accounts may be issued by all depository institutions. Currently the M_1 measure of the money supply includes NOW accounts.

Some economists prefer an expanded definition of the money supply that includes time deposits (that is, savings accounts) at commercial banks and other interest-bearing accounts. This expanded concept of the money supply is called M_2 and includes currency, checking accounts, NOW accounts, savings accounts, and other interest-bearing accounts. Milton Friedman is a leading proponent of this definition of the money supply. At the end of 1985, M_2 was $2564 million—more than four times the value of M_1. Friedman and others feel that the use of the M_2 definition better explains consumption and other decisions made in the economy. Additional definitions exist for broader concepts of money and liquid assets that are measured by the federal government and often used by economists in analyzing the economy. Other economists, however, believe that the Federal Reserve—when reflecting on policy actions that will result in changes in the money supply—really looks at the availability of credit in the economy rather than any precise M_1 or M_2 definition. For example, if the Fed feels credit is too tight, it will take measures to increase credit availability by increasing the supply of money in the economy.

Although the Fed is responsible for initiating changes in the money supply, individual banks allocate the money to the public, and to a large extent their allocation reflects the rates of interest in the economy. If interest rates are low, banks are reluctant to lend large quantities of money and to risk being locked into a low-yielding asset. On the other hand, if interest rates are high, the banks will be more willing to lend money *if it is available to them* (or if the Fed has allocated additional moneys by increasing the money supply). Constructing a money supply curve can be quite simple. Again, place the price of money, or the rate of interest, on the vertical axis and the quantity of money on the horizontal axis, as in Fig. 20.7.

The supply and demand curves for money can be illustrated together with the intersection of the two curves signifying equilibrium in the money market, as shown in Fig. 20.8.

At point E the quantity demanded for money is equal to the quantity supplied at an interest rate of r_0. There is no excess demand or supply in equilibrium.

If the Fed allows the money supply to increase, then the M_{s_0} curve will shift to the right (M_{s_1}), resulting in a lower rate of interest (r_1) in the economy, as in Fig. 20.9.

A decrease in the money supply will shift M_{s_0} to the left (M_{s_2}) and increase the interest rate (r_2). In Chapter 21 we will look at the tools with which the Fed changes the money supply. First we will examine the process by which commercial banks "create money" and how this money works within the Keynesian model.

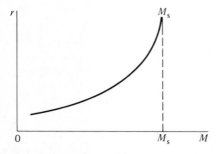

Figure 20.7 The money supply function.

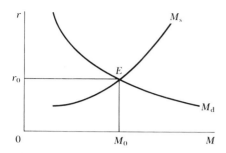

Figure 20.8 Equilibrium in the money market.

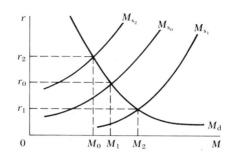

Figure 20.9 A change in the money supply.

THE MYTH AND MYSTIQUE OF MONEY

In the following excerpt from "Commercial Banks as Creators of Money," Yale economist James Tobin tries to "steal our thunder" in explaining the multiple **money creation** process in a principles text.

Perhaps the greatest moment of triumph for the elementary economics teacher is his exposition of the multiple creation of bank credit and bank deposits. Before the admiring eyes of freshmen he puts to rout the practical banker who is so sure that he "lends only the money depositors entrust to him." The banker is shown to have a worm's-eye view, and his error stands as an introductory object lesson in the fallacy of composition. From the Olympian vantage of the teacher and the textbook it appears that the banker's dictum must be reversed: depositors entrust to bankers whatever amounts the bankers lend. To be sure, this is not true of a single bank; one bank's loan may wind up as another bank's deposit. But it is, as the arithmetic of successive rounds of deposit creation makes clear, true of the banking system as a whole. Whatever their other errors, a long line of financial heretics have been right in speaking of "fountain pen money"—money created by the stroke of the bank president's pen when he approves a loan and credits the proceeds to the borrower's checking account.

    In this time-honored exposition two characteristics of commercial banks . . . are intertwined. One is that their liabilities—well, at least their demand deposit liabilities—serve as widely acceptable means of payment. Thus, they count, along with coin and currency in public circulation, as "money." The other is that the preferences of the public normally play no role in determining the total volume of deposits or the total quantity of money. For it is the beginning of wisdom in monetary economics to observe that money is like the "hot potato" of a children's game: one individual may pass it to another, but the group as a whole cannot get rid of it. If the economy and the supply of money are out of adjustment, it is economy that must do the adjusting. This is true, evidently, of the money created by banker's fountain pens as of money created by public printing presses. On the other hand, financial intermediaries other than banks do not create money, and the scale of their assets is limited by their liabilities, i.e., by the savings the public entrusts to them. They cannot count on receiving "deposits" to match every extension of their lending.

The commercial banks and only the commercial banks, in other words, possess the **widow's cruse** [an expression implying unending supply; emphasis added]. And because they possess this key to unlimited expansion, they have to be restrained by reserve requirements.

—Tobin, J., "Commercial Banks as Creators of Money," in *Banking and Monetary Studies*, D. Carson, ed. (Homewood, Ill.: Richard D. Irwin, 1963 ©). Reprinted by permission of the publisher.

Commercial banks create money on the basis of a **fractional reserve system** of deposit balances. The Fed requires that every bank hold a certain percentage of its total deposits in its vault or in the nearest Federal Reserve Bank to ensure safety and an ability to meet deposit withdrawals. These **reserve requirements** vary according to the size of the bank's assets, and the exact percentage to be held may be changed by the Fed at any time. The limits within which the Fed can set reserve requirements were specified most recently by Congress in 1973; they are as follows:

Time (savings) accounts   min. 3 percent, max. 10 percent

Banks with demand deposits > $400M   min. 10 percent, max. 22 percent

Banks with demand deposits < $400M   min. 7 percent, max. 14 percent

In 1984, reserve requirement rates in effect were as shown in Table 20.1

8. Why isn't there a 100 percent reserve requirement?

An example of the money-creation process should aid in clarifying what happens to a deposit in a commercial bank. For simplicity's sake, we shall use a 10 percent reserve requirement for demand deposits and begin with a $1000 deposit. New deposits in the banking system increase by $1000 and required reserves increase by $100. This, then, leaves the bank with $1000 minus $100 or $900. The prudent (profit maximizing) banker would undoubtedly make use of the $900 by generating loans and investments of an equal amount. Perhaps you are in the market for a $900 loan. If our friendly, neighborhood banker decides you are credit worthy, you may receive the "extra" $900. If you spend the $900 on new stereo components, there is a pretty good chance that the full $900 will enter the banking system when the Stereo Shack deposits its daily balances. The banking system then has another deposit, this time one of $900. So, 10 percent of $900 or $90 must be held as the reserve requirement on the *new* $900 deposit. Total new deposits are now $1900 and total new reserves are $190 in the banking system. And what will happen to the $900

Table 20.1 RECENT RESERVE REQUIREMENTS

TYPE OF DEPOSIT	BEFORE IMPLEMENTATION OF THE MONETARY CONTROL ACT MEMBER BANKS RESERVE REQUIREMENTS (PERCENTAGE)
Demand deposit (in millions)	
The first $2	7
From $2 to $10	9.5
From $10 to $100	11.75
From $100 to $400	12.75
Over $400	16.25
Time deposit	
Savings	3
Other time	
0 to 5 million	
Maturing 30–179 days	3
180 days–4 years	2.5
4 years or more	1
Over $5 million	
Maturing 30–179 days	6
180 days–4 years	2.5
4 years or longer	1

TYPE OF DEPOSIT	AFTER IMPLEMENTATION OF THE MONETARY CONTROL ACT DEPOSITORY INSTITUTION RESERVE REQUIREMENTS (PERCENTAGE)
Net transaction account (in millions)	
$0 to $28.9	3
Over $28.9	12
Nonpersonal time deposit (by original maturity)	
Less than 1½ years	3
1½ years or more	0
Eurocurrency liabilities	3

Source: Federal Reserve Bulletin, July 1984, Table A–7.

minus $90 or $810 left in the bank? Of course, potential increases in loans and investments. The final result of the initial $1000 demand deposit can be seen in Table 20.2.

Rather than carrying this process to its final result as above, we can more easily find the total amount of money "created" by the following formula

$$\Delta R \times \frac{1}{r_{dd}} = \Delta DD,$$

where ΔR is the original change in reserves, r_{dd} is the reserve requirement on demand deposits, and ΔDD is the total change in demand deposits. In our example, this becomes

$$\$1000 \times \frac{1}{1/10} = \Delta DD,$$

$$\$1000 \times 10 = \$10,000,$$

$$\Delta DD = \$10,000.$$

From $1000—with the stroke of a pen, as Tobin says—banks can "make" $10,000, or $9000 of new money. There are, however, several things that must be pointed out before accepting this fountain pen magic. The first is that an individual bank acting alone cannot create money. The process must operate throughout the whole banking system. We can perhaps more easily understand this by looking at a single bank that might try to expand or create money on its own. For example, if the first bank tried to make loans of $9000 based on the $1000 increase in its reserves

Table 20.2 MONEY CREATION

POSITION OF BANK	NEW DEMAND DEPOSITS	NEW LOANS AND INVESTMENTS	NEW RESERVES
Original bank	$ 1,000.00	$ 900.00	$ 100.00
2nd bank	900.00	810.00	90.00
3rd bank	810.00	729.00	81.00
4th bank	729.00	656.10	72.90
5th bank	656.10	590.49	65.61
6th bank	590.49	531.44	59.05
7th bank	531.44	478.30	53.14
8th bank	478.30	430.47	47.83
9th bank	430.47	387.42	43.05
10th bank	387.42	348.68	38.74
11th bank	348.68	313.81	34.87
12th bank	+ 313.81	+ 282.43	+ 31.38
Sum of 12 banks	$ 7,175.71	$ 6,458.14	$ 717.61
Sum of remaining banks	+ 2,824.29	+ 2,541.86	+ 232.39
Total for system as a whole	$10,000.00	$9,000.00	$1,000.00

(Totals may not be accurate
  due to rounding.)

with the $1000 deposit—what happens to that bank when someone comes to "withdraw" or use the funds the bank has just lent? As one might imagine, many problems can result, one being the bank's inability to maintain its reserve requirement.

9. What other difficulties might this bank run into?

So now we too have triumphantly explained the multiple creation process. What else makes the process not quite so grand as it seems? A second point to remember is that the multiple creation process "works" only if there are no leakages in the system. Leakages may occur in several places. Individuals may decide to place their funds elsewhere, either outside the banking system or in hoards. If the funds are not redeposited, then there is no "new money" to expand upon. Some funds may be placed in time accounts by consumers. This will lead to an even greater expansion of the money supply, since there is a lower reserve requirement placed on these funds and thus a larger money multiplier.

Another leakage may appear within the banking system itself. Bankers may decide that greater profits are to be made in asset holdings other than those of a loan or investment variety. Perhaps bankers feel their liquidity is too low and desire to place their remaining funds (or excess reserves) in more short-term types of assets (such as government bonds). In either case, there is a leakage of funds, funds that do not reenter the demand deposit flow for an indefinite period of time. Indeed, the amount of assets that banks hold in loans or investments is approximately 60 percent of their total portfolio. So caution should be the byword when examining the money-creation process. Nevertheless, the process does suggest that the commercial banking system has the ability to expand the money supply by "creating" demand deposits. In addition, the simple formula, $\Delta R \times 1/r_{dd} = \Delta DD$, approximates the amount of money that can be created from a new deposit in the banking system.

10. What happens to the money supply when people take $1000 out of their bank deposits?

But is it just money creation? Are commercial banks the only intermediaries that "create money"? In his article "Commercial Banks as Creators of Money," James Tobin concludes that other nonbank intermediaries aren't very different from commercial banks and may affect credit expansion and contraction as well, especially today because NOW accounts are legal at all commercial banks and savings institutions. In fact, other financial intermediaries are much like commercial banks and with monetary deregulation have become even more so. That is why the Fed will begin imposing reserve requirements on these other depository institutions. By July 1987 all depository institutions will possess "money creation" power.

11. How do savings banks enter into this process? What about a life insurance company?

MONEY AND THE KEYNESIAN SYSTEM

Money can be an integral part of the Keynesian system, as it was developed by Keynes and as it has been extended by post-Keynesian economists. You will recall from the last chapter that the "general gist" of the Keynesian system is that changes in consumption, investment, and government spending may be effectively used to expand or lower the level of income in the economy. Money can and most often does work within the Keynesian sphere to allow income changes as well. Changes in the money supply often directly influence both the business and household sectors in their investment and consumption decisions.

We know from our earlier discussion that an increase in the supply of money will lower the rate of interest (Fig. 20.10), just as (ceteris paribus) any increase in supply will decrease the price of a product. As money becomes "cheaper," investors will reconsider their present levels of investment.

Low interest rates will encourage businesses to borrow from banks and to spend these funds on new plants and equipment (i.e., investment); high rates, on the other hand, deter investment decisions. This is expressed graphically in Fig. 20.10 as an inverse relationship between the rate of interest (r) and the level of investment (I), or $I = f(r)$. As the interest rate falls from r_0 to r_1, investment (in housing, equipment, or plants) will expand from I_0 to I_1.

Returning to the Keynesian model developed in the last chapter, let's look at the effect of an increase in investment, this time stimulated by a reduction in the rate of interest, which resulted from an increase in the money supply (see Fig. 20.11.)

We find that as the money supply is increased from M_{s_0} to M_{s_1}, as in Fig. 20.9, the interest rate decreases from r_0 to r_1, and as this occurs, investment is increased from I_0 to I_1 (Fig. 20.10), and finally, this increased investment, working through the multiplier, generates a new higher income level, Y_1, as in Fig. 20.11. (Remember, $I_1 - I_0 = \Delta I$, $Y_1 - Y_0 = \Delta Y$, and the $\Delta Y = k \times \Delta I$.)

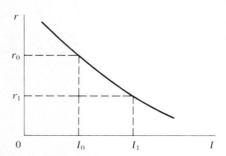

Figure 20.10   The interest–investment relationship.

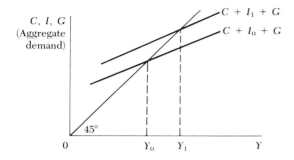

Figure 20.11   Income response to a change in investment.

12. **What happens when the Fed decreases the money supply? What happens to interest rates? The level of investment? The level of income? Employment?**

Keynes relied more on fiscal policy for the stimulation of aggregate demand in *The General Theory* because he felt that during times of depression the economy would operate in the area of the liquidity trap. In this area, no matter how much the money supply was increased, the rate of interest would fall no lower. And because of grim expectations of the future, the business community would not be tempted to further its investment activity, even with low rates of interest.

We can see in Fig. 20.12 that changes in the money supply within the range of the liquidity trap will have no effect on interest rates. And if interest rates are unchanged, the levels of investment and income will also remain the same, yielding no effect on aggregate demand.

Keynes also believed that business and consumer expectations could change during depressions, thereby thwarting the effect of monetary policy. It is for these reasons that the analogy is often made that increasing the money stock is much like pushing on a string.

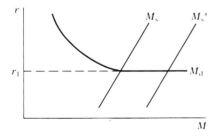

Figure 20.12   Money supply increase in the liquidity trap.

Since severe depressions have not been the dominant feature of our economy, we should examine the tools with which the Fed can and does alter the supply of money to change the level of income in the economy. This will be done in Chapter 21.

KEY CONCEPTS

money	Monetary Control Act
financial intermediaries	M_1
money supply	M_2
transactions demand	NOW accounts
precautionary demand	money creation
speculative demand	widow's cruse
liquidity preference	fractional reserve system
liquidity trap	reserve requirements
Federal Reserve System	

REVIEW QUESTIONS

1. Why would the Fed want control of the largest banks in the country? Why does the Fed want to control the reserves of savings and loan associations?

2. Explain the differences among the transactions, precautionary, and speculative demands for money. List five factors that influence your demands for money.

3. Why is a barter economy unsuitable for today's world?

4. Define NOW accounts. Why might they be a problem for the banking system?

5. What is the difference between M_1 and M_2? Why is it important to distinguish between them? Does it really matter what the money supply is? Discuss.

6. Suppose you discovered $40,000 of 1901 dollars stuffed in a mattress in your dorm. (a) What would be the effect of the $40,000 of "new money" on the banking system? Explain. (b) What would be the effect if you "blew" the money on a new Mercedes? (c) What if you stuffed the money back into the mattress?

SUGGESTED READINGS

John Kenneth Galbraith, 1975. *Money: Whence It Came and Where It Went*, Houghton Mifflin. For Galbraith addicts. An account of money throughout history, from the beginning to Keynes to now.

George Goodman (alias Adam Smith), 1972. *Supermoney*, Random House, Maybe even better than *The Money Game*. Goodman amusingly tells how "big money" operates and reports on the grim world of cocoa futures.

Martin Mayer, 1974. *The Bankers*, Ballantine Books. A "bestseller" that's really informative. It gives interesting behind-the-scene accounts of banking happenings.

Lawrence S. Ritter and William L. Silber, 1984. *Money*, Basic Books. An excellent *and* amusing account of how money works in the economy.

Adam Smith (alias George Goodman), 1967. *The Money Game*, Random House. A very well-written and readable account of how money works on Wall Street and, more important, an insight into the human side of money.

Monetary Policy

INTRODUCTION

In *The General Theory*, Keynes expressed substantial doubt about the ability of **monetary policy** to rescue the economy from a severe depression. Yet, during the past three decades we have seen the power of monetary policy to affect the levels of aggregate demand in the economy. During this period the active role the Fed has played in the determination of aggregate demand has often been challenged and criticized, but monetary policy has nonetheless continued to be an important tool for economic stabilization. Some critics have argued that the Fed is too powerful and too independent. Others believe that the money supply is much too important to be left to the discretion of mere mortals. In this chapter we shall first examine the tools that enable the Federal Reserve to control the supply of money and credit in the economy. Next we shall outline the philosophy and principles of the school of economists known as the monetarists, and finally we shall examine recent Federal Reserve policy and the interaction between monetary and fiscal policy.

MONETARY POLICY—TOOLS OF THE TRADE

The Fed has at hand several tools that may be used to affect the level of income in the economy: (1) *reserve requirement changes*, (2) *open-market operations*, and (3) *discount rate changes*. During World War II several *selective credit controls* on home mortgages and consumer credit were implemented by the Fed. The only credit control regularly utilized is the margin requirement for stocks, which stipulates the percentage of payment that must be in cash on any security purchase. In March of 1980 the Fed responded to President Carter's request for a greater tightening of credit in the nation to help quell the inflationary trends by announcing new controls on consumer and business credit. These controls were quickly withdrawn when it became evident that they were dramatically worsening the recession of 1980.

Reserve Requirements

Required reserve levels may be changed at any time by the Board of Governors. In general, the central bank views its ability to change **reserve requirements** as its most powerful tool and uses this tool with utmost discretion. Critics claim that it works like an axe rather than a scalpel. Since only a 1-percent change in reserve requirements alters the monetary situation geometrically, changes in reserve requirements tend to be infrequent. This tool has been used since 1935 and has been altered only a few times in Federal Reserve history. One can see why this tool is unpopular with bankers in the following example. Assume that the Fed wishes to restrict economic activity by reducing the money supply (e.g., to fight inflation). If banking assets are at $400 billion with 10-percent reserve requirements, some $40 billion are being held as reserves. If reserve requirements are increased by 1 percent to 11 percent, some $44 billion must be held. This takes $4 billion out of the money supply immediately as loans and investments are called in to increase reserves to the new level.

1. **In the example above what might happen to interest rates? Why?**

2. **What would happen if reserve requirements were lowered by 1 percent? How much would member banks be required to hold? What would happen to the "extra" money (or excess reserves)?**

An increase in reserve requirements can absorb large changes in *excess reserves*, such as those that occurred during the 1930s when substantial amounts of gold flowed into the country. A reserve-requirement reduction may offset a large loss in reserves. In either case, a change in reserve requirements announces a change in Fed policy to the public as well as to the banks. Critics of the Fed suggest that other means are more appropriate for the announcement of policy changes.

Open-Market Operations

The Fed is engaged daily in **open-market operations** through the activities of the Federal Reserve Open Market Committee. Activities in the open market involve the actual *purchases and sales* of government bonds, bills, and notes at the New York Fed. These actions will affect the money supply as well as the interest rates. To increase the money supply (and economic activity, e.g., to combat recession) the Fed

The Fed is responsible for the nation's monetary policy. (Photograph by Robert Bostwick.)

will actively *buy* bonds (Treasury issues). Buying bonds takes them out of the hands of the banks and the public and exchanges them for money (a check or cash from the Fed), thus increasing the money supply. If, on the other hand, the Fed desires to draw down the money stock, it will step up bond *sales* to commercial banks and other financial intermediaries, this time increasing the stock of bonds at commercial banks and decreasing their stock of reserves.

The effect on interest rates by these bond sales and purchases is inversely related to the money supply (a section on this follows). When the money stock is reduced by bond sales, interest rates must increase in order to attract businesses as well as households to the bond offerings. Otherwise, these funds would be invested or saved in something other than bonds. Bond sales, then, encourage interest rates upward as they compete with other assets for the public's cash balances. The interest rate will also rise because of the shortage of money—once the bond sales have been made.

Open-market operations are the Fed's most important and powerful tool. They take place on a day-to-day basis, and the Fed's Open Market Committee meets regularly to decide what impact they want open-market operations to have on the money supply and interest rates.

3. How do bond purchases affect the interest rates in the economy? Why?

INTEREST RATES AND THE MONEY SUPPLY

We can use the following example to illustrate the relation between the purchase of a bond by the Federal Reserve as well as the relationship between the price of bonds and the rate of interest. First, assume your grandparents give you a $100 government bond for your birthday. If you read the fine print on this particular bond, you will find that the U.S. government will pay you $100 at the end of 10 years. Obviously your grandparents did not pay $100 for a bond that is worth $100 at the end of 10 years; they paid something less. We can find how much they paid by examining a present-value table. The present value is the amount that the $100 bond, which is payable in 10 years, is worth today, or more generally, what a dollar at the end of a specified future year is worth today. By examining the abbreviated present-value table below, we find that if the interest rate is 10 percent, your grandparents paid $38.50 for the bond, with this 10-year bond yielding a 10 percent rate of interest. If the interest rate on the bond is 15 percent the present price of the bond would be $24.70. As you can see, as the interest rate rises (from 10 to 15 percent) the price of the $100 bond falls (from $38.50 to $24.70). There is an inverse relation between the rate of return or interest rate and the price of the bond.

PRESENT-VALUE TABLE FOR $100.00*

YEAR	7%	10%	15%
1	93.50	90.90	87.00
2	87.30	82.60	75.60
3	81.60	75.10	65.80
4	76.30	68.30	57.20
5	71.30	62.00	49.70
6	66.66	56.40	43.20
7	62.30	51.30	37.60
8	58.20	46.60	32.60
9	54.40	42.40	28.40
10	50.80	38.50	24.70

*The formula for finding the present-value entries in the table is $P = R/(1 + r)^t$: the present value P equals the future return R (in this case $100), divided by $(1 + \text{rate of interest})^t$, where t is the number of years to maturity (in our example, $t = 10$ years).

When the Federal Reserve purchases bonds in the open market in order to increase the money supply, the demand for bonds increases and

(continued)

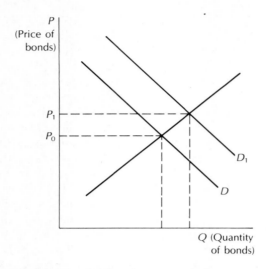

so the price of bonds rises (see figure). We know that as the price of bonds rise, the interest rate falls due to the inverse relation between the two. Thus, as the Fed buys bonds increasing the money supply, interest rates fall.

The Discount Rate

The **discount rate** is the rate at which a member bank can borrow from the Federal Reserve. Banks often borrow from the Fed to protect their reserve position. Most often collateral of bonds is presented by the banks and they are discounted by the Fed for short-term borrowing purposes. To increase the money supply (and economic activity), the Fed should lower the discount rate, making borrowing more attractive for the commercial banks. The banks can then pass the funds along to households and businesses by increasing the availability of loans. The discount rate should be increased when the Fed desires tight money, making the discount window available only when it is absolutely essential. The discount rate was lowered several times between 1980 and 1986, both to increase the money supply and to signal concern about economic activity. It is also used in "emergency" situations with the Fed serving as "the lender of the last resort."

Lags in Monetary Policy

As with fiscal policy, lags and delays are inherent in monetary actions. These lags have been classified by economists into two major types, the *inside lag* and the *outside lag*. The inside lag comprises the *recognition lag* and the *action lag*. The time it takes for the Federal Reserve authorities to recognize that there is indeed a problem in the economy has been dubbed the recognition lag. Between that time and the time some policy is implemented is the action lag. These lags are usually a function of measurement and forecasting. After the action takes place, there is a lag before impact (either partial or total) is felt in the economy. The length of these impact lags is a subject of dispute among economists and economic models. Monetarists argue that the impact lag with monetary actions is much shorter than do their Keynesian (fiscal) counterparts. Several econometric models have been used to estimate the effectiveness of policy actions. According to the St. Louis Fed economic model, monetary policy is significantly felt in the economy four months after action, while the Fed-M.I.T.-Penn model indicates that a much longer period is needed for the impact to be felt. To more fully examine the differences in these two models, we need to explore the world of the monetarists.

MONETARISM

The monetarists trace their roots directly to the classical economists and to the quantity theory of money. This relationship, which was discussed in Chapter 17, is the identity $MV = PQ$, where M is the quantity of money, V is the velocity, P is the price level, and Q is the volume of physical output. In the equation of exchange the relationship between M and P was of primary concern. Unlike the Keynesians, the monetarists see the money stock as the major stimulus for economic activity. Although their model is more sophisticated than the one of the classical economists, today's monetarists still use the velocity of money as the major link between money and the GNP (or output). They have found "direct and reliable links" between the two, as well as evidence indicating the stability of the velocity of money over time. With a stable velocity, the monetarists argue that economic growth (or decline) can be gained by altering the money supply. The monetarists agree that the velocity of money has changed over time, as we can see in Table 21.1. As income has increased since 1950, people have chosen to hold less money *relative* to their incomes. From 1880 through 1950, however, velocity declined steadily. The monetarists believe that there are long-run trends and short-run lags for which velocity must be adjusted. Once these adjustments are made, the relationship between GNP and the money held by the public (GNP/M) is stable. It is stable enough to predict changes in aggregate demand with given changes in the money supply, according to the monétarist argument. Thus, levels of aggregate demand, or GNP, can be targeted.

With the relation $MV = PQ = $ GNP, $V = $ GNP/M, monetarists believe that the GNP/M ratio will stabilize with increases or decreases in the money supply. The value of V changes as the money supply is altered, but will readjust to its former level. The transmission mechanism, then, is velocity, not the rate of interest as in the Keynesian system.

Table 21.1 and Fig. 21.1 show that velocity had a predictable growth rate through the past three decades. In 1982, however, velocity fell.

Some downturn in velocity would have been expected during the 1982 recession. When the economy is weak people fear the worst and tend to keep larger amounts of money in a checking account so that they can get to it quickly if some

Table 21.1 THE INCOME VELOCITY OF MONEY

YEAR	GROSS NATIONAL PRODUCT, GNP (IN BILLIONS)	MONEY SUPPLY, M_1 (IN BILLIONS)	VELOCITY, GNP/M_1
1947	$ 232.8	$113.1	2.05
1950	286.2	116.2	2.46
1955	399.3	135.2	2.95
1960	506.0	144.2	3.51
1965	688.1	171.3	4.02
1970	982.4	219.8	4.47
1975	1528.8	295.4	5.18
1976	1702.2	313.8	5.42
1977	1899.5	338.7	5.61
1978	2127.6	361.5	5.89
1979	2368.5	384.8	6.20
1980	2631.7	414.9	6.35
1981	2954.1	441.9	6.70
1982	3000.0	480.5	6.41
1983	3304.5	525.3	6.20
1984	3774.7	558.5	6.76
1985	3992.5	626.3	6.37

Source: Economic Report of the President, 1986.

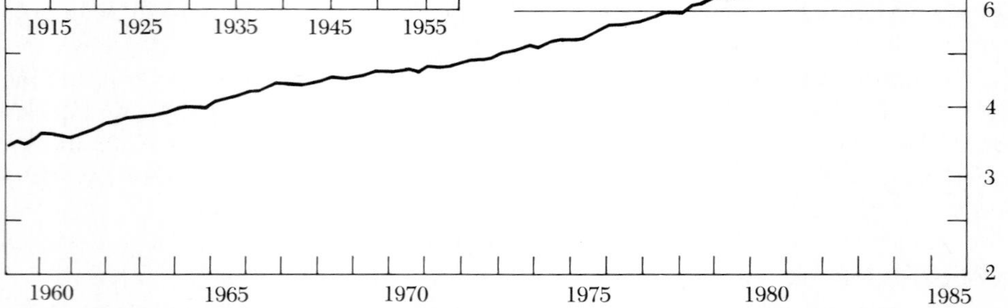

Figure 21.1 The income velocity of money (seasonally adjusted, quarterly). *Source: 1983 Historical Chart Book,* Board of Governors of the Federal Reserve System, p. 5.

misfortune such as job loss strikes. For the level of GNP then, people will hold more money, M_1, and so velocity, GNP/M_1, will fall. The problem in 1982 was that the fall in velocity was much sharper and longer than expected.

For a monetarist, one could say "*Only money matters.*" Monetarists essentially believe that inflation as well as recession can be and must be controlled through monetary policy. Monetarists argue that the only fiscal actions that have any impact at all on the economy are those financed by new money or by Treasury borrowing from the Federal Reserve. Any other means of financing, such as borrowing from the public through deficit financing, merely takes money from one sector and gives it to another. This, again, would be an example of the government's crowding out private expenditures through increased government borrowing from the private sector. Monetarists such as Milton Friedman who have studied the historical trends of the U.S. economy, believe that fiscal policy per se can shape the trends and paths of the economy, but that it has no predictable effect on inflation or unemployment. For example, monetarists argue that the fiscal policy of the 1964 tax cut was effective not because of the tax cut itself but because of the expansion in the money supply that accompanied the tax cut.

Friedman, the leading monetarist, has severely criticized the Fed for its "erratic" policy toward money creation. Friedman argues that more problems have been created by the discretionary actions of the monetary authorities—pumping money into and pulling money out of the economy—than a **monetary rule** would have created. Friedman's rule would allow the money supply to grow at a constant rate yearly and would eliminate the need for a Federal Reserve. According to Friedman, periods of inflation would be eliminated since the money supply would not be permitted to grow at a rate that would fuel the fires of inflation. Recession would be averted because a guaranteed supply of money would be available for investment purposes at all times, and businesses could be confident that the economy would not be tightened intentionally.

MONETARISM AND THE FED

The Fed has tremendously powerful tools, and the independence given to the Fed means that it has the authority to carry out the monetary policy it views as best. During the 1950s and 1960s the Fed followed its collective instinct in managing money matters. After economists severely criticized this policy in the mid-1960s, the Fed began to target interest rate levels in adjusting the nation's money supply. This type of policy, despite outcries from monetarists, continued until the fall of 1979. Monetarists believe that control of the nation's money supply is far more important than control of interest rates. Indeed, if you examine the preceding section, you will find no reference to interest rates, yet if you skim back over the last chapter, you will see that the Keynesians rely heavily on interest rates to transmit the effects of monetary policy to the economy.

Monetarists had argued since the 1950s that the Federal Reserve should stabilize the growth rate of the money stock to ensure economic growth without inflation. The lesson fell on deaf ears until the fall of 1979, when Paul Volcker, newly appointed chair of the Federal Reserve, called on the Fed to institute an essentially monetarist policy to bring down the 18-plus percent inflation that prevailed at the time. The Fed slashed monetary growth rates from 8 percent in 1979 to 5 percent by 1981. The results were spectacular. Inflation dropped to 4 percent and the unemployment rate rose to 10.5 percent. One thing that both the Fed and monetarists counted on and predicted was a decline in the rate of interest, but that decline failed to occur (see Fig. 21.2). Interest rates remained high throughout the recession, as financial markets demanded high interest rates to hedge their bet that inflation would not fall despite monetarist policies of decreased money supply growth. In fact, real interest rates increased dramatically. The real rate of interest is the nominal (published) rate minus inflation. Inflation fell much faster than interest rates until 1984. The Fed began increasing the growth rate of the money supply in June 1981, but again, monetarist and Fed predictions failed as the nation lingered in deep economic recession. It took nearly two years of higher monetary growth rates, of up to 13 percent, before the economy began to recover. Efforts to sharply reduce interest rates were thwarted by huge federal deficits. This period also taught us that velocity is not completely predictable, and consequently the Fed cannot be confident about how a given growth rate of the money stock might affect the economy.

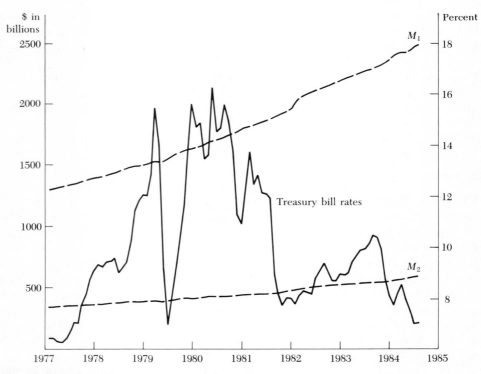

Figure 21.2   The money supply and Treasury bill interest rates.

With the period of monetarist experimentation, few still have confidence in their predictions of the forecasted results. Milton Friedman, monetarist *extraordinaire*, gives us his explanation of the failure of monetary variables and his forecast for future inflation as the economy responded to the rapid money growth in the 1981–1983 period.

INFLATION ISN'T BEATEN

Milton Friedman

During the 1980 Presidential campaign, both Democrats and Republicans proclaimed inflation the nation's No. 1 problem. "Double-digit inflation" became a household term. During the current campaign, the inflation issue is notable by its absence—except for Republican boasting about conquering inflation. And, indeed, the reduction in inflation has been remarkable. In the summer of 1980, consumer prices were rising at more than 12 percent per year; in early 1984, at 5.5 percent.

In the main, the candidates, the public and the press take it for granted that inflation is under control—though doubts are beginning to surface. In my opinion, the declaration of victory is premature. It looks more and more as if inflation will soon once again be the No. 1 economic problem.

Inflation over any substantial period is predominantly a monetary phenomenon. Prices rise in response to a more rapid increase in the quantity of money than in the output of goods and services. The response is not immediate. Indeed, for at least the past century, it has taken about two years in the United States and Britain for a monetary explosion to be reflected in higher inflation, and for a monetary slowdown, in lower inflation. Moreover, neither the timing nor the size of the response is uniform. Inflation is affected by many other forces, especially the public's perceptions about future inflation. In the early stages of an inflationary episode, prices tend to rise less rapidly than the quantity of money. As the public becomes aware of what is happening, inflation tends to feed on itself, and prices rise more rapidly than the quantity of money. Conversely, when monetary growth slows; inflation at first often responds sluggishly, but once the public becomes persuaded that inflation is headed down, that too feeds on itself and inflation falls much faster than monetary growth.

Both propositions are illustrated by recent experience. From the fourth quarter of 1977 to the fourth quarter of 1979, the quantity of money grew at the rate of 7.8 percent per year. Two years later (1979–1981), inflation

(continued)

hit 9.4 percent. From 1979 to 1981, monetary growth slowed to 6.2 percent; two years later (1981–1983), inflation slowed to 4.2 percent.

The more drastic slowdown in inflation than in prior monetary growth partly reflects the usual tendency for a reduction in inflation, like an acceleration, to feed on itself. But an additional factor was also at work. The monetary slowdown was exceptionally erratic and, as a result, so were interest rates and the economy. Increased uncertainty enhanced the public's desire to be liquid, which, on the one hand, produced the unusually severe and long recession of 1981–1982, and, on the other, the sharp slowdown of inflation.

The rate of monetary growth over the past two years explains why the declaration of victory in the war against inflation is premature. Over those two years, monetary growth jumped to 9.5 percent—higher than in any other two-year period since at least the end of World War II. Higher inflation is sure to follow. As in other episodes, prices may at first rise less rapidly than money—but even that is not certain. The public is far more sophisticated about inflation than ever before and it may well react more quickly than in earlier, more tranquil decades.

The early signs are already here. Consumer prices rose at the rate of 3.3 percent in the first half of 1983 and 4.8 percent in the second half; and of 5.5 percent in the first two months of 1984. Other broad price indexes show a similar pattern. We shall be fortunate indeed if prices are not rising in the 7 to 10 percent range by the fourth quarter of the year and in double digits by 1985.

If that unfortunate development does occur, a newly elected or reelected President, under great pressure to stop the inflation, will have no easy out. A monetary squeeze would ultimately stop the inflation but in the meantime it would stop the boom in its tracks and produce a recession. A siren call for price and wage controls would once again befoul the air. The public's memory is short—and so is the politician's planning horizon. By 1985, it will have been 14 years since Richard M. Nixon imposed price and wage controls to stop an "unacceptable" 4.5 percent inflation in consumer prices; more than a decade since the controls collapsed in a burst of inflation that topped 15 percent. It will be only four years since the monetary squeeze that ended the most recent inflation produced a long and severe recession. A Democratic President elected on a platform of full employment and low interest rates would be especially tempted to repeat a Republican President's greatest mistake. Irony, yes—but, more important, a potential national tragedy.

Now, Democrats and Republicans alike call for continued monetary growth to sustain current levels of growth. The monetarist experiment of the early 1980s was not a pleasant one. Admittedly inflation was reduced, but it took a heavy toll. At a call by monetarists to continue strict monetary growth, Chairman of the House Banking Committee, Fernand J. St Germain responded "This Congress will not tolerate a return to flinty-eyed monetarism, high interest rates, and recession. Our citizens have suffered under three years of miscreant monetarism, and the time to stay with the recovery is upon us."

4. **Why can't the Fed target both the money supply and interest rates?**

5. **Plot what has happened to interest rates and to the money supply since this book has been published. What does the Fed appear to have been targeting? (This information is published monthly in the *Federal Reserve Bulletin.*)**

6. **Why is Friedman upset with the Fed?**

7. **Are you convinced that there is a relationship between the money supply and prices? Why?**

8. **Has Friedman's predicted inflation occurred? What is the inflation rate?**

A CRITIQUE OF MONETARISM

Cambridge economist Joan Robinson launched one of the more severe attacks on monetarism. This former colleague of Keynes challenged the monetarist theory that inflation is created by too much money and recessions by too little. She stated:

> The alternative hypothesis that inflation is caused by an excessive creation of money does not pass the first test of logical consistency, for it seems to rely upon the statistical correlation between the stock of money and the flow of money income without explaining what mechanism connects them. It's easy enough to understand how a rise in PQ (from $MV = PQ$), the money value of the flow of transactions, causes M, the stock of money, to increase, for an increase in working capital calls for an increase in bank credit. And it is easy to understand that if MV fails to increase sufficiently, a restriction of credit will reduce activity, but no one has ever shown how causation is suppose to operate in the reverse direction.*

> *From *A Guide to Post-Keynesian Economics,* edited by Alfred S. Eichner. M. E. Sharpe, Inc., 1979, p. xix.

Other critics have raised questions about various models used by the monetarists, arguing that the models don't explain why or how an increase in the money supply changes income; they just show that it does. This "Black Box" approach fails to satisfy a number of Keynesian skeptics. They also believe that monetarist models oversimplify the process of economic change by focusing on monetary causes rather than real causes. So, the monetarist-Keynesian debate continues, with the majority of economists taking the middle position that both monetary and fiscal policy are important for economic stabilization.

THE EFFECTIVENESS OF MONETARY POLICY

It was noted earlier that the econometric model developed by the Fed, M.I.T., and the University of Pennsylvania indicates that in one year a $1 billion government expenditure is worth $3 billion of GNP. The same model also predicts that in one year a $1 billion increase in the money supply will lead to a $2.5 billion increase in the GNP. The St. Louis Federal Reserve model, on the other hand, shows that a $1 billion increase in government spending has *no* effect on GNP at the end of one year. (Some increase in GNP is seen within six months after the spending increase but is entirely wiped out by the end of the year.) At the same time, the St. Louis model predicts a $5 billion increase in GNP with a mere $1 billion addition to the money stock.

These models give such different results because of the underlying assumptions each uses. The monetarists emphasize velocity as the mode of transmission, and the Keynesians stress the rate of interest. Monetarists assume that there can be no effective fiscal policy unless it is accompanied by an increase in the money supply. Why? The government *must* finance its expenditures with increases in taxes or by debt issue. In either case, money is being transferred from one sector of the economy to another. As government spending proceeds and GNP increases, if there has not been an increase in the money supply, consumers and investors will find themselves short of cash and will begin to try to increase their liquidity by selling their financial holdings. This will have the effect of increasing bond sales even further, driving the price of bonds down and the interest rate up. As the interest increases, business investors are crowded out of financial markets by the government so that GNP doesn't change. Spending is just transferred from one sector to another.

Keynesians, however, would argue that the reason for government spending is to stimulate an economy in which neither business *nor* households *are* spending—so that the government at least got the process started. This would encourage spending by these sectors in the future. What we find is that monetary policy is very effective at slowing the economy, but not very effective when used to stimulate economic activity.

Shortcomings of Monetary Policy

Several additional factors can prevent monetary policy from being totally successful in its efforts to regulate and stimulate the economy. Five of these factors follow.

1. *Private offsets.* Policy can be thwarted by the actions of banks, specialized financial institutions, and private corporations outwitting Fed policy. Such things as borrowing from the Eurodollar market have caused disruptions in the past.

2. *Cyclical asymmetry*. Policy can be victimized by changing conditions in the economy. This is a problem of timing. A policy is designed to treat a specific condition but when the policy does take effect, the problem may be totally different. This is a problem of "lags" and policy backfiring.

3. *Velocity*. Monetary policy is often frustrated by the tendency of changes in velocity to jeopardize targeted goals of the money supply.

4. *Cost-push inflation*. Monetary policy does not effectively affect the causes of inflation that lie on the cost or supply side of the market.

5. *Investment impact*. Some argue that the Fed's policies have a marginal impact upon consumer spending. Others argue that the impact of the Fed policy on the investment process is overstated since many corporations finance their investments internally.

The Future of Monetary Policy

While monetary policy has strengths as well as weaknesses in achieving desired economic ends, recent changes in both supply and demand factors for money, caused by **financial deregulation** and **innovation,** have caused concern about the future effectiveness of monetary policy. Recent discussion among macroeconomists has been over the effects of the deregulated financial markets and innovations on monetary policy. Not only is the institutional framework that facilitates financial transactions changing rapidly, but money itself has been changing with the advent of money market accounts and others. Changes in the responsiveness of expenditures to interest rates variation and/or the amount of money demanded at various levels of income might occur as a result of these financial innovations. John Weinninger, an economist at the Federal Reserve Bank of New York, stated the problem clearly: "If relationships between key variables are changing then it simply is not practical for policy to focus in some mechanical way on any single variable, whether it be M_1, GNP, interest rates or even reserves themselves." If the predictability and the stability of known relationships deteriorate because of these recent changes and innovations, monetary policy cannot be as reliable or as predictable as it has been in the past. This will impose additional problems on policymakers as problems of recession and inflation arise.

MONETARY AND FISCAL POLICY

Monetary and fiscal policy provide a rather powerful punch when used together to fight inflation or stimulate economic recovery. One problem that arises, however, is in the coordination of the two policies. Since the Fed determines monetary policy, and fiscal expenditures are in the hands of Congress, there have been in the past and will be in the future policy decisions that either offset each other or are not complementary. The Fed reacted to the high inflation rates of 1980 by attempting to reduce the money supply in order to decrease aggregate demand. On the other hand, Congress decreased taxes, which increased aggregate demand. High interest rates created by the tight money supply tended to counteract the desired investment effects from lower tax rates. Although the chair of the Federal Reserve Board now regularly informs Congress of impending Fed action so that there are no surprises, policies may still offset each other.

Some people have called for a reduction in the independence of the Fed in order to achieve greater coordination of monetary and fiscal policies. Critics of this suggestion argue that to have the Fed controlled by either the legislative or the executive branch of the government would make the money supply a political tool—as surely as many fiscal expenditures and taxing decisions already are. They argue that we could regularly expect increases in the money supply in election years and decreases after elections. Whatever the solution, it is clear that monetary and fiscal policy must at least be aimed in the same direction in order to have effective economic policy.

9. **What is the Fed doing today to "defeat the forces of inflation"? Is policy being coordinated with the executive branch?**

10. **What kinds of "political mischief" might occur if the monetary authority were controlled by the executive branch?**

A SUMMARY—MONETARY AND FISCAL POLICY TOGETHER AGAIN

Thus far we have surveyed the major macroeconomic issues and problems, examined the theoretical basis for the Keynesian system, and studied the framework and behavior of the U.S. banking system. We have also devoted special attention to fiscal and monetary policy. All of this can be reviewed and summarized in the schematic outline in Fig. 21.3.

KEY CONCEPTS

monetary policy   monetarism
reserve requirements   monetary rule
open-market operations   financial deregulation
discount rate   innovation
lags

REVIEW QUESTIONS

1. How do the demands for money relate to Keynesian income and employment theory?

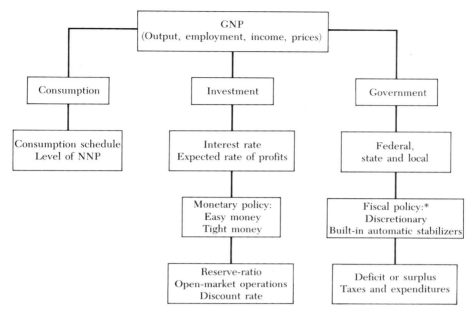

*Note: Fiscal policy can affect all types of spending—C, I, and G.

Figure 21.3 Monetary and fiscal policy.

2. Which of the monetary policy tools is used most actively by the Fed? Under what situations would the Fed's other tools be used?

3. What are the basic differences between a monetarist and a Keynesian?

4. Why do monetarists argue that fiscal policy is ineffective in adjusting the economy?

5. How do monetarists propose to eliminate the problem of inflation?

6. Of the basic monetary policy tools the Federal Reserve can utilize, which do you think is the most effective? Why?

7. What are some of the factors that inhibit the successful implementation of monetary policy?

8. Do you think the Fed ought to be "independent"?

9. In what kinds of situations is fiscal policy more effective than monetary policy? In what kinds of situations is monetary policy more effective than fiscal policy?

10. What would be some of the complications of finding the proper mix of monetary and fiscal policy?

11. If the economy were experiencing high unemployment and moderate inflation, what would be the appropriate monetary policy? Why?

SUGGESTED READINGS

Milton Friedman, *An Economist's Protest*, 1972. Thomas Horton. Chapter 3 is a repeat of *Newsweek* articles of the Nixon era on Fed actions.

Milton Friedman and Rose Friedman, 1980. *Free to Choose*, Avon. The master of conservative economic theory and monetarism explains his view of the world.

Thomas Mayer, 1968. *Monetary Policy in the United States*, Random House. Mayer discusses the advantages and the disadvantages of monetary policy as a tool for economic stabilization.

J. Huston McCulloch, 1975. *Money and Inflation: A Monetarist Approach*, Academic Press. More complex than the others mentioned, it is by no means too difficult for those seeking more on the monetarists' methods.

William Poole, 1978. *Money and the Economy: A Monetarist View*, Addison-Wesley. Monetarist theory, evidence, and policy are brought together for budding economics students.

22

Chapter

Aggregate Supply

To this point our analysis of macroeconomics, both theory and policy, has focused on aggregate demand. We must, however, recognize that in developing macroeconomic theory an analysis of supply has always accompanied one of demand. Indeed, one of Keynes's harshest criticisms of the classical economists was directed toward their view of supply or output in the macro economy. Keynes revised this classical view and to a large extent it remains the core of the analysis for those advocating a **supply-side approach** toward economic policy. This group is currently known as the supply-siders.

Aggregate demand has served as the center of economic theory and policy for the past four decades, while Keynesian solutions have remained at the helm of economic thought and have been preferred by policymakers. During the 1980 presidential campaign, we heard a lot about the economics of supply and a severe criticism of policies designed to increase aggregate demand to shore up a flagging economy. Rather, these upstarts suggested, the focus of government policy should be on increasing the **aggregate supply** of goods and services, or national output. Using the basic analysis of supply and demand developed in the section on microeconomics, an increase in supply had a great benefit over an increase in demand as a policy tool. Not only would output increase, but prices would fall—*not rise*, as they would with increases in demand (see Fig. 22.1).

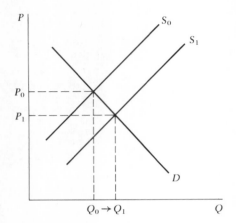

Figure 22.1 An increase in supply.

In this chapter, we will develop a simple analysis of aggregate supply, which Keynes extended from the classical theory. We will then focus on determinants of aggregate supply at the national level in our attempt to understand why supply policies are so very precarious. The labor market has a lot to do with the aggregate output or supply, and there have been many developments in labor markets over the past several decades. Finally, we will turn our attention to supply-side policies, or what some have dubbed *Reaganomics* (although in reality the policies of the Reagan Administration have been traditionally focused on increases in aggregate demand.) We will find out how supply-side economists viewed the situation and the results of supply-side policies during the Reagan Administration.

THE CLASSICAL ANALYSIS OF AGGREGATE SUPPLY

The Production Function

The earliest writers of economic principles observed that production of goods and services, or output, depends upon the inputs of the factors of production. In equation form, we can write this as a *production function:*

$$Q = f(L,N,K,T),$$

where Q is output at some point in time, f is the functional notation, L represents land or natural resources, N is the labor force, K stands for capital, and T represents advances in technology. At any moment in time, L, K, and T are constant. Great technical advances don't occur from day to day. New additions to capital—that is new plants, additional equipment, and inventories—do not appear overnight, and our natural resources remain fixed. Labor, however, is subject to change in the short run. New entrants may arrive at the workplace; the workforce may suddenly increase due to trends, income, or training; or some people may simply want to work more. Thus L, K, and T are assumed to be constant at a point in time. So at that point in time,

$$Q = f(N).$$

Graphically, we can represent this relationship between output and the labor force as shown in Fig. 22.2. In this production function,* output increases with the addition of each new worker until some maximum output Q_{max} is reached with the amount of labor, N_1. With the addition of just one more worker beyond N_1, output will fall.

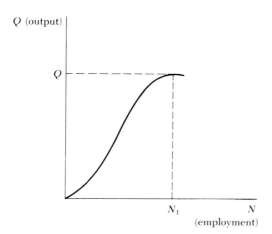

Figure 22.2   A production function.

The Classical Labor Market

The following analysis oversimplifies both the classical and more modern views of the **labor market,** but serves to help us understand its influence on aggregate supply. In the minds of the classical economists, the demand for labor was based on the **real wage** or W/P, where W represents wages divided by P, or the price level. The supply of labor was also thought to be based on W/P. Thus

$$S_N = f(W/P),$$

$$D_N = f(W/P),$$

$$D_N = S_N.$$

The labor market is illustrated in Fig. 22.3. We can see equilibrium in the labor market at point E, with the employment of N_1 workers at a wage W/P_1.

This is where the classical model differs from the later Keynesian changes. In the classical model point E was proclaimed not just equilibrium but *full employment* as well. This equilibrium at full employment was the only equilibrium to be found in the classical analysis.

*This production function represents the concepts of increasing, diminishing, and negative returns discussed in Chapter 11. Beyond N_1 we see the area of negative returns.

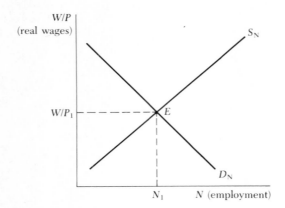

Figure 22.3 The labor market.

We know that in the Keynesian model this equilibrium level of employment might be at full employment, at greater than full employment, or at less than full employment. We need to remind ourselves in the following analysis that we are interested in equilibrium, not in whether or not it occurs at full employment.

1. **What does the amount of labor you are willing to supply to an employer depend on? Plot your own labor supply curve at the various wage rates below.**

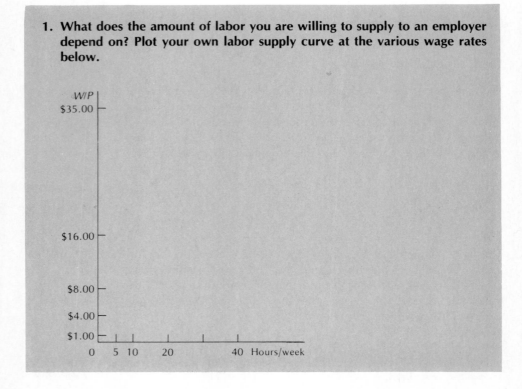

An important assumption for Keynes's analysis was that money wages or **nominal wage** rates (W) are fixed in the short run. Today, we know that wage rates are not fixed, but that they do lag and they tend to rise slower than prices. For example, when there is an increase in demand for goods and services, there will be a price increase. An accompanying increase in the demand for labor will occur (to produce the additional output), and nominal wages will rise. Nominal wage (W) increases, however will tend to be slower and less than the price increase (P) that occurred when demand rose.

By combining the production function, shown in Fig. 22.4(b), and the labor market analysis, shown in Fig. 22.4(a), and using Keynes's assumption of stable or less rapidly rising wages in the short run, we can see how an upward sloping aggregate supply curve is derived. The aggregate supply curve, shown in Fig. 22.4(c), represents the relationship between output (Q) on the horizontal axis and prices (P) on the vertical axis. We can graphically derive this curve by examining combinations of Q, output, and P, prices. We use just the labor demand curve in our

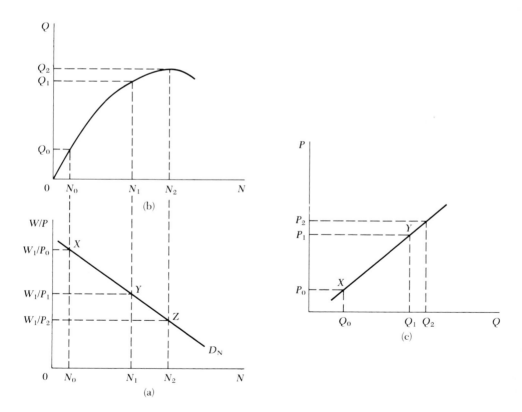

Figure 22.4   Derivation of an aggregate supply curve.

analysis, and examine the relation between real wages and employment (N). Note that nominal wages (W_1) remain the same at each point on the labor demand curve (D_N), and that prices (P) change to show that the real wage (W/P) is falling along the labor demand curve. This makes sense since employers will demand more workers if the real wage they must pay is lower. That means that each price level represented is different and that P_2 is greater than P_1, which is greater than P_0.* At point X, real wages are W_1/P_0 and employment is at N_0, in Fig. 22.4(a). At employment N_0, output is at Q_0 in Fig. 22.4(b). If we plot point X at the price (P_0) and quantity (Q_0) in Fig. 22.4(c), we have one point on our aggregate supply. At point Y on the labor demand curve D_N in Fig. 22.4(a), real wages stand at W_1/P_1 and employment at N_1. Output will be at Q_1 when employment is at N_1, in Fig. 22.4(b). Again plotting point Y in Fig. 22.4(c), we have price at P_1 (which is greater than P_0) and quantity at Q_1 (which is greater than Q_0).

> **2. Plot point Z on Fig. 22.4(c). Label points P_2 and Q_2. What is the relationship between price and quantity on the aggregate supply curve?**

The upward slope of the aggregate supply curve is partly due to diminishing returns, and partly due to resource and factor costs rising less rapidly than prices when demand for additional output increases. Moving along the aggregate supply curve illustrates the effect of increased aggregate demand at different levels of output and different price levels. Thus the aggregate supply curve shows us the price level associated with each level of output.

Shifts in Aggregate Supply

Many factors can cause the aggregate supply curve to shift, including changes in the labor market, supply shocks, and government policies that affect supply. Positive factors that cut costs, such as technological innovations, will cause the aggregate supply curve to shift outward to the right, while negative factors, such as rising costs, will cause the shift to be up and to the left. Let's examine some conditions that will cause such shifts.

Labor market forces have had and continue to have effects on the aggregate supply curve. Increases and decreases in the labor force are obvious factors that would cause such a shift. We know that over the past two decades men and women have entered the labor force in record numbers, so the impact of this supply factor has certainly been felt. Increases in the labor supply will, of course, increase aggregate supply and shift the curve to the right. Any factor that makes people want to work less—from attending school, higher taxes, or gaining more leisure—will cause a shift to the left.

---

*This must be the case since $W_1/P_0 > W_1/P_1 > W_1/P_2$. Each successive denominator must be larger in order for real wages to fall.

Supply Shocks

Forces now known as **supply shocks** are also factors in determining the position of the aggregate supply curve. These were particularly apparent during the decade of the 1970s, when the United States and the world economy experienced a variety of supply shocks, which sent prices soaring. A supply shock occurs when there is a dramatic increase in the cost of producing a wide variety of products. This will cause an upward shift of the aggregate supply curve and thus push prices upward. As the name implies, some type of unexpected shock occurs to aggregate supply.

The most noteworthy supply shock occurred in 1973 and 1974, when **OPEC** placed an **embargo** on oil exports. The reduced supply of oil products to many nations of the world severely curtailed production and increased prices. (As you can see in Fig. 22.5, the price level is raised for each level of real output.)

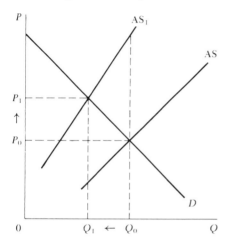

Figure 22.5 A supply shock.

Other less noteworthy supply shocks have also affected the prices and output of many goods and services throughout the world. Raw materials and/or agriculture products have often been the cause of these shocks.

During 1983–1984, as U.S. interest rates continued to increase, the interest payments owed by developing nations on their debts soared. Such added interest costs also serve as a supply shock to the economies of Brazil and Argentina, increasing their debt by $600 million instantly.

3. **List other possible shocks to a nation's aggregate supply.**

4. **List some factors that would be the reverse of shocks, and would increase the nation's supply.**

5. **List five ways that the government might increase production of the supply of goods and services to the public.**

Productivity

Another source of aggregate supply curve shifts comes from increases and decreases in labor productivity, or output per hour. During the past few years economists and politicians have become increasingly concerned with the apparent decline in the growth rate of the nation's productivity. Productivity is defined as output per person-hour worked. As productivity is currently measured by the government, it appears that the rate of gain in productivity in the United States is quite sluggish. Between 1948 and 1973, output per capita grew at an average annual rate of 2.2 percent, while between 1972 and 1978, industrial productivity in the United States increased by only 1 percent per year and has averaged 0.8 percent between 1979 and 1985. During the earlier period productivity increased by more than 4 percent annually in Germany and by more than 5 percent in Japan.

Measurement of productivity is a difficult task. Time periods simply aren't comparable since productivity usually increases during booms and falls during recessions. Another problem in the measurement of productivity concerns actual output. As the nation's labor force has shifted from industrial production to service activities, physical output has become more difficult to measure. Only 20 percent of the nation's workers produce a tangible product. The rest produce services that can be measured in dollars only by examining the number of hours worked. Increasingly, the underground economy* poses a problem in productivity measures. If one doesn't report an activity to the IRS, it isn't counted as part of the nation's output. Contractors and others who report only a part of a job add to the sluggish appearance of the nation's productivity figures.

If in fact there has been a slowdown in the productivity of the U.S. worker, what can be done to reverse the trend? The media portray the solution as supplying additional carrots and sticks to cajole and prod workers, but economists see the root of the problem as a slowdown in innovation and technological change. An "end of the decade" economic report from Manufacturers Hanover Trust states:

> Americans had come to take innovation for granted; the laboratories could be counted on to churn out new ideas year after year. But something has broken down. Thirty years ago the electronics industry was innovating with sophisticated computers and family television. Today the industry is innovating with electronic games. The American automobile is virtually unchanged, technologically, for at least twenty, and more likely thirty, years. It is now changing gradually, partly in response to our energy predicament and partly because of foreign competition.
>
> There is no intention here to say that innovation has stopped. A technological society that could in a decade advance space exploration as we did retains significant innovative urges. Our telephone and communications

---

*The underground economy comprises individuals who do not report income on services they render or products they produce. Barter exchange also takes place in this economy (e.g., a lawyer informally agrees to give legal services to an architect who designs a summer home for the lawyer).

industry continues to astound us. And behind the scenes, not visible to the typical citizen, there is a steady stream of large and small innovations that encourage productivity growth. But the number of important innovations appears to have dwindled. For example, what new products are on the horizon that might provide a lift to the economy in the years ahead? If a person could think of some he might properly be asked: "If you're so smart, why aren't you rich?" The fact remains that in both consumer and industrial products, the recent innovations tend to be marginal changes in existing products and processes that do not require major new capital expenditures.

—Tilford Gaines, "The End of a Decade," *Economic Report,* Manufacturers Hanover Trust, December 1979.

On the other hand, Zvi Griliches, an economist at Harvard, has suggested that there are numerous reasons for the slowdown in productivity, among them "the decline in research and development expenditures; decreases in the rate of investment in new capital equipment; changes in the labor force, with more young people and women; government regulations; the rise in energy prices [in the 1970s], inflation, and errors of measurement." Griliches states that although each has contributed to the problem, together they don't account for the observed size of the decline. He suggests that inflation, energy costs, and errors are the most likely villains for the declining growth rates of productivity.

> **6. Why would inflation and increased energy costs contribute to decreases in productivity?**

Labor, however, views the concern over productivity to be simply an excuse to "make fat cats fatter." Corporations would suggest tax cuts for business to stimulate capital investment and other incentives for research and development, and thus shift the aggregate supply curve down and to the right, providing lower prices at each level of output.

Now that we have developed the theory of aggregate supply, let's examine how this theory relates to public economic policy.

SUPPLY-SIDE ECONOMIC POLICY: THE RATIONALE

In 1975 a handful of academic economists and politicians began to reexamine the problems of the U.S. economy from a different perspective than mainstream Keynesian economics. The focus of this reexamination was on the "supply side." As we have seen previously, the orthodox Keynesian approach to the problems of inflation and unemployment focused on the demand side of the economy. If the economy showed signs of recession or depression, the verdict was that the economy was suffering from insufficient aggregate demand. If there were inflationary trends, then aggregate demand was too robust. There was a tendency for those policies to be inflationary, since once the government had initiated spending for particular programs, it was hard to reduce the spending.

Although neither Keynes nor the classical economists totally ignored the supply side of the market in their analysis of the economy, economic policies designed to deal with recurring economic ills were predominately aimed at either shoring up a weak aggregate demand or calming one that was excessive. To them, income or output was a function of aggregate demand.

Proponents of the supply-side approach argued that federal, state, and local governments have stifled production and incentive in this country during the past decade with their emphasis on Keynesian-type policies, which have led to increased spending, taxation, and regulation. They argue that higher tax rates and increased government regulation reduce incentives, while spending fuels inflation. Progressive taxes are particularly onerous since the marginal tax rate rises with income.

Increases in tax rates inhibit production and reduce output for several reasons. First, as tax rates increase, people begin to substitute leisure activities for productive activity. As more and more of one's income is taken in taxes, there is less monetary return for work; therefore people begin to take more and longer vacations, opt for early retirement, and turn down overtime opportunities. Each of these lowers the productive output of the nation.

Second, as taxes on personal income increase, people may begin to do more work in which they have less skill. This reduces the time spent in more productive economic activities and leads to an inefficient allocation of economic resources, since both market exchange and specialization are reduced. The do-it-yourself movement is an example of this rationale. For example, consider a pilot earning $50 per hour and paying taxes in the 50-percent bracket who wishes to have some carpentry work done in her home. If skilled carpenters work for $35 an hour, the pilot might easily decide that it is cheaper and more economical to borrow a couple of carpentry books from the library and do the work herself. The pilot would then spend less time in the productive activity in which she is skilled (flying) and more time in one which she is not (carpentry), since the work is nontaxable. For the pilot to "break even" in hiring a carpenter, her wages must increase to $70 per hour, with the tax bracket remaining at 50 percent. The productivity of the carpenter is also reduced in this example because of the prevailing tax conditions. Economic efficiency is affected by higher marginal tax rates that reduce wages, salaries, and profits, and thus work, investment, and output.

Third, one finds that tax-deductible goods may be less desirable than those that are nondeductible. Because of the tax advantage, however, they are purchased anyway. Business-related expenditures such as limousines, three-martini lunches, and business vacations at high-priced resorts are substituted for something that might be more desirable—like money. High-priced luxury business expenditures are indeed produced at a high cost to society, but their relative cost is considerably lower to business firms, given the tax deductions that accompany them.

Another reason for concern about excessively high tax rates is the intensive effort that develops to avoid them. Young people at some point begin examining the world in which they live in order to make career decisions. As taxes become higher and tax laws become more complex, many of them choose professions in the tax-shelter industry. Tax accountants, lawyers, and investment counselors are in great demand by people and firms seeking ways to avoid excessive taxation. In addition, all workers may find themselves spending more time seeking ways to reduce their own tax bills and, therefore, less time on professional or productive activities, thus reducing the total product of the economy. Finally, those advocating a supply-side approach point to the declining productivity in the United States arguing that lower tax rates would generate more business investment and thus increase productivity in the country.

Increased savings and perhaps increases in the rate of saving is a residual of this theory. Supply-side economists argue that lower tax rates will induce more saving in the private sector, which will make additional investment funds available if such saving is accompanied by reductions in government spending. Since people have more income because of the tax reductions, they have more income from which to consume and more income from which to save. This increased saving will provide more funds available for investment. This should lead to lower interest rates, increased investment, and economic growth.

In summary, then, advocates of the supply-side approach to economic policy see tax rates as extremely important in determining total output in the economy. They believe that decreases in tax rates will cause a substitution of such productive activity as work, investment, and specialization for nonproductive activities. This results, they argue, in a more efficient allocation of resources. Total economic output would rise with lower tax rates.

THE LAFFER CURVE: CUTTING TAXES AND RAISING GOVERNMENT REVENUES—OR, ON EATING ONE'S CAKE AND HAVING IT TOO

At the heart of the supply-side analysis is the **Laffer curve,** developed by economist Arthur Laffer of the University of Southern California. The Laffer analysis was first used during the California tax-revolt movement in 1978, when home-owners sought vast property-tax reductions. As the tax-revolt movement has spread through the country, we find the use of the Laffer curve even more popular. The argument does suggest that one can eat one's cake and have it, too. In his analysis, Laffer relates the tax rate to government revenues, suggesting that lower tax rates might in fact increase government revenues.

In Fig. 22.6, point A indicates a very high tax rate. At point A, the level of production is very low, an indication that corporations and individuals are overtaxed and have lost their incentive to produce. Consequently they decrease production. This in turn lowers government tax receipts. If the tax rate is lowered—for example, to B—not only are production and output increased, but this tax rate generates the same revenue, R_1 that was generated by the higher tax rate, A. Tax rate E (which may

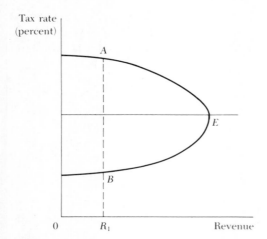

Figure 22.6   A hypothetical Laffer curve.

or may not be 50 percent since there are no numbers on the graph) is the "optimum" tax rate. That is, it is the tax rate that maximizes government revenue without decreasing production. Since any increase or decrease in that tax rate would lead to lower tax receipts by the government, they are inferior. The key, of course, is correctly *guessing* which rate is the optimum for the economy. And no one, not even Arthur Laffer, knows what that is.

7. **What could happen if the economists guessed wrong about the proper tax rate? How would they know they were at the optimum rate? Why might people differ over what the optimum rate is?**

SUPPLY-SIDE POLICY AND INFLATION

In tackling the inflation dilemma supply-side economists advocate **tax cuts.** Using the logic that inflation is simply due to an excess of demand over supply, supply-siders argue that the most painless way of dealing with the problem is not by reducing demand by means of tax incentives, but by increasing the supply of goods and services as a result of reducing tax rates. This will provide the incentive for businesses and individuals to invest and to increase production, thus increasing the supply of total goods and services available. With increased supply, there will tend to be lower prices, which should increase spending.

8. **How do taxes directly affect supply? Illustrate on a graph of supply and demand how a tax cut works.**

Some economists, such as Herbert Stein, a former chairman of the Council of Economic Advisors under Presidents Nixon and Ford, sympathize with the notions put forth by advocates of the supply-side approach but agree with Stein when he states:

> What we can do on the supply-side is not big enough to solve the problem. We have demand growing by about 12 percent a year and supply growing by about 2 percent per year, which yields 10 percent inflation. To increase the rate of growth of supply by 50 percent, from 2 percent a year to 3 percent a year, which is a difficult task, would still leave an enormous inflation, especially if the increase of supply is accomplished by means of cutting taxes, which at the same time increases demand.
>
> —Herbert Stein, "Some Supply Side Propositions," *The Wall Street Journal,* 19 March 1980.

We do not know whether Stein's argument would hold because inflation was not reduced by increases in supply and growth, but by recession and decreases in demand due to lower levels of income.

Another supply-side argument that has come under fire states that lower tax rates will provide incentives for people to work more, since they can "keep" more of their income. Critics of this notion argue instead that higher tax rates have forced some people to work *more* than they would like to simply to maintain their standard of living. These people already have two jobs or work overtime to keep the same level of income in the face of high tax rates. It is hard to conceive of these people's working more, yet easy to envision their working less if the tax rate falls.

Tax cuts for businesses have critics as well. Although in theory the cuts should stimulate investment, the critics question whether these funds will in fact be spent on new, productive activities. They cite the growing number of corporate mergers, such as the purchase of Montgomery Ward by Mobil Oil, as examples of corporate investment that create no new jobs or productive output for the nation.

Finally, the supply-side approach tends to shift the distribution of income. Wealthy individuals will benefit far more than middle- and lower-middle-income groups, and in absolute dollar amounts, the benefit to those earning less than $10,000 a year is minimal, if not negative. In Chapter 23 we will in fact discover this has happened. Reagan Administration policies have skewed the distribution of income in favor of the higher income groups. Between 1980 and 1984, for the bottom quintile of families, real disposable income decreased 7.6 percent, while the top quintile of families gained 8.7 percent in real disposable income (see Fig. 22.7).

REAGANOMICS AND THE SUPPLY SIDE

President Reagan's advisors at the Office of Management and Budget and in the Cabinet have been avid supporters of the supply-side approach to fiscal policy, working for tax cuts, expenditure cuts (except for military spending), rollback of federal social regulations, decontrol of the energy industry, and a monetarist

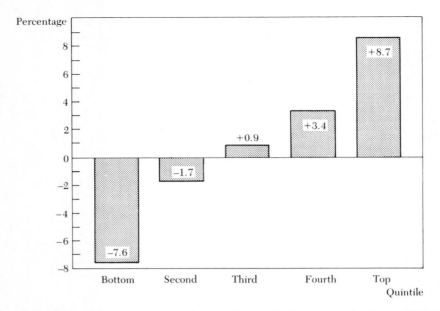

Figure 22.7 Percentage change in real disposable income for families, 1980–1984.
Source: Urban Institute household income model.

approach to monetary policy as a package of comprehensive measures to deal with the economy. Each of these policy recommendations supports a supply-side approach to fiscal policy. Resources were supposed to be shifted to the private sector as government spending was reduced and taxes fell. The program was designed to stimulate economic growth and to reduce inflation. But, we know that while the policy did significantly reduce taxes, government spending rose. Both provided expansionary effects, but not enough to counteract the recessionary effects of monetary policy.

The tight monetary policy employed by the Federal Reserve sufficiently halted growth of the money supply, creating the worst recession since the Great Depression. Double-digit unemployment replaced double-digit inflation, with 10 million of the work force out of work in 1982. In 1983–1984, while growth accelerated and inflation fell, aided by lower oil and raw materials prices, the Reagan Administration was still unable to control the growth of government spending. Most social programs were cut to the bone, but rising military expenditures and Social Security and federal pension increases made the Reagan Administration expenditures larger, as a percentage of GNP, than those of any previous administration.

The recovery of 1983–1984 was set in motion by the Federal Reserve pumping up money supply growth rates in 1982, along with the legislated increases in military spending and tax cuts. This stimulated a demand-led, rather than a supply-led, recovery, although business tax cuts did kick in higher levels of investment as the recovery mounted. Only time will tell the full effects of these policies. If budget deficits can be reduced without affecting economic growth, the decade of the 1980s should produce moderate levels of economic growth. If, however, deficits are not controlled, the decade may well be plagued by recession. We shall more fully examine the results of supply-side policies in Chapter 23. Now, however, let us look at two views of the supply-side revolution. The first is a review of Barry Bosworth's book *Tax Incentives and Economic Growth* detailing the theory and impact of supply-side policies. The second article, by University of Massachusetts economics professor Samuel Bowles, presents a critical view of supply-side and Keynesian policies. Bowles reviews the costs and benefits of the tax cuts enacted under the guise of supply-side fiscal policies.

DISSECTING SUPPLY-SIDE THEORY

John M. Berry

The economic policy mix adopted in 1981 to promote long-term economic growth was "exactly the opposite" of what was needed, according to a new book by Brookings Institution economist Barry Bosworth. . . .

The idea was that tax incentives could have a broad, powerful effect on economic activity. For instance, a cut in marginal tax rates for individuals would increase the after-tax return on invested savings and therefore encourage people to save and invest more.

The increased investment would boost the nation's productive capacity and, thus, the "supply" of goods and services. Ultimately, the higher level of activity was supposed to increase tax revenue despite the lower tax rates, the supply-siders said.

In an understated way, the book describes the shaky theoretical and empirical grounds on which the program was based. Bosworth acknowledges the problems that mainstream economists have had constructing an adequate theory to deal with the primary problem of the 1970s: inflation and slow economic growth. And he notes that economic policy-makers were focusing not on supply but on trying to manage the level of total demand, in order to stabilize the peaks and troughs of business-cycle fluctuations. . . .

He says that the large and continuing federal budget deficits are a sign of those inconsistencies and a principal reason that, in the end, the policies will not produce the added long-term growth desired.

Bosworth cites a number of studies showing that the level of total saving in the U.S. economy is quite stable at about 16 or 17 percent of the gross national product throughout the postwar period, and that "there is no evidence of a decline during the 1970s and early 1980s. What has changed is the composition of private saving: corporate saving has in-

(continued)

creased, while saving attributed to the household sector—which includes nonprofit institutions and unincorporated business—has declined."

The supply-side program was supposed to increase saving, which has not happened so far. Nor would an increase in saving necessarily lead to more business investment as the supply-siders claim, Bosworth says. If it occurred, it more likely would flow first into housing, because investment in that sector is more sensitive to interest rates—more saving ought to lower rates—than into the business sector.

As it has turned out, the major increment to U.S. saving has been a massive inflow of foreign capital matched by a huge deficit in trade in goods and services.

Bosworth goes on to suggest that, not only did saving not decline in the United States, but that there is little evidence there was a shortage of saving to finance desired levels of investment. If there had been such a shortage, companies would have had to pay more for the capital they were seeking, but, in fact, the inflation-adjusted returns on capital declined steadily during the 1970s, he says.

As for investment itself, Bosworth cites studies saying—quite contrary to supply-siders' contentions—that the effective tax on new investments declined in the 1970s. "If there was an increase in the real cost of investment during the decade, it was the result of increased financing costs rather than higher taxes," he says.

"Depreciation allowances for new investments have been liberalized by several legislative actions, and the size of the investment tax credit has been raised. In addition, the provision that allows firms to deduct nominal interest costs in computing taxable income became increasingly important during the period of high inflation. Thus, the effective corporate tax rates on new investment fell from 55 percent in 1969 to 33 percent in 1980, and the 1980 and 1981 tax acts will reduce that rate to about 15 percent in the 1983–86 period," Bosworth declares.

The problems with the supply-side approach are, if anything, more evident in terms of labor supply, he says. There, a reduction in marginal income tax rates cuts two ways. The higher after-tax return for an additional hour of work will make some people want to work more—the income effect. The same higher return, however, also will mean that the worker has more after-tax income than before for the hours he or she already is working, and, if that is more than is needed, may decide to work less—a substitution effect. Which of these effects is stronger is not fully known, but it is clear that they work in different directions.

Equally important, if you want to cut taxes on income from capital, then taxes on labor income must be raised to achieve a given level of spending, Bosworth points out. The only alternatives are to cut expenditures to cover the reductions in taxation of capital or, in the current circumstance, to cover the cuts in the taxes on both labor and capital in-

(continued)

come. But that was not done, and deficits are the result. And that is why Bosworth concludes that the policy mix was perverse if the goal was greater long-term economic growth.

"Given the evidence that private saving is rather immune to manipulation by government, government should expand the incentives for domestic investment and provide the required financing directly by reducing its own budget deficits," Bosworth argues.

"This can be achieved by pursuit of a budget policy that aims for a surplus (or, at worst, a balance) of revenues over expenditures. Meanwhile, monetary policy should be directed to maintain investment demand sufficient to reach the desired level of aggregate output."

Instead, the Reagan program moved in the other direction. "Tax reductions motivated in part by a desire to increase private saving and investment have, in combination with higher government spending, increased government dissaving. The final result may be perverse in that national saving and domestic capital formation will be reduced rather than increased . . ." he warns.

Most of all, Bosworth's book, which for the most part is easily understandable even without a detailed knowledge of economics, provides a survey of what economists do and don't know about these issues. Supply-siders won't care for it very much, but the debate would be advanced if they were to meet the challenge implicit in this 208-page volume: provide the missing theory and empirical data to back up the supply-side case.

THE TRICKLE-DOWN FAILURE

Samuel Bowles

Trickle-down economics has been tried, and it has not worked.

The poor know it. Their numbers soared to record levels last year, up 40 percent since 1978.

The rich know it too. The wealthiest 400 families in the US chalked up record incomes in 1982 (the year after the Reagan tax cuts), receiving incomes averaging 3000 times those of the typical American family. . . .

The current recovery has a long way to go before it can make up for that recent recession. In the four years from 1980 through 1983, the US lost more than $900 billion in total output (in 1983 prices), or more than $11,000 per household.

(continued)

Reprinted courtesy of the *Boston Globe*.

Many economists, certainly including those in the Reagan Administration, argue that such devastation was a necessary evil, a period of "cooling off" required to "break the back of inflation" and to rid the economy of accumulated fat.

Did such harsh medicine have its intended effects? Did the long, cruel winter of 1980–82 cure the US economy of its chronic stagflation?

The Reagan Administration has taken credit, at the least, for having whipped inflation. There is no doubt that inflation slowed—and slowed dramatically.

But anyone can reduce inflation by plunging the economy into a long and deep enough recession. The Great Depression was even more effective at combatting inflation than Reaganomics. Prices actually declined from 1929 to 1933, for example, but people hardly applauded Herbert Hoover for his skill at economic management.

Thus, the only meaningful test by which to measure the effectiveness of anti-inflationary policy is whether the reductions in inflation are achieved at an acceptable cost. The US economy was experiencing deepening trouble during the 1970s because it took a higher and higher rate of unemployment to achieve a tolerable rate of inflation. For the Reagan Administration to have "broken the back of inflation," it would have had to reverse this trend, reducing the rate of unemployment necessary to bring inflation within acceptable limits.

This is exactly what Reaganomics promised—that monetary restraint would have little negative effect on the level of output and employment but would systematically slow the rate of inflation. It did not work. Rather than improving the inflation-unemployment trade-off, the Reagan Administration simply traded lower inflation for high unemployment in the same unfavorable terms as in the late 1970s.

There is another test of the success of Reaganomics—one which, at least at the outset, they themselves proposed. The Republican Administration promised in 1981 that it would revive investment and get the economy moving again—if Congress would only agree to liberate the wealthy and corporations from the yoke of excessive taxation. Congress rushed to comply with the "Economic Recovery Act of 1981." Thus liberated, did investors respond to such public munificence?

The first year after the tax cuts was hardly auspicious. Real fixed nonresidential business investment fell from 3.3 percent of the net national product in 1981 to 2.3 percent in 1982. In 1983, this figure hit a post-war low of 1.5 percent. The 1984 Economic Report of the President states that "investment as a percentage of GNP was still lower in 1983 than in 1980, or than the average since 1970." Although investment has finally turned around, it will have a long way to go to regain the level it had reached before the tax cuts.

The "recovery" of 1983, indeed, was fueled . . . by the size of the government deficit—itself a product of soaring military spending and the

(continued)

ill-conceived 1981 tax-cuts. The irony was now complete. Ronald Reagan arrived in Washington as a champion of supply-side economics and a militant foe of the "big spenders." He would complete his first term as the biggest-spending military Keynesian of the postwar period.

Military Keynesianism has done little more than provide us with a respite from recession: it has done nothing to alter the basic pattern of decline. Since the mid-1960s, each of three successive business cycles has been worse than the last. Inflation at the peak has been higher and unemployment at the trough has been higher.

We can also compare the historical record of the economy's failure to achieve its potential levels of output by calculating the potential output lost between the business cycle peak and one year after its trough. After the peak of late 1969, the economy suffered a 5 percent loss in potential output. During the comparable period after the business cycle peak of late 1973, lost potential output totalled 10 percent. From late 1979 through one year after the trough of the most recent recession, lost potential output was a quarter of the peak year output.

Reaganomics has been begrudgingly accepted by many as mean-spirited but necessary medicine. The last three years have taught us differently. Trickle-down economics is not only unfair, it is a flop.

9. What makes Bowles conclude that supply-side economics was a flop?

KEY CONCEPTS

supply-side approach	supply shocks
aggregate supply	OPEC embargo
labor market	Laffer curve
real wage	tax cuts
nominal wage	trickle-down

REVIEW QUESTIONS

1. What are the incentives that supply-side policies attempt to improve? Are incentives important in economic analysis?

2. Explain the relationship between supply-side tax policies and "demand-side" policies. Are the two interrelated? Explain.

3. Why is it so difficult to increase output and thus expand economic growth through supply-side policies?

4. How does the classical model explain the impact of supply-side policies? Trace through each step in the process.

5. What are some of the reasons for the slowdown in productivity in the late 1970s and early 1980s?

6. Why are wages fixed or "sticky" in the short run?

SUGGESTED READINGS

Barry Bosworth, 1984. *Tax Incentives and Economic Growth*, The Brookings Institution. This account of supply-side theory discusses the way in which the taxes relate to work, saving, and investment decisions. Bosworth finds shortcomings in the supply-side theory and what economists know about these relationships.

William Greider, "The Education of David Stockman," *The Atlantic Monthly*, December 1981. A bold, honest, and rather embarrassing account of how the Reagan economic program was constructed and forced through Congress. Here we see how Stockman failed to deal successfully with the Pentagon for cuts in the military budget. "Trickle-down" became the buzzword for Reaganomics as the result of this article. A "must read."

Bruce W. Kimzey, 1983. *Reaganomics*, West Publishing Company. An account of the background, logic, and historical foundations of Reaganomics.

John L. Palmer and Isabel V. Sawhill, 1984. *The Reagan Record: An Assessment of America's Changing Domestic Priorities*, Ballinger Publishing Company. This volume is the result of the Urban Institute's attempt to measure the effect of Reagan Administration policies on domestic priorities. Theory, empirical evidence, and economic forecasts are presented along with an assessment of Reagan Administration policies.

Thomas R. Swartz, Frank J. Bonello, and Andrew S. Koraks (eds.), 1983. *The Supply Side: Debating Current Economic Policies*, Dushkin Publishing Group. Many articles on supply-side theory and policy are presented in this book of readings. One can select topics that are of particular interest.

23

Chapter

Unemployment, Inflation, and Stabilization

INTRODUCTION

The previous chapters dealing with macroeconomic theory and policy have touched only slightly on the controversy that surrounds most problems in policy decisions. Only hints have been made that there is some conflict between the monetarists and the Keynesians about solving the problems, and that there might be some **trade-offs** between the macro goals. Conservatives, liberals, and radicals see different sorts of problems and different sets of solutions. One of the most heavily debated issues that we shall focus on here is the trade-off between unemployment and inflation. An even more troublesome situation results when inflation and unemployment occur at the same time, resulting in **stagflation.** Continued high unemployment levels have left growing numbers of the population poor. Income distribution, unemployment, and inflation will be examined in the context of Keynesian and supply-side policies. How effective have these policies been in promoting employment, reducing inflation, and making life better for our citizens?

THE TRADE-OFFS: UNEMPLOYMENT AND INFLATION

If you've learned your Keynesian lessons well to this point, you should recognize a flaw within the system. Given the economic goals of price stability, full employment, and growth, Keynesian policy prescriptions tells us that increased spending is necessary to attain full employment. On the other hand, if inflation is to be attacked with Keynesian measures, income will be reduced—but so will employment. We seem to be between a rock and a hard place. But an even more difficult problem emerges when the economy develops high inflation as well as high unemployment rates.

There was a time when economists believed they had a rather simple answer to questions dealing with the trade-off between full employment and price stability. A British economist, A. W. Phillips, had studied the British economy over the past century and found that a rather stable relationship existed between increases in the wage rate and the rate of unemployment. High rates of unemployment were associated with low wage increases, and since there also appeared to be a relationship between wage increases and the general rate of inflation, people began to conclude that inflation and unemployment were inversely related. High rates of inflation were associated with low unemployment rates and vice versa. This relationship came to be known as the **Phillips curve.** If the Phillips curve represented a valid concept, then the matter of priorities seemed to be rather straightforward. Economists could present a menu of the various trade-offs that were possible: 4 percent inflation with 5 percent unemployment, 2 percent inflation with 6 percent unemployment. The democratic process would then be utilized to determine which combination the electorate desired, and the policymakers would "fine-tune" the economy to obtain this trade-off. If the economy had 5 percent inflation and 4 percent unemployment but the electorate and policymakers desired 4 and 4.5 percent, then economic policy should be ever so slightly more restrictive.

Those were heady days, and during the 1960s things seemed to be working according to this approach (see Table 23.1 and Fig. 23.1). We had,our longest period of uninterrupted economic growth during the Vietnam War, inflation was kept to an average of around 2 percent (although accelerating to over 5 percent by the late 1960s), and the unemployment rate went from 6.7 percent in 1961 to 3.5 percent in 1969. But the 1970s seemed to destroy all of this. In 1971, the unemployment rate moved to above 5.9 percent while the inflation rate rose to nearly 5 percent. By 1983 the unemployment rate was 9.5 percent, and inflation was 3.2 percent. In reducing inflation to 4 percent, unemployment reached 10.5 percent in 1982 and 7.4 percent in 1984. The concept of a simple trade-off between inflation and unemployment had broken down. It takes increasingly higher levels of unemployment to reduce inflation by increasingly smaller amounts. (By "connecting the dots," or each annual point plotted between 1960 and 1985 on Fig. 23.1, you will see an upward spiral, indicating the upward trend of the trade-off.) The world has grown more complex. Most economists hold that inflation and unemployment are still inversely related. As the rate of unemployment decreases, price pressures will tend to increase; and conversely, as unemployment increases, price pressures will tend to abate, but, for a variety of reasons, the trade-off has worsened. Before looking at the trade-off controversy we should examine some of the causes and the characteristics of inflation and unemployment.

INFLATION

Inflation may be defined as a rise in the general price level. One expects some increase in prices to accompany a growing, viable economy, but at some point the increase gets out of hand. It no longer accounts for productivity increases or growth in real output and is simply inflationary. During the past two decades there have

Table 23.1 PHILLIPS CURVE AND U.S. ECONOMY, 1960–1985

	PERCENT CHANGE IN CONSUMER PRICE INDEX	PERCENT OFFICIAL UNEMPLOYMENT (CIVILIAN WORKERS)
1960	1.6	5.5
1961	1.0	6.7
1962	1.1	5.5
1963	1.2	5.7
1964	1.3	5.2
1965	1.7	4.5
1966	2.9	3.8
1967	2.9	3.8
1968	4.2	3.6
1969	5.4	3.5
1970	5.9	4.9
1971	4.3	5.9
1972	3.3	5.6
1973	6.2	4.9
1974	11.0	5.6
1975	9.1	8.5
1976	5.8	7.7
1977	6.5	7.0
1978	7.7	6.0
1979	11.3	5.8
1980	13.5	7.0
1981	10.4	7.5
1982	6.1	9.5
1983	3.2	9.5
1984	4.3	7.4
1985	3.6	7.1

Source: Economic Report of the President, 1986.

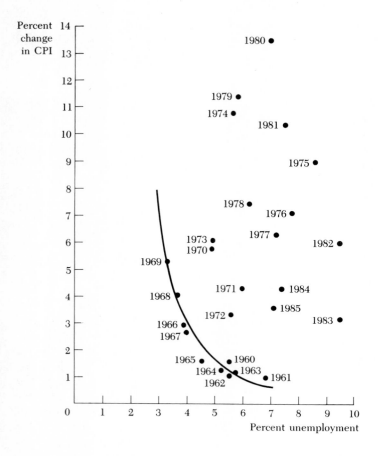

Figure 23.1 Phillips curve and the U.S. economy, 1960–1985.

been two prevailing theories of inflation. They are demand-pull inflation and cost-push, or supply, inflation.

The **demand-pull** explanation of inflation is very compatible with Keynesian economic analysis. If it was a flabby aggregate demand that created unemployment and recession, then an excessive aggregate demand was surely responsible for inflation. One can look at this view graphically in Fig. 23.2, where S represents aggregate supply, D represents different levels of aggregate demand (Y), Q represents real output, and P represents the general price level. Each shift of the aggregate demand curve increases both prices and output.

As income levels increase in the economy, the demand for goods and services will increase. Normally this will increase output and prices. These increases in demand give us the logic behind our Phillips curve analysis. As demand increases, prices are bid up and output will normally increase. (If the aggregate supply curve is perfectly inelastic, output will not rise, but prices will.) Still, as prices are bid up,

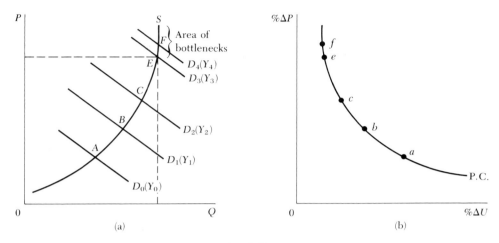

Figure 23.2   (a) Demand-pull inflation. (b) Phillips curve.

output, and thus income increases. There are more jobs created and so unemployment falls. As we move from point A to point B in Fig. 23.2(a) and aggregate demand increases, we likewise move from a corresponding point a to point b on our Phillips curve in Fig. 23.2(b). Thus a shift in aggregate demand increases prices and causes a movement along the Phillips curve.

But what happens when the increase in the demand for goods and services, raw materials, and labor exceeds the capacity to generate new output? Prices rise, but output does not—or it increases at a slower rate. Because of a more inelastic aggregate supply, we reach an economic "bottleneck", or as Keynes puts it, "as output increases, a series of 'bottle-necks' will be successively reached, where the supply of particular commodities ceases to be elastic and their prices have to rise to whatever level is necessary to divert demand into other directions. It is probable that the general level of prices will not rise very much as output increases, so long as there are available efficient unemployed resources of every type. But as soon as output has increased sufficiently to begin to reach the 'bottle-necks', there is likely to be a sharp rise in the prices of certain commodities"—e.g., point E to F in Fig. 23.2(a) and e to f in Fig. 23.2(b). One of the times this condition will be reached is when the economy reaches full employment of its resources.

Cost-push, or supply, inflation puts the responsibility for the price increases on the costs of production that push prices up. You might recall from the analysis of demand and supply in Chapter 10 that as costs increased in the production process, the supply curve would shift to the left, leading to higher prices. (Wages, raw material prices, interest rates, and profits are a few of the cost factors that might cause a shift in the supply function.) We see from the graph in Fig. 23.3(a) not only increases in price as a result of higher costs but also a reduction in output. Cost increases can, of course, come from many places. One of the earliest groups to be blamed for such increases were unions because their collective bargaining abilities gained wage increases for their members. It should be remembered that wage increases are inflationary only when the increase in output falls behind the increase in wages. There is, in addition to this **wage-push,** a **profit-push** from the entrepreneur. As market structures have become more concentrated, it has become easier for large corporations to increase or **administer prices** for their own benefit—which in most cases means to increase profits.

During the 1970s resource shortages pushed the prices of some goods upward. The lack of supply creates a bottleneck in the production process with very little of the raw materials forthcoming, even at higher costs. For aggregate demand inflation, the simple remedy was to cut back, on spending and on the money supply. For cost-push or supply inflation there is, unfortunately, no very simple remedy. Resource shortages are difficult to prevent. Cartels that withhold raw materials are hard to bargain with. Wage and price controls or some other types of incomes policy don't seem to work very well, when viewed in a historical context. Indeed, controls often lead to contrived shortages themselves, as suppliers hesitate to continue production when costs, which cannot be recouped, increase.

It is from this analysis of supply-led inflation that we can explain our shifts in the Phillips curve analysis. Now we see that as aggregate supply falls and the aggregate supply curve shifts up and to the left, from S_0 to S_1, prices increase and at each price level output is lower (at each level of output, prices are higher). As output falls, income falls and unemployment rises. We can see this on Fig. 23.3. Now, as we move from point A to point B in Fig. 23.3(a), with the decrease in aggregate supply, there is a corresponding adjustment from point a to point b in Fig. 23.3(b) illustrating the higher rates of inflation and unemployment brought about by lower output and higher prices.

Demand-pull and cost-push inflation can also work together and form a **wage-price spiral.** As spending and wages increase, so does demand for goods and services, which increases prices, which in turn results in demand for even higher wages.

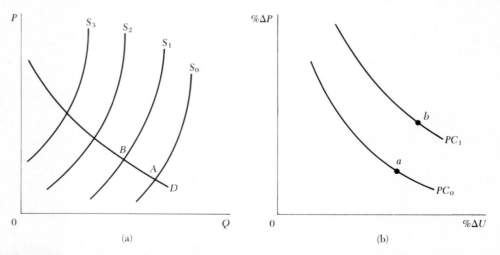

Figure 23.3 (a) Cost-push inflation. (b) Phillips curve.

Although the cost-push and demand-pull theories of inflation account for two rationales for the driving up of prices, it has become increasingly apparent that another factor affects both aggregate supply and aggregate demand. That factor is the *expectations* of future inflation. Inflationary expectations are critical in explaining inflation because each time we expect inflation, we generate that inflation. Indeed, William Nordhaus, an economist at Yale, has stated, "Inflation is a highly inertial process. It will go along to whatever rate it has been going at until it is shocked to a different level. From 1973 to 1980 we had 6 to 9 percent inflation built into the wage and price system. There were some months when the average annual inflation rate reached 15 percent in 1979. It was built into contracts. It was built into expectations. The recession [1980–1982] beat it down to 5 percent and now we have lower inertial rates." Aggregate supply is directly affected by inflationary expectations. As wages increase because inflation is expected by workers, costs to firms increase. Firms then pass these increased costs on to consumers in the form of higher prices. On the demand side, expectations of higher interest rates generate consumer and business borrowing and expenditures. This, of course, increases aggregate demand and drives up prices. In times when inflationary expectations are low, inflation is easier to moderate with monetary and fiscal policy. In the 1970s, when inflationary expectations were high, monetary and fiscal policy were largely ineffective. The results were increased unemployment without significantly lower inflation. Inflation does affect us all—and some more than others. Those on fixed incomes are hurt, as are creditors. Borrowers in general are helped.

1. **How is a person who borrows money helped by inflation? Is this always so? Do you know of any banks losing money? Which ones? Why?**

2. **What effect will "bottlenecks" have on the trade-off between inflation and unemployment, for example, when unemployment is increasing?**

Inflation: The 1970s and 1980s

During the 1970s the United States experienced record levels of inflation due to demand, supply, and expectations factors. The 1980s have brought an ebbing of inflationary pressures. As we might guess, demand, supply, and expectations are again responsible. The 1970s inherited the rising prices of the late 1960s as the government increased expenditures for the Vietnam War and the Great Society program. The Federal Reserve pursued an easy monetary policy in 1965, and between 1967 and 1969, taxes were not increased to finance the rising government expenditures and the economy boomed. The momentum of rising prices carried into the 1970s, with President Nixon temporarily freezing prices and wages in 1971. Incomes rose in the early 1970s as the result of expansionary monetary and fiscal policies between 1971 and 1973. Several unexpected forces entered into the scenario, all of which heightened the problem of inflation. The first round of oil price increases came in 1973 with the OPEC embargo. Energy prices soared and this supply shock caused the general price level to rise and output to fall. The Fed held the growth rate of the money supply to low levels to avoid more inflationary pressures. Fiscal policy remained essentially noncommittal until a tax rebate was passed in 1974. During the 1973–1975 period the nation experienced a severe recession—but one in which inflation averaged between 9 and 11 percent. There were shortages and price increases in food, metals, and other primary materials. The early 1970s also brought the fall of the Bretton Woods agreement, which had dictated the rules of international trade since World War II. This meant that the cost of goods imported into the United States increased, again yielding an upward pressure on prices, even during a recession. Between 1975 and 1979, the economy grew, with unemployment falling slowly but prices again rising at greater-than-normal rates.

The 1970s also ushered in a new period of government regulation. This time, instead of antitrust legislation, we saw the government act to regulate various aspects of our living and working environments, and to promote equal opportunity. While the social benefits of these regulations are widespread, they are also expensive. Costs increase with increased regulation, and these costs initially came on board during the 1970s.

It has been estimated that all of these shocks and increased costs have added a significant amount to the underlying rate of inflation. Accelerated government expenditures resulting from the Vietnam War are estimated to have added 3.25 percent to the underlying inflation rate, while the surge in oil prices, first in 1973 and again in 1979, added 4.75 percent. These factors alone explain an inflation rate of 8 percent.

In 1979 the second oil shock again sent prices upward, but as we know, in October the Fed acted to severely restrict the growth rate of the money supply. At the same time other events eased inflationary pressures. The price of oil began to drop as production increased and demand fell. The prices of other raw materials declined as well due to overproduction in many of the developing nations. Needing dollars to service their growing debt, these Third World nations hoped to sell more by increasing output. The result was an increased supply and lower prices.

Deregulation of a number of industries got into high gear in the early 1980s. Less regulation increased competition and lowered prices in the trucking, airlines, financial services, and telecommunications industries. In addition, the value of the dollar reached record highs against foreign currencies (see Chapter 24), which meant that prices of imported goods were very low. This helped to keep inflation low in the United States by providing a supply of cheaper imports and by keeping domestic prices in check as U.S. producers struggled to remain price competitive. Wages remained stable as productivity rose. Labor had made many concessions during the 1980–1982 recession and these "givebacks" now kept wages from rising. There were no bottlenecks in the economy pushing prices up. Supply-side economics mandated large cuts in spending on domestic programs, tax cuts, and increases in military expenditures. Unemployment soared, inflation abated, and huge deficits remained.

Economists at the Urban Institute assert that the early 1980s was a good time to be president. When Mr. Reagan entered office in 1980 the inflation rate was 12.4 percent. By December 1983 the inflation rate had fallen to 3.8 percent, or a

Table 23.2 DECLINE IN THE CPI, 1980–1983

	POINTS	PERCENTAGE OF TOTAL DECLINE
Homeownership measurement bias (changes in measurement of CPI between 1980 and 1983)	1.6	18.6
Food, energy, the dollar	2.9	33.7
Economic slack	4.1	47.7
Total	8.6	100.0

Source: Palmer and Sawhill, *The Reagan Record,* p. 80.

difference of 8.6 percent. As shown in Table 23.2, Urban Institute economists account for the 8.6 percent difference or the decline in inflation by changes in the measurement of housing in the CPI (1.6 percent), the decline in raw material prices and surge in the value of the dollar (2.9 percent), and the 1980–1982 recession (4.15 percent).

Table 23.3 indicates what has happened to prices in the past quarter century. Note the rates of inflation in recent years.

3. **On the average, how much would something that cost $200 in 1967 cost in 1984? How much inflation has there been since you were born?**

4. **Does any information in the table surprise you? Which category affects you most? Is it higher or lower than average?**

UNEMPLOYMENT

The Department of Labor defines those people who are over the age of 16 and actively seeking work as unemployed if they do not have a job. A little less than half of the population is in the labor force, and it is on this base that the unemployment estimates are made. By 1980 almost 100 million of the 219 million people in the United States were in the labor force.

Economists have defined five basic **types of unemployment.**

1. *Frictional unemployment* is caused by the temporary mismatching of people with jobs because workers change jobs, employers are constantly seeking new workers, and new people are entering the labor market. All labor markets have such frictional unemployment; even during World War II, when there existed a severe labor shortage, unemployment was still about 2 percent.

Table 23.3 CONSUMER PRICE INDEX* AND PERCENTAGE CHANGES FOR URBAN WAGE EARNERS AND CLERICAL WORKERS (1967 = 100)

YEAR	CPI	YEAR TO YEAR PERCENTAGE CHANGE IN CPI	YEAR	CPI	YEAR TO YEAR PERCENTAGE CHANGE IN CPI
1948	72.1	7.8	1967	100.0	2.9
1949	71.4	−1.0	1968	104.2	4.2
1950	72.1	1.0	1969	109.8	5.4
1951	77.8	7.9	1970	116.3	5.9
1952	79.5	2.2	1971	121.3	4.3
1953	80.1	0.8	1972	125.3	3.3
1954	80.5	0.5	1973	133.1	6.2
1955	80.2	−0.4	1974	147.7	11.0
1956	81.4	1.5	1975	161.2	9.1
1957	84.3	3.6	1976	170.5	5.8
1958	86.6	2.7	1977	181.5	6.5
1959	87.3	0.8	1978	195.4	7.7
1960	88.7	1.6	1979	217.4	11.3
1961	89.6	1.0	1980	246.8	13.5
1962	90.6	1.1	1981	272.4	10.4
1963	91.7	1.2	1982	289.1	6.0
1964	92.9	1.3	1983	298.4	3.2
1965	94.5	1.7	1984	311.1	4.3
1966	97.2	2.9	1985	322.2	3.6

*The Consumer Price Index (CPI) measures changes in the "cost of living."

Source: Economic Report of the President, 1986, pp. 318 and 320.

2. *Seasonal unemployment,* as the name implies, results from changing seasonal demand and supply for labor. Students seeking jobs in the summer and farm workers laid off in the winter are both part of this seasonal unemployment.

3. *Structural unemployment* presents a more serious problem than the previous types of unemployment. It is the unemployment that results from permanent displacements of workers due to shifting product demand and/or technological changes that require new skills. The shift in demand from natural to synthetic fibers created problems of structural unemployment for places such as Fall River, Massachusetts. The mechanical picking of tomatoes has caused many migrant workers to become structurally unemployed. Such unemployment is a function of geographic, as well as skill-level, mobility.

4. *Cyclical unemployment* is due to the decreased demand for labor that is a result of the business cycle. The high unemployment of the 1930s was basically a problem of cyclical unemployment.

5. *Hidden unemployment* is probably the hardest concept both to define and to measure. There is growing evidence that many people would like a job if they thought one was available, but many have become so discouraged by their past failures to find employment that they have literally given up trying. Technically, such people are outside the labor force, but in fact they are unemployed. One sign that such hidden unemployment exists can be seen from the fact that in the early stages of economic recovery, the labor force participation rate (i.e., the proportion of the total population seeking jobs) rises. More people seek jobs as the number of jobs increases, and the question arises as to why they were not part of the labor force when the unemployment rate was higher. In addition, there are many people who work part-time but would prefer to work full-time. These people are now counted as being employed. (We might also add a group of people that work but earn incomes that are below the poverty level.)

Table 23.4 shows selected unemployment rates for workers from 1948 to 1985.

5. Does it surprise you that married men typically have the lowest unemployment rates? Why or why not?

By 1983, 10.7-plus million people in the United States were unemployed. The fact of unemployment is an economic problem, both for the individual and for society. Beyond that, however, there are also problems in even counting and defining the unemployed in our economy.

Counting the Unemployed

Many economists are now beginning to use a new method of calculating the level of unemployment in the United States. David Gordon* from the New School of Social Research has proposed that we focus on **underemployment** rather than our traditional notion of unemployment in order to arrive at a more realistic and meaningful statistic. This statistic would give us better information and would be more instructive to policymakers trying to combat high rates of underemployment. How is this concept different from the one currently utilized?

Gordon defines underemployment as the statistic that calculates the number of people who fall into the following four categories:

*David M. Gordon, *Problems in Political Economy* (2nd Ed.), D. C. Heath, 1977, see pp. 70–75.

Table 23.4 SELECTED UNEMPLOYMENT RATES, 1948–1985

YEAR	ALL WORKERS	BY SEX AND AGE			BY COLOR		BY SELECTED GROUPS					
		BOTH SEXES 16–19 YEARS	MALES 20 YEARS AND OVER	FEMALES 20 YEARS AND OVER	WHITE	BLACK AND OTHER	EXPERIENCED WAGE AND SALARY WORKERS	HOUSE-HOLD HEADS	MARRIED MEN	WOMEN WHO HEAD FAMILIES	FULL-TIME WORKERS	BLUE COLLAR WORKERS
1948	3.8	9.2	3.2	3.6	3.5	5.9	4.3	—	—	—	—	4.2
1949	5.9	13.4	5.4	5.3	5.6	8.9	6.8	—	3.5	—	5.4	8.0
1950	5.3	12.2	4.7	5.1	4.9	9.0	6.0	—	4.6	—	5.0	7.2
1951	3.3	8.2	2.5	4.0	3.1	5.3	3.7	—	1.5	—	2.6	3.9
1952	3.0	8.5	2.4	3.2	2.8	5.4	3.3	—	1.4	—	2.5	3.6
1953	2.9	7.6	2.5	2.9	2.7	4.5	3.2	—	1.7	—	—	3.4
1954	5.5	12.6	4.9	5.5	5.0	9.9	6.2	—	4.0	—	5.2	7.2
1955	4.4	11.0	3.8	4.4	3.9	8.7	4.8	—	2.8	—	3.8	5.8
1956	4.1	11.1	3.4	4.2	3.6	8.3	4.4	—	2.6	—	3.7	5.1
1957	4.3	11.6	3.6	4.1	3.8	7.9	4.6	—	2.8	—	4.0	6.2
1958	6.8	15.9	6.2	6.1	6.1	12.6	7.2	—	5.1	—	7.2	10.2
1959	5.5	14.6	4.7	5.2	4.8	10.7	5.7	—	5.6	—	—	7.6
1960	5.5	14.7	4.7	5.1	4.9	10.2	5.7	—	3.7	—	—	7.8
1961	6.7	16.8	5.7	6.3	6.0	12.4	6.8	—	4.6	—	6.7	9.2
1962	5.5	14.7	4.6	5.4	4.9	10.9	5.6	—	3.6	—	—	7.4
1963	5.7	17.2	4.5	5.4	5.0	10.8	5.5	3.7	3.4	—	5.5	7.3

1964	5.2	16.2	3.9	5.2	4.6	9.6	5.0	3.2	2.8	—	4.9	6.3
1965	4.5	14.8	3.2	4.5	4.1	8.1	4.3	2.7	2.4	—	4.2	5.3
1966	3.8	12.8	2.5	3.8	3.4	7.3	3.5	2.2	1.9	—	3.5	4.2
1967	3.8	12.8	2.3	4.2	3.4	7.4	3.6	2.1	1.8	4.9	3.4	4.4
1968	3.6	12.7	2.2	3.8	3.2	6.7	3.4	1.9	1.6	4.4	3.1	4.1
1969	3.5	12.2	2.1	3.7	3.1	6.4	3.3	1.8	1.5	4.4	3.1	3.9
1970	4.9	15.2	3.5	4.8	4.5	8.2	4.8	2.9	2.6	5.4	4.5	6.2
1971	5.9	16.9	4.4	5.7	5.4	9.9	5.7	3.6	3.2	7.3	5.5	7.4
1972	5.6	16.2	4.0	5.4	5.0	10.0	5.3	3.3	2.8	7.2	5.1	6.5
1973	4.9	14.5	3.2	4.8	4.3	8.9	4.5	2.9	2.3	7.0	4.3	5.3
1974	5.6	16.0	3.8	5.5	5.0	9.9	5.3	3.3	2.7	7.0	5.1	6.7
1975	8.5	19.9	6.7	8.0	7.8	13.9	8.2	5.8	5.1	10.0	8.1	11.7
1976	7.7	19.0	5.9	7.4	7.0	13.1	7.3	5.1	4.2	10.0	7.3	9.4
1977	7.0	17.7	5.2	7.0	6.2	13.1	6.6	4.5	3.6	9.3	6.5	8.1
1978	6.0	16.3	4.2	6.0	5.2	11.9	5.6	—	2.8	8.5	5.5	6.9
1979	5.8	16.1	4.1	5.7	5.1	11.3	5.4	—	2.7	8.3	5.3	6.9
1980	7.0	17.8	5.9	6.4	6.3	13.1	6.9	—	4.2	9.2	—	—
1981	7.5	19.6	6.3	6.8	6.7	14.2	7.3	—	4.3	10.4	—	—
1982	9.5	23.2	8.8	8.3	8.6	17.3	9.3	—	6.5	11.7	—	—
1983	9.5	22.4	8.9	8.1	8.4	17.8	9.2	—	6.5	12.2	—	—
1984	7.4	18.9	6.6	6.8	6.5	14.4	7.1	—	4.6	10.3	—	—
1985	7.1	18.6	6.2	6.6	6.2	13.7	6.8	—	4.3	10.4	—	—

Source: Economic Report of the President, 1977, p. 221; 1980, pp. 237–238; 1986, p. 293.

Table 23.5 COUNTING THE UNEMPLOYED, SELECTED YEARS, 1970–1981

	1970		1975		1980		1981	
	NUMBER	PERCENT*	NUMBER	PERCENT*	NUMBER	PERCENT*	NUMBER	PERCENT*
Expanded labor force (labor force and discouraged workers who are not counted in the labor force)	85,528	100	96,546	100	109,537	100	111,418	100
1. Unemployed	4,093	4.8	7,929	8.2	7,637	7.0	8,273	7.4
2. Discouraged workers	639	0.7	1,093	1.1	993	0.9	1,103	1.0
3. Involuntary part-time (who couldn't find full-time work)	2,443	2.8	3,983	4.1	4,398	4.0	4,751	4.3
4. The working poor (households whose income is below the poverty line†)	2,763	3.2	2,601	2.7	3,027	2.7	3,603	3.2
Total underemployment	9,938	11.6	15,600	16.2	16,055	14.8	17,730	15.7

*Percentages may not add to 100 as a result of rounding.

†In 1983, the poverty line for an urban family of four was $10,866.

1. *Unemployed* people who are actively looking for work but unable to find a job.

2. *Discouraged workers* who are unemployed and want work but have given up in frustration because they believe no jobs are available.

3. *Involuntary part-time* people who actually want full-time work but are unable to find it.

4. *Underemployed* people who are working *full-time* but earning *less* than the poverty level of income as specified by the Bureau of Labor Statistics (1983 for an urban family of four, $10,866 per year; a person working full-time at the minimum wage in 1983 would earn approximately $6968 per year).

Using this methodology, we calculated underemployment between 1970 and 1981, as shown in Table 23.5.

In 1981, the level of underemployment of 15.7 percent is far greater than the "official" figure of 7.5 percent.

6. **Do you anticipate unemployment in your future? Why or why not? What are your "odds"?**

7. **Does it make any difference for economic policy how we count the unemployed?**

Over 10 million people (on the average) were unemployed during the recession of 1980–1982. The economic reality of unemployment often has direct social consequences for individuals and their families as well as for the communities enduring closed factories, unemployment lines, and discouraged workers. In the following article we see how the recession of the early 1980s sorely affected the workers and families of the Monongahela Valley and other areas of the country.

LEFT OUT

Peter McGrath with Richard Manning and John McCormick

They were the princes of industrial America. Now their factories are closed, their jobs gone and their dreams of prosperity are shattered—perhaps forever.

Bad news in the Monongahela Valley comes as a ripple of voices across the shop floor: another mill gone down, another brigade of workers on the street, another pack of wolves at their families' doors. So it was on the

(continued)

grim December day in 1981 when U.S. Steel announced the closure of its fabled Edgar Thomson Works in Braddock, Pa., the birthplace of big steel. That was the day Tom Medved, then a 39-year-old roller in the slab mill, found himself abruptly out of work, after 19 years and 364 days at E.T., as the plant is locally known. Since his layoff, Tom Medved has not held a regular job of any kind—and he's beginning to wonder if he'll ever work again. . . .

Tom Medved is not alone. All over America's industrial heartland, from the steel country of western Pennsylvania to Michigan's automobile towns, from the machine-tool factories of Illinois to the red iron-ore pits of Minnesota's Mesabi Range, the national faith in prosperity forever is fading. In its place are the brute realities of silent machinery and boarded-up storefronts, of once proud men waiting in welfare lines and leaden-eyed women staring from their windows. Recovery will come to the rest of the country, but the Midwestern depression belt and other pockets of traditional industry from Baltimore to Birmingham, Ala., will be left out. Not anytime soon will American automakers build 9.7 million cars a year as they did a decade ago; never again will American steel employ 650,000 workers.

The Midwest once was the bedrock of the wealth that made the United States the envy of the world. Here Andrew Carnegie produced the rails that tamed the West. Here Henry Ford invented the assembly line, along with the unheard-of wage of $5 a day, and made modern industry possible. And with modern industry came economic mobility: the ore-laden freighters and around-the-clock factories lifted many blue-collar Americans into the middle class—upward movement on a scale never seen before.

Civic pride flourished. Carnegie gave Braddock the first of the thousands of free public libraries he was to endow throughout the world, with turreted towers and beveled-glass windows, an indoor swimming pool and two bowling alleys. Flint, Mich., received from General Motors moguls a limestone cultural complex that would be the envy of any city twice the size; the Sloan Museum there testifies to American industry's exuberance with an exhibit of free-spirited experimental car models. Hibbing, Minn., astride an iron-ore lode described as 110 miles long and billions of dollars deep, boasted a municipal zoo, the country's first bookmobile, and a public-school auditorium with crystal chandeliers. The police wore imported Panama hats. In 1920, with a population of only 15,000, Hibbing managed expenditures of $3.3 million—almost as much as the budget for the entire state of Rhode Island that year. By 1947, President Harry Truman would say, with only slight exaggeration, "I know Hibbing; that's where the high school has gold doorknobs.

No more: as Hibbing's best-known son, Bob Dylan, wrote in a song about hard times in his hometown, ". . . the cardboard filled windows,

(continued)

and old men on the benches,/Tell you now that the whole town is empty."
The town is empty, too, in places like Braddock, where Edgar Thomson's
140 acres lie in sarcophagus silence; even with the firing-up this week of a
blast furnace, the mill employs only 650 workers, compared with 4,400 at
the peak of its activity. The town's population has dwindled to 6,000, from
a postwar high of 22,000, and municipal services are almost nonexistent.
Last year, the fire department disbanded and the volunteer crew that took
its place said it would be unable to answer emergency ambulance calls;
10 days later a woman in labor, stranded, had her baby in the kitchen
sink. The schools, like Carnegie's grand Romanesque library, are closed,
and the main streets are all but deserted. Braddock is dying, and the rest
of the Monongahela Valley is not far behind. Says 35-year-old Mark
Wasik, a laid-off steelworker from the neighboring borough of Homestead,
"I don't think the layoff will ever end. The handwriting's on the wall."

The handwriting *is* on the wall, and it reads HELP WANTED: NONE and
SORRY, NOT HIRING. The official unemployment rate in Flint is 24.6 percent,
reflecting the loss of 20,000 jobs at General Motors. Hibbing claims a job-
less rate of 28.4 percent, but local officials privately put it closer to 40
percent. Rockford, Ill., a toolmaking town whose factories serve factories
elsewhere, lost 17,000 manufacturing jobs in the last three years. "We
now have 23,000 people classed as unemployed," says Rockford labor analyst Charles Sinclair. "There was a time in 1966 when we only had 50
people actually drawing unemployment benefits." In 1981 the steel industry alone laid off 86,000 workers in the Monongahela Valley.

FATHERS AND SONS

The burden falls most heavily on the younger workers. At the General
Motors warehousing center in Flint, only workers with 18 or more years on
the job still punch the clock. Everyone hired after 1965 has been laid off.
At Flint's Chevrolet manufacturing plant, nobody with less than 14 years is
working—and people with less than five years have no hope of ever being
called back. Seniority sets the rules: a 35-year-old worker with a family of
five gets less consideration than a worker of 55 whose children are grown.
Even with an economic recovery, says Mayor Dick Nordvold of Hibbing,
"there are miners who won't make the callback. They're the young people.
They're going to have to be retrained, or they're going to have to leave."

It was never meant to be this way. In years past, factory employment
was a family tradition, passed from fathers to sons, from mothers to
daughters. "My father worked at E.T. for 40 years," says Tom Medved.
"My uncles and cousins all worked there. It was the natural thing to do."
A job in the industry meant security, presumably for life: "I used to get out
to the mine 30 or 45 minutes early, maybe talk with the guys or play
cards," says Steve Makarrall, 28, a laid-off heavy-equipment operator at

(continued)

the U.S. Steel ore mine outside Hibbing. "It was the best job I ever had. I loved it. I was going to stay there till I was 65, and go live on a lake somewhere. All of a sudden, the bottom drops out. . . ."

A GROWING DESPAIR

Now what will happen to me? The wording suggests an uncharacteristic passivity, even despair. But the lesson of the past several years is that taking charge doesn't always yield results. . . .

Mostly, workers on layoff kill time. Don Brooks volunteers for projects at his church. Others scrounge part-time work, almost as much to have something to do as for the money. Some find themselves in strange roles: men accustomed to leaving at dawn for an early shift now walk their children to the school-bus stop and hang shyly from the lampposts, waiting for the bus to come. Others help out at union halls, organizing a food bank, or fielding questions about welfare. In tapped-out towns like Braddock, the food bank is a lifeline: more than 700 Braddock families each month take home three pounds of hamburger, one dozen eggs, four cans of vegetables and a pound of cheese or margarine—not a lot, but in too many households the difference between eating and going hungry.

Hunger is a new and humiliating experience. "At first I felt really depressed about having to come here," says former Chevrolet worker Dave Anderson, 25, over a bowl of barley gruel at the Northside soup kitchen in Flint. But I'd run out of food stamps if I didn't." Even the Gospel missions, traditionally the refuge of drifters and drunks, are filling up with out-of-work factory hands and their families. "When the money runs out, we have to rely on the mission," says Michael Hartwell after a dinner of mashed potatoes and ham at the Flint Rescue Mission with his wife Lynn and four-year-old son Shawn. "The boy needs to eat and we need to eat. When it's time, it's time. . . ."

Pride prevents many of the new unemployed from taking advantage of either public or private assistance. Says Don Thomas, the president of the Steelworkers local in Braddock, "I've had guys say to me, 'You're crazy if you think I'm going to stand there for food . . .' Honestly, I don't know what some of these people are going to do." Bill Adkisson, the United Auto Workers' liaison with United Way charities in Flint, says he has had to "physically force" laid-off workers into his car to get them to the food bank. "One guy said to me that if it hadn't been for the Salvation Army, his wife and four kids would not have eaten in the last three or four weeks," Adkisson says. "There are so many others like that, but who are just too pigheaded to ask. . . ."

Daytime drinking is on the rise throughout the industrial states, and one of the predictable results is an increase in family abuse. "They sit in the tavern all day and then head home to kick the wife and kids around a

(continued)

while," says Don Brooks's wife, Diane. "I don't know whether there is more violence, but I do know the severity has increased," adds Jo Sullivan of Range Women's Advocates in Chisholm, Minn. "It's no longer the pushes and shoves and slaps. Now it's the stitches, the wired jaws, the broken ribs."

Unemployment may mean more togetherness than is good for a family. Says Paul Kapsch, the director of the psychiatric-services unit at the Central Mesabi Medical Center in Hibbing, "Now dad's home, making comments about mom's cooking and childrearing methods and other things he never noticed before. He's feeling inadequate, and if he's like most males, he's having difficulty expressing that." Instead, the housebound husband erupts in anger. "If the husband is home all the time, he can control the car and the phone," says Sullivan. "Women we'd been working with now tell us they can't go out for counseling, they can't meet with support groups and they don't want us to call. They're scared. And I'm sure there are women not even making initial contact with us for the same reason."

EASING THE BURDEN

Even more disturbing in the long run is the resentment and cynicism growing within the next generation. When older children are forced to look for work to help their families scrape by, there is "a great deal of tension," according to Carl Robertson of the Pittsburgh area Christian Family Services. "The kids feel, 'You had your chance, and you took it. Then you blew it. Now I'm being forced to pay for your mistakes'." Alternatively, many children may respond by lapsing into a permanent hopelessness. "I'm worried that the children will get the idea that life isn't worth living, that they'll be on welfare for the rest of their lives," says Maj. Alvin R. Nelson, coordinator of the Rockford Salvation Army services.

On welfare for the rest of their lives: it is an idea no industrial worker could even have conceived of 20 years ago, when American factories were pouring forth an endless stream of finished goods, and you could walk out of a job one day and have your pick of two others the next. There were recessions now and then, of course, but they seemed no more than momentary stumbles in the economy's ever-upward march. Of all the damage this last recession has inflicted on the industrial heartland, none is more worrisome than its undermining of the old optimism, for optimism is a precondition of economic health. Without it, people stop planning, stop saving, stop cooperating with each other. Without it, they tacitly concede defeat in the growing global economic competition.

What could produce a revival of optimism? The recovery now apparently under way will help, though it will not bring many jobs back to the Monongahela Valley or the Mesabi Range. Of the 21,000 workers General Motors is recalling in the coming months, not one will go back on
(continued)

the line in Flint, Mich. Extensive job-retraining programs would also help, giving dislocated workers some hope that they will find new niches in an evolving postindustrial economy. It will not be easy, however; even in Rockford, with its highly skilled, sophisticated work force, Mayor John McNamara says that worker re-education will mean lower standards of living for many and will take at least a generation to complete. Perhaps more helpful would be a retooling of basic industries—by whatever mix of tax and trade policies is necessary—to make them more competitive with their counterparts in Europe and Japan. For national-security reasons alone, the United States probably cannot turn its back on steel and automobiles in the rush toward fashionable high-tech industries.

Most of all, however, it would help if the new unemployed were not conveniently forgotten as the country begins at last to feel the blessings of recovery. An entire generation of workers, those now in their 20s, 30s and 40s, has been at the very least disabled—if not wiped out. They did not do this to themselves; they are victims of outmoded industrial practices and obsolete plants in an era of cheaper foreign products. But they and their fathers before them made the United States the powerful, wealthy nation it is today, and they are owed something. In the short term, they deserve a decent cushion in the inevitably painful transition to a less affluent way of life. In the long term, they deserve no less than their fathers earned: the satisfaction that comes from an honest day's work and an honest day's pay.

8. Can economists deal with social ills? Is it their job?

9. Would you hire 39-year-old Tom Medved?

10. If you were unemployed, what do you think your attitude would be?

11. What are the economic and noneconomic costs of unemployment?

SOLUTIONS—THE DILEMMA

The dilemma of the mid-1980s is what to do—what to do about high levels of unemployment, government deficits, high interest rates, and the myriad of other economic problems that surround us. Traditional Keynesian remedies have been declared deficient by economists of all bents. While the creation of a recession to bring down inflation is not very appealing to politicians or the public, it nonetheless works, and now efforts continue to keep price expectations low, even during a period of economic growth. More devastating to Keynesian policies has been the recurrence of inflation and unemployment in spite of stabilization policies. The post–World War II game rules seem to have changed with the collapse of the Bretton Woods agreement (see Chapter 24) and the challenge of increased international trade and exchange.

Alternatives such as wage and price controls have faded from sight as means to combat inflation or reduce unemployment in the Reagan Administration. Yet every president since and including Harry Truman has at some point flirted with controls or guidelines. Outside of the political machismo derived from controls, there has been little past evidence that the particular types of controls instituted have been effective.

Another group of economists, called the post-Keynesians, recommend the adoption of an **incomes policy** to determine an annual noninflationary rise in all types of income. This would involve controls over the rates of increase in personal and business income. Tax incentives would assure compliance. The post-Keynesians believe that government and business decisions for long-run public and private investment should be made jointly, and that employment and growth policies are central to a recovery and economic restructuring.

Nevertheless, it is supply-side fiscal policies that are being touted as the answer to our economic problems by some. Others believe that the large tax cuts designed to increase supply and trigger economic growth were simply excuses to improve the lot of corporations and the wealthy, since they are the ones who have benefited most from the cuts.

CONCLUSION

Increasingly, a problem that must be faced is that the traditional solutions to unemployment and inflation simply are outdated. New solutions must be found within the context of the existing U.S. and world economies, solutions that are significantly different from those of the past. To return to the "good old days" is simply not possible because of the current industrial and service structure. The U.S. economy is far different from what it was in the glory days of yore. The work force is no longer just white and male, and the economic base, which was continually regenerated through economic growth, is no longer solely industrial. Additionally, policy decisions must reflect the fact that the U.S. economy in the 1980s is greatly dependent on the other nations of the world. As government leaders plan for economic recovery and growth in the United States in the late 1980s, they must do so within a world context. Today more than 10 percent of the products we produce are exported to other nations. Exports plus imports were some 20 percent of the U.S. GNP in 1983, compared with 12.4 percent of GNP in 1970. If the economies of our trading partners are not healthy, we cannot expect ours to remain vigorous.

This chapter completes our discussion of macroeconomics. We have seen that the Keynesian approach to economic policy has carried us a long way from the classical approach. And yet problems still exist and new approaches may be needed to deal with future problems. Many of these issues are increasing our attention toward macroeconomics and the functioning of specific markets. Traditional macroeconomic policies for controlling inflation and achieving full employment do not seem to be working. Indeed, the two have coexisted throughout the 1970s and 1980s and have been dubbed, as we mentioned earlier, stagflation. It has been a failure in Keynesian economics to deal with this phenomenon. We will discuss this problem in significant depth in Chapter 30, but before we do, we need first to broaden our perspective and see what is happening in international economics, since an understanding of this arena is necessary to appreciate the complexity of the problem. As you might have guessed, if you think the problems we've been dealing with so far are complicated, "you ain't seen nothin' yet."

KEY CONCEPTS

trade-offs	profit-push
stagflation	administered prices
Phillips curve	wage-price spiral
demand-pull	types of unemployment
cost-push	underemployment
wage-push	incomes policy

REVIEW QUESTIONS

1. What is the basis for the trade-off between inflation and unemployment? Why can't there be zero unemployment and zero inflation?

2. Do you think fighting inflation is more important than fighting unemployment? Why?

3. What two competing theories explain inflation in the economy?

4. What structural elements in the economy limit the effectiveness of fiscal and monetary policies?

5. How does avoiding a boom avoid a recession? What is the resulting impact on inflation?

6. List the five types of unemployment. Which of these can be aided by macroeconomic policies? What sorts of policies would alleviate these types of unemployment?

7. What is the difference between unemployment and underemployment?

8. Why have the Reagan tax cuts helped upper-income taxpayers more than lower-income taxpayers?

SUGGESTED READINGS

Michael H. Best and William E. Connolly, 1976. *The Politicized Economy*, D. C. Heath. An attempt to suggest the problems for economic theory in the modern context and a prescription for the future.

Frank J. Bonello and Thomas R. Swartz (eds.), 1978. *Alternative Directions in Economic Policy*, University of Notre Dame Press. Views from liberals, conservatives, and radicals on the economic values of the future.

Robert Aaron Gordon, 1974. *Economic Instability and Growth,* Harper & Row. An economic history of the recent postwar performance of the American economy, focusing on macroeconomic goals and policy.

Walter Heller, 1976. *The Economy,* W. W. Norton. A leading liberal economist's attempt to lead us out of the woods.

Robert Lekachman, 1976. *Economists at Bay,* McGraw-Hill. An interesting and easy-to-read account of the failure of modern economists to deal adequately with economic issues.

Robert Lekachman, 1973. *Inflation,* Vintage Books. This is an interesting and well-written examination of the process and causes of inflation. Lekachman also gives five solutions to the dilemma.

Abba P. Lerner, 1973. *Flation,* Penguin Books. Lerner examines many of the complexities involved with the inflation–deflation problem.

Howard Sherman, 1976. *Stagflation: A Radical Theory of Unemployment and Inflation,* Harper & Row. One radical's attempt to explain the modern phenomenon of stagflation.

Lester Thurow, 1980. *The Zero-Sum Society,* Basic Books. In examining recent economic experience in the United States, Thurow suggests that we can no longer trade off our economic ills without severe hardship to certain groups.

Raburn Williams, 1980. *Inflation! Money, Jobs and Politicians,* AHM. Put in a crisis framework, this book reviews the ills creating inflation as well as the results of inflation.

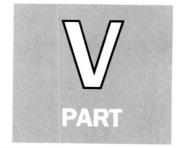

INTERNATIONAL ECONOMICS

With each passing decade the nations of the world grow increasingly dependent on one another. When considering various policy options, U.S. decision makers must take international economic conditions into account. In the past these decision makers were concerned simply with the value of a nation's currency, or its exchange rate, the balance of payments, and perhaps protectionist tendencies that might exist in the world economy. Today, however, more complex questions arise involving floating exchange rates, the effect of the OPEC cartel on the oil-importing nations, the changes in various international institutions, such as the IMF, the effect of the demands of the developing nations through a "new international economic order," and the overall increase in the level of world trade.

It is to this world economy that we now turn. First we shall examine the implications of increasing international interdependence. Next we shall look at the theory behind international trade. This will be followed by a survey of the incredible arena of international finance. Finally, we shall turn our attention to the developing nations of the world to examine the problems and the challenges that they face in the future.

24

Chapter

International Economic Interdependence

INTRODUCTION

Interdependence among nations is a major feature of the modern world economy. This interdependence will be a salient theme throughout the remainder of this book. It is necessary for us to be more specific about this concept if we are to understand it properly and apply it to the crucial problems we will be examining.

By the term **economic interdependence** we mean simply that all countries are affected by the events of an economic nature that occur in many other countries. For example, many industrialized nations rely on the developing nations for basic food and raw materials needs; in turn, many developing nations import manufactured finished goods from industrialized nations. The degree of interdependence is, of course, different for every nation. For example, Japan is severely affected by OPEC price increases yet relatively unaffected by Costa Rica's decision to increase banana prices. On the other hand, Costa Rica, also strongly affected by an oil price increase, has the flexibility to shift its imports of television sets from the United States to Japan. As we have defined this concept, it is purely economic. It is meant to be descriptive of the complex international flow of goods, services, *and* capital among nations.

The nature of this contemporary interdependence involves not only the exchange of goods and services but technology transfers, financial capital movements between countries, and factors affecting the international division of labor.

Pounds, pounds . . . nothing but pounds. Haven't you got any
deutsche marks?

Because of this growing interdependence, nations must be aware of com-
promising situations. In the following excerpt from *The Lean Years* by Richard
Barnett, we can see how potential conflicts can arise between our economic needs
and our belief in human rights.

MINERALS: THE ROCKS OF CIVILIZATION

Richard J. Barnet

A region that geologists call "High Africa," stretching from Transvaal in
South Africa to Shaba in Zaire and Angola, has the world's largest concentration of manganese and chrome (chromium). Manganese is absolutely essential for the production of iron and steel. The U.S. has no manganese
reserves. South Africa has more than 2 billion tons and sells the U.S.
about 10 percent of what it uses every year. The rest comes from Brazil,
Gabon, and Australia. Chrome is almost equally critical. There is no
known substitute for chrome in making steel, although for many common
industrial uses, there are substitutes for steel. A generation ago Stalin
asked, "How many divisions has the Pope?" Today the question that will

(continued)

decide the power balance on the continent of Africa is this: "How dependent is the industrial world on the manganese and chrome reserves of South Africa?"

Although chromite was discovered in Maryland in 1827 and the United States was briefly the principal world supplier, domestic production ceased in 1961. When the Bureau of Mines notes that chrome is "one of the Nation's most important strategic and critical materials," it is indulging in understatement. South Africa and Rhodesia have 97 percent of the known world's chrome reserves. The USSR is the next largest producer, but the extent of its reserves is secret.

Nature has been exceptionally bountiful in storing all sorts of resources under U.S. soil, but the world distribution of chrome is dramatic evidence of the limits of self-sufficiency. There is a certain irony in the fact that in a recent year the U.S. imported 31 percent of its requirements from its major antagonist, the Soviet Union; 27 percent from South Africa, the focus of what promises to be the major international political struggle of the 1980s; 18 percent from the Philippines, one of the most defiant violators of human rights; and 12 percent from Turkey, with which the U.S. has had strained relations since the Turks invaded Cyprus.

In its study *Contingency Plans for Chromium Utilization,* the National Research Council concluded that within twenty-five to seventy-five years South Africa and Rhodesia will have a monopoly on world chrome reserves. We should bear in mind, though, that *reserves* is a deceptive term. The size depends upon where and how hard one looks. If companies stopped looking in South Africa and turned their attention elsewhere, reserves would grow where the exploration was conducted and South Africa's would diminish. Recently, U.S. intelligence agencies have expressed concern that because of the boycott of Rhodesian chrome under a U.N. resolution, the Soviet Union has become America's major supplier. Thus the armor in one out of three new American tanks facing the Warsaw Pact forces on the Elbe River is probably fortified with Soviet chrome.

There are possible alternatives to the huge dependence on southern Africa—conservation measures, alternative technologies, increased exploration and mining elsewhere. But, as in the case of petroleum, the transition is the problem. It would take, according to the National Research Council, from five to ten years to adjust to a cutoff of chrome and manganese from southern Africa. The black African states lack a common minerals policy, as well as the technology and capital to develop their own reserves. They are dependent on South Africa to make their minerals industry work. Thus Zambia has had to use the South African transport system to ship its copper. Angola sells its diamonds through South Africa's Central Selling Organization, as indeed does the Soviet Union.

Minerals dependence on South Africa is real enough. In addition to possessing the indispensable steel-related minerals, chrome and manganese, South Africa has about one-third of the world's uranium supply (if

(continued)

you include Namibia). There is enormous interest in the U.S. and West Europe in the incredible riches of South Africa. For example, the British-based multinational corporation Rio Tinto-Zinc—in collaboration with a German company, Urangesellschaft, and a French government subsidiary, Total Compagnie Minière et Nucléaire—has been a partner with South Africa in developing the world's richest uranium mine at Rossing in Namibia. But there is also an ideology of minerals dependence that South Africa uses as a weapon. Just as oil companies have derived power from their exclusive knowledge of oil and natural gas reserves, warning of scarcity or celebrating abundance as their marketing strategies and public relations dictated, so these governments and some of the multinational corporations with investments in South Africa exaggerate the minerals dependence of the industrial world on South Africa.

"We now have a bargaining position equal to that of an Arab nation with a lot of oil," Louw Alberts, vice president of South Africa's Atomic Energy Board, boasts. In "Africa and Western Lifelines," a 1978 article published in the U.S. military journal *Strategic Review,* W. C. J. Van Rensburg, professor of energy economics at the Rand Afrikaans University, Johannesburg, argues that the West has no choice but to embrace South Africa, because it cannot do without her minerals. South Africa alone has, he reminds us, 86 percent of the platinum reserves, 83 percent of the chrome, 64 percent of the vanadium, 40 percent of the gold, and 48 percent of the manganese. (South Africa's mineral power is even greater because of its hold on the mineral economies of the surrounding black African states.) With the exception of the Soviet Union, South Africa is probably the most self-sufficient mineral producer in the world. The Soviet Union's increased interest in Africa of recent years is part of a plot, he suggests, to deny the West access to the minerals of southern Africa one way or another. Once the source of supply is cut off, the dependence of the U.S. and Europe on Soviet chrome and Soviet gold becomes nearly total. The South African analyst warns of the effects not only of "direct Soviet interference in the flow of strategic raw materials" but also of "economic strangulation," terrorism, or incursions by the neighboring black African states on the industrial order of the West. The message is clear: The industrial nations cannot afford to shun or to punish South Africa. Boycotts, blockades, and support for the forces of liberation and change—all will backfire. The beleaguered white regime is the international tar baby, as it was known in the Kissinger White House.

These views have dominated official NATO thinking for ten years. Numerous examples of military collaboration between South Africa and NATO countries have come to light over the years despite rather elaborate efforts to keep them secret. The U.S., in what surely must be one of the most shortsighted decisions of recent years, supplied South Africa with about 100 pounds of highly enriched uranium—enough to produce at least five atomic bombs. Giving in to the feelings of the outraged but impotent

(continued)

black states of Africa, it is argued, would expose the West to mortal danger. Eighty percent of Europe's oil and 70 percent of its strategic minerals use the sea lanes around the Cape of Good Hope. The supertankers heading for America—one leaves every thirteen minutes—use the same water routes. A prolonged struggle to control that strategic real estate or the emergence in power of a more humane but less cooperative regime would mean endless trouble for the U.S. economy.

On the other hand, a recent study for the State Department by Robert Dean Consultants, of the mineral potential of countries neighboring South Africa, concludes that "the strategic dependence of the West on mineral supplies from South Africa can be lessened" by investing in the mineral economies of the black regimes despite the problems of inadequate transportation and lack of skilled workers. There is no comparison between the escalating investment that has been pouring into the minerals industry of Rhodesia and South Africa since the end of the last century and the trickle of funds to Mozambique, Zambia, Botswana, Lesotho, and Malawi.

How dependent the U.S. and Europe are on South Africa, how interested the Soviet Union is in denying these minerals to the West, and how significant is the mineral potential of the black states all depend on bits of politicized fact which serve as missiles in the information war. There is no "objective" answer to any of these questions, for each of these important issues depends upon the behavior of governments and corporations. If reducing U.S. dependence upon South Africa were a serious objective, the design of materials conservation policies and the massive investment in the development of alternative sources would also have to be a higher priority. It is ironic that the United States should have tied its economic health so closely to two of the most anachronistic regimes in the world, Saudi Arabia and South Africa. The more the U.S. identifies with the wrong side in South Africa—wrong morally and wrong politically because eventually the white minority will lose—the more it will cut itself off from the majority of nations and peoples on whom it must increasingly depend. If the rate of mineral consumption requires policies that compromise human rights standards and friendly relations with nonracist regimes, then prudence would dictate retooling our economy rather than fanning the flames of war in southern Africa.

1. **What will happen to "national sovereignty" as this process of increasing interdependence unfolds?**

2. **What is the U.S. policy toward South Africa today? Is the United States dependent on South Africa?**

3. **Are there other nations in "a bargaining position equal to that of an Arab nation with a lot of oil"?**

With an understanding of this concept—economic interdependence—let us now raise two key questions and then develop an economic tool to help us answer these questions. First, what is the nature of this interdependence in the contemporary world? And second, how has this interdependence evolved historically, especially since 1945?

In order to handle these questions with any degree of sophistication, we need to develop an understanding of what is referred to by economists as the **balance of payments.** It is a tool of economics that will help us to understand international interdependence.

THE BALANCE OF PAYMENTS

All nations must eventually adjust their national economic policies to meet the demands of the international trading and financial system. The mechanism commonly used by a nation for keeping track of these demands is the balance-of-payments accounting system. A balance-of-payments account is a statement of a nation's aggregate international economic transactions over a period of time, usually one year. The balance-of-payments account attempts to estimate all of the international transactions of a country's citizens and businesses, as well as the government. It helps a government keep track of and to some extent control the flow of goods and services between its country and the rest of the world. In this accounting statement, all international economic and financial transactions must have either a positive or a negative effect on a nation's balance of payments accounts. For example, Fig. 24.1 shows how this occurs in five selected categories.

The balance-of-payments accounting statement is divided into four major classifications: (1) the current account, (2) the capital account, (3) the errors and omissions account, and (4) the official reserves account.

The **current account** includes the import and export of all goods and services during a year. Exports of goods and services create a receipt of income, while imports of goods command payments abroad resulting in an outflow of income. Payments subtracted from receipts are noted under the *Balance* column of Table 24.1.

Positive credits (+)	Negative debits (−)
1. Any *receipt* of foreign money	1. Any *payment* to a foreign country
2. Any *earnings* on an investment in a foreign country	2. Any *investment* in a foreign country
3. Any sale of goods or services abroad *(export)*	3. Any purchase of goods and services from abroad *(import)*
4. Any gift or aid *from* a foreign country	4. Any gift or aid *given* abroad
5. Any *sale* of stocks or bonds abroad	5. Any *purchases* of stocks or bonds from abroad

Figure 24.1 Credit and debits in a nation's balance of payments.

Table 24.1 U.S. BALANCE OF PAYMENTS, 1982 (IN BILLIONS OF DOLLARS)

TRANSACTIONS	RECEIPTS	PAYMENTS	BALANCE
Current account			
Merchandise	211.217	247.606	−36.4
Investment income	84.146	56.842	27.3
Net military			.2
Net travel and transportation receipts			−2.1
Other services, net			7.8
Remittances, pensions, and other unilateral transfers			−8.0
Balance on current account			−11.2
Capital account			
U.S. capital outflow, net			
Government assets			−5.7
Private assets			−107.3
U.S. capital inflow, net			
Official assets			3.2
Private assets			84.7
Balance on capital account			−25.2
Balance on current and capital accounts			−36.4
Errors and omissions (statistical discrepency)			41.4
Official settlements			
U.S. official reserve assets			−5.0
Allocation of Special Drawing Rights			—

Adapted from *Economic Report of the President*, 1984, pp. 332–333.

By far the largest category under the current account is the export and import of merchandise—cars, steel, raw materials, machines, etc. In 1982, U.S. exports totaled $211.2 billion, and imports totaled $247.6 billion. The merchandise balance, often referred to as the **balance of trade,** for 1982 was −$36.4 billion. In the merchandise category, payments were larger than receipts, resulting in a negative "balance." Besides merchandise trade, the current account records investment income and services of various types. When all of the transactions in the current account are totaled, we get the balance on current account. For 1982 this balance was −$11.2 billion.

The **capital account** includes all capital flows in and out of the United States. U.S. capital outflow represents the purchase of capital assets outside of the United States by the government, citizens, or corporations. To purchase these assets, dollars flow out of the country. In return, the government, citizen, or business now owns an asset abroad. If the U.S. government buys a bond issued by the French government, this represents a payment (debit) in the capital account of the United States. In 1982, the U.S. government increased its ownership of assets abroad by $5.7 billion—an outflow of $5.7 billion in the balance-of-payments accounts. In the same way, American citizens or businesses might make bank deposits in other countries, purchase foreign stocks and bonds, or even buy foreign productive facilities (plants, office, etc.). All of these activities produce an increase in U.S. assets abroad, or an outflow of dollars—a payment in the balance of payments. On the other hand, if Americans were to sell their foreign assets and bring the proceeds back home, this would be recorded as a receipt. In 1982, the net outflow of U.S. private capital amounted to $107.4 billion, which represented payments in the capital account. Capital inflow into the United States occurs when foreign governments, institutions, corporations, or individuals increase their assets in the United States.

Adding the current account and the capital account together, we get a balance on current and capital accounts. For 1982, this was –$36.4 billion. This is simply a net sum of all of the international economic transactions of U.S. citizens and corporations and the government during a particular year, as measured by the balance-of-payments accounts. As we shall soon see, however, the balance of payments always "balances" because whatever surplus (net inflow) or deficit (net outflow) these transactions generate is offset by the use of official reserve assets of the U.S. government and by the errors and omissions account.

The errors and omissions category, in one sense, is an accounting mechanism for "balancing" the accounts. For example, in 1982, the balance on current and capital account showed a $36.4 billion deficit, but the errors and omissions account was +$41.4 billion. Together with the –$4.973 billion in the U.S. official reserve assets, these produce a balance. However, there is another sense in which this account balances the overall international payments position of the United States. The totality of U.S. international transactions is incredibly complex and widespread. There is no way on earth that the government could accurately measure all of these transactions. There is thus some reality to the errors and omissions title; it is simply an acknowledgment that some transactions, both legal and illegal, will escape measurement. For 1982, this could mean a variety of things, or a combination of all of them. If the United States had a $36.4 billion deficit in its balance on current and capital account, it means that there was a large outflow of dollars. This would put downward pressure on the dollar, reducing its value and "balancing" the deficit. Alternatively, other nations could hold on to the dollars that they had received because of U.S. imports from their countries or U.S. capital flows to their countries. They might want to hold these dollars for future use. This action also serves to "balance" the accounts. Finally, in late 1979 the United States raised interest rates, in part to protect the value of the dollar; this led to a massive inflow of foreign capital (much of it unmeasured) into the country in short-term bank deposits in search of high interest rates. High interest rates continued to attract short-term capital through 1984. In conclusion, we can say that the errors and omissions category relates to the imprecision involved in attempting to measure all international economic activities and serves to balance mechanically the international accounts.

The final component of the balance-of-payments accounts is the government's official reserve assets. These are in the form of gold, foreign currencies, reserve positions at the International Monetary Fund, and Special Drawing Rights. Basically, if the United States reduces its holdings of reserves, it will do so in exchange for dollars. This might occur if foreigners wanted to get rid of their dollar holdings. For example, the United States might give up gold for dollars; this produces a receipt in the balance-of-payments accounts. On the other hand, an increase in reserve assets will appear as a payment in the balance-of-payments accounts. For 1979, the official reserve assets account was –$1.1 billion, denoting an increase in the U.S. official reserves and an outflow of dollars to pay for them. At the same time, however, the United States was also receiving $1.1 billion worth of Special Drawing Rights, which are, in essence, international money. These cancel each other and leave the overall international transactions in balance. The balance of payments between 1970 and 1984 is shown in Table 24.2.

Table 24.2 U.S. BALANCE OF PAYMENTS, 1970–1984 (IN BILLIONS OF DOLLARS)

TRANSACTIONS	1970	1975	1979	1980	1981	1982	1984
Current account	+2.3	+18.2	−.8	+.4	+4.6	−11.2	−107.4
Merchandise	+2.6	+9.0	−29.4	−25.5	−28.1	−36.4	−114.1
Investment income	+6.2	+12.8	+32.5	29.6	+33.5	+27.3	+19.1
Net military	−3.3	−.7	−1.3	−2.3	−1.4	+.2	−1.8
Net travel	−2.0	−2.8	−2.7	−1.4	−.6	−2.1	−9.0
Other services, net	+2.2	+4.6	+5.8	+7.2	+8.1	+7.8	+9.8
Remittances, pensions	−3.3	−4.6	−5.7	−7.1	−6.9	−8.0	11.4
Capital account	−5.4	−23.3	−23.0	−23.0	−24.7	−25.2	+80.0
U.S. capital outflow							
Government assets	−1.6	−3.5	−3.8	−5.1	−5.1	−5.7	−5.5
Private assets	−10.2	−35.4	−56.8	−72.8	−100.3	−107.3	−11.8
U.S. capital inflow							
Official assets	+6.9	+7.0	−14.3	+15.6	+5.4	+3.2	+3.4
Private assets	−.5	+8.6	+51.8	+39.3	+75.2	+84.7	+93.9
Balance on current and capital accounts	−3.1	−5.1	−23.8	−22.6	−20.2	−36.4	−27.4
Errors and omissions	−.2	+5.7	+23.8	+29.6	+24.2	+41.4	+30.5
Official settlements							
U.S. official reserve assets	+2.5	−.8	−1.1	−8.2	−5.2	−5.0	−3.1
Allocations of Special Drawing Rights	+.9	—	+1.1	+1.2	+1.1	—	—

Note: Figures may not add exactly due to rounding.
Sources: Adapted from data in *Federal Reserve Bulletin*, April 1981. p. A52; and *Economic Report of the President*, 1984, pp. 332–333 and 344–345.

4. If investment by Canada in the United States results in a "receipt" or positive effect on our balance of payments in the capital account, does this mean that it is necessarily good for the United States to have this investment? Why or why not?

5. What would be an example of a merchandise export? A government transfer payment? If you took $1000 out of your bank and put it in a bank in London, what effect would it have in the balance of payments accounts?

Further Notes on the Balance of Payments

When reporters, economists, and politicians speak of balance-of-payments "deficits" (outflows of dollars) and "surpluses" (inflows of dollars), they are referring only to the transactions in the current and capital accounts—and not in the balancing cash, gold, or bond accounts. Often this is referred to as the **basic balance** and includes the balance on the current account added to the long-term capital movements. This basic balance will normally show a payments deficit (payments > receipts) or surplus (receipts > payments).

If one looks only at the merchandise balance in the current account, which is called the **balance of trade,** one finds that the U.S. "balance" has often been a surplus. In other words, exports were greater than imports for every year from 1893 until 1971. In the 1970s and 1980s, however, the balance of trade has shown deficits—large ones in the late 1970s—and enormous trade deficits through the mid-1980s. The trade deficits of the early to mid-1970s were primarily due to the large increase in the price of imported oil. During the 1980s the trade deficits have been caused by a very strong dollar, which has made U.S. goods much more expensive than imported goods. This has decreased U.S. exports and increased foreign imports. If these conditions continue, trade deficits will continue to increase above the record $125 billion set in 1984.

These trade deficits have also increased the deficit in the basic balance. Now there is a deficit in *both* the current and capital accounts, creating even larger deficits in the basic balance. The capital account is usually heavily in deficit since it shows U.S. corporate investment in foreign nations. A high value of the dollar stimulates imports and restricts exports, slows economic recovery through the rest of the world, and promotes import restraint among the debt-plagued Third World nations. Let's examine how the value or the exchange rate of the dollar is determined and how it influences the balance of payments.

One of the problems that a nation encounters in trade, just as in life, is that it must pay for the goods and services received. In your own case, you can use either cash or an IOU. In the international sphere there are several alternatives. Payments are accepted in cash (dollars), gold, or Special Drawing Rights (of which, we will learn more in Chapter 26). If your country's exports exceed its imports, it will have attained a balance-of-payments surplus. The reward for this is increased employment and income at home. The penalty is higher prices. Why? As we export more and more of our goods and services, income (Y) and hence GNP increase. As income increases, consumption increases. (Remember your basic macro model?) As consumption increases, more dollars are competing for fewer domestic goods, and prices will tend to rise.

A payments *deficit* (imports greater than exports) earns your nation's economic and political leaders severe criticism. Contrary to popular opinion, great bolts of lightning will not be fired down from above, but deficits do have their disadvantages. Strains are placed on a nation's gold supply and on its currency with respect to the other currencies. If these strains become too severe, the country's currency will depreciate (be worth less) with respect to other stronger currencies. This means that imported goods will cost more, but that exports will become more attractive to foreign nations.

One final comment should be made on the balance-of-payments statement. It should not be thought that since a particular item is "big," a deficit would be done away with if we removed or reduced that item. For example, opponents of foreign aid have argued that this expenditure was the reason for deficits in the basic trade balance for so many years. This is not true. Over 80 percent of foreign aid is "tied"; that is, it must be spent on goods produced in the United States. So if we cut foreign aid by $1 billion, our exports would be reduced by $800 million! The gain would be very small indeed. Many of the items in the balance of payments are related to other items in this way.

It is, however, legitimate to note that since a particular item is in surplus, the country has the freedom to run up a deficit in some other item without creating pressure against its currency. This sort of situation can be created in either of two ways: (1) there may be items that in the working out of "basic economic forces" generate a surplus, or (2) other countries in the world economy may "allow" deficits to exist without exerting pressure for policy measures that would reduce them. An example of the former is the flow of investment income into the United States. The net income on U.S. investments abroad allows the United States, among other things, to increase its ownership of factories and mines in other countries and finance military expenditures abroad.

THE BALANCE OF PAYMENTS AND THE VALUE OF THE DOLLAR

During the 1970s the U.S. dollar experienced a spectacular decline, and the period between 1980 and 1985 found the dollar experiencing an even more spectacular rise. The decline in the 1970s reflected major weaknesses in the U.S. economy. Economic growth had slowed and Germany and Japan had with some success challenged the United States for economic leadership. This challenge, plus rapid and continuing inflation, made the dollar a currency to avoid. Currency prices, like the prices of goods and services, are determined by supply and demand factors. Since nations were demanding increasing amounts of German and Japanese products, those currencies were in demand and were thus rising in value. At the same time the

United States experienced trade deficits, which, with the exception of 1975, have grown larger each year. This is significant, since one would expect that the lower value of the dollar would have stimulated U.S. exports and reduced imports. High inflation rates in the United States made institutions and investors skeptical about the long-term stability of the currency, so that the demand for marks and yen increased as well.

The value of a nation's currency, or the currency's **exchange rate,** is determined by supply and demand factors. Supply factors are generally controlled by the central bank, but demand for a nation's currency is determined by a number of things. The most obvious are the demand for a nation's products and the prices of those products. The lower the price of the product(s), the greater the demand, and thus the greater the demand for the nation's currency, since currency is needed to purchase the product(s). Other determinants of demand would be tastes and preferences, population, prices of substitute and complementary goods, and income levels. In Fig. 24.2 an increased demand for German-produced BMW's in the United States increases the demand for marks, and thus increases the exchange rate of the mark in terms of dollars. Each dollar will purchase fewer marks as the price of marks in dollars rises.

Given the current trade deficits, it would seem that the value of the dollar should be falling with respect to many other currencies, since the demand for U.S. exports is low and the demand for imported goods is high. But, there are other factors affecting the demand for a nation's currency. Nontrade pressures, or things that aren't influenced by the demand for a nation's products, are dramatically influencing the value or the exchange rate of the dollar. Currencies are used not only to purchase goods and services, they are also used to make money—that is, to earn a rate of return, or interest. The Fed's tightening of monetary policy in the fall of 1979 did curb the growth rate of the money supply, but the resulting higher interest rate and a growing confidence that the United States was a "safe haven" for assets created a

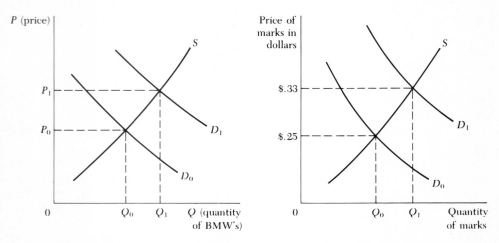

Figure 24.2 Supply and demand for marks and BMW's.

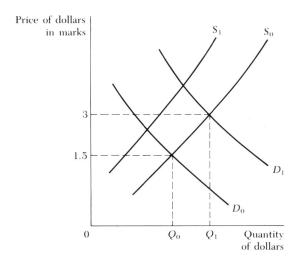

Price of dollars
in marks

Figure 24.3   Supply and demand for dollars.

demand for dollars among foreign corporations and investors. In Fig. 24.3 the Fed's reduction in the growth rate of the money supply is shown by the shift in the supply curve from S_0 to S_1. The higher interest rate attracts foreign investment and thus increases the demand for dollars from D_0 to D_1.

In our example (Fig. 24.3) we see that the dollar is very strong. That means that it will command or purchase a larger quantity of other foreign currencies and thus more foreign goods and services. Here we see that prior to the Fed's contractionary monetary policy $1 would purchase only 1.5 marks. With increases in demand, $1 now purchases 3 marks. German products are now relatively cheaper for U.S. consumers. That will tend to increase German (foreign) imports, which increases the tendency for the balance of trade to run a deficit. At the same time, 1 mark now commands fewer dollars. Initially 1 mark could command or purchase $.66, or 66 cents worth of U.S. products. Now 1 mark can purchase only $.33. This means that each U.S. product now costs German consumers more. Even though the prices of our products have not changed in absolute terms, for a German consumer they are relatively higher since the dollar-purchasing power of the mark has been reduced. This, of course, means that fewer U.S. goods are exported since their prices are higher to foreign consumers. And this leads to further deterioration in the balance of trade.

Since the fall of 1979 the dollar has been on an upward roll, reaching new highs against most European currencies each day in early 1985 (see Fig. 24.4). Clearly, many other factors have been responsible for the sustained value of the dollar, including the high U.S. budget deficits. In the following article Martin Feldstein, former Chairman of the Council of Economic Advisors under Reagan, accounts for these and summarizes how trade and the balance of payments has reacted to the value of the dollar during the early 1980s.

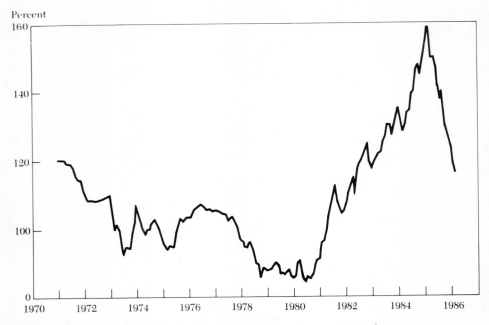

Figure 24.4 The trade-weighted value of the dollar. *Source:* Federal Reserve Bank of Cleveland, *Economic Commentary*, March 15, 1986.

WHY THE DOLLAR IS STRONG

Martin Feldstein

Since 1980, the exchange value of the dollar has increased nearly 50 percent relative to the other major currencies of the world after adjusting for differences in inflation. Why has the dollar risen so much? There is no single reason, but I believe that the primary cause has been the mix of fiscal and monetary policies: the large projected budget deficits combined with the expectation that the Federal Reserve will not permit the deficits to increase the rate of inflation in the United States. Both aspects of the fiscal-monetary mix are important, though several other factors have contributed to the strength of the dollar.

SOME BASIC IDEAS

To explain the effects of fiscal and monetary policies on exchange rates, it is necessary to begin by establishing some basic ideas about international

(continued)

Reprinted with permission of M. E. Sharpe, Inc., publisher, Armonk, NY, from January/February 1984 *Challenge.*

finance. The most fundamental of these is the distinction between the *nominal* exchange rate and the *real* exchange rate. To be specific, let me discuss the exchange rate between the dollar and the German mark. The nominal exchange rate is simply the number of German marks that can be purchased per dollar. The real exchange rate adjusts this ratio of currency units for different movements in the price levels within the two countries. Thus, in 1980, $100 could be exchanged for 182 German marks. In contrast, at the beginning of last October, $100 could be exchanged for 262 German marks. The nominal exchange value of the dollar relative to the mark thus rose 44 percent.

The effect on international trade of this rise in the number of marks per dollar depends on what happened to domestic prices in Germany and the United States during the same period. If the level of German prices had risen by 44 percent relative to the level of American prices during these three years, the rise in the nominal exchange value of the dollar would only have offset the change in relative domestic prices. The purchasing power of a dollar in the United States relative to its purchasing power in Germany would not have changed. In the language of international finance, the real exchange rate would not have changed; therefore, the incentives to import and export would not have changed.

In fact, the price level in Germany did not rise relative to the level of American prices during the past three years. Since 1980, the U.S. price level has risen 22 percent and the German price level has risen 16 percent. Adjusting the dollar's 44-percent *nominal* appreciation relative to the mark for this shift in domestic prices implies that the dollar's *real* value relative to the mark has risen 51 percent since 1980. This means that a dollar now buys some 51 percent more in Germany, relative to its purchasing power in the United States, than it did in 1980.

It is the rise in the real exchange value of the dollar relative to the other major currencies of the world that is the main reason for the substantial trade deficit that the American economy is now experiencing. (The other reasons for the trade deficit now are (1) the relative cyclical position of the United States and our major trading partners and (2) the contraction of imports by the OPEC countries and by the debtor nations. . . .) These trade deficits reflect a substantial decline in U.S. exports and a large rise in U.S. imports. Both of these trends are doing very substantial damage to major segments of American industry. Moreover, to pay for these huge trade deficits, the United States is being forced to reduce our stock of overseas investments and to borrow abroad. . . .

TRADE PREFERENCES

The changes in real exchange rates reflect changes in either trade preferences or investment preferences. To focus first on changes in trade prefer-

(continued)

ences, assume for the moment that there is no change in foreigners' desire to hold U.S. assets or in the rate of return on those assets.

If foreigners increase their demand for American goods, the dollar will rise; if Americans increase their demand for foreign goods, the dollar will decline. It is perhaps easiest and most natural to think of this change in the dollar's value as a direct result of the change in the demand for dollars or for foreign currency. There is another and perhaps clearer way of explaining why the dollar falls when Americans spontaneously increase their demand for foreign goods. The resulting increase in American imports causes a trade deficit. Since a trade deficit cannot persist indefinitely, something must change to make American exports more attractive to foreigners and foreign products less attractive to Americans. That change is a fall in the value of the dollar.

During the period when imports by Americans do exceed our exports to the rest of the world, foreigners must accept additional dollar securities in exchange for our excess imports. In different words, we finance the excess imports by borrowing from the rest of the world or by selling U.S. assets to foreigners. This accommodating flow of credit or capital to the United States is an inevitable corollary of the trade deficit.

INVESTMENT PREFERENCES

Consider now the effect of a change in investment preferences that causes Americans or foreigners to want to shift the mix of their investments between the United States and the rest of the world. (To focus on this change in investment preferences, assume that there is no change in trade preferences for American or foreign goods.) A change in investment preferences that causes an increase in the real value of the dollar might come about because investors consider the United States to be a safer place to have their investments, or because the real rate of return on dollar investments rises. In either case, investors will sell foreign currencies and buy dollars, thereby raising the dollar's value.

Note that a consequence of the dollar's higher value is to make U.S. exports less competitive and foreign goods more attractive to American buyers. The dollar's higher value thus worsens a trade deficit. Once again, the excess imports are financed by a flow of credit or capital from the rest of the world to the United States. The increase in the U.S. trade deficit equals the net increase in the capital inflow to the United States. But this time, the change in investment preferences is the basic cause and the trade deficit is the accommodating flow of goods.

THE DOLLAR IN THE '80s

The increase in the real exchange value of the dollar since 1980 has been due to a change in investment preferences rather than a change in trade

(continued)

preferences. The dollar has strengthened because investors want to hold dollar investments and the strong dollar has induced an accommodating trade deficit.

One possible reason for the increased attractiveness of U.S. investments has been the sense that the safety of investing in the United States may have increased relative to the safety of investing elsewhere. This in turn may reflect such things as a greater confidence in American resistance to inflationary pressures and the increased turmoil in many less developed countries. It is difficult to know how much weight should be attributed to this, especially since recent political developments in several European countries have increased investor confidence in those countries as well.

A second reason for the increased attractiveness of dollar securities and the rise in the real value of the dollar has been the substantial decline in the expected rate of inflation since 1980. Although the main long-term effect of a lower rate of inflation is to reduce the ongoing erosion of the dollar's *nominal* value, leaving its *real* value unchanged, the reduction in inflation and in the expected future rate of inflation do have significant short-term effects on the dollar's real value. When inflation began to fall in 1981, the real rate of interest in the United States temporarily increased significantly. The higher real rate of interest here relative to that in other countries attracted investments from other currencies to dollar assets, thereby causing the real value of the dollar to rise temporarily. Of course, the effect of the decline in the inflation rate on the real interest rate is only temporary. It cannot explain a continued persistence of high real interest rates.

Investors worldwide are confident that, despite the large projected U.S. budget deficits, the Federal Reserve will not pursue an inflationary monetary policy. This confidence prevents deterioration of both the real and nominal exchange rates. A perceived shift by the Federal Reserve toward an inflationary monetary policy would be likely to cause an immediate decline in the nominal and real values of the dollar and a continuing erosion of the dollar's nominal value.

Inflation expectations are thus the key to understanding the apparent paradox that the U.S. budget deficit has strengthened the dollar while in so many other countries large budget deficits have been associated with falling currency values. In other countries, budget deficits have often been monetized and accompanied by inflation and by falling nominal currency values. It is the often substantial and persistent fall in *nominal* exchange rates that causes the public to associate budget deficits with declining currency values. Moreover, budget deficits abroad have often been associated with periods of excessive domestic demand that cause a rise in imports and decline in exports, directly reducing the real exchange rate. Once this is understood, there is nothing surprising about the fact that the dollar has appreciated in the face of enlarged budget deficits.

(continued)

SAVING AND INVESTMENT SHIFTS

The third major source of the enhanced appeal of dollar investments has been the shifts in the balance between savings and investment in the United States and in other countries. Unlike changes in the rate of inflation, shifts in the balance between saving and investment can cause sustained changes in real rates of return. When these shifts cause the real rate of return on U.S. securities to rise relative to the return on securities abroad, investors will be attracted to dollar securities and the exchange value of the dollar will rise. Indeed, the dollar's value must rise by enough so that its expected subsequent decline will balance the higher risk-adjusted return on dollar assets.

The real rate of return on U.S. securities has risen substantially since 1980. The interest rate then on commercial paper averaged 12.3 percent and the inflation rate, measured by the Consumer Price Index, was 12.4 percent, implying a real interest rate that was approximately zero. Now that same commercial paper pays an interest rate of about 8.9 percent but consumer prices have risen at a rate of only 4.7 percent for the past six months. The implied real interest rate is thus about 4 percent. Such a real rate is very much higher than the American economy has seen in the past several decades. . . .

Moreover, while the real interest rates on comparable dollar securities and German mark securities were previously very similar, the real yield on dollar securities is now much higher. Although the inflation rates in Germany and the United States are now very similar, a three-month Eurodollar deposit yields 9.4 percent while a comparable Eurocurrency deposit in German marks yields only 5.8 percent. The yield differentials are similar on other types of assets and longer maturities. . . .

At the same time, European saving rates have remained relatively high, putting downward pressure on the potential rate of return in Europe. . . . [The] increasing . . . gap between the return on dollar investments and other investments has been [caused by] the sharp decline in net national savings in the United States.

The rise in the U.S. budget deficit has of course been the basic cause of the decline in our national saving rate. For the three decades from 1950 through 1979, the total savings of households, businesses, and state and local governments, net of economic depreciation, averaged 7.6 percent of GNP. During these years, the federal government had deficits averaging less than one percent of GNP, leaving net national savings of 6.9 percent of GNP. Since 1980, the net savings rate of households, businesses, and state-local governments has been somewhat lower than in the past, averaging 6.8 percent of GNP. But the federal deficit rose to 3.6 percent of GNP in fiscal year 1982 and 6.1 percent of GNP in fiscal year 1983. Net national saving fell from its customary 7 percent of GNP to only 1.5 per-

(continued)

cent of GNP in 1982 and 1.5 percent of GNP in the first three quarters of 1983. In addition, and of particular importance, the large budget deficits that are projected for the next five years and beyond if no legislative action is taken mean that our net national saving rate will continue to remain far below the previous level.

That is the essential explanation of the strong dollar: the high real long-term interest rate in the United States, combined with the sense that dollar investments are relatively safe and that American inflation will remain low, induces investors worldwide to shift in favor of dollar securities. Moreover, the unusually high real long-term interest rate here relative to the real rates abroad is now due primarily to the low projected national savings rate caused by the large projected budget deficits.

THE DOLLAR WILL DECLINE

What about the future? Even if there is no change in policies, the real value of the dollar will eventually decline under the weight of accumulating trade deficits and a growing volume of foreign investments in the United States. Since there is some limit as to how much in U.S. securities foreigners will be willing to hold, the dollar must eventually fall enough to balance the current account (i.e., the merchandise trade deficit minus U.S. earnings on foreign investments, services, and transfers).

A decline in the dollar's real value would help reduce the very large trade deficits that now hurt many industries. Exports would increase and imports would decline. Even before the trade flows adjusted significantly to the dollar's decline, the dollar's more competitive value would renew confidence among American firms engaged in international competition and therefore reduce the tendency of such firms to establish branches abroad or to look for foreign sources of inputs for U.S. products.

In the absence of a change in economic policy, no one can be sure how long it will take for the dollar to decline and whether it will proceed smoothly or by a sudden shift induced by a loss of confidence. For example, although the futures market implies that the dollar is expected to fall only about 4 percent relative to the mark over the next twelve months, it would not be surprising in the volatile foreign exchange market to see the dollar decline by more than 10 percent next year—or even to see the real value of the dollar continue to rise.

A change in policy could, of course, increase the likelihood of a more rapid shift of the dollar toward its long-term sustainable level. Some changes that could speed the dollar's decline—such as policies to reduce the safety of investing in the United States or a shift toward a more inflationary monetary policy—would clearly be against our best interest. The main hope for reducing the dollar's real value and thereby stimulating U.S.

(continued)

net exports is to increase the net national saving rate in the United States by increasing private savings or by reducing the budget deficit.

More precisely, since the dollar's value reflects real long-term interest rates and therefore the expected future balance of domestic saving and investment, an increase in expected future private saving or a decrease in the expected future budget deficit would cause a current decline in the dollar's real value. Those who sense the urgency of shifting the dollar's value to a more competitive level will recognize the need for immediate policy action to raise expected future national savings by substantially shrinking future budget deficits or increasing future private saving.

6. **What would be the effect on the exchange rate if the Fed followed a policy of monetary ease that led to rapid inflation? Explain.**

7. **List three reasons the dollar was so appealing for foreign investors during 1980–1985.**

8. **How does a federal budget deficit affect the balance of payments? Why is the savings rate important?**

9. **What do you expect will happen in the near future to the current account balance for the United States vis-à-vis Western Europe? How about the capital account balance with the poor countries?**

10. **Would you rather see the dollar strong or weak? Which way would General Motors rather see it? Explain.**

Since this article was written in 1984 the predictions made by Feldstein have come to pass. In early 1985 the dollar peaked and started a downward decline, particularly against the German mark and Japanese yen. In September of 1985, the Group of Five (the United States, the United Kingdom, France, West Germany, and Japan—also known as G5,) agreed to intervene in foreign exchange markets to lower the value of the soaring dollar in order to promote a more even-handed economic growth. By April 1986, the dollar had reached its post–World War II low against the yen as interest rates in the United States and oil prices continued to fall. The Bank of Japan was compelled to purchase dollars for a while to halt the upward pressure on the yen. The period between 1971 and 1986 then shows a complete cycle of exchange rate movements that respond to domestic inflation, interest rates and intervention in currency markets.

TRADE AND THE INTERNATIONALIZATION OF PRODUCTION: ELEMENTS OF ECONOMIC INTERDEPENDENCE

Trade and Interdependence

One of the major ways to examine economic interdependence is by looking at the nature of international trade. By examining relevant trade data and identifying the major trade trends since 1950, we can begin to appreciate the nature of contemporary interdependence. The following observations and generalizations can be made from these data.

Between 1950 and 1970 most nations exported increasing shares of their GNPs. This affirmed the notion that nations tend to increase exports as percentage of their GNPs as they develop. Between 1965 and 1980 all categories of nations increased exports as a percentage of gross domestic product (GDP),* although the less developed nations' share increased substantially less than the exports share of GDP in more developed economies (see Table 24.3). The U.S. share of total world trade is also increasing and that trade is approximately 17.3 percent of our GDP.

These observations demonstrate clearly that the role of international trade is growing with respect to national economies. However, the *magnitude* of the trade among nations is not necessarily the best indicator of international *interdependence*. More often the specialization and composition of trade among nations demonstrates its importance. For example, agricultural trade and trade in technology have recently highlighted the economic interdependence among many nations, while a decade ago petroleum trade was more significant.

Internationalization of Production and Interdependence

A second major way to examine economic interdependence is to look at the **internationalization of production.** This dimension of interdependence can be analyzed by examining the capital flows among nations (rather than the flows of trade).

Table 24.3 EXPORTS OF GOODS AND SERVICES AS A PERCENTAGE OF GDP

	1965	1970	1981
Low income nations	8.0	8.7	9.0
Middle income nations	14.2	17.7	28.4
Industrial market nations	11.7	13.4	19.8

Source: World Tables: Economic Data; Washington D.C.: The World Bank, 1983, p. 500

*Gross domestic product (GDP) is the sum of the production inside the geographic boundaries of a nation.

Some of these capital movements have taken the form of foreign investment and have included the process of the internationalization of capital and labor. This process is more readily understood by tracing the history of the operations of multinational corporations. It is these institutions more than any others that have created a new international division of labor on a global scale.

The multinational corporation (MNC) is a feature of this century, having matured in the post–World War II period. A typical U.S. multinational's history might read: The corporation begins its initial production for the U.S. market only; next it creates a factory abroad because of inexpensive labor and the accessibility of raw materials; and finally, the new foreign subsidiary's production is distributed in the local economy, and some is exported back to the United States. When a U.S. firm either builds a production facility or takes over an existing facility in another nation, direct investment occurs.

The modern expansion of the operations of MNC's has lead to an internationalization of production on a global scale. People in many countries are now dependent on decisions made in boardrooms of corporations in New York, Stuttgart, or Tokyo for their jobs and the products they consume. Individual MNC's based in the U.S. are increasingly dependent on other countries for their labor, resources, and markets to a far greater extent than that suggested by the U.S. export/GNP ratio. As this one major institution internationalizes, so must social, economic, political, and cultural institutions.

MNC-related capital movements gradually transfer the control of the accumulation and allocation of capital from institutions that are essentially national in character to MNC's and financial institutions that are global in their orientation. Each national economy is more thoroughly integrated into the world capital market and is increasingly affected by events that take place in other national economies. Multinationalization breeds increasing interdependence. Many are reluctant to grant so much freedom of operation to one private-sector institution. State and provincial governments have called for the control of MNC's. Plans to regulate MNC's abound. The MNCs' vision of one, homogenized world of consumers, all with similar tastes and life-styles—Coca-Colanization, as it is called—is a cause for concern. This concern, in fact, is part of the desire of some countries to create a "new international economic order."

The next two chapters treat the historical evolution of international trading and financial relations, as well as the major body of theory economists use to examine this interdependence. The topics in this chapter should be kept in mind when we examine the problems confronting the developing nations of the Third World and their demand for a "new international economic order."

KEY CONCEPTS

economic interdependence	balance of trade
balance of payments	exchange rate
current account	exchange rate determinants
capital account	internationalization of production
basic balance	

REVIEW QUESTIONS

1. How has increasing international interdependence since 1945 affected the nature of the relationship between industrial nations and the Third World?

2. If you were Minister for the Economy in a developing nation, how would you respond to the advice of a development economist from the United States that your country's best strategy for economic growth was to "fit itself" into the liberal world economic order?

3. What are the linkages among nations that have been most important in increasing interdependence in the world economy today?

4. When we say that the world economy is characterized by interdependence, does this mean that all nations are equally dependent on other nations, or are some nations more dominant and others more dependent? Why is that so?

5. What effect does a balance-of-payments deficit generally have on the value of a nation's currency? What effect does a surplus have?

6. What factors determine the rate of exchange between two currencies?

7. How can the decline in the value of the dollar in the 1970s and its subsequent rise in the 1980s be explained in the face of an increasing trade deficit?

8. How do multinational corporations lead to greater economic interdependence among nations?

SUGGESTED READINGS

Dave E. Apter and Louis Wolf Goodman, 1976. *The Multinational Corporation and Social Change*, Praeger. An excellent series of essays exploring every facet of MNC behavior. Especially recommended is Chapter 8, "The Multinational Corporation and Development: A Contradiction?" by Harry Magdoff.

Richard J. Barnet and Ronald E. Muller, 1974. *Global Reach*, Simon and Schuster. One of the most authoritative studies on multinational corporations. Part I gives an overview of the historical development of the MNC. Part II treats the impact of the MNC on the Third World. Part III analyzes the impact of the MNC on the United States and concludes with some thoughts about how to reform the MNC.

Jagdish N. Bhagwati (ed.), 1972. *Economics and World Order: From the 1970's to the 1990's*, Macmillan. A collection of essays dealing with global interdependence. We recommend the introduction and Chapter 2, "Global Perspectives." Also, we strongly urge you to look at Chapter 4, "The Multinational Corporation and the Law of Uneven Development."

John Deverell and the Latin American Working Group, 1975. *Falconbridge—Portrait of a Canadian Mining Multinational*, Lorimer. An excellent biography of a MNC.

Anthony Sampson, 1974. *The Sovereign State of ITT*, Fawcett. Another "biography" of a prominent MNC and its effects on economic interdependence.

Joan Edelman Spero, 1981. *The Politics of International Economic Relations*, St. Martin's. A good summary of international economic events and their consequences in the post–World War II period.

25 Chapter

International Trade and Protectionism

INTRODUCTION

International trade continues to be one of the more intensely discussed areas of economics. Political parties have at times justified their existence by campaigning for or against **free trade.** The logic behind this debate has kept economists bickering for the past two centuries. It is the question of comparative advantage: how nations have actively pursued specialization in a few lines of production for export, thus imposing on themselves a dependency or absolute reliance on others for products that may be crucial to their style and standard of living. Of course, this has not been done frivolously or out of allegiance to some obscure political philosophy. The theoretical payoff from specialization and exchange among nations is that world output will be maximized and that this maximum output is possible through free unhindered trade. The benefits of free trade were not, however, immediately apparent to people, and once free trade was adopted by England in the latter half of the 19th century, a countermovement toward **protectionism** soon developed.

This chapter examines the theory behind international trade and presents some of the more convincing arguments for protection. It concludes with a look at the current confrontation between free traders and protectionists.

THE MODERN THEORY OF INTERNATIONAL TRADE

1. How will you be matched with the work you will do for your working life? What will be your "specialty"?

The very same question is confronted for the world economy as a whole. How does an individual nation "fit into" the world economy? Why does one nation specialize in production of ground nuts; a second, textiles; a third, aircraft; and a fourth, financial services? Adam Smith was the first economist to deal with this question meaningfully, and in 1817 David Ricardo refined Smith's ideas. It is this general approach that we still use today. The basic concepts are **absolute** and **comparative advantage.** The model of trade follows from these concepts.

Who Trades What? And Why?

A comparative advantage means that one nation can produce a product relatively, not absolutely, more efficiently than another nation, while a nation with an absolute advantage can produce a variety of products more effectively than another. Trade is expanded when nations produce products with which they possess a relative or comparative advantage.

In the following example we can see what happens to total output of two goods (here, units of wheat and cloth) when trade occurs. We can also use a production possibilities curve to help us understand the effect of trade on total output. We don't know the sizes of these countries' labor forces so we can't calculate total output precisely, but it would be consistent with our hypothetical costs and rates of exchange to assume the following:

	TOTAL COUNTRY PRODUCTION		
	WHEAT		CLOTH
U.K.	2000	or	1000
France	2400	or	800

If each country has no international trade and uses half of its resources to produce each good to meet its own domestic demands, total world output will be:

	TOTAL WORLD OUTPUT (WITHOUT TRADE)	
	WHEAT	CLOTH
U.K.	1000	500
France	1200	400
Total	2200	900

This example is illustrated in the production possibilities curves in Fig. 25.1

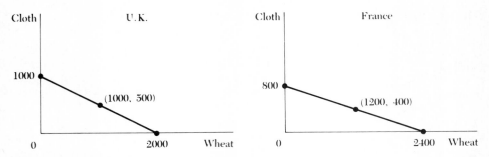

Figure 25.1   Production possibilities without trade.

But if France specializes in wheat production and the United Kingdom special-izes in cloth, and if each exchanges some of that good for its needs of the other commodity, then world output becomes:

TOTAL WORLD OUTPUT
(WITH SPECIALIZATION AND TRADE)

	WHEAT	CLOTH
U.K.		1000
France	2400	
Total	2400	1000

France produces wheat and uses some for domestic consumption and exports the rest. The United Kingdom produces cloth and uses some for domestic consumption and exports the rest. After trading, we might get a result like the following:

	WHEAT	CLOTH
U.K.	1200	500
France	1200	500
Total	2400	1000

Figure 25.2 shows the production possibilities curves of the United Kingdom and France with trade.

2. Who has gained what through specialization and trade?

Thus if each nation specializes in the product in which it has a comparative advantage, world output of both commodities is increased—in this case by 100 units

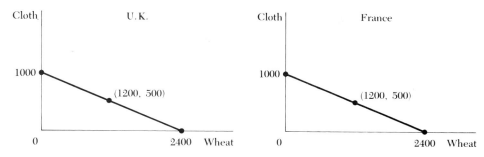

Figure 25.2   Production possibilities with trade.

of cloth and 200 units of wheat. If there is a reasonable distribution of this gain from specialization and trade, both countries are better off than they would be in the absence of trade. This is the essence, then, of the argument for free trade.

We now turn to a consideration of free trade theory and then we will examine the case for restricted trade—or protectionism.

CLASSICAL LIBERALISM AND FREE TRADE

The philosophy of classical liberalism was the first to advocate international as well as domestic free trade. The classical liberal belief in self-regulating markets was projected to the international level, where, again, laissez-faire prevailed. The development of this argument, it should be remembered, took place in the context of increasing international economic activity accompanying the emergence of capitalism in Western Europe. Free traders compiled an impressive list of benefits that should accrue to society as a whole if their policy were to be adopted. In general, proponents of free trade argued and *still* argue (1) that world output will be increased through a more "rational" and "efficient" use of the world's resources and (2) that the increase in production be equitably shared among all who participate in free trade.

RESTRICTIONS TO FREE TRADE—PROTECTIONISM

Free trade exists if there are no barriers to the export and import of goods and services. Though most economists have argued hard and long for some 200 years for free trade, nations have nonetheless felt impelled for just as many years to erect barriers to inhibit free international exchange. There are many types of trade restrictions that a nation might utilize, but the most common have been tariffs and quotas. **Tariffs** are simply *taxes* on the goods imported or exported, while **quotas** are limits on the *quantities* of goods imported or exported.

There are many reasons for establishing tariff and quota barriers between nations. Most often they are designed to protect some interest in the home country. In general, tariffs are successful in their objective—they protect a special interest at the expense of the whole population. In other words, a few people are helped a lot while all citizens are hurt a little as a result of paying higher prices for the goods and services on which tariff duties are imposed.

Special interest groups often appeal to Congress for a protective tariff. The textile industry has asked and received protection from cheaper foreign textile products. These tariffs increase the price of all textiles in the United States. The U.S. consumers are, in effect, subsidizing an inefficient industry—one in which we do not possess a comparative advantage.

During the Depression, the Smoot-Hawley tariff was levied to keep money in the country and to keep wages and employment levels as high as possible. Would the economy be led to high levels of income and employment and would money remain in the country with the extremely high Smoot-Hawley tariff? Let's see how economists use the Smoot-Hawley era to express their frustration toward protective tariffs. In 1971 several thousand economists signed a petition against the Burke-Hartke Trade Bill. This was an attempt to move the country toward a policy of increased protection for domestic producers. In arguing their case the economists referred to the Smoot-Hawley Tariff of the 1930s.

> Forty years ago, in the midst of a growing economic crisis at home and abroad, Congress enacted and the President signed the highest tariff in the nation's history. This curbed the ability of foreign nations to sell to us and hence their ability to buy from us. Our higher tariffs induced other democracies to *retaliate* with higher tariffs against our goods, notably farm products and machinery. Our exports shrivelled, intensifying our unemployment and deepening the Depression. The dollar weakened. The fabric of international cooperation further unraveled. Economic depression spread. Democracy floundered in many parts of the world. These were the seeds of World War II.

The same scenario, they argued, would unfold if the nation reversed the post–World War II trend of tariff reduction that had by the 1960s alleviated the trade hardships created by the Smoot-Hawley tariff.

But included in the protectionist's argument is another reason for tariff levies—retaliation. Tariffs have been increased many times in response to tariff increases by trading partners. The Smoot-Hawley tariff, for example, set off a worldwide round of tariff increases. This "do unto others as they have done unto you" philosophy has also been used simply for the sake of self-esteem. As a result, consumers in both nations pay the higher price. And, at worst, such **retaliation** can compound recession into worldwide depression.

At times there are proposals that Congress should levy tariffs for the purpose of raising revenue since the proceeds from the tax are collected by the government. This is well and good, but there are many ways of raising revenue that are more effective. Besides, if the tariff prices the imported good above that of the domestic product, no revenue will be collected since the consumer will be priced out of the import market and will purchase only the domestic product.

Another protectionist argument centers on the need to reduce the competition of cheap foreign labor. In the 1950s, a Houston oil and cotton magnate responded to the free trade argument by stating, "The only thing that made our country great is the protective tariff to protect us from the cheap labor abroad. Those people haven't developed in two thousand years. They've been letting the flies eat their children's eyes out all that time. If they take our tariff off, it's just a matter of time before the American people will be living like them."

3. **How do you think the "cheap labor abroad" would respond to this argument? Do you think they might be concerned by the financial service exports of the United States? Would they, too, argue for protection?**

Other arguments on trade policy have run from the rather dry and abstract to the invective. The "national defense" argument falls into both categories. The merchant marine and the oil industry have argued for protection since they are essential in times of national emergency. The cotton industry also requested a tariff for these reasons, presumably on the basis that no decent nation could run the risk of having an army forced to fight in the nude for want of good cotton clothing.

4. **The oil industry was protected for "defense" reasons by import quotas during the period from 1954 to 1973. How did these protective quotas, designed to encourage U.S. oil production, work during the oil embargo of 1973?**

NEOMERCANTILISM

What we are witnessing today is the fundamental clash of national policies which are primarily oriented towards solving domestic political and social problems. . . . Multilateral discussions are at a standstill. There has been a rise in mercantilist sentiment in most of the world. . . .

This neomercantilism is a profoundly disruptive force in international relations. It takes many forms. . . . In the case of the Common Agricultural Policy [of the European Economic Community] for example, the Europeans have taxed imports, thus reducing import sales while gaining revenues. The revenues are used to push domestic surpluses onto world markets, further taxing the exports of competitors by depressing their potential profits elsewhere. All exporters thus end up paying part of the cost of Europe's social program for its rural population. The American textile restriction program has a similar effect. It penalizes Asian exporters and American consumers in order to provide special benefits to Southern mills in areas of low wages and high availability of black labor. Neomercantilism, sector by sector, whether aimed at industry relief or rural poverty, must inevitably repress the interests of other countries, in particular sectors, in particular regions.

Harald B. Malmgren, "Coming Trade Wars?" *Foreign Policy* (Winter): 1970–1971, 115–143.

5. If a nation does encourage free trade, what happens to the "Southern mills," "low wages," and "black labor"?

In the post–World War II period, there has been a marked movement away from the excessive protection of the Depression years. This has been accomplished primarily through international negotiations in organizations such as the **General Agreement on Tariffs and Trade (GATT).**

There have been, of course, disagreements between nations on goods that should be exempt from tariff reductions and on tariff levels that should be aimed for; although the enthusiasm of reductions of the 1960s has given way to protectionist sentiments of the 1970s and 1980s, noteworthy accomplishments have been made.

The protectionist tendencies were particularly prevalent during 1975 and 1979 as the impact of severe recessions were felt throughout the world and as countries competed for a shrinking export market. Yet calls for protection did not cease during the 1983–1984 recovery. Many industries still reeling from the severe recession and threatened by growing imports continued to press for sanctions. The U.S. steel industry lobbied for protection from imports. So did the automobile industry, tobacco growers, clothing manufacturers, and even the mushroom and clothespin industries. Other nations also received complaints from their industries along with requests for greater tariff protection. The cry that has been raised is "Let's stop exporting jobs and stop importing products that compete with our industries."

The most recent attempts to reduce barriers to trade were the Multilateral Trade Negotiations, or the Tokyo Rounds. They were concluded in 1979 after five years of negotiation over tariff reductions and the elimination of nontariff impediments and distortions to trade. Some 99 nations participated in these talks. The agreements included a surprising amount of protection for various special-interest groups, leading some observers to suggest that if trade barriers are to be reduced in the future, it will be important to make sure that industries receiving protection are really in need of it, and that they are making attempts to adjust to competition from imports. Efforts must also be made to eliminate foreign subsidies and discrimination that injure U.S. firms.

Neomercantilist Industries: Autos and Steel

Neomercantilist proposals for the last 15 years have been in favor of quotas over tariffs for protection. Tariffs allow the consumer the choice between cheaper domestic goods and more expensive imported products, and allow the quantity purchased by the consumer to be determined by market factors, albeit with an added tax. These taxes go into government coffers since they are assessed and collected by the government. Quotas and so-called voluntary restraints are nonmonetary barriers that absolutely or quantitatively limit imports and thus limit the choice between imported and domestic goods. Importers reap the profits from the higher prices commanded by the limited supply (assuming that there is an inelastic demand for the product). The U.S. Toyota dealer gains from the limits placed on the export of Japanese automobiles.

The estimated consumer cost of all tariff and nontariff restrictions ranges between $10 and $15 billion annually. The cost to consumers of the quota placed on automobiles in 1980 was calculated to be $5 billion.

If trade were liberalized and more imports flowed into the country, domestic production would be replaced. According to the theory of international trade, labor and capital would move out of the affected industries. Unemployment would increase for a period of time, but workers would find their way into more productive areas of employment. Many argue, however, that the costs of underutilized workers and plants, the relocation, and the expense of additional capital all generate large social costs, and that these costs outweigh the price benefits of freer trade.

Protected industries have had a habit of not modernizing as rapidly as they might. Recently, however, the auto industry gained protection when they argued that short-term limits to Japanese auto imports would allow them time to modernize their factories. Japanese auto imports accounted for 10 percent of the market in 1960 and by 1980 reached 25 percent. In 1980 voluntary trade restraints were accepted by the Japanese on automobile exports. Only 1.68 million cars per year were exported between 1981 and 1984. This gave the U.S. auto industry time in which to modernize. By 1984 the U.S. auto industry not only had adjusted, but also had accumulated record profits. These voluntary quotas have cost American consumers dearly. Not only are many desirable Japanese imports unavailable, but importers are successfully adding a premium to the sticker price.

During the time the voluntary restraints have been in place, Japanese automakers have not been idle. They have been modernizing their factories as well, with the expectation of succeeding in the more expensive luxury auto market. The Japanese have always been quick to enter new markets when other markets have been closed to them. This has often meant hardships for additional industries in the protected country. When trade restrictions were placed on steel imports, the Japanese began entering the speciality steel market, one in which the U.S. producers had been dominant. Now, U.S. speciality steel producers are requesting protection since the Japanese have entered that market in full force.

The 1984 Democratic party platform called for the passage of domestic content legislation. This type of legislation would ensure that some components of foreign-made automobiles, and perhaps other foreign-made products, would be produced in the United States. While Japanese auto imports continue to capture increasing shares of the U.S. market, such legislation would ensure that some U.S. workers contribute to some phase of Japanese auto production, and thus be assured of jobs and income.

6. Would domestic content legislation introduce a new form of protectionism? Explain.

The U.S. steel industry has also felt the pinch from Japan, the EEC, South Korea, and Brazil. During the past decade nearly half the jobs in the American steel industry have been lost due to plant closings. Some 243,000 workers have been affected, as have the communities that house the steel industry. The closures have reduced steel-making capacity by 16 percent, but imported steel has more than made up for the reduction, now capturing some 33 percent of a declining market. Industry analysts predict more closings will be needed if the United States hopes to become competitive in the industry in the future, and hold little hope for modernization of old factories and efficient production of old products. Only movement to the production of high-quality steel products will save the industry, according to these analysts.

The steel industry has reacted by calling for quotas on imported steel. They argued, as did the auto industry, that this would give them time to modernize production. The industry, in fact, persuaded the Reagan Administration to limit steel imports from 1980 to 1985.

INTERNATIONAL TRADE AND PROTECTIONISM

During the past decade there have been a number of instances of controversy surrounding international trade and protection. Nations are quick to subsidize and protect their own industries and to criticize the efforts of other nations who do the same. And there is always the undercurrent of possible retaliation and trade wars similar to those of the 1930s, during which international trade almost disappeared. The following article by Steven Greenhouse traces the history of protectionism and points out the growing number of our nation's industries now calling for some sort of protection.

THE MAKING OF FORTRESS AMERICA

Steven Greenhouse

In recent months, industry after industry has lined up at the President's door asking for help against imports. . . . Steel, copper and machine tools are all waiting for President Reagan to aprove the import quotas they say they need to survive.

They have seen the President award import protection to the nation's textile manufacturers, to Detroit's auto makers, to Milwaukee's Harley-Davidson motorcycle company and to Pennsylvania's specialty steel producers and even its mushroom growers. And now they feel their time has come for relief. While they have turned to the White House, the nation's wine makers and manufacturers of telecommunications equipment have

(continued)

taken a different route, marching to Capitol Hill to demand special trade legislation.

Indeed, with imports at record levels . . ., the pressures to beat back the wave of foreign-made products "are probably the worst they've been since at least 1970," said Robert E. Baldwin, an economics professor and trade expert at the University of Wisconsin.

Product by product, industry and labor are trying to build ever higher the wall against imports. They have filed 200 petitions for relief from imports with the International Trade Commission, which recommends import action to the President. The number of petitions has tripled in just five years.

"What we're seeing is just the beginning," said Stephen P. Magee, a professor of international management at the University of Texas. "The U.S. is going to get more and more protectionist."

President Reagan has responded vigorously to the protectionist pressures. He has gotten Japan to agree to restrict auto shipments to the United States, and the Common Market to cut back steel sales. In addition, he has ordered stiff tariffs on motorcycles and quotas for specialty steel. . . . Administration officials [also] said that they would tighten restrictions on textile imports.

"If you add autos and steel and the tightening on textiles and odds and ends like motorcycles and specialty steel, you're talking about a heck

(continued)

THE REAGAN RECORD ON TRADE—MAJOR TRADE RESTRICTIONS IMPOSED SINCE PRESIDENT REAGAN TOOK OFFICE IN 1981

INDUSTRY AND DATE	ACTION TAKEN
Automobiles January 1981	Three-year agreement limiting import of Japanese autos to 1.65 million per year. New deal in 1984 raises annual ceiling to 1.85 million cars for one more year.
Steel November 1982	Common Market countries agree to U.S. steel quotas and Japan agrees to informal import restraints.
Motorcycles April 1983	A sharp increase in import duties imposed on large motorcycles.
Specialty Steel June 1983	Quotas imposed on imports of high quality, high alloy steel products.
Textiles September 1984	New agreement will tighten the 'rules of origin thereby increasing existing protection for domestic textile producers.

of a lot of trade," said Harald B. Malmgren, a Washington-based trade consultant and a deputy trade representative under Presidents Nixon and Ford. "That's more of an increment in protection than has occurred at any time since 1929–30 and the Smoot-Hawley tariff. It's a very substantial increase in protection."

In granting trade relief in response to protectionist pressures, Mr. Reagan is behaving much like his predecessors—Richard Nixon, Gerald Ford and Jimmy Carter. When he took office, a host of restrictions was already on the books for such goods as sugar, shoes, meat and apparel. In fact, trade rules of one degree or another now protect one-third of all American-made products from foreign competition. And Walter Mondale, the Democratic candidate for President, has indicated that he, too, would continue to build the wall against imports.

Indeed, many trade experts say that the push for protection—and awards of protection—will continue at least for a decade. For months, the strong dollar has made imports less expensive than similar American-made products, and many experts predict that it will remain strong. They add that newly industrialized countries like South Korea, Taiwan and Brazil will continue to operate as highly successful export machines. Only a decade ago these countries were buying steel, appliances and other products from the United States; now they are manufacturing these products and exporting them to America.

"We're losing our competitive advantage in many hard-goods industries," Mr. Magee of the University of Texas said. "As the third world industrializes, they'll be pumping out goods at an astronomical rate. As more and more industries get bombarded, there will be more demands for protection. What we see in automobiles and steel will be mirrored elsewhere."

In fact, some Administration officials say the biggest surprise is not that there are so many calls for protection, but that there are not many more. "When you look at the number of industries that have sought relief, the question should be, 'Why haven't there been more of them?" said Bill Brock, the United States trade representative.

Mr. Brock, who negotiates many of the Administration's trade agreements, takes umbrage at those who charge that by awarding relief against imports, the Administration has turned the United States into an enemy of free trade and a bastion of protectionism.

"We are more open than any other industrialized nation," he said.

That may be, but in the view of many trade experts, the new American protectionism could open up a chamber of economic horrors. Protectionism, they say, is pushing up the price of protected American goods and is taking the pressure off domestic companies to become more efficient. The experts add that it is raising the threat of retaliation against major United States exports, such as soybeans and corn.

(continued)

But the Administration and its friends do not apologize for President Reagan's forays into protectionism. "The Administration has been on a tightrope," said Barber B. Conable Jr., an upstate New York Republican, who is ranking minority member on the House Ways and Means Committee . . . "They're trying to keep Congress from enacting legislation that would be inflexible and irreversible by taking pragmatic steps to head off some of the pressures for protectionism."

Mr. Conable argued that the Administration's use of bilateral agreements and pressure to get trading partners to reduce shipments to the United States are preferable to special tariffs or quotas, which he said are too rigid and inflationary. "I'll give the Administration credit for pragmatism," he said.

Today's protectionism stirs memories of the infamous Smoot-Hawley Tariff of 1929, which, most economists agree, helped tumble the world into Depression. Smoot-Hawley's high tariff barriers generated retaliatory barriers from Europe, which helped cripple trade and industry and helped take the roar out of the Twenties.

Learning from their mistakes, the guardians of international trade lowered trade barriers bit by bit from the Great Depression until the early 1970's. Speaking about the decades of liberalized trade, Sir Roy Denman, the Common Market's ambassador to Washington, said in speech last week that "the enormous progress" in reducing barriers to world trade had coincided "with the greatest increase in prosperity the world has ever known."

But the movement toward liberalization began to grind to a halt after oil prices skyrocketed in 1973. As industrial growth slowed, partly in response to the energy crisis, nation after nation started to erect protectionist barriers.

"The only obvious thing to blame the shift on is the massive disruption of the industrial economies in the 1970's," said Richard E. Caves, a professor of economics at Harvard University. "In the 1960's, we had a run of luck with no major macroeconomic disturbances that tended to fuel protectionist pressure."

The slow growth of the 1970's fanned the protectionist flames. President Carter got Taiwan and South Korea to limit shoe and color television exports to the United States for several years.

Protectionist pressures continued in the first two years of this decade, but only since 1982 have they exploded. Ironically, this surge has coincided with the nation's economic recovery—a recovery that has turned out to be less of a boon for import-battered industries such as steel and copper than for other businesses.

Above all, trade analysts attributed the explosion in protectionist sentiment to the dollar's record strength. "There is great pressure on the entire trading-goods sector due to the overvaluation of the dollar," said Alan W. Wolff, a trade lawyer in Washington and a deputy trade represen-

(continued)

tative under President Carter. "Since 1979, it has gone up nearly 50 percent. Everyone but the President and the Secretary of Treasury agree that it is overvalued by more than 25 percent. This means an import subsidy of 25 percent and an export tax of 25 percent."

And Mr. Brock, the trade representative, added: "The explosion in the price of the dollar has made life more difficult than all the trade barriers in all the countries of the world put together."

But he said the dollar was not the only cause of today's protectionism. "People seeking relief from imports are seeking relief from change," he said. "The world is in the fastest mode of industrial change that it's been in since the industrial revolution began a century ago. That's going to be with us, and it's going to cause a good deal of pain and anguish."

Part of that industrial change is taking place in American factories, with automation replacing workers. Knowing that it is extremely difficult to fight against automation, unions look to one area where they feel they can score victories in their struggle to save jobs: the protectionist front. They are trying to keep out products that their members make.

Industrial change is also sweeping through third world countries. Low wages are helping turn some of them into industrial powerhouses that can undersell their American competitors. For instance, steelworkers in Brazil and South Korea earn less than 25 percent of what American steelmakers earn.

Because many developing countries are plagued by debt problems, their governments—to the chagrin of American manufacturers, but to the delight of American bankers—are pressuring their industries to increase export earnings. Aggravating matters, many countries subsidize their export industries, which makes it easier for them to undersell American-made products.

"We are an internationalized economy now," said Paula Stern, chairman of the International Trade Commission. "We weren't as internationalized in 1974, when protectionist pressures were not very great."

When companies and unions see that other industries can win import relief, they feel an additional incentive to push for protection. And early in his Administration, President Reagan showed that he was not deaf to appeals for protection.

Even though the International Trade Commission rejected a petition for import restraints brought by the United Auto Workers, President Reagan got Japan to agree in 1981 to limit its auto exports to the United States to 1.68 million cars a year for three years. Last November, Japan agreed to a one-year extension of that controversial agreement, which many say is the main reason for Detroit's record profits this year.

"I've been surprised by the amount of protection they've granted," said Professor Magee of the University of Texas. "I think the Republicans

(continued)

are trying to woo the blue-collar bunch. They're trying to break up the old Democratic coalition in the unionized, labor-intensive industries."

Such labor-intensive industries as autos, steel and textiles, which have large, sophisticated unions, seem to be the most frequent petitioners for protection. In response to pressure from both industry and labor, the Administration has gotten the Common Market to agree formally and Japan, informally, to each limit steel shipments to the United States to 5 percent of the domestic market. . . .

"The Administration's free trade principles have been very seriously compromised," said William R. Cline, senior fellow at the Institute for International Economics in Washington. "They have often been bowing to political reality. It's very difficult to ignore two million apparel workers, hundreds of thousands of steelworkers and nearly a million automobile workers. . . ."

Explaining why the Administration veered away from free trade in these decisions, Lionel H. Olmer, Undersecretary of Commerce for International Trade, said, "We do not live in a world characterized by free trade. Many nations embrace the notion, as we do, of the desirability of free trade and the necessity of moving toward liberalization. But to do that, you need the support of your industries, but you will lose that if you refuse to compromise with that ideal in order to find practical solutions."

In recent years, a few economists have challenged the idea that free trade is necessarily healthy. They say that free trade is not the best way for industrialized nations to preserve jobs and standards of living when technology can easily be moved to export-oriented developing countries that have far lower wages.

"No country in the world other than the United States believes that it's good to be injured by imports," said Lee Price, an international economist with the United Auto Workers. "The Japanese economy is the most protected of any industrial country, yet look at how successful it has been in maintaining economic growth."

But most economists attack protectionism as inflationary. They say, for example, that the agreement to restrict Japanese auto imports has increased prices of American cars by $1,000 on average. And critics say that protectionism does not save jobs because the higher prices that result from protectionism siphon consumer dollars away from non-protected industries to protected ones. That, they say, causes job losses in non-protected industries.

"Protectionism is dreadful," said Gary C. Hufbauer, a Washington-based trade expert and former Treasury Department economist, "because it eliminates price competition and orients industry toward thinking how to get the next round of protection, rather than how to become more efficient."

(continued)

Industry, on the other hand, often asserts that temporary protection is needed to increase profits so that money will be available to modernize. But, critics charge, industries are reluctant to make long-term investments when they know protection is temporary. Besides, temporary protection often becomes permanent, critics say, because inefficient industries—the steel industry is repeatedly cited—become dependent on protection.

Even protectionist labor unions criticize industry for not doing enough when protected. The U.A.W.'s Mr. Price criticized Detroit for having used its four years of protection to arrange to import and distribute foreign-made small cars rather than produce more of them in the United States.

Some free traders acknowledge that their protection may occasionally be appropriate, however. "The most reasonable argument for protection," said Barry P. Bosworth, a senior fellow at the Brookings Institution, "is, yes, certain industries are going to decline, but abrupt change imposes enormous costs on communities and workers. When 50-year-old workers lose their jobs, it's hard to employ them in other areas. Protection shouldn't be used to reverse the declining trend in those industries but to slow it down to a rate that imposes less social costs."

---

7. **Do you support import quotas for the steel industry? Why? If one of your parents worked in the steel industry would you feel differently? If you lived in Bethlehem, Pa., would you feel differently?**

8. **Do you support quota extensions for the auto industry? Why?**

9. **Is protectionism "dreadful"? Why?**

Less developed countries (LDC's) are especially concerned about growing protectionist tendencies. They need to increase their exports in order to earn much-needed dollars and foreign currencies with which to repay the enormous debt that they have accrued during the past decade. Any quota on imported steel would greatly affect a nation such as Brazil, which relies heavily on steel exports to earn foreign exchange.

The LDC's also have learned to play the game of protection. Import controls as well as export subsidies are being used by several of the LDC's to improve their trade positions. This trend has been caused by a minimal weakening of inflationary activity and the persistence of high unemployment levels.

Protection or free trade? Retaliation? Negotiated trade agreements? In his 1977 presidential address to the 12th biannual convention of the AFL–CIO, George Meany declared, "free trade is a joke and a myth, and a government policy dedicated to 'free trade' is more than a joke—it is a prescription for disaster. The answer is fair trade—do unto others as they do unto you—barrier for barrier, closed door for closed door."

KEY CONCEPTS

free trade
protectionism
absolute advantage
comparative advantage
tariff

quotas
retaliation
General Agreement on
    Tariffs and Trade (GATT)

REVIEW QUESTIONS

1. What factors other than comparative advantage might induce nations to trade?

2. Are you a believer in free trade or protectionism? Why? For the United States? For the world?

3. What arguments have been put forth in support of protectionist policies?

4. Even though protectionist policies impose costs on all consumers, such policies still receive a great deal of support. Who supports protectionist policies, and why?

5. How would you explain a reduction in tariffs to a textile worker in South Carolina?

6. What is the proper international trade policy for a nation experiencing a deep recession in its domestic economy?

7. Do you believe in free trade or fair trade? Explain.

8. Do you see any possibility of a relaxation of protectionist trends in the near future? Why? What would have to occur to bring about such a trend?

9. In the long run, what do you foresee as the effects of protectionism on the U.S. economy?

SUGGESTED READINGS

David P. Calleo and Benjamin M. Rowland, 1973. *America and the World Political Economy*, University of Indiana Press. Calleo and Rowland examine the postwar economic growth of Western Europe and Japan and their challenge to U.S. supremacy. They question the viability of the world economic system based on the old liberal order.

Anthony Harrison, 1967. *The Framework of Economic Activity: The International Economy and the Rise of the State in the Twentieth Century*, Macmillan. A history of the international economy from the rise and fall of the gold standard and economic liberalism to the managed world economy of the 1950s and 1960s.

Harry G. Johnson, 1965. *The World Economy at the Crossroads,* Oxford University Press. A renowned international economist deals with the history of trade and monetary and institutional organizations, with a special section devoted to the problems of the developing countries.

Jan Wororoff, 1984. *World Trade War,* Praeger. This book examines the recent trends toward neomercantilism, focusing on the trade policies of Japan vis-à-vis the United States.

26

Chapter

The International Financial System

INTRODUCTION

Thus far we have considered the theory and the recent history of international trade. We shall now turn our focus to the world of **international finance** that, as its name implies, deals with money flows between nations. These money flows are the consequence of decisions by citizens or institutions of a given nation to lend to or borrow from foreigners and to import or export goods and services. In recent years, the subject has a reputation for being so esoteric that only central bankers and the "gnomes of Zurich" could understand its complexities. Some economists and bankers believe the rules have broken down and have been ignored since 1971. This chapter briefly examines the history of international finance through 1944, when the Bretton Woods System was established. The Bretton Woods System is examined to understand how a fixed exchange-rate system functioned until its destruction in the early 1970s. The chapter helps us examine international finance during the late 1970s and 1980s, a period characterized by floating exchange rates and continuing problems, culminating in a financial crisis among debt-laden Third World nations.

THE GOLD STANDARD

Some type of international financial system is required as a result of the "imbalances" in the balance-of-payments positions among nations. If the United States, for example, has an overall balance-of-payments deficit with the rest of the world, some mechanism must exist for "balancing" that deficit. Throughout the history of modern world capitalism, several different systems have existed for accomplishing this task. The first of these that we will examine is the **gold standard.**

Gold served as the external form of payment in the international system from the Middle Ages until the 20th century. Under a gold standard, a country's currency was convertible into gold at a fixed price. The price of the currency expressed in terms of gold was known as its **parity value.** The mechanism worked in the following way. Both the United States and the United Kingdom, for example, defined their currencies in terms of gold. As a result, surpluses and deficits in the balance of payments were equivalent to a certain amount of gold. If the United States had a surplus in its balance of payments with the United Kingdom, then the U.K.'s deficit would be settled by the shipment of the appropriate amount of gold to the United States. British pounds, having demanded American goods and services, would have accumulated in the United States. The United States would then convert its "unwanted" pounds into gold from the United Kingdom. In this way, the U.K.'s deficit would be "balanced."

This mechanism was relatively simple and had some other attractive results. The flow of gold from the United Kingdom would reduce the money supply in the United Kingdom and increase it in the United States. As an automatic reaction, prices would fall in the United Kingdom and rise in the United States—since less (more) money would tend to force prices downward (upward) and since gold was a part of the money supply. Consumers in each country would then respond to these price changes—exports of U.S. goods would tend to fall and those of the United Kingdom would tend to increase. Consequently, the balance-of-payments surplus of the United States would tend to decline (all without any intervention of the government!). Thus under the gold standard, where gold flowed freely and was part of the money supply, there was an automatic mechanism for settling balance-of-payments imbalances and, in addition, imbalances would tend to be automatically eliminated.

However, there were some practical problems with the gold standard that eventually led to its replacement and, in the interim, created problems for the operation of the international financial system and, hence, for international trade. Under the gold standard, gold created the liquidity necessary to finance international trade and the resulting deficits for some countries.

The concept of **liquidity** is vital to trade in that some standards of "moneyness" must be universally accepted for transactions to occur. One must have this liquidity if trade is to take place. If there are not enough gold reserves (or gold mines) to facilitate trade or if output of goods and services outstrips the output of gold, a *liquidity crisis* emerges. In this situation, the health of domestic economies was at the mercy of the ability of the world to produce gold. For example, if the United Kingdom could not get enough gold to finance its deficit with the United States then it could not import goods and services from the United States. As a result, while the United States might have a balance in international accounts with the United Kingdom, domestic production levels would be restricted. The gold standard, then, limited the amount of international trade that could be financed and tended to restrict some domestic economies. And as nations and trade grew, the limited gold resources could not satisfy the needs of world trade.

Furthermore, following the turmoil, destruction, and economic havoc of World War I, the gold standard operated in such a way as to depress economic activity in Western Europe as these countries attempted to maintain the parity values of their overvalued currencies. (Overvaluation of a currency tends to limit the ability of a country to export its goods and to enhance its ability to import goods, thus tending to create international payments deficits.)

Feelings of nationalism and the need for *independent national* monetary and fiscal policies relegated the size of international reserves to a secondary position. People were more concerned with internal price, income, and employment levels than they were with the state of the currency on the international market. These along with other pressures of the age left a rather precarious international system to face the events of 1929. The system struggled and eventually failed. The high Smoot-Hawley tariff of 1930 and those made in retaliation to it ensured the demise of the gold standard and a virtual end to international trade for the duration of the Depression. Nations began abandoning gold as sailors might a sinking ship—even first-class seats offered no security. Gold was no longer used as a mechanism to settle balance-of-payments deficits.

Several international conferences led to draft resolutions, but the tremendous instability of *all* currencies permitted no permanent international economic structure to develop during the 1930s. As various agreements were being reached and order was being regained, World War II began and then the system went into chaos once again. This time, however, negotiations were occurring throughout the war years to allow the birth and formation of a new international economic system.

THE INTERNATIONAL MONETARY FUND AND THE BRETTON WOODS SYSTEM

The framework for the system that forms the official organizational structure for today's international financial negotiations was formulated in 1944 at a conference in Bretton Woods, New Hampshire. The economic arrangements made there are referred to as the **Bretton Woods system,** although today's system of financial arrangements is significantly different. Many arguments were advanced concerning the shape that the world monetary system should take at the conclusion of the war. The institutional arrangements settled on were to be overseen by a new organization, the **International Monetary Fund (IMF).** The IMF was established for five major purposes.

The first was to provide an institutional framework for monetary cooperation and consultation when problems arose. Member nations purchased subscriptions to the fund in accordance with their standing in world production levels. Policy was then heavily influenced by Western nations. In 1944 the United States contributed one-third of the Fund's stock of gold and currency and received one-third of the votes in major policy proposals. Today the U.S. annual quota is about 20 percent; and when an 80 percent majority vote is needed on a major policy issue, the United States has veto power.

The second goal of the IMF was to facilitate expansion and balanced growth of trade with high levels of domestic income and employment. A system of *fixed exchange rates* was established to accomplish this goal. Under the fixed exchange system, currencies were defined in terms of one another. Consistency was assured, with each nation also defining its currency in terms of gold and the U.S. dollar. In 1973 the system established a floating exchange regime that replaced the fixed exchange system in order to better achieve this goal in an even more interdependent world.

The third objective was to provide stable exchange rates between currencies. The U.S. dollar maintained a passive role in the Bretton Woods system because it was chosen to serve as the *key* or **reserve currency** that would be as acceptable as gold in international transactions. Currencies were defined in terms of the dollar, and the dollar became an acceptable means of international payment.

The maintenance of sufficient liquidity to finance world trade was the fourth goal. Liquidity was guaranteed through a multilateral payments system. Under the Bretton Woods system, gold, U.S. dollars, and IMF balances were the major sources of liquidity. A nation could also borrow from the IMF on a short-term basis if additional liquidity was needed. As we shall see shortly, insufficient liquidity became a problem during the 1960s. To provide additional liquidity with which to facilitate world trade, the Fund created **special drawing rights** (SDR's) in 1968. Between 1970 and 1972, $10 billion in SDR's was allocated for use. These were distributed to each nation on the basis of IMF quotas or voting rights. SDR's were created to substitute for gold as an ultimate means of settling balance-of-payments deficits and to substitute for dollars as an international reserve currency. The growth in international reserves could not be more stable with this bookkeeping currency. While SDR's are in fact used, they have not been as important to liquidity as economists assumed they would be in 1970.

Finally, as the fifth goal the IMF was charged with overseeing and correcting disequilibrium conditions in balance of payments. Countries were expected to utilize both monetary and fiscal policy to correct imbalances. For example, deficits would be corrected by limiting economic activity and hence imports. If this was insufficient for the necessary adjustments, the Bretton Woods system provided for a change in the exchange rates. When a devaluation occurs, the currency that goes down in value is said to have **depreciated,** while the currency going up has **appreciated.**

1. When a country's currency depreciates, it is worth less in terms of other currencies. What effect will this have on that country's exports? Its imports? Its balance-of-payments position?

If the parity rate has changed in terms of gold (more dollars buying the same amount of gold), the currency is said to have experienced a **devaluation.**

WHAT WENT WRONG? INTERNATIONAL MONETARY CRISIS

The IMF was created and designed to guarantee the working of the Bretton Woods system, and so the question that naturally arises is what went wrong? Why are we constantly reading about and hearing of new problems in the world economic arena? It is clear that the system was capable of dealing with many of the financial problems of the past four decades, but other problems have sent the scheme into periods of chaos, never quite fulfilling the dreams of its creators.

An examination of the collapse of the Bretton Woods system shows the recurrence of two fundamental shortcomings:

1. There was no mechanism designed within the system to *force* countries to change their exchange rates, even though they might be substantially overvalued or undervalued.

2. There was no *consistency* included in the system. National monetary policies were not necessarily compatible with the exchange rate system, which was in turn not necessarily compatible with international liquid assets.

During the 1950s the demand for dollars was very high, particularly in Europe, where U.S. dollars were needed to purchase the goods and services essential for the postwar rebuilding process. Dollars, however, were in very short supply at that time. The United States rose to the occasion, supplying dollars where shortages existed. Dollars began pouring into Europe. Some $37 billion had entered during the war under the Lend-Lease program, and some $130 billion continued to be shipped in for aid between 1945 and 1967. Perhaps the most politically and economically significant program was the Marshall Plan, initiated in 1948. Under the act that established this plan, $10 billion was designated for European "recovery." This program was significant to the self-interest of the United States. After all, what good was the U.S. productive capacity if there were no nations with which to trade? If Europe couldn't buy our goods and services, who could? European economic stability, both internally and externally, as well as increased European productivity, was necessary for the United States to achieve its optimum economic goals.

Part of the program was designed to protect the domestic stability and capitalist structure of Western Europe. The Truman Doctrine, designed to halt the spread of communism in Greece and Turkey, was extended to ensure political stability within Europe. During the Cold War, the United States provided military aid, troops, and bases to various countries. No doubt this program encouraged many U.S. firms to invest their funds in these rebuilding nations. Indeed, the returns to investments made in Europe were expected to be much larger than those made in the United States because production costs were lower and there was a newly emerging "consumption market" to be tapped. So it was that U.S. dollars flowed into Europe and turned the **dollar shortage** of the 1940s into the **dollar glut** of the 1960s.

This dollar glut meant that an excess supply of dollars was being held by Europeans, and these dollars were not being "recycled" for U.S. goods and services. New markets were now opening to the Europeans, and the demand for U.S. products was decreasing because of their higher prices. Also, as the dollar outflows continued and the *balance-of-payments position worsened,* economists wondered about the strength of the U.S. economy relative to nations that were no longer weak but were by now strong, viable, and competitive economies. It was here that the Bretton Woods system failed. According to the system, exchange-rate adjustments should occur in cases of persistent balance-of-payments difficulties—yet because the dollar was the reserve currency and essential for international liquidity, necessary dollar adjustments were avoided. The trouble lay deeper than this, however. There were extremely few realignments in currencies under the Bretton Woods system. Many felt depreciation was a sign of national weakness, while appreciation was viewed not as a sign of strength but as a compromise to a weaker economic position. Exchange rates of a number of nations were out of kilter since they were essentially the same parity rates that existed right after World War II.

Multinationals and Eurodollars

Dollars continued to flow abroad during the 1950s to purchase the new, relatively cheaper European goods and services and to seek the higher returns from European investments. As these investments spread and U.S. firms began locating business operations in these countries and buying European corporations, new and diversified institutional frameworks were needed. The **multinationals** required more convenient financial markets within the European host countries to facilitate capital flows. The dollars deposited in European banks by these multinational corporations were soon dubbed **Eurodollars.** Eurodollars have grown from total obscurity to a position of prominence in both world and national financial affairs during the past decade. The sudden and astounding rise of this market is without precedent in modern financial history. Estimates in 1979 place the current volume of Eurodollar funds at about $445 billion and Eurocurrency funds at $610 billion. Large quantities of petrodollars (from the increased value of oil sales) were recycled into this market and led to developing nations needing foreign exchange with which to purchase oil. As we mentioned earlier, the Eurodollar market developed as a response to real needs of the international financial community rather than as some freak money market discovery made in trying to decide how funds might be used more profitably. Eurodollars are U.S. dollar–denominated deposits at commercial banks outside the United States. They derive all of their characteristics from the U.S. dollar. The only difference between dollars and Eurodollars is their geographic location. This geographic difference means that Eurodollars are *not subject to U.S. governmental control.* Eurodollar banks are *not subject to legal reserve requirements* but are subject to regulation by the country in which they are located.

Eurodollars are created, for example, when a New York investor decides to switch funds from New York to Zurich. To do this, the investor simply writes a check on the New York account. The investor now holds dollar deposits in a bank in Zurich.

Another creation occurs when a U.S. firm borrows $1 million from a Zurich bank. Just as in the multiple creation of demand deposits in the United States, the bank in Zurich has now increased the number of dollars held by increasing the account of the firm by $1 million. Why is there so much banking interest in Eurodollars and other Eurocurrencies? Why are U.S. banks interested in establishing branches in foreign countries? Right both times! Profits! There is considerably more interest-rate competition in Eurobanking than there is in domestic banking, but because costs are lower, profits will be higher. Investors prefer holding Eurodollar deposits because they can receive higher interest on their funds with no higher risk (except perhaps political risk).

U.S. central bankers are concerned about the size of the Eurodollar market and their lack of control over it. They become frightened at the thought of a $1 billion transfer from a U.S. bank to a Swiss bank going through the multiple expansion process and ending up increasing dollar deposits abroad by four- or five-fold. This would obviously reduce the effectiveness of the central bank in controlling the money stock because dollar loans could be obtained from the Eurodollar market—even at a time of strict money policy. Eurodollars, therefore, contribute to worldwide inflation by increasing the availability of money on an international scale.

U.S. Policy in the Crunch

Despite these developments, along with ever-increasing deficits in the balance of payments, U.S. policy remained much the same during the 1960s. During this period the IMF virtually conceded its operations to the **Group of Ten**, the ten most economically powerful countries. At their meetings they discussed and acted at any indication of weakness in currency operations—but *prompt realignment* of parity rates was not forthcoming! A system of emergency capital flows was used instead, with funds being shuttled from one weak currency to the next. This led only to greater instability within the Bretton Woods system. By 1968 it was readily apparent to most economists that the system was preparing for collapse—but still it hung on.

Early in 1971 there were large movements of "interest-sensitive" capital from the United States to Europe. Speculation against the dollar grew, and as more and more dollars were dumped on the foreign exchange markets, more deutsche marks and yen were demanded to take their place in individual and corporate portfolios. In Fig. 26.1, we can see how this affected the U.S. dollar. As the supply of dollars increased in the European markets, their price was driven down in terms of (in this case) deutsche marks.

Pressure was put on the dollar, and it should have been revalued under the Bretton Woods system. But because the U.S. dollar was a reserve currency, the change was not forthcoming. To avoid the appreciation of the mark and yen at that time, both the German and Japanese central banks began buying dollars with the hope of absorbing enough to avoid realignment of the two currencies. By doing this, they hoped to keep German and Japanese exports at high levels and thus maintain high levels of employment in the two countries. Figure 26.2 illustrates the short-run results of the action of the two central banks. Because Germany and Japan bought

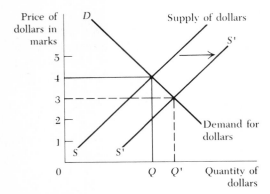

Figure 26.1   The pressures on the dollar.

dollars, the demand or dollars was increased from D to D', thus keeping the old exchange rates in effect.

2. **Would you have bought dollars if you were a central banker in Germany?**

3. **Why were the German and Japanese bankers so hostile to an appreciation of the mark and the yen in terms of the U.S. dollar? Doesn't appreciation signify strength?**

By mid-1971 the German central bank decided that it was spending too many of its valuable marks to support the overvalued dollar, and so it stopped dollar purchases and allowed the mark to **float.** Floating occurs when the exchange rate of the currency is determined strictly by market supply-and-demand factors. This means that the value of the currency could change from day to day.

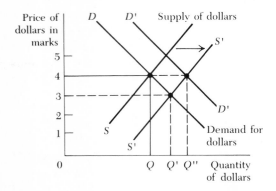

Figure 26.2   Keeping the value of the dollar up.

4. What are some factors that might change the demand for the mark? The supply? Review the determinants of supply and demand to help you with your answer.

By the time of the German decision to float the mark, a U.S. congressional subcommittee reported that the dollar was overvalued and called for a general realignment of exchange rates. Needless to say, this report caused even more speculation against the dollar, driving its value down even further. (The Japanese also soon abandoned their policy of buying dollars.)

In August of 1971, President Nixon introduced the New Economic Policy (NEP), which, along with domestic wage and price controls, called for a temporary 10 percent surcharge on all imports as well as a "temporary" halt in the convertibility of dollars into gold. (This temporary condition still exists, and it is now understood that August 15, 1971, marks the complete end of the gold exchange standard. Although U.S. citizens have not been able to exchange their dollar holdings for gold from the U.S. Treasury since 1934, foreign holders could until this suspension.)

By winter of 1971, pressures on the dollar continued to rise because of the war in Vietnam. Under the burden of the tremendous costs of and inflation from the war, the U.S. balance-of-payments deficit was larger and more pressing than it had been at any time in the nation's history. Both private and government capital flowed into Southeast Asia for investment as well as defense purposes. Although the U.S. balance-of-payments position had been precarious during the 1960s, these new pressures made the condition impossible.

FLOATING EXCHANGE RATES

On December 18, 1971, President Nixon committed what a few years earlier would have been political suicide and devalued the dollar. The "historic" Smithsonian agreement called for an 8 percent devaluation of the dollar and a realignment of other currencies reflecting the lower value of the dollar. Currencies were then pegged so that the market exchange could fluctuate within a 2.25 percent band (up or down) from the new rates. Again, as at so many times in the past, this solution did not deal with the *structural* problems of the Bretton Woods system. Superficial adjustments were once again made, working within the system to solve the mounting world financial difficulties.

The Float

In 1973, the world became aware that the "band-aid" solutions instituted in 1971 were not working at all well. Speculation pressures were again being brought against the dollar. The result of these new pressures and instability was the abandonment of the fixed-rate monetary system associated with both the Bretton Woods and Smithsonian agreements. A system of *floating exchange rates* emerged as a temporary settlement until "a more permanent solution to the chronic problems of the world's monetary system could be developed." The IMF has lost most of the strength and clout it once had in the arena of foreign exchange. Now the monetary systems are joined by a series of floating rates and linked floating rates that are sometimes called "joint floats." An example of this is the Common Market currencies, which float together against the world. One sometimes hears of **dirty** or **managed floats,** which are encountered when governments intervene in the currency markets to keep the floating currencies within desired bounds.

After 1973, the rules were changed so that de facto depreciation or appreciation could occur without official IMF sanction. It was by such a method that the United States "adjusted" the balance-of-payments deficit encountered during and after the OPEC oil embargo. The once overvalued dollar was now allowed to seek its own worth in the somewhat free international currency markets. In the current context, when the United States experiences a deficit, this deficit is "settled" through a combination of other countries' holding their dollar balances and some amount of decrease in the value of the dollar.

The Jamaica agreement in 1976 amended the articles of agreement of the IMF and signaled national and regional bias to the multilateral management of the system. The amendment, dealing with liquidity and adjustment, became effective in April of 1978. The objective of the amendment was to make the SDR the primary reserve asset of the international monetary system. At the same time the official price of gold within the IMF was abolished, thus ending transactions in gold between the IMF and its members. The IMF was also given the power to "oversee the exchange rate regime, adopt principles to guide national policies and encourage international cooperation."

In the years since the introduction of floating exchange rates, the international monetary system has found itself adjusting surprisingly well, even though the central banks of most major industrial countries have intervened at one time or another to "manage" their exchange rates. Until the early months of 1976, there had been no attempts at competitive depreciation to gain an advantage in product export, but in the spring and summer of 1976, the British pound was allowed to fall to much lower levels than its worth. This increased the demand for British goods throughout the world and boosted tourism to the United Kingdom. Other European countries have also been accused of a bit of competitive devaluation, and nations are reminded that if every country devalues, few if any gains are made.

The float has presented special problems for the less developed countries (LDC's). Because few of these nations had well-developed currency markets, they simply pegged their currency to that of their major industrial trading partner. An LDC whose currency was pegged to the British pound also found that its currency depreciated by almost 25 percent between May of 1975 and the end of 1976.

These kinds of exchange-rate movements can cause severe inflationary pressures in LDC's in which inflation is a persistent problem. Some of the OPEC nations have linked their currencies to the SDR to guard against inflation resulting from exchange rate changes.

INTERNATIONAL FINANCIAL ISSUES OF THE 1980S

"Currency jitters" seems to sum up the feeling in the 1970s as disarray mounted in the currency markets. Many nations, with an inherent fear of floating, kept looking for new stability. The 1980s have found nerves, if not international exchange markets, calmer. There have been two major characteristics of international financial markets in the 1980s. Third World debt has repercussions on both the developed and the less developed countries, as does the high value of the dollar in international financial markets.

The Soaring Dollar

In 1978 and again in 1979, U.S. policies were changed to respond directly to the weakness of the dollar abroad. In November 1978, President Carter outlined a domestic program designed to cut some federal expenditures and to tighten the money supply in order to bring down domestic inflation rates and to strengthen the dollar abroad. In October 1979, Paul Volcker, Chairman of the Federal Reserve's Board of Governors, launched a policy that targeted the money supply and sent interest rates soaring. This policy too was designed to curb inflation and to strengthen the dollar. Both policies, triggered by international considerations, had the effect of decreasing domestic economic activity. Revenue cuts and expenditure increases by the Reagan Administration produced federal budget deficits that continued the upward pressure on interest rates. We have seen in Chapter 24 how the value of the dollar continued to rise through 1985 in response to these developments. Record trade deficits have been the result of the high value of the dollar, slowing economic growth throughout the world, and increasing Third World debt levels.

Third World Debt

A second major characteristic of the late 1970s and early 1980s has been the sizable growth of Third World debt (see Table 26.1). While a strong dollar helps Third World nations increase their exports to the U.S., the high interest rates that sustain the value of the dollar increase the debt burden to the developing nations. The size of the Third World debt is largely the result of the oil price increases of the 1970s. OPEC nations responsible for the oil embargo and the quadrupling of oil prices recycled the increased income that flowed into their countries by depositing the proceeds in European, Asian, and American banks. Third World nations, however, were forced to borrow funds from these banks in order to finance their purchases of desperately needed energy supplies. These nations are now heavily in debt to both the banks and to international organizations from whom they have borrowed. Each time interest rates increase in the United States, the Third World debt mounts, since repayment is tied to market rates of interest. These interest increases all but eliminate the gains made by Third World nations in increasing their exports and instituting painful austerity measures at home.

Table 26.1 THE *WALL STREET JOURNAL* DEBT WATCH LIST, 1984

COUNTRY	FOREIGN DEBT (IN BILLIONS OF DOLLARS)
Argentina	45.3
Brazil	93.1
Mexico	89.8
Philippines	26.4
Poland	27.0
Turkey	23.9
Chile	18.6
Peru	12.5
South Korea	40.1
Ivory Coast	9.4
Indonesia	29.5
Yugoslavia	19.5
Nigeria	17.0
Israel	29.3

Source: The Wall Street Journal, June 22, 1984.

Third World debt is estimated to reach $1.3 trillion by 1990. This, coupled with trade deficits and the strong U.S. dollar, places the international financial scheme in a precarious position in the 1980s. The following article from *Dollars & Sense* traces the interrelationship between these problems and integrates the concepts we have developed throughout this section.

CRACKS IN THE EMPIRE

U.S. ECONOMY FACES INTERNATIONAL PRESSURE

Governments of less developed countries have long been forced to hammer out their domestic policies in response to changes in the international economic scene. Their economies have been constrained by the whims of multinational investors, erratic world commodity prices, and institutions like the International Monetary Fund (IMF).

Since its emergence as a world economic power, the U.S. has been relatively free of such constraints. U.S. economic policy has been formulated on the basis of national priorities, with very little regard for the rest

(continued)

Reprinted with permission from *Dollars & Sense,* 38 Union Sq., Somerville, MA 02143. Subscriptions $16 per year.

of the world economy. Quite simply, the U.S. has dominated the rest of the world—not the other way around.

But it seems the tables are turning. Currently, and for the foreseeable future, the major economic problems facing the U.S. trace their roots to international issues: the trade deficit, the value of the dollar, and third world debt. Regardless of the ideology of the next wave of U.S. policymakers, their domestic programs will have to be wrangled out in response to the instability of the international financial system.

LOSING U.S. BUSINESS

The huge trade deficit is the most urgent international issue confronting the U.S. During 1984, the U.S. imported about $128 billion more in goods and services than it exported. (The total value of imports was about $344 billion and of exports about $216 billion.)

From the turn of the century through 1971, the U.S. maintained a trade surplus, selling more goods abroad than it imported. Many years during the seventies saw trade deficits, peaking at $34 billion in 1978. But these deficits were largely accounted for by the growing bill for imported oil. During the last three years, the huge increase in the trade deficit—from $36.5 billion in 1982, to $61 billion in 1983, to $125 billion in 1984—has instead represented a general inundation of the U.S. market by foreign goods, and a general failure of U.S. businesses to increase exports.

The domestic ramifications of the trade deficit are grave. Many sectors—especially heavy industry—haven't shared in the recent economic recovery. The U.S. steel industry, for example, once dominated the world market. Yet now the U.S. imports about 25% of its steel. Farm equipment companies, like Caterpillar Tractor, were heavy exporters in recent decades; now they are being driven out of foreign markets. The shoe industry, apparel, and even machine tools are further examples of industries in difficulty because of foreign competition.

Boosting the trade deficit is the very high value of the dollar, which renders imports cheaper and makes it harder to sell exports. Though the strong dollar is a problem that could be reversed, the trade imbalance that results from the strong dollar creates other, longer term, problems.

Once U.S. manufacturers have lost their markets to foreign competitors, they will face an uphill battle to win them back. Shifts in market shares are not easily or quickly reversed. When U.S. producers controlled many markets at home and abroad, they had widely known brand names, and were able to establish long term supplying and servicing relations with their customers. Now that foreign producers have broken into these markets, they too have established relations with customers and are securing the positions of their brands. U.S. producers might succeed in halting their slide, but will have a hard time regaining their dominant position.

(continued)

With unemployment at home remaining high, especially in the industrial heartland, the U.S. government will be under continuing pressure to do something about the trade deficit. A number of policy options could be pursued. One choice is an industrial policy aimed at retraining workers and beefing up exports. Another would be for the government to consciously try to bring the value of the dollar down. Yet another alternative is to implement new tariffs and quotas in order to protect industries hurt by imports. . . .

To institute an industrial policy would require major institutional changes, such as establishing a national investment bank, and . . . would depend on a national consensus on the role of government in the economy.

Although the government could intervene directly to manipulate the value of the dollar, those policies might cause further problems. . . . In the end, the U.S. finds itself caught in the same old debate over protectionism versus free trade.

Even as the government has preached a free trade philosophy, it has moved in the direction of protectionism. In mid-1984, the Reagan Administration claimed it was refraining from restricting steel imports, for example, but at the same time it established "voluntary" quotas that would reduce foreign steel's share of the markets from 25% to 18% over the next five years.

The immediate impact of further protection would be to save many U.S. jobs. But protectionism holds the potential for negative consequences as well. First, protection without price controls almost always translates into higher prices, since domestic producers don't need to compete with lower-priced foreign goods. A further danger lies in retaliation: if other countries were to respond by erecting barriers against goods imported from the U.S., American exports would suffer. The result would be a general decline in world trade and losses all around.

THE SHADOW OF A DEBT

One factor contributing to the weakness of U.S. exports has been the debt crisis centered in Latin America and affecting much of the third world. Because of their growing debt burden, these countries are no longer able to spend money on importing goods from the U.S.

Debtor nations like Mexico, Brazil, and Argentina have not been able to get sufficient new loans to finance further economic growth. Moreover, simply to get the funds they need to stay afloat, governments of these nations have been forced to adopt programs that cut wages and consumer spending, reduce government spending, and curtail imports. Also, in order to pay back foreign bankers, governments throughout the third world are pushing exports. Countries pursuing such policies are hardly good custom-

(continued)

ers for U.S. exporters. Indeed, last year the U.S. ran a trade deficit with Mexico and Brazil of over $10 billion and of some $25 billion with all non-OPEC third world countries.

A lack of markets, though, is actually the least of the economic problems emanating from the accumulation of third world debts. Probably the most ominous of these is the possibility of an international financial collapse stemming from widespread defaults. Such a collapse, with governments and corporations unable to pay off their debts, could lead to bank failures and a worldwide shortage of funds for investment. The result would be a disastrous slowdown of production and employment that could pile up into a serious international recession.

That scenario, however, is not a likely one. The U.S. government, governments of other wealthy nations, and the IMF have all made it clear through their actions of the past two years that they will take whatever action they can to protect the viability of the international financial system.

But a collapse *could* happen, and there's the rub. As long as collapse and lesser defaults loom on the horizon, banks will insist on higher interest rates to compensate for the risks involved in lending. Moreover, as long as the large debtor nations are unable to reestablish economic growth, preventing defaults will continue to require a huge flow of funds—through governments, the IMF, and banks. This demand for funds will add further upward pressure on interest rates.

In late 1984, while none of the debtor nations appear to be on the immediate verge of default, neither is the prognosis very optimistic. . . .

For the U.S. the third world debt crisis means weak markets for exports, and growing pressure on interest rates. Yet there is little initiative toward attacking the problem. The IMF and the governments of the wealthy nations move from crisis to crisis, without any attempt at a long term program that would resolve the difficulties.

THE DOLLAR DILEMMA

The most important factor creating high interest rates, however, is not the debt problem of the third world. U.S. government policy—huge government spending deficits combined with relatively tight restrictions on the money supply—has been the primary force keeping interest rates at such high levels.

U.S. interest rates are currently about twice as high as those in, for example, Japan, Germany, and Switzerland. While the prime interest rate stands at around 12% in the U.S., it is 6% or less in those three other centers of international finance. High interest rates, combined with the strong expansion and high profits in the U.S. economy, have attracted a huge volume of foreign investors to the U.S.

(continued)

This flow of funds into the U.S. is the other side of the trade deficit coin. It amounts to a huge demand for dollars, forcing the value of the dollar up relative to other currencies. The result has been an "over-valued" dollar, which has made U.S. goods more expensive relative to goods produced in other countries and has contributed to the trade deficit discussed above. . . .

While the trade deficit has been doing wide damage to the economy, foreign investment in the U.S. has been a great boon. To a significant extent, foreign investment financed the U.S. recovery during 1983 and 1984. Foreigners purchased a substantial share of the government's debt, allowing the U.S. to stimulate growth without raising interest rates even higher than they are now.

It is impossible to determine whether the negative impact of the trade deficit has been outweighed by the positive impact of investment flowing into the U.S. Either way, foreign investment and the high value of the dollar will present the U.S. government with some sticky problems in the near future. If, as is widely anticipated, the growth of the economy slows down in 1985, it is likely that a smaller volume of funds will flow into the U.S. and the value of the dollar will begin to fall. If this process is slow and moderate, it would not present any great difficulties.

Yet because so much foreign investment is in relatively liquid assets—like government securities—foreign funds could move out of the U.S. very rapidly. Policy makers would then be faced with a dilemma.

A sharp outflow of funds, without any U.S. government response, would push interest rates even higher, and an economic slowdown could be transformed into a severe recession. Under the current circumstances, any set of events leading to higher interest rates is especially dangerous because of the third world debt crisis and the specter of defaults.

If, however, the government did respond to a sharp outflow of funds, other problems might arise. To keep interest rates down, it would be necessary to expand the supply of money, a course of action that would likely be inflationary.

The point of reciting all these dilemmas, actual and potential, is not to argue that all the impulses from abroad are necessarily negative, nor that the U.S. economy is about to fall apart. The overvalued dollar, associated as it is with a large flow of funds into the U.S., has helped spur economic expansion; it may continue to do so. . . . Further growth in the U.S. economy would be a strong antidote to trade problems, might stave off protectionism, and could ease European and third world stagnation.

Whether or not things develop favorably, the point is the same: because of widespread instability in the international economy, the options for domestic economic policy are constrained, and the course of the U.S. economy in the coming period is highly uncertain.

5. Why is the Third World debt such a problem?

6. What is the "dollar dilemma"?

Clearly, these issues confound the simple Keynesian solutions to macroeconomic problems. The 1980s will continue to present challenges to policymakers to find real solutions in a variety of economic arenas.

KEY CONCEPTS

international finance	depreciation
gold standard	devaluation
parity value	dollar shortage
liquidity	dollar glut
Bretton Woods system	multinationals
International Monetary Fund (IMF)	Eurodollars
reserve currency	Group of Ten
special drawing rights	float
appreciation	dirty float

REVIEW QUESTIONS

1. If you had been a minister of finance in 1944, would you have encouraged your nation to join the IMF? Explain your reasoning.

2. Is gold useful today, or is it simply a barbaric relic?

3. How did the United States finance its post–World War II international deficits?

4. Why do nations hesitate to float? Who gains? Who loses?

5. What impacts have the Arab nations had recently on the international financial system?

6. Should the U.S. government more vigorously attempt to lower the value of the dollar? Why or why not?

7. If the United States sold some of its hoard of gold, what would be the effect on the value of the dollar?

SUGGESTED READINGS

Robert A. Aliber, 1983. *The International Money Game*, Basic Books. A witty yet excellent discussion of the international money markets and the international financial system.

William Ashworth, 1975. *A Short History of the International Economy since 1850,* Longman. A historical perspective on the evolution of foreign exchange systems, international transactions, and international economic relations.

Paul E. Erdman, 1973. *The Billion Dollar Sure Thing,* Scribner's. A novel of suspense and intrigue surrounding international finance by a former Swiss banker. Erdman has also written *The Silver Bears* and *The Crash of '79.* Be prepared, as well, for a significant amount of sexism.

Herbert G. Gruebel, 1984. *International Monetary System: Efficiency and Practical Alternatives* (4th ed.), Penguin. This book presents the theoretical background of the changing international monetary system, from the gold standard through floating exchange rates.

Ronald I. McKinnon, 1979. *Money in International Exchange,* Oxford University Press. More complex than Aliber, but okay for students ready for the challenge.

Adam Smith (Paul Goodman), 1981. *Paper Money,* Summit Books. A normally gleeful Smith confronts the 1980 international financial situation and discovers why Americans should be very nervous.

Robert Triffin, 1968. *Our International Monetary System: Yesterday, Today, and Tomorrow,* Random House. A thorough discussion of the underpinnings of the Bretton Woods system and proposals for international monetary reform.

Economic Problems
of Developing Nations

Development processes are both cruel and necessary. They are necessary
because all societies must come to terms with new aspirations and
irresistible social forces. Yet the choices they face are cruel because
development's benefits are obtained only at a great price and because, on
balance, it is far from certain that achieving development's benefits makes
men happier or freer.

—Denis Goulet, *The Cruel Choice* (New York: Atheneum, 1975).

DEVELOPMENT AND UNDERDEVELOPMENT: WHAT'S THE
DIFFERENCE? WHY DOES IT MATTER?

The United Nations's world population projections indicate that by the year 2000,
world population will be 6 billion. Of these 6 billion human beings, 4 billion will be
living in the less developed nations of the Third World. Two-thirds of humanity will
be experiencing a standard of living barely above subsistence. For these people, life
at the margin of existence is horribly ugly, agonizing, and destructive. The statistics

503

so often quoted to illustrate the objective poverty of the Third World are themselves cold and empty when juxtaposed with the harsh everyday reality of the struggle for survival.

What does it mean to live in a country in which the following factors characterize a person's existence? (1) **GNP per capita** is less than $750 per year, (2) unemployment in the rural and urban areas is over 35 percent, (3) the annual rate of economic growth is consistently less than 3 percent, (4) population growth rates are 3 percent per year, (5) over 70 percent of the population is engaged in agricultural production, (6) there are few if any schools or hospitals easily accessible to the majority of the population, (7) houses are without running water and other sanitary fᵃcilities, (8) infant mortality rates are ten times those in the developed world, (9) life expectancies are 35 years for males and 42 years for females, and (10) millions of children suffer constantly from hunger and malnutrition.

The Reality of Underdevelopment

Among the developing nations there is a tremendous diversity, not only in geography but in language, race, culture, politics, and economic systems as well. Various indicators are used to examine and contrast the levels of **economic development** for

Table 27.1 THIRD WORLD BASIC INDICATORS FOR 1982

COUNTRY	POPULATION (IN MILLIONS)	GNP PER CAPITA (IN 1982 DOLLARS)	ANNUAL ECONOMIC GROWTH RATE, 1960–1982 (IN PERCENTAGE)	LIFE EXPECTANCY (IN YEARS)
Bangladesh	92.9	140	0.3	48
Burma	34.9	190	1.3	55
Tanzania	19.8	280	1.9	52
Somalia	4.5	290	−0.1	39
Sri Lanka	15.2	320	2.6	69
Kenya	18.1	390	2.8	57
Sudan	20.2	440	−0.4	47
Indonesia	152.6	580	4.2	63
Honduras	4.0	660	1.0	60
Nigeria	90.6	860	3.3	60
Ivory Coast	8.9	950	2.1	47
Jamaica	2.2	1330	0.7	73
Tunisia	6.7	1390	4.7	61
Jordan	3.1	1690	6.9	64
Algeria	19.9	2350	3.2	57
Yugoslavia	22.6	2800	4.9	71
Hong Kong	5.2	5340	7.0	75
Singapore	2.5	5910	7.4	72

Source: World Bank, *World Development Report*, 1984, pp. 218–219.

Table 27.2 SELECTED LDC'S COMPARED WITH THE UNITED STATES

COUNTRY	POPULATION (IN MILLIONS)	GNP PER CAPITA	AVERAGE LIFE EXPECTANCY (IN YEARS)
Chad	4.6	$80	44
India	717	260	55
China	1,008.2	310	67
El Salvador	5.1	700	63
Nicaragua	2.9	920	58
Mexico	73.1	2,270	65
United States	231	13,160	75

Table 27.3 HIERARCHY OF NATIONS

NATIONAL CATEGORY	GNP PER CAPITA
Low-income economies	$280
Middle-income economies	1,520
Lower-middle	840
Upper-middle	2,490
High-income oil exporters	14,820
Industrial market economies	11,970

Source: World Bank Annual Report, 1983.

countries in Africa, Latin America, Asia, and the Middle East. By examining them it is possible to appreciate the dimensions of underdevelopment compared with the affluence of the advanced industrialized world.

By examining Table 27.1 it is possible to see the range of differences among nations. If we select a few nations at random, we can more clearly see such distinctions. Look at Table 27.2 and note the comparative data.

To compare the relative standard of living for the nations of the world, the World Bank has organized a set of categories based on each nation's GNP per capita. Looking at Table 27.3, we can see the rather dramatic distinctions. For example, low-income economies are those with an average GNP per capita of $280 (in 1982 dollars), while middle-income economies had an average GNP per capita of $1520 in 1983. The industrial market economies had an average GNP per capita of $11,970 in 1983.

Everyday Life

The following article by Joseph Collins attempts to communicate what the daily life of a 17-year-old Nicaraguan would have been like in 1977 before the overthrow of the dictator Anastasio Somoza by the Sandinistas in 1979.

IMAGINE YOU WERE A NICARAGUAN . . .

Joseph Collins

Imagine it's 1977 and you are a 17-year-old Nicaraguan. Your family, like two-thirds of all rural families, has either no land at all or not enough to feed itself. If yours is "lucky" enough to have a little plot of land, half or even more of what you grow—or a steep cash rent—goes to the landowner in the city.

Last year you watched helpless as your little sister became repeatedly ill with diarrhea. Your parents saw her losing her strength but there was no one to help. In all of rural Nicaragua there are only five clinics with beds. The first few times your sister pulled through. But by then she was so weak that when measles hit, you watched her die after four painful days. The year before your brother died right after birth; your mother and father have lost five of their children.

You cannot remember a day when your mother was not worried about having enough food for your family—and, of course, you never really did have enough or your little sister wouldn't have died from measles. You heard once on a neighbor's radio that Nicaragua was importing more and more corn, beans, and sorghum. And you've heard about the incredible *supermercados* in Managua. But without money you can't buy food no matter how much there is.

The seven people in your family share a single-room shack, divided by a thin partition. The floor is dirt, there is no electric light, no toilet, no clean drinking water. You are outraged when you hear Somoza boast to some American reporters that "Nicaragua has no housing problem because of its wonderful climate."

You hardly know anyone who can read and write—except the priest, of course, but he's from Spain. You'd like to learn but there is no school. Anyway, you must work.

To buy a few simple tools, some cooking oil, sugar, salt, and kerosene, your father has to borrow money. But the only source of credit is the local moneylender who makes him pay back half again as much and sometimes much more. Not surprisingly, your family is forever in debt.

Locked in debt and without land to grow enough food, your family is forced to labor on the coffee, cotton, or sugar estates. But such work is available only three to four months a year at harvest time. Since the pay is miserable everyone in your family must work to try to bring in enough: your mother, your grandmother, your older sister—about 40 percent of the

(continued)

From *Nicaragua: What Difference Could a Revolution Make?* Institute for Food and Development Policy, copyright 1985, Food First Books.

coffee and cotton cutters are women—and your father and brother. You had to start picking coffee when you were six. For filling a 20-pound bucket you earn only 16 cents. Working sunup to sundown, you might earn a dollar.

Your "home" during the harvest is a long, windowless barrack built out of unpainted planks or plywood. With the other exhausted workers— men and women, old people and children, sick and well—you sleep on plywood slabs, called "drawers" because they are stacked four or five high with only a foot and a half of space between them. There is no privacy for there are no partitions. There is no flooring, no windows, not a single light bulb. The only toilet is the bushes. Filth all the day long. For three to four months a year this is home for you and for over 400,000 other Nicaraguans.

Working on the coffee estates is bad, but picking cotton is even worse. You found that out one year when your family had to travel even further, down to the Pacific coastal cotton estates, to find work. At least coffee grows in the cooler regions. But on the coastal lowlands the blinding tropical sun hangs in a cloudless sky, bringing temperatures to well over 100 degrees. You had nothing to protect you from the cotton branches, the pesticide-saturated fields, and the maddening swirl of gnats and jiggers.

Placing your baby sister on the edge of the hot, dusty field, your mother picked cotton as fast as she could, filling her sack and rushing to the weighing station so she could hurry back to nurse. She didn't know that tests would probably have shown that her breast milk had over 500 times the DDT considered safe for consumption by the World Health Organization, a frightening contamination due to twenty to forty aerial DDT sprayings a year of the cotton fields.

In the harvests, too, hunger is a constant companion. All you get are small portions of beans and fried bananas and, rarely, some rice or corn tortillas or a bit of smoked cheese in place of the bananas. Yet for this food, about three hours' wages are deducted from your pay. Even here, you're sure the owner makes profits. You only see meat on the final day of the harvest when the patron and his family put on a "feast."

As you grow older, you realize that even though your family has no land, it is not because your country lacks land. You learn—quite likely through a Catholic priest—that there are more than five agricultural acres for every Nicaraguan, and potentially twice that. The problem is that most of the land is owned by the few big landowners. The richest 2 percent own over 50 percent of the land, while the poorest 70 percent of landowners—and that doesn't include your father, who only rents his miserable plot—own only 2 percent of the land.

Not only do the rich own most of the land, you discover, but clearly they've got the best land. Their soil is most fertile and flat. Yet they waste

(continued)

its potential, using it mostly to graze cattle. By the 1970s, in fact, 10 out of 11 million acres used for export production were being devoted to cattle grazing.

While you are constantly hungry, you discover that 22 times more land goes to produce for export than to grow food for Nicaraguans. And much of the food-growing land is so poor and hilly that it should be in pasture. . . .

The history of your family, like tens of thousands of Nicaraguan campesino families, is tied to coffee. But you wonder where all the endless fields of cotton came from.

Your father explains that while he heard some talk of cotton when he was a boy, it was only in 1950, just ten years before you were born, that "white gold fever" hit Nicaragua. In only a few years the white puff balls took over the Pacific plain as far as you could see, north to south and right up to the base of the volcanos. The cotton plants wouldn't hold down the rich volcanic soils and soon the region became plagued with dust storms.

By the mid-1950s, cotton topped coffee as Nicaragua's biggest export. Somoza saw to it that the cotton investors got cheap bank credit, for he personally reaped millions of dollars on the cottom boom. It's completely unfair, your father tells you, that the rich export farmers don't even risk their money; he and the other campesinos grow what people really need most—basic foods—yet they can't get even the smallest bank loan.

In the cotton bonanza, campesinos, most of whom did not have any papers for their lands, were bought out for next to nothing; failing that, they were forced off the land. Absentee landowners returned to evict their campesino tenants and rent out their lands to cotton entrepreneurs.

When campesinos resisted, the National Guard burned their homes and crops and pulled up the fences. Indeed, some of the cotton speculators themselves were high officers in Somoza's National Guard, Nicaragua's army and police set up by the U.S. Marines. You understand more than ever why your father and all his friends hate the Guard.

Cotton took over the land that had been growing corn and beans, rice and sorghum, all the basic food crops of the people. The tens of thousands of displaced peasant producers at best wound up as sharecroppers and cash renters on plots of earth too small and poor to support them.

Some of the campesinos run off the land by the cotton invasion pushed east and north into the "agricultural frontier." There, just like your great-grandparents had done, they cleared trees and brush on the huge cattle haciendas only to be forced onto new uncleared land by cattlemen seeking to cash in on the next export boom—the 1960s boom in beef exports to the United States.

Pushed even deeper into the mountainous interior, these tens of thousands of campesinos are even poorer than your family. Almost half

(continued)

the year they are entirely cut off from the rest of the country: even a burro can't get through the muddy trails and dirt roads. Few have ever seen a doctor, even though the area teems with disease, including malaria and adult measles.

You think about all of this—what the priest says, your sisters and brothers needlessly dying, the stories of your grandmother and of your father, and what Somoza claims—every time you look down from your family's little hillside cornfield at the cattle grazing on the fertile valley plains of Somoza's lawyer.

---

1. From reading this article, how would you describe the nature of a rural peasant economy in prerevolutionary Nicaragua?

Underdevelopment is truly a shocking phenomenon. When one is placed in the midst of this condition, it is impossible not to be stunned by the poverty, disease, and squalor so prevalent throughout the developing world. Indeed, as Denis Goulet, the author of *The Cruel Choice,* has said, "Chronic poverty is a cruel kind of hell."

Once one confronts the physical and objective conditions of underdevelopment, it is not long before the emotional and psychological factors become evident and imposing. Underdevelopment breeds impotence, hopelessness, and vulnerability. Yet at the same time, it creates the preconditions for action, hope, and independent self-determination. As we shall see, to move from underdevelopment to development is a revolutionary and dialectical process.

Assume that we have a general sense of what it means to be underdeveloped: What, then, does it mean to be developed? Western economists have traditionally preferred to view development strictly in economic terms. Thus a nation able to increase its GNP per capita would be able to improve its standard of living. This requires increasing GNP and curbing population growth. In most cases, economic development would be characterized by an evolutionary process through which the developing nation becomes more and more like the advanced developed nations in the Western world today.

In recent years, this simplistic linear thinking has come under attack. There are several reasons for questioning the traditional viewpoint. First, in the developed world today, there is little agreement as to what it means to be developed. In fact, some are putting forth the notion of "overdevelopment" when describing the advanced nations. This is in part related to the issues surrounding the "quality of life" as the material standard of living increases. Second, there is a growing awareness of the multidimensional nature of development. In this context, economic development cannot be viewed as coincident with social development. It is necessary to examine the other institutions and processes of change in order to fully understand and appreciate the development process. We must also carefully investigate the political, social, and cultural institutions related to economic development. This point of view has been articulated by E. F. Schumacher, a British economist:

> Economic development is something much wider and deeper than economics. . . . Its roots lie outside the economic sphere, in education, organisation, discipline and, beyond that, in political independence and a national consciousness of self-reliance. It cannot be "produced" by skillful grafting operations carried out by foreign technicians or an indigenous elite that has lost contact with the ordinary people. It can succeed only if it carried forward as a broad, popular "movement of reconstruction" with primary emphasis on the full utilisation of the drive, enthusiasm, intelligence, and labour power of everyone. Success cannot be obtained by some form of magic produced by scientists, technicians, or economic planners. It can come only through a process of growth involving the education, organisation, and discipline of the whole population. Anything less than this must end in failure.
>
> —E. F. Schumacher, 1973. *Small Is Beautiful,* Harper & Row, pp. 192–193.

As we discuss the economic problems of developing nations, let us remember Schumacher's message and the human dimension of the subject. Also let us keep in mind the fact that, although we group the nations of the developing world together for the purpose of generalization, these nations are incredibly diverse. Their diversity is reflected in their geography, language, culture, customs, religion, political and social institutions, history, and natural resource endowments.

THE QUEST FOR ECONOMIC DEVELOPMENT

The quest for economic development by the Third World (Asia, Africa, and Latin America) is, as Goulet suggests both "cruel and necessary"—indeed, unavoidable. As we have noted, economic development has become synonymous with Western industrialization. For years, particularly during the 1960s (labeled the "Development Decade" by the United Nations), it was believed by most Western economists that the only way for a developing nation, or underdeveloped nation, to modernize was to follow the development model and experience of the now powerful and industrialized Western nations. The only real alternative to this model was the relatively new yet impressive model of socialism as practiced in the Soviet Union. However, the atrocities of Stalinist Russia and subsequent Cold War tensions made most nations skeptical of the Soviet model, even though by the mid-1960s the liberalized planning and market system of the Soviet economy had demonstrated its ability to produce rapid industrialization.

Many developing nations by the late 1960s and early 1970s had begun to realize that their quest for economic development and modernization was beginning in a period quite different from those that produced the success stories of the United States, Western Europe, and Japan. They have slowly come to the conclusion that this time period calls for a different strategy and a model more closely related to their own particular conditions and needs. It is important to recognize that they did not arrive at this conclusion overnight. It was reached after years of experience filled with trial and error and the failure to develop. Nevertheless, for those developing nations that have come to this conclusion, their present realities make it very difficult to change the course of history in midstream. On the other hand, there are some who are still committed to following the Western industrialized model.

As we saw in the last few chapters, in terms of international trade and finance the developing nations are having their share of problems in constructing a development model and strategy in a very competitive and often hostile interdependent global environment. In order to better understand their plight, let us now consider several crucial questions: (1) What is different about this particular historical epoch for the developing nations? (2) What basic problems and obstacles block them from achieving genuine economic development? (3) What are the basic economic schools of thought used to analyze their problems, and what policy prescriptions emanate from the different economic paradigms?

> **2. *Why* is it important for the developed world to understand the problems of the developing world?**

THE MODERN CONTEXT FOR DEVELOPING

The developing nations are launching their development schemes at a critical historical juncture. The emerging global awareness of resource scarcity, especially with respect to energy, has cast a dark shadow on industrialization dreams in terms of Western affluence. (Of course, oil-exporting developing nations such as Venezuela face a different set of future options.) What is hard to accept is that development requiring high-cost energy and capital-intensive technology is just not possible for every nation. Availability and cost considerations prohibit the continued use of and reliance on such methods of production in the long-term future. Second, developing nations begin their bid for modernization in a world with great disparities of wealth and power. In the world political economy, the developing nations are weak, fragile, vulnerable, and dependent vis-à-vis the advanced nations. A few nations have some leverage because of their control over scarce natural resources needed by the advanced nations, but most do not have this power. Finally, the developing nations, many of which were once the colonies or possessions of the advanced nations, cannot themselves gain colonies or possessions to supply them with the inexpensive labor and raw materials necessary for their own industrialization.

BASIC ECONOMIC PROBLEMS

Given these qualifying considerations, what then are the most basic economic problems facing the developing nations? Over the past several years each and every international conference related to this broad topic has inevitably identified *five* areas of concern: (1) population growth and rates of economic growth; (2) the distribution of income; (3) inflation and unemployment; (4) balance of payments difficulties, unequal terms of trade, currency instability, and mounting debt problems; and (5) questions of external control and influence, and human rights. Let us look briefly at each one of these basic problems.

1. Population growth rates alone make the prospect of meaningful economic development difficult. With the population growth rates in many developing nations greater than 3 percent a year, it would require unprecedented rates of economic growth to make any progress whatsoever. For example, it would require a real GNP growth rate of 8 percent to achieve a net growth rate of 5 percent in GNP per capita if population growth were 3 percent a year. At present, many developing nations are experiencing real GNP growth rates of less than 2 percent a year. Against these empirical data, the future is indeed grim. It would appear that a successful population control effort is a necessity for most nations. The growth of population, in addition to influencing the economic growth rate, also puts great pressure on the cities as the rural-to-urban migration trends continue to result in overcrowded, congested, and polluted urban environments.

2. The distribution of income is a continuing problem for the developing nations. First, there is the problem of the growing gap between the developed and the developing nations in terms of income distribution. A recent U.N. study on the future of the world economy made the following point: "If the minimum targets of growth for the developing countries, as set by the International Development Strategy, were implemented continuously throughout the remaining decades of this century, and if the growth rates prevailing in the developed countries during the last two decades were to be retained in the future, then the gap in per-capita gross product between these two groups of countries, which was 12 to 1 on the average in 1970, would not start diminishing even by the year 2000."

   In addition to this growing "gap" between the rich and poor nations, there is the problem of *internal* unequal distribution of income. The economic growth that has taken place has resulted in a highly unequal distribution of income and wealth such that the bottom 60 percent of the population has not benefited at all from this growth. In fact, it is the top 20 percent of the population in most developing nations that accumulates the income and wealth produced (see Table 27.4).

3. Added to the problems of population and income distribution are the problems of inflation and unemployment. Inflation has resulted in a declining standard of living and currency instability. It is not uncommon to see rates of inflation in developing nations ranging from 25 to 300 percent a year.

   Accompanying the high inflation and sluggish growth rates is the problem of unemployment. Unemployment in most developing nations ranges from 15 to 40 percent. This problem is exacerbated by the con-

Table 27.4 INCOME DISTRIBUTION: LDC'S VS. THE UNITED STATES

COUNTRY	YEAR	LOWEST	2ND	3RD	4TH	HIGHEST	TOP 10 PERCENT
United States	1978	4.6	8.9	14.1	22.1	50.3	33.4
India	1976	7.0	9.2	13.9	20.5	49.4	33.6
Sri Lanka	1970	7.5	11.7	15.7	21.7	43.4	28.2
Mexico	1977	2.9	7.0	12.0	20.4	57.7	40.6
Thailand	1976	5.6	9.6	13.9	21.1	49.8	34.1
Costa Rica	1971	3.3	8.7	13.3	19.9	54.8	39.5
Kenya	1976	2.6	6.3	11.5	19.2	60.4	45.8

Source: *World Bank Annual Report,* 1983.

centrated nature of the urban population. Thus Mexico City with a population of 14 million can have an unemployment rate of 35 percent.

4. The problems of international trade and finance are many. Highly unequal terms of trade and commodity price instability typically result in balance-of-payments difficulties. These balance-of-payments problems then trigger off foreign exchange and currency instability problems. Sooner or later, the developing nation out of desperation is forced to borrow money from any one of a number of sources (International Monetary Fund, World Bank, Agency for International Development, Export-Import Bank, private banks and financial institutions, etc.). This act of borrowing creates a debt burden for the developing nation. This process initiates a "vicious circle" that effectively makes the development effort more and more difficult. With the added burden of the OPEC price increases in 1973 and 1979, the developing nations increased their combined debt to over $950 billion in 1986. Experts are now debating the possibility and consequences of defaults on these debts on the international financial system.

5. The last of the five basic problems is the issue of external control, influence, and human rights. A truly frustrating and contradictory dilemma exists for any developing nation today. It is impossible to attain economic development in isolation. Like it or not, global interdependence is a reality. Most nations admit that they need help in many ways from other nations. Yet assistance in whatever form is difficult to receive without also accepting some degree of external control and influence. Ideally, most nations would like to solicit assistance in a form and manner consistent with their goals of independence, autonomy, and self-determination. The reality is certainly far from this ideal. Given the nature of the major international financial institutions, nation-states and their nationalistic behaviors, multinational corporations, global technology, communications systems, etc., the possibility of interacting with others without being controlled and influenced by

them becomes almost impossible. The most recent evidence of this is the "human rights" issue. There is great pressure on the major Western nations and their institutions that deal with the developing nations not to grant aid or loans to nations that "violate basic human rights." Some developing nations, such as Argentina, Brazil, and Chile, have reacted strongly against this kind of political leverage by the Western nations.

COMPETING VIEWS OF UNDERDEVELOPMENT: THREE MODELS

We have seen that there are many different kinds of developing nations with similar problems that differ only by degree. Economists have debated for years why nations are underdeveloped and what should be done to overcome this condition. Three basic models are used to answer these questions: the diffusion model, the structuralist model, and the dependency model. Let us examine each of these models.

The Diffusion Model

The **diffusion model** most closely represents the orthodox or mainstream economic school of thought. It posits at the outset the following crucial assumptions: (1) progress is related to the spread of modernism to backward, archaic, and traditional areas; (2) the primary catalyst for development is the diffusion of advanced technology and foreign capital from the advanced nations to the developing nations, for example, through MNC's; (3) underdevelopment is a condition that all nations have experienced; (4) traditional cultural and behavioral values need to be transformed into modern cultural and behavioral values; (5) economic development means essentially industrialization and diversification; (6) economic development requires political stability and limited government; and (7) the process of economic development is a gradual evolutionary process.

Basically, the diffusion model claims that the developing nations lack capital, technical knowledge, and the proper cultural perspective. It is usually further argued that the institutions of capitalism—private gain, private property, markets, and individualism—will be best able to create economic development.

The Structuralist Model

The **structuralist model,** a second school of thought on development, evolved in the 1960s during the United Nations Development Decade. This school was pioneered by Raul Prébisch, an economist with the United Nations Economic Commission on Latin America.

This model argues that the lack of development in the Third World (particularly Latin America) is due to "structural" deficiencies of the capitalist-oriented economic systems of the developing world. The capitalist diffusion model does not deal with what Prébisch and others felt were the fundamental obstacles to development, such as: (1) the inefficient systems of land tenure in the agricultural sector, (2) the excessive reliance on a single-crop economy, and (3) the concentration of economic wealth and power in the hands of elite classes, resulting in persistently unequal distribution of income.

The structuralist model rejects the analysis of the diffusion model. For example, as Prébisch points out, the diffusion model implies that specialization and division of labor should form the basis of exchange between nations in such a way that all nations tend to benefit by trading with one another. The question remains, why is it that advanced nations are supplied with raw materials at low prices and, in return, the developing nations receive capital and manufactured goods at high prices? Commodity pricing and the unequal terms of trade are basic issues analyzed in the structuralist model.

The structuralist model also questions the capitalist diffusion model's reliance on the market system to meet the needs of the developing nation's economy. Given the unequal distribution of income and wealth, the insufficiency of supply compared with demand, and the luxury consumption of the elite classes, the uncritical reliance on the market system to allocate and distribute goods and services equably is totally incomprehensible. The structuralists argue that the use of the free-market mechanism, given these institutionalized imperfections, becomes irrational in the context of the developing world.

The most important contribution from the structuralist model is that economic theories developed in advanced nations should not be blindly transferred to the developing nations, each of which has unique problems.

Uneven development: Mexican affluence. (Photograph by Steve Stamos.)

To conclude, the structuralist model would like to see the capitalist diffusion model reformed. If the structural constraints were removed, then the unfettered diffusion model would be an excellent development strategy for the developing nation. This would require, among other things, major land reform, the redistribution of income and wealth, the diversification of production, commodity price stability and equality, and a variation of orthodox economic policies designed specifically for the needs of the developing nations.

The Dependency Model

By dependence we mean a situation in which the economy of certain countries is conditioned by the development and expansion of another economy to which the former is subjected. The relation of interdependence between two or more economies, and between these and world trade, assumes the form of dependence when some countries (the dominant ones) can expand and can be self-sustaining, while other countries (the dependent ones) can do this only as a reflection of that expansion, which can have either positive or negative effect on their immediate development.

> —Theotonio Dos Santos, in Charles K. Wilber (Ed.), *The Political Economy of Development and Underdevelopment.* New York: Random House, 1973, p. 109.

The **dependency model** was developed out of the analysis of underdevelopment in Latin America. However, its proponents believe that the model also has general applicability for the rest of the developing world. As general dissatisfaction increased over the inability of the "structuralist" school to explain continuing stagnation and uneven development throughout the 1960s, radical economists developed this model as a modern Marxist model of imperialism. What made this model a more relevant extension of the original imperialist model was the inclusion of a concrete analysis of the multinational corporation and major international financial institutions as the major vehicles of modern imperialism.

The dependency model is based on a number of essential assumptions and postulates:

1. Underdevelopment is not an original state from which every country begins its quest for development.

2. Contemporary underdevelopment has been "created" by the process of global capitalist development and expansion.

3. The economies of the developing nations have been integrated into and shaped by the needs of the advanced nations' economies in such a way that the developing nations become "dependent" on the advanced nations.

4. This dependency is created by foreign penetration of the developing nation's banking system, manufacturing sector, retailing sector, communications system, advertising, and educational sector.

Uneven development: Mexican poverty. (Photograph by Steve Stamos.)

5. The developing nation's economic surplus is systematically drained out of the nation and is transferred to the advanced nations.

6. Foreign investment by the multinational corporation in particular is the primary vehicle for the penetration of the economy and the extraction or appropriation of the economic surplus. Foreign investment may increase the GNP but results in the outward flow of capital, foreign control of the internal economy, and investment decisions made according to the various criteria of profitability rather than domestic employment and production needs.

7. As the conditions of uneven development and dependency deepen, the developing nation is forced to seek aid, grants, and loans from international financial institutions, governments, and private lending agencies. This process eventually puts the developing nation into the situation of being controlled by outside institutions while becoming more and more dependent as debts mount because of excessive borrowing to pay off current debts and finance future development projects.

8. Dependency theorists claim that "authentic" development and the elimination of the state of underdevelopment requires the elimination of foreign capital and penetration, and the creation of democratic socialism. This will allow for the following: economic sovereignty, production and distribution of

basic necessities according to the needs of the people, the production and use of the economic surplus for continued authentic development and social and political equality.*

> 3. **Which of these brief sketches of the schools of thought on underdevelopment seems most helpful to you in understanding underdevelopment? Why?**

THE FUTURE OF DEVELOPING NATIONS

Making prognostications about the future of the developing world is not an easy task. Certainly it would be easy either to speak optimistically or to speak of obstacles and impossibilities. We shall for the moment do neither. It is our feeling that some optimism and some skepticism are not only warranted but necessary and healthy in order to develop a rational and mature perspective.

In our minds, we observe a world fraught with complex changes being brought about by a myriad of forces all interacting simultaneously. It is possible to say that the developing nations are fast approaching a truly unique historical watershed. Out of this apparent chaos is emerging a "new awareness" evidenced in recent years by the repeated demands on behalf of the leaders of the developing world for a **new international economic order.** The people of the developing world, while certainly not united in their stands on such issues, nevertheless share a common belief that one day they will have a future characterized by authentic development defined in their own terms. What this future will be and what role a new international economic order will play in it is mere conjecture at this time. Nevertheless, the dialogue going on now between the industrialized nations and the Third World must be examined in more detail. It is to this task that we now turn.

The Call for a New International Economic Order (NIEO)

The developing nations have come increasingly to realize that the international economic system based on the principles of free trade and the international division of labor has resulted in an unequal distribution of total global wealth. They perceive the nature of their present integration into the global economy as being detrimental to their dreams of genuine development. This position of inequality and dependency has been viewed as intolerable and unacceptable. The developing world is no longer willing to acquiesce to a system in which it sees no hope for the future.

The increasing collective consciousness of the nonaligned developing nations in the late 1960s and early 1970s produced extensive debate and dialogue centered on the need for a global restructuring of the international economic and financial

*See Ron Chilcote and Joel Edelstein, *Latin America: The Struggle with Dependency and Beyond*, Schocken, New York, 1974, Part I.

systems. These discussions resulted in the Sixth Special Session of the United Nations in April of 1974. At this session of the U.N. General Assembly two resolutions were drafted and adopted. The first called for the establishment of a New International Economic Order. The second resolution outlined a Programme of Action to bring about the creation of the New International Economic Order.

With these actions, the **Group of 77** (the developing nations) evidenced a new global posture vis-à-vis the developed world. They substituted "defiance for the deference of the past."

On December 12, 1974, at the regularly scheduled 29th Session of the U.N. General Assembly, the call for an NIEO was reaffirmed in the adoption of the "Charter of Economic Rights and Duties of States." Later in 1975 the U.N. called for the "full and complete economic emancipation" of the developing world.

The following excerpt is from the May 1, 1974, "Declaration of the U.N. General Assembly on the Establishment of a New International Economic Order."

DECLARATION ON THE ESTABLISHMENT OF A NEW INTERNATIONAL ECONOMIC ORDER

We, the Members of the United Nations,

Having convened a special session of the General Assembly to study for the first time the problems of raw materials and development, devoted to the consideration of the most important economic problems facing the world community,

Bearing in mind the spirit, purposes and principles of the Charter of the United Nations to promote the economic advancement and social progress of all peoples,

Solemnly proclaim our united determination to work urgently for THE ESTABLISHMENT OF A NEW INTERNATIONAL ECONOMIC ORDER based on equity, sovereign equality, interdependence, common interest and co-operation among all States, irrespective of their economic and social systems which shall correct inequalities and redress existing injustices, make it possible to eliminate the widening gap between the developed and the developing countries and ensure steadily accelerating economic and social development and peace and justice for present and future generations, and, to that end, declare:

1. The greatest and most significant achievement during the last decades has been the independence from colonial and alien domination of a large number of peoples and nations which has enabled them to become members of the community of free peoples. Technological progress has also been made in all spheres of economic activities in the last three decades, thus providing a solid potential for improving the

(continued)

well-being of all peoples. However, the remaining vestiges of alien and colonial domination, foreign occupation, racial discrimination, *apartheid* and neo-colonialism in all its forms continue to be among the greatest obstacles to the full emancipation and progress of the developing countries and all the peoples involved. . . .

2. The present international economic order is in direct conflict with current developments in international political and economic relations. Since 1970, the world economy has experienced a series of grave crises which have had severe repercussions, especially on the developing countries because of their generally greater vulnerability to external economic impulses. . . .

3. All these changes have thrust into prominence the reality of interdependence of all the members of the world community. Current events have brought into sharp focus the realization that the interests of the developed countries and those of the developing countries can no longer be isolated from each other, that there is a close interrelationship between the prosperity of the developed countries and the growth and development of the developing countries, and that the prosperity of the international community as a whole depends upon the prosperity of its constituent parts. . . .

CONCLUSION

The period from 1974 to the present has been filled with many lessons and harsh realities for most developing nations. The United Nations proposal for a New International Economic Order, passed with great optimism, has been met with a decade of poor economic conditions and increasing political tension throughout the world—both of which have virtually eliminated the essential climate of global cooperation necessary for the NIEO proposals to be effective. In particular the 1980s have seen these dreams and hopes fade away as the Cold War posture of the Reagan Administration fueled the arms race and escalated tensions between the United States and the Soviet Union. The United States chose to view the problems of the developing nations in strictly ideological terms. The continuing economic problems of the West pushed each nation further into protectionist policies, thereby excluding most developing nations from the potential gains of free trade. The **debt crisis** has become a major issue in the 1980s and no long-term solution appears to be forthcoming. Most experts agree that what is needed is sustained economic growth in the Western advanced economies and structural changes, guided by creative leadership with popular support, in the developing nations themselves.

KEY CONCEPTS

GNP per capita
Economic Development
diffusion model
structuralist model

dependency model
new international economic order (NIEO)
Group of 77
debt crisis

REVIEW QUESTIONS

1. Define in your own words the term "economic development." What are the basic obstacles to economic development in most developing nations?

2. Compare the diffusion and dependency models.

3. What moral and ethical issues and questions are there in the development process?

4. What do you think would be an appropriate response by the United States to the original demands for a NIEO at the end of the 1980s?

SUGGESTED READINGS

Joseph Collins, 1982. *What Difference Could a Revolution Make?* Food First. An excellent book about the agricultural transition in Nicaragua from 1979 to 1982.

Darrell Dalamaide, 1984. *Debt Shock,* Anchor Press. An excellent historical analysis of the international debt crisis.

Walter LaFeber, 1983. *Inevitable Revolutions: The United States and Central America,* Norton. A detailed historical analysis of U.S. involvement and foreign policy in Central America. The author makes the case that present and future revolutions in the region are rooted in the poverty and political oppression of the majority of people and not in external influences.

Bhasker P. Menon, 1977. *Global Dialogue: The New International Order,* Pergamon Press. A good introduction to the U.N. dialogue about the NIEO in the mid-1970s. This book contains the original transcripts of the major resolutions passed by the U.N. on the NIEO.

Michael Todaro, 1986. *Economic Development of the Third World* (3rd ed.), Longman. An excellent textbook on economic development.

Charles K. Wilber, 1984. *The Political Economy of Development and Underdevelopment,* Random House. A fine book of readings on development from a political economy perspective.

28
Chapter

Comparative Socialist Systems

INTRODUCTION

In this chapter, we will briefly review the differences between capitalism and socialism as economic systems. Then we will survey three societies undergoing socialist transition. First, we will examine the historical experience of the Soviet Union. Next, we will look at the experience of the People's Republic of China; and, last, we will analyze the Cuban experience. Our primary objective is to learn about the similarities and differences among societies attempting a socialist transformation. In addition, we want to keep in mind that there are many different kinds of economic systems in the world. All of these economic systems fall within the framework of the polar opposites of capitalism and socialism.

SOCIALISM VERSUS CAPITALISM

Socialism and capitalism present themselves as the two basic kinds, or models, of economic systems in the world today. While **capitalism** is characterized by the essential features of private ownership of the means of production and reliance on the market system (prices and profits), **socialism** is normally associated with the public (social) ownership of the means of production and reliance on some form of planning, either centralized or decentralized. As should be obvious by now, these two systems have very different approaches to accomplishing the basic fundamental economic tasks common to any society: (1) determining what is to be produced, (2) determining the level of production, (3) allocating scarce resources efficiently, and (4) distributing the goods and services produced. While this general description of each system usually serves to distinguish one system from the other, it is possible to define each in greater detail (see Tables 28.1 and 28.2).

While different property relations (ownership forms) distinguish capitalism and socialism, there is another major feature—ideology. Capitalism is based on the primacy of the individual. It is characterized by the private accumulation of income and wealth. The competitive assumptions made about human beings in the context of the private market economy naturally produce inequalities among individuals and classes. The ideology of socialism emphasizes the cooperative spirit of human beings. This ideology seeks to promote an egalitarian pattern of income distribution and eliminate the exploitation of human beings by each other for private gain.

These ideal types of systems do not exist anywhere in the world today in their pure theoretical forms, yet every nation in the world today is a reflection of some combination of these two systems and their ideologies. For example, we merely have to point to the following examples to appreciate this fact: (1) the French socialism of François Mitterand in the early 1980s; (2) the African socialism of Julius Nyerere in Tanzania; (3) the welfare states of the Scandanavian countries, particularly Sweden; (4) Eastern Bloc nations such as Bulgaria and Romania; (5) the dynamic capitalist economy of Japan; (6) the economy of South Africa; and (7) West Germany. Each example is testimony to the fact that the world's two great economic systems have successfully given birth to many different offspring. Usually what differentiates these systems from each other, aside from basic ideology and property relations, are the roles of the market and the state in the economy.

Table 28.1 CAPITALISM

1. Private ownership of the means of production
2. A market in labor
   a. Workers are divorced from ownership.
   b. Workers are without control over the process of production or choice of product produced.
   c. The price of labor (wage) is determined by the supply and demand for labor.
3. A market for land and natural resources
4. Income distribution is based on market-determined returns to owned factors of production (land, labor, and capital).
5. Markets in essential commodities (basic needs)
6. Control of the means of production (capital) and the production process by owners of capital or their managerial representatives

Table 28.2 SOCIALISM

1. Public (social) ownership of the means of production
2. Labor markets are determined by planning decisions.
   a. Workers participate in self-management and/or shared decision making.
   b. The price of labor is determined by planners in accordance with a market wage (supply and demand) in combination with a social wage that incorporates the free provision of many basic needs (i.e., health, education, transportation, housing, etc.).
3. Government allocation of land and natural resources
4. Income distribution is based on a market-determined wage, guided by government planning, in accordance with a social wage and government goals of reducing inequalities in the distribution of income. Income is not related to the ownership of capital or the exploitation of labor.
5. Provision of basic needs is free or at government-subsidized prices (**social wage**); goal is to maximize public welfare.
6. Full employment of human resources, utilizing **moral and material incentives** for increasing output and efficiency, guided by planning

A socialist economy generally relies on either centralized or **decentralized** planning (**market socialism**) to accomplish the basic economic goals and objectives. The centralized model utilized in the Soviet Union is based on long-term **economic planning,** usually five-year plans in which targets and goals are set and synchronized. Socialists believe that the planning process offers the opportunity to overcome the problems of cyclical instability endemic to capitalism, as well as being more efficient than the unregulated market. In the case of the Soviet Union, the planning, for the most part, progresses from the top down. Once appropriate information is gathered and sent up from the elaborate industrial and agricultural structures and merged with other significant data from vital sectors, the Soviet planners put together an input–output model that identifies all of the necessary inputs required to meet the desired goals for the five-year plan. In contrast, the decentralized market socialist model characteristic of Yugoslavia uses self-adjusting markets combined with greater freedom of decision making for individual firms to determine the pattern of production, level of output, and the allocation of resources; but the State does play a very prominent role by actively intervening in the economic process to ensure that the goals and objectives of individual firms can be met and that the national public welfare will be achieved.

In both the centrally planned and the decentralized market socialist economy, the state is engaged in the determination of the level of economic activity, the rate of growth of the economy, the level of investment (use of savings), and the determination of prices and wages.

As previously mentioned, one of the most interesting and successful market socialist economies has been Yugoslavia. By 1949, Yugoslavia under the leadership of the late Marshal Tito had broken away from the dominance of the Soviet Union. While rejecting the Soviet model of socialism, Yugoslavia was dedicated to the development of a genuine socialist nation. The alternative path to socialism became known as democratic market socialism. This model of socialism stressed the importance of **workers self-management.** If the workers themselves were directly involved in running their own enterprises, it would not be necessary to have a large dominating bureaucracy planning every facet of the society. The goal of bringing democracy to the workplace was at the center of the Yugoslav experience with market socialism. The historical experience of Yugoslavia has been an invaluable example for all nations.

Let us now turn to an examination of the Soviet experience.

THE SOVIET UNION

Marx's prediction that socialism would develop out of the state of advanced capitalist development was proven incorrect by the experience of the Soviet Union. In the latter part of the 19th century and the early years of the 20th century, the Soviet Union was a backward, semifeudal society. In the place of Marx's nonexistent urban proletariat was a peasant agrarian population suffering under the yoke and domination of an autocracy ruling a stagnant feudalistic society.

The early outbreaks of protest culminated in the October 1917 victory for the Bolsheviks, spearheaded by the leadership and doctrines of Lenin and Trotsky. This revolution changed the course of history for much of humanity.

During the early years of the revolution, a civil war lasting from 1917 to 1921 resulted in the adoption of a policy developed by Lenin called "war communism." This policy was executed primarily for the purpose of controlling and regulating capitalism in the urban areas and nationalizing large factories. Throughout the nation these policies were met with resistance, particularly in the countryside. Although Lenin proposed the socialization of production, administration of production by worker organizations, and equalization of salaries, the Bolshevik's authoritarianism fueled the compound problems of the civil war. In order to survive, Lenin found himself oscillating, displaying inconsistencies between his theory and his policies. After the end of the debilitating civil war period, Lenin instituted the New Economic Policy (NEP) program in an effort to recover and begin anew the process of socialist transformation. The first priority was the increased development of the forces of production. The material base for socialism did not exist and was consequently hindering progress on other fronts.

During the years of the NEP (1921–1923), Lenin managed to hold the economy and society together. Lenin died in 1924. After his death the Soviet leadership engaged in a power struggle to claim his vacant seat. This power struggle evolved into what is now called the "Great Debate," which centered around the issue of industrialization. The basic questions were how best to industrialize as fast as possible, and what was the relationship with the peasantry going to be during this industrialization drive?

The peasantry were the key to successful industrialization. The necessary economic surplus for investment in the capital-intensive urban industrial sector had to come from increased levels of agricultural production and savings. To generate a sufficient surplus, the peasants had to produce more output than ever before, while having their meager levels of consumption stay the same or even decrease. This was a great burden to lay upon the rural peasantry. They were far removed from the revolution and many did not really know what the difference was between their new leaders and the overthrown czar. Trotsky, leader of the left wing of the Communist Party, argued for the "Big Push" strategy—whatever the cost, to industrialize as fast as possible, utilizing sound economic planning. Opposing Trotsky was Bukharin, leader of the right wing of the Communist Party. He argued for a policy of "gradualism" expressing concern for the peasants. In the middle, representing the center faction of the Communist Party was Joseph Stalin. Initially, he sided with the Bukharin position in order to overwhelm and defeat Trotsky, but then he swung around to an ultraleft program. The Stalinist solution began to surface in the years 1927 to 1929. His solution was to forcibly collectivize the peasantry on state farms. This way, through the elimination of rich farmers (kulaks) and the collectivization of all other peasants, it would be possible to decrease consumption, increase production, and thereby generate the economic surplus for industrialization. This policy and its enforcement were met with considerable violent reaction.

Beginning in 1928, the Soviet Union embarked on a series of five-year plans, the third of which was interrupted by World War II. During this period, the Soviet Union was able to flex its muscles at the world. Emphasis on investment in heavy industry dominated the priorities of the central planners. By 1926 over 90 percent of the peasants were collectivized. Between 1926 and 1939, urbanization increased twofold. In 1927, 80 percent of industrial output came from new investment or improved machinery. The Soviet Union had emerged from a backward, agrarian, feudalistic society to a growing industrial world power. Under Stalin the material preconditions for socialism were being created at the expense of the workers and the peasants.

The Germans invaded the Soviet Union in 1941, occupying primarily the eastern regions, rich in raw materials and resources. The occupied territory contained 70 percent of the coal, 60 percent of the iron, 50 percent of the steel production capacity, and 33 percent of the grain production. The war dealt the Soviet Union a tremendous blow not only in halting economic growth but also by destroying much of the production base of the nation. In addition there were over 25 million people killed (mostly males).

After the war, with aid from the United States and other nations, the reconstruction process began. By the early 1950s substantial progress had been made. The fifth five-year plan (1950–1955) saw an astounding 80 percent increase in producer goods and a 65 percent increase in consumer goods.

After the war, tensions between the Soviet Union and the United States increased, evolving into the "Cold War" period. In addition, the Western defense perimeter established under the framework of the Truman Doctrine, along with the growing dissatisfaction of Marshal Tito of Yugoslavià with the dogmas of Stalin, created external pressures on the Soviet Union by the end of the 1940s. Meanwhile, in 1949, Mao Zedong had taken power in China.

In 1953, with the end of the Korean War, the riots of workers and students against the East German government and the general dissatisfaction throughout the rest of Eastern Europe created a dynamic backdrop for the death of Stalin. After Stalin's death, Nikita Khrushchev assumed the Soviet leadership. With him came a gradual liberalization of policies, reflecting a need to achieve a better balance of growth between the industrial and agricultural sectors.

A critical juncture in Soviet history was reached on February 25, 1956, when Khrushchev, in a speech to the 20th Congress of the Soviet Communist Party, openly criticized and attacked Stalin. During his speech, he praised the work and legacy of Lenin, while denouncing the policies of Stalin. From the mid-1950s to the mid-1960s, tensions between the United States and the Soviet Union further intensified. The dramatic Cuban missile crisis—coming in the midst of the space race, the arms race, and the competition to produce the greatest growth in GNP—dominated the time, energy, and resources of both nations at that time. Foreign relations were strained by the Sino-Soviet split as well as support for wars of national liberation throughout the developing world, especially Southeast Asia. Closer to home, in the Eastern Bloc countries, trends were in motion that would apply more pressure upon the Soviets.

Through 1965, the Soviet Union had been operating within the framework of a centralized bureaucratic planning system. This method of running the economy had indeed produced impressive growth rates, especially in heavy industry. The liberalization programs in Yugoslavia put pressure on Soviet planners to adjust to current needs and trends, and throughout the Eastern Bloc there was a movement toward decentralization. This movement was in part a demand for greater worker participation and the use of some market incentives to make the production system more productive and efficient. So, the Soviet Union began its own subtle process of decentralization. Evsei G. Liberman instituted a series of economic reforms (under Kosygin). These reforms allowed for the use of profitability as the criterion for efficiency in production, a free input mix, a bonus for managers meeting established targets, and some material incentives for workers. By the late 1960s, the Swedish economist Jan Tinbergen advanced a proposition arguing that the economic systems of the United States and the Soviet Union were on a "convergence" path and would in time become indistinguishable.

The Soviet economy is centrally planned. The government draws up five-year plans such as the one for 1981–1985 depicted in Table 28.3. In this plan, estimates (forecasts) are made in terms of targets or goals, for example, to expand agricultural output by 12–14 percent over the five-year period. This planning effort requires that the inputs to production be aligned with the desired output. Soviet planners use very sophisticated input–output analysis to achieve their goals. Looking at Table 28.4, it is possible to see the relative mix of GNP allocated to consumption, fixed investment, other investment, and defense for the period 1960–1980. Looking at the perfor-

Table 28.3 SOVIET FIVE-YEAR PLAN, 1981–1985

	ANNUAL PERCENTAGE INCREASE
National income	18–20
Total industrial production	26–28
Electric power	21
Steel	16
Machines and manufacturing	40
Agricultural output	12–14
Productive fixed capital	26–28
Consumer goods	27–29
Per capita real income	16–18
Retail trade	22–25
Average monthly wage	13–16
Collective farmers' income from the communal sector of collective farms	20–22

Source: Daniel Fusfeld, *Economics: Principles of Political Economy,* Scott, Foresman, & Company, 1982, Chapter 35, p. 611.

mance of the Soviet economy since 1961, it is interesting to see in Table 28.5 the behavior of GNP over this period. The 1960s were years of strong growth, averaging 5.1 percent. The 1970s, though, have registered an uneven track record, with very low growth.

The 1970s and 1980s have revealed a Soviet economy with growth rates of 0.8% in 1979 and an anemic 1.4% in 1980. The agricultural sector has not been able to expand and produce the basic foodstuffs for its people. Indeed, the United States, ideological tensions and political rhetoric aside, has become the "bread-basket" for the Soviets. This apparent contradiction is easily explained by the dependency of U.S. farmers in the Midwest on the Soviets for our grain exports. (Consider the

Table 28.4 PERCENTAGE OF SOVIET GNP ALLOCATED TO CONSUMPTION, INVESTMENT, AND DEFENSE

	1960	1970	1980
Consumption	58	54	53
Fixed investment	20	23	26
Other investment	4	5	7
Defense	18	18	14

Source: Central Intelligence Agency, *Handbook of Economic Statistics,* 1981, Table 37.

Table 28.5 SOVIET GNP

YEAR	GROWTH RATE (PERCENTAGE)
1961–65	5.0
1966–70	5.2
1971–75	3.7
1975	1.7
1976	4.8
1977	3.2
1978	3.4
1979	0.8
1980	1.4

Source: Central Intelligence Agency, *Handbook of Economic Statistics,* 1981, Table 45.

impact on our trade balance and our balance of payments if we halt shipment of grain to the Soviets.) In addition to agricultural problems, the Soviets have diverted enormous human and physical resources to the military. This has produced the same distortions that the U.S. economy experiences from our massive military expenditures. For the Soviets this opportunity cost shows up most dramatically in the absence of consumer goods. Most economists who study the Soviet economy tend to emphasize the worst features of it and usually combine their economic critique with political judgments oriented toward the lack of individual freedom and human rights abuses. Certainly the writings and testimony of such notable figures as Alexander Solzhenitsyn and Andrei Sakharov serve as a constant reminder of the past and present transgressions against those who have spoken out against the Soviet system.

By the mid-1980s there was tremendous concern about the prospect of nuclear war in both major countries. There was great tension surrounding the Soviet's invasion of Afghanistan. Soviet-watchers continue to point out the failures of the economy and argue that things do not seem to be changing much even after the death of Chernenko and the ascendancy of Gorbachev.

THE PEOPLE'S REPUBLIC OF CHINA

China in 1949 under the leadership of Chairman Mao Zedong set out to transform itself from a backward feudal agrarian society into an evenly balanced socialist society. The early years of the Chinese Revolution witnessed massive land reform in the primarily peasant agricultural society. The decade of the 1950s was devoted to agricultural development and some gradual industrial development with substantial support and assistance from the Soviet Union. In 1958, the Great Leap Forward was launched in order to fully institute the complex Chinese commune system in the agricultural sector while at the same time implementing an industrialization program of "walking on two legs" that essentially gave light, medium, and heavy industry equal treatment. The Great Leap Forward was somewhat successful but resulted in general disappointment. From 1959 to 1961 the "Crisis Years" set in, resulting in the Sino-Soviet split and internal ideological power struggles over the "correct" path to pursue in the future. The New Economic Policy, designed to revitalize the Chinese economy, involved the application and practice of policies termed capitalist and similar to those being implemented in the Soviet Union by the liberal reform economist Evsei Liberman. Great debate raged during these years, as some argued that Mao's way was the only way to avoid the road back to capitalism that Mao and his followers argued that the Soviet Union had traveled. There was fear that uneven development with too rapid industrialization would result in a privileged minority running a vast bureaucracy, thus abandoning the goals of the revolution. This running debate culminated in the Cultural Revolution, reaffirmed Mao's position, and guided the country into the early 1970s. In 1971 the first Western visitors made their way into the People's Republic of China and subsequently made their findings and impressions public. They were incredibly impressed by what they found and awed at what the Chinese people had accomplished in so little time. In 1970, the Stanford economist John Gurley wrote the following:

> The truth is that China over the past two decades has made very remarkable economic advances (though not steadily) on almost all fronts. The basic, overriding economic fact about China is that for twenty years she has fed, clothed, and housed everyone, has kept them healthy, and has educated most. Millions have not starved; sidewalks and streets have not been covered with multitudes of sleeping, begging, hungry, and illiterate human beings; millions are not disease-ridden. To find such deplorable conditions, one does not look to China these days but, rather, to India, Pakistan, and almost anywhere else in the under-developed world. These facts are so basic, so fundamentally important, that they completely dominate China's economic picture, even if one grants all of the erratic and irrational policies alleged by her numerous critics.

China in the 1970s went through a series of internal political power struggles following the death of Mao. As the leadership changed hands, debate raged over two issues: (1) Was Mao's legacy and strategy for Chinese socialist development beyond public criticism? (2) What kinds of changes were needed to continue the march toward socialist development? It was not long before severe criticism of Mao's practices and policies was initiated in public. In particular, Mao's critics focused on the excesses of the Cultural Revolution. This public criticism of China's legendary leader ushered in a period of liberalization—or "enhanced democracy," as Western observers described it. With a trend toward more conservative policies, the public criticism of Mao's period intensified, as exemplified by the attack on "The Gang of Four." Mao's widow and three others were arrested and charged with crimes against the people because of their role in carrying out policies that are now unacceptable to the new Chinese leadership.

It is self-evident that China is taking a different direction in its quest for socialist development. Experts debate among themselves whether the new direction is jeopardizing the gains made in the past or slowing down the progress made in the past, or whether it is simply a period of adjustment and transition necessary to lay the foundation for China's renewed efforts toward the continuation of socialist development. Whatever position is preferred, there is no debate over the fact that China has changed and will continue to do so throughout the 1980s.

In the 1980s, China began to "readjust, restructure, consolidate, and improve," with the long-term focus on the modernizations in industry, agriculture, science, technology, and defense.

In an article in *Scientific American* in 1980, Chinese economist Ding Chen described the basic components of the new Chinese approach to development. Since 1949, China has emphasized the development of heavy industry, but now it will increase the resources that it devotes to light industry, agriculture, and investments in human capital. In the past, there was central management of the economy through a national economic plan. Under the four-modernizations program, the Chinese hope to rely primarily on the planning mechanism to direct economic activity and development but will also rely on the operation of markets for goods and services. They hope to accomplish modernization through increasing the autonomy of firms and communes with respect to decisions about products, pricing, and marketing. The democratic management of firms by workers and managers will be promoted through linking rewards to work performed and allowing firms to retain some portion of their "profits." Finally, China intends to increase its use of foreign capital and advanced technology to advance its ability to produce economic growth while maintaining its self-sufficiency. Chen concludes his article with the following optimistic conclusion about the future of Chinese socialism.

> The four modernizations define the program for establishing China as a socialist power within the next two decades. Our nation, with its long history, its continental domain and its large population, is already a world power. In terms of our people's living standards, however, we are still only starting on the road to affluence and are some way behind the economically developed nations. Internally we now have a stable, unified political situation; internationally conditions have never been so favorable. By the end of the century the economic development of China will quantitatively, qualitatively and powerfully prove the superiority of the socialist way of ordering human affairs.

The four modernizations in the 1980s under the leadership of Deng Xiaoping (over 80 years old) have been influenced by the pragmatism of the Politburo and the State Council. Some of the changes toward decentralization were significant enough to allow President Reagan to visit China in 1984 and applaud what he and many Western journalists perceived to be the early signs of the emergence of free enterprise in China. Even though the Chinese leadership has approved and implemented a number of economic reforms aimed at decentralization, these reforms, contrary to the wishful thinking of many in the West, are still taking place in the context of a society deeply committed to building a socialist society.

In the following article by Christopher Wren, we can see and better understand the extent to which some of Deng's economic reforms have been very successful, particularly those related to incentives.

CHINA STEEL PLANT FLOURISHES—INCENTIVES SPUR OUTPUT

Christopher S. Wren

When Zigong's steel-casting plant reopened in 1975, it was so short of funds that the management could not afford to buy some bamboo sleeping mats.

The factory had been moved from Shanghai to Sichuan Province in 1965 to help spur the economy of south-western China. Then the Cultural Revolution began and production of steel valves was suspended while the plant's Maoist factions quarreled. For the next nine years, nothing was manufactured there.

"There were no roads and people had to make their own way," said Wang Zizhen, now the factory director, recalling his arrival with a team to reopen the plant. "Water was flowing into ditches and the place was covered with scrap metal."

A MODEL OF REFORMS

From a paralyzed bastion of leftist ideology, the factory in Zigong, a city of 500,000 best known for producing salt, has developed into a model of the industrial reforms promoted by China's leader, Deng Xiaoping. The factory presents a case study of the kind of production incentives being attempted in heavy industry, which enjoyed an unchallenged priority in the allocation of capital and raw materials under the late Mao Zedong. . . .

"At present, the central task in the structural reform of the urban economy is to eliminate the practice of making no distinction between well-run and badly run enterprises or between employees who do more work and those who do less," Mr. Zhao, now China's leading technocrat, told the National People's Congress in his annual report last May.

INCENTIVES FOR MANAGERS

Under the new program, state-owned enterprises are taxed according to how well they meet production quotas. They are allowed to keep some of the money they earn, and managers are allowed some leeway—and thus

(continued)

some responsibility—in spending it. Normally, the Government simply collects all earnings and covers all losses, eliminating any incentive for the managers to press for higher profits.

In addition, the new program establishes a series of tests and bonuses under which more skilled and productive workers may earn more money. And it seeks to break with the old practice of guaranteeing state jobs for life, no matter how poor the worker's performance.

The first task in 1975, Mr. Wang said, was to restore order at the Zigong factory and resume production. "We launched mass criticism of anarchy and bourgeois factionalism," he said, meaning that the radical troublemakers had been warned to behave themselves. That year, the plant met its first output target ever.

When Zhao Ziyang introduced his economic reforms in Sichuan in 1979, many factories were hesitant to try them out.

"At that time, people had different ideas about reform," said Mr. Wang, who was then party secretary at the Zigong plant. "Some well-managed enterprises were afraid that they would suffer a loss. And those enterprises not properly managed were afraid they could not meet the profit targets set up by the state."

ZIGONG FACTORY TESTED

Once the Zigong factory began moving from what Mr. Wang called backward to advanced, it was selected to try out the reforms.

At first, the factory was allowed to keep 5 percent of the profits from its quota and to keep 20 percent of whatever it produced above this norm. The value of its output quadrupled, to more than $300,000, within a year.

The plant now pays 60 percent of its profits in taxes to the state. It keeps the rest to invest in the facilities or dispense in wages and bonuses. The new system of taxing earnings instead of collecting them has been so successful that Prime Minister Zhao announced in May that it would be phased in at all state enterprises starting in October.

The Zigong factory made its 1,600 employees responsible for their performance. The workers, who had never worried about shoddiness or waste, were told to improve their products and to measure consumption of energy and raw materials.

The wage system was also revised to encourage initiative. "Workers got low wages and the distribution was inflexible," Mr. Wang said. "The basic factory wage has been doubled, to about $50 a month, but this is on a floating basis that can vary by 15 percent, depending on performance."

A worker who exceeds his targets and passes a skills test will make more money. Bonuses are issued more selectively and can be as high as a third of the basic wage. A worker who misses quotas will not only have

(continued)

his pay docked but may also be declared ineligible for a raise the following year. The criteria have been extended to the supervisors.

The percentage of wage increases is based on the extent that production targets are exceeded. If output falls short of the targets, no raises are given and previous raises can be revoked.

GREATER AUTONOMY SOUGHT

As the plant's director, Mr. Wang would like even greater autonomy than the current system provides, including the right to pick his own management team and negotiate with the state for a larger share of the profits if production keeps rising. The output is expected to reach 10,000 tons of semifinished castings next year.

Mr. Wang conceded that the reforms were unpopular with people who missed the lackadaisical way of doing things. "We faced resistance from the very beginning," he said.

Mr. Wang, who is a party member, feels that ideological education has not kept up with the industrial reforms. "We tell workers to love their country and factory and to work hard," he said, "but we also teach them that they should try to become wealthy."

1. **Why do you think the economic reform of taxing earnings in lieu of collecting them was so successful?**

2. **Do you think it is a contradiction in socialist ideology for Mr. Wang, the plant's director, to encourage teaching the workers to become wealthy? Why?**

CUBA

Cuba in the past 25 years has been an interesting example of an underdeveloped nation overcoming centuries of colonial domination by implementing a socialist transition. To understand the complexity of contemporary Cuba, it is necessary to view it in a historical context.

Columbus discovered Cuba on his first voyage in 1492. Soon thereafter, Cuba became a staging ground for the Spaniards' expeditions to the Mexican and North American mainland. Cuba's indigenous population, descended from immigrants from the Greater Antilles and the Bahamas, did not survive the first century of the Spanish colonization. By the 19th century, Cuba became important for its agriculture, especially coffee, tobacco, and sugar. The necessary labor supply was imported from Africa. Between 1800 and 1865 over 600,000 slaves were brought to Cuba. (Slavery lasted until 1886 in Cuba.) By 1860, Cuba produced one-third of the world's sugar supply. The sugar industry was dominated by U.S. firms. By 1928, American-owned firms produced 75 percent of Cuba's sugar.

Cuba's economic development was based on a monocultural, slave, export-oriented agricultural society. Nationalist Cubans rose up in revolt in the bitter Ten Years War (1868–1878) but were ultimately defeated by the Spanish troops. In 1878, José Marti, a revolutionary poet-lawyer exiled in New York, began plans for the next attempt at independence. A new revolt broke out in 1895. This war was brutal and dragged on for three years. The United States, with its investment interests and disdain for the brutality of the Spanish, took advantage of the sinking of the U.S.S. *Maine* in April of 1898 to declare war on Spain. The "splendid little war," as Teddy Roosevelt called it, lasted only seven months. A brief transition period resulted in the Platt Amendment being passed in 1901 and lasting until 1934. The Platt Amendment gave the United States the right to oversee the Cuban economy, veto international commitments, and intervene in domestic politics at Washington's discretion. Essentially, Cuba was an American protectorate. With sugar being responsible for 80 percent of Cuba's foreign exchange earnings and the United States buying (until the early 1950s) over 75 percent of Cuba's sugar production, Cuba was highly dependent on trade with the United States.

From 1933 to 1958, Cuba was ruled directly and indirectly by Fulgencio Batista. Batista was a brutal and corrupt dictator, who until the last days of his administration was supported by the United States. By the early 1950s, criticism and resentment began building against Batista and those he represented.

Fidel Castro, a nationalist lawyer from the middle class, directed a group of 165 youths in storming the provincial army barracks at Moncada on July 26, 1953. Castro was arrested, tried, and sentenced to 15 years in prison. During his trial, he gave his famous "History Will Absolve Me" speech. To appease public sentiment and improve his image, Batista granted Fidel (and his brother Raul) amnesty and exile after 11 months in prison. In 1956, Castro returned to Cuba from Mexico on an old yacht, the *Granma*, with 82 men. Tipped off by a peasant, the army greeted Castro and his men. Seventy men were lost and the remaining 12 vanished into the Sierra Maestra mountains in eastern Cuba. The rest is history.

In time, Fidel and his guerilla comrades were joined by thousands in the mountains and their support throughout the country grew, especially in urban areas. These revolutionaries did not have any preconceived idea of building a socialist society. They were unified and motivated by their common desire to rid themselves of the despot Batista.

Castro marched into Havana in 1959. He and his followers were seeking genuine independence and social justice. The transition was difficult. By 1960, there were four dominant trends in Cuba: (1) the slow but progressive nationalization of the economy, (2) the influence of the Soviet Union, (3) the emergence of a popular yet authoritarian regime, and (4) the implementation of egalitarian socioeconomic policies.

Again, none of these early trends was tied directly and consciously to any articulated vision of socialism. In April, 1961, anti-Castro exiles supported by the

CIA under John F. Kennedy staged the famous "Bay of Pigs" fiasco. This failed attempt to overthrow the young government of Castro, along with the harsh trade embargo imposed on Cuba by the United States forced Castro to look for help. Thus, the Soviet Union was in a strategic position to establish trade relations with Cuba and grant credit and aid in exchange for the opportunity to strategically position itself in our hemisphere.

By December of 1961, Castro formally announced that he considered himself to be a socialist and that he intended to lead Cuba along the path of socialist development. The famous Cuban "Missile Crisis" of October 1962 further exacerbated relations between Cuba and the United States.

The decade of the 1960s saw Cuba grow at an average rate of 3 percent per year. A debate raged between 1963 and 1965 over the use of material versus moral incentives. Ché Guevara (later killed in Bolivia in 1967) argued that the use of moral incentives would be the most effective way to increase production and at the same time transform the consciousness of individuals to develop into what he called the "new socialist man." The spirit and ideals of the revolution would spur people on to work harder, sacrifice personal consumption and gain, and work for the common welfare, according to his philosophy. Others argued against this thinking and urged Castro to utilize material incentives, rewarding those who work and those who work the hardest even if it meant having inequality in the society. In 1966, Castro decided to side with Guevara. After two years, it was a very mixed experience. The political socialization and mass consciousness of the people did seem to develop but at a great cost to the economy. Cuba decided to focus on sugar production and to rapidly expand that sector. Castro set a goal of 10 million tons of sugar for the 1970 harvest. The harvest (*zafra*) goal was not met: Sugar production was only 8.5 million tons. This disappointment ushered in a new period of sober pragmatism.

For Cuba, the 1970s produced very impressive economic growth. The period from 1971 to 1975 registered an annual average growth rate of 8.8 percent; and the period from 1976 to 1980, in spite of a very deep global recession, produced an annual average growth rate of 4 percent. What was primarily responsible for this improvement in the 1970s?

Experts point to five major factors to explain this impressive decade of economic growth: (1) the use of material incentives and greater reliance on market mechanisms; (2) the use of profits and greater income inequalities, so that firms and individuals were rewarded by their output, performance, and skill levels; (3) decentralization; (4) the promotion of mass participation of unions and local organs of popular political power; and (5) the expansion of foreign trade with the West and the adoption of Western technology.

Since the 1970s, Cuba has been following a path of economic development that has been categorized as dependent socialist development—dependent because of the major reliance upon the Soviet Union for trade, aid, and credit. In the mid-1980s, Cuba's trade with the Soviet Union represented 70 percent of its total trade. In 1984, 86 percent of Cuban trade was with the Soviet Bloc. Cuba's foreign debt has been steadily increasing in spite of more than $4 billion a year in economic aid from the Soviets, or about 25 percent of Cuba's total GNP. In addition to this dependence on the Soviet Union, Cuba still suffers from the dependence on sugar. While sugar production has been increasing in recent years, sugar prices have been extremely volatile. Sugar prices peaked in 1975 at $.76 per pound but had plunged to less than $.05 per pound in 1984 (one-third of the cost to produce). Fortunately for Cuba contracts with the Eastern bloc accounting for over 75 percent of Cuban sugar production insulate the country from low sugar prices. In 1983, for example, contract prices were set at $.38 per pound. But it is sugar exports to the West that are vital for hard currency (dollar denominated) to pay the increasing foreign debt.

The early years of the 1980s produced mixed results for the Cuban economy. The five-year plan instituted for 1981–1985 projected annual growth rates of 5 percent per year. In 1981, a growth rate of 12 percent surprised everyone, but the severe international economic recession in 1982 took its toll on the Cuban economy, which grew at a rate of only 3.1 percent (yet, the other nations of Latin America in that year had a negative growth rate, of –3 percent).

Thus far, Cuba has made impressive gains in increasing the standard of living in material terms for the majority of its citizens. Gains in health, education, and housing have been particularly impressive. The changing role of women has been one of the areas acknowledged by visiting experts; it is a goal of Cuban socialist development to make women equal participants in the society. Cuba has also made significant strides to reduce inequality in the distribution of income since the early 1950s.

Looking at Table 28.6, we can see that in 1959, at the time of the revolution, the bottom 20 percent of the people received only 5.7 percent of total income, whereas the top 20 percent received 54.6 percent. The bottom 60 percent received only 27.1 percent of the total income in 1959. By 1978, the bottom 20 percent received 7.8 percent of total income, and the top 20 percent received 33.4 percent. The bottom 60 percent received 39.9 percent of total income. The data after 1959 must be read with some caution. Cubans after the revolution have received a social wage that reflects the multitude of benefits and services provided free or heavily subsidized by the government. For example, Cubans receive free health care and education. Housing is either free or at a minimal rent. In addition, there is essentially full employment without inflation, both of which make the income distribution data

Table 28.6 INCOME DISTRIBUTION: CUBA, 1959–1978

	PERCENTAGE RECEIVED (CUMULATIVE PERCENTAGE)			
QUINTILE	1959	1962	1973	1978
Lowest	5.7 (5.7)	6.2 (6.2)	7.8 (7.8)	7.8 (7.8)
Second	8.9 (14.6)	11.0 (17.2)	12.5 (20.3)	12.4 (20.2)
Third	12.5 (27.1)	16.3 (33.5)	19.2 (39.5)	19.7 (39.9)
Fourth	18.3 (45.4)	25.1 (58.6)	26.0 (65.0)	26.7 (66.6)
Highest	54.6 (100.0)	41.4 (100.0)	35.0 (100.0)	33.4 (100.0)

Source: Claus Brundenius, *Economic Growth, Basic Needs and Income Distribution in Revolutionary Cuba*, 1981, Research Policy Institute, University of Lund.

more impressive. As a part of the planning process, wages and prices are set. While in recent years, policy has allowed larger disparities in income and wages, the ratio of the highest and the lowest possible salaries is still very low, in keeping with the goal of the socialist egalitarian ideology.

While these gains and successes have been applauded by those sympathetic to the Cuban revolution and objectively acknowledged by critics, Cuba has indeed had its share of failures and problems. The agriculture sector has been neither as diversified nor as productive as planners have hoped. There are problems with a pent-up demand for consumer goods. (In fact an underground black market exists for many popular Western consumer goods.) In addition, critics of the Cuban revolution point out human rights abuses (especially for political prisoners) and the virtual absence of any organized political dissent capable of challenging the power of Castro and the Communist Party.

CONCLUSION

Given the tremendous diversity of economic systems in the world today, we chose to focus briefly on three nations attempting socialist development. While each is distinguished from the others in many ways, there are basic characteristics common to all three, being socialist nations. These case studies have allowed you to compare a few socialist nations with a capitalist nation such as the United States.

For those of us in the West, it is often difficult to allow ourselves to view objectively the socialist experience of nations such as the Soviet Union, China, and Cuba. Given our own socialization and life experience as well as the constant ideological attack on socialism from our government, we have difficulty understanding why anyone could possibly think that socialism is or could be better than capitalism; yet, for a complex set of historical, political, and economic reasons, many nations and hundreds of millions of people have embarked upon this alternative.

In order to think more deeply about socialism, let us finish this chapter with the following excerpt by Robert Heilbroner, a distinguished economist from the New School for Social Research, from "Reflections on the Future of Socialism," from his book *Between Capitalism and Socialism*.

> Socialism is, at its root, the effort to find a remedy in social terms for the affront to reason and morality in the status quo. As such it is not limited to any particular place or time in history, but adapts its programs and its objectives to the indignities against which it fights. If socialism today in the United States derives its impetus from the spectacle of concentrated wealth, the commercial manipulation of human beings, or the indifference of the established power structure to the plight of the poor, . . . in the Soviet Union a genuinely socialist movement would (and some day will) take its organizing impulse from the concentration of political power and from the imprisonment of mind and spirit by communist authorities and doctrines alike. In each and every nation the presence of power and privilege thus establishes the fortresses against which socialism presses its attack.

It may well be that each attack succeeds only to fail; that new walls of power and privilege are built as rapidly as old ones are torn down; that the ultimate goal of a transformed—indeed, transfigured—man is only a chimera. Yet the vitality of socialism seems unlikely to be daunted by that possibility. For taking socialism seriously means more than acknowledging its difficulties as a political movement. It means understanding as well that socialism is the expression of a collective hope for mankind, its idealization of what it conceives itself to be capable of. When the fires of socialism no longer burn, it will mean that mankind has extinguished that hope and abandoned that ideal.

KEY CONCEPTS

capitalism   decentralization
socialism   market socialism
social wage   economic planning
moral and material incentives   workers' self-management

REVIEW QUESTIONS

1. What are the essential characteristics of capitalism and socialism as economic systems?

2. Compare the ideology of socialism with that of capitalism.

3. How is a market socialist economy different from a centrally planned economy?

4. What is the difference between moral and material incentives? What has been Cuba's experience with each? China's?

5. What kind of economic reforms are being implemented in China today?

6. Do you think the dependence of Cuba on the Soviet Union is similar to the dependence developing nations experience with the United States? Explain.

7. Do you think it is true that political freedom and individual liberty are not possible in a socialist society? Explain.

SUGGESTED READINGS

Claus Brundenius, 1981. *Economic Growth, Basic Needs and Income Distribution in Revolutionary Cuba,* Research Policy Institute, University of Lund, Sweden. An excellent piece of empirical research on Cuba.

Gil Green, 1983. *Cuba at 25: The Continuing Revolution,* International Publishers. A very readable polemic about the successes of the Cuban revolution. In spite of the bias of the author, it is filled with interesting antecdotes.

Ramon H. Myers, 1980. *The Chinese Economy: Past and Present,* Wadsworth. A good text for a general treatment of China.

Alec Nove, 1980. *The Soviet Economic System*, George Allen & Unwin. An excellent survey and overview of the Soviet economy.

Alec Nove, 1983. *The Economics of Feasible Socialism*, George Allen and Unwin.

Martin C. Schnitzer and James W. Nordyke, 1983. *Comparative Economic Systems*, South-Western Publishing Company. A fine elementary systems textbook with brief chapters on all of the major nations.

Martin Schrenk et al., 1979. *Yugoslavia: Self-Management Socialism and the Challenge of Development*, Johns Hopkins University Press. A good historical treatment of the Yugoslav experience.

PART VI

THE FUTURE

The future can rarely be predicted with precision; and the future of such a complex phenomenon as the world economy is particularly difficult to anticipate or even to visualize. When nothing is known about such a phenomenon nothing can be proven to be impossible. But as the actual state of the system and its structural properties become known and the forces and relations that govern its development and change become better understood, many of the originally envisaged futures are eliminated from the range of realistic possibilities. At the same time the distant outlines of the possible emerge more clearly and in more detail as increased knowledge and understanding are brought to bear on the subject.

However, even if the inner workings of the world economic system were fully understood and the external factors which will affect its development possibilities over the next quarter of a century were fully known, a gradual elimination of the options that first appeared to be open but upon further examination turned out to be closed cannot reduce the originally envisioned wide range of possibilities to a single inevitable path. One reason for this is that some of the factors upon which the course of future developments can be shown to depend will be controlled by purposeful national or international action guided by more or less rational choices.

—Wassily Leontief et al., *The Future of the World Economy,* Oxford University Press, 1977, p. 13.

In this final section of the text, the focus will be on the current and future economic issues. In Chapter 29 we will examine several examples of market failure in the context of crucial questions related to economic growth and the availability of scarce natural resources. Then, in Chapter 30 we will take a final look at the historic performance and behavior of the U.S. economy, building upon the inclusion of the international sector as well as the vital issues related to energy and the environment. Also, in this chapter we will consider a radical analysis of the economy and critically examine several alternative perspectives on the future.

Economics of the Environment

THE PROBLEM IN HISTORICAL PERSPECTIVE

Human beings have always been aware of and sensitive to the interrelationships among economic growth, resources, and the environment. This recognition, though, has manifested itself in different ways in different historical epochs. There have been those who feared the worst and predicted catastrophe and doom; on the other hand, there have been the eternal optimists, confident that somehow human beings will exercise their great natural creativity and ingenuity to develop the appropriate response to a given problem at a given time.

These different points of view have been permanently etched into the world's cultures by the works of artists, poets, musicians, architects, scientists, engineers, philosophers, and social scientists. Going back to the early 1700s in the midst of the great Scientific Revolution, we began to see the Western world transform its view of societal development, time, space, nature, labor, and resources. Societal advancement became associated with greater specialization, division of labor, and reliance on science and technology to greatly develop and expand the productive potential of society. This was a period of increasing secularization and materialism. Success was defined in terms of economic categories—particularly individual income, business profit, and total social output. The ideas of Adam Smith in *The Wealth of Nations* played an important role in encouraging this overriding concern with economic growth. Yet, in the midst of this period, which prepared the foundation for the Industrial Revolution, there were voices of caution and despair. One of the early classical liberal economists, the Reverend Thomas Malthus, an Englishman, predicted that geometric increases in population would eventually outstrip the available food supply, which increased only arithmetically. The result could only be widespread famine unless growth trends were checked by positive and preventative measures. This pessimism of the Malthusian theory, though ignored by many in his time, has resurfaced in recent years as a warning to modern society.

As the Industrial Revolution in Western Europe gained momentum, many people reflected on the general environmental degradation associated with urbanization, industrialization, the advancement of science and technology, and economic growth. One has merely to browse through *The Condition of the Working Class in England* by Friedrich Engels or *Hard Times* by Charles Dickens to get some sense of this reaction to the slums, the pollution, and the poverty.

In this context, controversy developed over whether growth was controllable or even desirable in the future. The political economist John Stuart Mill wrote about a "stationary-state" economy and looked forward to its coming.

> It is scarcely necessary to remark that a stationary condition of capital and population implies no stationary state of human improvement. There would be as much scope as ever for all kinds of mental culture, and moral and social progress; as much room for improving the Art of Living and much more likelihood of it being improved, when minds cease to be engrossed by the art of getting on.
>
> —J. S. Mill, *Principles of Political Economy* (Volume II), London: John W. Parker and Son, 1857, p. 326.

1. John Stuart Mill in this excerpt is optimistic about the possibilities "of mental culture, and moral and social progress" as well as "for improving the Art of Living" in a stationary-state economy. Do you agree with him? Why?

At about the same time, Karl Marx spoke of the inherent dynamics of capitalist growth that resulted in periodic cycles of prosperity and stagnation and would ultimately result in the collapse of the system itself. For the most part, Marx's analysis and warnings were met with hostility and were ignored. By the end of the 19th century and the beginning of the 20th century, the Western world was firmly committed to a philosophy of achieving greater economic growth at whatever cost. The mastery over nature, made possible by the marvels of science and technology, was legitimized by the economic and psychological motivations of self-interest, greed, profit-seeking, and capital accumulation. These forces set in motion a veritable "growth machine" with virtually no limits, ethics, or morals.

THE MODERN CONTEXT

Indeed, the need for raw materials and cheap resources to fuel the growth process sent the competing nation-states of Europe all over the globe. Each hoped to acquire and control whatever resources and markets it could to ensure and maintain its own growth and development goals. In the process, they carved out portions of Latin America, Asia, and Africa for themselves. This period of colonialism, accompanied by two World Wars, left the global arena in a precarious state by 1945. While Europe entered a period of reconstruction, the United States and the Soviet Union were locked into an "ideological" struggle. This "Cold War" mentality manifested itself in a competitive contest between the two nations. Economic growth and military power became the two major indexes of ideological strength and performance. This competition legitimized the emphasis on growth per se and military power in particular in both the United States and the USSR. While the two superpowers were so engaged, important events were taking place elsewhere. The early 1960s ushered in a period of decolonization and independence for the nations of the Third World. Yet the political independence of these nations did not mean automatic economic independence. The end result for most nations was a new stage of "neocolonialism." The interdependence of the colonial system persisted. The advanced nations maintained control over the raw materials and resources needed for their growth and prosperity.

Growing affluence in the United States blinded the majority of Americans (and economists) to a concern about the inherent costs and contradictions of such prosperity. Attention was first brought to the problems of a society obsessed with economic growth when John Kenneth Galbraith published *The Affluent Society*. Galbraith criticized our materialistic consumerism. He scoffed at the way the public was manipulated by the twin levers of advertising and salesmanship. In his critique, Galbraith challenged the orthodox economist's view of consumer behavior. He argued that the consumer depicted in economic theory—the person with insatiable wants who independently and rationally decided preferences—did not exist. Galbraith suggested that consumer behavior was determined by other forces and put forth a different explanation:

> As a society becomes increasingly affluent, wants are increasingly created by the process by which they are satisfied. This may operate passively. Increases in consumption, the counterpart of increases in production, act by suggestion or emulation to create wants. Or producers may proceed actively to create wants through advertising and salesmanship. Wants thus come to depend on output. In technical terms, it can no longer be

assumed that welfare is greater at an all-around higher level of production than at a lower one. It may be the same. The higher level of production has, merely, a higher level of want creation necessitating a higher level of want satisfaction.

—Edwards, Reich, and Weiskopf, *The Capitalist System*, Prentice-Hall, 1972, pp. 375–376.

2. Do you agree with John Kenneth Galbraith's analysis and critique of orthodox consumer behavior theory? Why? (Attempt to answer this question by reflecting on your own experience.)

Several years after Galbraith's contribution, a young Catholic priest named Michael Harrington set off across the United States to see how the American people were living in this period of prosperity. Upon his return, he wrote *The Other America*, documenting the widespread poverty he found amidst the affluence. As his book gained notoriety, people became shocked and embarrassed that this condition existed in such a great nation. Pressure was put on policymakers to draft legislation and implement programs to eliminate this condition. Although a few programs were started, the real solution for poverty and income inequality was believed to be more economic growth. This would mean more employment and income, as well as more goods and services to distribute. Such a natural and permanent solution was greatly preferred to the temporary and costly government intervention suggested by some policymakers.

In the midst of the chaos and unrest of the 1960s, the issues of ecology, environment, and growth continued to cause concern. With material prosperity, some people began to question the "quality of life" they were living. Clean air and water became just as important as having a high-paying job and a luxurious, leisure-oriented life-style. As cities grew and suburbanization accelerated, the larger and more mobile population witnessed the progressive deterioration of the natural physical environment. Resource use, particularly of nonrenewable fossil energy fuels, escalated at unprecedented rates. Some Americans began to recognize the fact that with only 6 percent of the world's population, they were consuming an unduly large share (over 30 percent) of the earth's finite resources.

Economists and members of the scientific community began to respond to this developing crisis. In 1966, Professor Kenneth Boulding suggested, in an article titled "The Economics of the Coming **Spaceship Earth**," that

We are now in the middle of a long process of transition in the nature of the image which man has of himself and his environment. Primitive men, and to a large extent also men of the early civilizations, imagined themselves to be living on a virtually illimitable plane. There was almost always somewhere beyond the known limits of human habitation, and over a very large part of the time that man has been on earth, there has been something like a frontier. That is, there was always some place else to go when things got too difficult, either by reason of the deterioration of the natural environment or a deterioration of the social structure in places where people happened to live. The image of the frontier is probably one of the oldest images of mankind, and it is not surprising that we find it hard to get rid of. . . .

The closed earth of the future requires economic principles which are somewhat different from those of the open earth of the past. For the sake of picturesqueness, I am tempted to call the open economy the "cowboy economy," the cowboy being symbolic of the illimitable plains and also associated with reckless, exploitative, romantic, and violent behavior, which is characteristic of open societies. The closed economy of the future might similarly be called the "spaceman" economy, in which the earth has become a single spaceship, without unlimited reservoirs of anything, either for extraction or for pollution, and in which, therefore, man must find his place in a cyclical ecological system which is capable of continuous reproduction of material form even though it cannot escape having inputs of energy. The difference between the two types of economy becomes most apparent in the attitude towards consumption. In the cowboy economy, consumption is regarded as a good thing and production likewise; and the success of the economy is measured by the amount of the throughput from the "factors of production," a part of which, at any rate, is extracted from the reservoirs of raw materials and noneconomic objects, and another part of which is output into the reservoirs of pollution. . . .

By contrast, in the spaceman economy . . . the essential measure of the success of the economy is not production and consumption at all, but the nature, extent, quality, and complexity of the total capital stock, including in this the state of the human bodies and minds included in the system. In the spaceman economy, what we are primarily concerned with is stock maintenance, and any technological change which results in the maintenance of a given total stock with a lessened throughput (that is, less production and consumption) is clearly a gain. This idea that both production and consumption are bad things rather than good things is very strange to economists, who have been obsessed with the income-flow concepts to the exclusion, almost, of capital-stock concepts.

—From "The Economics of the Coming Spaceship Earth," in Henry Jarrett (ed.), *Environmental Quality in a Growing Economy*. A Resources for the Future book published by the Johns Hopkins University Press. Copyright © 1966 by the Johns Hopkins Press.

Although most mainstream economists ignored Boulding's analysis and frightening description of possible future scenarios, a talented biologist, Barry Commoner, was busy writing *The Closing Circle*, which, along with Rachel Carson's *Silent Spring*, had an astounding impact on the scientific and academic communities. Commoner analyzed the environmental crisis and asked that we understand the future consequences of our short-sighted urge to indulge ourselves. He challenged the capability of our market system and the "profit" motive to respond quickly and creatively to the emergent environmental crisis: "The lesson of the environmental crisis is, thus, clear. If we are to survive, ecological considerations must guide economic and political ones."

The Limits to Growth

Following close on the heels of Commoner's book was the controversial report for the Club of Rome's Project on the Predicament of Mankind. *The Limits to Growth*, published in 1972, predicted that the human race faced an uncontrollable and disastrous collapse within 100 years unless a "global equilibrium" was established in which population and industrial growth were severely limited. A computer simulation based on five variables plotted a series of "possible" future scenarios. These variables were (1) resources utilization and availability, (2) population growth, (3) food per capita, (4) pollution, and (5) industrial output per capita. Two of the scenarios can be seen in Figs. 29.1 and 29.2. The first illustrates the "Growth and Collapse: Doomsday Model" and the second the "Stability-Stagnation Model."

> The "standard" world model run assumes no major change in the physical, economic, or social relationships that have historically governed the development of the world system. All variables plotted here follow historical values from 1900 to 1970. Food, industrial output, and population grow exponentially until the rapidly diminishing resource base forces a slowdown in industrial growth. Because of natural delays in the system, both population and pollution continue to increase for some time after the peak of industrialization. Population growth is finally halted by a rise in the death rate due to decreased food and medical services. . . . [Fig. 29.1]
>
> Technological policies are added to the growth-regulating policies of the previous run to produce an equilibrium state sustainable far into the future. Technological policies include resource recycling, pollution control devices, increased lifetime of all forms of capital, and methods to restore eroded and infertile soil. Value changes included increased emphasis on food and services rather than on industrial production. [Fig. 29.2]
>
> —Dennis L. Meadows et al., *The Limits to Growth*, Washington: Potomac Associates, 1972, pp. 129, 168.

Figure 29.2 thus illustrates that a stable society can be attained with major adjustments to the primary variables.

3. What changes are required to achieve a stationary-state economy? What are the basic strengths and weaknesses of this strategy?

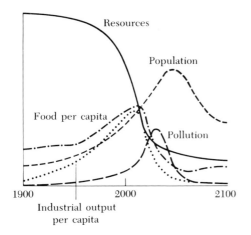

Figure 29.1 Growth and collapse: A doomsday model.

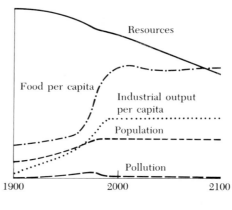

Figure 29.2 The stability–stagnation model.

Before the global community had time to fully digest these ideas, two other events reinforced the previous prognostications of ecologists and environmentalists. In October 1973, against the background of the Arab-Israeli conflict, the OPEC nations agreed to an oil embargo and a subsequent price increase that quadrupled the price of oil. This show of force by the OPEC cartel spelled dire consequences for the advanced Western industrialized nations and the oil-importing nations of the Third World. It signaled a fundamental change in the power relations of the global political economy.

In the same year, E. F. Schumacher, a British economist, published *Small Is Beautiful: Economics As If People Mattered*. This popular book advanced another critique of the growth fetishism of the modern Western world. Schumacher criticized the waste and squandering of resources and the overreliance on capital and energy-intensive technology in Western production methods. He criticized as well the behavioral traits and value system that allowed this process to continue. He challenged people to reexamine their values and life-styles. Indeed, for Schumacher the fundamental transformation necessary is a change in thinking and consciousness—a change from thinking that "more is better" to "small is beautiful." Schumacher's message made a great deal of practical sense as people recognized the immediate reality of energy shortages due to the market power of OPEC; it made even more sense in the context of the long-run future, when energy supplies are going to grow ever scarcer.

Yet with all of this mounting criticism and evidence, the advocates of slower growth, conservation of resources, and protection of the environment were met with fierce resistance. The Western industrialized world by 1973 had already entered into a widespread recession that was tremendously exacerbated by the OPEC embargo and eventual price increase. As the global recession intensified in 1974 and carried into 1975, some critical "rethinking" evolved on how to best accommodate environmental and resource concerns with a stagnating world economy and with critical energy resources firmly controlled by a handful of nations and multinational corporations.

It came as little surprise to onlookers that the Club of Rome at a conference in April of 1976 changed its conclusions from those of the report issued three years earlier. Because of the prolonged global recession, the Club of Rome had little choice but to conclude that only further economic growth could provide the stimulus for an economic recovery, thereby reducing world poverty and threats to world peace as well. In addition, at this conference, the Club of Rome previewed the conclusions of a report they had commissioned from economist Jan Tinbergen, Nobel laureate of the Netherlands, on the creation of a new international order. The thrust of the Tinbergen report pinpointed the need for international economic planning as a substitute for the uncontrolled play of market forces. Growth should be *planned* to avoid the catastrophes hypothesized in the *Limits to Growth* argument.

THE CARTER YEARS

From 1976 to 1980, President Carter seriously advanced the cause of environmental protection. He was actually the first president to fully embrace the goals and ideals of the National Environmental Protection Act, passed in 1969. Under his administration, funding and staffing for the Environmental Protection Agency steadily increased. The scope of the activities of the E.P.A. expanded as well. Having to provide environmental leadership at a time of continued economic stagflation was difficult because most people were willing to trade off environmental quality for economic growth. In addition, the pressures and consequences of developing a national energy program complicated the task of protecting the environment. Oil and coal companies wanted access to offshore tracts and public lands to explore for new supplies of oil and coal; on the other side, environmentalists were quite concerned about potential environmental impacts from these activities.

By the mid-1970s the environmental movement in the United States had successfully created a group of professionals working in government and the nonprofit private sector who were dedicated to keeping the nation moving toward an enlightened environmental awareness. But two events in the late 1970s served as catalysts and generated national attention. In August 1978, in Niagara Falls, New York, 240 families were evacuated from their homes to avoid further contamination from a toxic waste dump used for decades by the Hooker Chemical Company, a subsidiary of the Occidential Petroleum Company. This incident at the famous Love Canal site created a tremendous public interest and alarm at this newfound environmental problem that existed on a scale few were willing to admit. As a result of this incident and many others like it around the nation, the Resource Conservation and Recovery Act (RCRA), originally passed in 1976, was amended in an effort to improve its ability to address this kind of problem. Eventually, at the end of the Carter Administration in 1980, the Comprehensive Environmental Response, Compensation and Liability Act was passed. This legislation provided for the creation of a department to focus entirely on the clean-up of hazardous waste sites around the nation, with $1.6 billion derived from taxes levied on the chemical industry. This "Superfund" was viewed as a major accomplishment by environmentalists.

The second event was the March 1979 near meltdown of the nuclear reactor at the Three Mile Island facility in Harrisburg, Pennsylvania. This event also created a new national awareness about nuclear power and the problems of radioactivity and wastes.

In 1977 Carter requested that a major study be done on the current status and future prospects of the global environment. While this study was still in process, the second oil price shock by OPEC came in 1979, doubling the price of oil. Once again, the ensuing recession made the trade-off between environmental quality and economic growth a very political issue.

In 1980, the study group produced its report for President Carter: *The Global 2000 Report to the President of the U.S.: Entering the 21st Century* presented a very serious and frightening analysis of the state of the global environment. The report concluded: "If present trends continue, the world in 2000 will be more crowded, more polluted, less stable ecologically, and more vulnerable to disruption than the world we live in now. Serious stresses involving population, resources, and environment are clearly visible ahead. Despite greater material output, the world's people will be poorer in many ways than they are today."

PRINCIPAL FINDINGS

Rapid growth in world population will hardly have altered by 2000. The world's population will grow from 4 billion in 1975 to 6.35 billion in 2000, an increase of more than 50 percent. . . .

World food production is projected to increase 90 percent over the 30 years from 1970 to 2000. This translates into a global per capita increase of less than 15 percent over the same period. The bulk of that increase goes to countries that already have relatively high per capita food consumption. Meanwhile per capita consumption in South Asia, the Middle East, and the LDCs of Africa will scarcely improve or will actually decline below present inadequate levels. At the same time, real prices for food are expected to double.

Arable land will increase only 4 percent by 2000, so that most of the increased output of food will have to come from higher yields. Most of the elements that now contribute to higher yields—fertilizer, pesticides, power for irrigation, and fuel for machinery—depend heavily on oil and gas.

During the 1990s world oil production will approach geological estimates of maximum production capacity, even with rapidly increasing petroleum prices. The Study projects that the richer industrialized nations will be able to command enough oil and other commercial energy supplies to meet rising demands through 1990. With the expected price increases,

(continued)

many less developed countries will have increasing difficulties meeting energy needs. For the one-quarter of humankind that depends primarily on wood for fuel, the outlook is bleak. Needs for fuelwood will exceed available supplies by about 25 percent before the turn of the century.

While the world's finite fuel resources—coal, oil, gas, oil shale, tar sands, and uranium—are theoretically sufficient for centuries, they are not evenly distributed; they pose difficult economic and environmental problems; and they vary greatly in their amenability to exploitation and use.

Nonfuel mineral resources generally appear sufficient to meet projected demands through 2000, but further discoveries and investments will be needed to maintain reserves. In addition, production costs will increase with energy prices and may make some nonfuel mineral resources uneconomic. The quarter of the world's population that inhabits industrial countries will continue to absorb three-fourths of the world's mineral production.

Regional water shortages will become more severe. In the 1970—2000 period population growth alone will cause requirements for water to double in nearly half the world. Still greater increases would be needed to improve standards of living. In many LDCs, water supplies will become increasingly erratic by 2000 as a result of extensive deforestation. Development of new water supplies will become more costly virtually everywhere.

Significant losses of world forests will continue over the next 20 years as demand for forest products and fuelwood increases. Growing stocks of commercial-size timber are projected to decline 50 percent per capita. The world's forests are now disappearing at the rate of 18–20 million hectares a year (an area half the size of California), with most of the loss occurring in the humid tropical forests of Africa, Asia, and South America. The projections indicate that by 2000 some 40 percent of the remaining forest cover in LDCs will be gone.

Serious deterioration of agricultural soils will occur worldwide, due to erosion, loss of organic matter, desertification, salinization, alkalinization, and waterlogging. Already, an area of cropland and grassland approximately the size of Maine is becoming barren wasteland each year, and the spread of desert-like conditions is likely to accelerate.

Atmospheric concentrations of carbon dioxide and ozone-depleting chemicals are expected to increase at rates that could alter the world's climate and upper atmosphere significantly by 2050. Acid rain from increased combustion of fossil fuels (especially coal) threatens damage to lakes, soils, and crops. Radioactive and other hazardous materials present health and safety problems in increasing numbers of countries.

Extinctions of plant and animal species will increase dramatically. Hundreds of thousands of species—perhaps as many as 20 percent of all species on earth—will be irretrievably lost as their habitats vanish, especially in tropical forests.

(continued)

The future depicted by the U.S. Government projections, briefly outlined above, may actually understate the impending problems. The
methods available for carrying out the Study led to certain gaps and inconsistencies that tend to impart an optimistic bias. For example, most of
the individual projections for the various sectors studied—food, minerals,
energy, and so on—assume that sufficient capital, energy, water, and land
will be available in each of these sectors to meet their needs, regardless of
the competing needs of the other sectors. More consistent, better-integrated
projections would produce a still more emphatic picture of intensifying
stresses, as the world enters the twenty-first century.

By 1980, the United States seemed to have a well-developed environmental
consciousness. The previous 20 years had taught many lessons and produced a wealth
of new knowledge. Air pollution, water pollution, noise pollution, congestion, waste
disposal, soil erosion, our coastal areas and wetlands, the use of chemicals in our
food, the fragility of our oceans—all of these became important issues. The in-
terrelatedness and complexity of the earth's vital support systems had slowly become
part of our national psyche. Yet the endless examples of oil tanker spills (Galveston,
Texas, in summer 1984), nuclear accidents and waste disposal problems, oil-drilling
accidents, toxic waste (Dioxin in Times Beach, Missouri), water resource feuds in
California and Colorado, acid rain, the "Greenhouse" effect of coal combustion, and
other endless examples have placed us in a cruel dilemma—less economic growth
with strict environmental controls and regulations, or unrestrained economic growth
with severe environmental consequences.

REAGAN'S ENVIRONMENTAL POLICIES

Carter's defeat in 1980 was related to a number of factors, not the least of which were
the deep recession of 1979 and Carter's foreign policy decisions related to the Iranian
hostage crisis. The narrow electoral victory by Reagan gave him a mandate to reduce
the role of government in our society. However, it is important to note that this
support for deregulation did not pertain to the environment. Public opinion polls
indicated that the environment was rated as so important that the public felt that
environmental protection laws had not gone far enough. When questioned about the
trade-off between economic growth and environmental quality, 58 percent of those
responding agreed that government regulations and requirements to protect the
environment were worth the extra costs, and 75 percent felt that it was possible to
maintain strong economic growth with high environmental standards.

Yet Reagan's commitment to deregulation and reducing government spending
had an incredible impact on the government's environmental programs. Between
1981 and 1983, EPA expenditures were cut by 21.1 percent. In addition, the staff of
the EPA was cut by 22.6 percent.

Reagan's approach to the environment and natural resources was a conservative, free-market philosophy. The "market" ought to be the maker of envi-

ronmental policy. Reagan felt that the government was already too involved in regulating the behavior of individuals and firms, and that this regulation was not only too costly but was also infringing on the rights of individuals and the property rights of firms. While not reflecting the majority public sentiment, his philosophy was essentially imposed on the nation. The deep recession in the early 1980s helped divert people's attention toward such issues as employment but many increased their involvement in the environmental issues of the nation as a consequence of Reagan's policies.

Before we examine several specific environmental problems of the 1980s, it is necessary to develop a few economic tools and concepts.

ENVIRONMENTAL ECONOMICS

In a market system based on private property rights, it is very difficult to induce behaviors on the part of firms and individuals that will result in protection of the environment. After hearing an appeal to good citizenship, firms and individuals can usually do whatever they please with their privately owned resources. For example, in the absence of environmental laws and regulations, a firm that produces plastics can dispose of its untreated waste water in a manner that can directly and seriously harm human beings who live many miles away. Let us suppose that a plastic manufacturer disposes of untreated water into a stream on its property that feeds a stream used by a wheat farmer. Suppose that this untreated water contaminates the farmer's irrigation water and his personal water supply. As a consequence, the farmer incurs crop damage, loss of income, and damage to personal health. In addition the crop could be contaminated, thus affecting consumers.

> 4. What kinds of issues and questions are involved in this hypothetical case? If you were a lawyer working on this case on behalf of the farmer, what would your position be? On behalf of the firm? On behalf of the federal government?

Using scarce resources to improve environmental quality, as with any other economic good, must be traded off against other possible uses of such resources. Environmental quality has an opportunity cost. As we shall see, and as is self-evident from the example of the plastics firm and the wheat farmer, the benefits and costs related to any environmental decision or policy are not always evenly distributed and are often hard to measure.

In the case of the polluting plastics firm, we have an example of a firm disposing of its untreated waste into a stream, creating an externality, or negative spillover effect, from its production process. This **negative externality** imposes a cost on the wheat farmer and possibly on the general public, since the water in the river can be considered a public good.

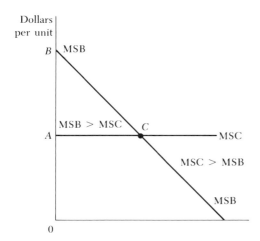

Figure 29.3 Pollution abatement.

Suppose, in this case, that the federal government decides to intervene and create a **pollution abatement** program to clean up the waste water before it enters the stream. Government tax revenues will be used to pay for the clean-up operation while the case is being litigated. How is the government going to decide on the amount of waste water to treat, the level of purity, and the cost to the public? Theoretically, we can answer these questions with the model in Fig. 29.3.

We need to assume two things: (1) each additional dollar spent results in one more unit of output of pollution abatement and is constant, and (2) the public values the first few units of pollution abatement more highly than subsequent units, i.e., there is a downward-sloping marginal social benefit (MSB) curve. The government will pay for the treatment of each unit of waste output (the marginal social cost, or MSC) up to the point at which the cost of the last unit of waste treated is equal to the marginal social benefit derived. In Fig. 29.3, MSC represents the cost of cleaning up each unit of output, and MSB represents the marginal social benefit derived from the program. From point B to point C, the MSB is greater than MSC, so in terms of efficiency the program will not pay for any further pollution abatement beyond point C.

ACID RAIN: AN INTERREGIONAL ENVIRONMENTAL ISSUE

One of the major environmental issues of the 1980s is the problem of acid rain, particularly for the states in the Midwest and the Northeast, as well as Canada. Acid rain (acid precipitation or acid deposition) is caused by the emission of sulfur dioxide and nitrogen oxides from the combustion of fossil fuels (especially from power plants). Aloft in the atmosphere, sulfur dioxide and nitrogen oxides are transformed into sulfuric acid and nitric acid, and air currents carry them hundreds and even thousands of miles from their original source. These acids are then deposited throughout our ecosystem, producing great cost and damage.

The politics and economics of acid rain are complicated. Determining an acceptable solution for the growing problem involves questions and issues unlike those of most other environmental problems. The Reagan Administration has successfully avoided taking a position on this issue, except to say that it ought to be studied further. Others, as the article below documents, have put forth specific proposals for dealing with the problem, but the interregional politics and economics are making it very difficult for any consensus to form around a national policy.

THE BITTER POLITICS OF ACID RAIN

Melinda Beck with Mary Hager, Marilyn Achiron, and Linda Brenners-Stulberg

Bronze statues in downtown Boston appear to be melting. In several Adirondack waters, the bass have completely disappeared. Half the spruce trees at Camel's Hump in Vermont's Green Mountains are withered and denuded. And across the border in Canada, the salmon in nine Nova Scotia rivers can no longer reproduce. The alleged culprit is acid rain—a catch-all term for sulfur dioxide and nitrogen oxides released by power plants, smelters and automobiles and carried hundreds of miles by the wind. "We're on the receiving end of an exhaust pipe for emissions across the country," says Matt Scott of Maine's Department of Environmental Protection.

Hardly a new phenomenon, acid rain is increasingly a political and economic issue with enormously high stakes. Acid rain is thought to cause as much as $5 billion in environmental damage annually, mostly in the Northeastern United States and southeastern Canada. But proposed controls on sulfur dioxide (SO_2) and nitrogen oxide (NO_x) emissions could cost $3 billion to $7 billion in higher utility rates and mean the loss of tens of thousands of jobs, mostly in the recession-swamped Midwest. The Reagan Administration insists that too little is known about the causes and effects of acid rain to warrant such harsh economic measures, but a growing number of scientists, lawmakers and environmentalists disagree. "We know more about acid rain now than we did about air pollution when the Clean Air Act was passed," says Maine Democratic Sen. George Mitchell, who has proposed a bill to reduce SO_2 emissions by roughly 50 percent in 31 states by 1990. . . .

There *is* scientific disagreement over some aspects of the acid-rain issue—including how SO_2 and NO_x emissions travel in the atmosphere and how far. One generally accepted theory is that tall smokestacks erected to limit pollution near emission sources have made acid rain worse by venting pollutants into the upper atmosphere. But all rainfall is slightly acidic,

(continued)

and some scientists say there is no evidence to suggest that a 50 percent cut in industrial emissions would create an equal reduction in acid rainfall. Moreover, while the killing effects of high acidity on forests and aquatic life are well documented, its impact on crops, buildings and human health is less clear.

Costs: What is certain is that some parts of the country are more vulnerable than others to acid rain because their soil and bedrock lack sufficient natural buffers. And the consensus for controlling emissions is growing with the number of areas that are thought to be endangered. A forthcoming congressional study suggests that as many as 9,000 lakes and 60,000 miles of streams in 34 states may be vulnerable. Officials in Wisconsin, Minnesota and Colorado already fear for local lakes with low alkaline levels, and even Los Angeles's infamous smog has been found to be heavily laced with acid-containing fog.

But as widespread as the effects may be, the industrial heartland would still bear the brunt of emission controls. Some Midwest utilities that burn high-sulfur coal say they would have to raise utility rates 20 to 50 percent locally to comply with the 50 percent reduction proposal. In addition, heavy industries such as steel, automobiles and rubber—the biggest users of electric power—would pass the costs on to consumers, further undercutting positions in international trade. What's more, switching to low-sulfur Western coal could deal a death blow to the high-sulfur Midwest coal industry. The United Mine Workers estimates that a 50 percent reduction plan could cost 80,000 coal-mining jobs, and perhaps three times as many in related service industries. Installing smokestack "scrubbers" instead could be even more expensive. It costs an estimated $69 million to $111 million to retrofit a single existing plant.

Industry spokesmen and some scientists argue that acid rain should be fought in the lakes and forests where it causes problems, not at the source. In the Adirondacks, experts are already neutralizing some acidified lakes with infusions of limestone. But "limiting" costs $100 to $150 per acre, and environmentalists see it as only a temporary "Band-Aid" gesture that falls far short of addressing the problem. "Here we have a chance to prevent a national problem," says Joshua Epel, a lobbyist for the National Clean Air Coalition, which is pressing for strong emission controls as part of a reauthorized Clean Air Act. "Isn't that what environmental protection is supposed to do?"

Predictions: The latest scientific studies support that view. A forthcoming report by the National Academy of Sciences is expected to back the 50 percent reduction, and momentum in Congress is building. Rep. Henry Waxman, chairman of a House subcommittee studying the Clean Air Act, plans to introduce legislation that would spread the costs of emission controls, perhaps by taxing all electricity generators to establish a nationwide emission-controls fund. In the Senate, Glenn's proposal would

(continued)

impose a nationwide surcharge on utility bills, amounting to perhaps $20 a year for the average family. Such share-the-burden solutions could neutralize much of the bitter regional resentment that stalled congressional action last year, but most experts will make no predictions. Politics has clearly eclipsed science in the acid-rain issue, and with such heavy economic interests at stake, its future is no more predictable than the weather.

5. According to the article, what are the politics and economics of the acid rain issue?

6. What do you think of the proposals put forth by Waxman and Glenn?

7. What is the present administration doing about acid rain?

NUCLEAR WAR: ENVIRONMENTAL IMPACT?

The last environmental issue we will briefly explore is nuclear war. This may at first seem odd, since it is an issue before us but not now affecting us. It is the prospect and possibility that we must confront. Obviously, the solution to this potential problem is not to have a nuclear war. Thus, the prevention of nuclear war becomes a major environmental policy.

The inability to ratify the SALT program in the late 1970s and the continued escalation of the arms race in the 1980s have generated enormous public interest and concern about nuclear war. The nuclear freeze movement made nuclear weapons a major issue in the United States in the early 1980s. Television specials and even movies, such as "The Day After," stimulated public interest and awareness. There have also been a number of books addressing this issue. Jonathan Schell in 1982 wrote *The Fate of the Earth* and in 1984, *The Abolition*. Each of these books make the point that nuclear war is a threat to humanity and the earth to a degree and magnitude that most of us have never really considered. With respect to the environment, Schell in *The Fate of the Earth* wrote the following about the likely environmental consequences of a large-scale nuclear war.

When vegetation is killed off, the land on which it grew is degraded. And as the land eroded after an attack life in lakes, rivers, and estuaries, already hard hit by radiation directly, would be further damaged by minerals flowing into the watercourses, causing eutrophication—a process in which an oversupply of nutrients in the water encourages the growth of algae and microscopic organisms, which, in turn, deplete the oxygen content of the water. When the soil loses its nutrients, it loses its ability to "sustain a mature community" (in Dr. Woodwell's words), and "gross

"Prometheus," by Mexican artist José Clemente Orozco. (Photograph by Steve Stamos.)

simplification" of the environment occurs, in which "hardy species," such as moss and grass, replace vulnerable ones, such as trees; and "succession"—the process by which ecosystems recover lost diversity—is then "delayed or even arrested." In sum, a full-scale nuclear attack on the United States would devastate the natural environment on a scale unknown since early geological times, when, in response to natural catastrophes whose nature has not been determined, sudden mass extinctions of species and whole ecosystems occurred all over the earth. How far this "gross simplification" of the environment would go once virtually all animal life and the greater part of plant life had been destroyed and what patterns the surviving remnants of life would arrange themselves into over the long run are imponderables; but it appears that at the outset the United States would be a republic of insects and grass.

KEY CONCEPTS

Spaceship Earth
Limits To Growth
Global 2000 Report
negative externality

pollution abatement
marginal social benefit
marginal social cost

REVIEW QUESTIONS

1. What is Galbraith's theory of consumer behavior?

2. Do you think Boulding's metaphor of "Spaceship Earth" is appropriate?

3. What are the five major variables in the *Limits to Growth* model?

4. What are the major conclusions and principal findings of the *Global 2000 Report?*

5. What is a negative externality? Given an example.

6. What is the economic logic of a pollution abatement program?

7. What is the MSC? Use the case of a hazardous waste polluter to illustrate.

8. Why is the creation of environmental policy with respect to acid rain so difficult?

9. Why does Schell feel that nuclear war would be the ultimate threat to the earth's environment?

SUGGESTED READINGS

John Allen (ed.), 1984. *Environment 84/85,* Annual Editions, Dushkin Publishing Group Incorporated. A nice collection of short articles on all aspects of the environment.

Gerald O. Barney, 1980. *The Global 2000 Report to the President of the United States: Entering the 21st Century,* Pergamon Press.

Robert H. Boyle and R. Alexander Boyle, 1983. *Acid Rain,* Shocken Books. An excellent introductory survey of the issue.

Lester Brown, 1981, *Building a Sustainable Society,* Norton; and 1984, *State of the World,* Worldwatch Institute.

Samuel Epstein, Lester Brown, and Carl Pope, 1982. *Hazardous Waste in America,* Sierra Club Books. See Chapter 5, "Dumping in Niagara Falls," which details the case study of Love Canal.

Jonathan Schell, 1982, *The Fate of the Earth* and 1984, *The Abolition,* Knopf. Two excellent books on nuclear war and its total societal and environmental impact.

Allan Schnaiberg, 1980. *The Environment: From Surplus to Scarcity,* Oxford University Press. A radical political-economy analysis of the environment.

Joseph J. Seneca and Michael Taussig, 1984. *Environmental Economics* (3rd ed.), Prentice-Hall. An excellent mainstream introductory environmental economics text.

Tom Tietenberg, 1984. *Environmental and Natural Resource Economics,* Scott, Foresman, and Company. An excellent intermediate-level text on environmental economics and natural resources, with some material on energy.

30 Chapter

What Has Become of the Keynesian Revolution?

What the bushy-bearded, heavy-handed German revolutionary did with malice aforethought and by frontal attack, the English aristocrat, a scholar of Eton and King's College, Cambridge, a director of the Bank of England, an advisor to the Chancellor of the Exchequer, a peer of the Realm, performed neatly, skillfully, and unconsciously, by flank attack.

—E. E. Hale

Now, it seems that the bastard Keynesian era is coming to an end in general disillusionment; the economists have no more idea what to say than they had when the old equilibrium doctrine collapsed in the great slump. The Keynesian revolution still remains to be made both in teaching economic theory and in forming economic policy.

—Joan Robinson

WHY THE QUESTION?

John Maynard Keynes published *The General Theory of Employment, Interests and Money* in 1936. In this book, as we have already learned, he attempted to diagnose the illness of capitalism in the midst of the Great Depression and to provide a prescription to cure the ailing system. More fundamentally, Keynes provided an explanation for the massive unemployment and some guidance as to how to reduce the gross inequalities in wealth and income characteristic of capitalism in the 1930s.

Many argue that the Keynesian Revolution was Keynes's formulation of a *new* economic theory breaking with the classical and neoclassical tradition. It was new economic theory more appropriate for the time period than a dated theory incapable of explaining existing economic reality. In another sense, as the American Marxist Paul Sweezy has said of Keynes's importance, his "mission was to *reform* Neo-classical economics, to bring to back into contact with the real world," with which it had lost touch since the 1870s.

Keynes posited that capitalism had reached the stage of development in which high levels of unemployment and stagnation of economic growth were logical out-comes of the natural operation of the system as it was then constructed. More important, he felt that it would not deviate from this path automatically over time in a "self-correcting" manner, as the dominant economic paradigm promised. In effect, Keynes proved that Say's law was incorrect. The real secret to the capitalist econo-my's health, viability, and stability was the level of aggregate demand relative to productive capacity. Keynes's new approach to the concepts and functions of saving and investment put to rest the myths of the previous economic paradigm. As he suggested, the only way to ensure full employment, price stability, economic growth, a positive trade balance, and an equitable distribution of income was for the govern-ment to take a more aggressive role in the economic system by utilizing the tools of fiscal and monetary policy. It could be argued that Keynes reintroduced the science of political economy into economics. By suggesting that government spend money to ensure the proper level of aggregate demand in order to maintain full employment, he raised indirectly the question "What should government spend the money on?" This question, as we will see, was answered over time by historical events and the exercise of political power and vested economic interest.

So there can be little doubt that there was such a thing as the "Keynesian Revolution" viewed as a new economic paradigm replacing the dying neoclassical body of thought. But many have since argued that the *real* Keynesian Revolution never occurred. Some economists maintain that what was truly revolutionary about *The General Theory* was never fully understood or articulated by Keynes or his disciples. The late E. E. Hale, one such critic who taught economics at the Univer-sity of Texas, argued that Keynes refused "to draw, or even to admit, the logical conclusions of the General Theory, but they are there nevertheless, and in plain sight for all to see." Hale further asserted that "Keynes's blindness at bottom results from his failure or refusal to recognize that he had hit upon the contradiction in the process of capital accumulation which Marx had so clearly pictured three-quarters of a century earlier." What, then, was this particular similarity between Keynes and Marx? Hale has summarized it as follows (as well as noting some differences):

> Keynes and Marx, indeed, have much in common. *The General Theory,* like *Das Kapital,* teaches that unemployment and depression are the norms to which the capitalist economy tends. Both Keynes and Marx were aware of deficient demand and oversaving, of the declining profit rate resulting from limited investment opportunities, of the unwisdom of capital exportation. Both were highly critical of the excesses of the capitalist

John Maynard Keynes, 1883–1946

> system. But Keynes was no socialist. For him the troubles of our society
> are due, not to the breakdown of a social system, but to a failure of
> intelligence. He is convinced that by the exercise of intelligence capitalism
> can be made more efficient for attaining economic ends than any
> alternative system yet in sight.
>
> —E. E. Hale (prepared by Ron Phillips), "Some Implications of Keynes' *General Theory
> of Employment, Interest, and Money,*" *Review of Radical Political Economics,* Vol. 8,
> No. 4, Winter 1976.

In retrospect, economic historians have concluded that essentially what **Keynes**
did was to rescue capitalism from its sickbed and reform it sufficiently so that it could
continue to function adequately. By administering Keynesian policy tools, those in
charge could tame the business cycle once and for all.

A BRIEF HISTORICAL OVERVIEW: WORLD WAR II TO THE PRESENT

It took several years after some initial reluctance for the United States to understand,
appreciate, and begin to implement the Keynesian doctrine. The United States
found (as did Hitler's Germany years earlier) that one way to achieve full employment was to engage in deficit spending to build a vast military machine. This can be
easily documented by the data in Table 30.1.

Adjustment to the postwar period for the United States was somewhat difficult
but nevertheless successful. There was a series of recessions in the time period 1949
to 1971, in which real GNP decreased and unemployment increased (see Table 30.2).

We can conclude from this that indeed the cyclical behavior of American
capitalism was not eliminated, but it was certainly curbed and mitigated. There were

Table 30.1

YEAR	UNEMPLOYMENT RATE	GOVERNMENT DEFICIT (BILLIONS OF DOLLARS)	TOTAL MILITARY OUTLAYS (BILLIONS OF DOLLARS)
1933	24.9	− 2.6	0.8
1939	17.2	− 3.9	1.4
1940	14.6	− 3.1	1.8
1941	9.9	− 5.0	6.3
1942	4.7	−20.8	22.9
1943	1.9	−54.9	63.4
1944	1.2	−47.0	76.0
1945	1.9	−47.5	80.5

Source: Economic Report of the President, 1977, pages 228 and 268; and "Statistical Appendix to Annual Report of the Treasury for the Fiscal Year Ended June 30, 1968."

recessions but no repeat of the depression experience of the 1930s. This is particularly impressive in light of the fact that the neoclassical-Keynesian synthesis did not really become popularly accepted theory until the publication of the first edition of Paul Samuelson's *Principles of Economics* in 1948. This spelled out in very elementary language and analysis the integration of the "Keynesian Revolution" with the then *revived* neoclassical theory. Yet it was not until the early 1960s that Keynesian economists were fully integrated into the policymaking institutions of the American economy. Most economists would point to the historic "tax cut" engineered by Walter Heller in 1964 as the real acceptance of Keynesian economics in the United States.

From the early 1960s to the early years of the 1970s, economists and the economics discipline were held in great esteem. An almost euphoric sense of confidence in the practice of Keynesian economics and the strength of the American economy filled the pages of textbooks, journals, periodicals, and newspapers, as well as the corridors of business and government. Keynesian economics was viewed as a

Table 30.2

YEARS	UNEMPLOYMENT RATE (PERCENTAGE)
1948–1949	5.9
1953–1954	5.5
1957–1958	6.8
1960–1961	6.7
1970–1971	6.0

Source: Economic Report of the President, 1977.

panacea for our economic woes of the past. The fragmented and persistent criticism by conservative monetarists and radical Marxists alike fell on deaf ears as the U.S. economy went breezing along. With strong economic growth, almost full employment, relative price stability and U.S. international hegemony, why should anyone doubt the universal applicability of Keynesian economics and its apparent immortality?

Much to the Keynesians' surprise, though, doubt did surface, and it became stronger and stronger over time. In the middle of the 1960s, the United States found itself committed to a land war in Southeast Asia, pouring hundreds of millions of dollars ($150 billion) into this effort, while domestically the nation was coming apart because of urban unrest, campus rebellion, and racial strife. Indeed, the Keynesian system found itself unable to deliver the promised goals and objectives under the pressure of *internal* and *external* demands that later proved to be contradictory in terms of the maintenance of the system's stability. Recessions occurred in 1970–1971 and again in 1973–1975. By the early 1970s, the U.S. economic system was experiencing great international pressures. The defeat in Vietnam followed by persistent balance-of-payments problems put such pressure on the currency that the Nixon Administration had little choice but to devalue the dollar twice within 18 months. This signaled to the world at large that one important institutional piece of the Keynesian synthesis in the capitalist world—the international monetary system—had collapsed.

Further exacerbating the emergent dilemma for the Keynesian system was the continued presence of a myriad of domestic problems that had surfaced in the mid-1960s. There was still poverty, racism, sexism, militarism, and environmental decay. A belligerent foreign policy still existed and caused complaint. In addition, new problems of inflation accompanied by high levels of unemployment, heightened global interdependence, the growing impoverishment of the developing world, and the growing concentration of political and economic power held by multinational corporations and the executive branch of the federal government all combined to bring additional pressures and problems to bear upon the ability of an economic philosophy fashioned to deal with a set of problems in the 1930s.

The 1970s brought forth the OPEC oil price shocks (1973–1974 and 1979) along with a mixture of ill-fated economic stabilization policies designed to arrest the tenacious stagflation that persisted from 1977 to 1980 during the Carter Administration. While struggling to fight inflation with rather conservative monetary policy, President Carter opted to allow unemployment to remain excessively high. The decline in economic growth accompanied by high unemployment generated huge government outlays and resulted in sizable government deficits. In 1980, the federal deficit soared to $59 billion (see Table 30.3). In retrospect, the 1979 OPEC oil price shock, the foreign policy consequences of the Iranian hostage crisis, and the recession induced by the strict monetary policies of the Federal Reserve Board under the new leadership of Paul Volcker in 1979 contributed to Carter's defeat and Reagan's election in 1980.

Reagan's campaign emphasized the failure of the Democratic Party's Keynesian economic policies. Reagan particularly criticized the irresponsible spending programs (the deficit) and the overall intrusion of government into the economy (regula-

Table 30.3

YEAR	UNEMPLOYMENT RATE	CAPACITY UTILIZATION IN MANUFACTURING	ANNUAL RATE OF INFLATION (CPI)	FEDERAL DEFICIT (MILLIONS OF DOLLARS)
1970	4.9	79.3	5.5	−2,845
1971	5.9	78.4	3.4	−23,033
1972	5.6	83.5	3.4	−23,372
1973	4.9	87.6	8.8	−14,849
1974	5.6	83.8	12.2	−4,688
1975	8.5	72.9	7.0	−45,154
1976	7.7	79.5	4.8	−66,413
1977	7.0	81.9	6.8	−44,948
1978	6.0	84.4	9.0	−48,807
1979	5.8	85.7	13.3	−27,694
1980	7.1	79.6	12.3	−59,563
1981	7.5	79.4	10.2	−57,932
1982	9.5	71.1	6.0	−110,609
1983	9.5	75.3	3.6	−195,407
1984	7.7	82.0	3.5	−183,689
1985	7.1	80.3	3.6	−212,300

Source: Economic Report of the President, 1985.

tion). Reagan promised to use the theoretical framework of supply-side economics to chart a new economic course for the nation. He promised to balance the budget, reduce inflation without recession, generate strong economic growth, and reduce the level of unemployment.

Toward analyzing and evaluating the performance of the Reagan Administration in the 1980s Leonard Silk situates the experience of the Reagan Administration in a historical context, beginning from the early 1960s and continuing up to 1984.

RECOVERING FROM THE ERA OF SHOCKS

Leonard Silk

The two decades after World War II have been called a "golden age" of growth and stability for the United States and the rest of the industrial world. "In the 'Golden Age' of the 1950's and 1960's," said Angus Maddison, a British economist, "economic growth in the advanced capitalist countries surpassed virtually all historical records."

(continued)

But, starting in the late 1960's, the United States economy was battered by a series of economic and political shocks that turned the golden age into an age of tin. First came President Johnson's "guns and butter" policy that bred inflation during the Vietnam war; then came President Nixon's surprise of Aug. 15, 1971, when he suspended convertibility of the dollar into gold, imposed wage-price controls and embarked on a highly stimulative fiscal and monetary policy. International financial chaos and the end of the Bretton Woods monetary system of fixed exchange rates hit the world economy in 1973, and the OPEC nations twice in that decade tipped the world into economic shock with monumental increases in oil prices.

As the United States economy careened from one shock to the next, inflation soared, productivity foundered, real growth slowed, several deep recessions battered industry and unemployment rose to the highest rates since the Great Depression. Internationally, mountains of debt, spawned by the explosion in oil prices, threatened to produce a world banking crisis.

But with the dawning of 1983, the darkness began to lift. The United States swung into a strong recovery, spurring weaker recoveries in other industrial countries. And now, a year later, some economists have begun to speculate that the nation—with inflation still low, unemployment high and industrial capacity ample—may even have an opportunity once again for a sustained period of economic growth reminiscent of the early sixties.

The Reagan Administration, . . ., has eagerly embraced that prospect. Its budget for the fiscal year 1985 and projections through 1989 are based on the President's belief that the nation has entered a long period of steady economic growth (4 percent a year during the second half of the decade), subdued inflation (3.5 percent measured by the deflator in 1989), lower interest rates (a 5 percent Treasury bill rate by then), and reduced unemployment (5 percent in 1989).

But has the United States truly entered into a postshock era of economic calm? Or will 1983 and 1984 turn out to be a brief interlude of growth, the prelude to another unsettling economic shock?

There is a great deal of skepticism among economists and businessmen about the dawning of a new era. Most expect 1984 to be a good year but are worried—primarily by the huge size of the expected Federal deficit—about what lies beyond the election year. . . .

There is a dissenting view, however, and not just at the White House. It is held by those who think that enough can be learned from studying the events and disappointments of the past two decades of economic history to mark a better course for the future.

One of the nation's most powerful economists, Paul A. Volcker, chairman of the Federal Reserve Board, asserted this view at last month's meeting of the American Economic Association in San Francisco. The United States, he said, may be able to reverse the experience of the 1970's

(continued)

and demonstrate that "an economy that seemed to be going downhill, with one adverse shock begetting another, can go up as well."

He saw an "enormous opportunity" to set in train a long period of growth and greater stability, but stressed that his "happy vision" would not come about if the nation sat back and simply hoped the "recent good news would produce a lasting momentum of its own."

There are new and unprecedented risks to sustaining progress, Mr. Volcker warned: the enormous budget deficits that loom ahead, the international debt problem, the gaping and still growing imbalance in the United States' international accounts, the strong forces of protectionism, and "not least," he said, "the temptation to return to behavior patterns bred in the years of inflation."

But he thought the threats could be met if the nation would act upon the lessons of the bitter past.

Even the skeptics might agree to that proposition. But what are the key lessons from history? Although economists and others may differ in degree about what these might be, there appears to be general agreement on a few key points:

Presidents must make the tough decisions on how to use limited national resources while there is time, not subordinate those decisions to immediate political advantage.

Inflation was kicked off in this country during the Vietnam War when President Johnson, with the economy approaching full employment, delayed, for political reasons, the difficult choice among three possible policies: raising taxes, cutting his Great Society programs or curbing military spending. And President Nixon gravely aggravated inflation a few years later with his New Economic Policy of Aug. 15, 1971, simultaneously launching a highly stimulative fiscal and monetary policy, clamping on wage and price controls, suspending the convertibility of the dollar into gold and embargoing sales of certain American agricultural products. When the controls were lifted after his electoral victory in 1972, the suppressed inflation burst forth.

There is a broad consensus among economists that President Reagan is taking undue risks of imposing inflationary strains on resources by his huge budget deficits, stretching, as David A. Stockman, director of the Office of Management and Budget, has put it, "as far as the eye can see."

If tight money is employed to keep those inflationary pressures from getting out of hand, the consequence, once again, is likely to be a shooting up of interest rates and another steep recession.

Economists differ on just how much time President Reagan has to put his budget in better order. Some see his so-called "supply-side" tax cuts as really Keynesian demand-side tax cuts that have, combined with an easier monetary policy, fortuitously helped to lift the economy out of the deep

(continued)

recession and should be allowed to push it even closer to full employment.

Thus, Gardner Ackley, professor of economics at the University of Michigan and chairman of the Council of Economic Advisers under President Johnson, told the economists in San Francisco: "For 1984, I see no reason to worry about the deficits. Rather, we should welcome them for their contribution to recovery. But I do worry about deficits of the size currently forecast if they extend much beyond 1984." His reasons: Unless curbed by tighter monetary or fiscal policy, the deficits threaten to reaccelerate inflation. And if excess demand were curbed primarily by tight money, as now seems likely, that could generate even higher interest rates and come at the expense of investment and growth.

Supply-siders, such as Alan Reynolds of Polynomics Inc., a consulting firm, still contend that concern about budget deficits is vastly exaggerated and that it would be foolish to try to reduce them by raising taxes. President Reagan, on that point, still marches with the supply-siders and is determined not to raise taxes if he can help it and not to reduce the planned rapid buildup of military spending.

But most of the President's own economic advisers . . . disagree. They fear a situation like Vietnam revisited—with military spending rising, taxes falling and the budget deficit widening. They believe, as do most economists, that with the economy in a recovery it is vital to bring down the deficit. Treasury Secretary Donald T. Regan, who believes the President should defer the tax issue until after the election, has laid out a list of options for Mr. Reagan to consider, if the President decides to increase revenues to reduce the fiscal year 1975 deficit from its expected $186 billion level, . . . "in 1984."

The United States must pay more heed to the international economy in setting its domestic economic policies. . . .

Mr. Volcker, in his address to the economists' convention last month, stressed that the need to close the budget gap and bring down interest rates was "pressing" for international reasons. The level of dollar interest rates, forced upward by the deficits, he said, "plainly aggravates the strains on the international financial system—strains apparent in the heavy debt burdens of many developing countries and in the persistent and growing flow of capital into the United States, with its counterpart of a widening trade deficit." Mr. Volcker said he did not share the comfortable assumption of some that working for better budget balance could wait a year or more.

C. Fred Bergsten, a former Assistant Secretary of the Treasury, warns that high interest rates and the huge American trade deficit—now threatening to reach $120 billion in 1984—could bring on a deluge of protectionism and wreck the world trading system as other countries retaliated.

(continued)

Foreign governments blame high American interest rates for holding down the European recovery and for draining the financial resources of developing countries like Brazil, Argentina and Nigeria almost to the breaking point.

But untangling this skein could itself be tricky. Geoffrey Bell, a leading international monetary expert and former British Treasury official, fears that at some stage the process of a strengthening dollar "will certainly be reversed and then the fall of the dollar could be very dramatic." That, however, could deal a new shock to the monetary system.

Tight monetary policy must be used with great caution.

There is no doubt any longer about the potency of monetary policy in checking inflation. But, in the process of squeezing inflation down over the past few years, tight money policy has taken an enormous toll in lost production, jobs, investment and growth.

There is a still a school of economic thought, led by Professor Emeritus Milton Friedman of the University of Chicago, that insists monetary policy should be properly applied by a simple rule: The money supply be increased year by year—or, if possible, month by month or day by day—at a rate consistent with the national growth of productivity. Following the rule, says Professor Friedman, will permit inflation-free growth over time—though it will not necessarily rid the economy of cyclical fluctuations in production, income and employment.

Since the fall of 1979, Mr. Volcker has experimented with what he calls "practical monetarism," heeding Professor Friedman's call for more attention to gradual growth of the money supply and less to the level of interest rates. But when tight money produced the recessions of 1980 and 1981–82, Mr. Volcker swung to much more rapid rates of monetary expansion than sanctioned by the Fed's "target ranges" and paid more heed to interest rates. Thereby, discretionary monetary policy was used as a powerful tool for getting the economy out of deep slumps. All but the most orthodox monetarists have cheered the moves.

As Prof. James Tobin of Yale, a Nobel laureate who eschews monetarism, put it recently, "Our Federal Reserve finally took mercy on the economy about a year ago and suspended its monetarist targets. Its easing of monetary policy saved the world financial system from dangerous crisis and averted further collapse of economic activity."

A better way must be found for combining high employment and growth with price stability.

With 8.2 percent of the labor force unemployed, this problem does not loom immediately ahead, but if the recovery continues into the mid-80's it will. Mandatory price and wage controls, last used by President Nixon, have proved rigid and inefficient. Resisting overstimulus while controls were in place proved impossible for the Nixon Administration. When the controls were finally lifted, inflation accelerated.

(continued)

But recessions are a costly way of undoing inflation, too. Thus, many economists have been on the prowl for years to devise a new form of voluntary "incomes policy" to hold back price and wage increases with less pain and less market interference. Arthur Burns, as chairman of the Federal Reserve, had been urging an incomes policy when President Nixon leap-frogged past him to mandatory controls.

Henry Wallich, a governor of the Federal Reserve Board, who in the past has favored an incomes policy based on tax incentives, offered a new idea in San Francisco. He suggested "taking a leaf from the wisdom of Japan" with a system of two-step wage increases, the second step of which is a bonus. "With a bonus in prospect," said Mr. Wallich, "the first step can be more moderate. The second step would reflect price and profit developments in the intervening period." He proposed a dialogue between business and labor, both of whom he thought had much to gain from such a plan.

Mr. Volcker also welcomed the new interest amongst both business and labor in profit-sharing arrangements or other ways of "rewarding workers when things are good, without building in an inexorably rising floor on costs."

This is just the top of the list of lessons to be learned from the past. Economists who share Paul Volcker's "happy vision" would argue that for the first time in almost two decades the United States and the rest of the world have at least a chance, however small, to profit from the harsh experiences of the late 60's and 70's and enter a period of stable and lasting growth.

Inflation, for the time being, has been battered down, unemployment is still relatively high, much industrial capacity is idle and after a rough run of recessions, American corporations have cut costs and improved profitability. Not since the Kennedy Administration in 1961 inherited an economy that had been through back-to-back recessions has there been such an opportunity for noninflationary growth.

At the San Francisco meetings Prof. W. Arthur Lewis, of Princeton University, the outgoing president of the economists, admonished his colleagues for failing to study history: "If our subject is lowering its sights, this may be because the demise of economic history in economics departments has brought us a generation of economists with no historical background."

Still, there is no simple formula provided by history to prevent the nation from being blind-sided again by another shock—or a series of them.

Moreover, even if economists fully agreed on the lessons to be gleaned from the troubled past, it does not follow that politicians would join in the agreement or enforce its prescriptions. Inevitably it is they, not their economic advisers, who will call the shots—or the shocks.

1. Silk makes four major conclusions (statements) about stabilization policy. What are they?

2. By 1984 what, according to Silk, were the major economic policy issues facing the Reagan Administration?

3. What has been the economic stabilization policy of the Reagan administration since 1984?

4. How successful have these economic stabilization policies been?

While most conventional economists have debated the efficacy of Keynesian economics, there also emerged in the late 1960s and early 1970s a radical perspective on the theory and practice of neoclassical and Keynesian economics.

RADICAL CRITIQUE: KEYNES AND THE BUSINESS CYCLE

Keynesian economics, in spite of all that it has done for our understanding of business fluctuations, has beyond doubt left at least one major thing unexplained, and that thing is nothing less than the business cycle itself.

—J. R. Hicks, from Joan Robinson, "What Has Become of the Keynesian Revolution?"
Challenge, Jan.–Feb. 1974, p. 6.

Since 1968 there has been a growing body of radical literature dealing with the intensified problems of American capitalism both domestically and internationally. This literature has been written primarily by members of the Union for Radical Political Economics. Many consider themselves Marxists since they adhere in general to the methodology and philosophy of Karl Marx. These radical critics have a different point of view and one that deserves, in our opinion, a detailed treatment.

Radical economists argue in general that the 1970s stagflation in our economy today was symptomatic not only of a failure of Keynesian theory and policy but also of a fundamental breakdown of American capitalism. Radical economists view American capitalism as experiencing a long-term *structural crisis*. They argue that the cyclical behavior of American capitalism since World War II (resulting in seven recessions) cannot be explained by "accidental forces" or factors external to the economy. It can be explained only by a systematic analysis of the behavior and operation of the capitalist economy. In a sense, the rediscovery and acceptance of the business cycle by orthodox economists has yielded common ground with radical economists. They all now agree that business cycles are inevitable in a capitalist economic system. The difference now appears to be between the orthodox economist's belief in the capability of Keynesian theory to tame the business cycle by "fine tuning" the economy and the radical's belief that it is becoming increasingly difficult to prevent and/or ameliorate the dislocations of business cycles.

In addition, the radical critique of Keynesian theory and policy challenges the "theory of the state" implicit in the Keynesian paradigm. Keynesian economic theory posits a view of the state as the legitimate arbiter of societal conflicts resulting from interest-group political behavior and lobbying. This view of political democracy is often termed "pluralism." In a pluralist society, the state (government) acts in a neutral capacity to provide for and protect the rights and interests of the majority as well as minorities. The radical economist's theory of the state is quite different. Radicals contend that the state is little more than the institutional apparatus that serves the interests and needs of the ruling class. There is no such thing as a *neutral state*. In a capitalist economic system, the political apparatus serves the dominant economic class by mediating societal class conflicts and arbitrating conflicts between members of the dominant class itself. This is the principal function of the state. The state's overriding goal is to preserve the operation and characteristics of the American capitalist system itself, with its emphasis on private ownership and free enterprise.

The radical view of the state can be best understood in the context of the "class-conflict" theory of the state as revealed in the radical theory of the **political business cycle.**

Radical economists argue that the state consciously guides the economy and cyclical instability in order to serve the needs of the dominant economic class: Cyclical instability serves a functional set of needs for the capitalist class. How do they explain this?

The business cycle describes the movement and performance of the economy as it passes through various stages of expansion and contraction. In the expansion phase, aggregate demand is high, total output of goods and services grows rapidly, and the economy approaches full employment and full utilization of productive capacity. In the contraction phase, aggregate demand is low, total output of goods and services is falling, and the economy experiences high unemployment and low levels of utilization of productive capacity.

Business cycles historically have been explained by orthodox economists in basically two different ways: (1) underconsumption or limited demand, and (2) overinvestment or overproduction. What radical economists have done is to combine the two different orthodox interpretations and forge them into one single theory of the business cycle. Their explanation is as follows: The primary motivation of the capitalist is the search for profits. This encourages the capitalist to invest and accumulate capital. This process stimulates economic expansion and conditions that encourage expectations of profit returns. In a way, an accelerator principle works to encourage greater and greater investment seeking higher and higher profit returns. As the expansion phase continues, distortions begin to appear. There may be overproduction of goods and services. Competition for capital results in the costs of capital increasing faster than other prices. In order to create the funds necessary for further investment capital, the capitalist must produce sufficient profits. This can be done by increasing prices for finished goods and services, thereby fueling inflationary pressures; by borrowing, thereby increasing the debt equity ratio and worsening the liquidity position of the firm; or by reducing payments to workers in the form of wages, thereby reducing their purchasing power and limiting total demand (i.e., underconsumption). This last option is difficult to do at the peak of an expansion because, as the economy approaches full employment, labor is in a stronger wage-bargaining position and more likely to demand and get high wage increases. The capitalist is faced with a "profit squeeze" from higher wage costs and higher capital costs and is thus forced, out of necessity, to alleviate these pressures by dismissing workers and reducing investment spending. This ushers in the contraction phase, or a recession. The contraction phase serves the function of curing the distortions of the previous expansion phase.

This "functional" analysis of the recession has been carefully summarized by economists Raford Boddy and James Crotty in the following manner:

> It is the economic function of the recession to correct the imbalances of the previous expansion and thereby create the preconditions for a new one. By robbing millions of people of their jobs, and threatening the jobs of millions of others, recessions reduce worker demands and end the rise of labor costs. They eventually rebuild profit margins and stabilize prices. During recessions, inventories are cut, loans are repaid, corporate liquidity positions improve, and the deterioration in the balance of payments position is reversed. All the statements of Keynesian economists to the contrary notwithstanding, *recessions are inevitable in the unplanned economy of the United States* because they perform an essential function for which no adequate substitute has *thus* far been available.
>
> —Raford Boddy and James R. Crotty, "Who Will Plan the Planned Economy?" *The Progressive*, February, 1975.

This, then, is the general description of expansion and contraction and the function of recession as viewed by radical economists. It is important to note that the cause is rooted in the structure of the economy and the behavior of the capitalist class. But there are other factors that normally intensify the business cycle. These are briefly (1) the psychological expectations of either optimism or pessimism, (2) the existence of monopoly power in the major productive sectors of the economy, (3) events or conditions related to the international economic and financial sector, and (4) speculation in money, credit, and commodity markets.

On the basis of the radical analysis of the business cycle, unemployment is perceived as being structurally "built-in" to the normal functioning of the capitalist system. Unemployment becomes a sort of cushion or "shock absorber" for the cyclical behavior of the system. Likewise, inflation becomes a structural characteristic of the system, having less to do with the rate of growth of the money supply than with the monopolistic pricing behavior of corporations with concentrated market power in the corporate sector.

In order to explain the continued existence of the business cycle and its *politicized* nature, radicals point to major structural changes in American capitalism since World War II that help to shed light on the present failures of Keynesian policy. First, they identify the growing concentration of production by corporate firms and their growing political and economic power. Another feature of the concentration of production is related to the international specialization and division of labor since 1945, carried out principally by multinational corporations and other international institutions. This increased global integration of capitalism not only has increased the concentration of production but has also made U.S. domestic stabilization policy difficult, as Keynesian economic policy is increasingly incapable of imposing controls and regulations on the multinational institutions. In fact, changes and events taking place in the international sector have become over time more and more troublesome for Keynesian policy to adapt to in promoting growth, price stability, and full employment. For example, the OPEC price increase in 1973–1974 completely upset the macro performance of the U.S. economy.

The last factor singled out by radical economists to explain the structural transformation of American capitalism since World War II is the growing symbiotic relationship between government and business. Radicals claim that this extensive "state–corporate" expansion prohibits the possibility of genuine democracy in America and clearly depicts an underlying class character of government functions and policies.

This, then, is briefly the radical view of the failure of Keynesian economic policy and the general crisis of American capitalism.

> **5. How would a radical (Marxian) economist analyze the early years of the Reagan Administration? Explain.**

THE REAGAN YEARS, 1980–1984: AN OVERVIEW

In September 1984, *Business Week* magazine ran an article entitled "Recovery Cheers the GOP." This article made the case that by the third quarter of 1984, the economy had demonstrated such a recovery that it was all but self-evident that the Reagan Administration would not have a difficult time defending its economic record in the re-election campaign. One could point to the following positive facts: (1) the 20-month-long economic recovery had produced an expansion that would produce a 6.5 percent rate of growth of real GNP in 1984; (2) the rate of unemployment had dropped from a peak of 10.7 percent to 7.5 percent by the end of 1984; (3) inflation was running at an annual rate of 3.5 percent in 1984 compared with 11.3 percent when Reagan took office; (4) productivity measured by output per hour worked had increased by over 3 percent in 1984; and (5) the U.S. dollar was at its strongest level in years. Yet there were still some major economic problems to be confronted and some very serious questions about whether this recovery could be attributed directly to the success of Reagan's supply-side theories and policies.

Reagan's economic program was characterized by a large expansion of defense spending, budget cuts, massive tax cuts, and a reliance on the Fed to fight inflation with strict monetary policy. Roger E. Brinner, an economist with Data Resources Incorporated, asserted that Reagan's budget cuts and tax cuts represented "a Keynesian revival" and not a supply-side miracle. The drastic reduction in inflation was said to be less the success of supply-side policies than the effect of harsh Federal

Reserve Board monetary policies inducing a deep and prolonged recession from 1980 to 1982, as well as such other factors as (1) slack labor markets resulting in a reduced rate of growth of wages; (2) an oil glut in the early 1980s that sent petroleum prices spiraling downward to $29 per barrel in 1984, compared with $34 in 1980; and (3) the sluggish recovery in Western Europe and the Third World, which kept commodity prices lower. The predicted explosion of investment spending and increased saving did not occur after the enactment of the 1981 Economic Recovery Act, providing for massive tax cuts for individuals and businesses. The recovery was first fueled by consumer spending (borrowing) and government deficits. Investment showed some sign of significant expansion by late 1983 but this came mostly from corporate profits (retained earnings) and some capital depreciation gains resulting from the tax act. In addition, large sources of foreign capital entered the country, chasing higher earnings and higher interest rates. This capital inflow provided an important means by which the huge federal deficits could be financed without drawing on domestic credit sources that would have driven up interest rates by the feared "crowding out" of credit. The strong dollar presented itself as a bit of a paradox: for buying imports and keeping inflation down it was a clear advantage, but it also hurt many sectors of the economy dependent on exports (farmers, for example) as well as contributing to the massive trade deficit of $120 billion in 1984. In addition, by mid-1982, with the recession having had a major impact on growth and unemployment, the Fed decided that the battle against inflation had been won and then chose to liberalize monetary policy to induce the recovery. Many economists argued that supply-side economics did not eliminate inflation without a recession and that the huge tax cuts did not produce huge tax receipts from growth to eliminate budget deficits. In fact after two years of spending restraint, tax increases in 1982 and 1984, and almost two years of strong economic growth, the deficit under the Reagan Administration went from a peak of $196 billion in 1982 to $174 billion in 1984. Reagan predicted that federal spending would be 19 percent of GNP in 1984, but in 1984 it was 23.5 percent of GNP.

In spite of these particular criticisms of Reagan's economic policy, the Mondale–Ferraro team focused more specifically on a set of basic economic issues. First, they raised the issue of "fairness" by charging that the tax cut, the spending priorities, and the monetary policy (induced recession) had negatively affected the poor and middle class and had benefited only the upper class of the nation. Indeed, the U.S. Commerce Department released data validating the fact that over 35 million citizens were living below the poverty line (over 15 percent of the U.S. population). A 1984 Senate Democratic Policy Committee Report concluded that "the poor and needy have become poorer and needier as a result of the Reagan administration's unfair budget policies." Second, the Mondale–Ferraro team pointed to the huge federal deficit(s) of $174 billion to indicate the failure of supply-side economics and the extent to which Reagan was jeopardizing the economic future of the nation by not bringing these deficits under control. Mondale and Ferraro charged that the only way to do this was by increasing taxes, but during the campaign Reagan would not in public support raising taxes (although many of his aides privately confessed that after re-election this would be necessary). Third, the Democratic Party's team pointed to the gigantic trade deficit of $120 billion in 1984 and challenged Reagan to lower interest rates and realign the dollar because it was overvalued and hurting many segments of the economy.

Many Keynesian economists took delight in pointing out that Reagan's supply-side economics did not work and that in fact what success he claimed was really attributed to good old-fashioned Keynesian policy. For example, Alan Blinder, Professor of Economics at Princeton University, in *The New York Times* (February 19, 1984), wrote, "Gradually, however, the force of events is showing that the new classical emperor, though resplendent in theoretical elegance, has no empirical clothes. . . . In sum, the supply-side experiment restored faith in Keynesian economics in a way that scholarly debate never can. . . . It may be premature to declare the Keynesian Restoration is upon us, but someone has to say it first."

In addition to Keynesians such as Blinder, Samuel Bowles, a radical economist from the University of Massachusetts at Amherst, was busy in 1984 editorializing about the failure of Reaganomics. In an article in the July 8, 1984 *New York Times*, Bowles argued the position of Blinder that "Keynes is Back, Thanks to Reagan." In another essay in *The Boston Globe* (April 17, 1984), "The Trickle-Down Failure," Bowles asserted the following:

> The "recovery" of 1983, indeed, was fueled . . . by the size of the government deficit—itself a product of soaring military spending and the ill-conceived 1981 tax cuts. The irony was now complete. Ronald Reagan arrived in Washington as a champion of supply-side economics and a militant foe of "big spenders." He would complete his first term as the biggest-spending military Keynesian of the postwar period. . . . Military Keynesianism has done little more than provide us with a respite from recession; it has done nothing to alter the basic pattern of decline. . . . Reaganomics has been begrudgingly accepted by many as a mean-spirited but necessary medicine. The last three years have taught us differently. Trickle-down economics is not only unfair, it is a flop.

This criticism and analysis of supply-side economics suggested that the U.S. economy would be continually plagued by the ups and downs of the business cycle, with its attendant economic and social costs. For many economists, the real issues of the late 1980s and early 1990s center around the theme of restructuring the economy to create sustained economic growth, full employment, and price stability with social justice.

AMERICAN CAPITALISM IN TRANSITION: REINDUSTRIALIZATION AND RESTRUCTURING

During the late 1970s and early 1980s many economists began to examine the problems of the U.S. economy from the vantage point of not only history but more specifically the structural foundations of the economy. Rather than focus on the specific policies of either the Carter or Reagan Administrations, many economists began to look at major historical forces thought to be changing the world itself and our economy in particular.

In terms of theory, Lester Thurow, an economics professor from MIT, wrote two important books during this period, *The Zero Sum Society* (1980) and *Dangerous Currents* (1983). In the first, Thurow argued that government had the responsibility of making moral and ethical value judgments about who would benefit and who would gain from any decision the government made in the realm of economics. The major issue was loss allocation. He argued for full employment, a guaranteed annual income, equality between the sexes, the fostering of new growth industries, and, to some extent, the socialization of the investment process. In the second book, Thurow debunked the conventional neoclassical market model (the price-auction model), demonstrated the theoretical failings of supply-side economics, and made the case for an enlightened and progressive Keynesian economics.

Barry Bluestone (economist from Boston College) and Bennett Harrison (economist from MIT) wrote *The Deindustrialization of America* in 1982, arguing that American capitalism was facing a deep and fundamental economic crisis. The economy had undergone a structural transformation and economic policy of the Keynesian variety was incapable of addressing the pressing task of restructuring the economy for reindustrialization. They argued that the globalization of production and the internationalization of labor had so transformed the world economy that corporations seeking to maximize profits move capital all over the world freely but at great cost to specific nations and particular communities within those nations. Their book documented this process of "capital flight" and its consequences. They suggested a number of general policies and programs to alleviate the consequences of regional dislocation and uneven development. They argued for (1) the reestablishment of the social safety net that Reagan had severely reduced; (2) an expansion of the government's regulatory system, especially in the area of plant closings; and (3) the development of democratic participation in the process of economic planning. Their ideas helped to spark a nationwide interest and debate about **industrial policy** and economic planning.

Robert Reich, a professor of government at Harvard's Kennedy School, furthered the debate in *The Next American Frontier* (1983). This book reinforced the historical analysis of the sweeping and massive changes that have taken place in the international economy and the resulting impact on the domestic economy of the United States. Reich charged that traditional Keynesian economics was not capable of responding to this situation, and neither was the supply-side doctrine, but he was not drawn to the kind of left-liberal thinking of Bluestone and Harrison. Reich argued for a new government posture oriented toward fostering new high-technology industries, or what he called "flexible system" enterprises. Reich implored us to find ways to restore American competitiveness without resorting to national economic planning or the state-corporativist model of Japan. Reich argued that we operate with a false dichotomy between what he called the "business" culture and the "civic" culture, i.e., making a distinction between the market and the realm of politics. He believed that the task before us is to merge social justice with private profit and private investment.

Others have written their own versions of strategies to overcome the crisis of

American capitalism. Gar Alperovitz and Jeff Faux, in *Rebuilding America* (1984), a book widely circulated among legislators in Washington, have presented a basic blueprint for restructuring the economy. Martin Carnoy, Derek Shearer, and Russell Rumberger wrote *A New Social Contract* (1984), focusing on the same kinds of issues and questions.

The most radical of the new literature addressing the issue of reindustrialization and restructuring was the book by Samuel Bowles, David M. Gordon, and Thomas E. Weisskopf—*Beyond The Wasteland: A Democratic Alternative to Economic Decline* (1983). This book was more theoretical and analytical than the others. It began by tracing the historical evolution of the economic crisis. Next, it analyzed the limits of trickle-down economics. It concluded with a very provocative "Economic Bill of Rights." The authors maintained that the choice before the American people is between a pro-business model/strategy for reindustrialization, and a democratic economics. The former would be characterized by a monetarist, corporatist, supply-side economics featuring profit-led growth, market-based allocation of goods and services, and the further militarization of the economy and society. The latter path would be characterized by wage-led growth, a needs-based allocation, and the conversion of the economy away from militarization. The democratic economic alternative would be based on the following as part of the "Economic Bill of Rights": (1) economic security and equity in conjunction with full employment; (2) a democratic workplace with respect to planning, investment, income distribution, and social relations; (3) democratic planning; and (4) the right to a better way of life, i.e., economic security, access to health care, democracy, and community.

This is but a sample of the work of economists on the general theme of American capitalism in transition and arguments for the need to fundamentally restructure the economy and move beyond traditional Keynesian economics and the recently popularized supply-side economics; as such, it gives a good idea of what will probably be the major issues of the late 1980s and 1990s.

In order to analyze more coherently the thinking of economists who are critical of the supply-side experiment under President Reagan and who feel that something more than a traditional Keynesian prescription is needed in the future, we have the following excerpt from Gar Alperovitz and Jeff Faux's *Rebuilding America* (1984). This selection is from the last chapter.

"REBUILDING AMERICA"

The American economy, the wealthiest in history, is rudderless. For roughly three decades following World War II we rode a wave of prosperity. That wave is spent. Buffeted by the pressures of a new economic era and succumbing to the illusion that the widening "trade-off" between unem-

(continued)

ployment and high prices represents the only reality, economic policy has careened between inflation and deflation, deepening stagnation and sporadic upturns. . . .

The failures of the conservative economic program in the first years of the 1980s have undermined some major ideological and political constraints that until now have prevented us from dealing with the realities of the new economic era. Conventional conservatism has had no more success in solving our economic problems than conventional liberalism. It is apparent that neither can deliver full employment and stable prices. We may well be living through what philosopher Hannah Arendt once termed an

> odd in-between period which sometimes inserts itself into historical time when not only the later historians but the actors and witnesses, the living themselves, become aware of an interval in time which is altogether determined by things that are no longer and by things that are not yet. In history, these intervals have shown more than once that they may contain the moment of truth.

The New Deal and the neoconservative counterreformation are no longer. Economic planning is not yet. This present interval may well be the moment of truth for democracy.

There are reasons to believe that our new economic conditions may themselves be paving the way for political change. The inevitable expansion of government responsibility for the economy brings with it an inevitable transformation of our perception of how the economic world works. . . .

As government's involvement in strategic economic decisions grows, the *way* in which it is involved must move increasingly to the forefront of awareness. To the degree that our capacity to influence the future becomes the context for political debate, the pressures for contending sides to produce practical rather than ideological answers must increase. The act of planning delineates choices and forces those involved to get specific. . . .

Any time of transition brings with it deep-seated stress. The eagerness with which we have embraced our new freedoms has matched a well-documented feeling of rootlessness and purposelessness. Yankelovich has also measured an increase in what he calls a *search for community*—"an intense need to compensate for the impersonal and threatening aspects of modern life by seeking mutual identification with others based on close ethnic ties or ties of shared interests, needs, background, age or values." Yankelovich finds a "large and significant" increase, from 32 to 47 percent, of Americans involved in this search.

In an age of alienating megasystems, impersonal technology, and forced mobility, whether we can expand democracy depends on the success of that search for community. The ideology that promotes greed and beggar-thy-neighbor individualism is rapidly becoming less relevant to both individual and national survival. Moreover, it is neither the case that capi-

(continued)

tal creates all wealth, as conservatism holds, nor that labor is the source of all value, as Marxism argues. The fundamental source of our common economy is the broader, inclusive entity we call the community—it sustains us, gives us our traditions, nurtures us over generations with ideas, information, and technology, and allows us to exchange and cooperate with each other. Without the community there is nothing but the isolated, lonely individual scratching out little more than his or her own sustenance—if he or she is lucky. Our task is to fashion the generally recognized mutual responsibilities of individual and community into a practical ideology appropriate to the new era. . . .

The concept of community also extends to other people. A strategy of sustained production is essential to the reinvigoration of the world economy that Third World and Fourth World nations so desperately need: as long as stagnation continues, they will continue to decline into decay, violence, and totalitarianism.

Overnight creation of economic planning aimed at sustaining community would be a recipe for economic and social disaster. We have neither the institutions nor the ideology to support it. Nonetheless, such planning is the only way we can hope to survive with our democracy and freedoms intact over the coming decades. Again, solving this paradox requires economic policies that deal with the immediate problems of inflation and unemployment *yet at the same time reinforce those individual values of cooperation and collective decision-making that increase our ability to plan competently.*

We have argued that only if solutions to our economic problems are anchored in shared human values can those solutions have a chance ultimately of overcoming the broker state's interest-group bickering and deal-making. Statisticians can debate national definitions of full employment, but in Youngstown the vast majority supported bold strategies for community jobs—making it impossible for major Ohio politicians, including even the conservative then governor, James Rhodes, to oppose their plan. Defining job strategies around the *local* paradigm of *community* full employment helps break the ideological deadlock around the issue of national full employment that all too easily isolates minorities and women. Similarly, emphasizing specific solutions to sectoral price problems bypasses an obsolete inflation politics that targets either social budgets, the poor, labor, or all together. Focusing on the necessities permits a principled coming together of the vast majority.*

The inflation issue is crucial; it is the Achilles' heel of Keynesianism, of the neoliberals, and of the Democratic Party. So long as there is no

(continued)

---

*In the midst of the Carter inflation, a precursor of such an alliance—"Consumers Opposed to Inflation in the Necessities"—a coalition of some seventy-eight labor, elderly, consumer, environmental, and religious groups—urged such a strategy as the alternative to budget cutting and recession.

well-understood alternative principle that confronts the neoconservative postulate that big government and unbalanced budgets cause inflation, then a mad politics of reducing government, cutting budgets, and inducing recession *must* dominate economic policy.

Such a politics in turn devolves into implicit or explicit racism. As economic pain deepens, it pits the blue-collar taxpayer against the black and brown unemployed worker and welfare recipient. Issues of crime, mandatory sentencing, and capital punishment put a violent, repressive political edge to an economic strategy that inherently isolates the ghetto.

Either a political regroupment of the vast majority around the problem of *managing the system* for sustained economic health will be achieved, or intensifying animosities will continue to divide individuals and groups. It is a dangerous illusion to think that Reaganomics' demise will mean an automatic return to middle-of-the-road Democratic politics. The world is not standing still. Neither is the Right. Kevin Phillips reminds us that a crisis alliance between the populist Right and the corporate planners could become a recipe for an American form of fascism.

History also suggests that in times of stress, leaders under pressure to distract attention from domestic failure all too often seek out foreign scapegoats. In the nuclear age it would be folly to imagine America as somehow immune to such pressures.

The most fundamental requirement of a politics of community is a bringing together of our public and private views of how to deal with the future. In our own lives we plan ahead, save money, educate ourselves and our children. Much of what we do concerns the future. Planning for tomorrow gives meaning to our lives today. A politics of community involves an extension of private responsibility to a concern for our neighborhoods, our cities, and the country. In the end, only if economic planning is seen as a process in which a steadily expanded capacity to plan is itself a primary product does it make sense.

"The making of a community is always an exploration," writes British social theorist Raymond Williams, "for consciousness cannot precede creation, and there is no formula for unknown experience."

> It is, in practice, for any man, a long conversion of the habitual elements of denial; a slow and deep personal acceptance of extending community. The institutions of cynicism, of denial and of division will perhaps only be thrown down when they are recognized for what they are: the deposits of practical failures to live. Failure—the jaunty hardness of the "outsider"—will lose its present glamour, as the common experience moves in a different direction.

A serious strategy must walk on "two legs." One leg is the principle that true social change can come only when people's attitudes and values

(continued)

change. The other is the principle that institutions can help shape the values that guide the way individuals behave. The process must be reciprocal; it involves both individual accountability to the community and community accountability to the individual. It is also incremental. We are concerned here not with the creation of a Utopia, but with the messy, day-to-day business of developing the conditions for a lasting social contract. Changing institutions changes people who will in turn change institutions, and so on, "people" being ourselves. In a democratic society political economics must be hospitable to that part of our character that accepts responsibility for the common good. To the extent that we build the spirit of democracy and cooperation into our economic institutions, in the neighborhood, workplace, and community, we get *practice* on how to be democratic and cooperative. And we desperately need the practice.

At the same time we must approach the future with humility and in a mature spirit of testing and learning as we go. Planning theorist John Friedman suggests that the archtypical citizen of the future will be neither the "economic man" whose values are greed and self-aggrandizement, nor the "socialist man," the saint who is always ready to sacrifice himself for the collective good. He will rather be the "learning man," constantly experimenting, practicing, progressing by trial and error in a self-conscious effort to create a better society and a better human being in himself.

Competent economic planning thus requires that we explicitly choose—along with employment levels and housing investment—the *values* we want to affirm. There is no getting around this responsibility. By whatever name we call it, we will have economic planning. Therefore we will have the choice of what values to support, whether we exercise that choice or not. We are responsible for the future; we become what we do, as individuals and as a society. The dying ideology obscures this truth by leaving the cultivation of individual character to the televised merchants of Pac-Man, new cars, and Club Med vacations. Ignoring the relationship between our economic system and our values does not mean that we leave it up to each individual to decide his or her values; *it means that we reinforce the corporate and bureaucratic values of the dominant economic institutions* whose interests are to keep us materialistic, self-absorbed, greedy, and apathetic. . . .

The recent past has also shown that Americans are capable of great national political efforts. In our own lifetimes we have seen a civil rights movement in which black Americans—after two hundred years of slavery, another hundred of oppression and servitude, and repeated prophecies of impossibility—suddenly demanded and achieved equal political rights in the space of a decade. Similarly, forty years after women's suffrage—when the tiny group of feminists had all but given up hope for a renewed fight for equality—American women were suddenly galvanized into an extraordinarily fervent and complex movement dealing not only with political

(continued)

or even economic equality but also with vastly more complex issues of personal and sexual relationships. The ecology movement, the antiwar movement, and the movement for nuclear sanity all brought millions of Americans into political activism, taking responsibility for the future of their community, country, and planet.

The list of efforts to which people have voluntarily dedicated their energies despite expert predictions of sustained apathy suggest that we have consistently underrated the individual's willingness to participate. Such participation is often seen as a disruption to the orderly processes of government and business; it is resisted by political and corporate leadership. Therefore it often becomes disorderly and disruptive. It should be read as people hungry to take responsibility for their community.

Each movement has its own unique history and politics. But the fact is that they occurred despite the lure of television and the assorted distractions of American life—and they have made a difference. We cannot help but ask: If grass-roots movements have risen to challenge successfully the most deeply felt personal attitudes about race and sex, is it too much to imagine that a politics can be fashioned to remove an obsolete and demonstrably unworkable economic ideology that is squandering our material well-being and destroying our experience of real community?

The decade of the 1960s was characterized by political involvement and a reaching out to take responsibility for the world. The 1970s—the time of the "me" generation—was characterized by concern with individual fulfillment and personal liberation. The symbols of *both* the 1960s and the 1970s—the demonstrator and the jogger—represent aspects of the modern American psyche that must be integrated in order to build a political economics of community. Such an integration can occur only if we move beyond abstractions to practical strategies—strategies that neither simply protest nor escape, strategies that *rebuild.*

Who among us will do what must be done? Go down the list: women and minorities, whose drive for equality is stalled by the stagflation strategy of conventional economics; working people, up to their necks in debt, suddenly not knowing where the next paycheck is coming from; small- and medium-sized businesspeople, whose tax cuts are meaningless without customers with money in their pockets; managers, who know the bureaucratic failings of corporate life; environmentalists, who are learning that unemployment, hunger for jobs, and pressures to reduce costs bring ecological disaster; young people, whose dream of owning a home is gone.

A meaningful vision of community is the only way to unite those who are now isolated and bring us all back into citizenship. The metamorphosis of the American economy continues. It is bringing us face to face with our responsibility for the country's future. The market does not choose. *We* choose.

6. What do the authors mean by the expression, "search for community"? Does this make sense to you? Why?

7. What are the advantages of economic planning? The disadvantages? Do you favor economic planning? Why?

WHAT HAS BECOME OF THE KEYNESIAN REVOLUTION?

By way of concluding this chapter and indeed the book itself, it is appropriate to ask once again, "What has become of the Keynesian revolution?" We have in this book demonstrated the importance of competing economic paradigms. In so doing we have studied the historical evolution of capitalism from feudalism, to Adam Smith and the classical liberal thinkers, to the utopian socialists and Marx himself. We saw the emergence of the neoclassical economics of the late 19th century and its modern-day manifestation in microeconomics. We analyzed the Great Depression and the emergence of the Keynesian Revolution. We saw how the Keynesian system was adapted to the U.S. economy. Beginning with the 1960s we surveyed the important role that the international sector played in the further development of the Keynesian system. The decade of the 1970s created turmoil with the international economy. The stagflation of the 1970s gave way to the deep recession of the early 1980s. At present we are in the early stages of an experiment with a modified version of Keynesian economics popularly known as supply-side economics.

Economists seldom if ever reach a consensus about anything. Disagreement and controversy characterize the economics discipline. This is what for many of us makes it challenging as well as frustrating. The present time period is no exception.

What about the Keynesian Revolution? There are a number of strong opinions. Many conservatives believe that the Keynesian revolution had run its course by the late 1970s. It was time for a new economic paradigm, more conservative in nature, to undo the damage of the Keynesian policies and chart a new course for the American economy based on the older and more lasting values of laissez-faire. "Let the free market unleash its powerful forces and the economy will explode with output and productivity" was the message of the supply-siders in 1980. Others, representative of the battered and much-maligned Keynesian paradigm, attempted to defend their system and suggest that unfortunate events (shocks) and some excesses on the part of government and business had produced some unfortunate results, yet the basic model was sound and merely in need of some "fine-tuning" and adjustment. Still others found themselves not satisfied with these two dominant points of view; a third category of economists were convinced that the Keynesian revolution had not fully taken place. They argued that Keynes was not properly understood and that the use of his ideas in the American context distorted the real Keynes. What was the real Keynes? According to scholars such as Hyman Minsky, author of *John Maynard Keynes*, Keynes, while no socialist, was still in favor of an advanced capitalism that would among other things be characterized by full employment, a more egalitarian distribution of income, and the socialization of investment. In addition many adherents of this view argue that changes in the global economy have made it imperative to radically adapt the basic Keynesian system to the modern world. Last, there are those economists who represent variants of the Marxian viewpoint. The range of opinion is quite wide, but in general these economists argue that the supply-side and Keynesian paradigms are not capable of resolving the fundamental nature of our economy's problems. What is necessary is some form of **economic democracy** or democratic socialism.

Granted that the futures of capitalism in general and Keynesian and supply-side economics in particular are uncertain, we need to anticipate the future now with the best theory and empirical evidence we can find. As we do this, a number of difficult but obvious questions and additional variables must be firmly and soberly *integrated* into our analysis. We are just now beginning to recognize the importance of the future implications of continued economic growth; of the availability and use of natural resources, particularly those related to energy; and of the use of formalized economic planning in our economic system. We will have to consider these seriously as we attempt to analyze and predict the future. Only by doing this can we possibly hope to construct a more humane economy, as described by Daniel Fusfeld:

> A humane economy requires more than prosperity and economic growth, more than efficient allocation of resources. It demands change in the framework of economic institutions to achieve greater equality and freedom. It requires dispersal of the economic power and governmental authority that support the present disposition of income, wealth, and power. It requires a social environment that brings a sense of community and fellowship into human relationships. It demands compatibility among man, his technology, and the natural environment. And all of these things must be done on a worldwide scale. These are the goals of the future, to which economists and everyone else will have to devote their energies.
>
> Daniel Fusfeld, "Post–Post–Keynes: The Shattered Synthesis," *Saturday Review,* January 22, 1972.

What will our future be? As we contemplate the issues before us, it is indeed awesome and frightening to consider the realities inherent in the arms race, nuclear war, international debt, resource shortages, environmental degradation, and on and on. One thing that we do know, however, is that there will be many competing perspectives slugging it out in the centers of learning, the legislative chambers of our representatives, our workplaces, and our communities. And you, having now concluded your first course in economics, will be a more knowledgeable and critically aware citizen taking part in the inherently human vocation of making history.

> The future need not necessarily correspond to the vision which results from what scientists and technologists describe by extrapolating dominant tendencies in the present and by applying laws of statistical possibilities to conscious human beings. On the other hand, there is little chance that the future will coincide with those dreams, no matter how noble and humane, which assume all possibilities are open and that we are absolutely free to choose among them.
>
> —Mihailo Markovic, *From Affluence to Praxis.*

KEY CONCEPTS

era of shocks
radical critique
political business cycle

industrial policy
economic democracy

REVIEW QUESTIONS

1. What is meant by the expression "The Era of Shocks?"

2. What is the radical critique of the business cycle? Does the argument of the functional nature of a recession seem to fit the experience of 1980–1982? Explain.

3. What were some of the economic successes of Reagan's first term in office (1980–1984)? What were some of the economic failures and problems of Reagan's first term?

4. What is the basic argument advanced by Alperovitz and Faux in their article? Critically analyze their article. Do you agree with them? Why?

5. What has become of the Keynesian Revolution?

SUGGESTED READINGS

Gar Alperovitz and Jeff Faux, 1984. *Rebuilding America*, Pantheon. An analysis of the transformation of the American economy and the need for progressive economic policies to restructure the economy and rebuild the society. This book has been used by many Washington politicians to educate themselves and others about the need for economic change.

Barry Bluestone and Bennett Harrison, 1982. *The Deindustrialization of America*, Basic Books. This book analyzes the global and regional restructuring of the economy, in particular focusing on the migration of capital and the resulting dislocation on communities and workers. The book elicits a call for a national industrial policy and some form of economic planning.

Samuel Bowles, David Gordon, and Thomas Weiskoff, 1983. *Beyond the Wasteland*, Anchor Doubleday. A Marxian analysis of the economic crisis, a critique of Reaganomics, and a blueprint for an economic bill of rights.

Martin Carnoy, Derek Shearer, and Russell Rumberger, 1984. *A New Social Contract*, Harper and Row. Another fine book analyzing the need for fundamental economic reform. In particular, the last chapter is an excellent statement of what the authors feel to be a desirable economic future.

Center for Popular Economics, 1986. *Economic Report of the People*, South End Press. An alternative to the *Economic Report of the President*.

Francis Fox Piven and Richard Cloward, 1982. *The New Class War*, Pantheon. A fabulous little book that analyzes the Reagan budget cuts, spending priorities, and induced recession of 1980–1982 in such a way as to argue that supply-side economics had as its major goal the breaking down of organized labor and the massive redistribution of income and wealth. The book develops this argument in an interesting historical framework.

Robert Reich, 1983. *The Next American Frontier,* Times Books. This well-documented and well-argued book makes the case for an industrial policy and application of economic policy that would make America competitive again and would not allow business to perpetuate its practices of historic preservation and paper entrepreneurialism, as well as halting government perpetuation of dead labor. Reich is one of the leading liberal thinkers of the 1980s.

Lester Thurow, 1983. *Dangerous Currents,* Random House. Thurow's latest book lucidly analyzing the theoretical shortcomings of neoclassical economics and the limitations of orthodox Keynesian theory. This book is a further justification for the kinds of policy proposals that evolved from his book *The Zero Sum Society* (1980, Basic Books). A bit advanced.

Charles K. Wilber and Ken Jameson, 1984. *An Inquiry into the Poverty of Economics,* University of Notre Dame Press. This excellent book develops the competing methodologies in economics in an historical context. The authors conclude by pointing out the need for a new economic paradigm, neither Marxian nor Keynesian. They call for the emergence of a Post–Keynesian–Institutionalist paradigm (PKI).

Glossary

absolute advantage In international trade, one nation has an absolute advantage over another nation on the production of a commodity if the same amount of resources will produce more of the commodity in the one nation than in the other.

aggregate demand curve The plot of all points corresponding to the total amount of goods demanded in the economy for a given aggregate price level.

aggregate supply curve The plot of all points corresponding to the total amount of goods supplied in the economy for a given aggregate price level.

alienation Refers specifically to the condition resulting from the separation of the producer from the means of production. Alienation from the producer's point of view results from (1) no control over the product, (2) no control of the means of producing it, (3) antagonistic relationship of workers and owners.

antitrust policy Laws that attempt to limit the degree of monopoly in the economy and to promote competition. In the United States, the passage, interpretation, and enforcement of antitrust laws have involved varying degrees of emphasis on (1) market performance, (2) market conduct, and (3) market structure. See *Sherman Act*.

appreciation of currency The relative strengthening of a currency in a flexible exchange-rate system. The appreciated currency rises in cost and value over the depreciated currency.

average cost Total cost divided by the number of production units.

average fixed cost Total fixed cost divided by total units of output.

average propensity to consume (APC) Total consumption divided by total disposable income. This is the average consumption income ratio.

average propensity to save (APS) Total savings divided by total disposable income.

average variable costs (AVC) Total variable cost divided by total output.

balance of payments A summary record of a country's transactions that typically involves payments and receipt of foreign exchange. Credit items and debit items must balance, since each good that a country buys or sells must be paid for in one way or another.

balance of trade The difference between the value of exports and the value of imports of visible items (goods).

balanced-budget multiplier When a balanced change in the budget occurs [that is, an increase (or decrease) in spending is offset by an equal increase (or decrease) in taxes], total output in the economy will increase (or decrease) by the amount of the increase (or decrease). The budget multiplier is always 1.

barriers to entry Obstacles to a firm's entry into new industries or markets. These obstacles may be political (such as tariffs or trade restrictions), economic (economies of scale or limited resources, especially in oligopolies), or legal (patents, copyrights, or monopoly).

Board of Governors Appointed by the President and approved by the Congress, the board coordinates and regulates the nation's money supply.

break-even point (1) The amount of income corresponding to consumption of the entire income. There is no saving or dissaving. (2) The amount of revenue corresponding to a production level for which revenues exactly equal costs. There are no profits or losses.

Bretton Woods Agreement (1944) The basis for today's international financial organizations. The economic arrangements negotiated between the Allied nations after World War II were to be overseen by the International Monetary Fund. Gold became the ultimate means of settling balance-of-payment deficits.

built-in stabilizers Automatic, nondiscretionary forms of fiscal policy that compensate for particular trends of aggregate changes in national income.

business cycle Recurrent ups and downs of business activity, shown in a host of business indicators. Expansion and contraction phases are both thought to have certain cumulative features. They may also contain the seeds of the turning points at the "peak" and "trough."

capital A factor of production, along with labor and land. Capital is the stock of a society's produced means of production, including factories, buildings, machines, tools, and inventories of goods in stock. Different from financial capital.

capital account All capital flows other than investment income.

capitalism An economic system in which the basic resources and capital goods of the society are privately owned. Decisions are usually made by individual units, which may be relatively small (pure competition) or quite large (monopoly/oligopoly). Profitability in the case of businesses, or economic self-interest in the case of individuals, helps guide the economic directions of capitalist society.

cartel An organization of producers designed to limit or eliminate competition among its members, usually by agreeing to restrict output in an effort to achieve noncompetitive prices. An example is OPEC.

central bank An operation of the Federal Reserve Board, *this* bank serves the nation's banks: Its major responsibility is control of the money supply along with some restriction, regulation, and investigation of the banking industry.

ceteris paribus Literally "other things being equal"; usually used in economics to indicate that all variables except the ones specified are assumed not to change.

class A concept used largely by Karl Marx. The basis of class in an economic sense rests on relations of production, i.e., the mode of production. Thus, as an example, under capitalism, Marx noted a class of people who worked the means of production (proletariat) and a class who owned the means of production (capitalists, bourgeoisie).

classical economics Usually refers to the doctrines of the British Classical School of the late 18th and early 19th centuries, especially those of Adam Smith and followers. They emphasized competition, free trade, and minimal state intervention in the economy.

commodity Marketable item produced to satisfy wants. Commodities may be either tangible goods or intangible services. Marx considered labor under the wage contract a commodity because it (1) orders wage contracts and (2) responds to supply-and-demand conditions.

communism An economic system characterized by socialization of labor, centralization of the ownership of the means of production, centralized coordination of production, centralization of credit policy through a central bank, and reduction of alienation and exploitation of the worker.

comparative advantage In international trade, a country's productive advantage with respect to commodity A is said to be comparative when it must give up fewer other commodities to produce a unit of A than another country would have to give up. It is this relative cost of production that is most significant in determining mutually beneficial patterns of trade among nations.

competition Exists theoretically in a perfect and an imperfect form, the former, known as perfect competition, the latter as monopoly/oligopoly or as monopolistic competition. Put simply, competition was predicated by Adam Smith as the "Invisible Hand" in capitalism. See *"Invisible Hand."*

conservative economists Those who advocate classical theory, classical liberalism, and classical economics, i.e., that government should intervene only when necessary, and then only minimally.

consumer price index This weighted average composite of goods and services commonly consumed by average families is an indication of inflation.

consumption Expenditures by households and individuals on consumer goods.

corporation A form of business organization with a legal existence separate from that of the owners, in which ownership and financial responsibility are divided, limited, and shared among any number of individual and institutional shareholders.

cost-push inflation Categorized as supply inflation because price rises are associated with increases in the cost of production.

crowding out Refers to the competition between economic units for the use of limited funds. Usually, specific reference is the federal budget deficit and the continuing borrowing practices of the U.S. Treasury. Funds used to finance fiscal spending deprive businesses of necessary capital, thus "crowding out" investment.

currency Any recognized material accepted as national money, almost always paper or coin.

current accounts Summarizes the flow of goods and services between the United States and the rest of world.

cyclical unemployment Due to decreased demand during the troughs of business cycles, output is correspondingly curtailed. Workers furloughed during this economic retraction are cyclically unemployed and will most likely be reinstated as the cycle moves upward.

deficit spending Generally refers to government spending when net government revenues are less than net government expenditures.

demand There are three distinct but closely related concepts: (1) quantity demanded; (2) the whole relationship of the quantity demanded to variables that determine it, such as tastes, income, population, price, etc.; and (3) the demand curve.

demand curve A hypothetical construction that tells us how many units of a particular commodity consumers would be willing to buy over a period of time at all possible prices, assuming that the prices of other commodities, money incomes of consumers, and other factors are unchanged.

demand, law of Concerning the relationship between price and quantity demanded, all other things constant, the lower the price, the higher the quantity demanded. Price and quantity demanded therefore are inversely related.

demand deposits Checking accounts in commercial banks; these deposits can be turned into currency "on demand," i.e., by writing a check. Demand deposits (M_1) are the main form of money in the United States.

demand-pull inflation An explanation for rising price levels that centers on increasing excess demand for a given level of output.

depreciation (1) Loss of value in capital equipment due to use or obsolescence, or (2) the loss of value in any valuable good or commodity due to use or market forces (such as currency exchange rates).

depression A prolonged downswing of economic activity exemplified by mass unemployment and a level of national income well below potential level; excess capacity is great. More severe and longer lasting than a recession. The economic breakdown of the industrialized world in the 1930s was called the Great Depression.

devaluation A downward revision in the value at which a country's currency is pegged in terms of foreign currency.

discount rate Interest rate charged on loans from the Federal Reserve Bank to its member banks. An instrument of Federal Reserve monetary policy.

discretionary fiscal policy Fiscal policies designed in response to a particular situation in the macroeconomy. These policies are implemented with specific goals in mind, usually high output, high employment, and stable prices.

diseconomies of scale The phenomenon of disproportionaly increasing costs as a firm's productive capacity grows. Simply put, the growth of production costs in an expanding firm outstrips the growth in production.

disintermediation A firm's direct involvement in resource allocation, particularly investment, to the exclusion of intermediary institutions such as savings and loans, banks, or brokerage firms.

disposable income Amount of personal income remaining after various federal, state, and local taxes and other nontax payments.

dissaving Deficit or negative spending; that is, dissaving consists of borrowing or drawing down other financial assets in order to consume.

distribution (of income) The division of the total product of a society among its members. The distribution is sometimes described by a classification according to income size or by a classification including factor payments.

division of labor Subdivision of a productive process into its component parts, which are then handled by specially skilled/trained laborers. Adam Smith believed it was a major source of increased productivity over time.

dumping Occurs when an exporting nation sells its product at a lower price in an importing country than it does in its own country. Such action tends to ruin the importer's domestic industry while strengthening the exporter's market share.

economic dependence Describes the relationship endured by the less advanced countries with the developed countries. The relationship is one of unequal interdependence, and thus is described as economic dependence. Put theoretically, a country is in a state of economic dependence if the expansion of its economy is dependent on that of another country. See *Imperialism*.

economic development Represents progressive changes in the ability of a society to meet its economic tasks of production and distribution. Development is characterized by increasing output and the growth of economic institutions, relationships and methods that facilitate society's abilities to cope with economic growth.

economic growth Increase in productive capabilities beyond the necessary elements of development. Expansion creates more jobs, goods, and income.

economic planning Is the planning of investment, consumption, etc., decisions by one or another bodies. Several variants (among which are corporate planning, command planning, and indicative planning) demonstrate that what is to be planned varies and that who does the planning also varies.

economic profits Return to capital above "normal profit," that is, profit remaining after opportunity costs have been taken into account.

economic theory Concerns a theory of economics or resource allocation. Marxist, classical, and Keynesian theory are examples. See *Theory*.

economics Concerns the allocation of resources and the manner in which these resources are allocated, as well as the method of production of these resources.

economies of scale The phenomenon of decreasing marginal costs in large-scale production (usually oligopolistic production). The growth of production in an expanding firm outstrips the growth in costs.

elasticity A function that describes the sensitivity of demand or supply for a product to changes in its price. Elasticity equals percentage change in quantity demanded (supplied) divided by the percentage change in price.

Employment Act of 1946 Created a council of economic advisors to advise the President on the state of the economy and on how the goal of full employment could best be achieved.

enclosure movement The feudal nobility fenced off or enclosed lands formerly used for communal grazing, serving to further destroy feudal ties and create a large, new "landless" labor force.

entrepreneur In the classical liberal sense, an owner of the means of production. In the modern corporate world, a businessman is often considered an entrepreneur.

equation of exchange Also, quantity theory of money, expressed as $MV = PQ$, where M is the money stock, V is velocity of money, P is price level, and Q is real national income. It is a tautology, because V is defined as PQ/M.

equilibrium A state of balance in which there are no endogenous pressures for change. Quantity demanded equal to quantity supplied at a single price is considered an equilibrium position.

exchange rate The price of a nation's currency in terms of another nation's currency.

exports (X) Any unit of production produced in country A that leaves country A for another destination is considered an export for country A and is registered accordingly in the balance of trade account.

externalities Costs of productive activity that the firm is not obliged to bear. The costs are born by the public—the social costs of production. Also known as third-party effect. Externalities may be detrimental (external costs) or beneficial (external benefits).

factors of production Any implement or agent whose services are used in the production of economic goods and services. Three basic factors are land, labor, and capital.

Federal Reserve Is instrumental in determining monetary policy for which its main weapons are (1) altering reserve requirements, (2) changing the discount rate at which member banks may borrow from Federal Reserve Banks, and (3) open-market purchases and sales of governmental securities.

feudalism The historical system that directly preceded capitalism. Relations of class were between lord and serf and were not mired in economics. Feudalism existed in a society in which tradition and ceremony played the major roles.

financial intermediation Use of financial institutions to deposit or acquire funds to or from the public. Such institutions pool numerous funds and then provide them to businesses, governments, or individuals.

firm Unit that makes decisions regarding the employment of factors of production and production of goods and services.

fiscal policy Governmental policy concerned with the tax and expenditure activities of the federal government, including the size of public spending and the balancing or un- balancing of the federal budget; designed to promote certain macroeconomic objectives, usually full employment, stable prices, economic growth, and balance of payments equilibrium.

fixed exchange rate Currencies are fixed (set) relative to either a universal exchange (gold) or to one another.

floating exchange rate Currency exchange rates float when they alter freely in response to the forces of international supply and demand.

fractional reserve system System under which commercial banks are not required to maintain reserves equal to their demand or other deposits, only a prescribed percentage.

free trade A situation in which all commodities can be freely imported and exported without special taxes or restrictions being levied merely because of their status as "imports" or "exports."

frictional unemployment Loss of jobs caused by temporary mismatching of laborers with jobs due to different needs of business and skills of labor.

full employment A condition under which those who wish to work at the prevailing wage are able to find work. In the United States full employment is reached at 4 percent unemployment, and this may rise to as high as 6 percent unemployment.

GATT (General Agreement on Tariffs and Trade) An association of 80 countries that "sets and regulates the code of international trade conduct."

Gini coefficient A measure of inequality derived from the Lorenz curve. It is calculated by dividing the difference in area between the diagonal line and the Lorenz curve by the entire area below the diagonal line.

gross national product Total output of funds, goods, and services produced in an economy in a given period of time, including gross investment.

Group of 77 Group of underdeveloped countries whose total number at present is in the neighborhood of 112, that through the United Nations and other international forums, demand that the developed world support their development.

historical materialism Developed by Karl Marx, is an in-depth historical study of material relations. Historical materialism forms the basis of social and economic change in class relations. The base, as Marx determined, rests on the mode of production, and all class struggle emanated out of the relations to the mode of production. The superstructure is determined by the base, and includes the philosophy, religion, ideology, etc., of the specific epoch.

imperialism Is a reflection of one country's economic, social, political, and cultural dominance over another country. Imperialism as developed by Lenin, Sweezy, Baran, Magdoff, and many others is a historical question and a historical problem, and is directly related to the growth and development of capitalism.

imports Any good absorbed by country A from another country is considered an import, and is registered accordingly as a deficit in the balance of trade.

income flow The path that income follows in the economy. Businesses pay out to households rent, wages, interests, and profits, which in turn provide land, labor, and capital for business to continue the flow. Households, in turn, spend their incomes for goods and services.

income velocity of money From the equation of exchange, the income velocity of money is GNP divided by the money supply.

incomes policy Governmental policies designed to limit inflation by various direct and indirect controls over prices, wages, profits, and other incomes.

index numbers A weighted average of a given variable with a specified base number, usually 100.

indirect business taxes Taxes imposed on the production and sale of goods—for example, sales tax, excise tax, custom duties, property taxes.

industry The collective group of producers of a single good or service or closely related good or service.

infant industry Industry that has recently been established in a country and has not yet had time to exploit possible economies of scale and other efficiencies. Such industries provide one of the traditional arguments for tariff protection.

inflation A general rise in the average level of all prices in an economy as defined by some index (consumer price index, wholesale price index, or GNP price deflator).

inflationary gap When aggregate demand exceeds the capacity of aggregate supply, prices rise but supply cannot expand. The inflationary gap is then the vertical distance from the 45° line at full employment to the demand curve. This is "too many dollars chasing too few goods."

infrastructure Concerns necessary conditions for development, such as transportation routes, social services, etc.

innovation A change for the better in technology or production. A "better" change involves higher efficiency and/or lower costs of production.

interest Reflects (1) the price of borrowing money and (2) the rate of return to owners of capital goods. The interest rate is the amount of interest expressed as a percentage of the initial sum.

international trade Buying and selling of goods and services across national borders. The country that sells is the exporter and the country that buys is the importer.

intermediate technology Is a middle-level, fairly labor-intensive technology. It currently is part of the Group of 77's demands from the developed world.

International Monetary Fund (IMF) Founded with the goal of encouraging trade by establishing an orderly procedure for stabilizing foreign exchange rates and for altering those rates in the case of fundamental balance-of-payments disequilibrium.

inventories Stocks of goods kept on hand to meet orders from other producers and customers.

investment An addition to a firm's or society's stock of capital (machines, buildings, inventories, etc.) in a certain period of time. In the Keynesian system, the total value of all goods and services produced by firms and not sold to customers.

"invisible hand" Adam Smith's term; it suggests that individuals who are motivated only by private (not social) interest will nevertheless be guided invisibly by the market to actions and decisions beneficial to the welfare of society.

Keynesian economics Theory characterized by its emphasis on macroeconomic problems, the special role of aggregate demand in determining national income, its stress on the possibility of unemployment equilibria, its attempt to synthesize real and monetary analysis, and its argument for a greater government intervention in the economy.

labor The physical and mental contributions of humans to the production process. Collectively, labor refers to all workers.

labor force participation rate Percentage of actual civilians participating in the labor force compared with the total number of civilians of working age.

labor theory of value Theory held by Marx (and Ricardo in differing form) that the value of a commodity is proportional to the labor embodied in its production.

Laffer curve The heart of supply-side economics. The Laffer curve relates the tax rate to government revenues. It suggests that there is an optimal tax rate for maximizing revenues.

laissez-faire Associated with Adam Smith, it is a doctrine that the state should largely leave the economy to its own devices.

land A means of production that includes raw materials and the land upon which productive activity takes place (i.e., factory, plant, farm).

law of diminishing returns On the production of any commodity, as more units of a variable factor of production are added to a fixed quantity of other factors of production, the addition to total product (marginal product) by each added unit of the variable factor will eventually begin to diminish.

liquidity Measures the ease with which an asset can be converted into cash. Considerations include the time necessary to acquire cash, the cost of conversion, and the predictability of value of the asset.

liquidity preference Demand for money as a function of the interest rate. Shows the willingness to hold money on hand.

liquidity trap In Keynesian theory, liquidity trap refers to the point in the economy when all economic agents desire to keep each additional dollar on hand. To them, the existing interest rate does not warrant the acquisition of bonds. The demand for money is thus perfectly elastic or horizontal. Monetary policy is completely ineffective in stimulating aggregate demand.

long run Any extended period, usually longer than 3 to 5 years. The long run is thought of as the period in which equilibrium is reached.

macroeconomics Concerned with large economic aggregates such as GNP, total employment, overall price level, and how these aggregates are determined.

Malthus, Thomas Developed a theory that population tends to grow at a geometric ratio while food supplies can, at best, grow at an arithmetic ratio. Thus, in Malthus's eyes, extreme poverty, famine, plague, and war would continually beset man.

marginal cost (MC) The increase in total cost resulting from raising the rate of production by one unit.

marginal physical product The additional output realized when one more unit of a variable input is used, assuming all other input levels are held constant.

marginal propensity to consume (MPC) The change in consumption divided by the change in income (MPC $= \Delta C/\Delta Y$).

marginal propensity to save (MPS) The change in saving divided by the charge in income that brought it about (MPS $= \Delta S/\Delta Y$).

marginal revenue (MR) The change in a firm's total revenue arising from the sale of one additional unit.

marginal revenue product The additional revenue realized when one more unit of a variable input is used, assuming all other input levels are held constant.

marginal revenue = marginal cost In microeconomics, the point at which profits are maximized for a firm.

market A concept with many possible definitions. First, an area over which buyers and sellers negotiate the exchange of a well-defined commodity. Second, from the point of view of a household, the firms from which it can buy a well-defined product. Third, from the point of view of the firm, the buyers to whom it can sell a well-defined product.

market economy An economy functioning largely due to market forces (i.e., supply, demand, etc.).

Marxian economics Aimed at understanding the conflicts between the class system (or private property system) of capitalism and the methods of production and commodity exchange under capitalism.

medium of exchange The function of money as intermediary. Since money is accepted in payment for goods and services and since it is valued for the goods and services it buys, money is a medium of exchange.

mercantilism A characteristic European economic doctrine in the 16th–17th centuries, emphasizing the role of money and trade in economic life and the desirability of active state intervention in the economy.

microeconomics Deals with the interrelationships of individual businesses, firms, industries, consumers, laborers, and other factors of production that make up the economy.

mixed economy An economy in which there are substantial public and private sectors, in which private enterprise and the market are significant determining factors, but in which the state also takes on certain basic economic responsibilities (e.g., full employment and business regulation). See *Capitalism*.

monetary policy Governmental policy concerned with the supply of money and credit in the economy and the rate of interest; designed to promote certain macroeconomic objectives, usually full employment, stable prices, economic growth, and balance of payments equilibrium.

monopolistic competition A market structure in which each firm is relatively small, but each has a monopoly on its particular version of the product in question. Competition in such a framework assumes the form of advertising, product differentiation, and other forms of nonprice competition.

monopoly A market structure in which there is a single seller of a commodity or service that has no very close substitutes.

monopoly capitalism Marks the dominance of imperfect competition; productive forces or factors are extremely concentrated, and markets are imperfect. See *Capitalism*.

multinational corporation One that operates within different national boundaries.

multiplier The number of dollars by which a $1 increase in spending (*C, I, G*) will raise the equilibrium level of national income. Its relation to

$$\text{MPC: } M = \frac{1}{1 - \text{MPC}} \quad \text{to MPS: } M = \frac{1}{\text{MPS}}$$

national income The total income of factors of production in the current productive period.

net national product (NNP) Total output of final goods and services produced in an economy in a given period of time, including net rather than gross investment. GNP = NNP + Depreciation.

new international economic order (NIEO) Part of the so-called north–south debate; the Group of 77 is calling on the United Nations for a NIEO, featuring greater support from the developed world toward the underdeveloped world.

oligopoly A market structure in which there are a few large firms that dominate the industry. Some of these industries produce an undifferentiated product, others a differentiated product. In either case, a special feature of oliogopoly is that the firms recognize their interdependence.

open market operations Federal Reserve purchases and sales of government securities on the open market. An important instrument of monetary policy. Sales of government securities reduce money supply, while purchases increase it.

opportunity cost The cost of an economic good can be measured in terms of the alternative goods one must forgo to secure it.

Organization of Petroleum Exporting Countries (OPEC) Organization of oil-producing nations, largely in the Middle East, for the purpose of controlling production, export, and price of petroleum.

paradox of thrift Identified by Keynes, an increase in the desire to save decreases output even though investment may increase. The moral: One must consume to have production.

peak (of business cycle) The height of the business cycle characterized by greatest economic activity and followed by contracting economic activity.

per capita income Total national income divided by total population.

petrodollars Dollars and currency in the form of monetary reserves being controlled by the oil-exporting (largely OPEC) nations.

Phillips curve Diagram showing relationship between inflation and unemployment.

political business cycle Distortion of the basic business cycle caused by the actions and policies of politicians bidding for reelection. Usually the cycle runs in four-year cycles in sequence with presidential elections.

political economy A social science dealing with political policies and economic processes, their interrelationships, and their mutual influence on social institutions.

possessions Personal possessions; examples: home, farms, tools, or any things we might own and use. Private property in contrast, reflects ownership of impersonal property not used by the owner except to collect rent on land, interest, and profits on capital, which is used (worked) by others.

postindustrial society Is a society that has encountered the processes of industrialization and has gone beyond industrialization in terms of benefits accruing to the people. Some people consider the United States as a postindustrial society.

praxis A term used by the young Hegelians and especially Marx; it was the equivalent of "practical activity with an added twist," i.e., the dialectical interrelation of thought and practice.

present value The current value of a future receipt or debt corrected for a prevailing or assumed interest rate.

prices Guide resource allocation. Reflect value of good or service. Transmitted by markets through which producers make decisions about what factors of production to use, and consumers decide what to consume.

price elasticity of demand Function that describes the sensitivity of demand for a product based on changes in its price.

price elasticity of supply Function which describes the sensitivity of supply of a product based on changes in its price.

price index (consumer) Is an evaluation of how consumer goods prices vary from one period to the next. The consumer price index is one means with which to gauge inflation.

price stability Price policy that aims to counter wide fluctuations in aggregate price levels. During a period of high inflation, for example, anti-inflationary measures such as credit withdrawal, higher interest rates, decreased government spending, etc., will be pursued (deflationary policies).

primitive accumulation Referred to by Marx, who claimed all methods of accumulation prior to socialist accumulation to be "primitive" since they all engender antagonistic classes. Socialism to Marx represented a break, for under it, class differences would dissolve.

product differentiation Close, but not perfect, substitute products retain some distinctive difference. Brand names, coloring, or packaging are means of differentiating products.

production possibilities curve Device that illustrates scarcity and opportunity cost by showing that whenever society chooses to have more of one type of good, it must sacrifice some of another type of good.

profits Excess of revenues over costs. Normal profits are equal to the opportunity costs of management. Economic profits are the profits above the normal profit. Theoretically, in pure competition, economic profits are equal to zero in the long run. However, in imperfect market structures, they are not.

progressive income tax Tax which claims ever-increasing percentage of income as the level of income rises.

property Tangible or intangible possession which may be used to produce some product or aid in the selling of the product. Certain legal rights are attached to this "private property."

property rights In capitalism, productive property is privately owned. Owners have rights to control the use of these productive resources. See *Possessions*.

protectionism Policy that institutes high tariffs on incoming goods, so as to preserve domestic industry. (See *Infant Industry, Tariff*.) Protectionism was a prevalent factor during mercantilism.

public debt The amount of outstanding federal debt held by individuals, and corporations, and nonfederal government agencies.

public goods Goods or resources that benefit the general public and are not necessarily directly paid for by all those who use them (i.e., street signs, public schools).

putting-out system Replaced the handicraft type of industry. In its earliest stages an owner would give the worker the materials and pay him to work them into a finished product. Marked the emergence of private capital.

quantity demanded The specific number of units of a product or products in the economy that are desired by economic agents at a given price level.

quantity supplied The specific number of units of a product or products in the economy that are provided by producers at a given price level.

quantity theory of money Monetarist theory that the quantity of money in the economy largely determines the level of prices. Stated as $MV = PQ$, where M is quantity of money, V is income velocity of money, P is price level, and Q is real national income. The theory postulates that V is largely determined by institutional factors and Q is determined by factor supplies and technology, hence changes in M will be reflected in proportionate changes in P.

radical economists Those critical of classical and neoclassical theory. Radical economics views the origins of economic problems as resulting directly out of the capitalist system itself, and thus the only serious relief to these problems is offered in a change of economic system.

rational expectations An economics-based theory about the nature of economic agents, stating that all agents are rational, logical, and aware of what is best for them and what the consequences of decisions and developments in the economy will mean for their well-being. Agents will act logically to take advantage of changes in the economy and enhance their position.

real wages Are wages measured from a specific point, i.e., wages that reflect the rate of inflation. Thus, if a worker's wage level increases 10 percent and inflation increases 10 percent in the same period of time, then we say that the real wage remains the same. Usually contrasted with money wages, which in the above situation would reflect only the 10 percent increase in the worker's wage.

recession A slowing down of economic activity, resulting in an increase in unemployment and in excess industrial capacity. Less severe than a depression. Sometimes defined in the United States in terms of a decline in GNP for two or more successive quarters of a year.

Regulation Q Legislated ceiling on interest rates payable by banks on deposits. This regulation will be phased out by the end of 1986.

rent (1) Payment for the services of the factor of production, and (2) payment for the services of any factor of production that is in inelastic supply, i.e., a surplus payment above that required to bring forth the supply of the factor in question (economic rent).

reserve army (industrial) A term developed by Marx to describe the functioning of capitalism. The purpose of the industrial reserve army, as Marx pointed out, was to decrease worker strength greatly, and only through being in constant motion (largely parallel to the cyclical change) could the reserve army be effective.

reserve currency A currency that is accepted in settlement of international exchanges.

reserve requirements In banking, the fraction of public deposits that a bank holds in reserves.

Ricardo, David One of the reformers of classical liberalism, developed by Adam Smith. Ricardo's analysis was based on an economy composed of many small enterprises.

savings All income received by households and not spent on the consumption of goods and services.

Say's law The doctrine (named after J. B. Say) that "supply creates its own demand." The production of one good creates an addition to both aggregate supply and aggregate demand. In this nonmonetary world, depression and mass unemployment are not possible.

scarcity Recognition of the fact that society's capacity to produce or secure goods is insufficient to satisfy all the wants, needs, and desires that people have for these goods.

services Duties (or work) for others that do not necessarily render a good but are nevertheless worth payment.

Sherman Act A major U.S. antitrust law passed in 1890, it prohibits "every contract, combination in the form of trust or otherwise or conspiracy, in restraint of trade or commerce," and prescribes penalties for monopoly.

shortage Disequilibrium situation wherein quantity demanded exceeds quantity supplied. In such a situation price will tend to rise until an equilibrium price level is established, with quantity supplied equal to quantity demanded.

Smith, Adam In 1776 published *The Wealth of Nations,* noting foundation of a new individualist philosophy, classical liberalism.

special drawing rights (SDR's) Created by the IMF to increase international liquidity, SDR's are drawn by each country in proportion to its original contribution.

specialization (of labor) Methods of production in which individual workers specialize in particular tasks rather than making everything for themselves.

speculative demand for money Function that describes the amount of assets held by households and firms in the form of money, related to the interest rate.

stagflation Term coined in the 1970s to describe the coexistence of unemployment (stagnation) and inflation afflicting the United States and other countries.

standard of deferred payment Characteristic of money based on mutual faith that it will be accepted as future payment.

state capitalism Involves the state as a major institution within the economy. Planning is often indicated, as is close cooperation between business and financial institutions and government. See *Capitalism.*

state economic planning In one particular context, state economic planning may take the form of state capitalism, in which the government plans the economy. State economic planning may also exist in socialist countries, such as China and Cuba. Russia may be argued to be either state capitalist or socialist.

stock Shares of ownership in a corporation (common stock, preferred stock).

store of value Use of money based on its characteristic as an asset that holds value into the future.

structural unemployment Type of rather permanent unemployment that stems from shifting demand and/or technological changes requiring new skills for workers. Disparities in geographic locations of workers and jobs are also part of this phenomenon.

supply The amount of goods or services produced and available for purchase.

supply curve The set of all points representing the amount of goods or services supplied at different price levels.

supply, law of Concerning the relationship between price and quantity supplied. All other things being constant, the lower the price, the lower the quantity supplied. Price and quantity supplied are positively related.

surplus A state of disequilibrium wherein quantity supplied supply exceeds quantity demanded. There will be a tendency for price to fall until an equilibrium price is established at which quantity supplied equals quantity demanded.

surplus value In Marxian terms, the amount by which the value of a worker's output exceeds his wage.

tariff A tax applied on imports.

terms of trade The prices of a country's exports in relation to its imports. Any improvement in a country's terms of trade means a relative increase in its export prices, while a deterioration in its terms of trade indicates a relative increase in its import prices.

theory A cogently expressed group of related propositions declared as principles for explanation of a set of phenomena.

total cost The cost of all factors of production involved in the production of one good.

total fixed costs Costs that do not change with varying output. Such costs will be incurred regardless of production levels.

total revenue The amount of funds credited to the firm for sales of its output; price multiplied by units sold.

total variable costs Costs that fluctuate due to the activity of the firm and the productive process. Labor and resources are the two major variable costs.

transactions demand for money Function that indicates the amount of money balances that individuals desire for purchasing purposes. Considered relatively constant given a level of income and consumption pattern.

transfer payments Payments made by the government to individuals that are not compensation for currently productive activity.

trough (in business cycle) The low point of the business cycle where business activity is the slowest. The cycle begins an upward swing following this low point.

unemployment A condition wherein workers who are ordinarily part of the labor force are unable to find work at prevailing wages. There are no fewer than five specific forms of unemployment: (1) frictional—all labor markets have this kind, due to workers changing jobs, etc.; (2) seasonal—results from changing seasonal demand and supply for labor; (3) structural—involves changing or shifting product demand, i.e., a function of geographic and job-skill mobility; (4) cyclical—results from changes in demand of labor during the business cycle; and (5) hidden unemployment—reflects frustrated potential workers who have given up looking for a job.

utility The ability of a product to satisfy a human want. Is closely related to use value. See *Value*.

value Every commodity has (1) a use value and (2) an exchange value. Use value is the expression of a utility relation. Exchange value exists only in commodity production, and it represents the social relation between owners and producers. The presence of exchange value points to a developed division of labor and a system of private production.

value added Strictly, the value of the final product less the cost of production. Loosely, the increase in value due to the labor input.

variable costs Costs that fluctuate due to the activity of the firm and the productive process. Labor and resources are the two major variable costs.

wage and price controls Mandatory regulation of wages and prices by the government; were applied in the United States to certain segments of the economy with varying force (Phase I–IV) from 1971–1974. Their purpose is to contain inflation.

wages The price paid for units of labor or service supplied in the market per unit of time.

World Bank Officially the International Bank for Reconstruction and Development (IBRD). Established after World War II by the United States to promote postwar reconstruction and development of underdeveloped countries. It assists poor countries through loans or by insuring private loans in the financing of development projects.

Indexes

Name Index

Subject Index

EXAM 2
  CHAPT 11 - 15, 29

WORKBOOK:
   7 - 14

ISSUES:
    1, 2, 7, 9